Zapando Sibirskaya Ravnina

P9-ARH-546

Omsk
Novosibirsk

R U S S I A

Vostachnyy Sayan

Yenisey

Ozero
Baykal

Astana

A l t a i

Karaganda

Ozero
Zaysan

Ulaanbaatar

KAZAKHSTAN

M O N G O L I A

Selenga

Ozero Balkhash

Shihezi

G o b i

Bishkek
(Frunze)

Almaty
(Alma-Ata)

Ürümqi

Jimsar

Shymkent

T I A N   S H A N

Hami

KYRGYZSTAN
Namangan

Ysyk-Köl

Aksu

Turpan

Anxi

Osh

Korla

Yumen

Khujand

Kashi
(Kashgar)

Tarim Pendi

Lop
Nur

CHINA

Wuwei

Huang He (Yangtze)

L ASIA

Taklamakan Shamo

Qiemo

Ruoqiang

Hotan
(Khotan)

K U N L U N   S H A N

C H I N A

Qinghai
Hu

Lanzhou

Xi'an

Kush

Gilgit

Karakoram

Qingzang Gaoyuan
(Plateau of Tibet)

Peshawar

Islamabad

H I M A L A Y A

Chengdu

Lahore

Sutlej

Indus

Lhasa

Chang Jiang (Yangtze)

Delhi
New Delhi

NEPAL

Kathmandu

Thimphu

Mekong

Lucknow

BHUTAN

Ganges

Brahmaputra

Kunming

BANGLADESH

Tropic of Cancer

Ahmadabad

Dhaka
(Dacca)

Narmada

Kolkata
(Calcutta)

Mahanadi

Mandalay

Ha Noi

MYANMAR
(BURMA)

Mumbai
(Bombay)

I N D I A

Hyderabad

Vishakhapatnam

Irrawaddy

Naypyidaw

Gulf of
Tongkin

VIETNAM

LAOS

Krishna

Bay
of
Bengal

Vientiane

Bangalore

Madras

Yangon
(Rangoon)

THAILAND

Mekong

Andaman
Islands
(INDIA)

Andaman
Sea

Bangkok

CAMBODIA

Gulf of
Thailand

Phnum
Penh

Ho Chi
Minh

Main Silk Road

Colombo
Sri Jayewardenepura
Kotte

SRI LANKA

Nicobar
Islands
(INDIA)

INSIGHT ⊙ GUIDES

THE SILK ROAD

www.insightguides.com/SilkRoad

◉ Walking Eye App

YOUR FREE DESTINATION CONTENT AND EBOOK AVAILABLE THROUGH THE WALKING EYE APP

Your guide now includes a free eBook and destination content for your chosen destination, all for the same great price as before. Simply download the Walking Eye App from the App Store or Google Play to access your free eBook and destination content.

HOW THE WALKING EYE APP WORKS

Through the Walking Eye App, you can purchase a range of eBooks and destination content. However, when you buy this book, you can download the corresponding eBook and destination content for free. Just see below in the grey panels where to find your free content and then scan the QR code at the bottom of this page.

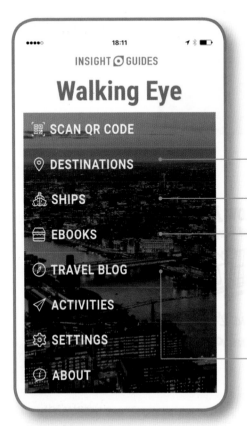

Destinations: Download your corresponding essential destination content from here, featuring recommended sights and attractions, restaurants, hotels and an A–Z of practical information, all for free. Other destinations are available for purchase.

Ships: Interested in ship reviews? Find independent reviews of river and ocean ships in this section, all available for purchase.

eBooks: You can download your free accompanying digital version of this guide here. You will also find a whole range of other eBooks, all available for purchase.

Free access to travel-related blog articles about different destinations, updated on a daily basis.

HOW THE DESTINATION CONTENT WORKS

Each destination includes a short introduction, an A–Z of practical information and recommended points of interest, split into 4 different categories:
• Highlights
• Accommodation
• Eating out
• What to do
You can view the location of every point of interest and save it by adding it to your Favourites. In the 'Around Me' section you can view all the points of interest within 5km.

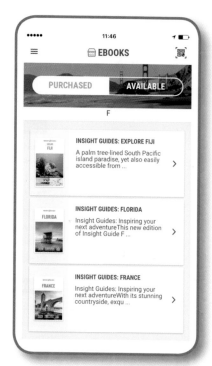

HOW THE EBOOKS WORK

The eBooks are provided in EPUB file format. Please note that you will need an eBook reader installed on your device to open the file. Many devices come with this as standard, but you may still need to install one manually from Google Play.

The eBook content is identical to the content in the printed guide.

HOW TO DOWNLOAD THE WALKING EYE APP

1. Download the Walking Eye App from the App Store or Google Play.
2. Open the app and select the scanning function from the main menu.
3. Scan the QR code on this page – you will then be asked a security question to verify ownership of the book.
4. Once this has been verified, you will see your eBook and destination content in the purchased ebook and destination sections, where you will be able to download them.

Other destination apps and eBooks are available for purchase separately or are free with the purchase of the Insight Guide book.

Contents

THE BEST OF THE SILK ROAD: TOP ATTRACTIONS

Ancient cities, some in ruins, some still thriving; huge mountain ranges, deserts, oases; and buildings to take your breath away.

△ **Mogao Caves**. These caves near Dunhuang lay undiscovered for centuries. They contain one of the world's greatest collections of Buddhist art. See page 160.

△ **Persepolis**. This great city was used to reaffirm the power of the Achaemenid kings. The western end of the Silk Road developed from the network of roads built to connect even the remotest corners of their Persian Empire. See page 325.

▽ **Registan, Samarkand**. A spectacular architectural ensemble, with fantastic Islamic designs and calligraphy etched into the facades of its mosque and madrassas. See page 279.

△ **Poi Kalon ensemble**. Consisting of mosque, madrassa and minaret, this is the focal point of Bukhara, one of the great centres of trade and scholarship along the Silk Road. See page 287.

△ **Isfahan**. This great city grew rich from the Silk Road trade linking with the Persian Gulf, resulting in some sublime architecture including the incomparable Imam Mosque. See page 327.

▷ **Karakoram Highway**. One of the world's most awe-inspiring roads, linking Western China and Pakistan across the mighty Pamir and Karakoram mountain ranges. See page 212.

◁ **The Turpan Oasis**. A sea of green surrounded by desert, is famous for its vineyards. The city of Turpan is also the base for excursions to ancient Silk Road sites and other attractions. See page 170.

△ **Lake Issyk-Kul**. The world's second-largest saline lake has a dramatic mountain setting. Meaning "hot lake" in Kyrgyz, it does not freeze, even in the depths of the Kyrgyz winter. See page 238.

▽ **Terracotta Army**. A legacy of China's First Emperor, Qin Shi Huang, who had it built to protect him in the afterlife. See page 142.

△ **Yurt living**. Experience the nomadic lifestyle amid the wilds of the mountain nation of Kyrgyzstan, at the heart of Central Asia. See page 232.

THE BEST OF THE SILK ROAD: EDITOR'S CHOICE

Linking two continents across 8,000km (5,000 miles), the Silk Road has much to offer. The following selection will provide inspiration to organise a trip.

A camel safari near Dunhuang in the Gobi Desert.

BEST LANDSCAPES AND JOURNEYS

Mingsha Shan and Crescent Moon Lake. Get a taste of the Taklamakan Desert by taking a camel ride in these great dunes near Dunhuang. See page 161.

Flaming Mountains. This is a major landmark near Turpan, enshrined in Chinese folklore. See page 174.

Lake Karakul. Just off the Karakoram Highway, the lake has great views of the Kunlun peaks of Kongur and Muztagh Ata. See page 199.

Heavenly Lake (Tian Chi). High in the Tian Shan to the east of Urumqi, at the base of Bogda Shan, this makes an invigorating escape. See page 201.

Kyrgyzstan jailoos. These are the upland pastures where the Kyrgyz nomads live during the summer. Visitors can stay in a nomad's yurt. See page 235.

Tajikistan's Pamir Highway. This is an amazing journey following the Silk Road across "the roof of the world", in the footsteps of some famous explorers. See page 254.

Iskander-Kul (Alexander's Lake). features on almost every trekking itinerary in Tajikistan's Fan Mountains. Legend has it that Alexander the Great appears riding on his horse through the water during a full moon.

Xi'an's bell tower lit up.

See page 265.

Hunza Valley, Pakistan. On the Karakoram Highway from China, this most beautiful of valleys is dominated by the enormous Rakaposhi. See page 212.

Northwest Iran. Dramatic mountains hid the infamous 'Assassin' murderers and protected ancient Zoroastrian fire temples such as Takht-e Suleiman. See page 332.

Pakistan's Hunza Valley.

BEST BAZAARS

Carpet-seller at Bazaar-e Vakil, Shiraz.

Sunday Market, Kashgar. Whether you want to buy a camel, a fat-tailed sheep or a horse, this is the place to come. An insight into the Silk Road of old. See page 195.

Peshawar, Pakistan. A maze of bazaars, the most authentic on the Silk Road. See page 216.

Siab Bazaar, Samarkand. A great place to meet the Uzbeks, and a bewildering array of produce. See page 282.

Tehran Bazaar. The mother of all markets, whose traders wield great power. See page 323.

Bazaar-e Vakil, Shiraz. One of Iran's most atmospheric markets. See page 324.

Grand Bazaar, Istanbul. The ultimate covered bazaar experience. See page 371.

BEST CITIES

Xi'an. The ancient capital of China, the eastern terminus of the Silk Road, famous for its city walls, pagodas and the nearby Terracotta Army. See page 135.

Kashgar. Major market town at a busy Silk Road junction, a hub of travel for Western China. Buy your camels here. See page 193.

Samarkand. One of the most famous Silk Road cities of all, with fantastic Timurid architecture and a 2,500-year history. See page 277.

Istanbul. The meeting point of Europe and Asia, Christianity and Islam, is the vibrant starting point of the Silk Road in the west. See page 370.

Herat. Dominated by the remains of a citadel constructed by Alexander the Great, this ancient Afghan city could become a major Silk Road destination again. See page 224.

Shiraz. The city that gave its name to the grape variety, and a centre of Iranian poetry. See page 324.

Isfahan. Once the showcase of Persian art and architecture, this has some breathtakingly stunning buildings. See page 327.

Ashgabat. Remarkable modern capital of Turkmenistan that few people have heard of, let alone visited. See page 300.

See-o-se Pol in Isfahan.

GREAT BUILDINGS

Jiayuguan Fort and the Great Wall. The Silk Road passes straight through this defiant building. See page 156.

Tash Rabat, Kyrgyzstan. A remote caravanserai in the wilds. See page 233.

Registan, Samarkand. The massive scale and intricate detail of the tilework is beyond compare. See page 279.

Gur-i-Mir, Samarkand. The tomb of the mighty ruler Timur (Tamerlane). See page 283.

Samanid Mausoleum, Bukhara. An architectural gem of Central Asia. See page 287.

Khiva city walls. The 17th-century walls of this oasis town feel frozen in time. See page 292.

Baltit Fort in Karimabad, Pakistan. This mountain fort was a key site on the frontier of the Great Game and has spectacular views. See page 213.

Minaret of Jam, Afghanistan. Isolated 12th-century minaret. See page 224.

Friday Mosque, Herat, Afghanistan. This great mosque features stunning tilework. See page 224.

See-o-se Pol, Isfahan, Iran. This bridge with two rows of 33 arches was commissioned by Shah Abbas I in 1602. See page 329.

Hagia Sophia, Istanbul. Remarkable religious building encompassing two faiths. See page 370.

Ishak Pasha Palace, Dogubeyazit, Turkey. Dramatic sandstone palace at the eastern edge of the Ottoman Empire. See page 361.

Khiva is an ancient Silk Road city.

Tomb of Ismail Samani, Bukhara.

SHRINES, TOMBS AND MONASTERIES

Tomb of Bakhauddin Naqshband, Bukhara. The founder of the Naqshbandi order of Sufism. See page 292.
Tomb of Khoja Ahmed Yassawi in Turkistan, Kazakhstan. Local Muslims believe making three pilgrimages here is equivalent to going on Hajj. See page 251.
Shrine of Hazrat Ali, Mazar-e-Sharif. One of Islam's holiest shrines.

See page 226.
Ismail Samani Mausoleum, Bukhara. Built for the founder of the Samanid dynasty. See page 287.
Labrang. The most important Tibetan monastery outside Tibet. See page 151.
Tomb of Mevlâna Jelaleddin Rumi, Konya. Home of the Whirling Dervishes. See page 367.

FESTIVALS

Silk and Spice Festival, Bukhara. Celebration of the food, fashion and folklore of Silk Road trade, held annually towards the end of May.
Nauroz (New Year). The spring equinox festival celebrated in Iran and Central Asian countries, deeply rooted in ancient Zoroastrian traditions.
Chinese New Year. The most important Chinese festival, which usually falls in late January or early February.

Central Asia Horse Festival, Kyrgyzstan. Watch the best of Central Asia's horsemen compete in horse races, horseback wrestling and *kok boru* – dead goat polo.
Muslim Festivals. The main ones are Id al-Fitr, held at the end of the fasting month of Ramadan; and Id al-Adha (the "Festival of the Sacrifice"), held to mark the culmination of the Hajj pilgrimage to Mecca.

ANCIENT SITES

Maijishan Shiku. One of China's four most important Buddhist temple groups, in a dramatic location. See page 146.
Mogao Caves, Dunhuang. The source of the world's most extensive collection of Buddhist statuary, paintings and manuscripts. See page 160.
Jiaohe Ancient City. The best preserved of Xinjiang's ancient Silk Road cities. See page 172.
Bezeklik Thousand Buddha Caves. There are few murals left here, but the caves are in a dramatic location. See page 175.
Penjikent. One of the great lost Silk Road cities of Central Asia, beautifully situated in the Zerafshan Valley of northern Tajikistan. See page 265.

Toprak Qala. Spectacular ruins from the Kushan era in the desert of Khorezm, Uzbekistan. See page 296.
Merv. Once the world's largest city, Merv was never to recover from its sacking by Genghis Khan. Its impressive ruins rise from the Darvaza Desert in Turkmenistan. See page 299.
Taxila. One of Asia's great archaeological sites, at a very important crossroads in Pakistan. See page 215.
Persepolis. One of the great cities of antiquity, a capital of the Achaemenid Empire. See page 325.
Nisa. The ruins of the ancient Parthian capital, spectacularly located at the foot of mountains on the outskirts of Ashgabat. See page 301.

Horseback games in Kyrgyzstan.

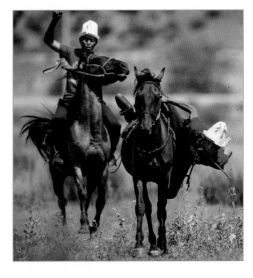

BEST MUSEUMS

Terracotta Warriors, Xi'an. An emperor's personal army – made for the afterlife. One of the great attractions of the Silk Road. See page 142.

Afrosiab Museum, Samarkand. A whole room of Sogdian murals has been recreated here; other rooms contain artefacts from the various periods in Samarkand's early development. See page 282.

Museum of the History of Uzbekistan, Tashkent. Fine exhibits from all the major sites including Buddhist remains. See page 276.

Ulug Beg's Observatory, Samarkand. The underground chamber of the famous astronomer's great sextant can still be seen cut into the rock. See page 283.

National Archaeological Museum, Tehran. Some fascinating exhibits from all eras across the Iranian world. See page 322.

Carpet Museum, Tehran. Some of the finest Persian carpets collected from Iran's weaving centres, demonstrating a variety of designs. See page 322.

Azerbaijan Archaeology Museum, Tabriz. An astonishing wealth of fascinating archaeological exhibits from the region, plus the so-called "Chelsea rewoven carpet" on the upper floor. See page 333.

Karakalpakstan State Museum of Art (Savitsky Art Gallery), Nukus. Remarkable collection of Soviet era avant-garde paintings and historical artefacts. See page 296.

National Museum of History, Ashgabat. Fabulous collection from early pre-Silk Road trading sites and the Parthian capital at Nisa. See page 300.

Silk Museum, near Beirut. Dedicated enthusiasts run this museum and keep the Silk Road dream alive in the modern world. See page 358.

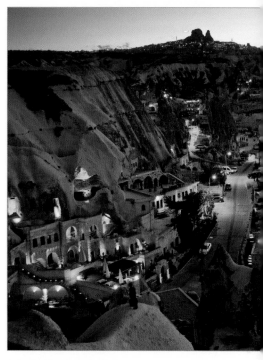

Cave dwellings in Cappadocia.

PLACES TO STAY

Uzbekistan. There are some fine places to stay in both Samarkand and Bukhara, with many hotels occupying traditional houses.

Turkey. Hotels cut into the rock are an unusual feature in Cappadocia.

Kyrgyzstan and Tajikistan. For those willing to rough it a little, homestays offer a viable alternative to hotels, and in some areas may be all that is available.

Yurts. Staying in a yurt is another exciting option, particularly on the jailoos of Kyrgyzstan. See page 232.

SILK ROAD AT A GLANCE

Where and how far?

The Silk Road starts in Xi'an in China and finishes at Antakya on the Turkish Mediterranean coast, or in Istanbul. It covers a distance of more than 8,000km (5,000 miles) and passes through 13 countries, which are (with their capitals):

China (Beijing), Kyrgyzstan (Bishkek), Tajikistan (Dushanbe), Uzbekistan (Tashkent), Kazakhstan (Astana), Paki-stan (Islamabad), Afghanistan (Kabul), Turkmenistan (Ashgabat), Iran (Tehran), Iraq (Baghdad), Syria (Damascus), Lebanon (Beirut) and Turkey (Ankara).

Geographical features

The Silk Road crosses some dramatic landscapes, including some of the world's harshest deserts like the Taklamakan and the Syrian Desert, and mountain ranges such as the Karakoram, Kunlun, Pamir, Hindu Kush and Tian Shan. The main rivers are the Huang He (Yellow River) in China, the Amu Darya (Oxus) and Syr Darya (Jaxartes) in Central Asia, and the Tigris and Euphrates in Iraq and Syria.

Why Silk Road?

Silk was one of its most valuable and important commodities, but the term Seidenstrasse (Silk Road) was only coined in 1877, by German geographer Ferdinand von Richthofen.

A camel caravan makes its way across the sand dunes near Dunhuang, China.

The magnificent tile work at the Tillya Kari Madrassa.

The remains of a caravanserai in Tash Rabat.

ANCIENT TRADE ROUTE

2,000 years ago the Silk Road developed as the world's greatest overland trade route, running from China to the Roman Empire.

Men at Kalon Mosque in Bukhara.

No trading route in the world has as much romance and adventure as the Silk Road, yet for centuries it remained little more than the stuff of dreams. Today, it is more accessible to ordinary travellers than at any time in its history and the "Silk Road" is no longer a purely historical reference to the overland trade route of antiquity. It is now increasingly applied to a re-established network of highways stretching right across Asia, linking East and West via harsh deserts and spectacular mountains, all awaiting the modern adventurous traveller.

Viewed from a Western perspective, these fabled settlements acquire an increased patina of romance the further east they lie: Antioch (modern Antakya), Palmyra, Balkh, Bukhara, Samarkand, Kashgar, Khotan, Dunhuang and countless others en route to Chang'an (modern Xi'an).

The same, semi-mystic quality is attached to the Silk Road when viewed from the East. Chang'an, the ancient Tang Dynasty capital, has long been a familiar name for the Chinese to conjure with, and Jiayuguan, the "Last Pass Under Heaven", traditionally marked the western limits of civilisation. Beyond lay the jade fields of Khotan, the Heavenly Horses of Fergana and – at the very edge of the western world – fabled Daqin, the ancient Chinese name for Rome. In between lay boundless deserts and insurmountable peaks thought to be inhabited by bandits and demons.

Marco Polo statue by the Great Wall.

Today, the restored Silk Road exercises an irresistible appeal on travellers from both East and West, as some sections of the journey become easier and more comfortable each year, whilst others have fallen to insecurity. The desert trip from Kashgar to Urumqi, which in 1940 took 40 days in an unsprung, camel-drawn cart, can now be accomplished in an air-conditioned sleeper bus in under 15 hours. The Chinese are proposing to build a high-speed-train line that would enable modern Silk Road travel from Beijing to Iran and Turkey. Moreover, as visitors bring new wealth, and long suppressed national pride burgeons, many ancient Silk Road sights and cities are being restored to their former glory.

The name "Silk Road" was coined in the 19th century, when explorers and archaeologists began to rediscover long-lost cities. The German geographer Ferdinand von Richthofen was the first to use the word *Seidenstraße*, in 1877. He was describing the overland export of one of the earliest and most valuable commodities carried from China to the Mediterranean – the direction of travel followed in this book.

Silk was not the only costly product to be traded across Asia, but it was unknown in the West and therefore highly prized. For centuries it was the most celebrated and profitable item transported along the caravan trails. Other valuable products, such as lapis lazuli from Afghanistan and jade from China, were traded, but not all the way.

The ancient ruins of Palmyra, as it was.

First produced in China 5,000 years ago, silk was symbolic of the link between continents as visionary rulers and merchants ventured further afield. Extending for around 8,000km (5,000 miles), the Road followed no single route – Central Asia in particular developed several branches – passing through different oasis settlements, depending upon the season and local political situation as much as the terrain. Water supply, earthquakes, desertification, or man-made events such as migration, wars and banditry all combined to make these intrepid merchants seek the safest and easiest course.

The Silk Road flourished throughout the first millennium AD, reaching its prime during the Tang Dynasty (618–907) and again in the 13th century under the Mongols. During the Ming Dynasty (1368–1644), land trade between China, Central Asia and the Middle East withered away, and by the time of the Ottoman and Qing supremacies, the Silk Road was little more than a memory, superseded by direct maritime trade between Europe and Asia and finally the arrival of the railways.

The Silk Road wasn't just a conduit for trade goods. As well as merchants, there were invaders, travellers, missionaries and pilgrims using the road and, crucially, spreading their ideas. The scientific knowledge, inventions, religions and foods that passed along the Silk Road transformed isolated countries into an interdependent global

Istanbul's Hagia Sophia mosque.

community. This made it the first, and perhaps the most important, information superhighway, helping to lay the foundations of the modern world.

Travelling along the Silk Road has never been easy: just as one route was cleared, another obstacle would arise. Today, most of the problems are not physical but ideological, and many people will think twice before travelling through countries such as Afghanistan and Iraq. On the other hand, new border crossings and passes have reconnected Central Asian states to their neighbours. Railway lines (the "Iron Silk Road"), oil pipelines and long-distance tour buses now follow former caravan trails.

The internet has been lauded as a "21st-century Silk Road". As researchers swap ancient documents online, it's clear that the idea of the Silk Road as a metaphor for international exchange is as valid today as it has ever been.

A camel silhouetted at sunrise.

THE INCREDIBLE JOURNEY

The Silk Road crosses some of the world's
most spectacular terrain, whose one-time
perils of deserts and mountains can now
be a delight for modern travellers.

The routes of the ancient Silk Road travel
through more than a dozen countries
between China and the Mediterranean,
crossing some of the most challenging and
inaccessible regions on earth. In classical times,
the arid deserts and freezing mountains were
incredibly hazardous to the long-distance
travellers, who hastened to their journeys'
end, pausing to rest only in the oases that had
grown up along the way. Today, travelling the
modern Silk Road, conditions are infinitely
easier and more pleasant. The same fertile and
hospitable oases remain, but the route between
them is so greatly improved that the traveller is
free to marvel at the natural beauty of endless,
shifting sand dunes and serried, snow-capped
mountains without fear of death through
starvation, thirst, frostbite or attack by bandits
(though modern hazards, notably motor
accidents, may still pose a threat).

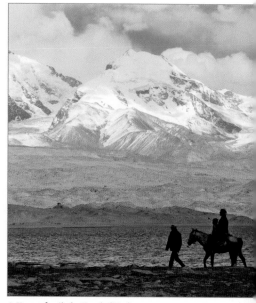

A Kyrgyz family by Karakuli Lake.

> It took 20 days to travel the first stretch of
> the journey from Xi'an to Lanzhou by pony,
> which until the 1930s was the only way to go.
> Today, by coach or train, it takes eight hours.

The highway from Xi'an

The Silk Road starts life in the great city of
Xi'an, formerly Chang'an, a modern metropolis,
capital of China's Shaanxi Province, and home
of the extraordinary Terracotta Army. From
here, National Highway 312 and the railway
trace the old route west to Lanzhou, capital of
Gansu province and the largest city in northwest China. Lying in a gorge, hemmed in by
steep mountains, its strategic location has long
made it an important garrison town. Surging

through its centre is the Huang He, coloured a
rich chocolate by the huge quantities of loess it
carries downstream.

Beyond Lanzhou the route continues through
the long, narrow Hexi Corridor in some of
the most dramatic terrain in all of China.
Extending for about 1,000km (620 miles) to
Yumen near the frontiers of Xinjiang, China's
westernmost province, this unwelcoming
landscape is punctuated by fertile oases that
form the basis for such old Silk Road towns
as Wuwei, Zhangye and Jiuquan. To the north
stretch the barren wastes of the Gobi desert,
and to the south the permanently snow-covered
peaks of the Qilian Mountains. They mark the
northern rim of the great Tibetan plateau,

product of the cataclysmic collision between India and Asia some 200 million years ago – a process that continues today, as the Indian plate presses into the Asian land mass at the rate of about 20mm (0.8in) every year.

The limits of China "proper"

Following the Old Silk Road, National Highway 312 is paralleled by the Lanxin Railway, and now carves its way west between these deserts and mountains, through a region that for centuries was seen by the Chinese as the limits of civilisation. Beyond Jiayuguan was alien territory,

the home of wandering desert ghosts and fierce nomads, a land bitterly cold in winter and intolerably hot in summer, where a lack of water meant only a few hardy plants such as the desert

> *"There are among them venomous dragons, which spit forth poisonous winds, and cause showers of snow and storms of sand and gravel. Not one in 10,000 of those who meet these dangers escapes with his life." Faxian (5th-century Buddhist) on the Pamirs*

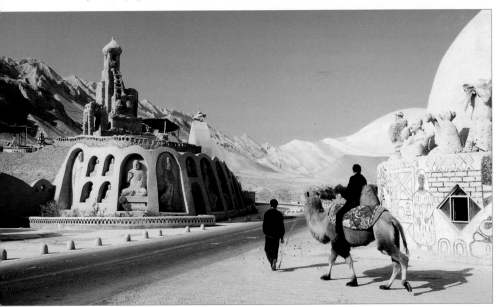

Seeing the sights on camelback at Bezeklik Thousand Buddha Caves in China.

THE TAKLAMAKAN

Of all the obstacles to progress along the Silk Road, the most fearsome was the Taklamakan desert. Its very name, *Takla makan*, means: "Go in and you will never come out". At 1,000km (620 miles) long and 400km (250 miles) wide, covering 270,000 sq km (105,000 sq miles), it is one of the world's largest sandy deserts.

The Taklamakan was a serious hindrance during the height of the Silk Road and it remains a perilous wilderness. The great Swedish explorer Sven Hedin (1865–1952) was nearly one of its victims when he spent two desperate weeks trudging through the sand only to realise he had been going round in circles. He was reduced to drinking camel urine and

only had the energy to crawl on all fours towards the forested edge of the desert. Two human companions and all but one camel died.

Winter temperatures can plunge to −20°C (−4°F). In 2008, snow was recorded right across the desert, reaching a depth of around 4 centimetres (1.6 in). With howling winds and desert ghosts, it is almost completely waterless, and comparable in terms of both harshness and beauty to Arabia's Rub' al-Khali or "Empty Quarter". Utterly uninhabited, the centre of the Taklamakan is filled with huge, shifting dunes, and it was only recently penetrated by two cross-desert highways built by the Chinese in their search for oil.

tamarisk and sagebrush could survive. Journeying along any section of the Silk Road was an epic undertaking: merchants spent months or even years waiting for the season to change or a war to end. Men couldn't travel faster than their feet, horse or camel could carry them, and steppe and mountains slowed their progress, forcing them to find navigable passes, food and watering holes.The oasis of Dunhuang, in Gansu Province, is the site of some of the greatest Silk Road discoveries. It marks the limits of China "proper" and the start of Central Asia, and is also where the route presents its first major division, offering three ways forward.

Highway 312 takes the Northern route, signposted with the ancient beacon tower at Yumenguan and heading for the oasis of Hami. The old Central Route goes via Loulan and a howling wilderness, the Desert of Lop, vividly described by Marco Polo. This route was abandoned more than 1,500 years ago and until 1996 China tested its nuclear bombs here. The third, Southern Silk Road heads southwest from the crumbling beacon tower of Yangguan, across the arid wastes of the Kum Tagh "Sand Mountains", home to China's only wild camel reserve.

The Chinese authorities are rapidly changing the ethnic map of their great western province of Xinjiang, the "New Frontier", allowing Han Chinese migrants to stream into the province where they now dominate Urumqi and the Dzungarian Basin in the north. But in the south, Uighur Turks and other related Turkic peoples are still predominant in many of the oasis towns that are strung like green jewels around the northern and southern rims of the Tarim Basin. On foot or by camel, the journey from Urumqi to Kashgar used to take about three months through the deserts of northwestern China. Men and camels died of thirst, lost among the dunes. When the railway arrived in the 1960s: the journey time fell to 24 hours. Today the flight time is 45 minutes. This is impressive country, centred on China's largest desert, the incomparable Taklamakan (see box).

Over the roof of the world

The Northern and Southern Silk Roads reunite at the old caravan city of Kashgar before climbing into the once-impenetrable Pamir Knot and leaving China via three routes. For centuries this transitional region marked the point where Chinese influence ended and the Silk Road passed

into western Central Asia. The most dramatic of these routes is the Karakoram Highway, a Chinese-built metalled road leading south and over the Khunjerab Pass (4,693 metres/15,397ft) to Pakistan. This is the highest paved international road in the world, and it descends through the awe-inspiring scenery of the Hunza Valley and within reach of Baltistan, home to five peaks in excess of 8,000 metres (26,000ft), including the world's second-highest peak, K2, and some of the world's longest glaciers.

Two other roads head north and west from Kashgar, going via the Irkeshtam and Torugart

A snowy section of Karakoram Highway in Xinjiang, China.

Passes respectively, to neighbouring Kyrgyzstan. At 3,752 metres (12,310ft), the Torugart Pass through the Tian Shan is lower than the Khunjerab, but the road is narrow and difficult, often being blocked by heavy snow and avalanches. The easiest pass is the Irkeshtam, rising to 2,841 metres (9,321ft) before descending, via a narrow mountain valley, to the Kyrgyz city of Osh and the fertile Fergana Valley, most of which lies today within Uzbekistan. This is the heart of the Central Asian region known in antiquity as Transoxiana – the region beyond the Oxus River. In fact the region is watered by two great rivers, the Oxus and the Jaxartes, which the Uzbeks call the Amu Darya and Syr Darya. To the north lies the endless steppe of Kazakhstan, and to the south the jagged peaks of Afghanistan's Hindu Kush mountains, crossed by the army of Alexander the Great in 326 BC.

In classical times a branch of the Silk Road passed south of the Oxus, through the sandy

> *Balkh in northern Afghanistan is one of the oldest Silk Road cities and is considered to be the first settlement to which the Indo-Aryan tribes moved from north of the Oxus River between 3,500 and 4,000 years ago.*

From Tashkent the main branch of the Silk Road continued southwest, passing through the narrow defile called the "Iron Gates" in the Buzgala Gorge and on to the fabled Silk Road cities of Samarkand and Bukhara. Beyond Bukhara the old Silk Road left the banks of the Zerafshan River, crossing the Oxus near Chardzhou – now the city of Turkmenabat in Turkmenistan – and continuing over the black sands of the Karakum Desert to the old oasis city of Merv on the desert's southern edge. The Arab historian al-Muqaddasi, writing in the 10th century, described Merv as "delightful,

Sunset over Bukhara's Kalon Mosque and Minaret.

wastes of northern Afghanistan, past the fabled city of Balkh – now little more than ruins – and Mazar-e-Sharif, the principal city of northern Afghanistan, before turning south to Herat and on to the great northeast Iranian city of Mashhad. There was another route to the north, via the Dzungarian Gate between northern Xinjiang and Kazakhstan, that avoided the Pamirs, but at the cost of travelling far to the north through territory controlled by fierce nomads.

So the main route continued west from Osh, through the settled Fergana Valley and the cities of Andijan and Kokand, to the former Sogdian centre of Chach – today the largely concrete city of Tashkent, the capital of Uzbekistan and the largest city in Central Asia.

fine, elegant, brilliant, extensive, and pleasant", but only the evocative ruins of the ancient city remain today.

Persia and the Arab heartlands

Merv was where the southern spur of the Silk Road running through Balkh rejoined the main route. Beyond it, the route led southwest across the modern Turkmenistan-Iran frontier to the ancient Persian city of Mashhad, a holy city of the utmost importance to Shia Muslims and distinguished by some of the finest Islamic architecture in Iran.

West of Mashhad the Silk Road continued across the semi-desert plains of Khorasan and northern Iran before traversing the foothills of the Elburz Mountains, dominated by the snow-capped cone of 5,671-metre (18,605-ft) Mount Damavand. From here it passed through the old Zoroastrian centre of Rey, a city long since surpassed by nearby Tehran, though the latter was not insignificant when the Silk Road was in its prime. To the south, en route to the Persian Gulf, lay the wealthy cities of Shiraz and Isfahan.

Next came the wild Zagros Mountains, the last serious upland barrier before the Mediterranean Sea. The road passed through Hamadan, a city dating back to 3000 BC that was formerly

> "One is not alarmed by robbers, but…by fierce tigers and lions who will attack passengers, and unless these be travelling in caravans of a hundred men or more…they may be devoured." Hou Han Shu (5th century Chinese chronicle)

the capital of the Achaemenids (559–330 BC) and, during the Silk Road's greatest period of prosperity, the summer capital of the Sassanids (AD 226–651). The surrounding mountains are home to Iran's Bakhtiari tribe, many of whom are still pastoral nomads.

After leaving the Zagros, the road descended to the plains of Mesopotamia, passing through Ctesiphon and – after its foundation by the Abbasid Caliph al-Mansur in 761 – Baghdad, the modern capital of Iraq and second-largest city in the Arab world after Cairo. The route then led northwest, between the Tigris and Euphrates rivers, to Dura Europos and the eastern frontiers of Syria. Today much of this territory is desert, but in the Silk Road heyday it was forested, and we know from Arab and even Chinese accounts that it supported large numbers of wild animals, including lions.

The next major population centre was the Graeco-Roman caravan city of Palmyra, sometimes called the "Queen of the Desert". Here the road split, the southern branch leading to the capital, Damascus, while the main, northern branch led through the age-old mart of Aleppo, a trading centre from 5000 BC, remarkable for its Old City, Citadel and souks until the terrible destruction wrought by the conflict of recent years.

As it neared the Mediterranean, the Silk Road branched out, like the delta of a river, from the Levant to Anatolia. One of the main end points was Antioch, today's Antakya, a somnolent Turkish port – still claimed by Syria – that was the capital of the Seleucid Empire in the 4th century BC. Across the Anatolian plains, the Seljuks secured trade by building a series of *hans* (caravanserais). Here the Silk Road largely followed the ancient Persian Royal Road before reaching its ultimate destination, the great city of Constantinople.

The distinctive landscape of Cappadocia in Turkey.

ARCHITECTURAL GEMS

The Chinese Silk Road offers awesome natural beauty, but rather less in the way of classical architecture. The ancient cities of the Tarim Basin are largely in ruins, and while Kashgar is justly proud of its great Id Gah Mosque it cannot compare with the architectural gems of Samarkand – the Registan, Bibi Khanum, Gur-i-Mir and Shah-i-Zindah – or Bukhara (with its Poi Kolon complex, Ark citadel and Samanid Mausoleum), or indeed the cities of Iran like Isfahan. In the ruins stakes, Iran also has Persepolis, while further to the west the great city of Palmyra in the Syrian desert was one of the greatest sights of the Silk Road.

Talk of the Road

In the bazaars and on the road, dozens of languages would be heard, but some were more dominant than others.

The Silk Road provided a cultural and commercial link between half of mankind, joining East and West and providing a constantly moving pathway for goods and ideas, peoples and entertainment.

An Iranian man reading the Koran.

Between Chang'an and the Mediterranean it passed through many diverse peoples and lands, which today include at least 13 countries, each with its own official language. How did people communicate with each other? Was there a universal *lingua franca*? Or did traders and cameleers employ interpreters, or resort to sign language?

The answer is, almost certainly, a bit of all three. Clearly merchants and caravaneers would have employed both sign language and the use of an interpreter, whenever and wherever it was necessary. And while there was no universal language employed between the Mediterranean and the Yellow River Valley (in the way that English is often used today), certain languages were more useful and more widely spoken than others.

Today, as in antiquity, China is the most unchanging political entity along the route of the Silk Road, and Chinese – generally the *putonghua* or "common speech" of Beijing and North China known as Mandarin in the West, as well as Xi'an and Gansu dialects – must have been, as they still are, the *lingua franca* of the Eastern Silk Road from Chang'an to Kashgar. Other languages spoken along the easternmost stretch of the Silk Road include Mongol and Tibetan, neither of which would have been much use to the west of the Pamirs, with the possible exception of Mongol during the Yuan Dynasty.

Turkic languages

Yet, even as far to the east as the Hexi Corridor in Gansu, Chinese was soon to be challenged by a second major world language group – Turko-Altaic. The Turkic linguistic group constitutes at least 30 related languages spoken across Asia, from the Salar population of southeast Gansu in the east, to the Anatolian Turkish of Turkey, parts of Bulgaria and parts of Bosnia Herzegovina in the west. These languages are different and yet cognate, and with a little bit of Turkish acquired in Istanbul or Ankara, it is possible to gain some understanding of simple conversations in, for example, Kashgar or Urumqi.

Next, to the west of the Pamirs, in Tajikistan, Iran, north and west Afghanistan, and the predominantly Tajik-inhabited Uzbekistan cities of Samarkand and Bukhara, Farsi, Tajik or other dialects of Persian are widely spoken and have had a major impact on Urdu and related languages of South Asia. In times past, when the Silk Road was at its peak, Chinese, Turkish and Persian must all have served as common means of communication between people in Chang'an and the frontiers of Iraq.

Further to the west, in antiquity at least, Greek and later Latin were the *common tongues* of the Mediterranean world and the Levant. During the time of Alexander the Great, and under the Graeco-Bactrian Kingdoms in south and central Asia, no doubt Greek functioned as a language of trade – with Greek letters used on coinage minted in Bactria and other distant outposts of the Greek world.

Yet Greek and Latin were, after the 7th century AD, abruptly replaced by a fourth, quite different linguistic group to add to Chinese, Turkish and Persian. This was Arabic, a Semitic tongue related to Hebrew and Syriac, which had long been spoken as a language of commerce throughout historic Jordan, Syria and Iraq, but which burst forth from the Arabian Peninsula in 622 following the revelation of Islam. Most significantly, the immutable Word of

God as revealed in the *Koran* was recited to Muhammad, according to Islamic belief, by the Archangel Jibril (Gabriel) in Arabic.

Arab influence

Within the short space of a hundred years, Arabic had become the dominant language of a huge swathe of territory extending from southern Spain and Morocco in the west to Iraq and the frontiers of Iran in the east. Most importantly, it was not just a language of trade, but also a language of religion. Although the Hanbali school of Sunni Islam, which predominates in the Turkic and Chinese Muslim

and Arabic – may be added a plethora of less widely spoken languages. Some of these, such as Sogdian, Tokharian and Syriac, have all but disappeared. Others, such as Burushaski, spoken by about 90,000 people in the Hunza Valley in Pakistan, are "language isolates", not readily linked with any of the major world linguistic families such as Indo-European, Semitic or Sino-Tibetan. Although clearly never important in the multinational trade of the Silk Road, Burushaski and other little-spoken tongues – Monguor in Qinghai and Gansu, Nuristani in northeast Afghanistan, Circassian in the Caucasus and Aramaic in Syria – are indicative of

A Turkmenistan family.

worlds, permits the translation of Arabic texts, including *Koran* and *Hadith*, into languages other than Arabic, Arabic remains the chief identifying mark of the *umma* or universal Muslim brotherhood – the language of prayer and, to a considerable degree, of religious education. As such, it spread far to the east of the Arab-speaking lands, to Central Asia, China and even as far as distant Chang'an. At the same time it was spreading by sea, through maritime trade, to India, Southeast Asia and southern China, most notably in Guangzhou. By 800 AD, Arabic was probably the most universally established language along the entire Silk Road, from Antakya all the way to Chang'an.

To the main "indigenous" languages of the Silk Road – Chinese, Mongol, Tibetan, Turkic, Persian

the vast ethno-linguistic and cultural territory spanned by the Silk Road.

Finally, mention should be made of more recent additions to the languages of the Silk Road – tongues which would have been little heard, or not at all, when the traditional Silk Road was at its peak, but which now serve as useful international languages the length of the route. Both are Indo-European, and both the result of European imperialism. The first of these is Russian, which now serves as a *lingua franca* in all the former Soviet Central Asian republics. The second is English, which has already become the single most indispensable language of the entire modern Silk Road, as likely to be understood in the Muslim quarter of downtown Xi'an as in the antique souks of Western Asia.

DECISIVE DATES

4000–3500 BC
Rise of civilisations in Mesopotamia and Egypt. First civilisations appear in the West.

3000–2500 BC
Early Chinese civilisation established on the Huang He (Yellow River); major urban developments in the Indus Valley.

3rd millennium BC
Lapis lazuli and rubies exported from Badakhshan west to Mesopotamia and Egypt. Sericulture is first developed in the Huang He valley.

2nd millennium BC
Phoenicians export cedar wood, gold jewellery, linen and purple Tyrian dye. Jade from Khotan is carried eastward to China.

Relief detail of Xerxes fighting a winged beast, Persepolis.

1st millennium BC
Coastal shipping routes develop between China, Southeast Asia and southern India. Improvement in overland trade routes.

7th century BC
The Medes establish an empire extending from Persia to modern-day Afghanistan, adopting the religion of Zoroaster.

c.550 BC
Persian Achaemenid Empire established by Cyrus the Great, who rule over a vast region extending from the Hellespont (Dardanelles) to the Indus.

521–486 BC
Cyrus is succeeded by his son-in-law, Darius the Great, who extends the empire to the Black Sea and orders the construction of the Persian Royal Road.

333 BC
Alexander the Great defeats the Persians at the Battle of Issus, forcing Darius III to flee eastwards. Alexander extends Greek power to the Pamirs.

241–210 BC
Qin Shi Huang, the First Emperor, unifies China and extends control south to the Pearl River Delta.

206 BC–AD 220
Qin Shi Huang's successor, Liu Bang, founds the illustrious Han Dynasty with its capital at Chang'an (modern Xi'an).

138 BC
Emperor Wu Di dispatches Zhang Qian west towards Central Asia. He returns over

Portait of a Terracotta Warrior, Xi'an, China.

13 years later, having made the first recorded crossing of the Pamir-Tian Shan ranges.

119 BC
Zhang Qian leads a second, successful expedition to the west, establishing diplomatic relations with Ferghana, Bactria and Sogdiana.

83 BC
The Romans occupy Antioch, which becomes the capital of the newly formed Roman province of Syria, the third most important imperial city after Rome and Alexandria.

53 BC
The Romans are defeated by the Iranian Parthians at the Battle of Carrhae. Possibly the first time the Romans saw silk – in the banners brandished by the victors.

Turn of 1st century
The Italian explorer Maës Titianus leads a party of merchants as far east as Tashkurgan in the Pamirs.

1st–3rd centuries AD

Silk Road trade is dominated by the Kushans, whose empire extends across Afghanistan, Uzbekistan and Tajikistan and into northern India. Buddhist monasteries are established in the Gandhara region.

97

Ban Chao leads an army of 70,000 across the Pamirs and the Tian Shan to protect the Silk Road against the fierce Xiongnu tribe.

220

The fall of the Han Dynasty allows China's old enemy, the Xiongnu, to start a war.

274

Queen Zenobia claims Egypt for Palmyra before being defeated by the Emperor Aurelian and dragged off to Rome in golden chains.

476

The fall of Rome to the Germanic tribes leads to the ascendancy of Constantinople, or Byzantium, capital of the Eastern Roman Empire.

A Roman mosaic showing a camel train.

552

Byzantine Emperor Justinian obtains silkworm eggs, smuggled to Constantinople across Persia by two monks. Silk gradually becomes a local Byzantine product.

618–907

The Tang Dynasty re-establishes full imperial control over the Eastern Silk Road.

c.610

Muhammad receives his first revelation from God, and begins teaching a strict monotheism aimed at driving idolatry from Arabia. This is the birth of Islam.

661–750

Under the Umayyad Caliphate, the Islamic Empire extends to Spain in the west and to the banks of the Indus in the east.

750–1258

Arab civilisation attains its classical Golden Age under the Baghdad-based Abbasid Dynasty, especially during the reign of the illustrious Harun al-Rashid.

751

At the Battle of Talas in modern-day Kyrgyzstan, the Arab forces of Ziyad ibn-Salih vanquish the Chinese forces of Gao Xianzhi, securing effective control over western Central Asia.

c.820

The Persian Samanids sever any direct Silk Road link between Tang China and the Abbasids. Samanid authority extends over Bukhara and Samarkand.

c.840

The Uighur are driven south by Kyrgyz raiders, and move into the Tarim Basin, settling in Kuqa and Aksu before spreading around the rim of the Taklamakan Desert.

907–960

As Tang power declines, outside interference in Silk Road traffic increases. The dynasty finally collapses and an era of disunity follows known as the "Five Dynasties and ten Kingdoms".

960

Rule of the Song Dynasty, the first government in the world to issue paper currency.

999–1211

The Karakhanid Turks take over the Tarim Basin. Islam gradually spreads across the region and into Gansu.

977–1186

The Samanids are replaced by the Turkish Ghaznavids, descendants of Turkic slave guards to the Samanids. The

Carved Palmyrene funerary head.

Ghaznavids control most of Persia, all of Afghanistan and Transoxiana.

11th century
Renegade Shia Muslims – the Assassins – disrupt trade along the Silk Road. Led by their fanatical leader Hassan-i Sabbah, they establish fortified settlements in Iran, Iraq, Syria and Lebanon.

800–1200
Communication between Tang China and the West withers. Trade on the Silk Road is disrupted by political uncertainties.

1206–27
Mongol expansion under the rule of Genghis Khan.

1258
Baghdad falls to the Mongols under Hulagu Khan, marking the end of the Abbasid Dynasty.

1271
Marco Polo sets out on his journey to China together with his father and uncle, and spends 17 years in the service of the Great Khan.

1272
Kublai Khan founds Beijing.

14th century
The disintegration of the Mongol Empire brings about the collapse of Silk Road prosperity as the political and cultural stability of *Pax Mongolica* disappears.

1336–1405
Reign of Timur (known in the West as Tamerlane), the

Han Chinese script.

Turkic-Mongol conqueror and founder of the Timurid Dynasty.

1299–1922
The Ottoman Empire is the centre of interactions between the Eastern and Western worlds for more than six centuries.

KEY PLAYERS

Abbasids second Muslim caliphate, based in Baghdad, AD 750–1000.
Achaemenids first Persian empire, created by Cyrus the Great.
Assassins murderous cult of Shia Muslims, 11th–13th century.
Assyrians ethnic group originating in Iraq, Iran, Turkey and Syria.
Byzantines successors to the Romans, based in Constantinople.
Han Chinese dynasty, 202 BC–AD 220.
Huns confederation of Central Asian nomads, 2nd–5th centuries AD.
Kushans ruled over Central Asia c. AD 100–250.

Mongols ruled the world's largest contiguous empire in 13th century.
Ottomans rulers of a Turkish empire, 1299–1922.
Parthians Iranian civilisation and empire, 247BC–AD224.
Phoenicians ancient maritime civilisation based in what is now Lebanon.
Romans the first Western customers for Chinese silk.
Samanids Persian dynasty of Central Asia, AD 819–999.
Sassanids Persian empire which succeeded the Parthians.
Scythians nomadic, highly cultured

people from the Central Asian steppe.
Seleucids Hellenistic successors to Alexander the Great.
Seljuks Turkish empire that united the eastern Islamic world, 1037–1194.
Sogdians people of Iranian stock who dominated trade in Central Asia.
Song Chinese dynasty, 960–1279.
Tang Chinese dynasty, 618–907.
Umayyads first Muslim caliphate, based in Damascus, 660–750.
Xiongnu feared nomads kept at bay by the Great Wall of China.

1368–1644
China's Ming Dynasty pursues isolationist policies.

15th–16th centuries
New maritime trade routes diminish the importance of the Silk Road. Christopher Columbus' discovery of the New World, Vasco da Gama's forging of the sea route around the Cape of Good Hope and Ferdinand Magellan's successful voyage to the Philippines revolutionise global trade.

19th century
Opium wars are fought along the Chinese coast, officially in support of free trade. Tea planted in India breaks China's monopoly. Central Asian states fall under the influence of Tsarist Russia as the Russian Empire expands south. Rivalry for the frontier lands between the Russian and British Empires is played out by spies, explorers and soldiers in the Great Game.

1900–79
Ottoman Empire collapses. Vast areas of Central Asia are swallowed up in the expanding but isolationist Soviet Empire. China turns Communist under the leadership of Chairman Mao. In 1979 the Soviets invade Afghanistan and the Shah of Iran is overthrown by Ayatollah Khomeini.

1979–91
Wars in Afghanistan and Lebanon paralyse both countries. Soviet Union tests hundreds of nuclear weapons in Semipalatinsk, Kazakhstan. In 1991 the Soviet Union collapses, causing political and economic instability for the newly independent Central Asian Republics.

1990s
A booming Chinese economy and the development of oil and gas resources in Central Asia and the Caucasus revitalise the Silk Road, with new roads, pipelines and rail links.

2000s
US-led invasions of Iraq and Afghanistan limit access for foreign tourists, as do revolutions in Kyrgyzstan (2005 and 2010) and civil unrest in Pakistan.

2011–2015
Civil war in Syria and Iraq and the rise of Daesh destabilise the Western Asia region. There is violence in Tajikistan during 2015.

2016–present
Palmyra is freed from Daesh control by Syrian regime troops but retaken in December 2016. Offensives bring the liberation of Mosul and Aleppo

Monument to Timur in Shahrisabz, Uzbekistan.

from Daesh ever-closer by the end of 2016, but at great civilian cost. In July 2016 an attempted military coup in Turkey fails. Lebanese parliamentary elections and Iranian presidential elections are scheduled for May 2017.

Exquisite tilework at the Sheikh Lotfollah Mosque in Isfahan.

A stone relief at Persepolis in Iran showing offerings being brought to Darius.

THE FIRST STEPS

As trade followed conquests, interconnecting routes began opening up, especially for such highly prized imperishables as lapis lazuli and jade.

t is impossible to state with any certainty when long-distance trade began, or indeed precisely where civilisations arose at each end of the Silk Road, but the west appears to have developed more significantly than the east, with both Damascus and Aleppo in Syria having substantial claims to be the oldest continually inhabited city on earth. They lie in the Fertile Crescent, an arc that stretches from the Persian Gulf to the Mediterranean, encompassing Mesopotamia and Egypt and producing the first civilisations in the west, from 4000 to 3500 BC, while those in the Indus Valley and China came later, between 3000 and 2500 BC.

Agricultural communities had already been active for several thousand years – the earliest granary yet discovered was built in the Jordan Valley around 9500 BC, and the granary at Mehrgarh just to the west of the Indus Valley in present-day Pakistan dates from 7500 BC. There was undoubtedly some limited bartering and communication between these Neolithic communities, who knew about weaving. But the later centres of civilisation had greater material needs, which meant trade links had to be established by land and sea. The former required domesticated, efficient pack animals, and none were better suited for crossing the deserts and vast steppes of Inner Asia than the horse and the camel, which became keys to the development of international relations and trade. High quality horses, necessary for both the military and for general transport, were in particularly short supply in China, and the need to ensure regular deliveries from Central Asia led to the formation of the Tea and Horse Commission in the 10th century AD, a government monopoly that ensured the Chinese state first pick of all horses entering China.

Stone Age granary from the Middle East.

The Silk Road was never static. Whilst policies such as the Pax Mongolica and infrastructure projects such as Darius' Royal Road brought certain routes to prominence, other roads fell out of use for protracted periods due to regional warfare, natural disasters, banditry and high taxation. Changing tastes, technologies and the availability of certain goods also dictated which cities flourished, while merchants, manufacturers and caravans turned their attention to places most likely to generate a profit.

Men of vision

Unlike local market trade, distant trade involved merchants and middlemen – entrepreneurs of vision, prepared to risk losses and endure delays in the hope of making a substantial return on their investment. Such speculative enterprises were dangerous, and goods carried ideally had to be small, light and as easily preserved as possible. In the 3rd millennium BC, for instance, caravans carried scarce lapis lazuli and rubies from the mines of Badakhshan west to Mesopotamia and Egypt; later precious jade from the rivers of Khotan was carried eastwards to China. Other goods included spices and perfumes, gold and silver ornaments, instruments in copper and bronze and, last but not least, luxury goods as gold jewellery, glass, linen and purple Tyrian dye.

During the 1st millennium BC, coastal shipping routes also developed between China, Southeast Asia and southern India. Within a hundred years it is likely that a system of coastal commerce connected, however indirectly, the Mediterranean world with that of the Far East, but direct voyages, made possible by the seasonal monsoon winds, were not widespread for at least another three centuries. Graeco-Roman trade goods may have reached the Far East, and Chinese trade goods have been found in the

Phoenician traders around 600 BC.

rich textiles, the most valuable of which was silk – bringing with it strange rumours of the worm that spins silken threads.

Coastal links

As well as overland trade, maritime trade also fostered links across the continents. In the west, the sophisticated civilisation of Mesopotamia had developed coastal shipping, and formed a link in a maritime chain connecting Egypt and the Mediterranean with the Indus Valley civilisation and South Asia. In the 2nd millennium BC the Phoenicians (from present-day Lebanon) dominated the Mediterranean; their merchants exported cedar wood for ship and house-building, as well as such

> *The first major trade routes followed the great rivers that formed the agricultural bases for the earliest civilisations, on the Nile, the Tigris and Euphrates, the Indus and Huang He or Yellow River.*

Mediterranean, but quantities were small, and the two centres of world civilisation knew little of each other.

The overland and maritime routes were not, however, separate entities. Cities such as Venice, Istanbul and Alexandria were meeting points for both types of traders. It was not until the discovery of the sea route around the Cape of

Good Hope by Vasco da Gama in the 1490s and, later, the opening of the Suez Canal in 1869, that journeys from Europe to the Far East could be made entirely by sea.

The discovery of silk

With only these tentative links, China developed in virtual isolation from the rest of the world. The fertile valley of the Huang He (Yellow River) was the heartland of Chinese civilisation, and it was here, in the 3rd millennium BC, that the cultivation of silk, known as sericulture, first developed. Empress Xi Lingshi,

> All the ultramarine paint in both Western and Eastern art came from the lapis lazuli mines of Sar-e-Sang, Afghanistan. The blue mineral has been prized and traded for more than 6,000 years.

wife of the Yellow Emperor Qin Shi Huang (2697–2598 BC, see box) is traditionally seen as the person who first turned the fibrous excretions of a caterpillar into a prized material.

Although initially reserved for Chinese royalty, some silk made its way west. The grave of a Celtic chieftain dating from about 500 BC, at Hochdorf near Stuttgart, Germany, was found to contain silk garments – this is some 300 years before the "official" start of the Silk Road, at the end of the 2nd century BC when Roman and Chinese traders made contact. Traces of silk of probable Chinese origin have also been found in the hair of an Egyptian mummy dating from 1000 BC.

Throughout the 1st millennium BC trade routes and communications by land continued to improve. Along the Euphrates River, ancient cities such as Ur and Uruk (also known as Akkad) had been developed by the Sumerians. Sumer was to be followed by the rise of the Assyrian cities of the Tigris and Euphrates rivers, in particular the prosperous city of Babylon, where the "Hanging Gardens" became one of the Seven Wonders of the Ancient World.

In the 7th century BC the Medes from the east of Iran made incursions into the region to establish the first Persian Empire and introduce new levels of horsemanship and horse-breeding. By 550 BC the region came under Cyrus the Great, whose Persian

Achaemenid Empire was the largest so far seen, stretching from the Hellespont to the Indus. Zoroastrianism, the world's first monotheistic religion, was established. It spread quickly along the early trade routes and was ultimately to have a massive influence on the development of Judaism, Christianity and Islam.

The Persian Royal Road

Cyrus was succeeded by his son-in-law, Darius the Great (521–486 BC), who extended the Persian Empire to the Black Sea and the Caucasus, venturing beyond the Oxus River.

The Yellow Emperor, Qin Shi Huang.

TYRIAN PURPLE

Tyrian Purple, also known as Imperial Purple, is a dye that was first produced by Phoenician craftsmen in the Lebanese city of Tyre. It occurs naturally in *Bolinus brandaris* sea snails found in the Mediterranean. The dye was highly prized by the Romans, who used it to colour ceremonial clothing. Only emperors wore the full purple robe, while senators had a strip of purple on their white togas. Pliny the Elder noted: "The Tyrian hue is considered of the best quality when it has exactly the colour of clotted blood, and is of a blackish hue to the sight, but of a shining appearance when held up to the light."

In order to administer this region more effectively, subdue revolt and actively promote trade, Darius ordered the construction of the Persian Royal Road, which ran for almost 3,000km (1,900 miles) from the Persian capitals at Susa (in southwestern Iran) and Persepolis to the Lydian capital, Sardes, close to the eastern shores of the Aegean Sea. It also connected with other important trade routes into North Africa, Arabia and eastwards to both India and Central Asia. The Royal Road built by Darius was of such quality that it became a core section of the future Silk Road in the west, and was still in use in Roman

"There is nothing in this world that travels more swiftly than the Persian couriers... Neither snow nor rain, nor heat nor darkness of night prevents them from accomplishing the task appointed to them with the uttermost speed." Herodotus

times. Darius also revolutionised the Persian economy: he followed the Lydian tradition of minting coins with his own system of gold and silver coinage. Trade was encouraged and routes

A gold Daric coin from the late 5th century BC, showing King Darius I.

THE LADY OF THE SILKWORMS

Once upon a time, Empress Xi Lingshi, chief wife of the Yellow Emperor Qin Shi Huang, observed the effect of hot liquid on a cocoon that accidentally dropped from a mulberry tree into her cup of tea. She deduced it would be possible to reel silk in a long, smooth unbroken filament. She is revered as the Lady of the Silkworms, and to this day, cocoons of *Bombyx mori* are immersed in hot water, a process that allows reeling. Sometimes she is also credited with inventing the loom, as one of a pantheon of deities connected with sericulture and silkworking, requiring propitiation and sacrifices to ensure good harvests.

were improved, linking this overland route with the parallel sea trade, connecting to the Persian Gulf and Euphrates and Tigris rivers.

Alexander the Great

The Greek states were united in the mid-4th century BC by Philip II of Macedon, but it was his son, Alexander the Great (336–323 BC), who conceived the ambitious idea of conquering all "the known world". For Alexander, a visionary and military genius, this meant, first and foremost, war with the Persian Empire. Soon after the death of his father, he gathered his loyal troops and crossed into Asia at the head of a 42,000-strong army that was to prove unstoppable. In 333 BC he defeated the main Persian army at the Battle of Issus, forcing Emperor Darius III to flee eastwards, abandoning his wife, mother and two daughters, as well as substantial treasure. He next drove south, capturing the Holy Land and seizing Egypt, before turning east against Mesopotamia. Here he again defeated Darius III, at the Battle of Guagamela in 331 BC, and captured the ancient city of Babylon. Next, following the Royal Road built by Darius I, he crossed the Zagros Mountains and captured the Persian royal capital at Persepolis.

Declaring his war against the Persian Empire over, Alexander adopted various conquering Bactria, Sogdiana and all of present-day Afghanistan.

At the height of his advances into Central Asia, Alexander seized control of the Fergana Valley in present-day Uzbekistan, in the foothills of the Tian Shan. Within just five years Alexander had crushed the Persian Empire and extended Greek power all the way east to the Pamirs and to the very edge of the frontiers of China.

Alexander's ambitions were boundless, and having married Princess Roxana of Balkh to cement his control over his newly conquered Central Asian Empire, he turned his attention

Alexander the Great riding into battle at Issus (333 BC).

Persian customs. As well as marrying into the former Persian royal family, he encouraged his Greek followers similarly to take Persian wives to ensure the unity of the two peoples. Meanwhile, he began a new campaign against Bessus of Bactria, advancing as far into Central Asia as the western flanks of the Pamir Massif,

About 70 cities and settlements were founded by Alexander. These include Alexandria in Egypt, Kandahar in Afghanistan, Alexandria on the Oxus, and Alexandria Eschate – "the furthest" – corresponding to Khojand in modern-day Tajikistan.

SYMBOLIC LANDMARK

Carved into the spectacular rock outcrop at Bisotun in western Iran, around which traders and invaders have had to pass for thousands of years, there is a life-sized bas-relief of Darius, attended by two servants, with his left foot on the chest of his opponent, the prostrate Gaumata. To the right stand ten 1-metre-high figures, with hands tied and rope around their necks, representing conquered peoples. The winged symbol of the Zoroastrian God, Ahura-Mazda, hovers above. The accompanying cuneiform inscription devoted to Darius' achievements is written in three different languages – Old Persian, Elamite and Babylonian.

towards India. Marching south into the Hindu Kush and then east across the Khyber Pass, he conquered southern Kashmir – the Kingdom of Gandhara – before attacking the Hindu King Porus (Raja Puru) in the Punjab. Again, Alexander was victorious, but his army of Greek and Persian mercenaries had had enough, and mutinied by the Beas River in the eastern Punjab – the furthest point east of all Alexander's conquests.

Returning to Babylon, Alexander died suddenly of a fever on 10 June 323 BC, one month before his 33rd birthday. In an unparalleled explosion of energy, he had conquered a vast swathe of land, linking Libya and Greece in the west with Transoxiana and the Punjab in the east. He knew little or nothing of distant China, and so he was in effect, and in his own eyes, a world-conqueror.

Alexander's campaign had forged new and strong links between Greece and Central Asia that were both cultural and commercial, including the spread of the Greek language and monetary system. Although his invading forces temporarily decimated regional markets and the political instability damaged overland trade, in the longer term the movement of

Map showing the conquests of Alexander the Great.

THE SCYTHIANS

The Scythians were a nomadic Indo-European people who dominated a vast area stretching from the Ukraine to Mongolia during the 7th–1st centuries BC. They developed highly skilled metalworking techniques, executed in bronze and gold with great skill. Designs featured bearded men, horses, stags and eagles, as well as griffins and other mythical creatures. From about the 3rd century BC they were increasingly influenced by contact with the neighbouring Greeks, producing a syncretic style which spread to the east, where Chinese jade-carvers began to adapt and borrow from Graeco-Scythian motifs.

troops spread knowledge and taste for a variety of consumer goods, many of which had to be transported east from the Mediterranean. His generals subsequently divided up the conquered lands, and each set about forging their own small empires, establishing the Antigonid Empire in Greece (301–168 BC), the Ptolemaic Empire in Egypt and Palestine (305–30 BC) and the Seleucid Empire in Persia and Mesopotamia (323–63 BC). The Alexandrian territories furthest east formed the Graeco-Bactrian Kingdom of Bactria and Sogdiana (250–140 BC), the Indo-Greek Kingdom of Gandhara centred on Taxila, and the Punjab (189 BC–10 AD). This unlikely but fruitful union of Greek and Indo-Buddhist civilisations would produce some of the most spectacular syncretic art forms of the ancient Silk Road, particularly when Indo-Greek influences were extended north, across the Pamir Massif, into the heart of Central Asia.

Alexander's Bactrian successors continued to expand eastwards, especially under King

Qin Shi Huang is famous not just for uniting China's warring clans; such was his ego that the First Emperor had a terracotta army of life-size warriors to guard him in the afterlife.

River in the south. The unification process was completed by Qin Shi Huang (241–210 BC), who became First Emperor, extending Chinese control south as far as the Pearl River Delta.

It was a question now of where else to expand: to the north was the barren desert where the hostile Xiongnu nomads had been held back since the 4th century BC by the construction of defensive fortifications that would eventually be combined to form the Great Wall. But another alternative existed in the direction of little-known Central Asia – source of precious jade.

The First Emperor's famous Terracotta Warriors at Xi'an.

Euthydemus (230–200 BC), who extended his control into Sogdiana on the Kazakh and Kyrgyz frontiers with present-day Xinjiang. The Bactrians crossed the Tian Shan into Chinese Central Asia, marking the earliest known direct contacts between China and Europe, around 220 BC.

China heads west

Meanwhile, far to the east and beyond the Pamir Massif, nascent Imperial China was similarly flexing its muscles. For the first two millennia of its existence, the Chinese state had gradually coalesced, establishing its control over an area extending from the Gobi Desert and Manchurian Plains in the north to the Yangtze

Qin Shi Huang was succeeded by Liu Bang, founder of the illustrious Han Dynasty that lasted from 206 BC to AD 220, and with his accession as Emperor Gaozu in 202 BC, the stage was set for China's imperial expansion westwards – and the first recorded crossing of the Pamir Massif to Central and Western Asia.

The Silk Road could not become a single thoroughfare linking east and west until the barrier of the Pamir Massif and the steppes of Central Asia were breached, linking the antique lapis lazuli trade routes west of the Pamirs with the almost equally venerable jade routes to the east. Once this was achieved, the path was open for direct trade between the Chinese and Mediterranean worlds.

Exotic fruits depicted at the Temple of Bel, Palmyra.

THE OPENING OF THE ROAD

The extraordinary adventures of the imperial envoy Zhang Qian into Central Asia created an eager market for China's luxurious silk.

Some 200 years after Alexander's adventures eastward, there was still no sign of China in the classical world. It was not until the ascendancy of the Han Dynasty that a unified and powerful Chinese state turned its attentions west. In 138 BC, Emperor Wu Di (141–87 BC) despatched his imperial envoy Zhang Qian to investigate the territories to the west, via the Hexi Corridor, towards Central Asia. If possible, he was to seek a military alliance with the Yuehzhi (the Indo-European Tocharians of the Tarim Basin and Bactria) against the powerful nomadic Xiongnu of the north. It was to be an epic journey, marking the first real beginning of the Silk Road.

Zhang Qian set out at the head of a delegation of around 100, mostly military officers, and one Xiongnu guide. A mural dating from the 8th century AD in the Mogao Caves at Dunhuang represents his departure, while another from the same era shows his patron, the Emperor Wu Di, venerating images of Buddha before starting his campaign against the Xiongnu.

Despite Zhang Qian's best efforts, he was captured by the Xiongnu and detained by them for 10 years before making his escape. He crossed over the Tian Shan into present-day Uzbekistan (which he called Dayuan), where he discovered many things unknown to the Chinese. There was the mundane (turnips), the intoxicating (wine), but above all were the legendary "heavenly horses" of the Fergana Valley (see box), which the Han Chinese were eager to obtain to help transform their cavalry for the wars against the nomads of the north.

Eventually Zhang Qian reached the long-sought kingdom of the Yuehzhi in Bactria, but they were not interested in joining a Chinese

Green-glazed tomb figure of a Fergana horse.

HEAVENLY HORSES

The "heavenly horses" of the Fergana Valley were prized above all other by the ancient Chinese. The Han Dynasty began the custom of importing great numbers of horses from Bactria and western regions, frequently in exchange for silk. At other times the Chinese used military invasions to secure supplies. In AD 102 they attacked Bactria and demanded that the defeated forces should supply the Han Empire with 100 of their finest horses for breeding purposes, and a further 3,000 to use as war mounts. According to Chinese tradition, the finest of the heavenly steeds sweated blood, earning them the sobriquet "blood-sweating horses".

campaign against the fierce Xiongnu. After a stay of one year, the intrepid Zhang Qian set out on a voyage for home, but was once again captured and held prisoner by the Xiongnu. He managed to escape again two years later

Wu Di was the seventh Han emperor and one of the greatest rulers in Chinese history. He is remembered for the vast territorial expansion China attained under his reign, as well as for organising a strong, centralised Confucian state.

Emperor Wu Di welcoming a man of letters, from a history of Chinese emperors.

and eventually returned to the Han court at Chang'an in 125 BC.

After an absence of more than 13 years, he had long since been given up for dead by Wu Di, who was delighted by his return. The mission to form an alliance with the Yuehzhi may have failed, but Zhang Qian had succeeded in making the first recorded crossing of the Pamir-Tian Shan ranges and brought back much valuable information about the regions to the west.

According to the Han annals: "The Emperor Wu Di learned of Dayuan (Fergana), Daxia (Bactria), Anxi (Parthia) and other lands, all great states rich in unusual products where people cultivated the land and made their living in much the same way as the people of Han. All these states were weak militarily, and prized Han goods and wealth."

Zhang Qian's reports also made reference – apparently second-hand – to even more distant regions, including Liuxuan (Turkmenistan), Yancai (Kazakhstan), Tiaozhi (Iraq) and Shendu (India). Finally, in the furthest west, lay the almost mythical land of "Lijian", thought to be the earliest reference in Chinese literature to the distant territories of Rome.

Diplomatic missions

Zhang Qian was heaped with praise and honours before leading a second, successful expedition in 119 BC to the west of the Tian Shan, effectively establishing diplomatic relations with Fergana, Bactria and Sogdiana, all of which sent ambassadors to Chang'an, beginning a process of regular diplomatic missions to the Chinese capital. Zhang Qian returned via the southern rim of the Tarim Basin, bringing with him a gift of exquisite Fergana horses for Emperor Wu Di. About a decade later another Chinese emissary returned the favour when he visited the kingdom of Anxi or Parthia, bearing with him gifts of fine silks.

The basis of future trade along the great Silk Road was thus put in place, with commerce portrayed in contemporary Chinese annals as gifts going west and tribute travelling east to the Han court at Chang'an. In this way Chinese embassies eventually penetrated as far west as Rome, perhaps during the reign of Emperor Augustus (27 BC–AD 14). According to the historian Florus "even those countries of the world not subject to imperial sway" sent embassies to Rome, "the great conqueror" of nations: "Thus even the Scythians and the Sarmatians sent envoys to seek the friendship of Rome. Nay, even the Seres came likewise, and the Indians who dwell beneath the vertical sun, bringing presents of precious stones and pearls and elephants... In truth it needed but to look at their complexions to see that they were people of another world than ours."

Zhang Qian died around 104 BC, but because of his remarkable achievements he still remains one of China's most revered national heroes, seen by many as the father of the Silk Road – the man who first opened the long route to Central Asia and the West.

Between 121 and 110 BC, Emperor Wu Di followed up his successful diplomatic and commercial initiative to the West by establishing military garrisons along the Hexi Corridor, thus ensuring control of the only practical road between Chang'an and the Tarim Basin. It also served to bind the future province of Gansu to "China proper" once and for all. Future generations of Chinese would make this distinction – as they still do today – by referring to the area east of Dunhuang as "the region within", while to the west lay "the region without". The new garrisons were designated prefectures, and to ensure Han Chinese hegemony of the previously sparsely populated region, large numbers of convicts were sent west to settle them.

The area between Dunhuang and the Pamirs, corresponding to today's southern Xinjiang, was dominated by the vast Taklamakan Desert, around which a number of oases were strung. The choice was to go north or south. The southern route left China proper via Yangguan, the Pass of the Sun, while the more northerly route left via Yumenguan, the Jade Gate Pass. Later a third route would develop still further to the north, running

Mural of Zhang Qian serving as an ambassador to the West located in the Mogao Caves at Dunhuang.

DUNHUANG – THE BLAZING BEACON

Famous for its Buddhist art, the desert town of Dunhuang began life as a key command post built as part of Emperor Wu Di's massive programme of wall-building to defend China's outer frontiers against the forays of nomadic tribes. Built between 121 and 110 BC, this part of the Great Wall stretched across the mouth of the Hexi Corridor, the narrow strip of fertile land sandwiched between the Qilian Mountains to the south and the Ala Shan and Gobi deserts to the north. Dunhuang's strategic importance at this natural gateway was thus clear; the name means "blazing beacon", and it was one of a series of beacons used to warn the Chinese of enemy encroachment.

Dunhuang continued as a garrison town for around 1,000 years. Once the Silk Road opened up, its location made it an important commercial and cultural centre, as well as a military hub. Early Buddhist monks arrived from Kashgar, and Dunhuang became a centre of pilgrimage and learning. A vast repository of Buddhist and other manuscripts was collected in the nearby Mogao Caves. Manuscripts and murals painted by the monks remained hidden in the caves. They were rediscovered by a Taoist monk in 1900 and then looted by international archaeologists such as Aurel Stein in the early years of the 20th century.

around the north rim of the Tarim Basin via the oases of Hami and Turpan, in the lee of the Tian Shan. Wu Di's control of this vast region was essential to hold back the nomads of the north – the Xiongnu and their successors – while maintaining the increasingly prosperous trade route with the west.

The conquests of Ban Chao

By the time of his death in 87 BC, Wu Di had almost doubled the size of Han territories, making China the largest and most powerful empire in the world – surpassing even contemporaneous Rome. Yet it fell to his successors, the Emperors Ming (AD 58–75), Zhang (76–88) and He (89–105) to truly consolidate Chinese control over the Tarim Basin and modern-day Xinjiang. These Western Han rulers all benefited from the services of one of China's truly great soldiers, General Ban Chao

"In the time of the Western Han there was Zhang Qian, In the Eastern Han there was Ban Chao." Chinese saying

The Great Wall near Jiayuguan.

THE CELTS IN CHINA

Although the Chinese were not to come west until the 1st century AD, there is significant archaeological and DNA evidence that Bronze Age Celts had already somehow made their way to Xinjiang's Tarim Basin. Burial pits unearthed in the Taklamakan Desert contain a significant number of mummies of European origin.

Dating back some 3,000 years, one of the earliest mummies is a 6-ft-tall male with reddish hair, high cheekbones, a long nose and a ginger beard. He was buried in a twill tunic and tartan leggings. Now preserved in the Urumqi museum, the mummy has been DNA tested and is undoubtedly of Caucasian heritage. His DNA and his dress link him strongly with the Celts

of France and Britain, but sadly offer no clue as to how or why he and his family might have reached China.

More than 400 such mummies have been discovered in the Tarim Basin, and there are also thousands of skulls. Thanks to the dry climate and alkaline soils, they are well-preserved: hair styles and make-up are still visible. Clothing is also in a sufficient state to be analysed, and some cloth samples have been shown to be of the same weave as those found on the bodies of salt miners in Austria. They date from 1300 BC.

These may not have been the only Europeans to find their way into China. There are accounts of Roman soldiers being taken as captives to Yongchang.

(AD 32–102), who crushed the Xiongnu and pushed west into the Tarim, eventually bringing the whole Tarim Basin under Chinese control.

In AD 97, Ban Chao led an army of 70,000 across the Pamirs and the Tian Shan to protect the now strategically vital Silk Road against the continuing depredations of the Xiongnu. Making an alliance with King Pacorus II of Parthia (AD 78–105), he advanced as far as the shores of the Caspian Sea, where he despatched an envoy to Rome – though he only reached the shores of the Black Sea before turning back. Nevertheless, with the advance of Ban Chao's

Pax Romana

As the Chinese expanded westwards, the Roman Empire was spreading its influence east. In 83 BC, they occupied the eastern Mediterranean city of Antioch and it became the capital of the newly formed Roman province of Syria. Such territories at the eastern end of the Mediterranean acted as a buffer zone against troublesome Parthians of Persia and the Nabataeans further south around Petra. Semi-independent client kings such as Herod the Great (37–4 BC) carved out mini-empires within a creaking Hellenistic

Roman colonnade at the city of Apamea in Syria.

armies to the borders of Europe and the Middle East, Chinese power, influence and prestige reached a high point in Inner Asia. The "Seres" (see box), for so long mysterious and distant from the West, were now neighbours who had come to stay.

At the same time, the Great Wall of China, first established as a series of defensive walls against the nomads of the north, was extended west towards Lop Nur in the Tarim Basin. China's current claims to these far-flung territories are based on their conquest and settlement in Han Dynasty times – fully 1,000 years before the Uighur Turks, Xinjiang's main "indigenous people" in modern times, moved into the region.

PARTING SHOT

At the Battle of Carrhae, the Parthians employed their trademark military tactic known as "the Parthian shot". Mounted archers would feign retreat, then turn around in the saddle and shoot at the pursuing enemy while galloping at full speed. The manoeuvre required skilled horsemanship, since the rider needed both hands to shoot the arrows. The gambit entered the English language as a "parting shot" – scoring points by having the last word or gesture. It is referred to by the satirist Samuel Butler in *An Heroical Epistle of Hudibras to His Lady* (1678): "You wound, like Parthians, while you fly/ And kill with a retreating eye".

structure, though always with an eye on developments in Rome.

During the stable *Pax Romana* period, a loose federation developed amongst 10 cities known

> *"I do not see how clothes of silk…can be called clothing… seamstresses labour that the adulteress may be visible through her transparent dress…her husband has no more knowledge than any outsider…of his wife's body." Seneca (3 BC–AD 65)*

Roman fresco from Pompeii depicting a silk-clad maenad (follower of Dionysus).

as the Decapolis, in what is today southern Syria and northern Jordan. Improved agricultural systems, particularly the use of traditional Persian methods of collecting and distributing water, turned the land into a valuable source of grain and olives. Some of these underground water channels remain in use today and are still known as *qanat romani*.

In the expanding world of trade, silk began to arrive in Rome, and though some of this may have slipped through from China, much of it came from a people called the "Seres", about whom little is known (see box). Despite Ban Chao's advances to the west, Rome remained largely ignorant of China. Romans believed that

silk was somehow "combed off leaves", while some contemporaneous Chinese sources state that asbestos cloth – obtained from the west – was "woven from the wool of sea sheep". It would not be long, however, before many of these misconceptions disappeared, for East and West were about to discover each other, not by coastal maritime trade, but much more directly, across the Pamir Massif and the steppes of Central Asia.

Silk banners show the way

Other great empires lay between Rome and China, most notably that of Parthia, which dominated the lands of Iran, Mesopotamia and Eastern Anatolia from 247 BC to AD 220. When the Parthians defeated the Romans at the Battle of Carrhae in 53 BC, survivors reported that the victorious Parthians had unfurled shimmering banners of an unknown material, embroidered with gold, which flashed like fire in the sunlight. This is widely interpreted as the first sighting of silk by Romans.

These three powerful empires finally enabled the Silk Road to operate effectively from around 100 BC. Though allied with Ban Chao against the nomads of the north, the Parthians were determined to maintain their role as middlemen between China and Rome, controlling all silk that came out of China and reselling it at fabulous prices.

As a consequence, no Roman armies penetrated beyond Parthia to China, and few Roman traders made it across the Iranian plateau to the Pamirs. One exception, however, was Maës Titianus, who at the end of the 1st century AD sent a party of merchants as far east as Tashkurgan on the very western frontiers of China. Almost nothing is known of Maës Titianus, but he was probably seeking to maximise his profits in the incredibly lucrative silk trade.

Silk was a mystery to the Romans, but it had captured the heart of the fashionable elite. The Senate, deeply troubled by the outflow of money to the east, tried several times to stem this trade through edicts prohibiting the wearing of silk. Yet Rome was gradually learning more about this desired material. Pliny the Elder (AD 23–79) had already established the fact that silk did not grow on trees, but that moths "weave webs, like spiders, that become a luxurious clothing for women, called silk". As this knowledge slowly spread westwards, China's monopoly on the rich silk trade would gradually begin to diminish.

Roman Ancestry

Today, the citizens of Yongchang wonder if they are descended from a group of Romans who might have reached China.

It had always been understood that until the time of Augustus, Rome and China had barely been aware of each other's existence. However, in 1957, American sinologist Homer Hasenpflug Dubs published a book suggesting that a group of captive Roman soldiers had been resettled at the modern town of Yongchang, near Wuwei, in the remote reaches of Gansu. Dubs was an Oxford don who specialised in Chinese history and philosophy by translating earlier texts.

Dubs' hypothesis

According to Dubs in his book *A Roman City in Ancient China* these lost legionaries were the last remnants of an army commanded by the Roman general Crassus that was defeated in 53 BC by the Parthians at Carrhae, near to the modern border between Turkey and Syria. Crassus' army of 42,000 was decisively routed, with 20,000 dead and around 10,000 escaping to fight another day. But more importantly there were reports that over 10,000 soldiers were taken prisoner. According to the Roman historian Pliny, these captives were resettled in Sogdiana where they were employed as Parthian mercenaries.

Roman prisoners

In 36 BC, a Chinese army led by General Kan Yanshou made a punitive raid against the Sogdian settlement of Zhezhe. The Han Dynasty annals record that the Chinese forces came up against a group of foreign soldiers who formed an unusual defensive formation like a tortoise, interlocking their shields above their heads – a military tactic of the Roman legions quite unknown to the Chinese. The actual Chinese description is 'fish-scale formation', an apt term for what we know as the *testudo*. Despite the unfamiliar tactics, the attackers were victorious, and took around 150 of the defeated soldiers with them to Chinese Central Asia.

Four decades later, in AD 5, Chinese chronicles mention a newly established settlement named Lijian – a contemporaneous Chinese

name for Rome – which was populated by assorted captives and convicts. Dubs suggests that the Roman soldiers captured at Carrhae, or their immediate descendants, were forcibly resettled at Lijian to help populate and defend the strategically vital Hexi Corridor.

Such an action would have been very much in line with frontier policy of the time, which had long sought to "use barbarians to control barbarians". Dubs died in Oxford in 1969 having stimulated interest in this field of study and his hypothesis is fascinating but not entirely convincing.

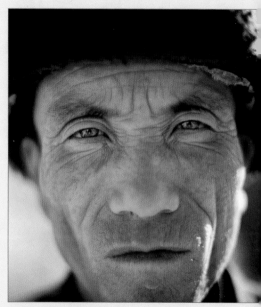

A green-eyed man from Yongchang.

True or false?

Unfortunately, DNA tests conducted at Yongchang, the modern town near Lijian, in 2007 found no genetic evidence to support claims of Roman ancestry among the town's overwhelmingly Han population.

Unconcerned with the findings, Yongchang remains proud of its supposed Roman heritage. Statues of a Chinese mandarin, together with two "Romans" – one male and one female – have been erected near the southern entrance of the town. These figures are more of a curiosity than a genuine attraction, but may well represent the easternmost limits of Roman penetration along the ancient Silk Road, if indeed it did take place.

Buddha preaching the law, in a painting from Dunhuang.

THE MIDDLEMEN

Specialist merchants kept trade flowing
along the Silk Road even after the fall of
both Rome and the Han Dynasty.

By the 1st century AD trade in both directions along the new Silk Road linking China with the Mediterranean was already well established, as were the diplomatic and tributary missions sent, with increasing frequency, between East and West. But China and Rome remained far apart, and few if any merchants would have made the long journey all the way from Chang'an to Antioch or to Rome itself. Local people took the caravans over the most dangerous and difficult sections of the journey. But, of course, this trade route was not just for silk. Towards Europe came exotic animals, furs, ceramics, jade and, most importantly, spices – cinnamon, balsam, cardamom and pepper. In the other direction went gold, ivory, pearls and precious metals.

Remote from the Greek heartlands, Bactria had a high level of Hellenic sophistication. Balkh and Ai Khanoum in northern Afghanistan had theatres, gymnasia and buildings with Corinthian columns.

Trade was dominated by Central Asian middlemen, who bought goods from the Chinese at Dunhuang or Kashgar, and from Mediterranean caravan merchants in Mesopotamia, Iran or Transoxiana. Central Asian trade was dominated by Tocharian and South Asian traders to the east of the Pamirs, and by Bactrian and Sogdian merchants to the west of the Pamirs.

The Kushans

The most important new Central Asian state to emerge during this period was the Kushan

Buddha in Greek garb from the monastery of Takht-i-Bahi in northern Pakistan.

Empire (1st–3rd centuries AD), which is linked by historians with the peripatetic Yuehzhi, thought to have been the Indo-European Tocharians of the Tarim Basin, who were driven westwards to settle in Bactria by the Xiongnu in the 2nd century BC. In the 1st century BC the Yuehzhi began to absorb Graeco-Bactrian territories to the south of the Pamirs, adopting elements of Greek culture.

At its height in the 2nd century AD, the Kushan Empire sat squarely astride the Silk Road, as well as the southern extension via Kashmir to India, controlling all Bactria, the western Tarim Basin and northern India, and dominating Silk Road commerce. Besides trade goods, the ever-expanding network of Central Asian trade routes also carried art and ideas between distant centres of civilisation. The Kushans were nothing if not eclectic, adapting the Greek alphabet to suit their own language. They also borrowed the

> *Lokaksema was a Buddhist Kushan from Gandhara. He is the earliest known monk to have translated Mahayana Buddhist scriptures into Chinese.*

Mural depicting Sogdian traders, at the Rudaki Museum in Penjikent, Tajikistan.

minting of coins from the Greeks, combining texts in Greek with South Asian Pali written in the Kharoshthi script. Their religion they took initially from Persia, embracing the heterodox ideas of Zoroaster, only to add a veneer of Buddhism from South Asia.

The Kushans established their summer and winter capitals at Bagram (Kapisa) in Afghanistan and Peshawar (Purushapura) in Pakistan, at the heart of the ancient Buddhist kingdom of Gandhara. They used part of the enormous wealth they derived from the Silk Road to sponsor the creation of Buddhist monasteries and stupas right across the territory, lavishly adorned with statues of

Buddha and bodhisattvas (future Buddhas) and narrative scenes both from the life of Siddhartha, the historical Buddha, and from the Jatakas, his previous births. From their position on the Silk Road the sculptors were able to draw on a range of artistic influences, and it was the particular fusion of Graeco-Roman and Indian styles that produced the distinctive and much acclaimed Gandhara art form. Significantly, it was at this time that a new form of Buddhism developed called Mahayana Buddhism, in which the image of the Buddha himself came to be worshipped, and a revolutionary feature of the Gandhara School was the successful representation of the Buddha in human form, often wearing a Greek-style toga. Kanishka, the greatest of the Kushan kings, appeared to have given his full support to the new ideas. The message of Buddhism was sent out to the world. Missionaries were despatched westwards into Central Asia and eastwards into China and Tibet via the Karakoram. The extraordinary flowering of Gandharan Graeco-Buddhist art that would stun Silk Road archaeologists in the late 19th century dates from this imaginatively syncretic period of Kushan rule.

Nomads of the north

The great settled empires – Chinese and Roman, Persian and Kushan – were not alone in dominating the Eurasian land mass. To the north of the Silk Road, extending from Manchuria and the Gobi Desert in the east to Dzungaria and the Kazakh Steppe in the west, the great, empty open spaces were dominated by very different peoples. These were the wandering nomads, who migrated seasonally and whose wealth lay in livestock, not grain or the precious goods of the cities. Yet this very peripatetic existence made the nomads of the north into fine horsemen and fierce fighters, unpredictable warriors who could move vast distances in short periods of time, difficult – almost impossible – to control and almost equally impossible to predict.

Decline of the Han Dynasty

Ban Chao's advance into Central Asia at the turn of the 1st century AD had projected Chinese power far west along the Silk Road to encompass the small independent kingdoms of the Tarim Basin. By the 2nd century AD, however, Han power was rapidly disintegrating. When the dynasty fell, in AD 220, a period of internal division began, with Chinese imperial power effectively ending at Dunhuang. In the face of this weakness, China's old enemy, the Xiongnu, although divided into northern and southern sections, once again took up the cudgels of war, capturing the ancient Chinese capital of Luoyang in AD 311, and the Silk Road capital of Chang'an five years later. By the mid-4th century, all of northern China was under Xiongnu control.

During this period the petty oasis kingdoms of the Tarim Basin succeeded in restoring their autonomy, but as vassals to a branch of the Xiongnu nomads known in the West as the Hephthalites – and soon to become more widely known and feared as the Huns, particularly under Attila (AD 406–53), the "Scourge of God". To the south and west, the Kushan Empire was similarly in decline, losing western territories to the Persian Sassanids (AD 226–651), as well as to the Xiongnu in the north.

Palmyra's ascendancy

The extremities of the Roman Empire were always under pressure as rivals sought to regain territory. The Parthians, based at Ctesiphon on the Tigris, were almost continually at war with Rome. By a quirk of nature, the route from Dura Europos ("Fortress of Europe" in Aramaic), on the Euphrates, through Syria to Emesa (Homs) was dramatically shortened by a natural spring at Palmyra, enabling the Silk Road to run straight through the inhospitable Syrian Desert. By charging huge taxes, the

city of Palmyra became extremely wealthy and formed a useful barrier between the Romans and Parthians. So wealthy did it become that many of the exotic goods never reached Rome, but furnished the ever-expanding demands of its own population. This independent state built a huge imperial city in the middle of the desert, much of which still lies buried, but the funerary objects and mummified silk remains testify to its great wealth.

The Parthians were replaced by the Sassanids in the Second Persian Empire (AD 226–651), who in AD 260 under King Shapur defeated

A camel carved in stone at Palmyra.

THE SOGDIANS, CONSUMMATE MIDDLEMEN

For centuries the cosmopolitan Sogdians dominated trade along the Central Asian Silk Road. As the route's consummate middlemen, their language became the *lingua franca* of trade for a thousand miles, as Sogdian communities enjoyed influential positions in cities from Samarkand to Xi'an. Masters of the production of iron armour and chain mail, they introduced the Chinese to the art of making coloured translucent glass and kept the Tang court supplied with its exotic delicacies.

The Sogdians lived mainly in the lands between the Amu Darya and Syr Darya, in modern Uzbekistan and Tajikistan. Much of what we know about them has come from archaeological finds and friezes unearthed

in the cities of Penjikent (east of Samarkand), Varakhsha (near Bukhara) and Afrosiab. Their palaces had some of the region's most sophisticated decoration, mixing Graeco-Bactrian, Sassanian and even Indian artistic influences. We know they used the Aramaic alphabet and were religiously tolerant, promoting Zoroastrianism alongside pockets of Manicheism and Nestorian Christianity. Much of what we know about their political life comes from a cache of Sogdian documents discovered by Aurel Stein in a Great Wall watchtower near Dunhuang.

Copies of the Sogdian friezes can be seen at museums in Penjikent and Afrosiab.

the Roman Emperor Valerian, and held him in captivity in Bishapur where he died. Palmyra's King Odainath, siding with Rome against this Persian dominance in the region, then defeated the Sassanids. His wife and successor was

> When Nestorian Christianity was outlawed by the Roman Church in AD 432, merchants took this faith along the Silk Road. The first Nestorian church in Chang'an was consecrated in AD 638.

The Beginning of the Silk Industry in Europe, engraved by Philip Galle, c.1600.

Queen Zenobia, who in AD 274 went on to claim Egypt for Palmyra before being defeated by Emperor Aurelian and dragged off to Rome in golden chains.

All this disruption in trade across the desert resulted in the development of another route further up the Euphrates, which made it only a short journey to Aleppo. This vibrant city had always been an important trading centre of the Levant, being on the edge of Asia, the Middle East, Europe and Africa. Silk and other luxury goods flowed naturally through its ancient souks and *khans*.

This branch of the Silk Road ended at Seleucia Piera, the port of Antioch, which became wealthy enough to indulge in the decadent pleasures of silk even before it became popular in Rome. St Paul had set sail from here for Cyprus on his first missionary journey around AD 48, and when emerging Christian sects were outlawed by the Romans during the first few centuries AD, Christianity also moved east.

The secret is out

The fall of Rome to Germanic tribes in AD 476 led to the ascendancy of Constantinople (modern Istanbul), capital of the Eastern Roman Empire, which had been founded by Constantine I (AD 306–77), the first emperor to convert to Christianity. By the mid-6th century, Emperor Justinian I (AD 527–65) had recovered Italy, southern Iberia and parts of North Africa, but the nature of this new Byzantine state had changed completely, with Latin abandoned and Greek adopted as the language of government. Justinian was also keen to strengthen his empire by expanding long-distance trade, and, in doing so, overcoming the Chinese and Persian Sassanid monopoly on silk.

For at least two millennia, even from the time of the legendary Yellow Emperor, Qin Shi Huang, China had managed to maintain a successful ban on the export of silkworms and the knowledge of sericulture. But no monopoly is foolproof, and no technology can be kept secret forever. The industry was defended by imperial decree, which imposed a mandatory death sentence on anyone attempting to export silkworms or their eggs, but this

PAPER TRAIL

The art of papermaking is thought to have developed in China during the 2nd century AD. One of the "Four Great Inventions of Ancient China" (others are the compass, gunpowder and printing), the Chinese kept the process a secret for hundreds of years, though it appeared in Korea in the 7th century. After the Battle of Talas in 751, the technology spread to Baghdad and Damascus, then east and south to Iran and India. The first paper mill in the Islamic world was founded in Samarkand; and in Europe the first was established at Valencia in Spain in 1120, probably as a direct result of the Battle of Talas, by way of Islamic Spain.

security was breached by the 2nd century BC, when knowledge of sericulture reached Korea and Vietnam. During the first half of the 1st century AD, the technology is thought to have reached the Han Chinese-dominated oasis of Khotan in the Tarim Basin – a centre of silk production today.

> A Chinese princess given in marriage to a Khotan prince is said to have carried the eggs of silkworms to her new husband concealed in her hair.

From Khotan, silkworms and knowledge of sericulture is thought to have travelled south to India and west to Sassanid Persia, then inevitably further to the west. But the Sassanids still had a monopoly on production. The breakthrough for Justinian came in AD 552, when he first obtained the elusive silkworm eggs. These were smuggled to him in bamboo tubes across Persia by two Nestorian monks. With their safe arrival in Constantinople, silk would gradually become a local Byzantine product.

The Eastern Silk Road

Nearly a century later the first Byzantine ambassador arrived at the Chinese court at Chang'an (Xi'an) and presented himself to the Tang emperor. Just as Rome had entered a period of decline, so had the Han Empire, following repeated nomadic invasions from the north. The Huns – a western branch of the same Xiongnu tribes troubling China far to the east – penetrated as far as the Alps and the central Balkans.

So it fell to the great Tang Dynasty (AD 618–907) to re-establish full imperial control over the Eastern Silk Road. The second Tang emperor, Taizong (AD 626–49), mounted campaigns against the Eastern and Western Turks to the north, before sending his forces into the Tarim Basin and re-establishing control over Turpan, Kashgar and Yarkand as well as Kuqa and Khotan.

However, even under the Tang Dynasty, China's control over the Eastern Silk Road was to prove tenuous. With the northern nomads temporarily at peace, a new challenge to Tang power arose from an

unexpected source – Tibet. It had no previous history of expansionism in Central Asia; indeed, it is hardly mentioned in the Chinese annals until this time. In AD 608–9, however, a Tibetan nobleman named Namri Lontsan united the fledgling Tibetan state and sent emissaries to the Chinese court. For the next four centuries the Tibetan Empire would play a decisive military role in Central Asia, its armies issuing forth from the Tibetan plateau to challenge Chinese control over the Silk Road in Gansu and, especially, in the Tarim Basin, where Tibetan forces seized

The Story of the Silk Princess, a wooden panel painting from the Khotan oasis, 6th century.

control of the Southern Silk Road between Dunhuang and Khotan.

Meanwhile, to the north of the Hexi Corridor and in the Gobi steppe and Dzungaria, a new power, the Gökturk Empire, arose to replace the Xiongnu. Between AD 552 and 745 the Gökturks succeeded in unifying the disparate Turkic tribes of Central Asia into a single powerful entity, playing the same role to the north of the Hexi Corridor as the Tibetan Empire to the south. By the mid-8th century, however, the power of the Gökturk khans was on the wane, and in AD 744 a new Turkic power, the Uighur Khaganate, took control of Mongolia and proclaimed itself leader of all the Turkic peoples of Central Asia.

The rise of Islam

By the 7th century Chinese power and prestige were once again established over much of the Eastern and Central Silk Road, with restive Turkic tribes to the north, and expansionist Tibetans to the south. The Middle East was generally under the control of the Sassanids, while Byzantium ruled much of the Mediterranean. But this established relationship would not survive much longer.

Sometime around 610, Muhammad, a prosperous Mecca-born merchant and trader, received his first revelation from God, and began teaching a strict monotheism aimed at driving idolatry from Arabia. In 622 he and his followers left Mecca on *hejira* or "migration" for the relative safety of nearby Medina; the Islamic Era is dated from this event. By the time

> "The house that contains pictures will not be entered by angels." This saying is attributed to the Prophet Muhammad, who believed only God could bestow life. Hence geometric patterns rather than figures in most Islamic art.

Muhammad died a decade later, in 632, most of Arabia had converted to the new faith of Islam, or "submission" to the will of God.

The new religion expanded at a phenomenal rate. Arab Islamic armies swept out of Arabia, conquering the great trade routes and cities of the Fertile Crescent, before advancing as far as Libya in the west and Afghanistan in the east. The emerging Arab civilisation chose Damascus as its first capital, and the Umayyad Mosque became the latest in a long line of religious buildings on this sacred site. Under the Umayyad Caliphate (AD 661–750) the frontiers of the Islamic Empire were extended to Spain in the west, while Bactria and Samarkand were conquered in Central Asia, and Muslim armies reached the banks of the Indus. The world had seen nothing like it before – Sassanid Persia was swept away in just over a dozen years.

In 750, the unpopular Umayyad Dynasty was replaced by the powerful Abbasid Dynasty. While the Umayyads were studiously Arab in their make-up, the new Abbasid rulers enjoyed a much wider power base in Baghdad that rested not just on Arab aristocrats, but on poor Arabs, non-Arab converts and even sectarian Shia dissenters.

The rise of the Abbasids brought a Golden Age for the Islamic Caliphate, lasting for just over five centuries until the Mongol conquest of Baghdad in 1258. Islam was a religion based on trade and wedded to both overland and maritime commerce. But before commercial, cultural and religious exchange between Tang China and the emerging Islamic Empire could be established, spheres of influence had to be sorted out. The testing ground would be

The tale 'Journey to the West', depicting the travels of Xuanzang.

ANCIENT TRIO OF CARAVANSERAIS

Perhaps the oldest trade route in the Middle East runs north from the Hejaz and Sinai through Jordan and Syria to the former Silk Road port of Antakya. Here it joined a desert route linking with Mesopotamia and the Persian Royal Road. As well as the cities of Damascus and Aleppo, three historic entrepôts straddle these routes, symbolic of an entrepreneurial past. Petra, Jordan's "Rose Red City half as old as Time" flourished 2,000 years ago and traded across the Syrian Desert with the city of Palmyra. Further to the east, on the banks of the Euphrates, Dura Europos formed the third of these famous desert caravanserais.

Central Asia, as both sides sought to take control of the opulent Silk Road traffic.

Tang versus Abbasid

The first clash occurred in 715, when Alutar was installed as king of Fergana with the reported backing of both Arab and Tibetan soldiers – a combination of enemies guaranteed to anger the Tang ruler, Xuanzong. Ikhshid, the deposed Fergana king, fled to Chinese-controlled Kuqa, where he appealed for aid. Xuanzong sent a force of 10,000 men under Zhang Xiaosong to restore Ikhshid to his throne, a task he accomplished successfully. Two years later Arab and Tibetan armies cooperated in besieging Aksu in the Tarim Basin. Once again the Chinese, led by General Tang Jiahui, were victorious.

China had successfully asserted its might over the Arabs on two occasions without effectively projecting its control to the west of the Pamir Massif in the vitally important Fergana Valley and across western Central Asia. In AD 751 Xuanzong determined to change this by challenging the first Abbasid caliph, Abu al-Abbas Abdullah, for control of the Syr Darya (Jaxartes) River and, more particularly, the Fergana Valley – home to those valuable "heavenly horses". The Arab forces of Ziyad ibn-Salih and the Chinese forces of Gao Xianzhi eventually met by the banks of the Talas River in present-day Kyrgyzstan. The Arabs won the day and they now had effective control over western Central Asia. The Chinese inflicted heavy losses on their adversaries, however, and these rare Sino-Arab clashes helped to establish clear spheres of influence, based on mutual respect

and in no way hindering Silk Road traffic or the exchange of ambassadors between the Tang and Abbasid courts.

As a result of the Chinese defeat at the Battle of Talas, an important technological transfer between East and West is thought to have taken place. After the battle, large numbers of Chinese prisoners of war were sent to Samarkand, where they taught their Muslim captors the art of making paper. By 794 this new skill had reached Baghdad, where a paper mill was set up, and eventually the technology of papermaking reached the West.

Tilework on the Jameh Mosque in Yazd, Iran.

XUANZANG

The peripatetic Buddhist monk Xuanzang (AD 602–64) remains the best-known and best-loved of all Chinese travellers on the early Silk Road, not least because of his fictional reincarnation in the celebrated 16th-century novel *Xiyouji* or "Journey to the West". The novelist Wu Chengen created a magical version of the Buddhist pilgrim's travels, accompanied by his companions Monkey, Pigsy and Sandy, to the realm of the "Queen Mother of the West".

The real Xuanzang set out from Chang'an (Xi'an) for India in AD 629, at a time when unauthorised travel to the western regions was forbidden. Travelling mainly by night to avoid soldiers and officials, he crossed the

Jade Gate Pass at Yumenguan and set out for the oasis of Hami, where he almost died of thirst in the desert. After a period of recuperation at Turpan, Xuanzang continued along the Northern Silk Road via Kuqa and across the Tian Shan to Transoxiana, before turning south to India. Here he studied at the Buddhist University of Nalanda for several years before continuing to visit historic Buddhist centres, spending a total of around 15 years in the subcontinent.

Later he returned to Chang'an, bringing with him 22 horses burdened with Buddhist manuscripts, written mainly in Sanskrit, as well as religious relics and precious Buddha images.

*Detail of an anonymous painting,
Banquet and Concert, showing life
at the Tang court.*

GLORY AND DECLINE

As the cities of the Silk Road prospered, Chinese and Arab culture enjoyed a Golden Age. But it would not last.

Between its inception in AD 618 and its ultimate fall in 907, Tang China came to epitomise the prosperity, sophistication and power most associated with the ancient Silk Road. Through judicious use of the overland and maritime trade routes – and in particular the Silk Road – the Tang grew wealthy and gained access to new technologies. From India, Central Asia, Persia, the Middle East and the Mediterranean world they acquired new ideas of fashion, glass-making, ceramics, medicines, perfumes, incense, spices, wines and new techniques of metalworking. Foreign ideas crept in – from sitting on benches and chairs to new forms of dancing and musical entertainment.

"Seek Knowledge, even though it be in China" Hadith (Traditions of the Prophet)

The Tang state wasn't always militarily successful, yet during the halcyon days of the late 7th and early 8th centuries the capital at Chang'an (Xi'an) was unsurpassed in wealth and style. At its peak in around AD 750 it was probably the largest and most populous city in the world. An estimated 800,000 to 1 million people lived within its walls, with another million or so living outside in the greater metropolitan area. The city walls were massive, rising 5.5 metres (18ft) in height, and extending for 35 km (22 miles) to form an elongated square with sides 8km (5 miles) by 9.5km (6 miles). As many as 25,000 foreigners, including Turks, Persians, Arabs, Mongols, Indians, Koreans, Malays, Japanese and Armenians lived there too, congregated mainly around the Western Market. Although the Tang state functioned as

The Tang emperor Wudi and his entourage.

a Confucian bureaucracy, other religions were widely tolerated, and Chang'an had Buddhist and Taoist temples, as well as places of worship for Manicheans, Nestorians, Zoroastrians, Christians and Muslims. It was a sophisticated, fun-loving city, with entertainers and courtesans from far and wide – though the dancers, tumblers, singers and musicians from the Tarim Basin city-states of Kuqa and Aksu were particularly popular.

Secondary trade routes branched off in all directions along the full length of the main Silk Road: north to Mongolia, south to Guangdong and the Chinese colony of Annam, southwest to Yunnan and the Tibetan plateau, and east to the fertile plains of the Yellow River. At the western end a route developed which ran northwest from Rey (now a suburb of Tehran) on a more direct route through Tabriz to the Black Sea and Constantinople.

Continued demand for silk

By the mid-8th century, China's monopoly on silk production had been definitively broken, but the best silks in the world still originated in China, and demand for them continued. Moreover, from Tang times China began to develop a new and important export to Central

Steppe and driven south by Kyrgyz raiders. The Uighur moved into the Tarim Basin, settling in the old oasis cities of Kuqa and Aksu before gradually spreading around the rim of the Taklamakan Desert. Here they underwent a major transformation, turning from pas-

"Uighurs are the best among Turks. Their language is called King's Turkish" Mahmud al-Kashgari, Dictionary of Turkic Languages (1072)

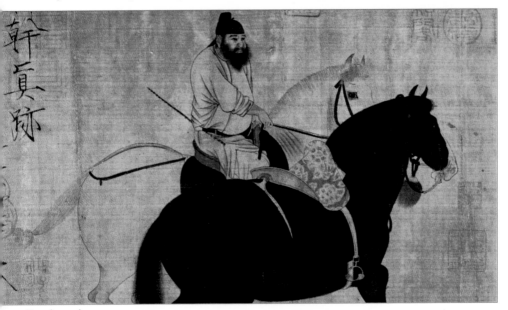

Tang-dynasty horseman.

Asia, Tibet and India – tea, which was easily carried when compressed and valuable enough to exchange for the warhorses that China always greatly desired.

During the Tang era, maritime trade also flourished and expanded. Chinese goods were shipped from Guangdong and the south China coast to India and the Middle East, generally aboard Arab and Persian ships. The same merchant navigators carried wine and incense, pearls and precious glass back to China.

The Turkic Uighur

Around AD 840 a group of Turkic people known as the Uighur were displaced from their ancestral homelands in the Mongolian

toral nomads into settled oasis dwellers and cultivators.

The newly settled Uighur seem to have practised Manicheism and Buddhism at this time, as well as writing in an adapted Sogdian script. It seems that they intermarried with the original Tokharian inhabitants of the oases, gradually giving the Tarim Basin the overwhelmingly Uighur nature of its indigenous population today.

The Songs of China

As Tang power and prestige declined, nomadic attacks on outlying garrisons and interference in the Silk Road's traffic increased. In AD 907, after almost three centuries in power, the dynasty finally collapsed and was followed by a period of disunity known as the "Five Dynasties and Ten Kingdoms" (907–60). The nation was only reunified in 960 with the accession of the Song Dynasty that would rule all China under the Northern Song (960–1127) and the southern part of the country under the Southern Song (1127–1279).

Song China was both wealthy and sophisticated. The state rested on a Confucian meritocracy, administering what became an increasingly free-market economy encompassing a massive population – for the times

the Song period, Gansu's Hexi Corridor represented the western limits of Chinese control, while in the Tarim Basin the scattered Uighur city-states came under the control of the Karakhanid Turks (999–1211).

It was during this period that Islam gradually extended its control across the Tarim Basin and into Gansu, changing the character of the northwest completely. No longer was Chinese Central Asia – the area today known as Xinjiang – a region inhabited by Tokharian Buddhists and Uighur Manicheans, but instead it became firmly Turkish-Muslim in culture.

The Kizil Caves near Kuqa, one of many Buddhist sites abandoned as Islam began to spread into the northwestern part of China.

– of about 100 million people that produced abundant food surpluses and other goods for trade. The Song was the first government in the world to issue paper currency (known as *jiaozi*). It also maintained the first standing navy of any Chinese state, introduced gunpowder warfare, new techniques of hydraulic engineering and the first movable-type printing machines.

For most of the Song Dynasty's three centuries, China was prosperous and relatively powerful – but unlike in Tang times, the Song polity looked south and east, sending ships to the Indian Ocean and trading with Southeast Asia, India and beyond, but not exercising great control over Central Asia. Indeed, for most of

THE TEA-HORSE ROAD

China's ancient Tea-Horse Road was a collection of tracks and trails leading from the tea-producing regions of Yunnan and Sichuan westwards to Central Asia and Tibet. Tea was in great demand among Mongols and Tibetans, for whom it represented an important dietary supplement, usually drunk with yak butter and salt. In exchange, the Chinese required swift and powerful steeds that they could not easily breed at home. The main Tea-Horse Road led from Yunnan, across the Chamdo region of Tibet, to Lhasa and Nepal. Other similar "tea for horse" roads paralleled the ancient Silk Road through Gansu and Qinghai provinces.

Arabic Golden Age

To the west of the Pamirs, Arab civilisation attained its classical Golden Age under the Abbasid Dynasty during the 8th and 9th centuries, most particularly during the reign of the fifth Abbasid caliph, the illustrious Harun al-Rashid (763–809). Harun was a learned scholar and poet who promoted science and the arts, and encouraged wise men and scholars to settle at his court in Baghdad. He maintained diplomatic relations with India and China, as well as with the Holy Roman Emperor Charlemagne (768–814). Relations between these two near-contemporaries seem to have been very good. Harun sent envoys bearing silks, brass, perfumes, slaves and ivory, as well as an elephant and a water clock, which made a great impression at Charlemagne's court in Aachen. In return he received fine Spanish horses, Frisian cloth and trained hunting dogs.

Harun was also a good soldier, and his relations with Eastern Christendom at Constantinople were by no means as good as his relations with Charlemagne and the Holy Roman Empire. Between AD 780 and 806 he led several large armies against Byzantium, which only prevented the capture of Constantinople by paying the Abbasids a substantial tribute in gold.

Following Harun's death, the Abbasid Caliphate entered on a long, slow period of decline. The rival Umayyads maintained their dynasty in Spain, and the North African provinces from Morocco to Egypt acquired de facto independence. Next, in about 820, the Persian Samanids asserted their control over Transoxiana and Khorasan, severing any direct Silk Road link between Tang China and the Abbasids. Samanid authority extended over Bukhara and Samarkand – the Mausoleum of Ismail Samani (892–907) in Bukhara was built during this time – and the Tajik people generally date their emergence as a nation from the Samanid period.

Harun al-Rashid.

The Turkic-Muslim states

After nearly two centuries, the Samanids in turn were replaced by the Turkish Ghaznavids, descendants of Turkic slave guards to the Samanids who, ultimately, overthrew their Persian masters. The Ghaznavids controlled most of Persia, all of Afghanistan and Transoxiana, and northern India as far as the Punjab during the period of their primacy (975–1187). The Ghaznavid state was the first major Muslim empire in Central Asia, and definitively marked the end of Arab and Abbasid influence in the region. By the mid-11th century, however, the Ghaznavids found themselves challenged to the west by the emergence of yet another Turkic-Muslim state, the Seljuk Empire (1037–1194), which established control over all the territory between Anatolia and Afghanistan, reducing the Ghaznavid state to the North Indian plains.

The Assassins

During the 11th century a small group of renegade Shia Muslims began to disrupt trade

---

FORBIDDEN SILK

Under the Abbasids the Arabs, too, were desirous of fine silks, despite the Prophet Muhammad's injunction against wearing silk clothes – at least for Muslim men. According to the Hadith or "Traditions of the Prophet", Muhammad addressed a group while holding a silk garment in one hand and gold in another, saying "These are prohibited to Muslim men, but permitted to Muslim women." The Koran states that those believers who enter paradise will be "adorned with gold bracelets and pearls, and their clothing will be of silk" (Sura al-Hajj), and believers "will wear green garments of fine silk and rich brocade" (Sura al-Insan).

along the Silk Road. They established a number of fortified settlements in Iran, Iraq, Syria and Lebanon, embarking on drug-crazed murdering sprees from their mountain hideouts, as instructed by their fanatical leader Hassan-i Sabbah. These *Hashisheen* (meaning "hashish-users"; from which we also get our word "assassin") threatened the safety of locals and traders alike, and even launched suicide murderers against their Sunni foes (see page 330). They also formed alliances for territory with Christian Crusaders who arrived to free the Holy Land from Sunni Muslim control.

successors, the Song, continued to produce and export millions of bolts of fine silk, but they were increasingly rivalled by Persian and Byzantine production.

> *"The best-preserved and most wholly admirable castle in the world"* T.E. Lawrence describing Krac des Chevaliers castle in Syria, built around 1030 to control the Homs gap, on one of several routes to reach the Mediterranean shore

Three assassins being prepared for their mission by the Old Man of the Mountain in Syria, from the Travels of Marco Polo.

China in decline

To the east of the Pamirs, China was in absolute decline, and a series of petty states and fierce nomad entities developed to disrupt trade. To the west, Abbasid decline and the emergence of contending Persian and then Turkish states did little to promote trade along the Silk Road with China. During this period, between AD 800 and 1200, the direct contacts that had been established between Tang China and the West withered. While caravans continued to traverse the Silk Road, trade was disrupted by political uncertainties, with the sea routes to China via the Indian Ocean prospering as a consequence.

Nor was silk the important commodity it had once been. Both the Tang and their

THE LAST OF THE ABBASIDS

Hulagu Khan (1217–65), grandson of the Mongol founder Genghis Khan, captured and sacked Baghdad on 10 February 1258. It was an event that marked the end of the Abbasid Caliphate and the Arab Golden Age. Muslims warned the victorious Hulagu that disaster would befall the Mongols if the blood of al-Musta'sim, the last Abbasid Caliph, were to be spilled. Hulagu took the warning to heart and had al-Musta'sim rolled in a carpet and trampled to death by horses to avoid bloodshed. Al Musta'sim's family were also executed, with the exception of the youngest son and daughter, despatched to Mongolia to become slaves to Hulagu's court.

THE MONGOL ERA AND RISE OF EUROPE

Genghis Khan ruthlessly brought the Silk Road under Mongol control, but overland trade declined as new sea routes opened up.

In the 13th century a new and unexpected power exploded onto the scene, rapidly conquering the entire length of the Silk Road from Chang'an in the east to Antakya (Antioch) in the west, bringing the whole of the passage under the umbrella of a single empire for the first time in history. This produced the last great flourishing of Silk Road trade before its final decline and gradual disappearance in the 15th and 16th centuries. The engine for this new empire was the drive for Mongol expansion, and the man who made it happen was a nomadic ruler called Temujin, who would later assume the title Genghis Khan (1206–27). His name is remembered with a shudder by all the settled peoples from Chang'an to Baghdad, and with fierce pride by the nomadic Mongols themselves.

> *The highly efficient Mongol shuudan or postal service used horse-relay stations similar to the US Pony Express. As most Mongol officers were illiterate, orders were communicated in verse so that instructions were transmitted correctly.*

He was born around 1162 not too far from Ulaanbaatar, the present capital of Mongolia. Despite enduring a difficult childhood and relative poverty, he showed remarkable willpower and military ability, gradually defeating his clan enemies until, in 1206, he united the feuding Mongol tribes under his sole leadership as Great Khan. He lived for a further 21 years, during which time his armies conquered the greater part of Asia, including the Silk Road between China and the Caspian Sea. On his

14th-century portrait of Genghis Khan (1162–1227), founder of the Mongol Empire.

death in 1227, the Mongol Empire is estimated to have encompassed 26 million sq km (10 million sq miles), an area about four times the size of the Roman or Macedonian empires at their peak. It covered 22 percent of the earth's land surface and lorded over 100 million people.

Despite his ruthless efficiency as a military commander, Genghis was remarkably enlightened in matters of religion and culture, allowing his many conquered subjects considerable freedom. He also set the seal on another aspect of Mongol policy – the encouragement of trade relationships between the increasingly far-flung corners of the empire. His rule generally brought destruction to most of Persia, including the removal of the Assassins, but spared certain centres, including the city of Tabriz, close to the border with Azerbaijan and Turkey.

This enlightened policy caused a brief but dazzling resurgence of the ancient Silk Road, as all merchants and ambassadors carrying proper documentation and authority were permitted, and indeed encouraged, to travel throughout the vast Mongol realm under imperial protection. As a consequence, overland trade between Asia and Europe greatly increased. During the 13th and early 14th centuries this policy encouraged hundreds, perhaps thousands of

notionally allied khanates. In fact, four rival kingdoms emerged. In the east, the greatest of all was the Empire of the Great Khan, soon to become the Yuan Dynasty of China. The greater part of Central Asia, including both Kashgar and Samarkand, became the Chagatai Khanate. Most of Persia and the Middle East became the Ilkhanate, centred on their capital at Tabriz. Finally the vast Russian steppe stretching from the Altai Mountains to Kiev was incorporated in the fabled Golden Horde.

This political division of the Mongol realms was soon to become a cultural divide as well.

Mongol mounted archer.

Western merchants to travel the Silk Road to China, the most celebrated of whom was Marco Polo (see page 66).

Division of the spoils

Genghis Khan was succeeded by several wise and highly competent rulers, notably his third son Ogedei Khan (1229–41) and his grandson Kublai Khan (1260–94). Kublai, who had studied Chinese culture, became the first emperor of China's Yuan Dynasty in 1271, and under his rule Mongol power and prosperity reached new heights. Yet the seeds of future imperial decline were already sown before Kublai attained manhood. In his will, Genghis had ordered the Mongol Empire divided into four separate,

RUSSIA'S CAPITAL DESTROYED

In 1246 Giovanni de Plano Carpini, papal envoy to the Mongols, gave an eyewitness account of the khan's ruthless methods: "The Mongols attacked Russia, where they made great havoc, destroying cities and fortresses and slaughtering men; and they laid siege to Kiev, the capital of Russia; after they had besieged the city for a long time, they took it and put the inhabitants to death. When we were journeying through that land we came across countless skulls and bones of dead men lying about on the ground. Kiev... has been reduced almost to nothing... and the inhabitants are kept in complete slavery."

Marco Polo

The description of the Italian's adventures to the court of Kublai Khan is one of the Silk Road's greatest historical records.

During the 13th and 14th centuries, Venetian merchants dominated much of the trade in rare and exotic goods trafficked between Europe and Asia by way of the Mediterranean and Red seas. It was a

Marco Polo in caravan.

source of great wealth to the tiny but prosperous Venetian Republic. But the lure of the Silk Road still attracted the interest of ambitious Venetian merchants who sought to profit overland as well as by maritime trade. Two such merchants were brothers Niccolo and Maffeo Polo, who set out to trade in the region of the Volga steppes.

Depending on one's interpretation, their luck was either bad or exceedingly good, as their venture coincided with the wars of conquest of the expanding Mongol Empire, which prevented the brothers' return home. Instead, in 1264, they decided to accompany a tributary mission from the Volga region to Khanbaliq, the seat of Kublai Khan, near present-day Beijing. They were well received and hospitably treated by the Great Khan, who

enjoyed religious and philosophical debate. At the end of their visit Kublai Khan sent them back to Venice under his protection with a request that they should return to China together with "one hundred learned Christians" able to debate and argue the cause of their religion at the Mongol court.

The second journey

In 1271 the Polo brothers set out on their return journey to Beijing accompanied by Niccolo's 17-year-old son, Marco, who would find especial favour with the Great Khan. The Polos travelled overland, by way of Central Asia, passing through Persia and staying three years in Bukhara before crossing the Pamirs into present-day Xinjiang. Here they took the Southern Silk Road via Kashgar and Khotan before passing through the much-feared "Desert of Lop", which Marco describes as a howling wilderness inhabited by malevolent demons intent on luring men and beasts into the sandy wastes of the Taklamakan Desert.

Marco Polo spent 17 years in China, much of it in the service of the Great Khan, before leaving for Europe in 1291. Interestingly his return route was a two year sea journey to the Straits of Hormuz and then overland via Trebizond on the Black Sea. He reached Venice in 1295, reportedly laden with concealed rubies and other jewels, but was captured and briefly imprisoned by the Genoese in 1298, during a short war between Venice and Genoa. While in prison, he dictated an elaborate account of his travels to a fellow prisoner, Rustichello da Pisa, which was subsequently published as *Il Milione*, known in English as *The Travels of Marco Polo*. The popularity of his journey gave many people the impression of merchants travelling the full length of the Silk Road, but in practice most traders covered much shorter sections before returning with exchanged goods.

The veracity of Marco Polo's account of his travels in China and beyond has been called into question by some authorities. Why, for example, does he not mention the use of chopsticks, or the Great Wall? Yet these apparently glaring omissions fade to almost nothing when compared with the information Marco did bring back, much of it arcane and arbitrary, but also clearly verifiable today. *Il Milione* was an immediate success, stimulating interest in the Orient across Europe. Christopher Columbus, who would discover the New World in his quest for a western maritime route to Asia, is known to have owned a heavily annotated copy.

Quite simply, the Mongols were overwhelmingly outnumbered by the settled peoples they now ruled, and they were also deeply influenced by the more sophisticated cultures they had conquered. Thus Kublai Khan, who founded Beijing in 1272, was an enthusiastic student of Chinese culture and rapidly became sinicised. The rulers of the Chagatai Khanate adopted Islam and were soon absorbed into Central Asian Turkic culture. To the west, the Ilkhans similarly converted to Islam and, renouncing all loyalty to the Great Khan, became deeply influenced by Persian and Arab mores.

to Muscovite Russia in the 16th century. The later Safavids, who established the first lasting Shia state in Iran, emerged from the northern Iranian city of Ardebil. They also set their capital at Tabriz, but it was always too close to the border with the emerging Ottoman Empire, so they moved to Isfahan.

> *"In all the other parts of the world light descends upon earth. From holy Samarkand and Bukhara, it ascends." Tajik saying*

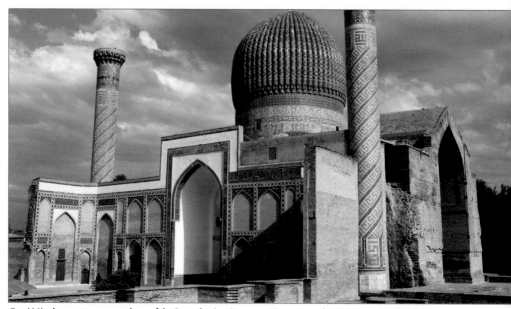

Gur-i-Mir, the sumptuous mausoleum of the Central Asian Conqueror Timur (Tamerlane), in Samarkand, Uzbekistan

Timur's glories

Meanwhile, to the north and west the Golden Horde fell increasingly under Tatar influence and abandoned its Mongol allegiance before being fatally weakened by the great Turkic-Mongol conqueror Timur (Tamerlane, 1336–1405). Timur was not only a military genius, but also a patron of the arts, and his rule inspired the creation of some of the greatest works of architecture ever built, including the Registan, the Bibi Khanum Mosque and his own tomb of Gur-i-Mir in Samarkand, as well as buildings in Bukhara, Shakhrisabz and elsewhere in Central Asia.

Timur's descendants would go on to found the Mughal Dynasty in India (1526–1867), while the Golden Horde finally succumbed

Decline and demise

The gradual disintegration of the Mongol Empire also brought about the collapse of Silk Road prosperity as the brief political and cultural stability of *Pax Mongolica* disappeared. The eastern part of the Silk Road passed from the short-lived Yuan Dynasty (1271–1368) to the sphere of the Ming Empire (1368–1644). At the same time, to the west of the Pamirs, the old Silk Road came under the control of various decentralised Turkic kingdoms, including the Chagatai, Timurid and subsequently Uzbek khanates, while the Middle East and Anatolia unified under the new power of the Ottoman Empire (1299–1922), which would become the centre of interaction between the Eastern and

Western worlds for more than six centuries. But the great trans-Asian highway that had for so many centuries served as a link between East and West was already fatally ruptured. Trade flourished in the East under the Ming, and in the West under the Ottomans, but overland

> *"Do not say that you were not warned in due time! Tremblingly obey and show no negligence!" Emperor Qianlong's message to King George III*

Chinese ships at anchor.

trade between the two was never fully re-established, due both to Central Asian instability and to two seminal changes that would irreversibly change the nature of commerce between Europe and China.

The first of these was the isolationism of the Ming Dynasty, which turned its back on Central Asia and fixed the limits of its territorial ambitions within the traditional Chinese cultural sphere. China increasingly became inwardlooking, despite being the richest, most populous and – for a time – the most powerful state in the world. Eventually the empire lost touch with reality and failed to keep pace with the startling changes beginning to sweep the West.

Exploration by sea

Secondly, an emerging Europe was hungry for spices and trade with the Orient, but often cut off from China by a Muslim world that treasured its trade monopoly and drove prices ever higher. The resultant European search for new routes to the Orient led to Christopher Columbus's discovery in 1492 of the New World, which he mistakenly thought was "The Indies". Just six years later, Vasco da Gama reached Cochin on the Kerala coast by sea, establishing a direct link for the first time between Western Europe and India. Both the Ottoman and the Chinese empires were about to be outflanked by merchant navigators from Spain and Portugal, closely followed by the Dutch and British.

In 1521 Ferdinand Magellan completed the work of Columbus when he reached the Philippines, establishing a direct link between Europe and Asia across the Pacific for the first time. With two direct maritime routes established between Europe and the Far East, it was not long before Chinese waters were dominated by aggressive European sailors, while China had no effective naval response.

The demise of the overland Silk Road owes much to the development of the silk route by sea, where it became easier and safer to transport goods in ships that were stronger and more reliable. Over the following couple of centuries trade centres were established along the Indian Ocean coastal route, opening up opportunities for the Europeans and making new contacts. The new Safavid capital at Isfahan, for example, prospered on a trade route that connected the Persian Gulf with the Black Sea.

China refused any trade with the British, and in 1793 Emperor Qianlong informed the Macartney embassy that "We possess all things. I set no value on objects strange or ingenious, and have no use for your country's manufactures". The emperor made it clear that he regarded the embassy as a tributary mission, and sent a message to King George III warning that British vessels putting ashore at any point other than Guangzhou would be immediately expelled.

The great powers at play

Less than half a century later, in 1842, China was resoundingly defeated by Britain in the First Opium War; maritime trade in the Far East was securely in European (and later American) hands. The great, ancient Silk Road, long ago abandoned and remembered only at the best-surviving oases, was all but forgotten.

Rivalry for these forgotten territories of Central Asia and western China resurfaced throughout the 19th century when Britain wanted to prevent Russia expanding its territories southward. Britain's manoeuvrings for control to halt this threat to India, its "Jewel in the Crown", became known as the Great Game. At a time when boundaries were becoming increasingly important, much of the area remained unmapped, which added to the uncertainty, but also offered opportunities to seize land regard-

creating a complex jigsaw of new nation-states and nationalisms in the process.

For almost 1,500 years, the Silk Road had held a unique role in Asian foreign trade and political relations, but today the story is far from over. Like a disused railway line given a new lease of life, a booming Chinese economy is giving the modern Central Asian republics an opportunity to reuse the Silk Road, with new roads, pipelines and rail links. They continue to carry the latest commodities (such as oil and gas) from one region to another, which has always been the main reason for the Silk Road.

Ambassador George Macartney and his delegation grovelling before Emperor Qianlong in 1793.

less. The impasse was superseded by the onset of World War I, as Russia and Britain found themselves allied against Germany.

At the beginning of the 20th century, vast areas of Central Asia were swallowed up in the expanding but isolationist Soviet Empire: the lands of the former Golden Horde and the khanates of Bukhara, Khiva and Kokand were divided up on ethnic rather than cultural lines, ensuring ongoing instability. But the end of World War I also saw the break-up of the Ottoman Empire, and the emergence of new identities such as Lebanon, Syria and Iraq. Equally momentous changes occurring at the end of the century led to the collapse of the Soviet ideal, once again freeing the Central Asian states and

CHINA TAKES THE SEA ROUTE

The third Ming emperor, Yongle (1402–24), was unique in the annals of Imperial China in that he pursued an active maritime policy, sending his favourite admiral, the Yunnanese Muslim eunuch Zheng He (1371–1433), to explore Southeast Asia and the Indian Ocean as far as the Red Sea and the East African Coast. Starting in 1405, Yongle sent Zheng He on six major naval expeditions at the head of a fleet of hundreds of "treasure ships". His purpose was to extend Chinese control over Nan Yang, the "southern seas", by imposing imperial control over trade and overawing the peoples of the littoral into paying tribute to the Ming throne.

The Great Game

As Britain and Russia headed towards each other in Central Asia, spies, skulduggery and derring-do brought tales of high adventure.

The 19th century saw the Russian Empire reach southwards towards India, Britain's "Jewel in the Crown", just as the British Empire expanded its grip into the northwest frontier and Afghanistan.

Alexander Burnes.

As the two empires inched ever closer, the need to map out the little-known areas between them and to gain influence with the various rulers in this buffer zone became imperative. The British in particular were terrified that the Russians would advance through Central Asia and into India in search of a warm-water port. The result was the Great Game, an imperial play of cat and mouse, incursions and espionage set in the deserts and mountains of Central Asia. It ranks as one of the most colourful periods of Silk Road history.

As listening posts in places such as Kashgar and Mashhad sent back reports to London and St Petersburg, a series of pundits, explorers, spies, diplomats and military officers (supposedly on "hunting leave") slipped into Central Asia, some in disguise, others in uniform at the head of armies. Those that returned brought reports of dastardly emirs, terrible deserts and ripping tales of derring-do. It was irresistible propaganda, and the public lapped it up in newspapers and at public lectures organised by the likes of the Royal Geographical Society.

Early disasters

The initial Russian forays south into Central Asia were disastrous. In 1717 a detachment of 4,000 Russian troops sent to Khiva were slaughtered to a man. In 1839 another winter march, this time to Khiva to free Russian slaves, was again forced to turn back, with the loss of 1,000 men and 8,500 camels and not a single shot fired.

In the meantime a series of intrepid British traveller-spies began to brave the deserts and slave-raiders of Central Asia, including William Moorcroft, Arthur Conolly (who travelled under the alias "Khan Ali") and Alexander "Bokhara" Burnes. Using charm and flattery, well-versed in local languages and dressed in local cloaks and turbans, these players of the Great Game wrote secret reports, reconnoitred military routes and (if they were lucky) returned home to publish a best-selling memoir.

It was a dangerous job. The Emir of Bukhara threw Captain Conolly and Colonel Charles Stoddart into a vermin-infested pit for two years before killing them. Alexander Burnes was hacked to death by an Afghan mob in Kabul and numerous others perished in remote valleys from disease or poisoning. All knew they would be coolly disowned by their governments should they be caught.

Russia advances

Russia's attempt to create a defendable southern border began with a line of forts across the Kazakh steppe, from Orenburg to Ak Mechet, and spread quickly as railway lines and steamer routes pressed deeper into Central Asia, bringing with them the double-edged sword of Russian trade and "protection".

The Russian conquest was gradual but unstoppable, largely because the emirates and khanates of Bukhara, Kokand and Khiva were too busy squabbling with each other to worry about the Russians. Russian troops took Shymkent (1864), Tashkent (1865), Samarkand (1868),

Krasnovodsk (1869), Khiva (1873) and Kokand (1875) within a decade. St Petersburg's assertion that the towns of Turkestan would be returned to local rule was a farce.

Such was the delicate situation when a young British officer unofficially came to see for himself. Captain Frederick Gustavus Burnaby of the Royal Horse Guards had only recently returned home from the Sudan and set off to travel to the next potential Russian objective of Merv in the middle of winter 1875–6. His efforts to avoid the Tsarist troops and survive the freezing desert temperatures with local tribal assistance meant that he ended up in Khiva instead. His account of the journey *A Ride to Khiva* remains a Victorian classic adventure read to this day.

As the Russians pushed south, the political temperature spiked. Russian troops crushed the Turkmen tribes at Gök-Tepe (1881) in a massacre that left 14,500 Turkmen dead. Three years later they took the oasis of Merv (1884), creating a panic that the British press wittily dubbed "Mervousness". The subsequent Russian advance to Pandjeh, the gateway to Herat, pushed the two sides to the brink of war, and 25,000 British troops rushed to Quetta. The sabres were only put away with the establishment of a Joint Afghan Boundary Commission in the border town of Sarakhs.

Afghanistan

The British endured an even rougher time in Afghanistan. The 1838 invasion ended in the massacre of 16,000 British troops, with just one man surviving to limp back through the Khyber Pass. The second Anglo-Afghan War, a result of an 1878 Russian mission to Kabul, was almost as disastrous as the first. The message was as clear then as it would be to the Russians more than a century later; no one invades Afghanistan and wins.

The British solution to their ongoing military failures in Afghanistan was to create a tripartite frontier: a directly controlled British territory in the Punjab; a belt of vassal states (the Pashtun-dominated Federally Administered Tribal Areas – FATA); and then the independent buffer state of Afghanistan. Britain's foreign minister, Sir Mortimer Durand, met with Amir Abdur Rahman in Kabul in 1893 to discuss which areas of the FATA should fall under their respective influences. The dividing line they identified became known as the Durand Line.

The focus of the Game now shifted to the Pamirs, a strategic vacuum where the Russian, British and Chinese empires converged. A string of Russian and British explorers (including Lord Curzon, Colonel Francis Younghusband, John Wood, T.E. Gordon and Ney Elias) mapped the rivers and passes in an attempt to pin down a border. Every now and then the two sides came face to face: Younghusband met his Russian counterpart General Gromchevsky in Hunza in 1889. Whatever their political affiliations, meetings required fine dinners accompanied by port, crystal and linens. The Great Game was, after all, a gentlemen's affair.

The Russians engaging the Emir of Bukhara's forces.

End game

Eventually the Joint Afghan Boundary Commission (1887) and Anglo-Russian Convention (1907) defused border tensions. Concerns over Russian influence on India lingered (and even prompted the Younghusband invasion of Tibet in 1903), but the height of Anglo-Russian rivalry was over. The Soviet army did not cross the Oxus until 1979, and Russian troops never even made it close to the thresholds of India. The Durand line marks a de facto border today, though it is still disputed. Some historians contend that the Great Game was more fiction than fact, owing more to Kipling's Kim than to historical events. The Russians themselves never used the phrase, referring only to a "Tournament of Shadows". But if parts of the Game were fiction, what a ripping yarn it was.

Expedition in the Taklamakan,
pictured by Aurel Stein.

REDISCOVERING THE ROAD

Another Great Game, but this time between explorers and archaeologists searching for long-lost Silk Road cities and their vanished treasures.

As Silk Road trade withered and China withdrew behind its wall, the ancient oasis towns of Chinese Central Asia grew increasingly isolated. Glacier-fed streams retreated, irrigation channels collapsed and the desert began to reclaim abandoned settlements. Half-buried temple complexes, garrison towns and Buddhist stupas were left to crumble undisturbed for centuries, preserved only in local legends of buried cities protected by desert demons.

Little by little, rumours of these lost cities began to funnel back to the listening posts of the British Empire. As the finds became more impressive, the trickle of interest turned to a flood, and soon archaeological teams from seven nations were involved in a frantic race to carve out spheres of influence in a rivalry that carried clear echoes of the Great Game.

The Finnish Baron Carl Gustav Mannerheim (who later became president of Finland) passed by Dunhuang in 1907 but decided to go pheasant shooting instead, thus missing out on one of the greatest treasures of the Silk Road.

Sculptures and murals inside the Mogao Caves, Dunhuang.

The archaeologist-explorers who braved the fearsome Taklamakan Desert first unearthed walls, then houses, monasteries and entire cities, all spectacularly preserved in the dry desert air. Paintings in a hitherto unseen blend of Greek, Iranian, Indian and Chinese styles resurfaced as fresh as the day they were painted, alongside documents in Sogdian, Tokharian and a dozen unknown scripts.

Over a period of 25 years, caravan-loads of booty were carted out of China and, for better or worse, ancient libraries, frescoes, statues, relics and entire temples were removed by the tonne. Slowly but surely, the forgotten commercial and cultural crossroad towns of Turpan, Kuqa, Miran and Niya were resurrected after 1,500 years of slumber.

The first steps

Long before the archaeological teams launched their assaults on Turkestan, individual spies, explorers, scientists and travellers had begun to pick up fragments of the past coughed up by the desert. In 1876–7 Nikolai Przhevalsky, Russia's greatest Central Asian explorer, wrote of finding a large deserted city in the deserts of Lop Nur. The following year the Russian botanist Albert Regel became the first foreigner to lay eyes on Karakhoja near Turpan, before the Chinese threw him out as a spy. In 1890 the French explorer Dutreuil de Rhins picked up terracotta figures and scriptures, and four years later was murdered on the Tibetan plateau.

The first reliable reports of Turkestan's lost cities had come from the *pundits* or *munshis*, Indian spies employed by the British Raj, but it was the arrival of the Bower Manuscripts in 1890 that really excited the British. Lieutenant Bower had purchased 51 pieces of birch bark in Kuqa (they were discovered by local treasure-hunters

Sven Hedin on a camel.

THE FORGER OF KHOATAN

One of the great archaeological hoaxes in history was perpetrated by Islam Akhun, an Uighur from Khotan. After years of duping European experts with his forged documents and scripts, Akhun came clean only after being confronted by Aurel Stein in Khotan in 1901. The enterprising forger would stain his documents with local tree dye and hang them over a fire to age them, finally adding sprinkles of sand for authenticity. Demand became so great that he had to block-print entire texts. By the time Stein exposed the fraud the documents were in museums across Europe, fooling the finest philologists and orientalists in their fields.

in a nearby stupa), while investigating the murder of Scottish trader Andrew Dalgleish. The eventual realisation that the Sanskrit documents dated from the 5th century – and thus were one of the oldest pieces of writing ever found – was a revelation. What were 1,500-year-old Buddhist documents written in an Indian script doing in the heart of Central Asia?

It was the Russians, led by Dimitri Klementz in 1898, who were first, with a purely archaeological expedition to the region. Klementz's haul of manuscripts, frescoes and photographs from the cave temples of Karakhoja (Khocho), Astana and Yarkhoto in the Turpan oasis set the archaeological community alight, giving birth to the brand-new academic field of Central Asian studies.

Sven Hedin

The true trailblazer of Silk Road rediscovery was the Swede Sven Hedin, perhaps the greatest of all the explorers to Central Asia. Fluent in seven languages and tutored by Ferdinand von Richthofen, the German geographer who in 1877 had coined the phrase "Silk Road" (Seidenstrassen), it was Hedin's three groundbreaking expeditions in the 1890s into the heart of the Taklamakan that proved travel in Chinese Turkestan was possible. But his expeditions regularly left a trail of dead camels, ponies and assistants in their wake.

Hedin's first expedition was a disaster that claimed several lives, and nearly his own. In February 1895, after a winter crossing of the Pamirs that included a failed summit attempt on 7,546-metre (24,75-ft) Muztagh Ata, 29-year-old Hedin travelled to the Yarkand River and set off into the desert equipped with a mobile larder of animals and more than 1,000 photographic plates tied to the sides of several camels. Two weeks later the expedition was dying of thirst, jettisoning baggage left and right in a desperate race to find water. One guide lost consciousness after drinking camel's urine, while Hedin himself became temporarily paralysed after drinking primus fuel. After six days without water, two men and all the camels except one were dead and all the surveying equipment lost.

Not one to let a near-death experience slow him down, Hedin set out again in 1899 for three months through the Taklamakan Desert on a boat up the Yarkand and Tarim rivers, before continuing on foot for three weeks across the desert to Cherchen and Lop Nur. Here he unearthed the Chinese garrison town of Loulan (Kroraina), lost to barbarians in the 4th century and already under the sands for a millennium by the time Marco Polo passed through in 1275.

Hedin returned to a knighthood, gold medals from the Royal Geographical Society and a fame that was compounded by subsequent trips across the Trans-Himalaya to map the headwaters of the Indus and Bhramaputra in western Tibet. By the time of his death in 1952, however, his achievements were largely forgotten, replaced by notoriety for his pro-German stance in both world wars.

For all his achievements, Hedin was an explorer and a geographer – "The scientific research I willingly left to others." The detailed unearthing of the Silk Road was left to the archaeologists, foremost among them Marc Aurel Stein.

Aurel Stein

In many ways Marc Aurel Stein is the father of Central Asian archaeology. Inspired by the journeys of Alexander the Great and Xuanzang (see page 57), the British-Hungarian scholar, archaeologist and cartographer mounted three great expeditions to Chinese Turkestan over the course of 16 years, racking up an estimated 40,000km (25,000 miles) of travel. His first journey, from Kashmir in 1900, was described as "the most daring and adventurous raid upon the ancient world that any archaeologist has attempted".

Accompanied by his terrier Dash, he battled sandstorms and frostbite (the toes of his right foot were amputated after a surveying trip to the Kunlun Mountains), navigating the Taklamakan sands with the aid of Hedin's maps and excavating at remote sites for weeks at a time. Hedin proved you could travel to Turkestan, and Stein proved you could excavate there.

After an inauspicious start in Khotan where he found nothing but "complete decay and utter desolation", the incredible first trip revealed the cities of Dandan Oilik, Niya, Endere, Karadong and Rawok. At Dandan Oilik he dug through 2 metres (8ft) of sand to unearth Gandharan-style temple frescoes and a 5th–6th-century Buddhist library. At Niya his discovery of Greek-influenced images of Athena, Heracles and Eros proved cultural links with Bactria, while

documents in Kharoshthi script tied the Southern Silk Road sites firmly to the Indian cultural sphere. Writing up notes in his tent late into the night until the ink in his pen froze, it was Stein who invented the term "Serindia" (from Seres, or Land of Silk) to describe the unique mix of Chinese, Indian and Gandharan styles that characterised Southern Silk Road art.

At Rawok, north of Khotan, he discovered a huge stupa half-buried in 8 metres (25ft) of sand. Over nine days he unearthed 91 Gandharan-style statues, only to rebury them. Five years later he returned to the site to find that

Aurel Stein in the field together with his guide and his terrier Dash.

> "To be hired by Hedin on one of his trips meant almost certain death for man or beast." Historian Frances Wood

tomb-raiders had smashed the statues in the hope of finding gold inside.

Stein sent his treasures back to George Macartney, the British Consul-General in Kashgar. Over the years Macartney's residence, Chini Bagh, became a clearinghouse for Serindian art, arranging discrete shipment and logistical support for Stein and others. Eight ponies carried the 12 crates of treasure over the mountain passes to Osh and Andijan, where they were placed on a train to Russia. News of Stein's finds preceded him, and by the time he returned to Europe the secret of Turkestan's lost cities was out.

The Germans

Spurred on by Stein's success and Klementz's reports, in 1902 the Germans launched the first of four expeditions to the relatively accessible oasis of Turpan. Over the next decade the expedition leaders Albert Grünwedel and Albert von Le Coq would send back 34 tonnes

Albert von Le Coq on an expedition.

HEROES OR THIEVES

While fêted at home as heroes, archaeologists like Stein, Pelliot and von Le Coq are viewed by most Chinese scholars as thieves. Accusations of exploitation are hard to avoid. At one point von Le Coq swapped rotten berries for a pile of priceless manuscripts, claiming the berries held rejuvenative powers. Even Stein privately described von Le Coq and his assistant as "little more than treasure-hunters". Archaeologists' claims to be safeguarding finds for posterity suffered a direct hit in World War II when seven Allied bombs struck Berlin's Ethnographical Museum and 28 of the Bezeklik murals were destroyed.

of antiquities to Berlin in 423 crates, including over 40,000 fragments of manuscripts.

At the time of the first expedition (1902–3) even getting to Central Asia took more than seven months, first by Trans-Siberian train, then steamer up the Irtysh River, and then by carriage to Urumqi, with von Le Coq sitting astride 12,000 roubles in gold (the expedition funds), brandishing a shotgun. The first expedition worked on Karakhoja (modern Gaochang), with modest results. Grünwedel was ill for the second expedition and leadership passed to von Le Coq, a museum volunteer and former wine merchant who had changed careers in mid-life to study Arabic, Turkish, Persian and Sanskrit. The string of breathtaking finds that followed included a Nestorian church and a 1.8-metre (6-ft) fresco of Manes (the founder of Manichaeism), the first such portrait ever found. Other finds included cloth paintings, further frescoes, illuminated manuscripts (including a Christian prayer book in Persian) and manuscripts in 24 different scripts, as well as the murdered corpses of 100 Buddhist monks.

It was Bezeklik ("Place of Paintings") that yielded the greatest finds, including six wall-sized Buddhist portraits and 15 giant murals of the Buddha. The chance discovery of the Bezeklik murals was a classic moment of Silk Road rediscovery. Von Le Coq's response to such splendour was to hack away at the straw-and-mud walls, cutting the largest frescoes into pieces and packing them with reeds and cotton wool to transport them back to Germany. It was a move that would later make the blood of Chinese scholars "boil with indignation".

By the time of the second German expedition in 1906 the race was really heating up, as rival international groups staked their claims. Stein was about to return, and the Russians and French (relative latecomers due to their excavations at Angkor in the French Protectorate of Cambodia) were both planning expeditions. Such was the heightened rivalry that Russian and German archaeological teams almost came to blows over the division of excavation rights in Kuqa.

The Germans headed straight for the Ming-oi or "1,000-chambered" cave temples of Kumtura and Kizil, on the Muzart River near Kuqa. At one stage, scraping off an inch of white mould, the team revealed a row of incredible 1,500-year-old Hellenistic images painted in a distinct Kuqan style. To this day the Kizil frescoes remain a highlight of Central Asian art and the Germans' greatest discovery. "What I have seen here", Grünwedel was moved to declare, "goes beyond my wildest dreams."

Tensions grew between von Le Coq and Grünwedel, who disagreed strongly over the cutting and removing of frescoes, but the expedition was immensely successful, amassing some 128 cases of treasures. It was such a haul that it was to be six years before they returned to Central Asia.

The discovery of Dunhuang

Back in Kashgar in 1907, a departing von Le Coq missed the arrival of his rival Stein by less than a week. For his second expedition Stein entered Central Asia through the Pamirs on what would be a two-and-a-half-year expedition, recounted in his book *Ruins of Desert Cathay*.

Stein's first target was Loulan, remotest of the desert sites. Travelling by night to avoid the heat, his caravan included 50 labourers and 25 camels, most of which were to carry huge blocks of ice for drinking water. Stein's analysis of documents and rubbish at Loulan revealed it as an outpost so remote that it was still paying a tribute in the name of an empire that had ceased to exist 14 years previously. Stein also found Hedin's measuring tape, which he returned to him at an RGS dinner in London.

From Loulan, Stein headed to Miran to uncover some fabulous murals, including one of classical winged angels signed by the Roman-sounding artist "Titus". He packed these off to Kashgar, two months' travel away, and headed for his most important discovery yet.

Rumours had long been echoing down the Silk Road about the cave complex at Dunhuang. Stein had heard of it from a Hungarian geological expedition who visited in 1879. Albert von Le Coq had considered visiting from Hami in 1905 and spun a coin to decide; it landed tails up and he returned to Kashgar. Stein arrived at Dunhuang in March 1907 to find the self-appointed guardian Abbot Wang (Wang Yuanlu) away. While killing time he discovered a series of watchtowers that he believed formed an extension of the Great Wall, and located the famous Jade Gate, or Yumen, through which all Silk Road

Abbot Wang of Dunhuang.

COUNTRIES WITHIN COUNTRIES

Although Tsarist Russia had begun colonising Central Asia in the 1890s, it was Stalin whose political policies were to have greatest regional impact. In creating new Soviet Socialist Republics (SSRs), he implemented a set of borders based on ethnic lines rather than cultural or geographical ones, and these ultimately became the borders of the new independent republics in 1991.

In practice this made no sense: ethnic communities did not live in discreet blocks and often intermarried. Consequently, the border lines wriggled between villages, including some fields and houses but not others. Enclaves and exclaves were created, regardless of whether or not they were entirely surrounded by

someone else's sovereign territory. There are four Uzbek exclaves in Kyrgyzstan alone, and another two belonging to Tajikistan. Kyrgyzstan too has exclaves in Uzbekistan and Tajikistan.

Stalin's border policy in Central Asia was one of divide and rule: he understood that constant border skirmishes between the various states would ensure ongoing instability in the region, preventing the states joining together (for example on the grounds of shared culture or religion) and challenging Moscow. In this respect, the policy was a great success: the Fergana Valley, where most of the enclaves are found, is the least stable part of Central Asia.

traffic had passed for centuries. Stein had to tread slowly to placate the nervous Abbot Wang, but finally won him over with their shared appreciation of Xuanzang. As Wang revealed the walled-up cave (Cave 17), filled with texts and hidden for 1,000 years, Stein wrote:

"The sight disclosed in the dim light of the priest's oil lamp made my eyes open wide. Heaped up in layers, but without any order, there appeared a solid mass of manuscript bundles rising to a height of nearly 10 feet and filling, as subsequent measurement showed, close on 500 cubic feet."

Paul Pelliot inspecting scrolls at the Mogao Caves, Dunhuang (Cave 17).

"Suddenly, as if by magic, I saw on the walls bared in this way, to my right and left, splendid paintings in colours as fresh as if the artist had only just finished them."
Von Le Coq on the Kizil frescoes

Stein bundled up 24 cases of documents and five cases of rare Tang paintings and secured the purchase of the priceless documents for £130. Among the 13,000 documents brought back to the British Museum was the *Diamond Sutra*, a giant scroll dating back to AD 868, making it the world's oldest dated printed book. Linguists spent the next 50 years translating the estimated 32km (20 miles) of scrolls. It was an archaeological scoop that would later be compared with the discovery of the Dead Sea scrolls.

Stein's finds in Dunhuang were incredible, but his inability to read Chinese was a severe hindrance. The brilliant (and Chinese-speaking) 29-year-old French linguist Paul Pelliot faced no such handicap when he arrived at the caves a year later, unaware that Stein had already visited. He spent three weeks in the tiny cave reading by candlelight through the remaining 20,000 manuscripts and sifting out the cream of the crop, which he then purchased for £90. Amongst Pelliot's finds was a 14-page section of *The Record to Five Indian Kingdoms*, a hitherto lost text by Hwi Chao, the Korean equivalent of Xuanzang who travelled through Turkestan to India from AD 713 to 741. Back in Beijing at the end of his two-year trip on horseback, Pelliot revealed some of the documents to local Chinese scholars, and orders were finally sent to seal up the caves. Pelliot had effectively closed the door on Dunhuang.

End games

As news of the spectacular finds from Dunhuang reached Europe, great rivalry came to the fore, and the race turned into an archaeological free-for-all. The British labelled their rival Japanese archaeologists as spies and shadowed them for more than a year. The Russians were also back, rediscovering the fortress citadel of Karakhoto (Black City) in 1908, while the 1909 and 1914 expeditions of Sergei Oldenburg, Russia's foremost Buddhist expert, explored more sites around Turpan and Kuqa. Moreover, by 1913 the Germans had returned, excavating once more at Kuqa and the important artistic centre of Kumtara. The following year Stein returned to Dunhuang to grab another five cases of documents, before continuing to Karakhoto, Bezeklik and finally the 5th-century tombs of Astana, where he carefully removed silks from dozens of 1,000-year-old corpses in an attempt to date them and trace the spread of silk designs across Central Asia.

Yet the times were changing. The Germans were forced to return early in 1914 due to the threat of war in Europe, and never returned to Central Asia. Hedin and Stein (then aged 67) both returned to Central Asia after World War I, but their expeditions were largely failures. China was by this time racked by political instability (every member of Hedin's team was issued with 800 rounds of ammunition), and foreign archaeologists were no longer welcomed. Only the American Langdon Warner, the Harvard professor who was a model for Indiana Jones, scored some success, travelling in 1923–4 to Karakhoto and Dunhuang, where he removed a dozen 8th-century cave murals in their entirety. But the world was now quite a different place, and the Chinese were about to slam shut the door. The race for Turkestan's treasures was over.

Soviet archaeology

Unknown to most Westerners, archaeologists from the newly formed Soviet Union were quietly unearthing some spectacular sites. One highlight was the discovery of the ancient Parthian capital of Nissa, in modern-day Turkmenistan, where digs revealed 40 ivory *rhytons* (drinking horns) and fragments of a marble Aphrodite.

Sergei Tolstov's later excavations in the wasteland of Khorezm between 1948 and 1957 revealed a rich oasis culture dating from the 7th century BC and centred around the desert castles of Toprak Qala and Koy Krylgan Qala. Focus then shifted to the spectacular Sogdian friezes of Penjikent, Varakhsha and Afrosiab.

In Turkmenistan the Greek-Russian archaeologist Victor Sarianidi has been excavating for half a century to reveal the civilisation of ancient Margiana. In the sun-baked mud flats of Gonur Tepe he brought to light a 5,000-year-old temple, palace and necropolis that may mark the birthplace of the Zoroastrian religion.

Unearthing Afghanistan's past

Archaeology in neighbouring Afghanistan had a relatively late start. Aurel Stein had long wanted to excavate in Balkh, but it was the French Archaeological Delegation in Afghanistan (FADA) that finally gained permission in the 1920s to excavate the country's rich trove of Bactrian and Kushan sites. Their most famous discovery was the 2,000-year old Bagram Treasure, unearthed in 1937–9. At the junction of the Indian, Chinese and Greek worlds, the Kushan-era court epitomised the cosmopolitanism of the Silk Road, with finds ranging from Indian ivories and Hellenistic bronzes to Graeco-Roman glassware.

The French followed this 30 years later with the Greek city of Ai Khanoum ("Alexandria on the Oxus"); the 2,300-year-old palace complex revealed Corinthian capitals and a statue of Heracles.

Recent finds

One of the great finds of recent years was the discovery in 1978 of six royal Bactrian/Kushan tombs at Tillya Tepe, near Sheberghan on the bank of the Oxus (Amu Darya). Over the course of nine years archaeologist Victor Sarianidi's "Golden Hoard of Bactria" has totalled 22,000 gold objects, from necklaces and bracelets to buckles and brooches in Greek and Scythian styles, alongside Indian ivories, Parthian coins and Chinese mirrors. The

Digging at Tillya Tepe in 1978 uncovered a hoard of gold objects.

find was rushed to Kabul Museum in 1979 to an uncertain future. Remarkably it survived, though Afghanistan's quarter-decade of civil war has taken a terrible toll on its museums and cultural heritage. The Taliban destruction of the Buddhas of Bamiyan in 2001 marked a low point in Silk Road archaeology, but Afghan archaeologist Zemaryali Tarzi claims to have found the fabled third Buddha of Bamiyan, a 300-metre (1,000-ft) -long sleeping Buddha mentioned by Xuanzang and thought to be east of the destroyed Buddhas.

The 1994 discovery of Djumbulak Kum, an unknown 2,000-year-old fortified city, showed that even the deserts of Xinjiang have yet to reveal all of their secrets.

TREASURES OF THE SILK ROAD

A treasure-trove of manuscripts, paintings, murals, statues and artefacts reveal a great deal about daily life and beliefs centuries ago.

A century of excavations along the length of the Silk Road have resulted in a spectacular array of finds, from stirringly beautiful 1,000-year-old desert murals to glittering caches of gold.

The Buddhist frescoes of Xinjiang and Gansu remain perhaps the most visually impressive, with frescoes from Bezeklik, Kyzil and especially Dunhuang most clearly illustrating the quintessential Silk Road blurring of styles – Greek, Indian and Chinese – that would eventually be termed Serindian or Gandharan art.

Less visual but perhaps more important historically are the contemporary documents that remain so vital in dating and contextualising the surrounding finds. The earliest documents were on birch bark or wooden tablets (paper did not find its way from China until AD 100). Equally fascinating are the mundane scraps recovered from ancient rubbish tips (everything from bills of sale and correspondence to ancient mousetraps), that offer revealing insights into daily life two millennia ago.

The spectacular caches of gold that signify royal tombs across the continent remain something of a mixed blessing. Though beautiful, it was the lure of these highlights of applied art that drove tomb-raiders and looters to ransack so many stupas and tombs in their search for treasure.

The real work of deciphering the Silk Road finds began back at home. Academics at the British Museum took 50 years to work their way through Stein's Dunhuang documents, and some silks were so fragile that it took seven years to open them! Research continues to this day.

Mural from the caves at Bezeklik depicting Uighur princes wearing Chinese-style robes and headgear, dating from 8th–9th centuries.

The Buddhas at Bamiyan were long one of the great treasures of the Silk Road, despite defacement by iconoclasts. They were finally toppled by the Taliban in 2001.

A griffin-headed bracelet from the Oxus Treasure, a 5th-century BC collection of gold and silver discovered on the borders of modern Tajikistan and Afghanistan in 1877.

Frontispiece of the Diamond Sutra, the world's oldest book. Dating from 868 AD, it was discovered in Dunhuang and is now in the British Library.

ONLINE TREASURES

It's surprisingly difficult to view the major art collections of the Silk Road. London's British Museum and British Library, Paris' Guimet Musée, Berlin's Museum of Indian Art, Tokyo's National Museum and Stockholm's Ethnographical Museum all have excellent collections, but only a fraction of these are on view at any one time.

Digital technology is now at the forefront of Silk Road research, and online collections present the best opportunity to view Central Asia's treasures up close.

Visitors to the British Museum's website (www.british museum.org) can view an online collection of paintings from Dunhuang. The British Library website (www.bl.uk) also has an online Silk Road feature, and even offers a 3D viewing of the Diamond Sutra (click on "Turning the Pages"). The new Silk Road Museum in Jiuquan has an excellent online collection showing artefacts excavated along the Silk Road dating from pre-history to the Ming and Qing dynasties (www.silkroutemuseum.com).

The website of Silk Road Seattle (http://depts.washington. edu/silkroad) is particularly useful for its links and overview of all the major Silk Road collections, including the wonderful Turfan (Turpan) collection.

Other sites include the Digital Silk Road Project (http://dsr. nii.ac.jp) the groundbreaking International Dunhuang Project (http://idp.bl.uk), which has a database of 100,000 digitised documents.

...he Mogao Caves at Dunhuang represent the richest collection ...f Buddhist statuary, paintings and manuscripts ever ...iscovered. This coloured-ink illuminated manuscript shows ...Aarici, the Buddhist Goddess of Light, and her two servants.

...actrian gold from Tillya Tepe. Uncovered in 1979 in ...lorthern Afghanistan, the Bactrian Hoard (1st century BC) ...as presumed looted until it resurfaced in Kabul in 2003.

Murals found at the Sogdian city of Penjikent in Tajikistan include this depiction of Rustam, the supreme hero of Firdausi's Shahnameh.

THE STORY OF SILK

Silk has been in high demand for thousands of years. Who would have thought a tiny caterpillar could create such a fuss?

No matter where you travel, you can find silk, a fabric that is as luxurious and desirable today as when it was discovered in China thousands of years ago. It is one of nature's most remarkable creations, and no man-made fibre has ever been found to challenge its supremacy.

Silk is a protein fibre produced by silkworms and akin to the spun filaments of spiders' webs, which are produced in a similar way. Silkworms are caterpillars of the order Lepidoptera (butterflies and moths). All Lepidoptera produce silk, but none can match the lustrous, long fibre created by *Bombyx mori*, a Chinese domesticated species that dominates silk production worldwide. Selectively bred over thousands of years, *Bombyx mori* has evolved into a species of blind moth that can flap its wings but cannot fly. Its only impulse is to reproduce. The female moth waits for her suitors to scent her pheromones and trundle towards her to fulfil their destiny, ensuring the next generation of silk-producing caterpillars.

Intricate work on an emperor's robe at Urumqi Museum, Xinjiang.

> *"Patience is power; with time and patience the mulberry leaf becomes a silk gown."*
> Chinese proverb

All Lepidoptera pass through the same stages of metamorphosis: egg (also called grain), caterpillar, chrysalis and adult. The eggs require an initial period of cold incubation, and usually hatch 6–12 weeks after being laid. Normally this coincides with the freshest supply of mulberry leaves, but scientists have also engineered other methods to bypass nature and maximise production.

Once hatched, the caterpillars start eating: cultivated silkworms increase their body weight 10,000 times in their 25- to 28-day lives. Their principal foodstuff is white mulberry, to which they are attracted by the odorant cis-jasmone, but they will also eat other plants of the Moraceae family such as Osage-orange. At first, the caterpillars spend more or less their whole lives eating. Periodically they sleep for about a day, wake up, wriggle out of their old skin and start eating again. After the final skin shedding, they cast a light web to anchor themselves. The caterpillar then rears up and moves its head in a figure-of-eight, as a liquid is extruded from two pairs of spinnerets or silk glands located below its mouth. The effect of air on the liquid solidifies it into a continual silk filament. Spinning a silk cocoon takes two to three days, and then the silk is secured by a gum called sericin. Once cocooned, the caterpillar can rest; its final caterpillar skin slips away and a chrysalis is formed.

When the adult moth is ready to emerge it will make a hole in the cocoon, but silk-makers do not want *Bombyx mori* cocoons to be broken, so the insects are stifled inside the cocoon either by steaming, baking or soaking in salt water. Then the sericin is removed by immersing the cocoons in hot water, while stirring constantly, to allow the unbroken silk filament to loosen. Then the cocoons are gathered, usually with revolving brushes, which pick up the end thread as it comes loose.

Depending on the thickness needed, the silk thread is twisted or plied with several others,

> *In ancient China, people worshipped silk deities, who were served by priestesses, and to ensure good harvests, human prisoners were sacrificed to the Silk Goddess.*

The silk moth, Bombyx mori, emerges from a cocoon

THE EXTRAORDINARY QUALITIES OF SILK

Silk is highly absorbent, which makes it easy to dye. This also means that it is an ideal material to wear, as it conducts moisture away from the body.

Silk is nature's strongest natural fibre and has a high tensile strength. It is stronger than a filament of steel of equivalent dimensions. This means that silk threads do not yield to breaking and are even stronger if twisted (plied) round each other. Silk was used in making Concorde's nose and early military parachutes, and the Tour de France often spins along on silk tyres, which give a smoother ride and better traction.

Silk threads can be stretched to 20–25 percent of their length, which makes them ideal for stockings.

Provided it is not overstretched, silk will recover its former shape immediately.

Silk will fold or crush to extraordinary degrees and it can also be worn multi-layered.

When woven, silk falls and drapes in ways particularly flattering to the human form, making it the fashion fabric par excellence.

Pure silk is difficult to burn.

Silk is hypo-allergenic. There are no known allergies to silk, which makes it extremely useful for surgical and medical purposes.

Silk is a good insulator, and has been used for the insulation of electric wires.

and reeled for the next stage. Other silks have different qualities and textures, but *Bombyx mori* silk is unique in that it can be reeled in this way, as a long, strong, continual filament.

Ancient silk production

Lady Xi Lingshi, chief wife of the Yellow Emperor, Qin Shi Huang, is revered as the Lady of the Silkworms and the inventor of sericulture. This was during the reign of the Yellow Emperor (2677–2597 BC). However, we know that silk-making was long established by then, as the oldest surviving silk fabric has been dated to the middle of the 4th millennium BC.

Cocoons were one of many natural fibres explored to see what practical use they may have; the Chinese realised that one particular type of cocoon, made by the wild ancestor of *Bombyx mori*, had superior qualities, being smoother, finer and rounder than that of other silk moths, which produce irregular, flattened filaments. Flatter threads tangle easily, and break if unwound, whereas the rounder filament can be reeled as a long, continuous, stronger thread.

Archaeologists in China have found silkworms made of jade, inscribed oracle bones, and tools for all stages of textile production, including fine bone embroidery needles. Evidence of woven and embroidered silks survives in the surface corrosion of ritual bronze vessels from the Shang period (*c.*1766–1400 BC), which were wrapped in precious silk. Shang literary sources are full of references to silk and sericulture; they even mention human sacrifices to a pantheon of silkworm deities to ensure good harvests of cocoons.

China guarded the secrets of sericulture for hundreds of years, and many colourful stories explain the dissemination of this knowledge, involving beautiful and resourceful princesses hiding silkworm eggs or cocoons in their hair when despatched to marry foreign princes. Chinese emigrants took sericulture to Korea around 200 BC, and Chinese annals record silk fabrics in Japan from about 28 BC. A series of Japanese envoys visited the Chinese court, and in AD 188 the Japanese emperor received a gift of silkworm eggs, evidently not the first, from a Chinese ruler.

India's wild silks

India's history of silk production is also thousands of years old. Very early references to Indian silk usually indicate native moths, which produce silks of different textures and qualities

from that of *Bombyx mori*. Silk found in the hair of an Egyptian mummy from the Ptolemaic period (around 300–30 BC) proved to be from one of the Indian Saturnidae moths, suggesting early export from the subcontinent, albeit on a small scale. Assam's Muga moths produce a distinctive golden-yellow silk, used undyed as embroidery threads, while silk woven from Assam's Eri moths is warm and durable, but it has short staple, which must be spun like cotton or wool. A certain amount of farming and domestication has been achieved to commercialise these silks, but they are not as easy to dye

Silk is ideal for dyeing.

or bleach as *Bombyx mori*, and their rougher, more robust texture is referred to generally as "wild silk". But India also has truly wild silk, produced by huge caterpillars guarded in the forests by little boys with big sticks, who protect them against birds. Silk was deemed by Hindus to be a pure substance; the Jains, who abhor the taking of life, produce silk from broken cocoons.

Commercial silk trading

The earliest known exports of silk from China were gifts from the emperor to those who had served him well or with whom he wished to form an alliance. The beauty and exclusivity of the product quickly made it much sought after, and a commercial industry was born.

The first silk workshops were set up during the Han Dynasty (206 BC–AD 220); from the Han capital, silk was traded as far as Antioch on the Mediterranean, and eventually onwards by sea to Rome, where laws were enforced to try to control overspending on this luxury. Queen Zenobia founded the breakaway city-state of Palmyra around AD 270 to try to wrest control of the lucrative silk trade from Rome – surviving funerary statues of Palmyrene high society, draped in jewels and swathed in silks, are reminders of this. Not all the silk that found its way west was woven. Silk yarn, to be dyed,

this distinctive motif were echoed by Sogdian weavers in Central Asia.

Byzantine silk

Sassanian-ruled Persia provided Byzantium with its silk, but political problems around AD 550 obliged Roman Emperor Justinian to seek other solutions to fulfil Byzantine silk requirements. By this time, a chain of Nestorian monasteries stretched as far as China's heartland, so he despatched two monks whose mission was to return with whatever was necessary to start independent Byzantine

The dragon pattern woven on a Nanjing brocade, also known as Nanjing Yunjin, or traditional jacquard silk. It was only used for the royal families of the Yuan, Ming and Qing Dynasties.

woven and used as the ultimate embroidery thread, was also transported and traded.

By the beginning of the 3rd century AD, the Parthian Dynasty (in what is now Iran) was making huge profits from customs duties levied on silk and other goods transported along the Silk Road. The Parthians were defeated in AD 224 by the Sassanians, whose weavers developed their own highly distinctive silk designs. These so impressed the Tang Chinese (AD 618–907) that they began to imitate them. Preserved Tang silks display typically Sassanian designs, such as repeated registers of single or confronting birds or animals, often with a central tree or flowering element. Variations on

sericulture. The monks returned carrying silkworm eggs packed in bamboo staves. At this time, Byzantine territories included Greater Syria, and it was here, and in the Morea (in modern Greece – *moria* is Greek for mulberry) that sericulture was established.

Silk and the Church

Silk production and trade in Byzantium and Christian Europe had a close connection with the Church, and was closely regulated by government decree. Clerics would wear silk garments, and altar cloths were made of silk. Sumptuary laws (which determined what people were entitled to wear according to their status) were important in maintaining the hierarchies of the imperial court and Church, and colour and design were an integral part of silk's symbolic status. "Royal purple" was the colour of Byzantium, a silk-ruled empire, and the best was obtained by Syrian dye masters from the murex shellfish, an industry developed by the Phoenicians. Syrian silk merchants were always accorded special privileges by the Byzantines. Byzantine rulers are depicted wearing silk garments with huge patterns, roundels containing lions, eagles, mounted heroes and heroic images, symbols seen also in older Near Eastern images.

> "A silkworm spins all its silk until it dies, and a candle won't stop its tears until it is burnt out." Tang poem.

Islamic influence

Following the tide of Islam that flooded out of the Middle East, sericulture and silk weaving was introduced into Spain in the 8th century, where new forms and patterns of silk weaving and embroidery developed. Sicily's conquest (c. 880) made it another centre of excellence for silk weaving. After the defeat of the Tang army by a Muslim army at the Battle of Talas in AD 751 (in present-day Kyrgyzstan), many skilled Chinese craftsmen and master weavers taken prisoner were sent to Iraq, where they taught local weavers their skills. The first dynasties of Islamic rule, the Umayyads in Damascus and the Abbasids in Baghdad, adopted the Sassanian *tiraz* system of textile production. This involved elegant calligraphy, and it became a feature of court silks and embroideries. Although under Islam the wearing of silk was not as restricted as in Byzantium or China, the *tiraz* robes of honour were made for caliphs and high-ranking nobles.

The Crusades brought exotic Near Eastern silks into European courts and churches. But the Fourth Crusade's sack of Constantinople (1202–4) ended the great silk tradition in Byzantium, although silks continued to be woven in Nicaea (present-day Iznik in northwest Turkey).

Pax Mongolica and Italian silks

Under the *Pax Mongolica* of the Yuan Dynasty (1260–1368), when the Silk Road was under the control of the Mongol Empire, Venetian explorer Marco Polo brought back "Tatar

Cloths" from the Far East. The most sumptuous of these silks were embellished with gold thread manufactured by gilding fine strips of membrane or parchment. An important Mediterranean trading centre for these cloths was Ayas, on the coast of Turkey, then in Greater Armenia. They became readily available to Italian merchants, and later featured in Quattrocento paintings and sculptures. They inspired Italian weavers to incorporate Far Eastern motifs.

As the Silk Roads approached the eastern Mediterranean, they multiplied – across Anatolia there were five main routes, and some 22

An Uighur woman with colourful silk headscarf.

SILK MUSEUMS

China National Museum of Silk, Hangzhou, http://en.chinasilkmuseum.com
France Musée des Tissus, Lyon, actually two museums: one for textiles another for decorative arts, www.musee-des-tissus.com
Italy Museo Didattico della Seta, Como, at the centre of modern silk manufacture, www.museosetacomo.com
Japan Yokohama, www.yokohamajapan.com
Korea Korea Silk Museum, http://mus.silktopia.or.kr
Lebanon B'sous Museum, in the hills above Beirut, www.thesilkmuseum.com
UK Silk Museum, Macclesfield, Cheshire, www.silkmacclesfield.org.uk

Information technology owes a lot to silk. Joseph-Marie Jacquard's silk-weaving loom, invented in 1801 using punchcards to make patterns, is seen as an important step in the development of computers.

beautiful early Ottoman caravanserais still mark their transit. The Turkish tribes that settled in Anatolia were traditionally weaving cultures, and motifs from further east – dragons, phoenixes, lotus palmettes, sinuous cloudbands – infiltrated Seljuk, and subsequently Ottoman, patterns.

Genoa and Venice competed energetically for the eastern luxury trade, and the availability of raw silk and the inspiration of glorious woven fabrics during the Pax Mongolica gave fresh impetus to the fledgling Italian silk industry, which seems to have begun in Lucca. Skills and techniques were jealously guarded, and workers were forbidden to travel in case they revealed weaving secrets to a competitor. The city-states developed their own styles and specialities. Venetian silks, which reached their peak in the 15th century, can sometimes be identified by ship or boat designs. Undulating patterns with pomegranates and pine cones, bifurcating stems and small blossoms gave drama to silks woven in rich colours.

Silk designs

Under the Ottomans, Bursa in northwest Turkey became an important centre for imported silk, weaving, and eventually sericulture. After their conquest of Constantinople, the Ottomans adopted the Byzantine guild system to regulate all aspects of silk production and commerce, and produced a wide range of glorious silks, many worked with gold thread.

In Persia, under the Safavid Dynasty, the palette of silks was one of tender shades of pale peach, pinks, almond greens, ivory and shades of blue, silver and gold, in delicate floral designs, with birds, butterflies and figures. Safavid silks include extraordinary figurative velvets and carpets.

Persian influence is also apparent in India, where Mughal looms adopted existing Indian techniques and patterns. Some Mughal rugs, with silk warps and wefts and pashmina pile, are so fine that they have been mistaken for velvets. Mughal style is predominantly floral, with underlying geometry. Though sharing common roots, each culture developed highly individual silks.

The most spectacular silks during this period incorporated gold and silver thread, and the most sumptuous are velvets woven in large-scale patterns. Richest to the touch, the most extravagant velvet was a Venetian speciality, *alto-e-basso*, velvet cut in two or more levels. To make these lavish textiles required huge quantities of raw silk.

French fashion seasons

Sericulture in France began round the papal city of Avignon, and flourished in the nearby hills of the Cévennes until the mid-1850s when disease devastated the silkworm stock.

Spools of shiny silk.

Tours was an important early centre, but Lyons became the silk-weaving heart of France. In 1667 Colbert, Louis XIV's Minister of Finance, directed manufacturers to produce new patterns on a regular basis, and by the end of the 17th century fresh designs were introduced twice a year. This led directly to the development of the fashion trade, and the twice-yearly showing of collections, which continues today.

Religious strife in Europe resulted in the arrival in England of Huguenot refugees. Many were weavers, and attempts were made to introduce sericulture, as well as silk weaving, to Britain. Silk weaving flourished, and Spitalfields silks, known as "flowered silks", became fashionable.

Silk production today

The first imperial silk workshops were established in Sichuan and Shandong. These traditional Chinese silk-producing regions have retained importance but whereas vast mulberry orchards were once needed to furnish supplies of fresh leaves to feed the voracious caterpillars, and production was seasonal, now genetically modified bushes produce four consecutive harvests of fresh leaves. Japanese scientists have also produced a synthetic diet which contains the necessary ingredients for nourishment and growth, so that caterpillars, and thus silk, can be produced year-round.

Silk today is produced and processed by more than 30 countries, and despite its high value accounts for just 0.2 percent of the global textile fibre market. Como is the silk centre of Italy, Europe's main producer country, processing raw material imported from the East. China produces more than 80 percent of the world's silk, employing more than a million workers. The country's silk production is around US$12 billion a year, and silk exports exceed US$5 billion. Both China and Japan are the main suppliers for *Bombyx mori* eggs, and silkworm technology is a thriving science.

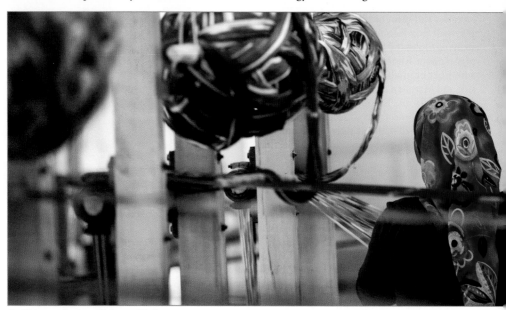

An Uighur worker in a silk factory, Xinjiang.

GLOSSARY OF TERMS

Brocade – fabric woven with discontinuous supplementary wefts. **Chiffon** – transparent silk woven like fine muslin, with a semi-dull lustre and grainy texture. **Crêpe, crêpe de Chine** – opaque, with a semi-dull lustre and smooth, slightly crinkly texture. **Damask** – self-coloured fabrics patterned in the weave, named after Damascus. **Dupioni** – rough silk reeled from double cocoons nested together. The threads are uneven and irregular. Italian Dupioni is the finest. **Figured silks** – fabrics of a single colour patterned in the weave (see Damask). **Gauze** – weaves with some interlacing and an open-work appearance. **Georgette** – crêpe silk, heavier than chiffon, with a wrinkled surface. **Ply** – twisting together of threads that are either spun or previously twisted filaments. **Satin** – a weave in which floating threads, either warp or weft, give a smooth, lustrous surface. **Sericulture** – silk farming. **Simple weave** – formed by one set of warps and one set of wefts. **Tabby** – simple, plain weave. **Taffeta** – a stiff, crisp, shiny silk, which creates a soft rustling sound when worn. **Throw** – to twist silk filament yarns. **Twist** – to spin or ply threads. **Twill** – weaves with floating threads in a diagonal alignment. **Velvet** – fabric with a napped or pile surface. **Wild silk** – silks made from one of the Saturnidae moths, whose cocoons have shorter staple fibres, giving interestingly textured yarns.

SILK PRODUCTION

How extraordinary it is that the filament spun by an unprepossessing caterpillar should be responsible for the world's favourite fabric.

Nowadays the majority of silk is made in large factories and most of these are in China. However, it is still possible to see traditional methods of weaving along the Silk Road. The two best-known places are at Khotan in Xinjiang, where there are a number of small factories spinning and weaving silk, and Margilan in the Fergana Valley, where visitors are welcome to tour the Yodgorlik Factory. In addition to these, from Xi'an to Istanbul there are numerous small-scale producers – artisan cooperatives in Bukhara and Khiva, for example, that produce beautiful hand-made silk carpets.

Whether large or small scale, the same fundamental principles are used to produce a silk item. The cocoon is produced by the *Bombyx mori* silkworm (see page 85) after it spends its short life munching mulberry leaves. The cocoon itself consists of a single filament of raw silk up to 1,000 metres (3,000ft) long. However, the individual filaments are very thin, and so they must be twisted together with other filaments to produce a silk thread. To draw out the silk successfully, the thread must be reeled smoothly and consistently – too fast and the silk breaks, too slow and it sticks to itself and becomes tangled. A form of Chinese exercise called "silk reeling" involves movements made in continuous, cyclic patterns performed at a steady speed with the same light touch needed to reel silk.

It takes approximately 5,000 silkworms to produce a pure silk kimono (the traditional garment of Japan, which literally translates as "something worn" in English). Roughly 110 cocoons are needed to make a man's tie, and 630 for a woman's blouse.

The mulberry tree provides food for the voracious Bombyx mori.

Weaving with silk on the loom in Kashgar in Xinjiang.

This is the start of the reeling process at the traditional Yodgorlik Silk Factory in Margilan, Uzbekistan, where the cocoons are immersed in hot water to kill the silkworms and make the cocoons easier to unwind. The filaments from several different cocoons are then combined to produce a silk thread.

Reeling wheel in an Uzbeki factory.

NOT THE REAL THING

As the world's most expensive fabric, silk has long had its imitators. It was not until the 19th century that these began showing any signs of success, with such inventions as the electric light filament developed by Joseph Swann. In 1892, a patent was taken out for viscose made from wood or cotton fibres by the French Count Hilaire de Chardonnet, and in the 1920s viscous rayon, the first man-made fibre, was produced in France from polymers derived from wood pulp. The technology was bought a decade later by the DuPont Company of America, who went on to develop nylon, made from polymers, which became a substitute for silk stockings. Cut off from Asian silk during World War II, the Americans also put nylon to military use, as a substitute material for silk in tyres and parachutes.

Today, artificial silks can be made in a variety of ways. Fake silk rugs are often made from cotton that has been mercerised, a process that strengthens the fibre and adds lustre. To tell the genuine article from an artificial one takes a practised eye. Real silk is warmer to the touch, is more tightly woven and, if you care to set fire to a piece, will turn into an ashen ball and smell like burning hair.

he silk worm in its fourth instar (stage of development), now bout 10,000 times heavier than when it first hatched.

Cocoons being harvested from mulberry branches in Uzbekistan. They will be taken to the factory to be sorted according to quality, size and colour. The actual cultivation of silkworms in Uzbekistan and elsewhere is a cottage industry, with individual farmers selling their produce on to massive state-run factories.

The start of silk production in a modern factory.

LIFE ON THE ROAD

Silk Road goods changed hands many times,
which made the bazaars and caravanserais
among the most exciting places on earth.

Trading along the Silk Road in either direction was no small undertaking, whether for the small-scale trader or merchant prince. The road was tough, often beset by bandits or dangerous animals, and suffered extremes of weather.

Along the road there was greater safety in numbers, and travellers would wait in urban centres or even at remote caravanserais to join major caravans that might include hundreds or even thousands of camels and horses, perhaps accompanied by armed guards. As well as merchants, possibly with their families, servants and translators, there were many specialists, including camel-drivers, doctors and vets, local guides, cooks and guards. Journeys could last for weeks or months, with the precise distance covered per day liable to the availability of water and the exigencies of the weather, nomadic raiders and local politics.

Merchant caravans were often joined by private individuals, whether itinerant traders, monks and religious teachers, entertainers moving between urban centres, adventurers or even criminals and escaped slaves. Musicians would travel east from Persia and Sogdiana, Khotan and Kuqa, while some travelled west from China into Central Asia, adding to the sounds of the journey, and though their songs are lost to us, we can see from murals and paintings the kind of instruments they played. Because of this mix of people, as well as for purposes of taxation, regulation and promoting peaceful commerce, passports and other forms of *laissez passer* were issued by various authorities, notably at times of dynastic strength. Again, only under the Mongols would a single pass, issued by the appropriate authority, have sufficed for the entire length of the Silk Road – and then

Samarkand's golden peach was highly valued at the Tang court.

only briefly. Examples of such bronze passports *(paizi)*, looking rather like medals, survive today; engraved in a special Mongol script called Phags-pa commissioned by Kublai Khan in 1269, these passports guaranteed unimpeded passage for diplomats and other official travellers throughout the vast Mongol realm. Marco Polo was issued with one of these on his journeys in the service of the Great Khan.

Merchandise

Although the Silk Road owes its name to the most significant article of merchandise to travel its entire length, in fact hundreds of different products were constantly on the move, carried on pack animals and traded at the markets en route. Other exports heading westwards included ceramics, bronze artefacts, spices and medicinal herbs. This meant that the caravaneers needed something similarly valuable to carry back in the other direction. Due to the difficulty and expense of long-distance commerce, and because of the challenging terrain, such goods needed to be light, compact, rare and valuable. Ideally, to suit such sophisticated and demanding tastes as those of the Tang court, they also needed to be both precious and exotic.

Dates from the Middle East.

Exotic food

The Golden Peaches of Samarkand may have been deemed "royal", but they were far from the only exotic fruits and foodstuffs valued by the emperors' court. Dates, unknown in China, were brought dried and sugared from the Middle East, while watermelons from Khorezm (in what is now Uzbekistan) and honeydew melons from Hami were transported east, preserved in lead containers packed with ice from the Tian Shan. Still more valued were the "mare-teat grapes" of Kuqa, brought east and planted at Chang'an in around AD 640. Grapes were a novelty to the Tang, a society that produced many types of alcohol from rice and other grains, but which soon learnt to plant vineyards and produce wine.

Pine seeds were imported, peeled and eaten as exotic snacks, as were pistachio nuts, which were not only deemed tasty, but thought to enhance male sexual vigour. Little cakes of sugar known as "stone honey" came from Bukhara and Samarkand, while both black pepper and long peppers, known by their Sanskrit name *pippali*, travelled overland from India. In the case of the latter, the annals comment: "Westerners bring it to us; we use it for its flavour, to put in food." Quite different was the betel pepper, also a highly valued product from the West, considered by Tang pharmacists to be "a tonic for loins and legs, and a digestive aid to abolish coldness in the stomach".

Aromatics, too, were carried to Chang'an. These included a scented resin called storax from Parthia – long thought by the Chinese to be dried lion's dung – gum guggul and benzoin from Gandhara, and myrrh and frankincense from southern Arabia and distant Somalia. The value of these rare substances was greatly increased by traversing the Arabian Incense Road between Yemen and Damascus even before starting the long journey east along the Silk Road to Chang'an.

Caravans travelling from west to east took gems, gold and other precious metals, ivory, amber and coral, as well as opium from the Middle East, which was introduced as a medicine in China 1,500 years before the West began pushing it as a narcotic.

Distant Khorezm (Uzbekistan) exported to China prized furs including sable, ermine, fox and marten. Rhubarb, too, came from the northwest; its root was highly regarded as a bowel tonic. Less valuable, but also transported east from the Hexi Corridor and Mongolia, came horsehides for use in making armour, and small coracle-like craft used on the Huang He and other rivers of north China. Sacred objects, such as Buddha images, relics and, of course, religious treatises and books of secular knowledge also entered China by caravan from the west and especially, via the passes across the Pamirs, from India to the south.

Among the most extraordinary examples of imported Tang exotica were ostrich eggs, sometimes set in precious metal and used as drinking vessels. The Chinese regarded ostriches – which they called "camel-birds" – with awe, believing they could run 500km (300 miles) in a day, fuelled by a diet of copper and iron.

Beasts of burden

Goods moved slowly across Asia, travelling about 40km (25 miles) a day, the distance typically covered by a fully loaded camel in about eight hours, depending on the terrain. On the flatter sections, camel-drawn carts would also be used. Few caravans – if, indeed, any – would have completed the

while in Central Asia and western China, harsh landscapes that endure long and bitter winters, the double-humped Bactrian was the camel of choice.

Caravans also employed asses, mules and even cattle to carry goods, depending on

> *"When I drink this wine, I am instantly conscious of harmony suffusing my four limbs. It is the true Prince of Grand Tranquillity." Emperor Muzong (821–4)*

A halt in the desert.

indeed, any – would have completed the entire journey between Chang'an and the Mediterranean. Instead, goods were moved in stages, passing through the hands of different caravan-drivers and on the backs of different beasts of burden from oasis to oasis, each transfer of ownership increasing the cost to the purchaser and enriching local merchants and transport guilds.

Perhaps the most important beasts of burden employed in the caravan trade were camels, which could be ridden by merchants and caravaneers, as well as being used to carry valuable trade goods. Far to the west, in the warmer lands of Syria and Mesopotamia, the single-humped dromedary was preferred,

GOLDEN PEACHES OF SAMARKAND

The American Sinologist Joseph Fletcher (1934–84) made the "Golden Peaches of Samarkand" symbolic of the trade in Tang exotica, choosing them as "deputies and proxies of all exotic goods in medieval China" because "they suggest, simultaneously, the Golden Apples of the Hesperides, the Peaches of Immortality believed by Chinese tradition to flourish in the far west, and James Elroy Flecker's poem *Golden Journey to Samarkand*. The peaches were sent by the Kingdom of Samarkand as gifts to the Chinese court. According to the Tang annals, "They were as large as goose eggs, and their colour was like gold."

the nature of the terrain. Large, fierce caravan dogs were valued, both to help drive off predatory wildlife such as leopards and cheetahs, and to deter sneak-thieves or warn

> "On large roads guards were posted at junctions to safeguard communications. Travellers and merchants had the right to demand that their wealth and belongings should be escorted by these guards, who were held responsible for any loss." Amir Timur.

of approaching groups of bandits. In the coldest and highest regions yaks might also be used as beasts of burden, notably in the mountains of Badakhsan and the Pamirs, across the Qinghai tablelands and on the icy Tibetan plateau.

assigned to an official called "Emissary of the Bright Camel", and used to carry the imperial mail. Other highly esteemed Bactrians were designated "flying dragon camels" and kept in the imperial stables.

Camels were not just used for transport, but also prized for their long manes, which made excellent cloth, while camel hump was considered a delicacy. Similarly yaks, as well as being used in transport, were valued for their milk, cheese and meat, as well as dung, which could be burnt as fuel. Their hair was spun into yarn for knitting warm clothing.

Caravanserai at Mylasa, Turkey, 1845.

Domestic animals

Domestic animals also formed an important part of the trade between west and east. The Chinese particularly valued the horses of Central Asia, and especially of the Fergana Valley (see page 270), which they exchanged for silk, but they also imported Bactrian camels, asses and sheep from the plains of Central Asia. Particularly swift and dependable camels were

Maintaining the road

Even at the height of its prosperity, the Silk Road was not a single track, except where it was forced through narrow defiles such as the Iron Gates at Tiemenguan near Korla and its namesake at the rather wider Buzgala Gorge in Uzbekistan, or across narrow passes in the Pamirs or Tian Shan. Rather, it was an interconnecting network of tracks, established over the centuries and familiar only in parts to experienced caravaneers who knew and understood the terrain. In sections and at times of imperial strength it was well maintained, for example the Persian Royal Road under the Achaemenids, and the Hexi Corridor under the Han and Tang dynasties.

Great empires and rulers of vision who appreciated the value of trade ordered the construction of garrisons and caravanserais at regular intervals, for example in the West under the Abbasids and Ottomans, in the East, again, under the great Tang Dynasty. At other times imperial control collapsed and chaos ensued, with caravans threatened by bandits and natural hazards. Only under the Mongols in the 13th and early 14th centuries was the entire length of the Silk Road briefly united under a single, efficient system, best exemplified by the Mongol shuudan or postal relay service, in which fast horses were maintained in prime condition at regular stations, ready to speed military orders and political news from one end of the empire to the other.

Most caravan transport was carried by road, but there were instances when boats, ferries or rafts were necessary – as, for example, in crossing the Oxus at Chardzhou or the great rivers of Mesopotamia, the Tigris and the Euphrates, in present-day Iraq. Elsewhere river transport could be a useful and economic way of transporting goods through difficult terrain where

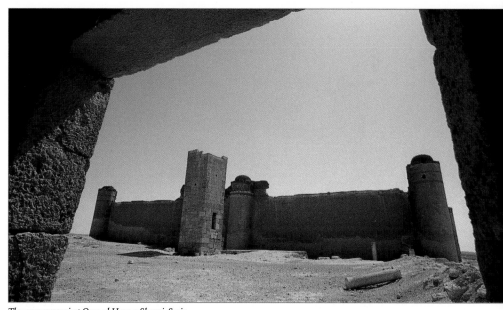

The caravanserai at Qasr al-Hayr a-Sharqi, Syria.

CAMELS, THE ESSENTIAL TRANSPORT

There are two kinds of camel. The dromedary, also known as the one-humped or Arabian camel, has a single hump and is native to the dry desert and upland areas of Western Asia. It was domesticated in the 3rd millennium BC and traditionally plied the trade routes in Iran, Iraq and Syria. The two-humped Bactrian camel is from Central Asia, where its long hair insulates it from the cold during the night and reflects the sunlight by day. The Bactrian, which was domesticated about 2,500 years ago, was preferred along the Chinese section of the Silk Road from Xi'an to Kashgar, as well as to the west of the Pamirs in Transoxiana. In fact Bactrians were not known in the West until Islamic traders began using the Silk Road. Dromedary-Bactrian hybrids are raised in Kazakhstan where they are called *bukhts*. They are larger than either parent, have a single hump, and make good draft animals.

Camels can go for four or five days without water (they can drink up to 60 litres/13 gallons in 10 minutes) carry heavy loads, and sustain speeds of up to 40kph (25mph), but they also produce milk and wool, and their dung can be used to make fires. There are an estimated 14 million dromedaries in North Africa and the Middle East, with a further 1.5 million Bactrians in Central Asia and Western China. They live for between 40 and 50 years.

roads were poor or dangerous, for example eastwards on the Wei River or the Huang He in Gansu, where rafts of inflated goatskins are still used today, or westwards on the Oxus in the region of Termiz.

> *A few caravanserais, such as the atmospheric Abbasi Hotel in Isfahan, have been turned into hotels. Others serve as markets or have been restored to provide service as restaurants.*

Bazaars and caravanserais

A series of overnight halts known as caravanserais or khans was established to provide food, water and security for the travellers and to promote and protect the trade that enriched their kingdoms. The word "caravanserai" comes from the Persian *karvan*, meaning a company travelling together, and *sara*, a living place, though in Persia it was also called a *khan*, in Turkey a *han*. Ideally these were roadside inns placed a day apart where travellers could eat, sleep and recover from the day's journey, with their animals securely tethered, watered and

19th-century sketch of the main bazaar in Kabul.

THE RELIGION OF TRADE

It is no coincidence that some of the great bazaars of the world are in Muslim countries, for much of the ethos of Islam revolves around commerce. Soon after the initial Arab conquests, it became advantageous for the conquered peoples to embrace Islam, both to avoid paying the tax levied on infidels, and to benefit from Islam's extended trade links. Muslim traders helped each other in ports, oases and city bazaars. Caravanserais sprang up along trade routes to serve the travellers, while mosques acted as places for Muslim travellers to rest, store goods safely and exchange information. In Islamic law, a mosque should be established in any community where there are at

least 40 believers. Resident Muslims, whether restaurateurs and innkeepers or religious teachers, required wives and readily intermarried with local women, bringing up the children of such unions as Muslims.

In this way Islam spread rapidly along the Silk Road – indeed along most trade routes – establishing small, self-propagating Muslim communities just about everywhere trade caravans or sailing dhows might stop. Islamic law requires that Muslims should only eat permitted, halal food, while non-Muslims, too, would happily consume Muslim fare. It's hardly surprising, then, that Muslims gradually acquired a monopoly in the accommodation and catering businesses.

> *"When wind is about to arrive, only old camels have knowledge of it…and bury their mouths in the sand. The men take this as a sign, and…cover their noses and mouths… If not, they would be in danger of sudden death." Bei Shi – Chinese Annals.*

fed, and their precious goods safely within walls. Of course, the harshness of the terrain and the great distances involved meant that inns of such quality were the exception rather than the rule, especially in the wilder reaches of the Middle Eastern deserts and Central Asian mountains.

Typically, caravanserais were built within a square or rectangular wall to give protection from attack as well as from the elements, excessive heat and cold, rain and snow, dust storms and hail. They were entered by a single, easily defended gate that was wide enough and high enough to permit fully laden camels to pass through. The central courtyard was open to the sky and lined with stalls for beasts of burden and rooms to accommodate travellers together with their merchandise. Well-organised caravanserais provided washing facilities, cooked food and fodder for animals, and sometimes contained small shops. In Muslim areas – which, by the 8th century AD, meant most of the Silk Road – there were rooms for prayer, orientated towards Mecca.

Bazaars, by contrast, were not established at regular intervals in the wild, but were naturally found in towns and oases, especially at large commercial crossroads such as Lanzhou, Dunhuang, Yarkand, Kabul, Bukhara, Mashhad, Rey and Palmyra. The very best were at Chang'an in the East, at Kashgar and Samarkand in the centre, and at Baghdad, Damascus and Aleppo in the West. The great souks of Damascus and Aleppo survived almost unchanged until their recent destruction in Syria's war. It seems entirely possible that a time traveller from the Abbasid period could find the spice bazaar or the gold market in many of the souqs in exactly the same location as it was during their lifetime.

In contrast to the simplicity of the caravanserai, essentially a transit stop where men and beasts rested overnight, layovers in the great bazaars could easily extend into weeks or even months. Trade was carried out in these locations, goods sold, purchased and exchanged for onward carriage or for local consumption. Specialists services such as money-changing, banking, interpreting and, of course, a gamut of entertainments ranging from music and theatre through to drinking and sex were also available to caravaneers and merchants.

The most difficult stages on the old Silk Road were those that crossed the Tarim Basin circling the barren central Taklamakan

A very old mosque near Turpan in Xinjiiang.

Desert and the passes across the Pamir and Karakoram ranges. Caravans would generally halt for a longer rest, perhaps for a week or two, before setting out to face these natural obstacles. An ingeniously crafted pair of goggles currently on exhibit at the Xinjiang Autonomous Region Museum in Urumqi, cut from metal a thousand years ago to permit tiny eye-slits, and lined with felt to keep out the driven sand, confirms the ever-present threat of sand-storms.This imparted particular importance to the bazaars at Dunhuang, Kashgar and Samarkand, all key bazaar towns on the Central Asian Silk Road, and further to the west at Palmyra and Petra in the Syrian and Jordanian deserts.

BAZAARS

Bazaars are the economic and social hubs of villages, towns and cities throughout Asia – and also great fun for visitors.

One of the modern thrills of travelling through any of the Silk Road countries is to experience the cut and thrust of shopping within the bazaars and souks. Traders along the Silk Road would traditionally stay overnight in caravanserais, which provided food, water and shelter for both man and beast. In the major towns and cities there would be a number of warehouses, each specialising in a particular item, such as gold, silk, leather, metal or spices, from which the local merchants would purchase their raw goods. It was then up to the merchant to work that raw material into a desirable item.

The system of each trade having its own section within a souk or bazaar is still obvious in some of the older souks such as Isfahan, Samarkand and Kashgar. It is still possible to see these central warehouses with the shops of the local merchants clustered nearby.

Most towns and cities have permanent bazaars open for five or six days a week, but there are some places that have special weekly markets attracting people to buy and sell. The most famous would probably be the Sunday market in Kashgar with traders even today travelling from other countries to attend. Simply observing is not an option as everyone gets carried along with the massive swell of people around the temporary stalls. The most interesting, chaotic and dusty area is the trading of animals, as goats, sheep, donkeys and camels are all systematically prodded, poked and inspected by potential buyers.

Spices are usually sold together in one section of the main bazaar. In Istanbul, there is a separate Spice Market, with a astonishing array of products in all the colours of the rainbo

To see how animals are traded in Central Asia, head for the Sunday farmers' market in Kashgar, China.

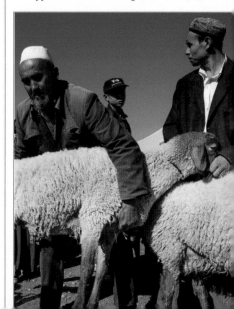

Smoking a hookah is part of teahouse life.

Taking tea in a chaikhana, sitting on "tea beds".

CHAIKHANA CULTURE

Perhaps the best place to soak up the local culture along the Silk Road is in a *chaikhana*, or teahouse. Although they vary across Asia, these crowded roadside meeting places are always part social club, part café, and provide respite from the modern world. In many Islamic countries, drinking alcohol is frowned upon and so tea is at the hub of the community's social life.

A *chaikhana* is to the Uzbeks, Uighurs and Iranians what a pub is to the British. Seats are generally on a *tapchan*, or "tea bed", with a low table placed on it. Green tea is the norm and *shashlyk* (kebabs) and local bread are generally available, though sadly the storytellers and jugglers of the past are now long gone. If you do partake in the local tipple, remember the following golden rules of tea etiquette: pour the first two *pialas* (cups) back into the pot to aid brewing; don't blow on your tea to cool it; and always keep a guest's teacup full. From Syria to Xi'an, identical scenes are played out each day, amid shouted orders, the clicking of dominoes and the drifting smoke from the waterpipes or hookahs.

zaars are organised by product, so the silks can be found gether. This trader is selling Chinese silks in the bazaar at iraz, Iran.

metalworker in the bazaar at Isfahan, Iran.

Uzbek bazaars tend to be dominated by women, most of whom wear the long silk dresses seen throughout the country.

THE SPREAD OF IDEAS

Not only goods travelled along the Silk Road.
Different cultures, religious beliefs, architectural
styles and technical developments were passed on.

In the courtyards of the caravanserais, around the sociable oases and in the excitable bazaars, conversations would have turned to many things. There would be a thirst for news of events and upheavals, a need to know the latest market prices of goods and the desire to learn of any bargains. People would tell of the adventures they had endured and enjoyed, and the extraordinary sights, both natural and man-made, they had seen. But perhaps it was during the long, monotonous days on the road in awe-inspiring landscapes and beneath vast empty skies that they would spend time mulling over the state of the world, what it should look like, who and what it was governed by, and where their destinies lay.

Religions and philosophies

Not surprisingly, it was the proselytising religions that travelled furthest. Flowing east were the monotheistic religions of Judaism, Christianity and Islam. Persian religious traditions such as Manichaeism and Zoroastrianism found audiences, too. South Asian religions, including Buddhism and some aspects of Hinduism, cut off from China by the Tibetan plateau, passed east along the Silk Road, and reached the Far East by sea.

In the other direction, Daoism and Confucianism made no real progress west along the Silk Road, except as practised by Chinese migrants – officials, troops and settlers – in the western regions. Daoism is a philosophical tradition based on abstract concepts such as the "flow of the universe", and Confucianism approximates more closely to a moral, ethical and philosophical social system. Neither offered a personal path to salvation in the way that Buddhism, Christianity and Islam did. Yet,

Craftsmen carving patterns on a wooden door board in a madrassa in Tashkent, Uzbekistan.

perhaps because of the dominant cultural role played by China in East Asia, Daoism and Confucianism did spread east and south from the Middle Kingdom to the kingdoms of Korea, Japan and Vietnam.

Zoroastrianism

This is a late 19th-century term for the religion based on the teachings of the Persian prophet Zoroaster, who was active around the 5th century BC. Also known as Mazdaism, it acknowledged one universal and transcendental god called Ahura Mazda. The best-known Zoroastrian symbol is fire, which is kept burning in Zoroastrian temples and represents radiance and purity. For this reason Zoroastrians have often been styled "fire worshippers" by proponents of other religions. At one time this monotheistic belief dominated much of the greater Iranian world, and had a significant impact on both Greek and Roman thought.

Under the Sassanids (AD 226–651), Zoroastrianism spread north to the Caucasus and east to Sogdiana, then along the Silk Road to Xinjiang and China. Zoroastrianism in the East centred on communities of Sogdian traders. Remains of their temples have been found in the Tarim Basin, notably at Dandan Oilik, and

The Cube of Zoroaster at Naqsh-e Rustam in Iran.

HALOS FROM THE EAST

The halo that first appears in Christian art in the 5th century is probably derived from the much older circular sun symbol associated with the Egyptian Sun God Ra. It was also used in Persian representations of kings and divinities. The symbol was carried east, perhaps by the Greek armies of Alexander the Great, and was subsequently used in Graeco-Buddhist representations of the Buddha from the 1st century AD, before spreading back west along the Silk Road to Christendom. The crown is merely a more sophisticated version of the halo, designed to represent the idea of light emanating from the head of a superior being.

further to the east at Dunhuang, Kaifeng and Zhenjiang in China. Significantly, there were at least four Zoroastrian temples in Tang Dynasty Chang'an (Xi'an).

Manichaeism

Derived from the dualistic teachings of the Persian prophet Mani (AD 210–77), who postulated the existence of two natures, lightness and dark, Manichaeism decrees that the universe is the temporary result of an attack from the realm of darkness on the realm of light. Mani proclaimed himself the last in a line of prophets that included Zoroaster, Buddha and Jesus – a position that won him no friends among the Zoroastrian Persian establishment, who had him killed.

Mani's teachings spread with remarkable speed, reaching Egypt in AD 244 and Rome by 280. But in AD 296 the Roman emperor Diocletian ordered his followers "be condemned to fire along with their abominable scriptures". Persecuted and proscribed in the West, Manichaeism fared rather better in the East, arriving in China by the mid-6th century. Manichaean churches were established at numerous locations along the Eastern Silk Road, including at Chang'an. The Uighur ruler Bugug Khan (AD 759–80) adopted Manichaeism, which became the state religion of the Uighur Empire for the following century. The last organised Manichaean communities seem to have died out in southern China in the 16th century.

The sacred texts of Manichaeism were originally composed in Syriac Aramaic, but as they spread west were translated into Greek, Coptic and Latin. To the east their history serves well to illustrate the multicultural nature of Silk Road society, as they passed through Iranian, Parthian, Sogdian, Uighur and Chinese translations.

Buddhism

This developed from the teachings of Siddhartha Gautama, the future Lord Buddha, who was born around 563 BC, a prince of the Shakya clan in the Kapilavastu Kingdom on the Indo-Nepal borderlands. Although raised amid the comforts of the royal court, Siddhartha was deeply troubled by the misery and poverty he encountered beyond the palace gates, and embarked on a long quest to identify the cause of suffering. Eventually, he discovered the Middle Way, a path of moderation that lies between indulgence and mortification, and results in enlightenment. The philosophy that he taught gradually spread across northern India and, under the Buddhist emperor Asoka (260–218 BC), beyond to Sri Lanka, Burma and

> *"Now have I seen him with my own eyes, knowing him in truth to be the wise Lord of the good mind and of good deeds and words." Zarathustra (Zoroaster)*

An embroidered silk banner of the Buddha Sakyamuni, with an almond-shaped aureole.

Bactria. From Bactria it gradually spread along the Silk Road west to the shores of the Black Sea and Mediterranean, and east to the Tarim Basin and China.

Buddhism reached China around the 1st century AD, but extensive contacts date from the 2nd century, with the establishment of the Buddhist Kushan Empire (see page 51). The earliest Buddhist missionaries to follow the Silk Road to China were Parthian, Sogdian and, later, Kuqan. This cultural traffic became a two-way exchange from the 4th century, when Chinese monks travelled west to the Tarim Basin and south, across the Pamirs to India, seeking Buddhist scriptures. The Silk Road transmission of Buddhism began to decline from about the 8th century, with the rise of Islam in Transoxiana and, subsequently, the Tarim Basin.

Once in China, Buddhism began to acquire broadly Mahayana characteristics, eventually spreading to Korea, Japan and Vietnam. In Southeast Asia it re-encountered Theravada Buddhism, which had been established in Sri Lanka and Burma during the reign of Emperor Asoka. Meanwhile, in Tibet and Mongolia, a third variant, Vajrayana, emerged.

Judaism

Judaism may have existed in China for as long as two millennia. A stele preserved in the city of Kaifeng in Henan Province suggests that Jews settled there as early as 231 BC, though there is no record of a synagogue until 1163. It is believed that the ancestors of this community migrated along the Silk Road from Central Asia, where a small community still survives in Bukhara. Over the centuries, the Kaifeng Jews became integrated within Chinese society and, in particular, with the local Chinese Muslim community.

Intermarriage and isolation from both Ashkenazi and Sephardic Jewish communities far to the west led to a loss of religious and ritual customs, as well as social and linguistic tradition. The Kaifeng synagogue collapsed in the mid-19th century, but by this time, it is said, all that survived of Jewish tradition were the injunctions to circumcise sons and to abstain from eating pork. So it is quite probable the last Kaifeng Jews were subsumed in the local Hui Muslim population.

Nestorianism

It is thought that Nestorianism penetrated China by way of the Silk Road as early as the 3rd century AD; a metropolitan see was established there by representatives of the Assyrian Church in 411, when Christianity was known as *Jingjiao* or the "Luminous Religion". The Syrian monk Nestorius (AD 386–451) taught that Christ exists as two persons, the human (Jesus) and the son of God (Logos). This view was condemned at the Council of Ephesus in 431, leading to the separation of the Assyrian Church of the East from the Byzantine Church.

Condemned as heretics in the West, Nestorians migrated east along the Silk Road, spreading their variant of Christianity to Central Asia, China, Mongolia and ultimately Japan. The Nestorian missionary Alopen arrived at Chang'an in AD 635 and was given a warm welcome by the Tang emperor Taizong

In AD 589 the Arab Muslim traveller Yan Zhitui recorded the use of toilet paper, noting with disapproval that the Chinese, unlike Muslims, used paper rather than water to clean themselves after visiting the bathroom.

Tomb of the 12th-century Sufi mystic Farid ud-Din Attar in Nieshapur, Iran.

(AD 626–49). The famous Nestorian stele was erected at Chang'an in AD 781 celebrating the accomplishments of the Assyrian Church in China. Murals from a Nestorian monastery at Khocho in Xinjiang from the 7th century also survive.

Islam

Islam, along with Buddhism, was one of the most successful of the great world religions to pass east along the Silk Road to China. The first Arab missionaries to Chang'an caused something of a stir, refusing to *ketou* ("kowtow" or "knock the head") except to the One God. They soon established communities across the empire, intermarrying and eventually becoming so Chinese that the only distinction between them and their Han neighbours was their religion. Today, officially recognised as the Hui minority, Chinese-speaking Muslims are to be found all over China, often still working in transport-related businesses like trucking and catering.

Other, non-Chinese minorities within China converted to Islam as it spread east, including the Uighur, Kazakh, Kyrgyz and Salar Turks, the Bao'an and Dongxiang Mongols, and the Persian-speaking Tajiks. Almost all, including the Hui, are Sunni Muslims of the Hanafi *madhhab*, the sole Islamic school of law to permit translation and recitation of the Holy Koran in languages other than Arabic – clearly a factor in the successful proselytising of Islam in Chinese and – in Turkic-speaking lands. Only the tiny Tajik minority in Xinjiang's far west are Shia, followers of the Ismaili Aga Khan.

Science and technology

Unlike religion and philosophy, which flowed chiefly from west to east, the transfer of science and technology was very much two-way traffic. In antiquity, and independent of Persian, Greek or Roman discoveries, Chinese scholars made significant advances in mathematics, medicine and astronomy, recording the earliest observations of solar eclipses, supernovae and comets, and developing acupuncture, herbal medicine and their own traditional Chinese pharmacopoeia.

The "Four Great Inventions" of ancient China are defined as the compass, gunpowder, papermaking and printing, all of which spread west along the Silk Road, making an immense contribution to both the Muslim world and medieval Europe. The Tang era (AD 618–906), in particular, was a time of great innovation, while technological and scientific exchanges continued along the Silk Road up to the end of the Yuan Dynasty, in 1368, and into the early Ming period.

Tang innovations included woodblock printing. The *Diamond Sutra*, discovered at Dunhuang and dating from AD 868, is the world's first known printed book, and it has both illustrations and text. The Buddhist monk Yixing (AD 683–727) developed an astrolabe powered by a waterwheel to be used in astronomical calculations as a rotating celestial sphere; the device had a mechanical bell that chimed the hours and a mechanical drum that beat the quarter-hours, becoming effectively the world's first astronomical clock.

More frivolous, but equally impressive in technical terms, was a mechanical wine pourer installed at the Tang court that used a hydraulic pump to siphon wine from dragon-headed taps, as well as tilting bowls that dipped when filled into a central wine lake – an interesting example of imperial indulgence serving scientific discovery.

Tang pharmacologists and doctors spared no effort in classifying all manner of herbs and drugs used in Chinese medicine. In AD 657 Emperor Gaozong commissioned a comprehensive *materia medica*, complete with full descriptive text and illustrations listing more than 800 medicinal substances derived from herbs, vegetables, fruit, animals and minerals. Alchemists, too, were active, compounding different chemical formulae for waterproofing, fireproofing and even repelling dust.

Cartography was another field in which the Tang made great advances. Chinese mapmakers developed grid systems and graduated scales, and in AD 785 Emperor Dezong commissioned the geographer Jia Dan (AD 730–805) to draw up a map of China together with its Central Asian territorial possessions – effectively the first complete map of the Eastern Silk Road. On completion, the map – now lost – measured 9 metres (30ft) in length and 10 metres (33ft) in height.

Chinese contributions to military technology that spread west along the Silk Road included gunpowder and cannon, as well as a kind of brass flame-thrower that forced incendiary material known in the West as "Greek fire" through a nozzle.

The Muslim contribution

Just as Chinese scientific discoveries were transferred to the Muslim world and, subsequently, to Europe via the Silk Road, so many Muslim inventions and discoveries passed the other way, from the Middle East and Central

Paper being made traditionally in China today.

SUFISM

It was not just trade that propelled Islam along the Silk Road, nor the invasions of Muslim armies. Just as important for the spread of the religion was the missionary activity of Sufi *pirs* (preachers), named for the clothes of wool *(suf)* that they wore as a badge of their having renounced the world to pursue a path of mystical realisation. These wandering mystics had a tolerant, sometimes revolutionary message, often scornful of authority. They taught that it was possible to attain a special closeness to God – sometimes described as unity with the divine – even during life. The idea caught on and spread widely along the Silk Road into Turkey, Central Asia and China, as well as southwards into

India, and it continues to thrive in all four areas today. The famous "whirling dervishes" of Turkey are Mevlevi Sufis, and many of the Sufi orders remain active.

The most enduring Sufi discipline has been the practice of listening to the singing of mystical poetry in the strongly rhythmic style called *qavvali*. Particularly encouraged by the Chishti order, this devotional music has always had immense popular appeal. The venue for *qavvali* performances will often be the courtyard of the shrine built over the tomb of a Sufi master, or saint. The musical tradition of the Uighurs has been particularly strongly influenced by *qavvali*; and a vital part of the cultural life of Pakistan.

Asia to China and Japan. This was an ongoing process from the Arab conquest of Transoxiana in 706, but as China enjoyed a time of great innovation under the Tang, so the Arabs went through a truly astonishing scientific and philosophical Golden Age at the time of the Baghdad-based Abbasid Caliphate (AD 750–1258).

When the Arabs first burst out of the Arabian Peninsula in AD 637 they were a desert people of relatively little sophistication. Over the next century, however, their conquests made them heirs to the accumulated knowledge of the

post-Ptolemaic model of planetary motion (without any epicyles) long before Galileo. Muslim scientists laid the foundations for later telescopic astronomy, developing astrolabes and other astronomical instruments to enquire into the position of the sun, planets and stars. In chemistry, Muslim scholars invented steam distillation and produced the first kerosene and solid soap, while in geography they developed techniques of triangulation to measure the radius of the earth, as well as the topographic coordinates of towns and other important localities.

This miniature by Avicenna (980–1037) on an Ottoman manuscript shows the preparation of medicines for the treatment of a patient suffering from smallpox in 17th century Istanbul.

ancient Middle East, Greece, Persia and India. Under the Abbasids, they systematically translated and classified this knowledge, developing and adding to it, transferring it east along the Silk Road, as well as ultimately, helping to fuel the European Renaissance. Without six centuries of Arab science and learning, it is quite possible, for example, that Greek philosophy might have been lost following the European "Dark Age" (c.476–1000).

In astronomy the great Tajik philosopher Abu Rayhan al-Biruni (973–1048) first proposed that the Milky Way was a collection of thousands of nebulous stars, while Ibn Bajjah (Avempace, 1095–1138) devised a new

In mathematics al-Khwarizmi (780–850) established algebra as an independent discipline in his treatise *al-Jabr wa-l-Muqabala* ("The Compendious Book on Calculation by Completion and Balancing"), a compilation and extension of known rules for solving quadratic equations and other problems. The mathematician al-Kindi (801–73) wrote a pioneering work on cryptology, while al-Karaji (c.953–1029) introduced the theory of algebraic calculus.

In mechanics Ibn Sina (980–1037), better-known in the West as Avicenna, discovered the concept of momentum as a precursor to Sir Isaac Newton's laws of motion, while in 1115, al-Khazini first proposed that the gravity of a body varied depending on its distance from the centre of the Earth, a phenomenon subsequently described by Newton's law of universal gravitation in 1687.

In medicine and pharmacology Muslim scientists made many ground-breaking advances, developing a mathematical scale to quantify the strength of drugs, pioneering urinalysis and stool analysis, and identifying smallpox and measles. Abu al-Qasim (936–1013) compiled a 30-volume medical encyclopaedia and invented numerous surgical instruments, including the first designed

Text and diagram from al-Biruni's treatise on the construction of the astrolabe.

specifically for gynaecology. His encyclopaedia, together with Avicenna's *Canon of Medicine* (1025) and *Book of Healing* (1027) remained standard textbooks in both Muslim and European universities until the 17th century.

Ibn Zuhr (1091–1161) performed the first known medical dissections and post-mortem autopsies, as well as being the first physician known to have used vivisection and animal testing. In 1242, towards the end of the Abbasid Golden Age, Ibn al-Nafis was the first to describe pulmonary circulation and coronary circulation.

Other Muslim medicinal discoveries include the immune system, the invention of injection by syringe, and the identification of more than 2,000 medicinal and chemical substances.

Architecture

The materials, engineering techniques and latest fashions for architecture were also passed along the Silk Road. Architects, engineers and skilled craftsman travelled to cultural centres – often the capital city – where wealthy patrons indulged every aspect of the creative arts. Architecture was particularly important as impressive buildings enabled a ruler to project his power to his subjects and rivals: construction flourished when a ruler was at his peak, and his buildings were the first thing to be significantly altered or razed and reconstructed once he fell from grace.

Artisans brought with them the skills and tastes of their respective homelands and, consequently, when they worked together on a structure, numerous influences brought a fusion of styles. The same thing happened when the building's patron changed. Exemplary is the Hagia Sophia in Istanbul. It began life as a Roman church but later builders added Hellenistic columns, the Byzantine dome and mosaics, four new buttresses, calligraphic inscriptions and Islamic minarets. The Hagia Sophia's structure mirrors the cultural shifts in each era of Istanbul's history.

Byzantine

Early Byzantine architecture was a continuation of Roman styles, but it also incorporated features found within the new territories of Constantine's Eastern Roman Empire: Asia Minor and the Near East. Churches began to be built in a cross shape (a tradition drawn from Greek Orthodoxy), and engineers developed the techniques necessary to support a dome on top of a square structure. Pillars taken from classical buildings were re-incorporated in both religious and secular buildings, most notably in Istanbul's Basilica Cistern, the Yerebatan Sarayi.

Exposure to the decorative conventions of Islamic architecture is evident in Byzantine design from at least the 11th century. The exteriors of buildings began to be decorated with geometric patterns, either executed in polychrome brickwork or through the addition of coloured tiles. Ornamental scripts, in imitation of Islamic calligraphy, also came into vogue.

Persian

The Islamic conquest of Persia in the 7th century AD brought the early Islamic design of the Middle East first to Iran and then to Afghanistan and Central Asia. In each of these regions it encountered indigenous artistic traditions, and evolved into new, syncretic forms.

Out of these encounters, two important developments emerged: elaborate funerary architecture, and the technical innovations that would enable the construction of giant domes. Improvements in dome buildings under the Ilkhanate, founded by Genghis Khan's grandson Hulagu Khan in 1255, included the creation of double-layered domes. Arches between the layers reinforced the structure, enabling the construction of a dome 50m high and 25m in diameter at Sulteniyeh in Iran by 1312 (see page 331).

Persian architecture experienced a renaissance in the 16th century under the Shia Safavid Emperor Shah Abbas. Designating Isfahan as his new capital, Shah Abbas set about constructing a city with dozens of colourful domes. The turquoise blue tiles were a tradition inherited from the Seljuks, but the Safavids were also

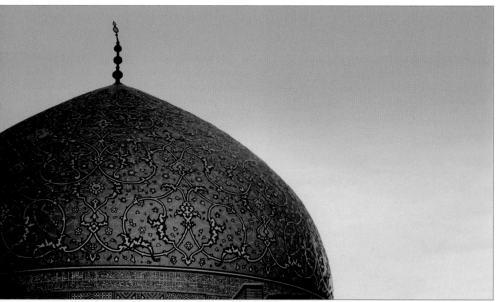

Sheikh Lotfollah Mosque (built in 1615).

ABU RAYHAN AL-BIRUNI, SILK ROAD POLYMATH

Abu Rayhan al-Biruni was born near Khiva in present-day Uzbekistan in AD 973, and died at Ghazni in Afghanistan in 1048. A Persian-speaking Tajik, he ranks as one of the greatest universal geniuses of all time, a true Muslim "man for all seasons". Although less well known in the West than such great Muslim scholars as Ibn Sina (Avicenna) and Ibn Rushd (Averroes), in the past century the full extent of his extraordinary contribution to human knowledge has become increasingly appreciated, and a geological feature on the moon, the Al-Biruni Crater, has been named in his honour.

As a young man, al-Biruni studied mathematics and astronomy under Abu Nasr Mansur. One of his colleagues was the great philosopher and physician Ibn Sina. He was a member of the court of Mahmud of Ghazni (971–1030), accompanying the latter on his campaigns in India where he developed an enduring passion for Indian science and philosophy. In addition to his native Persian, al-Biruni mastered Arabic, Greek, Sanskrit and Syriac. During his long and active life he wrote no fewer than 146 works in Arabic and Persian on many subjects.

He was the first Muslim scholar to study India and the Brahmanical tradition, and is remembered as the father of Indology, as well as the founder of experimental mechanics and experimental psychology.

able to glaze tiles in gold, white, dark blue and a myriad of patterns, having recently invented the *haft rangi* (seven colours) technique for colouring and firing tiles.

> "By the favour of Ahuramazda I built this Gateway of All Nations. I built many other beautiful things in Persia. I built them and my father built them…by the favour of Ahuramazda." Inscription at Persepolis by Xerxes I (r. 486-65 BC)

Mughal

The Mughal emperors were Timurids, and their familial lands were in the Fergana Valley. Various attempts to control Samarkand, and a lengthy exile with the Safavid Shah Tahmasp in Herat, had exposed them to masterpieces of Persian architecture and this was to heavily influence the structures they built across Afghanistan, Pakistan and northern India.

The Mughals were, however, a religious and ethnic minority within their empire, and under the leadership of Akbar (r.1556–1605) they began to integrate the local elite and project themselves as the legitimate rulers of not only their Muslim subjects, but Hindus, Jains and other religious groups as well. The architecture they created in this period consciously drew from a variety of architectural influences, including Hindu and Jain temples.

A prime example of Mughal syncreticism is the Badshahi Mosque in Lahore, built by Emperor Aurangzeb in 1671. The red sandstone of its construction was a popular building material for mosques and temples across the subcontinent, but was rarely used further west. Whilst the onion domes show Persian influence, the cupolas and arches atop the minarets are an Indian design. The ornamental merlons have their origins in Roman battlements, and the lotiform motifs are derived from Hindu and Buddhist sources.

Indo-Saracenic

From the late 18th century, British imperial architects pioneered the Indo-Saracenic or Mughal Gothic style. It took aspects of Mughal and Hindu architecture and combined them with Gothic revivalism and neo-classicism. There was a belief that although

architectural forms originating in the colonies had a certain charm, they could be significantly improved with the application of European forms and engineering.

Structures built in the Indo-Saracenic style were predominantly those associated with the state: railway stations, courthouses, government colleges and public museums. Their grand scale and impressive facades were intended to remind colonial subjects of the superiority of their British masters.

It was not only in the colonies that Indo-Saracenism took off, however. Asian exoticism

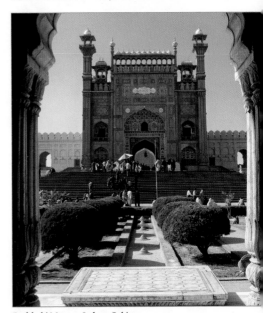

Badshahi Mosque, Lahore, Pakistan.

> The walls of the mausoleum are decorated with multicoloured gilded inlay…the tomb is made of inlaid ebony, with silver-studded corners, and three silver lamps are hung inside" Ibn Battuta describing the tomb of Kusam ibn Abbas in Samarkand

was a hot topic in the fashionable drawing rooms of London and Paris, where wealthy patrons commissioned homes and pleasure gardens styled with an oriental twist. The Royal Pavilion in Brighton, with its bulbous domes, minarets and chinoiserie interiors, is an excellent example.

Colourfully-dressed Uzbeks.

PEOPLE AND THE ENVIRONMENT

Scarce resources have always dictated the best places to live. Political demands and environmental degradation continue to force migration.

The history of the Silk Road is a history of peoples on the move. Traders journeyed along the road as they transported their goods, but at some time or other almost every community living along the Silk Road has moved in pursuit of land, food and opportunities, or been driven into new territories by natural disasters, war or political upheaval. The movements of these people transcends the boundaries of modern nation states, and the decisions (political, economic or environmental) made in one country often have repercussions felt far beyond their borders.

Ethnographic research suggests that the Kyrgyz and Native American peoples have the same ancestors, a group of people who lived in Siberia at a time when Asia was linked to the Americas by a land bridge, between 12,000 and 20,000 years ago.

A Chinese Uighur man in Xinjiang.

Peoples of the Silk Road

The peoples of the Silk Road can be categorised in numerous ways – by their ethnic roots and languages, their religions or their cultural traditions. The identification of a specific group can often be a challenge, not least because of their migrations, the many different historical names used for them both by themselves and by outsiders and, of course, because of intermarriage and assimilation. That said, two umbrella groups have been identified, through their common ancestry, related languages and customs and also, more recently, through DNA testing. These groups are the Turks and the Kurds.

The largest group of peoples along the Silk Road are Turkic: they speak languages belonging to the Turkic group and, to a greater or lesser extent, share some historical background and cultural traits. Although it is the Turkish in Turkey who most readily bear the Turkic name today, Kazakhs, Kyrgyz, Turkmen, Uzbeks and Uighurs are all part of the same ethno-linguistic group, as were past civilisations such as the Seljuks, Ottomans, Mamluks and Timurids.

Though now spread across Europe and Asia, it is thought that the first Turkic people lived in the Altay Mountains (between modern Kazakhstan and China) and spread as far as Siberia. They were nomadic herdsmen with a clan-based society. These nomadic tribes were united under the Göktürk Empire (AD 552–745) but the unity was undermined by dynastic conflicts. When the empire finally collapsed, the competing groups migrated to different territories including Eastern Europe, Iran and Anatolia in the west, Russia in the north, and Mongolia in the east. Recent DNA studies have confirmed the shared Siberian origins of these migrants' modern descendants.

A second significant ethno-linguistic group is the Kurds, whose 30 million members are found in significant numbers in Armenia, Iran, Iraq, Syria and Turkey but are most concentrated in Kurdistan, a historical region not widely recognised by modern nation states. The Kurds are rooted in tribes at least 4,000 years old, including the Lullubi, Guti and Medes.

Kurdish nationalism arose after World War I and the collapse of the Ottoman Empire. During the war Kurds had been victims of ethnic cleansing and deportations, and more conservative members of the community deeply opposed Ataturk's secularism. Some Kurdish groups sought political autonomy and although a number of Kurdish states existed for brief periods in the 20th century (notably the Republic of Ararat in Turkey, the republic of Mahabad in Iran, and the Kingdom of Kurdistan in Iraq), all were short-lived.

Modern migrations

Josef Stalin was responsible for one of the greatest upheavals of people that the Silk Road has ever known – the so-called Soviet "purges". In the late 1930s and '40s as many as 6 million people were deported from their homelands: not only political dissidents and those he wished to punish but also groups who might sympathise with Nazi Germany or Japan, farm labourers to cultivate the "Virgin Lands", and Russians and Eastern Europeans who might "civilise" the nomads of the steppe.

Between 1941 and 1949 alone, some 3.3 million people were deported to Siberia and the Central Asian republics. An estimated 43 percent of this resettled population died from malnutrition and disease, but those that survived had to start new lives in an unfamiliar and

Portrait of a Wakhi nomad woman, Afghanistan.

THE 40 TRIBES OF MANAS

The legendary hero Manas (see page 231) is at the heart of Kyrgyz national identity for unifying 40 tribes against the Khitans. The very name "Kyrgyz" recalls this event – it is derived from the Turkic word for 40.

Although the government espouses that the Kyrgyz are one people, this origin myth proclaims the opposite: tribal or clan-based allegiances remain exceptionally strong. There are three main clan groupings in Kyrgyzstan today: the Ong (from southern Kyrgyzstan), the Sol (from northern and western Kyrgyzstan) and the Ichilik (who are from the south but also include some non-Kyrgyz groups). The Sol incorporates seven clans including the Buguu and the Sarybagysh, the clan from which the country's first President, Askar Akayev, was drawn.

Clan affiliation plays a significant role in both business and politics and has the power to topple governments: regimes in Kyrgyzstan have been strongest when there has been a balance of clan power, perception of an external threat, a legitimate power broker and a pact between the clans of the north and the south. Clan alliances make introducing a functional democracy in the country a considerable challenge: block voting is common, it is hard to reach a consensus and each side is accused of promoting their protégés and rotating them continually between key political posts.

often hostile land. Ironically, the deportations meant that the Central Asian capitals became amongst the most cosmopolitan cities in the USSR: in a single marketplace you'd find not only ethnic Russians and local people, but also Volga Germans, Crimean Tartars, Poles, Greeks, Chechens, Lithuanians and Koreans – and so on. Significant numbers of indigenous communities fled the Soviet Union, migrating to China and Afghanistan.

A politically significant migration of recent times is that of the Han Chinese into Xjinjiang and, more recently, into southern Russia and Central Asia. Since 1949, the percentage of Han Chinese in the population of Xinjiang has risen from 6 percent to as much as 45 percent. The majority of this population influx occurred since the 1990s as the Chinese government sought to rapidly industrialise the province.

The greatest humanitarian disaster of recent times in the region is the ongoing Syrian refugee crisis. Since the outbreak of violence in Syria in March 2011, roughly 50 percent of Syria's 23 million people have been displaced, of which about 5 million have fled outside the country to an uncertain future. The neighbouring countries of Turkey, Lebanon and Jordan are all struggling to cope with the huge numbers involved, especially as they had already received hundreds of thousands of Iraqi refugees fleeing a series of even longer conflicts. Various armed groups and militias have used the instability to further their own agendas, causing even more chaos. Whenever the wars end, it will be many years before there is any semblance of normality for these once beautiful countries and their hospitable people.

Environment

The geography of the Silk Road encompasses everything from glaciers and alpine lakes to some of the most arid landscapes on earth. Whilst the need for resources has always kept people on the move, man's interference in his environment (sometimes deliberate, sometimes accidental) has put more pressure than ever before on water supplies, land, food and mineral resources.

Water

From the *New Statesman* to the BBC, environmental commentators agree that the bitterest conflicts of the 21st century will be

fought over water: the Silk Road may well be their battleground. Melting glaciers cause first dramatic floods and then drought; misuse of water supplies creates saline soils where nothing can grow, sinking water tables and disappearing seas.

The Aral Sea disaster dates back to the early 1960s. It had been the fourth-largest inland sea in the world, fed by the Amu Darya and Syr Darya rivers. Soviet planners, keen to expand Central Asia's cotton production, ordered the building of canals across Uzbekistan and Turkmenistan, diverting the rivers' water into the

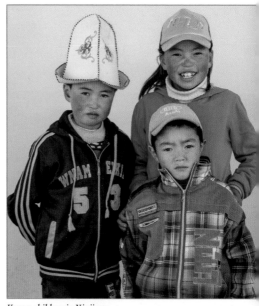

Kyrgyz children in Xinjiang.

KAZAKHSTAN'S GHOST PORT

The Aral Sea has shrunk to such an extent that the waters are up to 100km (60 miles) from harbour of the once-rich fishing port of Aralsk. The roach, bream, sturgeon and carp that were once caught by the thousand are but a distant memory, the empty canneries and rusting cranes seem to mock their former workers, and the skeleton ships sit rotting into the sands.

There are still 35,000 people living in Aralsk, largely supported by NGOs. The young have left in search of work, and the old sit on steps around the town and wait in the forlorn hope that the waters will one day return.

fields. Cotton output boomed, but the Aral Sea began shrinking.

By the mid-2000s the inland sea was a quarter of its original size. The fishing industry was decimated because ports were cut off from the sea; the water's salinity increased to a level at which

> *Radiation tourism is on the rise in Kazakhstan. Local companies offer tours to the Polygon, but in order to participate you must bring your own radiation suit and Geiger counter.*

Surveying the Aral Sea in Uzbekistan.

the fish could no longer survive; biological warfare agents dumped on islands in the sea were now exposed; and dust and sandstorms ripped across the region, often carrying with them the toxic pesticides and fertilisers used in the cotton fields. Whereas the sea once played a moderating role in the local climate, now summers are shorter and drier, winters longer and colder. Rainfall has decreased and growing seasons are significantly reduced, leading to a fall in agricultural output.

About 5,000km (3,000 miles) to the east, the Hexi Corridor (see page 152) has begun suffering from the opposite problem: sudden floods are wreaking havoc, washing away villages and crops. The glaciers above the corridor are melting because of climate change and are

expected to have disappeared entirely by 2050. In the short term this means that the springs on which people depend for drinking water have swollen, particularly during the winter months. More than 1,000 families have had to evacuate in recent years, and both Zhangye and Jiuquan have flooded repeatedly.

Perhaps even more concerning is what will happen once the glaciers have gone. There are an estimated 30 million people living in the Hexi Corridor and, as precipitation in the region is only an annual average of 125mm/5ins, when the glacier-fed springs dry up, there will be no alternative source of water. The competition for water resources is not without its political consequences, particularly as water consumers in one country are often dependent on water supplies in another country. In 2009 the Russian government gave the Kyrgyz $2 billion in loans to build hydroelectric stations and water-management systems. The Kremlin was confident the Kyrgyz would default on their repayments (which they duly did), putting the new infrastructure under Russian control. Kyrgyzstan's rivers flow directly into Uzbekistan, and the hydroelectric power generated is not only a key power source for Kyrgyzstan but is also exported to Uzbekistan and thence to Afghanistan. The ability to turn off the tap is a powerful bargaining chip indeed.

Minerals

Lapis lazuli has been mined in northern Afghanistan for at least 5,000 years, and the mountains of Central Asia are rich in gold, copper, uranium, rare earth metals and precious stones. Soviet geologists mapped mineral deposits in the mid-20th century and their exploitation makes up a significant proportion of the region's economies. A single gold mine in Kyrgyzstan, Kumtor, accounted for 55 percent of the nation's industrial output in 2011 alone.

Though gold and other metals are valuable commodities and other minerals have vital industrial applications, their extraction is not without significant environmental impact. Open pit mines leave vast craters in the earth; highly toxic chemicals are used to leach metals from their ores; and huge quantities of waste products (known as tailings) are generated in the process.

The gold-mining industry in Kyrgyzstan makes an ideal case study. Though the country's main mines are run by fairly reputable international companies and strict environmental controls are observed, mines still have a detrimental effect on the environment. Sodium cyanide is used in large quantities to extract the gold from granular ore. In 1998 a truck transporting the cyanide to the mine plunged into a river, contaminating the water supply and poisoning 2,500 people downstream. Spills of nitric acid and ammonium nitrate have also been recorded. It is estimated that the mining sector in Kyrgyzstan has generated 100 million m3 of waste products, 2 percent of which are radioactive. Though currently stored behind dams, there is constant concern that if any one of these dams were to rupture (which is relatively likely given that the region is prone to earthquakes), the waste would pour down into the valleys below.

Nuclear testing

The Silk Road has the unenviable distinction of being home to two of the world's largest nuclear-test sites: the Chinese site at Lop Nur, and the Soviet site at Semipalatinsk in Kazakhstan (called the Polygon). Around 500 nuclear tests took place at the two sites between 1949 and 1989.

The Polygon, which lies in northeast Kazakhstan, covers around 190,000 sq km (70 sq miles) of steppe land. The city of Semipalatinsk is 150km (90 miles) to the west, and a number of small villages are even nearer. Until 1991 the full impact of radiation exposure was kept hidden; it has even been alleged that populations were not evacuated from the fallout zone so that scientists could observe the long-term effects of radiation poisoning. Health studies since the

test site was closed suggest that it has had a direct and detrimental impact on the health of 200,000 people, many of whom are suffering with cancers and thyroid abnormalities.

> *Kazakhstan's President Nazarbayev has spoken against nuclear testing, by preventing the USSR expanding the Polygon in the 1980s and encouraging the UN's General Assembly to establish August 29th as International Day Against Nuclear Tests.*

A coal seller in Kashgar

KYRGYZSTAN'S KOREANS

In 1935 there was one known Korean living in Kyrgyzstan – a middle-aged woman named Pak. Two years later Stalin began mass deportations from the far east of Russia to Central Asia, displacing almost 40,000 families. An unknown number of people died on their forced march west, but today some 200,000 Koreans are living in Kyrgyzstan, the descendants of these same refugees.

Unlike other countries that established policies to repatriate their nationals after the fall of the Soviet Union, South Korea had no such programme. Instead, the Korean government has encouraged ethnic Koreans to learn about Korean culture through local

institutions (such as the Korean Center for Education, opened in Bishkek in 2001) but also to fully integrate with other communities in Kyrgyzstan. There are several popular Korean restaurants and grocery stores; and marriage between Koreans and other ethnic groups is increasingly common.

In recent years, Koreans in Korea have taken an interest in Kyrgyzstan. South Korea opened a full diplomatic mission in Bishkek in 2008, Korean missionaries have established a number of small churches for Korean Christians, and Korean businesses are investing in a variety of Kyrgyz industries including potato processing, shoe making and mobile phone assembly.

A family travelling by carriage in Kashgar.

A Pakistani jeep driver in his ornately decorated cab in the Baltistan capital, Skardu.

Footsteps in the sand in Maranjab Desert, Iran.

THE SILK ROAD EXPERIENCE

Modern transport has made travel along the Silk Road much easier today, and yet the sense of adventure is not diminished.

Enjoying coffee in Turkmenistan.

Most of the silk trade flowed in an east–west direction, the route followed by this guide, which covers the whole road and some of its most important tributaries from Xi'an to Antakya (ancient Antioch) on the Mediterranean coast, ending at the western hub, Istanbul.

In the same way that original journeys along the Silk Road would have been divided into logical sections, so too is this book. The first section is devoted to China, the second to Central Asia and the third to Western Asia. The borders of modern nation states are a relatively new construct, but for ease of planning, the three main sections correspond to countries, and within China, provinces. Each chapter includes information about border crossings, so that readers wanting to cover whole stretches of the route can still see what's involved. But even today it isn't always easy. Just obtaining the required visas to travel from one Central Asian country to another can be particularly difficult. But negotiating local bureaucracy was always a requirement for Silk Road travellers (except during Mongol times when you were given a passport which covered the whole route), and the challenges of dealing with border guards, for example, are part and parcel of the Silk Road experience.

Karakoram Highway in China.

There are a number of countries on the route that can be considered dangerous for visitors from the West. Travellers should consult updated advice from their own governments and agencies, and think twice before heading into war-torn Iraq, Afghanistan, Syria or even Pakistan and Tajikistan, for example. However, all countries share that same vital ingredient without which the Silk Road could never have blossomed, namely hospitality. A mural found at the ancient site of Penjikent in Tajikistan depicts the rituals of hospitality as practised by the Sogdians back in the 7th century AD. The vast majority of people and places will still give the traveller an equally warm welcome today.

The view atop Xi'an's City Wall.

CHINA

The journey through China from Xi'an to Xinjiang,
covers almost half of the Silk Road, encompassing
an extraordinary cultural heritage.

Buddhist murals in the Mogao Caves.

Sericulture, or silk cultivation, was first developed between 3,000 and 5,000 years ago in the Yellow River region that forms China's traditional heartland. From here, it spread east to Korea and Japan, and south to Vietnam, but most famously west, along the ancient trade route that would come to bear its name.

Through deserts, mountains and oases

The Silk Road starts in old Chang'an, today the great city of Xi'an, capital of Shaanxi Province. From here it heads west through the spectacular gorges of the Wei River to the old garrison city of Lanzhou, at the eastern end of the Hexi Corridor. To the north is the Gobi Desert and to the south are the snow-covered peaks of the Qilian Shan, but the road passes from oasis to oasis through Gansu Province until it reaches Yumenguan, the "Jade Gate" that traditionally marked the western limits of China proper.

Here the Silk Road enters China's largest province, once known as Chinese Turkestan or Eastern Turkestan, but today designated Xinjiang, the "New Frontier". This vast and inhospitable region, bitterly cold in winter and baking hot in summer, and the size of Western Europe, comprises a sixth of China's territory, but is home to less than a sixtieth of its population. The Silk Road continues west, passing along the northern and southern rims of the Tarim Basin, which forms one of the most extraordinary geographical features on earth. At its centre lie the shifting sands of the Taklamakan Desert, surrounded by the snow-capped mountain ranges of Kunlun Shan, Tian Shan and Pamir.

One of the famed Terracotta Army.

Around the Tarim Basin lie a series of fertile, poplar-lined oases, fed by the icy runoff from distant glaciers, until the two branches of the trade road again conjoin at the venerable oasis city of Kashgar, the pivot of the antique Silk Road at the heart of Central Asia.

Kashgar lies at the foot of the Pamir and Tian Shan ranges and marks the western limits of Chinese territory. To the south the Karakoram Highway leads past the glaciers and ice-covered peaks to the high Tajik settlement of Tashkurgan and across the Khunjerab Pass to South Asia. To the west the main branch of the old Silk Road crosses a lower but formidable spur of the Pamirs, passing into Western Turkestan and the fabled caravan cities of Samarkand, Khiva, Bukhara and Balkh.

Ornate architecture in Kashgar.

Peoples, cultures and religions

China has always been a land-based rather than a maritime power. From the time of unification under Qin Shi Huang in 221 BC, its major territorial imperative has been westward, towards Central Asia, always pitted against the primarily nomadic peoples of the northwest – Turkic, Tibetan and Mongol. At times of Chinese strength, notably under the Han (206 BC–AD 220), Tang (618–907) and especially Qing (1644–1912) dynasties, Chinese imperial power has been projected into western Central Asia.

At times of Chinese weakness – notably during the Tibetan and Mongol periods – the nomads surged back, retaking the north-west and briefly conquering China itself. This back-and-forth process culminated in the Manchu conquest of China in 1644, but the resultant Qing Dynasty, soon became sinicised and adopted a Han policy of conquest and control across the northwest.

The establishment of the People's Republic in 1949 and subsequent large-scale Han migration into the region, coupled with major improvements in transport, has strengthened the links between the northwest and the rest of the country. Nevertheless, Han Chinese cultural influence diminishes the further west one travels towards distinctly Turkic cities like Yarkand and Khotan.

Travelling China's Silk Road today

In large part because of Chinese control and Beijing's determination to bind its distant western provinces ever more closely to the centre, it has never been easier to travel between Xi'an and Kashgar. New roads and railways are under construction, in particular the addition of a high-speed passenger line between Lanzhou and Xinjiang, and even the much-feared Taklamakan Desert, once considered quite impassable, has now been penetrated by surfaced, cross-desert highways.

As elsewhere in China, prosperity has increased rapidly in recent years. In predominantly Han cities such as Urumqi and Aksu, felt boots and sheepskins have long since been replaced by Gucci and Armani – even if most are illegal copies – and the bazaars are filled with more DVDs and computer games than rare spices and hand-woven carpets.

Uighur men discussing cattle at the market, Yarkand.

There are practical advantages to such globalisation. The visitor can now travel in a comfortable minibus along a carefully maintained, surfaced highway between Kashgar and Lake Karakul in a few hours. The scenery is magnificent, and the glaciers and snow-capped peak of Muztagh Ata, the "Father of Ice Mountains", are still reflected in translucent waters. If you venture this far, you may see a noble Kyrgyz horseman clad in furs edge his mount into the shallows to allow it to drink – just before his mobile phone rings.

Guards dressed in *Qin Dynasty* style at the ancient city gate, Xian.

SHAANXI

Xi'an, known previously as Chang'an, or "Enduring Peace", offers iconic city walls, pagodas, Muslim quarter and the world-famous Terracotta Warriors.

L ying near the geographical heart of China, Shaanxi has also long been at the centre of Chinese civilisation. The Huang He or Yellow River, traditional cradle of Chinese civilisation, forms the eastern frontier with Shaanxi province, and its principal city and current capital, Xi'an, or "Western Peace", is one of the four great ancient capitals of China (together with Beijing, Nanjing and Luoyang). Even today Shaanxi lies near the centre of China's vast communications network, linking Beijing with the Southwest, and Shanghai with Xinjiang. It is a province whose political, cultural and historical significance can scarcely be overstated or overlooked.

Xi'an

Xi'an served as China's capital for more than a thousand years, most notably under the illustrious Tang Dynasty (618–907). Located near the heart of China's traditional Yellow River and Wei River valleys, yet far enough to the west to exercise effective control over the great overland trade routes between East and Central Asia, the city emerged as the western gateway (or eastern terminus, depending on geographical perspective) of the fabled Silk Road.

As early as 5000 BC a sophisticated agricultural society had developed in the area, firing clay pots and domesticating animals. Relics of this early civilisation, called the Yangshao Culture,

can best be seen at Banpo, to the east of today's city.

Xi'an became the political and cultural centre of China in 1027 BC, when the Western Zhou Dynasty established its capital at Fenghao, about 15km (9 miles) southwest of the present-day city centre. Next, under the short-lived Qin Dynasty (221–206 BC), Emperor Qin Shi Huang (246–210 BC) ordered the construction of a great tomb, guarded by a Terracotta Army, befitting the founder and "Commencing Emperor" of the first unified Chinese

Main Attractions

City Walls (Xi'an)
Muslim Quarter (Xi'an)
Great Mosque (Xi'an)
Forest of Stelae Museum (Xi'an)
Pagodas (Xi'an)
Shaanxi Museum of History
Terracotta Warriors

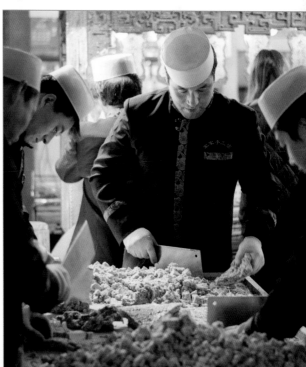

Find halal foodstuffs on Beiyuanmen in Xi'an.

TIP

Easier and faster than walking around the city walls is to rent a bicycle, and there are some available at the city gates, especially the Southern Gate. Alternatively, electric buggies operate on top of the walls, and will carry passengers along the parapets for a small fee. Even for a short section, the views across the city are impressive.

Crowds on Beiyuanmen.

state. The magnificent tomb survives at Xianyang, the location of the former Qin capital, 36km (22 miles) to the east.

Xi'an prospered greatly under the Han Dynasty (206 BC–AD 220), and began to develop as a great cosmopolitan city, the capital of China and also the chief beneficiary of the developing Silk Road, the overland corridor connecting the Chinese heartlands with Central Asia and the distant Mediterranean world. The city prospered further under the magnificent Tang Dynasty (618–907), when Xi'an, now renamed Chang'an, emerged as the largest and most culturally diverse city in the world, attracting businessmen, traders, artisans, courtesans, mendicants and holy men from all over Asia and beyond. Xi'an lost its position of national prominence after the fall of the Tang Dynasty in 907, with subsequent imperial capitals moving to Kaifeng and, under the Mongols, to Dadu – later renamed Beijing. Xi'an prospered under the Ming Dynasty (1368–1644), when a new city wall was built by Emperor Hongwu in 1370. Tellingly, however, the new wall

enclosed a much smaller city than the earlier Tang city at Chang'an. Despite its former size and pedigree, Xi'an would remain something of a western outpost, removed from the power and influence of Beijing, until the completion of the strategic east–west Shanghai–Lanzhou Railway in the 1930s.

Since that time Xi'an has expanded as a major industrial centre. The walled central area contains most of the more interesting sights, while the extensive suburbs conceal such historic locations as the remains of the former Weiyang Palace to the north, the complex of religious buildings such as Little Wild Goose Pagoda and Big Wild Goose Pagoda to the south, and the presumed "Start of the Silk Road" near the current junction of Zaoyuan Lu and Daqing Lu to the west of the city walls – this latter supposedly corresponding to the site of the former Western Market, once the terminus of the ancient Silk Road in Tang Dynasty Chang'an.

Within the walled city

Perhaps the most distinctive feature characterising present-day Xi'an is

ENTERING AND LEAVING SHAANXI

Xi'an, the capital of Shaanxi and eastern terminus of the Silk Road, is readily accessible by air, train and bus from Beijing and most Chinese provincial capitals. (See page 374 for more on transport in China.)

Deluxe and express trains run between **Beijing** and Xi'an via Shijiazhuang and Taiyuan, on a daily basis, as do express bus services. The simplest and most comfortable way to reach Shaanxi from Beijing overland is by overnight sleeper, though a daytime bus journey through the middle Huang He area is an interesting experience.

Deluxe and express trains run between Xi'an and Lanzhou in **Gansu** province several times a day, as do express bus services. The journey by train is swift and comfortable, and the superhighway, opened in 2010, allows motorists to complete the journey in around four hours.

Soft- and hard-sleeper express trains run between Xi'an and Chengdu in **Sichuan** province on a daily basis, as do express bus services. The bus journey is spectacular as it climbs through the Qin Ling range to the south of Xi'an, and across the easternmost outriders of the Tibetan plateau.

A similar range of rail services operates between Chongqing and Xi'an on a daily basis, as do express bus services. Both the railway line and Highway 210 run directly between the two cities, cutting through the forested Qin Ling Mountains to reach the vast Sichuan Basin.

its iconic walls. Known in Chinese as **Chengqiang** (City Walls; daily 7am–10pm, shorter hours in winter; charge), they date back more than six centuries and extend for more than 14km (8 miles), creating one of the largest defensive systems in the ancient world. The walls are in truly remarkable condition – the best and most complete medieval city wall anywhere in China. They are 12 metres (40ft) high and up to 18 metres (60ft) across at the base, quite wide and smooth enough to permit a comfortable four-hour stroll around the perimeter. It is also possible to hire bikes by the hour to cycle the same route. The 5,984 crenellations and periodic watchtowers, as well as **Nanmen** (the Southern Gate), are illuminated at night with rows of red lanterns and spotlights that reflect attractively in the waters of the surrounding moat.

Near the very centre of the walled city, the 14th-century **Zhonglou** (Bell Tower; daily 8am–9pm, shorter hours in winter; charge) was restored under the Qing Dynasty in the 18th century and is today in excellent condition,

offering fine views across the city's central junction and busy Drum Tower Square. Also dating from the 14th century and having benefited from an 18th-century Qing restoration, the nearby **Gulou** (Drum Tower; daily 8am–9pm, shorter hours in winter; charge) is open to the public and offers good views, as well as a chance to examine some of the biggest drums you are ever likely to see. Musical performances featuring – hardly surprisingly – bells and drums are held at both the Bell Tower and the Drum Tower each morning (9–11.30am) and afternoon (2.30–5.30pm, variable).

Immediately to the north and east of Drum Tower Square lies Xi'an's sizeable **Muslim Quarter**, a direct link with the city's culturally diverse Silk Road past when itinerant Muslim merchants and religious teachers settled in the city from the time of the Tang Dynasty onwards. Today some 50,000 Chinese-speaking Muslims, officially recognised as the Hui minority nationality, live within the narrow streets of the Old City. A prosperous community, easily recognised by the simple white caps

TIP

Visitors can climb the stairs inside the Little Wild Goose Pagoda, but it was never constructed for this purpose. Some of the dark passages are narrow and low, only just allowing people to pass, and it's difficult to see or to take photographs from the small and rather inaccessible windows.

Bird cage for sale.

Xi'an

Almost completely Chinese in design, the Xi'an Great Mosque is somewhat reminiscent of a Confucian Temple of Literature, but built along an axis facing west, towards Mecca, rather than south. Most of what can be seen today is from later Ming and Qing dynasties, but its origins are from the Tang period.

The Bell Tower.

of the men and the modest head veil worn by some – but by no means all – of the women, the local Muslims have converted **Beiyuanmen**, to the north of the Drum Tower, into an "Islamic Walking Street", where street stalls and restaurants serve a wide range of halal (Chinese: *qingzhen*) foodstuffs, ranging from the ubiquitous *rouchuan* kebabs (beef, mutton or chicken) and toasted Hui flat breads called *bing*, to fresh fruits, raisins, walnuts and pistachios. Other shops offer an eclectic selection of souvenirs aimed chiefly at local tourists (including apparently endless models of Terracotta Warriors as chess pieces or bookends), different varieties of specialist teas and tea-related paraphernalia, and Islamic sign-writing in both Chinese and in the unusual and rather eccentric Arabic script favoured by the Hui.

A left (west) turn along bustling Xiyangshi Jie gives onto a narrow alleyway leading to Xi'an's **Qingzhen Da Si** (Great Mosque; daily 8am–7pm, shorter hours in winter; charge for non-Muslims). One of the oldest and most unusual mosques in China, it was originally founded in 742 during the Tang Dynasty, though in its present form most of the buildings date from Ming or Qing times. Much of the charm of this lovely building lies in its apparent heterodoxy, featuring a large spirit screen to the west of the main gateway, as well as representational art forms in the shape of huge stone tortoises hunched unexpectedly in the carefully maintained mosque gardens. Eaves are sharply upturned, and the pillars and interior of the Five Room Hall and the Phoenix Pavilion are lacquered in deep red and gold. The minaret – in fact a three-storey pagoda-like structure – owes little indeed to Islamic architecture. But over doors and gateways, in curvilinear Arabic script, the Oneness of God and the Prophethood of Muhammad are constantly proclaimed as reminders to the faithful. The prayer hall is closed to non-Muslims.

Also within the city walls, the **Beilin Bowuguan** (Forest of Stelae Museum; daily 8am–6.30pm; charge), once a Confucian temple, is located just to the east of **Nanmen** (Southern Gate).

The main attraction here is the collection of more than 1,000 inscribed stone stelae, including the earliest extant Nestorian Christian tablet, dating from AD 781. A sculpture gallery featuring Buddhist images dating from the Tang Dynasty and before is similarly evocative of Xi'an's former position as the beginning – or end – of the Silk Road.

The western section of the city walls houses the **Xi'an Tang Hanguang Entrance Remains Museum** (8am–5.30pm; entrance fee), is a pleasant place to visit. Some of the oldest and most fragile sections of the city wall are preserved within the museum, protected from the elements, alongside stone tablets, oracles, clay seals and Chinese calligraphy.

Beyond the walls

Immediately south of the city walls, about 1.5km (1 mile) beyond Nanmen, **Xiaoyan Ta** (Little Wild Goose Pagoda; daily 8am–6pm; charge) stands in the grounds of **Jianfu Si** (Jianfu Temple). Dating from AD 684, this temple was dedicated to the deceased Tang Emperor Gaozong (649–83). Between 707 and 709 Gaozong's successor, Zhongzong, ordered the construction of the Xiaoyan Ta to house Buddhist scriptures brought back from India and Srivijaya by the itinerant Chinese monk Yi Jing (635–713). In all, Yi Jing is reported to have collected more than 400 Buddhist manuscripts over 25 years of travel, and these were lodged in the Little Wild Goose Pagoda for safekeeping and translation.

In its original form, the ochre-yellow pagoda rose through 15 storeys, though an earthquake in 1487 is said to have split the pagoda in half. A subsequent earthquake brought the two halves of the pagoda back together again – in fact no signs of the former split are visible – but the top two storeys were destroyed, reducing the pagoda to its current 13 levels. There is a small *stelae* garden to the east of the pagoda.

About 2km (1.2 miles) to the southeast, on Yanta Nanlu, **Dayan Ta** (Big Wild Goose Pagoda; daily 8am–6.30pm; charge) is an iconic landmark for the City of Xi'an that was constructed in AD 652 on the orders of Emperor Gaozong. Like the slightly more recent Little Wild Goose Pagoda, it was built to house Buddhist sutras and texts brought back to Xi'an by the Buddhist monk Xuanzang (602–64). Xuanzang is said to have asked the emperor for a solid stupa of the kind he had seen on his travels in India, but Gaozong built a hollow wood-and-stone structure, which was originally called Scripture Pagoda. Initially five storeys high, it was raised to 10 storeys in 703, then subsequently reduced to the current seven storeys by fire. The pagoda stands in the grounds of **Daci'en Si** (Temple of Grace; daily 8am–6.30pm; charge included with Dayan Ta), also established by Gaozong in 647.

Just to the northwest of Big Wild Goose Pagoda on Xiaozhai Donglu, **Shaanxi Lishi Bowuguan** (Shaanxi Museum of History; daily 8.30am–5pm; charge) is one of the better museums in China. The 300,000 exhibits follow

Xi'an is home to some 50,000 Chinese Muslims.

Little Wild Goose Pagoda.

Life in Old Xi'an

In the 8th century, the Tang capital was at its most powerful and one of the greatest cities in the world.

Xi'an lived and prospered by trade during the Silk Road's heyday, and naturally attracted communities of merchants from all over the known world. Many such traders from groups as diverse as Arabs and Turks, Sogdians and Persians, Tibetans, Mongols and South Asians settled within the city walls, often close to the great Western Market where most long-distance trade occurred.

The city was known as Chang'an until the start of the Ming dynasty and at its peak it had a population of more than 2 million. Contacts with Central Asia and the Far West meant that troops of musicians and dancers from the Tokharian Oases of Xinjiang and celebrated "tumbling dancers" from Sogdiana performed nightly in the city's entertainment area. Restaurants and teahouses served delicacies and cuisines from regions as diverse as Guangzhou and Bukhara, while wine shops were well stocked with intoxicating liquors from the four quarters of the known world.

Ladies of the court enjoying a banquet.

Hardly surprisingly, Chang'an catered to the sexual needs of its itinerant merchant population, as well as to the foibles of its local citizens, rich and poor. There were recognised brothel quarters and taverns with friendly serving girls, and there was even a gay quarter in the northwest of the city where those who enjoyed "the way of the cut sleeve" (as homosexual love in China was called) could indulge themselves.

A city of culture

Many musical traditions were represented in the singing houses of Chang'an, but perhaps the most famous and most admired was that of Kuqa, characterised by four-stringed lute and drum-playing orchestras. The Emperor Xuanzong (712–56) was particularly fond of Kuqan music, and is reported to have maintained 30,000 musicians and dancers at the imperial palace. Kuqan dance seems to have been strongly influenced by Indian traditions, placing emphasis on hip movements and hand gestures, flashing eyes and stylised facial expressions. Dance troops from India, Burma, Sogdiana and Southeast Asia competed with the popular Kuqans for custom.

In addition to music and dance, Chang'an was famous for its poets, painters and other artists. Two of China's most prominent classical poets, Du Fu (712–70) and Li Bai (701–62) lived in Chang'an during its primacy. Other, less intellectual pastimes and entertainments included cock-fighting, horse-riding and polo. We know from painted pottery figures that women paid great attention to fashion, in terms of their clothing, make-up and elaborate hairstyles.

The people of Chang'an celebrated many holidays and festivals, the most important of which then (as now) was Lunar New Year. This was a seven-day festival characterised by the ritual consumption of "Killing Ghosts and Reviving Souls Wine", which was believed to guard against illness during the coming year. Particularly beautiful was the Lantern Festival, held on the 14th, 15th and 16th days of the first lunar month, when the city's night-time curfew was lifted and citizens could stroll through the streets, competing with each other in the size and splendour of their lanterns. Three-day carnivals were also frequent, with much merrymaking involving eating, drinking, street parades and sideshows. Such carnivals were not tied to fixed events, but were called to celebrate good harvests, military victories and other auspicious events.

Chinese history from the earliest semi-legendary period on the ground floor, via Han Dynasty (206 BC–AD 220) artefacts on the second floor, to significant Sui and Tang Dynasty (581–907) displays in the last section of the museum. Characteristic Silk Road objects include bronze bells, murals and ceramic figurines of braying camels, dancers, musicians and local Xi'an women with elaborate Tang Dynasty hairstyles.

Weiyang Palace

North of the Walled City, about 2km (1.2 miles) northwest of Xi'an West Railway Station, are sections of wall and moat that mark the site of the former **Weiyang Gugong** (Weiyang Palace), built by the first Han Emperor Gaozu (247–195 BC) to grace his new capital at Chang'an. Originally extending over 5 sq km (3 sq miles), and with a wall 8,800 metres (5.5 miles) in circumference, this area was at the heart of Han and subsequently Tang Chang'an. Said to have been the largest palace ever constructed on earth, historic sources claim it was 6.8 times the size of Beijing's Forbidden City, or 11 times the size of Vatican City, though there is little to see there today. Instead, with the massive local tourist market very much in mind, a huge 67-hectare (165-acre) **Tang Paradise Theme Park** (Datang Furongyuan; daily 9am–10pm; charge) seeks to recreate an idealised version of Tang Dynasty Chang'an for enthusiastic Chinese visitors. Everything from the food to the music fits with the park's theme.

Around Xi'an

There are many historic sites in the Wei and Jing river valleys around Xi'an, and it is quite common (as well as practical) for visitors to take the readily available day tours that are on offer at hotels and travel agencies across the city. The most popular tour is the **Dongxian Youlan** or Eastern Circuit, which takes in the Tomb of Qin Shi Huang, Banpo Neolithic Village, Huaqing Hot Springs and – most impressive of all – the Army of Terracotta Warriors. Less popular but still very entertaining is the **Xixian Youlan** or Western Circuit, which includes visits to Famen Temple, the Imperial

The interior of Little Wild Goose Pagoda, one of Xi'an's most popular sites.

Tombs, the Tomb of Emperor Jingdi and Xianyang City Museum (Xianyang Shi Bowuguan).

From a Silk Road perspective, the most significant of these outer sites are those associated with **Qin Shi Huang** (r. 221–210 BC), the first emperor of a unified China who, despite his ruthless and autocratic rule, also introduced far-reaching improvements in administration and infrastructure. He also sought to protect China from the restless nomads of the Northwest, ordering the construction of a single defensive wall – Changcheng, the fabled "Great Wall"

Terracotta Warriors

The most impressive memorial to Qin Shi Huang, a site that has made Xi'an internationally celebrated and also earned the city a Unesco World Heritage Listing in 1987, is undoubtedly **Bingmayong** (The Terracotta Army; daily 8.30am–5.30pm; charge). Although it was widely believed that Qin Shi Huang was entombed in the area, no trace of the celebrated Terracotta Army was known to exist until March 1974, when local farmers

The emperor's bronze chariot, part of the Terracotta Army.

digging a well to the east of Li Mountain uncovered traces of terracotta soldiers and horses. Subsequent archaeological excavations have revealed a total (to date) of 8,099 life-sized terracotta figures arranged in ranks, as well as 130 terracotta chariots and more than 600 terracotta horses. It's now generally accepted that their function was to help Qin Shi Huang continue his autocratic rule over a spirit empire in the imperial afterlife.

The statistics behind the Terracotta Army are impressive enough to be somewhat mind-boggling. Building of the mausoleum began in 246 BC and is supposed to have taken an army of 700,000 workers four decades to complete. Qin Shi Huang was interred after his death in 210, amid great pomp and expense. According to the historian Sima Qian (145–90 BC), the First Emperor was entombed with great quantities of treasure amid a jewelled model of the universe complete with flowing rivers of mercury and assorted crossbows and other booby traps designed to repel tomb-raiders. Despite these precautions, it seems likely that General Xiang Yu,

THE FIRST EMPEROR

The first emperor of a united China, Qin Shi Huang, inherited the throne of the State of Chin in 247 BC and set about conquering the surrounding states with a view to uniting all China under his leadership. He attained this goal in 221 BC and announced himself "Commencing Emperor". A tyrant who burnt books and persecuted Confucianism, sometimes burying his opponents alive, he nevertheless assumed colossal status after his death in 210 BC. Among his monumental achievements were the building of the Great Wall, the foundation of a network of roads and canals, the standardisation of weights, measures and currency, and the establishment of a national legal system. He remains a central figure in Chinese history and culture.

who looted the tomb just five years after Qin Shi Huang's death, started a conflagration that lasted for three months and destroyed large parts of the complex.

Nevertheless, large numbers of terracotta figures, of both men and horses, survived, although their wooden weapons and most of their chariots have by and large burnt or rotted away. From these figures it is apparent that their production was almost on an industrial scale, with specific body parts being manufactured and fired before being arranged in subterranean vaults in careful order of rank and duty. The completed figures were both life-sized and lifelike, and it is famously claimed that no two figures look exactly the same.

Seeing the Terracotta Warriors requires a degree of patience because of the sheer numbers of visitors queuing to share the experience. In fact the authorities have made an excellent job of preserving the serried ranks of warriors in three separate covered pits, the largest of which – **Pit 1** – contains nearly 6,000 equine or human statues in various states of repair, their original brightly coloured lacquer finish on faces and clothing now having almost completely faded. **Pit 2** contains around 1,800 warriors, as well as several perfect specimens that have been preserved in glass display cases at room level to permit visitors an opportunity to get "up close and personal" with some of Qin Shi Huang's warriors and their mounts. **Pit 3**, the smallest yet excavated, is thought to represent the army headquarters, with 72 warriors believed to be of senior rank, together with weapons and horses.

The actual **Tomb of Qin Shi Huang** (Qin Shi Huang Ling; daily 7am–6pm; charge) is located about a mile to the west of the Terracotta Warriors complex, and remains unexcavated pending, perhaps, the development of more sophisticated archaeological preservation techniques in the future. A distinct low hill marks the spot where, according to legend, the deceased emperor was entombed together with all the artisans and workmen who had helped in its construction, buried alive to take their secrets with them, quite literally, to the grave.

Ranks of terracotta warriors.

Sand dune hiking at Dunhuang.

GANSU

Gansu marks the first leg of the journey through the Hexi Corridor to the Jiayuguan Fort and caves of Dunhuang.

The long, narrow province of Gansu, shaped like a cartoon drawing of a dog's bone, extends northwest from the Shaanxi frontier all the way to Yumenguan, the "Jade Gate Pass" that marks the western limits of China proper and the start of China's vast Central Asian province of Xinjiang, the "New Frontier".

Gansu is the very essence of the Eastern Silk Road. A narrow corridor created by the tectonic upheaval of India's collision with Asia, it passes between the high mountainous Tibetan plateau to the south and the bleak Gobi of the Mongolian Steppe to the north, growing harsher and less "Chinese" with each stage further west. In times past it offered merchants and long-distance caravaneers the opportunity to grow rich and prosper. Yet to officials who were exiled here far from the central plain around China's capital, the distance was measured in despair; after all they were almost halfway to the Jade Gate Pass and total banishment from China.

Modern times

Today Gansu remains one of China's poorer provinces, with an economy based largely on agriculture and mining, and a population that is about 75 percent rural. Unlike Shaanxi, which is almost entirely Han Chinese,

Gansu is home to numerous minority nationalities including Hui, Tibetan, Dongxiang, Mongol, Kazakh and Salar, comprising almost 10 percent of the population. This ethnic diversity, combined with the province's ancient archaeological treasures, make Gansu an essential destination in following the ancient Silk Road. Here, at the end of the narrow Hexi Corridor, is the mighty fortress of Jiayuguan, which marks the "first and greatest pass under heaven", and the ancient oasis town of Dunhuang, where the Mogao

Main Attractions
Maijishan Shiku
Labrang
Silk Route Museum, Jiuquan
Jiayuguan Fort
Overhanging Great Wall
Dunhuang
Mogao Caves
Yumenguan
Yangguan
Yardang National Park

Fearsome clay figure at the Buddhist grottoes of Maijishan Shiku.

Caves – also dubbed the "Caves of a Thousand Buddhas" – are a major Silk Road highlight.

Southeastern Gansu

Despite the incredible importance of the Eastern Silk Road in the past, communications across China's great northwest have always been poor, and notwithstanding titanic feats of engineering currently under way, the road across Gansu between Shaanxi and Xinjiang remains slow and difficult in many places. Until a motor road was built between Xi'an and the Gansu capital of Lanzhou in the 1930s, this 720km (447-mile) stage of the Silk Road took about 20 days to traverse by mule track. Communications were further improved with the completion of the Xi'an–Lanzhou Railway in 1954, and the new superhighway along the same route, opened in 2010, has significantly reduced travelling times.

Taking the old and more photogenic road route, the first half of the journey westwards to Tianshui is fast and easy along the dual carriageway of Route 310 as far as the industrial

Lanzhou on the Yellow River.

town of Baoji near the western frontier of Shaanxi. Beyond this point the Wei Valley narrows dramatically as the river is forced through a steep defile between the Qin Ling and Liupan ranges. Here the road is reduced to a single carriageway, winding precariously through the gorge in marked contrast to the Xi'an–Lanzhou Railway, which drives through tunnel after tunnel and crosses soaring viaducts in an almost straight line.

Maijishan Shiku

Tianshui or "Heavenly Waters" is the second-largest city in Gansu, with a population of almost 400,000. Confusingly, it is divided into two urban areas connected by a freeway. The industrial area in the east is the place from which to catch a minibus or taxi to **Maijishan** or "Wheat Stack Mountain", about 35km (22 miles) southeast of town.

Maijishan Shiku (Maijishan Grottoes; daily 8am–6pm; charge) are one of China's four most important Buddhist temple groups (the others being Datong, Luoyang and the famous Mogao Caves at Dunhuang, further

ENTERING AND LEAVING GANSU

Gansu is a long and narrow province and, as such, most visitors not flying directly into Lanzhou or Dunhuang will enter from Shaanxi to the east or Xinjiang to the west. (See page 374 for more on transport.)

Deluxe and express trains run between Lanzhou and Xi'an in **Shaanxi** province several times a day, as do express bus services. Improved road links have reduced the journey to a little over eight hours.

The celebrated Lanxin railway links Xi'an with Urumqi in **Xinjiang**, passing through most of the main Eastern Silk Road destinations, as does the Lanzhou–Xinjiang High-Speed Railway. Regular buses ply National Highway 312 between Lanzhou and Urumqi, but given the distances involved it's still faster and more comfortable to travel by train.

It's possible to reach Chengdu in **Sichuan** province directly by train from Lanzhou, but it's much more interesting and popular to travel by bus or car across the mountainous Tibetan-inhabited uplands via Linxia, Langmusi and Songpan, making a side visit to the important Tibetan monastery of Labrang, at Xiahe.

Hard- and soft-sleeper carriages (equipped with oxygen) travel daily from Lanzhou to Lhasa in **Tibet** on the Qingzang Railway, via Xining and Golmud (around 23 hours). Long-distance buses are not a terribly comfortable option for onward travel to Tibet (20–25 hours between Golmud and Lhasa). Tibet permits are required in advance.

west along the Silk Road). Starting during the Northern Wei (386–535) and Northern Zhou (557–81) dynasties, pious Buddhists cut caves into the sides of a startling red outcrop rising from the surrounding foliage-covered hills. Figures of the Buddha, bodhisattvas and disciples were carved in harder rock brought from elsewhere, and installed in the caves; it is thought that well-to-do merchants involved in the Silk Road trade acted as patrons, putting a percentage of their profits into endowing and expanding the cave complex, both to give thanks for their good fortune and to ensure future success in the material and spiritual worlds. At their height, the Maijishan Grottoes are believed to have numbered almost 800, but they suffered serious damage during an earthquake in 734. This event, combined with the exigencies of time, has reduced the number of extant caves to 194 – still no small number, making a visit to Maijishan a very worthwhile day trip.

A great part of the attraction of visiting Maijishan lies in the striking setting of "Wheat Stack Mountain",

which rises unexpectedly out of the surrounding hills. The red rock face is pitted with caves and grottoes large and small, as well as two large carvings of the Buddha attended by bodhisattvas. The entire complex is reached by a confusing and apparently precarious (though in fact quite safe) series of steps and catwalks set into the side of the cliff – this is no place for sufferers from vertigo – leading through or past series of caves, many of which are locked, though it is possible to peer in. The surviving sculptures and murals reflect a wide range of artistic styles, with some of the earlier images clearly reflecting South Asian influences, while later images are more distinctively Chinese.

Lanzhou

West of Tianshui, Route 316 continues through hilly countryside for about 250km (150 miles) to **Lanzhou**, the largest city and provincial capital of Gansu. Due to its strategic location by the Huang He (Yellow River) in a narrow gorge dominating all traffic between central China and the

A bullet train on the Lanzhou-Xinjiang high-speed railway.

THE LANXIN RAILWAY

Until the Lanzhou–Xinjiang High-Speed Railway (Lanxin Second Railway) opened in 2014, the Lanxin Railway (Lanzhou–Xinjiang) was the only rail link joining Xinjiang to the rest of China. It was constructed in 1952–62 and runs for 1,904km (1,183 miles) from Lanzhou, closely following the route of the old Silk Road via Turpan to Urumqi. In the 1980s a 477-km (296-mile) extension was added to reach the Kazakh frontier at Alashankou, the link-up with Kazakhstan Railroads forming a route across Central Asia. In 1999, the South Xinjiang Branch of the Lanxin Railway was completed between Urumqi and Kashgar. Future projects may include extensions to Osh in Kyrgyzstan and to Pakistan via the Karakoram Highway, an ambitious plan that would link the Chinese and South Asian rail systems for the first time.

TIP

Most people leaving Binglingsi return directly by boat to Yongjing, but it is possible to take a small speedboat down the Yellow River and across the Liujiaxia Reservoir to the pier at Lianhuatai, where it's easy to catch a taxi for the 50-minute trip to Linxia, a convenient place to overnight on the journey south to Xiahe and Labrang Monastery.

northwest, Lanzhou has long been a vital garrison town that has expanded rapidly in recent decades to become a major city of more than 3 million people. With an economy based on heavy industry and petrochemicals, Lanzhou isn't a particularly appealing town, but it sits squarely astride east–west communications, and remains as vital a transport hub today as it was during the Silk Road era. Long and narrow by virtue of its geography, sandwiched between steep hills, it is a very cosmopolitan city, with a noticeable Hui Muslim presence.

As well as good hotels and restaurants, Lanzhou has a few attractions to appeal to visitors, not least of which is the fast-flowing Huang He, already a major river though still about 1,500km (900 miles) from the East China Sea. The best way to see the Yellow River is to take the cable car across the chocolate-coloured, loess-rich waters up **Baita Shan** (White Pagoda Hill; daily 6.30am–8.30pm; charge), where fine views across the city can be augmented by a cold drink and a snack. Near the cable-car station, by the

bank of the Yellow River and facing westward towards Central Asia, stand the **Journey to the West** (*Xiyouji*) statues featuring the celebrated Buddhist monk Xuanzang and his legendary companions, Monkey, Pigsy and Sandy. Nearby is **Waterwheel Park** (Shuicheyuan; daily 6.30am–8.30pm; charge), where two giant, reconstructed waterwheels revolve in the waters of the Yellow River. Introduced as an irrigation technique from Yunnan in the 16th century, these two wheels are all that remain of an estimated 250 waterwheels in the Lanzhou area in the early 20th century. Also in the same downtown area, the Daoist **Baiyun Guan** (White Cloud Temple; daily 7am–5.30pm; charge) offers a tranquil and attractive retreat from the city bustle.

Finally, in the northwest of the city not far from the West Train Station, the **Gansu Provincial Museum** (Gansu Sheng Bowuguan; Tue–Sun 9am–5pm; charge) is definitely worth visiting for its unsurpassed collection of Silk Road artefacts including, most famously, the "Flying Horse of

Transport options on the Liujiaxia Reservoir to Binglingsi.

YARDANGS

Yardangs are strange-looking, wind-eroded outcrops formed by the elements over many millennia. The name is Turkic in origin, meaning "steep banks". Yardangs form in areas where water is scarce and prevailing winds are strong and abrasive. These harsh winds erode low-lying areas into parallel ridges and distinctive mounds that take on a unique shape reminiscent of the upturned hull of a ship. The process gradually yields a field of yardangs of roughly the same size, commonly referred to as "a fleet" due to their uniquely characteristic shape. Yardangs occur most commonly in Xinjiang, the Tibesti region of the central Sahara, and in Arizona in the American West. Recently, huge yardang formations have also been discovered on Mars.

Gansu" found at Wuwei in 1969, and a 2ndcentury silver plate showing Dionysus, the Greek god of wine, found near Lanzhou but clearly originating far to the west and carried overland to China at some stage during the early Silk Road era.

Thousand Buddha Caves

Lanzhou may have relatively few attractions, but the city serves as a gateway to some of the most interesting Silk Road sites in eastern Gansu.

Binglingsi Shiku (Thousand Buddha Caves; usually accessible June–October; charge) is a remarkable collection of caves and grottoes set in an inaccessible canyon by the Yellow River about 80km (48 miles) upstream from Lanzhou. To reach them, take a bus or car to the small town of Yongjing, then catch a ferry (four hours) or a speedboat (90 minutes) along the Liujiaxia Reservoir to Binglingsi. There is no direct road access, and during winter months – approximately November to May – water levels in the Yellow River fall, making access by boat impossible.

Yet it is this very isolation that has protected and preserved Binglingsi, not least from marauding Red Guards during the Cultural Revolution (1966–76). The first Buddhist grottoes at Binglingsi date from the Eastern Jin Dynasty (c.317–420), and construction continued for well over 1,000 years throughout the Tang, Song, Ming and Qing eras. As was the case with nearby Meijishan, the Binglingsi Caves were often sponsored by wealthy patrons investing some of their Silk Road profits and accruing merit for this life and the next. A total of 183 caves, together with nearly 700 carved stone statues and 82 terracotta sculptures, survive, many showing very clear evidence of South Asian Buddhist artistic influences – indeed, art experts agree that Binglingsi is a stylistic midpoint between the former monumental Buddhas of Bamiyan in Afghanistan and grotto complexes further east within China at Datong and Longmen.

The setting is indeed spectacular. Travellers arrive by boat at a steep dock by the banks of the Yellow River in extraordinary eroded sandstone

Carving of Maitreya, the Buddha of the future, at Binglingsi.

Xuanzang and his companions on their Journey to the West.

country, with tall peaks hemming in the cave complex in a narrow valley known as **Dasi Gou** or "Big Temple Gully". The caves are dominated by a giant carving of Maitreya, the Buddha of the future, which is almost 27 metres (90ft) tall. Green-painted wooden catwalks lead up the cliff to a point above the image's head, but these are generally closed to visitors, both for reasons of safety and to protect the images. A one-hour hike up the narrow canyon (or 15 minutes by jeep, apparently specially brought in by boat) leads to a small but active Tibetan monastery, together with a Tang Dynasty cave sheltering a Buddha image holding the *dharmachakra* or "wheel of life".

Detour to Labrang

Linxia, formerly known as Hezhou, is a little-visited but economically significant town on a southern spur of the former Eastern Silk Road leading to the Tibetan plateau and, ultimately, to Lhasa. Nowadays a city of 300,000 people, it is a predominantly Muslim town, the capital of **Linxia**

The beautifully situated Labrang Monastery.

Hui Autonomous Prefecture and home to an Islamic-majority population comprising Chinese-speaking Hui Muslims, Mongol-speaking Dongxiang Muslims, and a few Turkic-speaking Salar Muslims who may have originally migrated from distant Uzbekistan. The town is an important Sufi centre for Muslim mystics (recognisable by their six-cornered hats), as well as a cultural meeting point for Han Chinese, Hui Muslims, Tibetan Buddhists and Dongxiang Mongols. Most visitors staying overnight in Linxia will be en route from Binglingsi to the great Tibetan monastery at Labrang. There's not a great deal to see, but there are a number of adequate hotels, and it's easy to find cheap and good Muslim food – lamian noodles, lamb and beef kebabs, toasted *bing* (flat breads) and the like – at the night market on central Minzu Square.

The countryside beyond Linxia is densely populated by Dongxiang Muslims – in fact they look very much like Hui, with whom they have lived and sometimes intermarried for many centuries – living in small, prosperous agricultural settlements raising livestock (but not pigs) and growing wheat, millet and a luscious selection of fruits including grapes, pomegranates, melons, apples and pears. Each village has at least one mosque surmounted by a row of three crescent moons, and the relaxing, pastoral atmosphere makes for a very pleasant drive.

After about an hour the road passes through two long tunnels linking Linxia Hui Autonomous Prefecture with **Gannan Tibetan Autonomous Prefecture**. Minarets give way to Buddhist *chorten (stupas)*, and the deep magenta and purple of Mahayana Buddhist monks' robes replace skullcaps and veils. This cultural frontier marks the beginning of the Tibetan plateau, and although part of Gansu province, local Tibetan residents make it quite apparent that they, at least, consider this to be a part of Tibet. The road rises steadily, and after about two hours enters a beautiful mountain valley. Here, attached to the predominantly Tibetan town of **Xiahe**, stands

Labrang Monastery (Labuleng Si; daily 8am–5pm; charge), one of the six major **Gelug** "Yellow Hat" monasteries in Tibetan Buddhism, and a major pilgrimage centre, attracting Tibetans from Lhasa and even Dharamsala (the Dalai Lama is a member of the "Yellow Hat" order).

Labrang, which is the most important Tibetan monastery outside the Tibetan Autonomous Region, was established in 1709. At its peak it held as many as 4,000 monks. Today's number of monks is around 2,000 and crowds of Tibetan pilgrims throng the prayer-wheel corridors in their very colourful best clothing. Increasing numbers of Han Chinese visitors also come to worship here, some even painstakingly completing the full 6km (4-mile) *kora* or pilgrimage circuit, constantly prostrating themselves full length as they go.

The large complex dominates the western part of the village. The white or ochre walls and gilded roofs are predominantly Tibetan in architectural style, though the occasional Chinese dragon also graces the eaves.

Gompa decoration.

Pilgrims in the prayer-wheel corridors around the perimeter of Labrang.

Confucius Statue at Wuwei Confucian Temple.

A sprightly Flying Horse of Gansu in downtown Wuwei.

In all there are 18 halls, six colleges, the **Gongtang**, a magnificent golden stupa bearing gilded bas-reliefs of the goddess Tara, and miles of prayer-wheel corridors.

The modern town of Xiahe, where the best accommodation and some surprisingly good restaurants are to be found, lies to the east. It's here that the Han Chinese and Hui Muslims have their shops, with many Hui shopkeepers selling all kinds of religious paraphernalia, including Buddha images and prayer wheels, to the visiting Tibetan faithful.

Hexi Corridor

West of Xiahe, old trade routes extended Silk Road traffic across the Tibetan plateau and beyond, as well as south to Sichuan and Yunnan. But the main route continues to the northwest from Lanzhou, through the Hexi, or Gansu, Corridor. This long, narrow strip of land, sandwiched between the snow-capped Qilian Mountains to the south and the Ala Shan and Gobi deserts to the north, has always provided China with its main overland access to Central Asia and the West. Compared to the harsh terrain to the north and south, travel was always relatively easy along the Hexi, with its series of interconnected oases.

Wuwei

Almost 280km (175 miles) due north of Lanzhou on Route 312, the city of **Wuwei** is "small" only by Chinese standards, with a population of around 500,000, mainly Han Chinese, but with visible numbers of Hui as well as Mongols and Tibetans. In earlier times it was called Liangzhou. Dominating the eastern end of the Hexi Corridor, it has long played a significant role on this major trade route.

Wuwei's most famous historic artefact, the celebrated Han Dynasty (206 BC–AD 220) bronze horse known as the **Flying Horse of Gansu**, was discovered here in a tomb beneath **Leitai Temple** (Leitai Si; daily 8am–6pm; charge) in the north part of town. The original is on display in the Gansu Provincial Museum at Lanzhou, but the horse's likeness is everywhere, most notably at the centre of Wuwei's downtown Wenhua Square.

Other sights to visit include the impressive and tranquil **Wen Miao** (Confucius Temple and Museum; daily 8am–6pm; charge), where stelae recording past academic achievements adorn well-tended gardens; and **Dayun Si** (Dayun Temple; daily 8am–6pm; charge), the ancient Bell Tower northeast of the city. Just beyond the restored Bell Tower, in an undistinguished courtyard, Daoist rites are often performed, with mediums covering supplicants with red cloths, ringing bells and shaking censers, vigorously casting out spirits and diseases in the heart of People's China. Finally, and related directly to the old Silk Road, **Luoshi Si Ta** (Kumarajiva Pagoda; daily 8am–6pm; charge) dates from the 7th century, when it was built to honour the Buddhist monk Kumarajiva (Jiumoluoshi, AD 344–413). Born into a royal household in Kuqa, he travelled to Kashmir and parts of India before returning to translate the Mahayana Buddhist sutras and other writings

he had collected. He lived at Wuwei from 386 to 403, and is remembered as one of the city's most illustrious residents. The temple, which is currently undergoing very extensive renovation and which will be quite splendid when complete, centres on the 1,300-year-old yellow brick pagoda dedicated to Kumarajiva.

Zhangye

Just 56km (36 miles) northwest of Wuwei, Highway 312 passes through the undistinguished little town of **Yongchang**. In 1957 an American sinologist, Homer H. Dubs, advanced the theory that a group of 145 Roman centurions captured by the Chinese in 36 BC were settled here (see page 49).

A further 250km (150 miles), or half a day's bus ride northwest of Wuwei, **Zhangye** is an important light industrial and agricultural centre at the heart of the Hexi Corridor, with a population of about 200,000. Like Wuwei, it was originally an important garrison town designed to protect Silk Road traffic and keep the troublesome nomadic invaders out of China proper.

The entrance to Dafo Si, the Great Buddha Temple, in Zhangye.

FLYING HORSE OF GANSU

In 1969 archaeologists were excavating at a tomb beneath Leitai Temple in Wuwei when they discovered, among more than 200 other relics, a 25-cm (10-in) -high bronze sculpture of a horse at full gallop, its raised head neighing and its rear right hoof resting lightly on the head of a startled swallow in flight. Believed to represent the "heavenly steed" of Central Asian tradition so greatly desired by the ancient Chinese, the "Flying Horse of Gansu" soon became an icon for the province and, increasingly, for China as a whole. Widely considered to be an artistic masterpiece, representing Chinese bronze work at its most sophisticated and elegant, the "flying horse" was cast by an unknown artist at the time of the Eastern Han Dynasty around 2,000 years ago.

FACT

Most of the people of Gansu speak a dialect of Mandarin Chinese, but in some outlying areas you can also hear Tibetan, Mongol and Kazakh. Salar is a Turkic language spoken by around 60,000 people who claim to have arrived in the 14th century from Samarkand. Mandarin, also called putonghua or "common speech", is understood by just about everyone.

Everything narrows in central Gansu as the northern **Longshou Shan** or "Dragon's Head Mountains" press south from the Gobi to sandwich all – the former Silk Road, the modern road, railway lines and the **Great Wall of China** itself – into a narrow corridor facing the mighty **Qilian Shan** or "Sky Mountains" further south. The Great Wall, which is mainly of compressed earth in these remote western reaches, stretches to the north of Highway 312 for about 150km (90 miles) before cutting across the road at Shandan and continuing, like a crumbling mud serpent, south of the highway towards Zhangye.

Zhangye is a more attractive town to stay in than either Wuwei or, further to the west, Jiayuguan. There are adequate shops and hotels, as well as Mingqing Jie, a reconstructed "Ming and Qing Dynasty" walking street that is lined with reasonably priced, clean restaurants. Cultural attractions tend to be clustered in the southwest of town, around Zhongxin Square, a large, paved walking area where local people gather to drink beer, chat or

Tu Ta (Earthen Tower) in Zhangye.

fly kites in the cool of the evening. Dominating the west of the square is Mu Ta (Wooden Pagoda; daily 7.30am–6.30pm; charge), a carefully restored octagonal pagoda dating originally from the 6th century. A short distance south is Xilai Si (daily 7.30am–6.30pm; charge), a small but active Buddhist temple with a resident population of monks.

To the southeast of the square stands – or rather, lies – a 34-metre (20-ft) -long Reclining Buddha, said to be China's largest. The image is housed in the main building of **Dafo Si** (Great Buddha Temple; daily 7.30am–6.30pm; charge), which is currently being restored. The Buddha image is impressive, but photography is forbidden. Further to the east in the temple grounds stands Tu Ta (Earthen Tower), a 20-metre (65-ft) -high Tibetan-style stupa.

Away from southeastern Zhongxin Square, the geographical centre of the city is marked by a fine **Gulou** (Drum Tower; open 7am–8pm; charge) that dates from 1507 and holds a large Ming Dynasty bronze bell. Finally and

KUMARAJIVA, THE GREAT TRANSLATOR

The renowned Buddhist monk and translator Kumarajiva, known to the Chinese as Jiumoluoshi, was born into the Kuqan aristocracy in AD 344. He was the son of a South Asian nobleman, Kumarayana, and a Kuqan princess, Jiva. His father was an Indian Buddhist monk who had crossed the Pamirs to Xinjiang before settling in Kuqa, where he became the royal priest, while his mother entered the Buddhist nunnery of Tsili near Kuqa when Kumarajiva was just seven years old.

Even by this age, the young Kumarajiva is said to have mastered several Buddhist texts and committed many sutras to memory, and during the two years his mother spent in the nunnery his studies continued apace. Aged 9, he returned to Kashmir to further his religious education. He spent three years in India before returning to Xinjiang, where he continued his studies at Kashgar, ordaining the son of the king of Yarkand while studying the Hindu Vedas.

Subsequently he moved to the Chinese capital at Chang'an where he eventually died in 413. During his long life Kumarajiva translated many texts, including the *Amitabha Sutra*, the *Lotus Sutra*, and the *Diamond Sutra*, but he is best remembered for his peerless rendering of the great *Maha Prajna Paramita Sutra*, or "Heart of Perfect Wisdom" Sutra into Chinese.

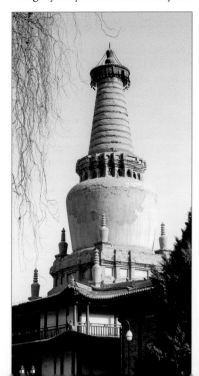

rather unexpectedly, in the northwest part of town near Ganquan Park, there stands a robed and distinctly Occidental statue representing the Venetian traveller **Marco Polo** (1254–1324), who is said to have spent a year here, together with his father Niccolo and his uncle Maffeo, towards the end of the 13th century.

Around Zhangye

Southwest of Zhangye a narrow road climbs into the foothills of the Qilian Shan, approaching a series of permanently snow-capped peaks rising to Mt Qilian at 5,547 metres (18,199ft). The road leads to **Mati Si** (Horse Hoof Monastery; charge), carved into sandstone hills some 65km (40 miles) from Zhangye. The monastery was once an important religious centre, but suffered badly at the hands of iconoclastic Red Guards during the Cultural Revolution. It is sobering to think that, had Binglingsi been more accessible, it too might have suffered irreparable damage. As things are, Mati Si is being restored, and in any case is worth visiting if time permits, as the countryside round about is wild and appealing for hikers, as well as being home to the Buddhist Yugur minority who are embracing tourism with some enthusiasm, offering horse-riding and accommodation in Yugur yurts together with such delights as *chang* (barley wine) and *shouzhua yangrou* or "hand-eaten lamb".

Beyond Zhangye Route 312 runs northwest for a further 250km (155 miles) to Jiuquan, passing through pleasant, fertile countryside sheltering poor, but not impoverished, villages of mud-walled, inward-looking domestic compounds. Few rural buildings are more than one storey high because of the threat of earthquakes. Grapevines hang in front of many houses to provide shade in the heat of the day, while flat roofs are covered with firewood or straw to guard against the bitter cold of winter. Livestock includes numerous sheep, goats and cows, but fewer pigs in this increasingly Islamic region. Everywhere are small trucks packed with tomatoes, big red chilli peppers, apples, melons, grapes and pears, tended by local people who – especially the high-cheek-boned Gansu women – all seem to sport rosy cheeks as a result of the strong, sometimes sandy wind and the hot Central Asian sun. The predominant colours of the surrounding countryside are green where irrigated fields and lines of poplars define the outskirts of villages, and a sere, dusty yellow reflected in the surrounding hills, scrubland and the surviving entrails of the Great Wall, still staggering towards the "Last Pass under Heaven" at Jiayuguan, the traditional terminus of the Ming Great Wall.

Jiuquan

Just half an hour before Jiayuguan, the old Silk Road city of **Suzhou** (not to be confused with Suzhou in Jiangsu province) has been reinvented around **Jiuquan** (population 350,000). Jiuquan is another old Silk Road garrison town, said to derive its name *jiu quan*

FACT

Jiuquan is widely known as China's aerospace city and was founded in 1958. The massive Jiuquan Satellite Launch Centre, which covers an estimated 2,800 sq km (1,081 sq miles) and may house up to 20,000 scientists and technicians, is in fact located in the nearby Alashan region of Inner Mongolia.

Mati Si.

or "wine spring" from a legendary incident that took place in around 120 BC, during the Han Dynasty's long wars with the Xiongnu nomads of the Northwest. The Han commander, Huo Qubing (140–117 BC) was sent a flagon of wine by the emperor, and deciding to share it with all his men, tipped the wine into a nearby spring, which was subsequently named Jiuquan. The spring – officially called Jiuquan Yuan or "Wine Spring Park" – still exists, and Jiuquan artisans still produce "night-glowing cups" of green Qilian Mountain jade which are said to glow when filled with wine and set in the moonlight. A nice story, but *caveat emptor* – they don't!

The modern town of Jiuquan is centred on a **Drum Tower** (Gulou) established in the 14th century when Suzhou was an important Ming garrison town guarding the western end of the Hexi Corridor, but dating in its present form from 1905. The original structure was praised by Marco Polo in his writings. Aligned with the cardinal directions, above each of its gates are inscriptions in Chinese proclaiming that "East is

Huashan" (in distant and desirable Shaanxi), "North is the Great Desert" and "South are the Qilian Mountains". Chinese soldiers stationed here over the centuries would hardly have needed the fourth reminder that: "West is Yiwu", the old name for Hami Oasis in Xinjiang, distant some 650km (390 miles) across some of the most bleak and arid desert anywhere in the world.

The town's newest attraction is the **Silk Route Museum** (www.silkroute museum.com; daily; charge), which opened in 2009 and is spread out across a huge site of 280 hectares (700 acres) The museum houses over 35,000 artefacts including well preserved frescoes from the Wei Jin tomb, fossils, Buddhist temple carvings and a large selection of jade figurines. The museum has a large fund at its disposal for ongoing acquisitions and has regularly changing exhibitions.

Around Jiuquan

There are two sites of interest shortly outside Jiuquan city, 3km (2 miles) to the west. The **tomb chamber** at Dingjiazha houses some of China's earliest wall paintings, dating from the East Jin Dynasty (317–430 AD). The tomb is thought to belong to a nobleman, and the murals include scenes of hunting and banquets, as well as an attractive depiction of the heavens.

The **Jiuquan Satellite Launch Centre** (Shuang Cheng Tzu) was China's first ballistic missile and satellite launch pad. The Centre is a part of **Dongfeng Space City**, which features test-flight facilities and a small museum.

Jiayuguan

Much closer to hand, just 20km (12 miles) or so from Jiuquan, stands the great fortress of **Jiayuguan**, the "First and Greatest Pass under Heaven", completed in 1372 on the orders of Zhu Yuanzhang, the first Ming emperor (1368–98), to mark the end of the Ming Great Wall – or, more specifically, the very limits of Chinese civilisation, and the beginnings of the

Dramatic rock formations around Zhangye.

outer "barbarian" lands. For centuries, the fort was not just of strategic importance to Han Chinese, but of cultural significance as well. This was the last civilised place before the outer darkness – those proceeding beyond, whether disgraced officials or criminals, faced a life of exile among nomadic strangers, before which they had to cross the ghost-infested wastes of the Gashun Gobi, a wind-blasted, arid wasteland hundreds of kilometres across where hapless travellers faced extremes of heat and cold by day and night. Jiayuguan was quite properly feared, and even today many Chinese associate the pass with exile and despair, bringing to mind the exiles' poem:

Looking westward, we see the long, long road.

Only the brave cross the Martial Barrier

Who is not afraid of the vast desert?

Should not the scorching heat of heaven make him frightened?

Soldiers stationed at Jiayuguan took a similarly bleak view of the location, but one that was perhaps rather more sanguine, as befits military men. In the mid-8th century the Tang poet Liu Zhongyong summed up their feelings in his verse "The Troopers' Burden":

For years, to guard the Jade Pass and the River of Gold

With our hands on our horse-whips and our sword-hilts

We have watched the green graves change to icy snow

And the Yellow River ring the Black Mountain forever.

Today **Jiayuguan City** is a modern, prefecture-level town of about 250,000 people – almost all Han Chinese – that makes a living from transport and heavy industry. The main interest for the tourist is its proximity to the great fortress, and its spectacular natural setting at the western end of the Hexi Corridor beneath the permanently snow-covered peaks of the great Qilian range. This strategic position has always attracted a lively mix of a dozen ethnic groups and today offers adequate accommodation and even a couple of rather good restaurants. In other words, it's a good base to visit the nearby fortress and various remains of the Great Wall, as well as the rather superior Great Wall Museum that opened in 2003.

Jiayuguan Chenglou (Jiayuguan Fort; daily 8.30am–7.30pm; charge) stands in the desert about 6km (4 miles) west of Jiayuguan City, overlooking the narrow entrance to the Hexi Corridor, at this point about 15km (9 miles) across, dominated by the icy Qilian to the south and the bleak, wind-blasted Mazong Shan, or "Horse-Mane Mountains" to the north. The fort, which has been fully restored and is in fine condition, is surrounded by walls 11 metres (36ft) high and about 750 metres (2,500ft) in length, being trapezoid in shape and pierced by three gates, the eastern **Guanghua Men** or "Gate of Enlightenment", the inner **Rouyuan Men** or "Gate of Conciliation" and the outer, western gate, sometimes imaginatively called the "Gate of Sighs", but

The impressively restored Overhanging Great Wall.

Reaching for the sky at the Jiuquan Satellite Launch Centre.

in fact bearing the Chinese characters **Jiayuguan Men**, or "Gate of the Pass of the Pleasant Valley". Each of the three main gates has 17-metre (55-ft) -high towers with curving, upturned eaves. Within the main courtyard, the restored **Residence of General Rui Neng** is a Ming Dynasty structure with realistic waxwork figures of the general's family, soldiers and domestic servants going about their business. The whole complex is surrounded by a lesser, outer wall, and the crumbling remains of the Great Wall itself march west from the fort's southwest corner to the nearby Taolai River, where it stops suddenly above a steep gorge.

Outside the fortress, but within the grounds of the park that surround it, **Changcheng Bowuguan** (Great Wall Museum; daily 8.30am–6pm; charge included with fort) features many aspects of the history of the Great Wall, as well as Silk Road exhibits and painted tiles from the **Wei and Western Jin Tombs** (AD 220–420) that lie scattered in the desert about 25km (16 miles) east of Jiayuguan. Outside the museum stand busts of **Feng Sheng**,

Jiayuguan Pass, with the Qilian Mountains in the distance.

the Ming general who drove the last Mongol armies westwards out of the Hexi Corridor in 1368, and of **Yi Kaizhan**, the legendary master engineer who oversaw the construction of the fortress soon thereafter.

Two other Silk Road-related sites worth visiting in the vicinity of Jiayuguan are the **Overhanging Great Wall** (Xuanbi Changcheng; daily 8.30am–7pm; charge) and the **First Beacon Tower** (Wanli Changcheng Diyi Dun; daily 8.30am–7.30pm; charge). The former is an impressively restored section of wall to the northwest of the fort, connecting its ramparts to the outliers of the Mazong range. The wall climbs straight up the mountain flank in a manner reminiscent of the Great Wall north of Beijing, offering fine views across the surrounding countryside. The latter marks the point where the Great Wall meets the Taolai River Gorge, and is marked by an abandoned beacon tower. A balcony of reinforced glass projects from the cliff and offers dizzying views of the waters of the Taolai River swirling through the gorge below.

FIRST PASS UNDER HEAVEN

For Han Chinese the great fortress at Jiayuguan marked – symbolically, at least – the westernmost limits of civilisation. Beyond lay only the demon-inhabited wastes of the Gashun Gobi and Taklamakan deserts, as well as the fierce and unpredictable nomadic tribes that posed a constant threat to China's settled security. Jiayuguan was the harshest and least popular station in the entire empire for those troops sent to guard the western frontier and the all-important Silk Road that lay beyond. It was also a place of terror and anguish for those banished from the realm, whether disgraced officials or common criminals, who were forced, unwillingly, through the "Gate of Sighs".

Those passing through the gateway, whether into exile or on imperial service in some distant "barbarian" oasis, would often leave despairing poems and other graffiti on the walls of the narrow passage leading to Jiayuguan Gate. Small pebbles were thrown at the wall to see if they bounced back or simply fell to the ground – a sign of whether the traveller would eventually return to the safety and civilisation of China, or might languish forever in a realm of malevolent spirits and "barbarian" nomads "stinking of rancid mutton". For merchant venturers, however, Jiayuguan represented a gateway to opportunity and the possibility of immense wealth.

Western Gansu

The fortress at Jiayuguan represents the end of the Hexi Corridor, but not quite the end of Gansu province and of China proper. The proximity of Central Asia is palpable, in the faces and clothing of the people, the aroma of grilling kebabs and spiced naan breads pervading the markets, even the dust storms that blow in all too frequently from the Gashun Gobi and Taklamakan deserts. Yet there is still some distance – nearly 400km (250 miles) – to the unprepossessing truck stop of Xingxingxia on the Gansu–Xinjiang frontier, and Western Gansu, freed from the crushing embrace of the Qilian Mountains now far to the south, opens out to embrace the antique oasis town of Dunhuang, as well as the celebrated Mogao Caves and two long-abandoned Han Dynasty passes, Yumenguan and Yangguan, that marked the traditional start of the Northern and Southern Silk Roads, respectively, via the Tarim Basin oases that skirt the unforgiving Taklamakan.

Yumen and Anxi

About 60km (37 miles) west of Jiayuguan, Highway 312 skirts north of the old city of **Yumen** or "Jade Gate", a name that hangs heavy with evocative nostalgia, but is today a rather uninspiring oil town. Continuing northwest, the road leaves the Qilians behind and enters bleak and arid wasteland. After a further 230km (140 miles) the town of **Anxi** or "Pacified West" marks an important junction on the former Silk Road, but was badly damaged during the 19th-century Muslim rebellions, and holds little appeal for the visitor today. The Silk Road divided here, with a northern branch heading across the Gashun Gobi to the oasis city of Hami in Xinjiang, and thence to Turpan and the northern Tarim Basin, while a southern branch led first to Dunhuang, and then across the dry Kum Tagh, or "Sand Mountains", to the remote oases of the southern Tarim Basin.

Both routes would rejoin at the distant caravan city of Kashgar, near China's westernmost extremity.

Dunhuang

Yumen and Anxi may be little more than transit points today, but **Dunhuang**, or "Blazing Beacon", more than makes up for this deficiency. As early as 117 BC, Dunhuang was made a prefecture by the Han Emperor Wu Di (141–87 BC). Wu Di recognised the strategic location of the oasis, both as the last major watering hole before the Taklamakan Desert, and because it sat astride the three main Silk Road routes running west. The Great Wall was extended into the desert to the west of Dunhuang, linking the settlement with the two main Silk Road gates, **Yumenguan** and **Yangguan**. By the 3rd century AD, Dunhuang dominated Silk Road traffic in the region and had become a prosperous town, with merchants and pilgrims sponsoring the construction of the nearby Buddhist **Mogao Caves**. Subsequently the town enjoyed mixed fortunes, being occupied by Tibet in

TIP

Dunhuang town is pleasant to see on foot, with the lake and dunes easily reached by bicycle or taxi. For Mogao Caves take a regular bus, minibus or taxi for the 30-minute journey from the centre of town. Once you reach the caves you are obliged to join a guided tour to see a selection of the caves.

Riding camels in the desert by Mingsha Mountain, Dunhuang.

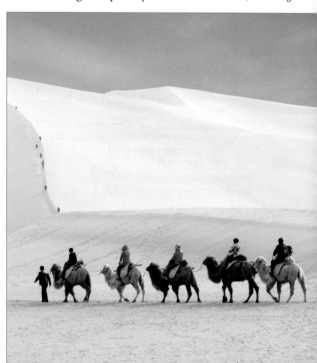

the 7th century but prospering under the Tang Dynasty (618–907) before being occupied, in turn, by the Xixia (1036) and the Mongols (1227). The city was re-established by the Qing in 1760, and once again became prosperous, enjoying – according to missionary sources – the Silk Road sobriquet "Little Beijing".

Today **Dunhuang** is a busy and, once again, prosperous little frontier town of about 100,000, mainly Han but also Hui, Uighur, Mongol and Tibetan citizens. Laid out in a simple grid pattern around a central traffic circle, the town is small enough to explore on foot. The atmosphere is relaxed and friendly. Busy **Shazhou Night Market** on Yangguan Donglu sells excellent food, while a string of small restaurants on nearby Mingshan Lu, near the main bus station, offer Sichuan and other regional cuisines often accompanied by – luxurious surprise – English-language menus! Accommodation is both plentiful and reasonably priced. All in all, Dunhuang is an excellent place to break a Silk Road trip for at least a

couple of days; as well as being congenial, there's plenty to see in the surrounding area. Not that there's much in town itself, beyond **Dunhuang County Museum** (Dunhuang Xian Bowuguan; daily 8am–6pm; charge), where rather average collections of Silk Road-related artefacts and Mogao Caves scrolls are displayed.

Around Dunhuang

The most important attraction in northwest Gansu, and the main reason most Silk Road travellers and Buddhist pilgrims visit Dunhuang, is the **Mogao Caves** (Mogao Ku; daily 8.30–11.30am, 2.30–6pm; charge). Located about 25km (15 miles) southeast of the town centre and accessible by taxi or minibus, the caves were cut into the soft rock face of the **Mingsha Hills** over a period of more than 1,000 years, from the 3rd to the 14th centuries. They represent China's – and probably the world's – most extensive collection of Buddhist statuary, paintings and manuscripts, though many of the original materials are now in foreign museums, especially in Europe.

Having suffered many depredations at the hands of robbers, warlords, iconoclastic Muslims and Red Guards over the years (but none so damaging to the Mogao Caves, at least, as their late 19th–early 20th-century discovery by archaeologist-explorers such as Aurel Stein – see page 75 – and Paul Pelliot) the cave complex is now extremely well cared for. Visitors cannot enter without a guide, photography is forbidden and generally the only illumination will be the guide's torch – to prevent the murals fading over time.

Almost 500 caves survive, set back against and cut into the cliff face, and connected by a series of ramps and walkways. Not all the caves are open to the public – even accompanied by an obligatory guide – and it may be necessary to make special arrangements (and payment) with the Mogao authorities to explore further such off-limits grottoes. An estimated 45,000

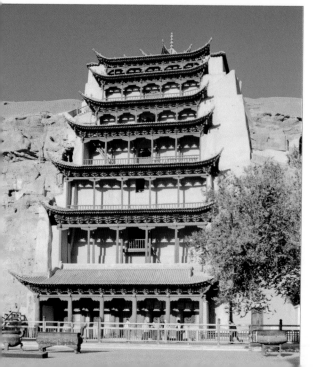

The entrance to the Mogao Caves.

sq metres (148,500 sq ft) of murals and more than 2,000 painted stucco figures can be seen (though it would take considerable dedication and several days to try to visit all of them). The years of darkness have kept the generally pastel colours fairly bright, and it is a wonderful experience, even to the lay person with limited knowledge of Buddhist art, to wander through the caves as the torchlight reveals image after image derived, variously and distinctively, from South Asian, Gandharan, Turkic, Tibetan and of course Chinese traditions. A well-presented museum in front of the caves features examples of the astonishing number of scripts found on manuscripts and other documents preserved at the caves, including writings not just in Chinese and Sanskrit, Tocharian and Tibetan languages, but also in various Turkic dialects, Persian and even Hebrew.

Less spectacular, but also less well known, the **Western Thousand Buddha Caves** (Xi Qianfodong; daily 7am–5.30pm; charge), located 35km (22 miles) west of Dunhuang City, are

also worth visiting. The supervision by guides is much less strict, and visitors can generally explore the six caves (of a total of 16) that are open to the public. The caves date from the Northern Wei Dynasty (4th century) through to the late Tang and beyond.

Also reminiscent of the Silk Road, about 4km (2.5 miles) due west of Dunhang, the nine-storey **White Horse Pagoda** (Baima Ta; daily; charge) is dedicated to the memory of the Buddhist monk Kumarajiva's horse, which died here in 384. The 12-metre (40-ft) –high, dun-coloured pagoda is made of baked clay decorated with stucco overlay.

After Mogao Caves, and perhaps even more popular with local tour groups, the biggest attractions at Dunhuang are the **Mingsha Shan** (Singing Sand Dunes; daily 6am–9pm; charge). Dominating the horizon about 4km (2.5 miles) south of town, these are the largest and most impressive sand dunes in China. The main dunes, which rise to between 250 and 300 metres (820ft–1,000ft), would not look out of place in the Grand Erg dunes

Camels make a popular photo opportunity.

The western end of the Great Wall at Jiayuguan.

FACT

Yangguan was once the major gateway to the west and an important toll point on the Chinese Silk Road. In the 7th century the eminent Buddhist monk Xuanzang passed through on his return to Xi'an from India, when Yangguan was a military strongpoint set in a small but flourishing oasis.

of Algeria, and are truly impressive. They're called "Singing Sands" because the shifting grains reportedly make a humming noise in powerful winds.

Set in the lee of the great dunes, **Crescent Moon Lake** (Yueyaquan; admission included with Mingsha Shan) is – as the name suggests – a small, crescent-shaped stretch of water that can look very blue at the right time of day and in good weather. The entire (admittedly lovely) area has become a kind of Silk Road theme park and funfair, with long teams of Bactrian camels carrying Chinese tourists wearing orange sand-boots and carrying mobile phones up the sand dunes. It's a great photo opportunity, but also rather deflating to find that – just off lens from that perfect sand dune and camel train image shot at sunset – there are another 250 camels carrying similar, long lines of tourists! Other very popular activities in the area include quad biking, paragliding and sand-surfing down the steep dunes.

Further afield, and directly related to the former Silk Road, are the remains of the two Han Dynasty gates marking the various Silk Roads running west, from Dunhuang to Kashgar and beyond.

Yumenguan

Yumenguan (Jade Gate Pass; daily 8am–6.30pm; charge) is about 90km (56 miles) to the west of Dunhuang City. It was established by the celebrated Han Emperor Wu Di around 120 BC to defend the western reaches of the empire and control trade and taxes. The Silk Road passing through Yumenguan divided west of the gate, a long-lost central route leading via Lop Nur and the former city of Loulan to Korla, and thence following the southern foothills of the Tian Shan around the northern Tarim Basin to Kashgar. An alternative northern route avoided Loulan altogether and swung northwest, across the Gashun Gobi to Hami, and then on to Turpan and Korla, where it rejoined the central route. Due to progressive desertification and the shifting of Lop Nur Lake, the pass at Yumenguan – really a kind of ancient toll gate – was probably abandoned by the 6th century, as

Reclining Buddha at the Mogao Caves.

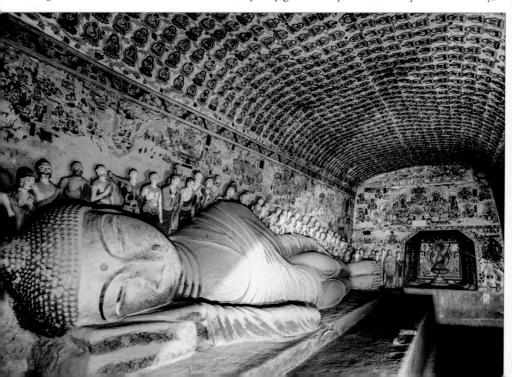

traffic increasingly followed the present northern route via Xingxingxia and Hami to Turpan.

Today Yumenguan is an isolated rectangular watchtower of rammed earth some 10 metres (33ft) high. It has two gateways, in the west and the north. A *ma dao* or horse ramp once allowed soldiers to lead their horses onto the tops of the crenellated battlements. The charge includes a small but worthwhile museum detailing Yumenguan's former importance on the Silk Road and postulating that the name "Jade Gate Pass" originated from the fine jade brought back to China via the toll gate from Khotan and beyond.

The Tang Dynasty poet Li Bai (701–62) immortalised Yumenguan in his poem "The Moon over Jade Gate Pass", which remains familiar to many Chinese and evocative of exile far from home:

A bright moon rises above the Mountains of Heaven,

Lost in a vast ocean of clouds.

The eternal wind, across thousands upon thousands of miles,

Blows past Jade Gate Pass.

Yangguan

Near Nanhu village, about 60km (37 miles) south of Yumenguan and a similar distance west of Dunhuang, stand the remains of **Yangguan** (Sun Pass; daily; charge). Like its twin at Yumenguan, Yangguan was erected by Wu Di in around 120 BC to control the Southern Silk Road to Kashgar, striking west through the arid wastes of the Kum Tagh "Sand Mountains" before reaching the ancient Silk Road settlement and fortress of Miran, some 75km (46 miles) northeast of Charklik. From here the southern route continued via the oases to the south of the Taklamakan Desert, and via Khotan and Yarkand, to rejoin the northern and former central routes at Kashgar.

Like Yumenguan, Yangguan is remembered in a famous verse of parting and exile, penned by the Tang poet Wang Wei (701–61):

A morning rain has settled the dust in Wei City.

Willows are green again by the tavern door.

Do not leave until we have drained one more glass of wine together –

To the west of Yangguan you will meet no more old friends!

Today the remains of Yangguan stand atop a low hill in the desert. In recent years it has been joined by a Silk Road Exhibition Hall at Yangguan Museum (Yangguan Bowuguan; daily; charge). Nanhu Village offers opportunities for snacks and cold drinks, as well as delicious locally grown grapes.

Finally, in the desert beyond, **Yardang National Park** (Yadan Guojia Dizhi Gongyuan; charge included with Yumenguan) is an extraordinary terrain of steep, wind-eroded outcrops on the edge of the Gashun Gobi. Set in an isolated, eerie wasteland, it's no wonder the local people traditionally considered it an "abode of demons". At twilight or in a dust storm the natural formations do indeed look strangely like the time-worn buildings of an abandoned, ancient city.

Old wagon at Yangguan Pass.

The oasis at Crescent Moon lake.

Subash Mosque near Lake Karakul.

XINJIANG

Xinjiang is archetypal Silk Road terrain: deserts, mountains, lost cities, bazaars, but with many surprises, such as the vineyards of Turpan.

Xinjiang is China's largest province, accounting for one-sixth of the nation's territory and, at 1,660,000 sq km (640,000 sq miles), equalling almost exactly the land areas of France, Germany, Spain and the UK combined. At a mere 20 million, the population is sparse but demographically diverse. In 1949, the inhabitants of this part of China were mainly Turkic Muslim, with Uighurs predominating in the south and Kazakhs in the north. Han Chinese, almost all of whom were officials or merchants from China proper to the east of the Jade Gate, numbered between 3 and 4 percent of the total population.

Since 1949, Han Chinese have migrated to Xinjiang in large numbers, and are now the second-largest ethnic group in the province, comprising around 41 percent of the total, compared to the Uighur at 45 percent. Smaller groups – ranging from the Kazakhs at 7 percent and the Hui at 5 percent down to the Persian-speaking Tajik minority at Tashkurgan in the far west, numbering a mere 0.2 percent of the population – are numerically less significant.

Xinjiang has been of immense strategic significance to China for more than 2,000 years. From about the 2nd century BC, when Han China first began to extend its influence over the area, it was called Xiyu or "Western Region". For centuries it was known

in the West variously as Eastern Turkestan or Chinese Turkestan. Following the Qing re-conquest of the area in 1884, it was renamed Xinjiang or "New Frontier" and given provincial status, before becoming the Xinjiang Uighur Autonomous Region in 1955.

The vast area is dominated by some of the highest mountains and most arid deserts in the world. In the east, the area around Hami and Lop Nur has long been strongly influenced by nearby China proper, and is dominated by Han and Hui Chinese with a scattering

Main Attractions
Hami
Turpan
Flaming Mountains
Bezeklik
Kuqa
Khotan
Kashgar
Lake Karakul
Xinjiang Autonomous
  Region Museum
Heavenly Lake

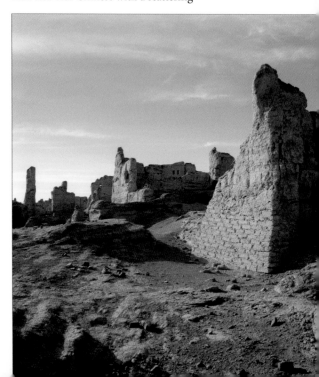

The ruins at Gaochang Gucheng.

of Uighurs. North of the Tian Shan, Urumqi is an overwhelmingly Han Chinese city, while the Dzungarian Steppe and Altai Mountains are home mainly to the province's Kazakhs. The Tarim Basin in the southwest, distinguished by a series of oasis towns surrounding the central Taklamakan Desert like beads on a necklace, is dominated by Uighur, though both Han and Hui continue to settle throughout the area, especially in the larger cities.

The Silk Road has defined Xinjiang for millennia, dividing into three main routes near Dunhuang and traversing the province before coming together again in Kashgar and continuing to Central Asia. The very transient nature of Silk Road commerce has forged Xinjiang's character as a marginal land, a meeting place of peoples and cultures as diverse as Chinese and Arab, Tibetan and Turk, Mongol and Manchu. The religions they brought – Buddhism, Manichaeism, Nestorian Christianity, Judaism and Islam, all left their mark and have contributed to the fascinating cultural and artistic heritage of the province.

Find large wholemeal naan breads in Xinjiang.

The former central route

Until the 4th century AD, the main Silk Road route west from Dunhuang led through Yumenguan, across the incredibly inhospitable Gashun Gobi, to the almost legendary city of Loulan on the shores of a lake called Lop Nur, before following the waters of the Konqi River northwest to the oasis town of Korla. By about AD 400, increasing desertification and the wandering nature of Lop Nur – dependent on the Tarim River system and the run-off of glacial waters from the Tian Shan, Pamir, Kunlun and Altun ranges – had combined to make this Central Route impracticable. It became easier to follow either the old, long-established Southern Route via Yangguan and Miran to Khotan, or the Northern Route, via the oases of Hami and Turpan, to Korla. Both routes converged in the west at Kashgar before continuing west to Samarkand, or south to Ladakh and Kashmir.

Ancient Loulan was rediscovered by Sven Hedin in 1899, then excavated more thoroughly by Aurel Stein in 1906 and 1914. It was rediscovered by the

ENTERING AND LEAVING XINJIANG

Travellers leaving China via Xinjiang for points further west on the Silk Road should apply for onward visas in their home country or in Beijing. It is not possible to get visas for any of the neighbouring countries on arrival at the land border. Check security advice for all routes. (See page 374 for more information on transport in China.)

Entering Xinjiang from **Gansu** is easy via either the Lanxin Railway, or National Highway 312. This runs south from Karghalik before heading across the **Tibetan plateau** towards Lhasa. It remains officially closed to foreign visitors, though increasing numbers of independent motorists and bus passengers do manage to take it.

The difficult, largely unpaved route from Dunhuang to Charklik on the Southern Silk Road in Xinjiang, is not recommended and is often snowbound in winter. There are four efficient overland crossings between Xinjiang and **Kazakhstan** at Korgas Alashankou/Dostyk, Dulata/Koljat and Bakhty, as well as a twice-weekly rail link at Alashankou to Almaty.

Two roads lead to **Kyrgyzstan**, the relatively easy Irkeshtam Pass to Osh and the less-frequented Torugart Pass to Naryn and Bishkek. It is only possible for foreigners to cross with private transport.

The spectacular Karakoram Highway via the mighty Khunjerab Pass leads to Gilgit in **Pakistan**. A regular bus service plies this route from May to October, but sometimes is closed to tourists.

Chinese authorities in the 1970s, and desultory excavations have continued in the area since that time. The best of the finds are on display at the Xinjiang Autonomous Region Museum in Urumqi (see page 200), and include a manuscript outlining the military strategies of the Warring States period, mummies and a 10-metre (33-ft) -high pagoda. The archaeological site at **Loulan Gucheng** (open 8am–4pm daily; charge) remains off-limits to ordinary Silk Road travellers. Four-wheel-drive vehicles and camels are necessary to visit, as well as a professional GPS system and – crucially – an expensive permit from the appropriate Chinese authorities.

One reason such permits are not readily obtained is the damage that has been done to the site over the years by robbers, vandals and others. Another, which should also discourage thought of a casual journey to Loulan, is that apart from its extreme aridity the **Lop Desert** has been extensively irradiated. China's first nuclear bomb test took place at Lop Nur in 1964, and was followed by a further 44 nuclear explosions until testing

was halted in 1996. Today the town of **Yuli** (Lop Nur), about 85km (53 miles) south of Korla on Highway 218 to Charklik, remains an important centre of China's nuclear industry, and is consequently not commonly a part of the Silk Road itinerary.

The northern route

With the decline of Lop Nur and the Central Silk Road, the importance of the longer – but better-watered – Northern Silk Road increased, until by the time of the Tang Dynasty (618–907) it also came to overshadow the older, Southern Silk Road. Since that time the road northwest via Hami and Turpan to Korla and Kashgar (followed by today's highways 312 and 314) has remained the most important east–west route across southern Xinjiang. It's no coincidence, also, that the railway from Jiayuguan to Kashgar, completed in 1999, also follows this route.

Hami

It's a long 621km (386 miles) from **Jiayuguan** to the isolated oasis of **Hami**, the first settlement of any size along

QUOTE

"If a stranger comes to [Hami] seeking hospitality he receives a very warm welcome. The host bids his wife to everything that the guest wishes…and stays away two or three days. Meanwhile the guest stays with his wife…as if she was his own wife. The women are beautiful and vivacious and always ready to oblige."

Marco Polo

People gathered at a butcher's shop and bakery in Khotan.

*Bixir's Tomb
in Kumul.*

*Taking part in the
Hami Melon Festival.*

the Northern Route in Xinjiang. At first Highway 312 crosses the bleak **Bei Shan** or Northern Mountains – in fact, little more than blackened, sun-blasted slag heaps – to reach the Xinjiang frontier post at **Xingxingxia**. There's little to see in this unprepossessing truck stop, but several of the hills overlooking the road where it passes through a narrow ravine are topped by old fortifications dating from the warlord era that characterised the Republican period (1911–49). Beyond Xingxingxia the highway becomes, if anything, still more bleak, as it passes through the endless flat wastes of the windswept Gashun Gobi, while the arid, saw-toothed peaks of the **Karlik Shan** range dominate the northern horizon.

The ancient oasis settlement of **Hami**, also known in Uighur as **Kumul**, sits in a fault depression 155 metres (510ft) below sea level and, like nearby Turpan, experiences extremes of temperature ranging from a scalding 45°C (113°F) in summer to a freezing -30°C (-22°F) in winter. Clearly, Silk Road caravans didn't visit Hami for its appealing climate – rather they stopped there for its fresh springs and water run-off brought by *karez* (underground canals) from the distant Karlik Tagh, for its fabled fresh fruit – Hami melons are famous across China today – and perhaps, if Marco Polo is to be believed, for the ready appeal and easy morals of its women. More importantly still, they stopped there because there simply was nowhere else to go. Hami was, and still remains, the only significant oasis in the Gashun Gobi, an essential stop on the long and difficult desert stages between Anxi and Turpan.

Hami's association with China goes back at least as far as 73 BC, when the great Han general **Ban Chao** first conquered the oasis and established a settlement there. Chinese rule was far from continuous, however, and between the 9th and 17th centuries Hami passed at various times under Turkic and Mongol control. During the Ming Dynasty (1320–1644) the local Uighur rulers of Hami generally paid tribute to Beijing, a practice that was continued under the Qing

LAST KING OF THE GOBI

Sometimes called "The King of the Gobi", Maqsud Shah was the last of the hereditary Uighur rulers of Hami, enjoying semi-autonomous powers under Chinese suzerainty, not unlike the contemporaneous Princely States in British India. In fact Maqsud was very sinicised for an Uighur Muslim, speaking Turkic with a Chinese accent, dressing in Chinese robes, and being proficient in the use of chopsticks. He also liked a drink or two, and the German archaeologist Albert von Le Coq was "astonished to find in the house of a Muhammedan prince an enormous quantity of Russian liqueurs and excellent French champagnes. He was continually drinking our health and seemed quite hardened against any of the ill effects of alcohol". Maqsud died in March 1930.

whenever circumstances allowed, eventually making Hami the most "Chinese" of all the Uighur oases. The local ruling family survived until 1930, when Maqsud Shah – known to his Uighur subjects as Khan Maqsud, to the Chinese as the Hami *wang* or king, and to his occasional European visitors as the "King of the Gobi" – died, leading Jin Shuren, the avaricious Chinese governor of Xinjiang between 1928 and 1933, to annex the khanate. The resultant rebellion led to the destruction not just of any vestigial Uighur power in the area, but also left most of the oasis in ruins.

Today Hami is a prosperous agricultural prefecture with about 500,000 people, around 70 percent Han Chinese, with less than 25 percent Uighur, the balance being mostly Hui Muslims. Although there isn't a great deal to see of historic interest, it remains an essential (and very convenient) stopping point along Highway 312, about equidistant between Dunhuang to the east and Turpan to the west. The main attraction, **Hami Wangling** (Tombs of the Hami Kings; daily 9am–8pm;

charge), is located in the southern part of town on Tuanjie Lu. A large complex encompassing the attractive old wooden tombs of the former rulers, the royal mosque, and what the Hami tourist office describe in English as "King Hui's Palace" – a misleading description both because the hereditary ruling house was Uighur and because the current building, a modern restoration designed to replace the palace destroyed in the 1931 rebellion, is very much a Han Chinese creation, owing little to authentic Uighur history or culture.

The centre of modern Hami, together with the best accommodation and restaurants, lies further to the north, near Renmin Park. There are several good hotels with Muslim, Chinese and "Western" restaurants available, while the bustling **Night Market** on Aiguo Beilu serves tasty and reasonably priced fare.

Turpan

On leaving Hami, Highway 312 runs through rich oasis farmland supporting orchards and extensive melon

Loulan ruins in Lop Nur.

LOP NUR, THE WANDERING LAKE

Lop Nur lake was the key to the flourishing caravan city of Loulan and the Central Silk Road between Yumenguan and Korla. When the lake began to dry up around 2,000 years ago, Loulan gradually declined and was eventually abandoned in the 5th century AD. Soon, as Silk Road traffic was redirected via the Northern and Southern routes, Loulan – together with other former caravan cities lost to the advancing sands of the Taklamakan – became little more than a legend, a rumour of lost splendour and wandering ghosts.

The ancient city was rediscovered by the Swedish explorer Sven Hedin in 1899. Hedin was the first to understand and explain how Lop Nur had "wandered", changing its location apparently at random over the centuries, but in fact due to the changing course of glacial rivers losing themselves in the heart of the Tarim Basin. In the 1920s Lop Nur dried up almost completely, and today there is little more than a small, seasonal salt marsh to indicate the presence of the former lake.

In the 1960s Lop Nur once again emerged from obscurity, when China exploded its first nuclear device, codenamed "596", in the area. China is now observing a de facto moratorium on nuclear testing, and has begun a project to divert water from Korla's Kongque River in an attempt to bring Lop Nur back to at least partial life.

DRINK

As befits a famous wine-producing area, good Turpan wines (dry red and sweet white dessert wines) are widely available in the town and a reasonably priced alternative to the local beer. "Loulan" is one of the better reds, while the strangely named "Scent of a Woman" dessert wine is also very refreshing.

Turpan traffic.

fields before, after about 15km (9 miles), re-entering unremittingly harsh, flat, stony desert – there are no graceful sand dunes here. To the north, the Karlik Tagh gradually give way to another eastern outlier of the Tian Shan, the **Bogda Shan**, dominated by the snow-crowned summit of 5,445-metre (17,860-ft) **Bogda Feng**. After a short climb into the Bogda Shan foothills, the road descends sharply into another basin, the Turpan Depression, before reaching the lush and attractive oasis of Turpan some 400km (250 miles) from Hami.

Turpan (called Tulufan by the Chinese) is about the same size as Hami, with a similar population of around 500,000, but in almost inverse ethnic proportion – about 70 percent Uighur and 20 percent Han, the remainder comprising mainly Hui Muslims. Long an economic backwater, its relative isolation to the south of the main Silk Road (and today of Highway 312) has helped to protect both the local Uighur culture and a considerable bucolic charm. Yet in times past Turpan Oasis was

a strategically significant centre on Xinjiang's Northern Silk Road, site of the ancient cities of Yarkhoto (Jiaohe) and Karakhoja (Gaochang).

Chinese armies first entered Turpan in the 2nd century BC, during the reign of Han Emperor Wu Di (141–87), when the oasis was a centre of Indo-European Tocharian culture. From about this time the city of Yarkhoto, known to the Chinese as Jiaohe, functioned as the capital until the 5th century AD when it was replaced by Karakhoja, called Gaochang by the Chinese, some 45km (28 miles) further to the east. From the mid-9th century the oasis became increasingly dominated by Uighur Turks migrating from the northern steppe, but Turpan retained a Buddhist character until the time of the Chagatai Khanate in the 13th century, when Islam gradually became the dominant religion. The Venetian Marco Polo passed through here in about 1271, and reported that the people of Karakhoja were "idolaters [Buddhists], but they include many Christians of the Nestorian sect and some Saracens [Muslims]".

A side road leads south from Highway 312 to Turpan, running through fertile fields watered, like those of Hami, by run-off brought by many *karez* (canals) from the mountains to the north. Important crops are wheat, cotton, vegetables and fruit of all kinds including mulberry, apricot, apple, pomegranate, fig and walnut. There's no doubt, however, that here the grape is king, as widely celebrated across China as Hami melons or Korla pears. The oasis is set in the **Turpan Basin**, at 155 metres (509ft) below sea level the second-lowest depression in the world (after the Dead Sea), and experiences great variations in temperature, ranging from 40°C (104°F) in summer to well below zero (32°F) in winter. Officially, it's the hottest place in China, once known as **Huozhou** or "Region of Fire", and the **Huoyan Shan** or "Flaming Mountains" to the northeast (see page 174) have long been infamous as a furnace-like wasteland. The lowest point in the depression is **Aydingkol Hu** (Moonlight Lake), a bleak, salt-encrusted pan where temperatures in midsummer can reach as high as 60°C (140°F).

Modern Turpan is a pleasantly relaxed small town centred on the downtown junction of Laocheng Lu and Gaochang Lu. Most attractions are located well out of town in the surrounding oasis, but **Turpan Museum** (Tulufan Bowuguan; daily 9am–7.30pm; charge) on Gaochang Lu is worth visiting. The second-largest museum in Xinjiang, it houses an intriguing collection of funerary goods, mummies, silks and painted figurines excavated at the Astana Tombs, some 40km (25 miles) to the east. Well enough known to have become a symbol of the city, the 18th-century **Sugong Ta** (Emin Mosque and Minaret; daily 7am–7pm; charge), the largest minaret in Xinjiang, is located just 2km (1.2 miles) southeast of the town centre and also merits a visit. One of the most impressive Islamic monuments in China – and very Central Asian in style – the mosque, made of simple, dun-coloured brick arranged in attractive geometric patterns, is dominated by its 44-metre (144-ft) -high minaret, built on the orders of the Turpan ruler **Emin Khoja** in 1777–8.

There's a good range of comfortable, reasonably priced accommodation in town, as well as restaurants serving Uighur, Chinese and an approximation of Western fare. A busy Night Market sells mainly Uighur and Hui food by the junction of Gaochang Lu and Wenhua Lu.

Grape Valley

There's a lot to see and do around Turpan, and it makes sense to spend a day or two here exploring either by local taxi or by one of the many private tours that just about every hotel and travel agent is happy to arrange. Some of the closer sights are easily accessible by bicycle, but others – notably the Flaming Mountains and Tuyoq – are rather too distant for biking, at least in the hot summer months.

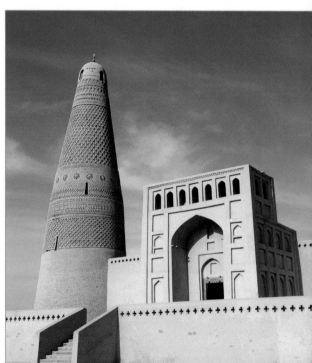

Turpan's Emin Mosque and Minaret.

To the northeast of town, **Putao Gou** (Grape Valley; daily; charge) is the most celebrated of Turpan's extensive vineyards and a must on every tour-group itinerary. Turpan has been cultivating grapes for more than two millennia, and today more than 100 varieties are grown, accounting for around 90 percent of China's seedless grape production. In times past the most valued variety of grape, known as *manaizi* or "mare's nipple" grapes, formed part of Turpan's tribute to the Chinese court at Xi'an and later Beijing. Today the grape harvest contributes substantially to the wealth of the oasis and its people, and vines are cultivated just about everywhere they can be grown, for fruit, wine and indeed shade. To celebrate this bounty, an annual **Turpan Grape Festival** is held each August and includes grape-eating competitions, folk dances and live music.

Yarkhoto

To the west of town the ruins of **Yarkhoto** or **Jiaohe Gucheng** (Jiaohe Ancient City; daily 9am–6pm; charge) are perhaps the best-preserved and most accessible of the ancient Silk Road cities anywhere in Xinjiang. Located just 10km (6 miles) west of Turpan town at the confluence of two small rivers, the ruins stand on a raised loess bluff. Yarkhoto was developed as an administrative centre and garrison town by the Chinese following the Han conquest of the area in the 2nd century BC and the city flourished under the Tang Dynasty (618–907), before eventually being abandoned early in the 14th century. The extensive ruins that remain today date mainly from the Tang era, when the population numbered in excess of 7,000, mainly Buddhist Uighurs.

The entire city is made of sun-baked loess soil, prompting the contemporary Chinese authorities to describe it as "the largest, oldest and best-preserved earthen city in the world". Overall, the city is 1,650 metres (1 mile) long by 300 metres (1,000ft) wide, with a main avenue leading north from the South Gate. In total it was home to about 700 households supporting 6,500 residents and 1,000

The ruins of the abandoned city of Yarkhoto (Jiaohe).

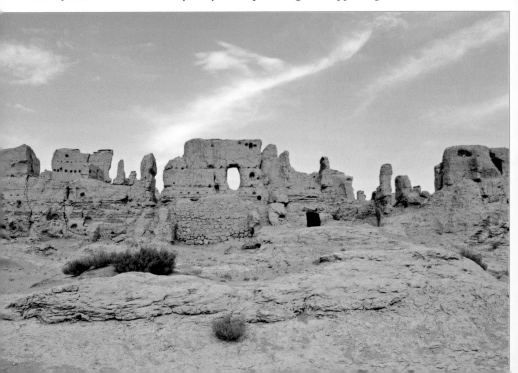

soldiers. The city was divided into three quarters, one for the common people to the west, one for the ruling aristocracy to the east, and one for religious observances to the north. At the end of the main avenue stands a Buddhist complex comprising a monastery, stupa and monks' cells. At the northern end of the city there is another, well-preserved stupa surrounded by tombs.

Yarkhoto was partially excavated by the Chinese authorities in the 1950s, and remains in excellent condition. Wooden boardwalks allow the visitor to explore the streets, private dwellings and temples without damaging the site. There are fine views from the top of the bluff across the valley; on the clifftops opposite stand numerous grape-drying houses used for producing Turpan's famous raisins. Guides are informative and many of the information boards are in English as well as Chinese.

On the way back to town, drivers will encourage you to visit an ancient underground canal or *karez* system (**Kanerjing**; daily; charge). Although heavily commercialised, this is an attraction worth seeing. For centuries Turpan has owed its lush agricultural produce and green oasis setting to an elaborate system of underground canals called *karez* that bring water from the nearby mountains. Turpan is watered by more than 400 such underground canals, with a total length of almost 5,000km (3,000 miles). In a complex and sophisticated process, water run-off from the mountains is carried by gently sloping tunnels accessed every few hundred metres by vertical maintenance shafts, substantially reducing evaporation by the blazing sun.

Karakhoja

Like Yarkhoto, the ruins of **Karakhoja** or **Gaochang Gucheng** (Gaochang Ancient City; daily 8am–5pm; charge) date from the initial Han Chinese conquest of the area in the 2nd century BC. Located about 46km (29 miles) southeast of Turpan on the edge of the Lop Desert, Karakhoja is larger than Yarkhoto, but rather less well preserved. Originally established as

Winter in Grape Valley.

Detail of a mural at Bezeklik, the "place where there are paintings".

Steps from the Astana Tombs.

a garrison town, it developed into a prosperous city by Tang times, before being eventually abandoned in the 14th century, probably due to a combination of endemic warfare and desertification. In its prime, Karakhoja was divided into three sections – an outer city, inner city and palace area. It was surrounded by a 5.5-km (3.5-mile) -long, 11-metre (36-ft) -high defensive wall of tamped earth, pierced by nine city gates, the best-preserved of which are to the west. Over the centuries local people have removed much of the crumbling loess buildings to use in new construction work but a fairly substantial Buddhist monastery remains in the southwest part of the city. A row of covered restaurants serving kebabs and other Uighur foodstuffs, as well as cold drinks, is situated by the Karakhoja ticket office, and you can explore the extensive site on foot or by donkey trap.

Astana Tombs

The **Astana Tombs** (Asitana Gumuqu; daily; charge) are located a short distance north of Karakhoja, about 40km (25 miles) from Turpan. Both rulers and citizens of Karakhoja were buried here, sometimes in elaborate splendour, in sealed subterranean burial places. Astana was excavated by the Chinese in the 1970s, and over 1,000 tombs were identified. The arid climate had preserved the bodies and many elaborate accompanying artefacts and murals almost perfectly, and the Xinjiang Autonomous Region Museum in Urumqi (see page 200) has a particularly fine collection of painted terracotta figurines showing scenes from contemporaneous everyday life. Little remains on display in Astana, however, though visitors can descend into three of the tombs via narrow flights of steps to view three mummified figures, as well as murals depicting auspicious Confucian figures.

Highway 312, leading back towards Hami, is the best and quickest way to reach both Astana and Karakhoja. En route, to the immediate north of the highway and running for a distance of about 90km (60 miles), the **Flaming Mountains** (Huoyan Shan; daily; charge) dominate the horizon.

JOURNEY TO THE WEST

Written in the 1590s and ascribed to the writer Wu Chengen, *Xiyouji* or "Journey to the West" is considered one of the four great novels of traditional Chinese literature. In the West, it is better known by the title *The Adventures of Monkey* or, more simply, *Monkey*, the name given by the English translator Arthur Waley. It presents a fictionalised account of the travels of the Buddhist monk Xuanzang (see page 57). On the instructions of the bodhisattva Guanyin, he is accompanied by three bodyguard-disciples, Sun Wukong or "Monkey", Zhu Bajie or "Pigsy" and Sha Wujing or "Sandy". Xuanzang is also provided with a celestial mount in the form of a dragon prince disguised as a horse.

As they progress westwards, the pilgrims are faced with all kinds of obstacles, including the Flaming Mountains near Turpan. They are unable to cross them because of the burning heat, until Monkey procures a magical palm-leaf fan from Princess Iron Fan, wife of the Ox Demon King, with which he extinguishes the flames. As an allegory, satire and travelogue, the text is deeply rooted in Chinese folk tradition. A large part of its continuing appeal is that it is also a great adventure story that has been adapted innumerable times for the stage, movies, comics, television soap operas and, most recently, computer games.

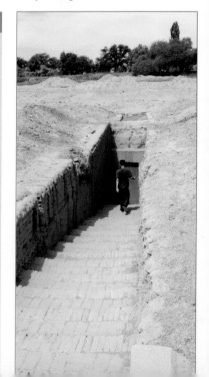

harging an entry fee to a range of ountains that few people in their ght mind would wish to enter may em an unlikely business venture, ut these are no ordinary barren hills. he Flaming Mountains are known roughout China as the place where e 7th-century Chinese Buddhist onk Xuanzang almost died of thirst, story immortalised by **Wu Chengen** his 16th-century allegorical account *iyouji* or "Journey to the West". As a onsequence, a stream of predomi-antly Chinese tourists queue to nter not the mountains themselves, ut an elaborate subterranean *Xiyouji* isneyworld featuring Xuanzang and is companions, Monkey, Pigsy and andy. Above ground – where it is deed generally blazing hot at noon the serrated, ochre-coloured flanks f the Flaming Mountains make a star-ing backdrop against which tourists an be photographed perched astride actrian camels.

ezeklik

he celebrated **Bezeklik Thousand uddha Caves** (Bozikelike Qianfo

Dong; daily 8.30am–5.30pm; charge) are set above the Murtuk Darya Gorge in the side of the Flaming Mountains some 60km (40 miles) from Turpan, and are easily accessible by road. "Beze-klik" means "place where there are paintings" in Uighur, with reference to a series of 77 caves once lined with pious Buddhist murals dating from the 4th to the 10th centuries. Sadly the surviving murals are but a shadow of what Bezeklik must once have been. Many of the finest were removed by the German archaeologist Albert von Le Coq at the beginning of the 20th century and subsequently sent to Ber-lin; others were reportedly damaged by iconoclastic Red Guards during the Cultural Revolution (1966–76). The caves and their mud-brick porticos are still worth visiting, however, not simply for a glimpse of the surviving murals, but for the caves' spectacular setting in the side of a cliff overlook-ing a narrow but lovely gorge.

Tuyoq

About 30km (19 miles) southeast of Bezeklik and 70km (44 miles) east of

The spectacularly located Bezeklik Caves.

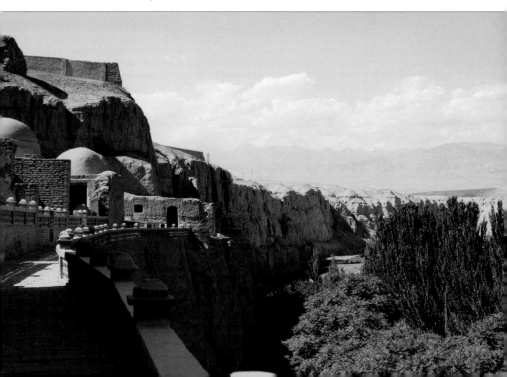

The 28-year-old peripatetic Buddhist monk Xuanzang passed through Kuqa as he followed his dream to travel all the way to India c.630. He noted that two 27-metre (89-ft) -high Buddha images stood guard at the city gates. It was 14 years before he passed through Kuqa on his return.

Turpan, near the eastern rim of the Turpan Basin, the traditional Uighur village of **Tuyoq** (Tuyugou; daily; charge) offers a fascinating opportunity to visit a remote and traditional Uighur village set in a narrow valley in the southern outliers of the Flaming Mountains. There are numerous caves set high into the steep mountainside above the village, but they are all but inaccessible, and such artistic treasures as they once held have mainly either been destroyed or dispersed to museums in China and Europe. Yet the appeal of Tuyoq is less these caves than the village's idyllic setting and bucolic charm. The **Tomb of the Seven Sleepers** dominates the hillside above the settlement and its green dome is an attractive feature on the otherwise low-rise skyline. The local Uighur people do not permit non-Muslims to enter either the shrine or the dusty cemetery that abuts it, but will grant permission to take photographs outside.

West of Turpan

West of Turpan, Highway 312 follows the former Northern Silk Road

for a further 46km (29 miles) befor branching off north to Urumqi an ultimately, via the Dzungarian Route to Kazakhstan on an old norther spur of the Silk Road that passes b the shores of the Issyk-Kul, to rejoi the main Silk Road near Samarkanc The main Northern Route to Kash gar branches off from Highway 31. near Toksun, becoming Highwa 314 and heading west all the way to Kashgar and, beyond, to Pakistan vi the Karakoram Highway. After cross ing the bleak Argaybulak Pass (1,78. metres/5,856ft) it descends throug the arid, 60-km (37-mile) -long **Ga Gou** or "Dry Ditch" gorge befor reaching the eastern fringes of th Tarim Basin by **Bagrash Kol** (Boste Hu). This 1,000 sq km (386 sq mile freshwater lake, located in **Bayingo lin Mongol Autonomous Prefec ture**, seems remarkably lush whe set against the surrounding Gobi, anc is home to many species of fish anc birds. Nearby is the small settlemen of **Yanqi**, today an unremarkabl town, but during the Han Dynast (206 BC–AD 220) it was better know

The anicent village of Tuyoq.

CLIMBING TIEMENGUAN

Located 7km (4 miles) northeast of Korla, the ancient strongpoint of Tiemenguan has now been bypassed by the 21st-century tarmac of Highway 314. Set amid incredibly barren, harsh and crumbling mountains that would not seem out of place in J.R.R. Tolkien's vision of Mordor, it's possible to understand the immense strategic significance of the "Iron Gate" pass by climbing the exhausting 1,497 steps to the summit. Here the tomb of Tzuhola and Tayir is set high above the narrow defile that once channelled the old Silk Road between two impassable rocky outcrops. A small path winds by a stream, far below – nowadays all but unused, but for at least two millennia a narrow artery for men, goods and camels passing between east and west.

as **Karashahr** or "Black City", capital of an independent Buddhist kingdom located between Turpan to the east and Korla to the west. Little remains to be seen today other than some tamped-earth city walls.

Beyond Yanqi the road enters another rocky defile, leading to the former stronghold and toll gate of **Tiemenguan** or "Iron Gate" (daily; charge). Because of its strategic location controlling the Silk Road as it passed south of the Tian Shan and into the Tarim Basin, Tiemenguan was easily defended by garrison troops and almost impossible for merchants and other travellers to avoid. The gate was destroyed during the Cultural Revolution (1966–76) but has since been rebuilt. Its significance for Han Chinese and Uighur is rather different, though it carries sad associations for both peoples. Han Chinese, understandably, considered a posting here akin to being banished to outer darkness. A traditional verse laments:

Iron Gate at the edge of the world
Few travellers are to be seen
One lowly official guards the gate
All day staring at stone walls
A mountain pass, a thousand dangerous steps
A narrow road winding between sharp cliffs
I climb West Tower to take a look
One glance and my hair turns white!

For Uighurs, however, the narrow pass is associated with tragedy in love. Long ago Tzuhola, an Uighur princess, fell in love with Tayir, a simple shepherd. Her father, the king, had intended the princess to marry a prince, and was greatly displeased. The two lovers fled into the mountains pursued by the king's troops, who had orders to bring them back. They fell to their deaths near Tiemenguan and the king, who was heartbroken, ordered the building of a twin tomb so they could be together in the afterlife. A statue of the two lovers in flight on horseback has recently been erected near the tomb.

Korla

The city of **Korla** (Kuerle) about 7km (4 miles) southwest of Tiemenguan is today one of Xinjiang's wealthiest cities, with a rich agricultural economy (in particular for the production of mulberries, white apricots, figs and musk melons) boosted by heavy industry and, in recent decades, oil production from the nearby Taklamakan Desert. Although it has a long history – it was occupied by the Han general Ban Chao in AD 94, and the head of the Korla king, together with the head of the king of neighbouring Karashahr were sent to be displayed in distant Luoyang – there is little of historical interest to see in town.

As in historical Silk Road times, Korla remains an important communications centre sitting astride the main road and rail links between Urumqi, Kashgar and Lanzhou, as well as Highway 218 south to Charklik, while Korla's Hualing Bus Station is the northern terminus for Desert Highway 312 to Niya on the Southern Route. Besides its significance as a transport hub, Korla is a pleasant

Ethnic Uighurs.

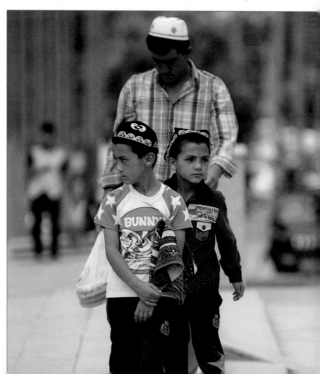

TIP

If at all possible, travellers should visit Kuqa's Old City on a Friday, when the market is at its colourful best, busy with hundreds of donkey traps and thousands of Uighur, male and female, old and young, bargaining over an astonishing selection of fresh fruit and vegetables, freshly butchered *halal* meat, sheep, goats, horses and cows.

enough place to stay. The Konqi River (*konqi* is Uighur for "abundant waters") flows through the centre of town on its way south from the Tian Shan, making for abundant greenery, while the nearby presence of oil ensures that Korla has some of the best hotels and restaurants in Xinjiang.

West of Korla, Highway 314 runs through arid desert in the lee of the Tian Shan, passing through vast wind farms, for 310km (190 miles) to the oasis of Kuqa. About halfway, at the small town of **Luntai** (Uighur name Bugur), the **Shamo Gonglu** (Desert Highway 312) branches off south across incredibly inhospitable shifting sand dunes to Niya, 522km (324 miles) distant. This modern road, opened in 1995, offers an opportunity to take a shortcut to the old Southern Silk Road, as well as to see the endless sand dunes of the much-feared Taklamakan Desert.

Kuqa

The ancient oasis town of **Kuqa** (Kuche), though now overshadowed by Korla to the east and Aksu to

the west, was once a key stop on the Northern Silk Road. It first came under Han Chinese control when it was conquered, in AD 91, by the indomitable General Ban Chao. By the 4th century it had emerged as an important centre of Tocharian civilisation, sitting astride not just the Northern Silk Road, but also lesser routes to Dzungaria in the north and Khotan in the south. The celebrated Buddhist monk Kumarajiva (see page 154) was born here, and travelled west on the Silk Road to study in Kashmir before returning east, to Wuwei, where he taught and translated Buddhist texts for 17 years.

The oasis reached its zenith during the Tang Dynasty (618–907), when the royal court at **Qiuci** was famed for its pious Buddhist monasteries with more than 5,000 monks, as well as its rather less pious musicians, singers and dancing girls, who were much appreciated in the distant Tang court at Xi'an. Kuqa took on an increasingly Uighur character from the mid-9th century, abandoning Buddhism in favour of Islam during the 13th century. For many centuries Kuqa was the most populous oasis in Xinjiang, but today only about 100,000 people live here, about 75 percent Uighur, with Han Chinese and Hui Muslims making up the balance.

Modern Kuqa is divided into two parts, the overwhelmingly Uighur **Old City** to the west, and the predominantly Han Chinese **New City** to the east. The former, a warren of twisting, narrow alleys, is both picturesque and home to the city's most interesting sights. The latter, a typical small, grid-system Chinese town, is the centre for transport, accommodation and dining. The two are separated by the narrow Kuqa River and an open area given over to the important **Friday Market**, which sells local foodstuffs including iced yoghurt and giant *naan*. Also lying between the two are the remains of **Qiuci Gucheng** (Qiuci Ancient

An Uighur woman and her child travelling by auto-rickshaw in Kuqa.

ity), though there is little to see
part from an ancient mud wall.

Most visitors will stay in the New
ity, but spend their time exploring
n the Old City. It's a 40-minute walk
r 10-minute drive between the two,
eading west along Wenhua Lu past
Maulana Ashidin Khoja Mazar, the
omb of an early Muslim missionary
ill venerated by local Uighurs. Little
nough is known of Ashidin Khoja,
aid to have been an itinerant Arab
eacher, except that some time after his
rrival in Kuqa, probably in the mid-
8th century, he killed a pigeon and
ubsequently dropped dead – surely
a story rooted in Qiuci's ancient Bud-
hist past rather than in Islam. The
imple wooden shrine, which was
estored in the mid-19th century,
tands next to a green-roofed mosque.
s is common in Central Asian Islam,
trips of cloth are attached to a tree
utside the shrine, indicating the pres-
nce of the tomb of a *pir* or Muslim
oly man.

Wenhua Lu continues west through
ne open market area to the Old City.
he market brims with all manner

of fresh produce, and some sections
of the market are given over to clothing of all kinds, others to Uighur hats,
equine equipment, knives, tools, rugs
and carpets, toys and even jewellery.

Beyond the market, an old bridge
leads over the Kuqa River and enters
the Old Town via **Laocheng Shih-chang**, the Old City Bazaar. Watch
out here for open-air barbers and hair-
dressers, kebab and *naan* bread sellers
– Kuche is famous in Xinjiang for its
unique wholemeal *naan* (flat breads),
much larger than elsewhere in the
province and covered with toppings
of chopped carrot, onion and sesame.
Immediately to the west of the bazaar
stands an old Qing Dynasty mosque
with Uighur elders known locally as
aqsaqal or "white beards" selling religious tracts and Islamic paraphernalia. One block further to the west is
Kuqa's **Great Mosque** (**Jama Masjid;
Qingzhen Da Si**; daily; charge for
non-Muslims), an attractive building
dating from 1923 with an imposing
gateway flanked by two tall minarets leading to a large, green-domed
prayer hall. The mosque is entirely

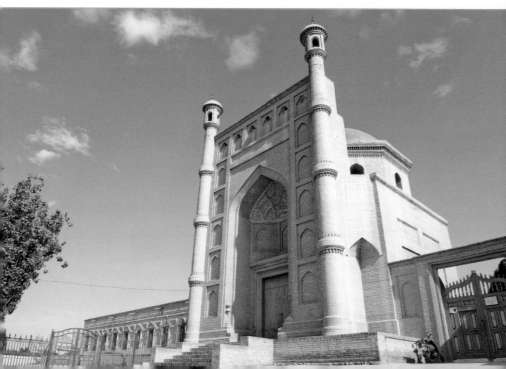

*Kuqa's Jama Masjid
(Great Mosque).*

Watching the world go by.

Kuqa is famed for its giant naans.

Central Asian in style, with none of the Chinese Islamic characteristics seen further to the east (and especially at Xi'an's Qingzhen Da Si). Beyond the Great Mosque, on Linji Lu, the **Kuqa Museum** (**Kuche Bowuguan**; daily; charge) houses an interesting collection of artefacts from old Qiuci and the nearby ruins of ancient Subashi.

While fresh and good street food is available in and around the Old City Bazaar, the best restaurants and hotels are to be found back in New Kuqa, clustered along central Wenhua Lu and on nearby Tianshan Lu. There is also a busy **Night Market** by the junction of Youyi Lu and Xinhua Lu that serves all the usual Uighur specialities as well as freshly squeezed juices – a welcome source of vitamin C.

Around Kuqa

Kuqa's once flourishing Buddhist past is best appreciated by visiting two ancient Silk Road-related sites that are readily accessible by taxi. About 20km (13 miles) northeast of town, the ruins of **Subashi Gucheng** (Subashi Ancient City; daily; charge) are

all that is left of the ancient capital of the Kingdom of Qiuci from the 4th century AD until it was abandoned sometime in the 12th century. After Yarkhoto and Karakhojo in Turpan Oasis, Subashi is one of the better preserved and more easily accessible abandoned ancient cities of the Tarim Basin. The city walls and a row of once-inhabited caves are all that remain, but they're spectacularly situated beneath snow-covered peaks.

Most impressive are the ruins of **Zhaoguli Buddhist Temple**, dating from the 5th century AD. The site was first excavated by Count Otani Kozui of Kyoto in the early 20th century. His most important find, a 6th-century *sarira* or relic box now held in the Otani Collection at Tokyo National Museum, shows paintings of Tocharian men in long robes. Another noted archaeological discovery from the city is the so-called "Witch of Subashi", a desiccated female mummy found wearing a tall and pointed black hat, now on display at the Xinjiang Autonomous Region Museum in Urumqi (see page 200).

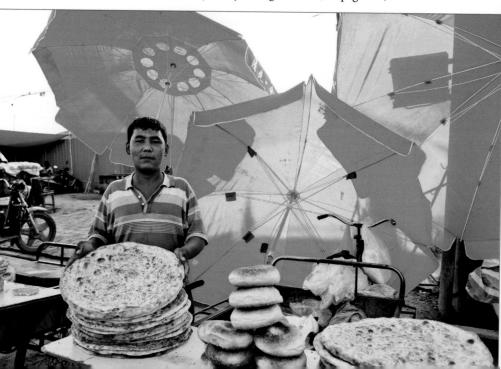

Located 75km (47 miles) to the northwest of Kuqa, the **Kizil Thousand Buddha Caves** (**Kezier Qianfo Dong**; daily 7am–7pm; charge) is a Buddhist cave temple complex dating from the 3rd to 13th centuries AD. Accessible only by taxi or private car, the road to the caves leads through **Yanshui Gou** or "Saltwater Gulley", an extraordinary landscape of eroded rock formations. The caves are set in the cliff face of a narrow gorge sometimes optimistically styled "Tian Shan Grand Canyon" by Kuqa travel agents. At its height, during the Tang Dynasty, the complex numbered 236 caves, though the travails of time and the destructive impact of Islamic iconoclasm and both Western and Japanese archaeologists have reduced the number to just 80 caves containing mural fragments – no statuary survives. The researches of Japanese Count Otani and German von Le Coq show that the caves once contained particularly fine examples of Gandharan Indo-Greek art, with some Persian but almost no discernible Chinese influence, but fully to appreciate this it is necessary to travel to Berlin's Ethnology Museum (*Museum für Völkerkunde*). Only nine caves are open to visitors at Kizil today, and these contain mere fragments of frescoes.

On leaving Kuqa, Highway 314 (as well as the Urumqi–Kashgar Railway) passes the isolated, 16-metre (52-ft) -high **Kizilgah Beacon Tower** about 6km (4 miles) west of Kuqa. This imposing structure, dating from the Han Dynasty (206 BC–AD 220), marks an antique Chinese garrison point on the former Northern Silk Road. Goats are the tower's most common visitors.

Aksu

Like the other oasis towns of southern Xinjiang, **Aksu** – which means "White Water" in Uighur – has a long history, though little survives to suggest this today. Like Kuqa and Korla to the east, it was conquered by the Chinese general Ban Chao in the 1st century AD, and visited by the monk Xuanzang in the 6th century. In the 14th century Tughlugh Timur, Khan of Moghulistan (1347–63), briefly made Aksu his capital, a position the

The Silk Road passes Subashi Gucheng.

city temporarily regained under the Mughal Khan Esan Buqa II (1429–62). After this time Aksu slipped into political obscurity, though it remained a significant caravanserai on the Northern Silk Road.

Today **Aksu** (Akesu) is an industrial city of about 400,000 inhabitants, the great majority of whom are Han Chinese; another 200,000 or so ethnic Uighurs farm the surrounding oasis. There is really nothing of historical significance for the visitor to see, but Aksu remains a convenient stopping place on the long road west from Kuqa to Kashgar, with a good choice of hotels and restaurants, as well as plenty of Uighur and Chinese street food in and around **Aksu Bazaar** (Aksu Shihchang). In October 2007 a **second desert highway** was opened, leading directly across the barren wastes of the Taklamakan to Khotan, 424km (264 miles) to the southwest. This has greatly increased Aksu's importance as a communications hub – but still, it seems few Silk Road travellers will choose to do more than stay overnight here.

Beyond the green fields and poplar-lined lanes of Aksu, arid, windswept desert resumes. Highway 314 continues west along the track of the old Northern Silk Road, hemmed in by the bare, rugged outliers of the Tian Shan to the north and the great sand dunes of the Taklamakan to the south. There are no major oases along the route between Aksu and Kashgar, but 214km (133 miles) west of Aksu, at the small oasis of **Sanchakou**, a small junction marks an old road south, following the Yarkand River through the traditional Uighur farming centres of Bachu and Markit, to **Yarkand** (see page 192) on the Southern Road. West of Sanchakou, Highway 314 continues for a further 213km (132 miles), passing through the small towns of Sugun and Artux, before terminating at the fabled Silk Road city of **Kashgar**.

The southern route

As we have seen, the antique Southern Route between Dunhuang and Kashgar started at Yangguan or "Sun Pass", near today's Nanhu village, about

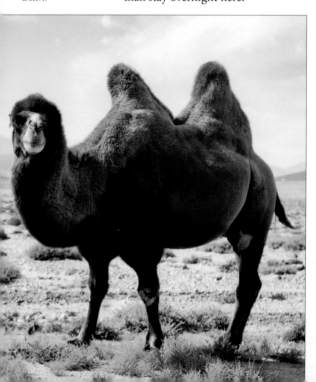

A Bactrian camel in the Taklamakan Desert.

60km (37 miles) west of Dunhuang. Probably older than the Northern Route, and still more arid and remote, it nevertheless had certain advantages, including being further from the nomadic raiders of Mongolia and the Dzungarian Steppe – though the Tibetans were nearer at hand, a people also not averse to raiding caravans or direct military conquest.

Having rested up and watered their beasts in Dunhuang, the caravaneers would leave China proper through the watchtower and toll gate at Yang-guan and head straight into open desert, leading their camels through the waterless **Kum Tagh** or "Sand Mountains" on the southern edge of the Gashun Gobi through a wind-blasted, lifeless wilderness in the lee of the mighty Altun Shan range. This route passed through the last, most remote fringes of western Gansu province before crossing into a still more barren corner of Xinjiang. Nobody, indeed nothing, could live here, except perhaps a few wild camels. Marco Polo passed this way in the 13th century, and noted: "Beasts and birds there are none, for they find nothing to eat." There were legions of ghosts, however, who would call out in spirit voices to lure travellers into the void, where they would inevitably perish:

Yes, and even by daylight men hear these spirit voices, and often you fancy they are listening to the strains of many instruments, especially drums, and the clash of arms. For this reason bands of travellers make a point of keeping very close together. Before they sleep they set up a sign pointing the direction in which they have to travel.

In fact travellers have posted "signs" to indicate direction along the Southern Route for centuries, using the skeletons of dead camels and other beasts of burden as markers. Over the intervening centuries the inexorable advance of the desert southwards has made this section of the route still more inhospitable. This is the most difficult and inaccessible stretch of the former Silk Road anywhere in China, and to all intents and purposes it is closed, both because of its poor condition and because of its proximity to the Lop Nur nuclear testing site. As

Fences made of reeds hold the sand to prevent desertification.

FACT

The ancient city of Endere (Endere Gucheng), dating from the 2nd–7th centuries, is buried in the desert to the northwest of Cherchen. It had a Buddhist monastery but was already abandoned when Xuanzang travelled through the region in AD644 on his way back from India. It is currently inaccessible except to authorised archaeological expeditions.

Barren scenery nearing Charklik.

As if in confirmation of this, a short distance west of Dacaotan, Highway 313 is blocked by a police guard post. Just about the only way to reach Miran and Charklik via this route is to arrange a four-day jeep safari with a specialist company in Urumqi – though this is an expensive option by any standards.

Dunhuang to Charklik

There are at present two alternative ways of reaching Charklik from Dunhuang – neither authentically part of the Southern Route, but until and unless the Chinese authorities improve and open the western section of Highway 313 between Dacaotan and Charklik, there are no other options.

The first alternative involves following the Northern Route from **Dunhuang** as far as **Korla** (see page 177). From here Route 218 runs south past China's nuclear research centre at Lop Nur (Yuli), following the rapidly diminishing waters of the Tarim River as it is gradually swallowed by the eternal sands. After the small desert settlement of **Tikanlik**, 216km (134 miles) south of Korla, the last waters disappear, and the road continues between the Taklamakan and Gashun Gobi deserts for a further 227km (141 miles) to Charklik. It's a long way round, but the road is good and there are regular buses between Korla and Charklik.

The second route between Dunhuang and Charklik involves travelling south along Highway 215 from Dunhuang to **Aksay**, then climbing into the vast, snow-capped Altun Shan and crossing into Qinghai province via the spectacular 3,519-metre (12,840-ft) **Dangjin Pass**. The road – now Highway 315 – continues across the bleak Qaidam Basin, through starkly magnificent scenery about as different to the Tarim Basin as might be imagined, to the ugly mining town of **Huatugou**. Although this route crosses some very harsh terrain and is often closed during winter months, buses ply between Dunhuang and Huatugou twice a day, and the journey is not as difficult as it sounds. Things becomes worse at Huatugou, a gritty, unappealing settlement where it is, nevertheless, generally necessary to stay overnight. Hotels and restaurants exist, but they are basic.

Huatugou may feel like the end of the world, but it isn't. That distinction should be reserved for the next stopover, **Magnai Zhen** or "Asbestos Mine", located about 70km (44 miles) further west on the Qinghai–Xinjiang border. Local minibuses run between Huatugou and this least attractive of places on a regular basis when full, covering the distance in about two hours. The route onwards to Charklik crosses the high Altun Shan, with the horizon to the left dominated by the 6,062-metre (19,890-ft) **Yusupalik Tag** ("Yusuf Ali Mountains"), before descending via narrow valleys and generally dry river beds to the small settlement of Yandaxkak and, ultimately, to the isolated – but very welcome – oasis.

Charklik

Once at **Charklik** (Ruoqiang), whether by way of Korla or Qinghai, the traveller is back on the authentic Southern Route. The isolated oasis has an overwhelmingly Uighur population of around 30,000. There's nothing to keep the visitor in Charklik, which centres around the long-distance bus station providing links north to Korla and west to Khotan. About 110km (68 miles) east, back along the original Southern Silk Road (Highway 215), the ancient site of **Miran** (Milan Gucheng; charge) is one of the more accessible "lost cities" of the Taklamakan – the ancient ruins are set in the desert about 15km (9 miles) southwest of the new town. To visit, a permit (charge) must be obtained from the local Charklik Cultural Relics Bureau, or – more expensively – can be purchased in advance in Urumqi. Travellers should take a bus to New Miran, 96km (60 miles) distant, then hire a taxi to Old Miran; alternatively, a taxi can be hired for the return trip in Charklik.

Miran was a flourishing trade centre on the Southern Silk Road between about AD 100 and 400. In the 8th century it was occupied and fortified by the Tibetans. The site was rediscovered by the American Ellsworth Huntington in 1905, and first excavated by Aurel Stein in 1907. Stein discovered rich examples of Gandharan art, the most easterly evidence of Graeco-Buddhist influence yet found. He took away many of the tempura murals he unearthed, some of which were richly gilded, and the best are now held in the National Museum in New Delhi. He also discovered numerous documents in Tibetan, Kharoshthi and Turkic scripts in a 1,000-year-old midden by the Tibetan fort, of which he wrote: "I have had occasion to acquire rather extensive experience in cleaning ancient rubbish-heaps, and know how to diagnose them. But for intensity of sheer dirt and age-persisting smelliness I shall always put the rich 'castings' of Tibetan warriors in the front rank". Today the main relics viewable at Miran include the 8th-century Tibetan fort, the remains of a 2nd-century

A Mao Zedong monument in Niya.

Buddhist stupa and the foundations of several Buddhist monasteries.

Cherchen

Highway 315 runs southwest from Charklik through sandy wastes for 350km (220 miles) to **Cherchen** (Qiemo). The oasis, which is predominantly Uighur, supports a population of 60,000, and is watered by the Cherchen Darya with snowmelt from the Altun Shan to the south. The most significant Silk Road site is at the village of **Zaghunluq**, 5km (3 miles) southwest of the town centre. More than 1,000 ancient tombs were discovered here in the 1980s, and one tomb, containing 14 mummified corpses that date back 2,600 years, is open to the public. Other finds from the tombs, including Zaghunluq grave artifacts, are preserved in the **Cherchen Museum** (Qiemo Bowuguan; daily; charge), located in a the former home of an Uighur warlord. About 10km (6 miles) to the northwest of town, **Old Cherchen** (Qiemo Gucheng; daily; charge) is accessible by taxi, but little remains for the casual visitor to see.

Niya

West of Cherchen, Highway 315 continues to follow the ancient Southern Silk Road for 314km (195 miles) to the small town of **Niya** (Minfeng), a predominantly Uighur oasis supporting a population of about 10,000. The southern terminus of the Desert Highway 312 from Luntai joins Highway 315 to the east of town, and the opening of this route in 1995 transformed remote Niya into an important communications hub. There is little to see in Niya itself, and the ancient town of **Old Niya** (Niya Gucheng), lost in the shifting sands of the Taklamakan some 130km (81 miles) to the north, is only accessible by camel caravan with special permission from the Chinese authorities. Niya has adequate hotels and restaurants, however, and is an ideal base for making a short excursion into the Taklamakan without crossing the entire 522km (324 miles) of the Desert Highway.

Around Niya

It is possible to make a fascinating day trip from Niya by taking a minibus

An Uighur barber in his Niya shop shaving the head of a client.

or taxi north into the desert, to the tiny and isolated Uighur village of **Kapakaskan** (Padishayimu) to see the **Imam Jafar Sadiq Mazar** (daily; charge), the so-called "Mecca of Turkestan". While the shrine is of interest, in particular its impressive brick entrance gate, it's the journey itself that really makes the trip worthwhile. To get to Kapakaskan head east along Highway 315 for 21km (13 miles) to the junction with Highway 312, then head north along the Desert Highway for a further 50km (31 miles), before turning west, into the desert, near kilometre marker 512. Kapakaskan is 12km (7 miles) to the west.

While more than 500km (300 miles) of Desert Highway – in fact a black ribbon of tarmac stretching through and around endless drifting sand dunes – can easily become tedious, the 50km (30-mile) journey to the Kapakaskan turning is ample to witness the extraordinary feats of engineering and desert control techniques employed by the Chinese in building this extraordinary road. It also allows the traveller to see something of the Taklamakan Desert without arranging a special caravan expedition. There are blue buildings with red roofs every 5km (3 miles). These are irrigation stations that pump water from aquifers beneath the desert to water the desert reeds and grasses planted to stabilise the sands in the immediate vicinity of the road. Each is manned by a single person or couple whose job it is to maintain the irrigation system – surely one of the loneliest jobs in the world.

Kapakaskan is a tiny oasis, watered by the rapidly diminishing flow of the Niya Darya, which loses itself in the desert sands about 35km (22 miles) further north. Surrounded by a veritable *shamo* or "sea of sand", the hamlet is an entirely Uighur settlement of mud-brick houses, with a single, concrete school. The shrine is a further 5km (3 miles) north of the village, set amid shifting sands. It's not clear who exactly is buried here, but it's not the celebrated Imam Jafar Sadiq, the sixth Shia imam and direct descendant of the Prophet Muhammad, whose tomb is in Medina, Saudi Arabia (though some local Uighur will tell you that it *is* his final resting place). Rather a simple structure, decorated with branches, skins, feathers and tied pieces of cloth, it is typical of similar small tombs, often of Sufi mystics, that can be found across Central Asia.

Keriya

Highway 315 continues from Niya through endless sandy desert to the oasis of **Keriya** (Yutian) 120km (75 miles) to the west. Another predominantly Uighur oasis, Keriya supports a population of around 160,000. Marco Polo visited in the late 13th century and noted that the oasis was "amply stocked with the means of life", with rich estates including orchards, vineyards and cotton, as indeed it is today. Even so, there's not a great deal to see here, though there are several reasonable hotels, as well as restaurants serving Chinese and Uighur cuisine. The oasis is watered

Enjoying a snack of saffron tea and bread in Keriya.

Remains of Melikawat near Khotan.

Silk drapery at the market in Khotan.

by the Keriya Darya, which rises in the high Kunlun Shan to the south and flows through Keriya before disappearing into the sands of the Taklamakan far to the north.

Around Keriya

A number of antique, sand-smothered sites lie to the north of Keriya. These include the former Buddhist centre of **Dandan Oilik** (Dandan Oilik Gucheng), meaning "the houses with ivory", uncovered by Sven Hedin in 1896, and **Karadong** (Karadong Gucheng), site of some of the earliest Buddhist murals. Further north still, about 220km into the shifting sands, is the former settlement of **Yuan Sha** (Yuan Sha Gucheng), abandoned as early as 130 BC. Like ancient Niya further to the east, these sites are generally off-limits without permission, requiring special equipment, including four-wheel-drive vehicles, camel caravans and global positioning systems. The tiny Uighur settlement of **Tongguzbasti**, 170km (102 miles) north of Keriya beside the rapidly diminishing Keriya Darya, must rank as one of the

most remote places in Xinjiang. It is said to stand on the ruins of the lost city of Keladun, and artefacts dating from the Han Dynasty (206 BC–AD 222) have been found here. Today about 50 families of Keriya Uighur live here in almost complete isolation, and they are known as the "lost tribe of the Taklamakan". It is possible to visit their undecorated wooden homes and also the village school.

Khotan

Highway 315 heads west from Keriya for 180km before reaching the substantial oasis of **Khotan** (Hotan), the first sizeable town (and first ATM or money-changing facilities) since Korla or Dunhuang. Here the minor oases of the Southern Route are at an end, and both facilities and accessible sights of interest increase markedly.

The Buddhist Kingdom of Khotan traces its history back at least as far as the 3rd century BC, when the eldest son of the Indian emperor Asoka is said to have settled there. It was long of great importance on the Silk Road, and is claimed to have been the first

FRUITS OF THE LOOM

Khotan has long been famous for its hand-woven carpets, and while quality may have declined over the past 50 years, it's still worth visiting the Carpet Factory (Gillam Karakhana/Ditang Chang) over the bridge on the east side of the Yurungkash River where women artisans weave by hand on looms. Another workshop of special significance for this old Silk Road city is Shatuo Silk Factory (Shatuo Sichou Chang; daily; fee for tour) in Laksui District, a short distance north of town. Here the visitor can see the entire process of silk manufacture before being led into a silk showroom and encouraged to make purchases. Less organised but perhaps more authentic is the Atlas Silk Workshop (Atlas Karakhana) in Jiya Village, about 13km (8 miles) northeast of Khotan.

place outside China to have cultivated silk. It sits astride the Karakash or "Black Jade" and Yurungkash or "White Jade" rivers, which here conjoin to form the Khotan Darya, and has been famous for its jade for well over two millennia. In times past trade routes crossed the desert to the north all the way to Kuqa, and as recently as 2007 this link has been re-established for the first time in centuries with the opening of a second Desert Highway leading to Aksu, some 424km (264 miles) to the north.

In 1006, Khotan was conquered by Uighur Muslims from Kashgar, and since that time the city has remained a very Uighur place indeed – seemingly the more so since the increased sinicisation of Kashgar in recent decades. It has an urban population of 150,000, good communication links with Aksu, Yarkand and Kashgar, plenty of good hotels and restaurants, and a great deal to see. The city – which in itself is ordinary enough – centres on **Tuanjie Square** (Tuanjie Guangchang), with Beijing Lu running north–south and Tanaiyi Lu

running east–west. Most hotels and restaurants are in the central area, and this makes it a good base for explorations further afield.

There isn't much left of old Khotan, though a few hundred metres of the crenellated city wall (Chengqiang) survive immediately to the northwest of the huge central square. Just to the south of Tuanjie Square – which is dominated by a statue of Chairman Mao Zedong shaking hands with an elderly Uighur man – is the excellent **Khotan Museum** (Hetian Bowuguan; daily; charge). The ground floor is devoted to regional archaeology and includes a fascinating diorama of the site of Old Niya, as well as two well-preserved 1,500-year-old mummies, jewellery, cooking utensils and remnants of silk. The second-floor exhibits are more recent, and include examples of local manufactures (jade, carpets, silk, musical instruments) and regional costumes.

Just south of the museum at the junction of Gujiang Bei Lu and Jiamai Lu is the **Khotan Jade Factory** (Hetian Yuqichang; free tours, but

Uighur women carpet-weaving.

naturally visitors are encouraged to make a purchase). The ground floor is a workshop where skilled jade carvers are at work, while the second floor is a large showroom filled with all kinds of jade sculptures for sale. Jade enthusiasts will also find a street of **jade shops** on nearby Beijing Lu, while a 4km (2.5-mile) walk or taxi ride east along Beijing Donglu leads to **Yurungkash River** where, during the winter months when the water level is low, you can join local jade prospectors in raking through the pebbles hoping to strike it lucky. Across from the jade factory is Jianshe Lu, leading to **Khotan Night Market**, a good place to find cheap and tasty Uighur food – just follow the aroma of grilled kebabs.

Slightly further afield, in the northeast of town by the attractive Jama' Masjid or Friday Mosque, **Khotan Bazaar** is a good place to watch local artisans – tinsmiths, silversmiths, goldsmiths, carpenters – at work, as well as to shop for fruit, spices, clothing, knives, carpets, silk and other handicrafts. The bazaar is at its busy

Taking a cow to market in Yarkand.

best on Fridays and Sundays. Khotan also holds a celebrated **Sunday Market** (Xingqitian Shihchang) which is similar to, but less touristy than, its celebrated Kashgar equivalent.

Carpet hunters should head to **Khotan Carpet Factory** (free) on the outskirts of the city (accessible by bus 5 or 10). The factory celebrates 2,000 years of carpet weaving in Khotan and features tours of the hand-weaving workshops and the option to purchase direct from the artisans.

Around Khotan

The Jiya township 23km (14 miles) northeast of central Khotan is home to the **Atlas Silk Workshop** (open 9am–4pm daily). Tours are in Chinese only but visitors are welcome to wander around and watch the hand-weaving. Whilst in Jiya, also visit the **Tomb of Imam Asim** (daily). In April and May pilgrims come here from across Xinjiang and it is possible to watch traditional storytelling, wrestling and music.

A number of ancient sites are scattered around Khotan and further to

QUEEN OF YARKAND

Queen Amannisahan (1526–60) was a noted poet in the Uighur language, penning two celebrated collections of poetry, which are both still widely read in this part of China – *Virtue* and *Poems of Amannisahan*. She also collected the "Twelve Muqam" of traditional Uighur music that follow the astronomical almanac and take around 20 hours to perform. Queen Amannisahan died prematurely in childbirth at the age of 34, and lies entombed in the blue-and-white-tiled mazar that bears her name in Old Yarkand. In 2005 her achievement was recognised when UNESCO designated the Twelve Muqam "a masterpiece of the Oral and Intangible Heritage of Humanity". She also features as the heroine of the popular 1994 Chinese film, *Amannisahan*.

the north in the Taklamakan Desert. The former Buddhist centre of **Melikawat** (Malikewate Gucheng; daily; charge) is just 28km (17 miles) south of the city and readily accessible by taxi, but there's much less to see than at Yarkhoto or Karakhoja in Turpan. Much more impressive is **Rawak**, site of a relatively well-preserved Buddhist stupa rising 9 metres (30ft) out of the desert sands about 32km (20 miles) northeast of Khotan. The site is open to visitors, but visits must be arranged ahead of time through the Cultural Relics Bureau at Khotan Museum. Similarly the old Tibetan fort at **Mazar Tagh**, 180km (112 miles) north of Khotan in the heart of the Taklamakan, may be visited, but only with the appropriate permit from the Cultural Relics Bureau. A visit to either of these sites, and especially the latter, requires special transport and can be expensive.

Highway 315 continues northwest from Khotan, following the Southern Silk Road through the towns of **Karakash** (Moyu) and **Guma**

(Pishan), to **Karghilik** (Yecheng), a distance of 226km (140 miles). In earlier times this small oasis was a stopover for trade caravans heading south from Yarkand to Ladakh and Kashmir by way of the difficult 5,575-metre (18,290-ft) Karakoram Pass. Today this route is decisively closed, as the Karakoram Pass lies in an area disputed by China and India, as well as close to the Siachen Glacier, the world's highest battlefield, where India confronts Pakistan.

Highway 219 follows part of the old trade route as it heads south from Karghilik, through Akmeqit, Mazar and Xaidulla, across the disputed Aksai Chin to Ali (Senge Khabab) in western Tibet. Although it is still officially closed to visitors, Chinese security has relaxed and it is becoming a popular (if difficult) way for travellers to reach Tibet from Xinjiang. Karghilik itself is a quiet little place with an attractive 15th-century Friday Mosque, a bustling bazaar and several reasonable hotels, making it a possible stopover on the journey between Khotan and Kashgar.

Yengisar is famous for its high quality knives.

A donkey cart and auto-rickshaws make up the traffic on this Khotan road.

Yarkand

Just 52km (32 miles) north of Karghilik, the important oasis of **Yarkand** (Shache) was once the seat of an ancient Buddhist kingdom and an important caravanserai on the Southern Silk Road. It was of particular importance as the northern terminus for the trade route over the Karakoram Pass to Ladakh, and by the 19th century its population outstripped even that of Kashgar. Today it is a predominantly Uighur city with a population of 375,000 producing cotton, wheat, corn and fruit (notably pomegranates, pears and grapes), as well as oil and natural gas. Modern Yarkand is divided into a mainly Han Chinese New Town and an overwhelmingly Uighur Old Town or **Altyn Shahr**. Most visitors will stay and eat in the former, which lies to the west along Xincheng Lu or "New Town Road", while exploring the narrow lanes and busy bazaar of the latter, which lies east of the town centre along – appropriately enough – Laocheng Lu, or "Old Town Road".

The Amannisahan Mazar in Yarkand.

A small section of the former **City Wall** (Chengqiang) survives in the west of town, but there's little else of interest here. To the northeast, however, there is a large and busy bazaar, packed with goods and businesses of every kind, as well as hole-in-the-wall places to eat and food stalls. Once a week this expands into Yarkand's picturesque Sunday Market. A short distance further east, in the heart of the Old Town, is the Friday Mosque, the 16th-century **Altyn Masjid** (Aqindian Qingzhen Si), as well as the **Amannisahan Mazar**, a blue-and-white tiled tomb that is the last resting place of Amannisahan, poet, musician and queen of Yarkand in the 16th century, who was a celebrated composer of Uighur *muqam* music. The adjacent **Cheeltanlireem Cemetery** houses the tombs of a number of Yarkand's former kings, including that of Amannisahan's husband.

Yengisar

Highway 315 continues for another 120km (75 miles) to the small Uighur-dominated oasis of **Yengisar**

Kashgar

0 _____ 1000 m
0 _____ 1000 yds

Yinbin Dadao

Nizawak Lu

Abakh Hoja Mazar
(Tomb of Abakh Hoja)

Qiniwake Binguan
(Chini Bagh Hotel)

Former
British
Consulate
Seman Lu

Binhe Lu

Tuman Lu

Yengi Bazaar
(Sunday Market)

Tuman Lu

Azirete Lu

ALTYN SHAHR

Seman Lu

Chengqiang
(Old Town
Walls)

Seman Binguan
(Former Russian
Consulate)

Masjid Id Kah
(Id Gah Mosque)

Youmulakexia Lu

Jiefang Beilu

(OLD CITY)

Renmin
Hotel

Mao Zedong

Renmin Donglu

Xiyu Dadao

Renmin Xilu

Renmin
Guangchang
(City Square)

Wenzhou
Hotel

Keziduewei Lu

**RENMIN
GONGYUAN
(PEOPLE'S
PARK)**

Tian Nanlu

Payinapu Lu

Donghu
(East Lake)

Binhe Lu

Kashgar Train
Station

Tuanjie Lu

Wenhua Lu

Tiyu Lu

Yusup Has Mazar
(Tomb of Yusup Has)

Keziduewei Lu

Saglam Lu

Jiefang Nanlu

Latbag Lu

Mal Bazaar
(Animal Market)

Yingjisha), known throughout Xinjiang for its production of handmade knives. It's worth stopping off to visit the **Small Knife Factory** (Pichak Chilik Karakhana/Xiadaochang) to see skilled local craftsmen producing fine knives with inlaid handles. Just about every Uighur man carries a knife, both as a sign of manhood and for the more utilitarian purpose of cutting up melons, and the most valued (and expensive) come from here. Beyond Yengishar, just 58km (35 miles) to the north, lies the important oasis and city of Kashgar, the western terminus of the Southern Silk Road, and also the point at which the Southern and Northern routes meet, having encircled the Taklamakan Desert.

Kashgar

Kashgar (Kashi) has been a key centre on the Silk Road for well over two millennia. The Northern and Southern roads that separated at Dunhuang rejoin here, linking up with mountain passes leading west to Samarkand and Bukhara, as well as south to Kashmir.

In times past, when caravans reached Kashgar, men and beasts alike drew breath and rested, secure in the knowledge that they had reached a safe haven near the very centre of the Silk Road.

Kashgar's physical centre may be the vast (and relatively empty) main square (**Guangchang**), dominated by a huge statue of Chairman Mao Zedong, but the city's spiritual heart lies a few hundred metres further to the north, at the **Id Gah Mosque** (Masjid Id Kah/Aiti Gaer Qingzhen Si; daily; charge for non-Muslims). "Id Gah" means "Place of Festival" in Farsi, and it is here that the city's Uighur Muslims congregate to worship every Friday, and also to celebrate the twin festivals of Id (or Eid) – Id al-Fitr, or "the celebration of the breaking of the fast" at the end of the holy month of Ramadan, and Id al-Adha, or "the celebration of sacrifice" marking the Hajj, or annual pilgrimage to Mecca.

Probably the largest mosque in China, the Id Gah Mosque was built in 1442 but it incorporates a structure

Getting a shave in Kashgar.

Busy streets in Kashgar.

Muhammad Yakub Beg

Yakub Beg was a Central Asian potentate during the Great Game, when British and Russians were vying for the region.

During the 19th and early 20th centuries a fierce, if clandestine, competition for political and military influence in Central Asia was played out between the British and Russian empires. As Britain extended its control across South Asia from the shores of Sri Lanka to the Himalayas, imperial Russia pressed south and east, across the great plains of Central Asia, to threaten the venerable khanates of Bukhara and Khiva. By the early 19th century only a few hundred kilometres of desert and mountains separated British from Russian forces, and both Afghanistan and Xinjiang emerged as unlikely settings for the Great Game between the Russians and the British in India.

In 1862 the great Northwestern Muslim Rebellion spread across China between Shaanxi and Gansu. Hui Muslims living in eastern

Muhammad Yakub Beg.

Xinjiang and Dzungaria soon joined in the general rising, cutting the Uighur oasis towns of southern Xinjiang off from China proper. The Uighurs, though Muslims, had very different aspirations to their Hui co-religionists, looking to Central Asia rather than to China as their natural spiritual home.

At a time of Chinese imperial weakness, there were opportunities for Central Asian adventurers, and one of the most interesting, Muhammad Yakub Beg, was to make himself emir of the "independent" Kingdom of Kashgaria. An Uzbek from the Kokand Khanate, he became commander-in-chief of the Khan's armies and fought against the Russians, albeit unsuccessfully, at Ak Mechet in 1853. On being defeated, his thoughts turned eastwards, and he crossed the Pamirs, making himself master first of Kashgar and Yarkand, then gradually of all the oasis towns as far east as Turpan and Hami.

Skilled negotiator

Yakub Beg was able to benefit from the *realpolitik* of the Great Game, appealing for British aid and recognition to act as a buffer state between the British, Russian and Chinese Empires. He issued his own currency, recognised the spiritual authority of the Ottoman Caliph in Istanbul, and sought arms from both Turkey and British India. He was not popular with his Uighur subjects, however, and as an Uzbek remained something of an outsider.

Yakub Beg did not long enjoy the fruits of his conquests. By 1877 the great Chinese general Zuo Zongtang had fought his way across Gansu and was engaged on a reconquest of the far west for the Qing authorities. Yakub Beg was preparing to resist the Chinese from his advance base at Korla, when he was either poisoned or died of a stroke on 30 May 1877. After his death all resistance in Kashgaria ceased, and Zuo Zongtang claimed the entire region, including Urumqi and Dzungaria in the north, for China. Zuo also gave this vast tract of land a new name: Xinjiang, or "New Frontier".

Yakub Beg's death and the re-establishment of Chinese power over Xinjiang didn't lead to the end of the Great Game, but rather drove it underground. Between the late 19th century and the Chinese Communist seizure of power in 1949, rival British and Russian consuls based at Kashgar alternately spied and schemed against each other on behalf of their imperial masters, or shared drinks and played cards together in this most remote of diplomatic destinations.

500 years older. It is said to be able to accommodate as many as 10,000 worshippers during the Id festivals (known as Bairam and Qurban in Turkish/Uighur). Yellow-tiled and very different to the Great Mosque in Xi'an (see page 138), the architectural style is definitively Central Asian and not Chinese, although – while impressive – it does not match up to the mosques of Samarkand and Bukhara. Still, this is clearly a cultural frontier, the end of China and the beginning of Islamic Central Asia.

Non-Muslim visitors may enter the mosque at will (except during prayers), but should dress modestly and observe the usual strictures such as removing shoes and (in the case of women) covering their hair. Tellingly, Han Chinese are far less likely to observe these restrictions than Westerners, much to the bemused and frustrated disdain of the Uighur custodians.

Kashgar is a city that is changing fast. Once ringed by crenellated walls and staunchly Muslim, today it is increasingly Han Chinese, as waves of settlers from the east – from "China proper" – follow the newly constructed railway from Lanzhou (1999) to seek their fortune in China's "Wild West". Much of the Old City (Altyn Shahr/Laocheng) has been demolished in recent years.Old Kashgar is best seen to the west of Id Gah Square – where parts of the Old City wall (**Chengqiang**) are still extant to the west of Seman Lu; alternatively, another section of the Old Town has been preserved to the east of Id Kah Square and is now actively promoted as a (paying) tourist attraction.

The Old City aside, Kashgar's main attraction is undoubtedly the **Sunday Market** (Yengi Bazaar/Xinqitian Shichang). In fact the market is daily, though at its busiest on Sundays – if you have time and opportunity, head out west of the Tuman River to Aizirete Lu early on a Sunday morning for the most authentic Kashgar market experience. Overwhelmingly Uighur (though Han Chinese, Hui, Kazakh, Kyrgyz and Tajiks are also present), expect everything from locally manufactured hats, furs and knives to carpets, clothing, boots and traditional aphrodisiacs – the dried scorpions look particularly appealing. Uighur foodstuffs, from kebabs to *naan*, are also ubiquitous. You'll see plenty of tourists as well, but – interestingly – most will be Han Chinese, who seem to know little of their Uighur fellow citizens, but are clearly fascinated by them.

Also best visited on a Sunday, the **Animal Market** (Mal Bazaar/Dongwu Shichang) is great fun and uniquely "Kashgari". Located in the southeast of town, some distance beyond the confines of urban Kashgar, it's packed with Uighur men buying and selling livestock of all kinds, from fat-tailed sheep to camels and yaks. This is serious business for the locals, and tourists are all but ignored as Uighurs in leather boots and *chapan* (long-sleeved Central Asian coats) weigh up and discuss the relative merits of livestock of all kinds, or "test ride" horses, camels

Stunning scenery forms the backdrop to the Tajik town of Tashkurgan.

The Id Gah Mosque in Kashgar.

SHOP

Upal (sometimes referred to as Opal) holds a busy market every Monday which is almost as photogenic, and far less visited by tourists, than the celebrated Sunday Market in Kashgar. If you can choose which day to visit Lake Karakul, make it a Monday and buy provisions at Upal market on the way.

and even yaks in the dusty surroundings of the vast, open market.

Roughly 5km (3 miles) from the city centre, on the northern outskirts of town, is the **Tomb of Abakh Khoja** (Abakh Khoja Mazar/Xiangheimu; daily 10am–7pm; charge for non-Muslims), also known locally as the **Tomb of Xiangfei**. Dedicated to the memory of Xinjiang's most celebrated Sufi mystic – a member of the Naqshbandi order and reputed *sayyid* or descendant of the Prophet Muhammad – the 17th-century sage is entombed here together with many members of his family, as well as Abakh Khoja's granddaughter, the Uighur woman Iparhan – better known in Chinese as Xiang Fei, the "Fragrant Concubine" – who was given as a wife to the Emperor Qianlong (1735–96) and immortalised in a painting by Giuseppe Castiglione (1688–1766).

Another important Uighur site is the **Tomb of Yusup Has** (Yusup Has Mazar; daily 10am–7pm; charge for non-Muslims). Yusup Has was the author of the Uighur text *Qutatu Bilik* or "Benefical Lore", one of the greatest works of Uighur literature, and together with Mahmud al-Kashgari remains among the most respected and revered of Uighur intellectuals.

During the late 19th and early 20th centuries, Kashgar was at the very centre of the Great Game (see page 70) for power and influence in Central Asia, with both the British and the Russians maintaining consulates in the remote but strategically significant oasis. The former British Consulate, known as Chini Bagh or "Chinese Garden", is located behind the **Chini Bagh Hotel** (Qiniwake Binguan) on Seman Lu, while the former Russian Consulate survives at the **Seman Binguan** (also now a hotel), also on Seman Lu. It's extraordinary to think that the diplomatic representatives of these two great powers lived and competed with each other in this remote oasis, plotting and planning each other's downfall while at the same time meeting for dinner and drinks on a regular basis, driven to friendship by isolation, while at the same time serving the interests

Bartering for sheep at the weekly Kashgar Animal Market.

of their different, distant masters in London and Moscow.

Around Kashgar

About 35km (21 miles) northeast of town lies the remains of **Hanuoyi Gucheng** (Ha Noi Ancient City) and **Mu'er Fota** (Mor Pagoda), both dating from the pre-Islamic period when Buddhism flourished in Xinjiang, and contemporaneous with other abandoned cities in the Taklamakan Desert like Niya and Karahoja. Thought to have flourished between the 7th and 12th centuries AD, there's little enough to see nowadays, though the remains of the Mor Pagoda are indicative of the Buddhist civilisation that once flourished here.

More interesting (and harder to get to) is the natural phenomenon known as **"Shipton's Arch"**. Remote, unique and astonishing – yet only 40km (24 miles) from downtown Kashgar – this is considered to be by far the largest natural rock arch anywhere in the world, rising to the same height as the Empire State Building. Discovered by British mountaineer

and Kashgar-based diplomat Eric Shipton (1907–77), it is located in the heart of the remote slot canyons of the inaccessible **Kara Tagh** or Black Mountains. Known in Turkic as **Tushuk Tash** or "Pierced Rock", and in Chinese as **Tiandong** or "Heavenly Gap", its location was completely forgotten in the troubled years following the Chinese Communist seizure of power in 1949, and the arch was only rediscovered (and permanently located using GPS technology) by a National Geographic expedition as recently as May 2000. It is possible to climb the arch, and ladders have been added to the lower section to make the scramble easier.

Leaving Kashgar

Beyond Kashgar, the old Silk Road continues westward to Kyrgyzstan and Uzbekistan via the **Torugart Pass** (3,752 metres/12,310ft) as well as the somewhat easier **Irkeshtam Pass** (2,841 metres/9,321ft) leading to Osh and the Fergana Valley – this is the poet James Elroy Flecker's *Golden Road to Samarkand*. The Irkeshtam

Stairs leading to Shipton's Arch.

Pass is the main route following the old Silk Road, and remains the main link between western China and the former Soviet Central Asian republics – the so-called "Stans".

Buses leave Kashgar for Osh, the first major town in Kyrgyzstan, twice a week from the **International Bus Station** (Guoji Chichezhan on Jiefang Beilu), or a taxi will take you to the Irkeshtam international frontier (250km/155 miles, about five hours). Crossing the Torugart Pass is more complex and requires a special permit or *xukezheng* from the Chinese authorities, and it isn't always easy to find onward transport from the Kyrgyzstan border to Naryn or Bishkek. It's best to make arrangements beforehand with one of the Kashgar travel agencies such as the Caravan Café, John's Café or CITS.

An alternative route following the old Southern Silk Road spur to South Asia leads via the Khunjerab Pass (4,693 metres/15,397ft) to Pakistan. This is the Zhongba Gonglu or **Karakoram Highway**, an engineering marvel that was opened in 1982 and remains the highest paved road in the world. Even if you're not going all the way to Pakistan, it's well worth travelling the 280km (175 miles) to Tashkurgan or "Stone Castle", the last town in China before the Khunjerab Pass. Fans of the 2007 film *The Kite Runner* may recognise the castle as many scenes were shot on location here in place of Kabul Fort.

An hour distant from Kashgar is the small town of **Upal** (Wupaer). On a bluff above the town is the **Mausoleum of Mahmud al-Kashgari** (Mahmud al-Kashgari Mazar; daily; charge). This renowned 11th-century linguist, poet and historian compiled the first comprehensive dictionary of Turkic languages. A statue of the great man stands in front of the actual mausoleum.

Lake Karakul

Beyond Upal, the highway climbs through stunning scenery, following the valley of the Ghez River (Ghez Darya) before passing through the weird Kum Tagh or "Sand Mountains", strange formations that look

The Karakoram Highway between China and Pakistan is the world's highest paved road.

as though they are made of wet sand. Before long the permanently snow-capped peaks of the Pamirs come into view, with **Kongur Tagh** (7,649 metres/25,100ft) and **Muztagh Ata** (7,546 metres/24,760ft) dominating the skyline. At an altitude of 3,900 metres (12,800ft), **Lake Karakul** (Karakul Gol/Kala Hu) must be one of the loveliest stretches of water in Asia. Renowned for its clarity and tranquillity, the huge mass of Muztagh Ata is clearly reflected in the waters. It's possible to see no fewer than 14 separate glaciers from the lakeshore. Two small settlements of Kyrgyz nomads lie by the side of the lake, and visitors can stay overnight in one of their mobile homes or yurts – Kyrgyz men will approach travellers as they arrive at the lake and offer to arrange this accommodation. It's cold at this height even in summer, so travellers intending to stay overnight should ensure that they bring sufficient warm clothing.

Those staying overnight will be able to experience the peace and tranquillity of Lake Karakul at dusk and at dawn, when the increasingly common tour buses have left or not yet arrived, and when the majestic scenery surrounding the lake is at its best. Yet despite its remoteness, Lake Karakul is changing fast as its fame percolates through to eastern China. The influx of tourists both here and at Tian Chi or "Heaven Lake" in the Tian Shan to the northeast of Urumqi has inevitably had an impact on the local herdsmen, and it's now common to see local tribesmen, richly clad and sitting astride magnificent horses, chatting with their neighbours across the waters by mobile phone.

Beyond Lake Karakul the road descends slightly to reach the small Tajik town of **Tashkurgan** (Taxkorgan), 260km (162 miles) distant from Kashgar. This ancient settlement was mentioned by Ptolemy in the 2nd century AD as the westernmost point in the "Land of Seres" or China. Xuanzang passed this way in the 7th century laden with precious Buddhist sutras he was carrying back from India to Xi'an. Today Tashkurgan is a quiet little place with a couple of fairly basic hotels and restaurants for travellers. Out of season the hotels may not have heating. The remains of a 6th-century stone fort – from which the settlement derives its name – stand just north of the town.

The Chinese border post of Pir Ali (Hongqilapu) is a further 54km (32 miles) beyond Tashkurgan, though the actual frontier is 50km (30 miles) beyond this point. The road climbs over the **Khunjerab Pass** via the Karakoram Highway before continuing to Sost and, eventually, to Gilgit in Pakistan.

The Dzungarian route

In times past a northern spur of the Silk Road led north of the Tian Shan crossing the Dzungarian Basin of northern Xinjiang before entering what is now Kazakhstan by way of the Dzungarian Gap. Today China's only rail link with Kazakhstan, as well as Highway 312 to Almaty, pass the same

A traditional yurt by Lake Karakul.

way. Truth to tell, there is little of Silk Road interest in the area today, though it's a convenient and relatively easy way of travelling between China and Kazakhstan – certainly more straightforward than using either the Torugart or Irkeshtam routes from Kashgar.

Xinjiang's capital and main city, **Urumqi** (Wulumuqi) lies this way, and while it's a relatively new city with few sites to see, it is a convenient hub for onward journeys by road, rail or air. The airport is well connected to other cities in China, and to most of the Central Asian capitals. In marked contrast to the Uighur oases of southern Xinjiang, it's a very Han Chinese city, with a population of 3.1 million, with Han making up 75 percent of the residents while Uighurs constitute a mere 12 percent. The balance is made up of Hui Muslims and Kazakhs.

Good hotels, restaurants and communications links aside, there is one very good reason to visit Urumqi. The **Xinjiang Autonomous Region Museum** (Xinjiang Zizhiqu Bowuguan; Tue–Sun 10am–6pm; free) is one of the finest museums in China and has some truly outstanding Silk Road exhibits, including the most famous of all, the Taklamakan Desert mummies, the 4,000 year old "Beauty of Loulan", "Cherchen Man" and the "Witches of Subeshi". The museum has undergone extensive renovation in recent years, including the addition of 10 new halls at a cost of $13 million, and exhibits including dioramas of some of the lost desert cities, a fine display of Buddhist frescoes from Kizil near Kuqa, and a stunning collection of artefacts from the Astana Tombs at Turpan, including remarkably preserved brocades. It's easy to spend a whole day here, and there's really nothing else to match it anywhere in the province.

Beyond Urumqi it's possible to follow the old northern spur of the Silk Road to Kazakhstan by either road or rail. Trains depart Urumqi for Almaty twice a week, but it's a slow journey, with long delays at the international frontier – reckon on six hours going through both sets of customs. Alternatively, sleeper buses run between Urumqi's **North**

The Urumqi International Bazaar is nestled in the heart of Uighur, Hui and Russian neighbourhoods and claims to be the largest bazaar in the world.

Bus Station (Changtu Qichezhan) and the border town of Korgas (12 hours); from here it takes a further 12 hours by bus to Almaty.

Around Urumqi

There are two outstanding natural beauty spots near Urumqi, and it's worth visiting at least one of them to see the Tian Shan or "Heavenly Mountains" up close, as well as to meet some of the region's nomadic Kazakhs who inhabit the high mountain pastures. **Tian Chi** or "Heavenly Lake" is 110km (66 miles) east of the city and can be reached in about 2.5 hours by bus or taxi. It makes an excellent day trip, though it's also possible to stay overnight in a Kazakh yurt – you'll certainly be approached with offers of accommodation on arrival, and it's also possible to book overnight accommodation through a travel agent in Urumqi.

The long, blue lake is at an altitude of 2,000 metres (7,000ft) and lies in the lee of permanently snow-capped **Bogda Feng**, "The Peak of God", at 5,445 metres (17,864ft) the highest mountain in the eastern Tian Shan. During the summer months Kazakh yurts cluster by the lakeshore, and there are plenty of tourists and day-trippers from Urumqi taking advantage of the truly beautiful scenery. In winter, however, it's simply too cold to visit, and even the hardy Kazakhs move down to lower pastures. It's difficult to overstate the pristine beauty of Tian Chi, though purists will cavil at the chairlift that now whisks passengers from the lower parking area to the shores of the lake several hundred metres above.

Also appealing are the "Southern Pastures" at **Baiyang Gou**, about 48km (30 miles) south of Urumqi. The main attractions are a 20-metre (66-ft) -high waterfall, the wooded slopes of White Poplar Valley and – once again – the distinctive circular yurts of the Kazakh nomads who live here. It's a popular day trip from Urumqi, and Chinese tourists enjoy themselves riding horses or camels and drinking *kumis*, the fermented mare's milk for which Xinjiang's Kazakhs are famous.

Heavenly Lake.

The ruins of ancient domes, Herat, Afghanistan.

CENTRAL ASIA

In Central Asia, the Silk Road offers a real
mix of adventure and high culture in cities
such as Samarkand, Bukhara and Herat.

A Kyrgyzstan felt rug.

Today's "Stans" have always formed the heartlands of the Silk Road, whether you call it Central Asia, Inner Asia, Tartary, Turkestan (the land of the Turks) or Transoxiana (the land between the Caspian and the Tian Shan). This meeting point of Europe and Asia forms the middle leg of the route, a resting spot and a place of transfer, whose spectacular cities have long attracted traders and invaders in equal measure.

Mountains, steppe and desert

With a huge land area of 6.45 million sq km (2.5 million sq miles), Central Asia is subcontinental in its scope. Kazakhstan alone is roughly the size of Western Europe. Mountains, steppe and desert characterise much of the scenery. To the north is the endless Kazakh steppe, the reason for 19th-century Russia's relentless drift south in search of a permanent defendable border. South of here, steppe turns to sand in the wastes of the Karakum (Black Sands) and Kyzylkum (Red Sands) deserts of Uzbekistan and Turkmenistan. Between them runs the Amu Darya (Oxus), Central Asia's great river of antiquity and the life source of the Khorezm oasis and the Aral Sea.

The southeast is dominated by the high mountains of the Tian Shan, Pamirs and Hindu Kush, whose remote, snow-capped ranges reach to 7,000m (23,000ft) and higher. Wrapped in the spurs of these mountains is the Fergana Valley and the great lake of Issyk-Kul.

Horses by Lake Issyk-Kul in Kyrgyzstan.

In the far south, the plains, mountains and deserts of Afghanistan mark the transition from Central Asia to the Indian subcontinent, with the northern regions of Herat and Afghan Turkestan oriented towards Central Asia and the Pashtun areas of the east and south pointed to Pakistan.

Empires and invaders

Central Asia's spectacular history is overwhelming in its richness and could fill several books of its own. The stars of the past stretch from the enigmatic settled cultures of the Sogdians and Bactrians to the nomadic lands of the Scythians, Kazakh hordes and Turkmen tribes, and the almost global empires of Alexander the Great, the Kushans, Tamerlane and Genghis Khan.

One major theme you'll recognise early on is that of the settler versus the nomad; the horsebound traditions of the Kazakhs and Kyrgyz versus the settled trading cultures of the Tajiks and Uzbeks. Central Asian history has been shaped for millennia by the cyclical nature of its empires:

from growth, expansion and brilliance to decadence, invasion and, ultimately, destruction. The region has been fought over by everyone from the Mongols and Arabs to the Persians and Russians.

Perhaps the most colourful period of history was that of the Great Game, the 19th-century imperial stand-off between the Russian and British empires. The Russians prevailed and their successors, the Soviets, changed the face of the region faster than anyone else since the Mongols.

Nanga Parbat reflected in a pond at Fairy Meadows, Pakistan.

Since the fall of the Soviet Union and the disappearance of such icons as Lenin, Central Asian leaders have been keen to promote new indigenous heroes to fill the ideological vacuum. Uzbekistan has rehabilitated its hero Tamerlane, Tajikistan has the Persian-speaking Ismail Samani (Ismoil Somoni in Tajik) and Kyrgyzstan has its epic hero Manas. Statues of Kazakh bards have popped up across Kazakhstan, and Turkmenistan has been turned into a shrine to its deceased leader Turkmenbashi. One set of myths has replaced another.

Silk routes – then and now

The silk routes criss-crossed Central Asia like a web. There were three main options: the northern route through the Dzungarian Gap into modern Kazakhstan; the central mountain routes over the Tian Shan to the Fergana Valley; or the Wakhan route through Afghanistan. Each had its own problems, but it was the great clearinghouses of Samarkand, Bukhara and Merv on the central route where caravans from Baghdad and Aleppo handed over their goods to merchants from Turpan, Kashgar, Yarkand and Khotan.

These days modern travellers can once again savour the Silk Road cities of Samarkand, Bukhara and Herat, but as with all worthwhile trips, some obstacles do remain. The oddly-

Bags of spices in Krygyzstan.

shaped modern republics are only now disentangling themselves after 70 years of enforced Soviet brotherhood, resulting in a bewildering array of visa regulations, travel permits, currencies and border crossings. The meeting point of this bureaucratic tangle is the Fergana Valley, which remains a political and security hotspot with ongoing violence and instability.

Much of neighbouring Afghanistan lies shattered after a generation of war, though a number of areas in the north of the country remain accessible and relatively safe.

A visit to Central Asia promises some marvellous moments and the spirit of the Silk Road can still be felt on a horse trek to a Kyrgyz yurt or while taking tea with a turbanned Uzbek in a *chaikhana*. The very names of cities such as Samarkand, Balkh, Herat and Merv still resonate with association, unequalled in their romance, centuries after their heyday.

Packing cotton in the fields, Uzbekistan.

A basic bridge suspended over the Hunza river.

PAKISTAN

The Karakoram mountains of the Hunza Valley, Baltistan and Khyber Pass offer some of the most dramatic scenery on earth.

The main Silk Road caravan routes from China headed due east to Central Asia. But there were also routes linking up with South Asia, notably through the Karakoram mountains to present-day Pakistan.

Pakistan is the Land of the Indus, and for millennia this great river that rises in Tibet and then slices through the Karakoram, before spilling onto the plains of Punjab and Sindh, has nurtured a succession of civilisations that have left behind a remarkable cultural legacy. The 5,000-year-old Indus Valley Civilisation centred in the south of the country produced the world's first large-scale urban planning, which can still be seen at Moenjo-daro in Sindh, one of the world's great archaeological sites. Later, the north, always strategically situated between South and Central Asia, found itself at the crossroads of civilisations, where the great city of Taxila became one of the most important centres of learning in the ancient world. Alexander the Great came here after crossing the Khyber Pass in 326 BC, and held philosophical discussions with resident intellectuals before dining in the great hall. Asoka nurtured Buddhism here in the 3rd century BC. Later, under the Kushans, Mahayana Buddhism became the buzzword as monasteries were created throughout Gandhara, and pilgrims such as Xuanzang (see page 57) took the new ideas north across the

Karakoram and into China, where they were further developed and studied in places like Dunhuang (see page 184). The significance of the region as a key player in Silk Road history cannot be underestimated.

In the days of the Silk Road, busy exchanges would have gone on with numerous visitors from foreign lands, something that in recent years modern Pakistan has found hard to emulate. The number of tourists had never been that great, but following 9/11 and all the uncertainties posed by media reports of

Main Attractions
The Karakoram Highway
Hunza Valley
Rakaposhi
Baltistan
Nanga Parbat
Taxila
Takht-i-Bahi
Peshawar
Khyber Pass

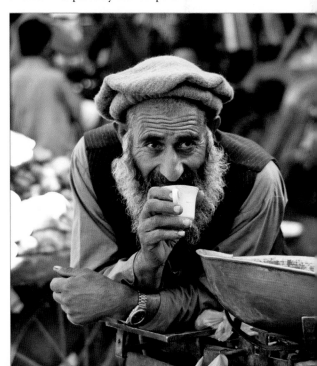

A local drinks tea in Gilgit's bazaar.

EAT

Hunza is famous for its delicious apricots, with no fewer than 24 varieties grown. Rich in vitamins and minerals, the apricots are central to a healthy local diet. Bags of them are piled high in the shops in the Karimabad bazaar and are also served up in local restaurants, in the delicious *bateringe daudo* (apricot soup).

Ladyfinger Peak.

lurking Taliban, the flow virtually dried up. Tourism remains at a low ebb due to ongoing terrorist attacks in Islamabad, Lahore and other prominent locations, and the city of Peshawar on the Khyber Pass is largely out of bounds. Foreigners travelling through Baluchistan are advised to take a police escort. Would-be visitors should take due note of official advice regarding their security and focus their plans on the large parts of Pakistan that are relatively safe. Most Pakistanis are fantastically friendly and welcoming of foreigners.

Karakoram – Hunza Valley

The Karakoram extend right across the Pakistan side of Kashmir, from Baltistan in the east to the **Hunza Valley** region. The range contains the densest concentration of big peaks on the planet, as well as nurturing the longest glaciers in the world outside the polar regions.

The very meaning of the word Karakoram – "black mountain" – conjures up an image of the precarious nature of a journey through this land. Today, following in the footsteps of early pilgrims and merchants, the traverse of the Karakoram is one of the world's great road trips. The Karakoram Highway (KKH), an engineering marvel built by the Chinese and opened in 1986, takes you from China into Pakistan via the Khunjerab Pass, the highest paved road border crossing on the planet. From the top of the Pass it's a gentle downhill journey through scenery that is impressive enough, but it isn't until you reach the fabled Hunza Valley that the Karakoram mountains reveal themselves in all their glory.

Near the north Hunza village of Passu is the snout of the Batura Glacier, a giant river of ice (58km/36 miles) that rises to the west and culminates in the beautiful Passu and Batura Peaks. On the east side of the Hunza river, a new road bridge provides access to the narrow confines of the remote **Shimshal Valley**, a paradise for trekkers heading for the pastures of Schwert, where the women of the valley tend huge numbers of yaks and goats in the summer. Just to the south, as the KKH veers west towards Central Hunza, are the mighty peaks of Trivor

ENTERING AND LEAVING PAKISTAN

Many visitors will arrive at one of the country's three main airports: Islamabad, Karachi or Lahore. Peshawar is also served by international flights from the Gulf. From Islamabad there are daily flights, weather permitting, to Gilgit and Skardu, both offering superb views of the mountains. Check travel and safety advice.

For Silk Road travellers, the journey to or from **China** will be via the Khunjerab Pass on the Karakoram Highway (KKH) from Kashgar. It is often snow-covered during the winter and is closed from 15 October to 1 May. Border posts are situated at Tashkurgan on the China side and Sost on the Pakistan side. Direct buses or jeeps link both sides, but this route can be closed to tourists.

The main border crossing to or from **Afghanistan** is the Khyber Pass, sometimes closed to tourists. The road through Pakistan passes through the Tribal Areas, so travellers require a permit and armed guard, obtainable in Peshawar from the Home and Tribal Affairs Office.

The other main route into Pakistan is from **India**, where the principal border crossing is at Wagah, just to the east of Lahore. This is crossed by the daily Samjhota Express train service and a four-times-weekly bus service operating between Delhi and Lahore.

Travellers coming from **Iran** will cross the Pakistan border at Taftan, but this is often out of bounds.

and Disteghil Sar, both of them just shy of 8,000 metres (26,000ft).

With mountains rising steeply on both sides and its tapestry of terraced fields fed by water channelled down from the glaciers, **Central Hunza** is an astonishingly beautiful place. The capital is the town of **Karimabad**, which lies just off the KKH, cowering under the vertiginous flanks of **Ultar Peak** (7,388 metres/24,240ft) that rear up just behind the village, alongside the lower Hunza Peak and aptly named pinnacle of Ladyfinger Peak. The village itself is dominated by the ancient **Baltit Fort** (daily Apr–Oct 9am–5.30pm, Nov–Mar 9am–4pm; charge), once the stronghold of the *mirs* (rulers) of Hunza and now a Unesco museum. The hereditary Mir of Hunza is today also the elected governor of the Northern Areas.

For centuries, the *mirs* controlled anyone with the nerve to pass through, their coffers regularly replenished by booty plundered from caravans plying their trade over the passes to and from Central Asia. The Baltit fort has been restored as a museum of local history and culture. Behind it, a track leads through the Ultar Nullah (ravine) on its way to **Ultar Meadow**, an idyllic spot for camping beneath the ramparts of Ultar Peak. Another good vantage point is the hamlet of Duiker, the so-called **Eagle's Nest**, situated on a knoll high above the valley at 3,200 metres (10,500ft) and offering spellbinding views. Wherever you are in Hunza, the gaze is automatically drawn to the dazzling serried buttresses of **Rakaposhi**, whose sloping northern face is the highest uninterrupted mountain face on earth, rising to a mind-boggling 7,788-metre (25,550-ft) summit straight from its base at only just over 2,000 metres (6,500ft).

From Hunza, the KKH accompanies the Hunza river as it squeezes through rocky defiles on its way to joining the Indus to the south. Just off the highway, the old fort at the village of **Chalt** is a reminder of the presence of the British in the area at the end of the 19th century. The British used Chalt as an important outpost of the Gilgit Agency. The garrison here provided support for expeditionary forces visiting the *mirs* of Hunza and Nagar in a bid to gain

TIP

Depending upon the security situation, a number of tour operators based in Gilgit and Islamabad can help organise trekking and jeep safaris to Fairy Meadows and beyond. Options could include a trek to Nanga Parbat base camp, Manthoka waterfall, Khaplu, Deosai, Shigar and Skardu, where most of the famous K2 climbing teams assemble crew and equipment.

Baltit Fort.

allegiances in the face of the much-feared advance of the Russians over the Hindu Kush at the height of the Great Game. The neighbouring village of Nilt was the scene of the final battle in 1891, by which all resistance to the British presence was crushed.

Gilgit

Situated at an altitude of 1,500 metres (5,000ft), Gilgit has always been a prosperous market town. With the establishment of links to China around 2,000 years ago, it was strategically placed to become an important trading centre along the Silk Road. Today it remains the focal point for the northern region of Pakistan, where the tradesmen of Central Asia and the plains to the south still meet. Since the opening of the KKH, the volume of goods and people passing through has increased dramatically; the influx of outsiders has brought much development but also exacerbated long-standing sectarian tensions between Shia and Sunni. The sound of the call to prayer from Gilgit's main mosque has a strange echo in this mountain environment as do the drums and clarinets of the local band attending the afternoon polo game. Polo fans come from across the world to watch Gilgit's team play against their arch-rivals, Chitral, at the **Shandur Pass**, the world's highest polo ground.

Baltistan

Rakaposhi may have the world's highest uninterrupted mountain face, but the Karakoram mountains are at their most unyieldingly dramatic in the region of **Baltistan** to the east, where the giant rock and ice spires of the inner Karakoram culminate in K2, the second-highest mountain in the world at 8,611 metres (28,250ft). No less than five of the world's 14 peaks over 8,000 metres (26,250ft) are clustered here at the head of the thundering Baltoro Glacier. The main centre of Baltistan, **Skardu**, can be reached along the daunting "Skardu Road", which follows the Indus as it recedes eastwards from the KKH just south of Gilgit, slicing its way through some of the most forbidding country on the planet. Suffice to say, this region also played a role in Silk Road history. To the west of K2, the Mustagh Pass was an ancient crossing used by local tradesmen crossing from Yarkand to Skardu, from where caravans would continue to Srinagar and Kashmir. Away to the east, out of Pakistani territory in northern Ladakh, the Karakoram Pass joined Yarkand with Leh, another important link in the Silk Road network of communications.

Nanga Parbat

The road follows the Indus south from Gilgit until it is forced west by the giant bulk of **Nanga Parbat**, whose 8,125-metre (26,656-ft) summit towers an awesome 7,000 metres (23,000ft) above the river. The huge dimensions of this mountain confirm that while not being quite the highest peak in the world it is undoubtedly the largest. Standing at the very edge of the monsoon belt, Nanga Parbat (Naked Mountain) always receives the final onslaught of the storm. It is the snow, the avalanches,

A jeep ride along the dangerous narrow road to Fairy Meadow in the Karakorum.

the collapse of ice and the yawning crevasses on its faces that have led to the mountain being renamed the Killer Mountain, as numerous expeditions have found to their cost. Access from the north side is via a rough jeep track from the Rakhiot Bridge, which goes as far as the village of Tato. From there it's a short trek up to the lush pastures of **Fairy Meadows**, where the whole of the North Face confronts the senses in a scene of unrivalled grandeur. For the experienced trekker, the flanks of Nanga Parbat provide unequalled possibilities: at 5,400 metres (17,700ft), the Mazeno Pass provides access to the southern part of the mountain and the Rupal Valley, above which a sheer face soars an awesome 4,500 metres (14,800ft) to the summit.

Rock art

West of Nanga Parbat, the KKH enters the forbidding gorges of Indus Kohistan, but before that, above the river near Chilas, is one of the greatest collections of rock art anywhere in the world. Engraved on boulders, more than 30,000 **petroglyphs** and inscriptions in more than a dozen languages testify to more than 10,000 years of human history, from prehistoric depictions of animals and ancient symbols, to Scythian merchants and pilgrims from Central Asia, to images of the Buddha and scenes from his life. Sadly all this, and 31 villages, will be submerged under a huge lake created by the construction of the massive **Diamer-Bhasha Dam** a little further downstream. The dam's foundation stone was laid in 2011 and it is expected to take 12 years to complete. Astonishingly, the dam will straddle the same major tectonic faultline – the collision zone between the Indian and Eurasian continental plates – that has been responsible for making this one of the most geologically unstable places on earth.

Taxila

The KKH continues through Kohistan, reaching the town of Besham before continuing down to the Thakot Bridge and across Hazara to the plains of Pakistan. Just to the west of **Rawalpindi**, the route that took pilgrims and merchants to and from China

TIP

If time and security allow, head for the glorious Chitral Valley in the far northwest of Pakistan. Dominated by Tirich Mir, the highest peak of the Hindu Kush, it is popular with trekkers and mountaineers, and just above Chitral Town is the Chitral Gol National Park, one of the most important sanctuaries for the elusive snow leopard.

Polo match at the Shandur Pass.

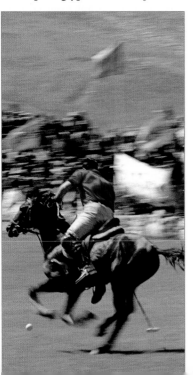

A PASSION FOR POLO

Polo actually originated in Central Asia and was developed into a competitive sport by the Persians. It spread to southwest Europe, where it eventually died out, and also east to the north of the Indian subcontinent, which is where the British rediscovered it. Polo in the Northern Areas has assumed its wildest and most untethered form. The unbelievably daredevil horsemanship of the players is almost matched by the bravery of the spectators who line the ground atop a low wall from which the ball, hit around at amazing speeds, rebounds into play. The pace of the game is controlled by the music, which increases in pitch as the contest continues. The horses have got to be admired for staying the pace.

The game used to be played all over the Northern Areas, but can now only be seen in those areas still wealthy enough to scrape a team together. It is still played in Gilgit and Chitral and some parts of Baltistan. The only rule seems to be that there are six players to each side, though even this seems to be overlooked on occasion. The first game of the season always comes with the Spring Festival towards the end of March. The old practice of sacrificing a goat and using the head as the ball has all but died out, but judging by the way the ball is hit around the ground it seems that it may still symbolise the skull of the devil.

meets the route that brought invaders via the Khyber Pass to the Indian subcontinent: the Grand Trunk Road ("GT Road") as the British came to call it. Persians, Greeks, Mughals, Afghans, as well as the British, all used this thoroughfare for their forays into and out of India.

Just at the intersection of this hugely significant crossroads lies the ancient Gandharan capital, **Taxila**, one of Asia's great archaeological sites, encompassing three major cities and numerous Buddhist *stupas* and shrines dotted around a delightful valley. The first city was Bhir Mound, where streets, lanes and foundations of houses and shops are still clearly visible. The later city of Sirkap was built on a grid layout by the Bactrian Greeks, Alexander the Great's successors, in about 180 BC, and highlights include Greek-style architectural details at the Shrine of the Double-Headed Eagle and the remains of the Royal Palace where St Thomas is said to have stayed in about AD 40 as he began his missionary work in India. There are also several temples in the vicinity with distinctly Greek-style features. Sirsukh

Suspension bridge across the Indus River.

dates from the Kushan period, the most frenetic time for Taxila, when numerous monasteries such as Jaulian were constructed in the valley. The Dharmarajika Stupa, the largest in Pakistan, was reputedly built by Asoka to house the relics of the Buddha himself.

GT Road and Peshawar

Taxila lies close to the present capital of Pakistan. Also planned on a grid system, **Islamabad** represents the modern aspirations of the country, with some striking architecture and pleasant residential zones and shopping centres. To the east of neighbouring Rawalpindi, the GT Road heads towards India. Babur, who founded the Mughal dynasty came this way and proceeded to capture **Lahore**, which subsequently became one of the pearls of the Mughal Empire and is well worth a visit for the Fort, the Badshahi mosque and much else besides. In the other direction lies the ancient city of **Peshawar**, the capital of Gandhara under the Kushans and a place that oozes history. This is one of the great cities of Central Asia, and its bazaars are probably the most authentic along the entire Silk Road. Depending on the latest security advice, take a walk along the Qissa Khawani – the "Street of Storytellers" – and peek into the jewellery shops of Andar Shehr before taking in the colours of the wonderful sabz bazaar (vegetable market) or trying a delicious kebab on the Namak Mandi.

North of Peshawar, on the way to the Malakand Pass, is **Takht-i-Bahi**. This is considered to be the most complete of all the Gandharan Buddhist monasteries, occupying a stunning site on the side of a hill overlooking the plain.

Just west of Peshawar lies the **Khyber Pass** itself, which is mostly within Pakistan. Depending upon the latest official travel advice and security situation, you might be able to stand on this pass between South and Central Asia, contemplating the great history that has unfolded here.

Gandharan Art

It is surprising to find such remarkable examples of ancient Buddhist art in the Islamic countries of Pakistan and Afghanistan.

Gandharan or Graeco-Buddhist art is the result of the fusion of Classical and Buddhist cultures in Afghanistan and, to a lesser extent, Pakistan and northern India, created from the time of the conquests of Alexander the Great until the arrival of Islam in the 7th century AD. Initially under the patronage of the Graeco-Bactrian kings (250–125 BC) in Bactria and Sogdiana, and then the Kushan emperors (c.30–230 AD), artists and architects created devotional and municipal works that drew heavily on Buddhist traditions but also had a classical twist. This ancient fusion has created a unique style.

Aspects of the Buddha

Gandharan art focuses heavily on the person of the Buddha. Episodes in his life, including his childhood, teaching, miracles and death, were exquisitely carved using a variety of media, usually bluish schist or stucco. Although the Buddha was the primary focus in these scenes, there were also supporting appearances from bodhisattvas and Maitreyas.

The living Buddha had explicitly forbidden images of himself. Despite this, the most significant contribution that Gandhara made to the development of Buddhism was the transformation of his image from an abstract symbol to representation in human form, a process that dates to the beginning of the 1st century AD. Early representations of the Buddha as the *chakra*, or wheel (symbolising the wheel of law), and the *triratna*, or trident (symbolising the three pillars of early Buddhism), changed to a new image, that of an idealised teacher.

Cosmopolitan ideas

Gandharan art was very much a result of the confluence of Silk Road ideas in cosmopolitan Afghanistan. The country's historic exports of lapis lazuli, rubies and other precious stones, and also its numerous communications routes to the surrounding countries, made it a veritable trading hub. Patrons and artisans alike were influenced by the latest fashions and developments in style and technique. Thus in Gandharan art we see syncretic depictions where the Indian Buddha, or another local figure, is shown wearing Roman dress and with the hairstyle of a classical general. Gandharan art was transported along the Silk Road to China and Tibet by pilgrims and merchants. It remained little known in the West, until its "discovery" at Dunhuang and elsewhere by European archaeologists following in the wake of the Great Game. Key artefacts are now preserved in the collections of the British Museum, Musée Guimet, the National Museum of Pakistan and Peshawar Museum, the largest such assembly in the world.

Some of the greatest Gandharan artefacts have proved to be too large to remove from the rocks in which they were carved or the cities where they were constructed. The survival of others has been determined largely by chance. Long-abandoned monasteries and stupas have been left to crumble, while the archaeological site of Taxila and the Takht-i-Bahi, both UNESCO World Heritage Sites, have been well-preserved. Numerous other examples have not been so lucky: most famously, the remarkable Buddhas of Bamiyan and Jehanabad were damaged irreparably by Taliban iconoclasts.

Buddhist ruins at the Jaulian Stupa and Monastery, Taxila.

Herat's Friday Mosque.

AFGHANISTAN

Afghanistan has an extraordinary cultural heritage:
from bustling Kabul to ancient Balkh, Herat,
and the ghostly empty niches of Bamiyan.

n recent years Afghanistan has become synonymous with the troubles of the world, from the unfinished business of the Cold War to the "War on Terror". But for most of its history, the country has been referred to as "the crossroads of Asia", a cosmopolitan centre where Central Asia, the Indian Subcontinent and the Middle East all meet.

Afghanistan has played a crucial role in the development of culture and empire, from a crucible for Buddhist ideas under the Kushans, to pride of place in the Timurid renaissance alongside Samarkand and Bukhara. It has also proved a tough nut for other empires to crack, including the British and Russians – only Genghis Khan truly made his mark here.

Modern Afghanistan is struggling to outgrow its history, and whilst the government is positive, it does not control parts of the country. Swathes of the south are no-go areas due to the Taliban insurgency. The north is relatively safe, but incidents do occur – a tourist bus was attacked by grenade in August 2016. If planning a visit, keep a close eye on events and official advice for the foreseeable future.

The Khyber Pass

The border post at Torkham (Towr Kham) would be a nondescript sort of a place, were it not for its location

at one end of the fabled **Khyber Pass**. The pass is mostly on the Pakistani side, from where you get a sense of the strategic importance of this winding mountain corridor.

The road from Torkham leads to the old Mughal city of **Jalalabad**, famous for its oranges and poetry. The region was important to the Buddhist Kushans, and you can still make out the cliff-side caves that served as monks' retreats on the far side of the Kabul River on leaving town. Near Jalalabad are the ruins of the ancient

Main Attractions
Kabul Museum
Babur's Gardens
Timur Shah's Mausoleum
Minaret of Jam
Herat Old City
Shrine of Hazrat Ali

Dried fruits and nuts for sale at a Kabul bazaar.

monastery of **Hadda**, an important and beautiful pilgrimage site reduced to rubble by Soviet bombardment in the 1980s.

Continuing from Jalalabad, the road rises through the **Tangi Gharu** gorge, before levelling out onto the Kabul Plain, and beginning its approach to the capital.

Kabul

Recently ravaged by war, Kabul has a long history of being fought over. The ancient Persians and Greeks had outposts here, the Kushans turned it into an important trading spur on the Silk Road, while the city was a Hindu outpost for several centuries before the arrival of Islam. It was the Mughal Empire (and in particular its founder, Babur) that made Kabul great, although it took the creation of modern Afghanistan in the 18th century to turn it into a capital.

Modern Kabul remains the vital heart of the country, but it has struggled after the shattering bombardments it suffered during the civil war of the 1990s. Its population has soared, and infrastructure has been unable to keep pace. There are signs of great poverty and wealth rubbing up against each other everywhere, from begging war widows to the profusion of new glass buildings. Security barriers are a sign of the times, as an often-weary population wonders in which direction Afghan politics will carry them next.

Kabul Museum

In the 1970s the **Kabul Museum** (daily 8am–4pm; charge) was one of Asia's best museums, and its diverse collection of artefacts from Greek coinage, Buddhist statuary and Islamic art was almost entirely collected from within the country. During the civil war the museum was looted mercilessly, and virtually razed to the ground. The Taliban smashed much of what remained.

International aid and the dedication of its staff have allowed a modest rebirth. The refurbished building has displays dedicated to several periods of Afghan history, most notably a large collection of wooden statuary from Nuristan. Other items include several Gandharan statues (some recently restored), coins and a huge carved marble mosque basin. Most of the museum's greatest remaining treasures, such as the Bactrian gold hoard from Shiberghan and many of the Bagram ivory carvings, have yet to be exhibited publicly in Kabul, but have toured museums in Europe and the US.

Opposite the museum is the empty shell of **Darulaman Palace**, once the royal residence but gutted during the civil war.

Babur's Gardens

First laid out in the 16th century, the hillside park of **Babur's Gardens** (daily 8am–sunset; charge) is thought to be the world's oldest extant Mughal garden. The emperor Babur (see page 272) was highly enamoured of Kabul, and dedicates much of his memoirs, the *Baburnama*, to descriptions of the city and its gardens.

The garden had been reduced nearly to scrub, and it has undergone a massive renovation project. The

old marble channels that send water cascading down the garden's terraces have been restored, and there has been plenty of replanting. The central terrace holds an old pavilion erected by Ami Abdur Rahman Khan. Above this is a white marble mosque, erected by the Mughal emperor Shah Jahan. Finally, and overlooking all of western Kabul, is Babur's surprisingly modest grave.

Also on the top terrace is the Queen's Palace, used for music and theatrical performances. The slope the gardens sit on is part of the Shir Darwaza mountain ridge that helps split Kabul in two. Above Babur's grave, and slightly to the north, is the **Noon Gun** lookout point, from where you can see most of the city, and also the **City Walls** with similarly remarkable views.

Sultani Museum

Within the grounds of the unremarkable **National Gallery**, the Sultani Museum (daily 8am-4pm; charge) is a private collection housing more than 3,000 well-displayed artefacts. Opened

An Afghan sheep herder.

ENTERING AND LEAVING AFGHANISTAN

Most cross-border routes are fairly straightforward in terms of paperwork, but check the security situation before attempting them.

The Khyber Pass between Peshawar in **Pakistan** and Kabul is the iconic route into Afghanistan (often closed to tourists), who also require a Tribal Areas permit and armed guard, obtainable in Peshawar from the Home and Tribal Affairs Office. Across the border at Torkham, plentiful shared taxis rush to Kabul.

It is possible to travel quickly from Mashhad in **Iran** to/from Herat, via the border at Islam Qala, either by shared taxi, in stages, or by direct bus between the two cities, but the Iranian side can be closed to tourists.

The remote border at Gushgy north of Herat is usually open, but entering **Turkmenistan** you'll need to be met by an official guide.

The border at Hairatan near Mazar-e-Sharif across the Amu Darya (Oxus) River to Termiz in **Uzbekistan** is open to all travellers holding visas. A new bridge at Shir Khan Bandar makes the **Tajikistan** border crossing north of Termiz a straightforward affair, with onward transport available to Dushanbe. There are two crossings in Badakhshan, at Ishkashim and Khorog. Both lead into Tajik Gorno-Badakhshan, which requires a special GBAO permit to travel; this must be arranged at your embassy or in Dushanbe prior to travel. The roads to the border at Khorog are often difficult to traverse due to winter snows.

in 2004, the pieces – which include beautifully illustrated Korans, stonework and gold – were all acquired by gold and antiques dealer Ahmad Shah Sultani while in exile in London during Afghanistan's civil war. Once security improves, Sultani plans to give his collection to the nation, and those items that came on to the international art market having been looted from the National Museum have already been returned.

Central Kabul

Near the heart of the central Shahr-i-Naw District, **Chicken Street** is Kabul's most famous bazaar street. Once a hub for travellers following the Hippie Trail, its shops can sell you anything from lapis lazuli to carpets and antiques of varying ages.

The occasionally green Shahr-i-Naw Park is just north of Chicken Street, and beyond this is the **European Cemetery** (usually dawn–dusk; donation requested). Built for the British dead of the Second Anglo-Afghan War, more recent additions include memorials to NATO soldiers killed

Relaxing in Babur's Gardens on a Friday, Afghanistan's day of rest.

in Afghanistan since 2001. The celebrated Silk Road archaeologist Aurel Stein is also buried here.

Tucked into the alleys off Jad-i-Maiwand near the blue-domed Pul-i Khishti Mosque, the **Bird Market** (Ka Faroshi) is one of the few corners of the city where life carries on as if the upheavals of recent history had never occurred. Keeping birds is one of the great Afghan pleasures, and flocks of doves are flown recreationally above the city every evening.

If you continue through the lanes north to the Kabul River, you'll reach **Timur Shah's Mausoleum**. The son of Ahmad Shah Durrani, Timur Shah moved the Afghan capital to Kabul in 1772, and his tomb has been the centre of recent renovation by the Aga Khan Trust for Culture.

Landmine Museum

Sitting near the foot of Teppe Maranjan hill, the OMAR **Landmine Museum** (daily 8am–3pm; donation requested) is one of the most unusual in Asia. It exhibits mines and ordnance recovered from every corner of Afghanistan, reminding visitors that the country is still one of the most heavily mined in the world. The museum also doubles up as a training centre for mine-disposal experts, and there's a roll call of OMAR staff killed during demining procedures.

Overlooking the museum, **Nadir Shah's Mausoleum** sits broken-faced on the top of Teppe Maranjan. The dilapidated mausoleum is the last resting place not only for Nadir Shah, but also his son, King Zahir Shah, who died in 2007, having returned from exile as "Father of the Nation" after the collapse of the Taliban.

Bamiyan and Points West

Driving north from Kabul to Bamiyan, the highway passes through the wide and fertile **Shomali Plain**, an area famous for its fruit, particularly grapes. Just above the plain is the ancient village of **Istalif**, whose artisans make appealing blue-and-brown pottery.

From the turning off the main highway at Charikar, the Bamiyan road deteriorates considerably in quality but the views, as it winds deeper into the mountains, are increasingly dramatic. Just before entering the Bamiyan Valley, the road meets the confluence of the Bamiyan and Kalu rivers, overlooked by the red fort of **Shahr-e-Zohak**. High on the cliffs, its capture by Genghis Khan from its Muslim Shansabanid rulers was the preface for the Mongol capture of the whole region.

Bamiyan first flourished as a Kushan trading centre in the first centuries of the Silk Road, and reached greater prominence after their eclipse. Under the White Huns in the 6th century, Bamiyan's Buddhist art tradition produced its greatest masterpiece, the two giant **Buddha statues** carved out of the valley's cliff wall. Bamiyan never fully recovered from its devastation by the Mongols, and when its Hazara inhabitants (who claim descent from those invaders) adopted Shia Islam, it placed Bamiyan further from the mainstream of Afghan history.

Destroyed by the Taliban in 2001, the massive empty niches of the

Pendant found at Tillya Tepe.

SCYTHIAN GOLD

The excavations by Victor Sariandi were hurriedly completed in 1979 at the Scythian royal burial ground of Tillya Tepe in northern Afghanistan, where he unearthed more than 20,000 gold ornaments, many lavishly decorated with turquoise and lapis lazuli. With the Soviet invasion looming, archaeologists were forced to hastily abandon the site, without having time to properly catalogue their discoveries. Artefacts were later removed to Kabul and secured in the vault of the National Bank by officials in the late 1980s. The keys to the vault were distributed among a number of trusted diplomats.

In 1996 the Taliban captured Kabul and attempted to force their way into the national vault, but without success. The bank manager even resorted to breaking off his key in the vault door in an attempt to stop the looters. During the invasion of Afghanistan by US-led forces, the Taliban made one last attempt to get their hands on the treasure by planting bombs on the vault door but were thwarted at the last minute. In 2003, after the Taliban had been expelled from Kabul, the safety of the Bactrian Hoard was finally secured.

A new museum is being planned in Kabul to house the Scythian gold and, in the meantime, highlights from the collection have been exhibited in the US, France, UK and Japan.

Only about 36 percent of Afghan girls receive an education and many challenges to this continue to exist, although the figure is a marked improvement on the years under the Taliban, when only 3 percent of girls went to school.

The extraordinary Minaret of Jam.

Buddhas entirely dominate the town. Known simply as the Large and Small Buddhas, the statues stood 55 metres (182ft) and 38 metres (125ft) high, respectively. The rough figures were cut from the soft sandstone, covered with mud plaster for detailing and finally painted. The faces wore gilded masks, although (like most of the decoration) these didn't survive to the modern period.

A series of passageways, monks' cells and rooms have been dug into the cliffs surrounding each niche. It is possible to climb to the top of the Large Buddha's "head", but it's only for those who have a head for heights.

On one of the hills on the southern edge of Bamiyan there is a scramble to the remains of another fort ruined by the Mongols, **Shahr-e-Gholghola**.

Four hours west of Bamiyan are the mineral lakes of **Band-e-Amir**, a series of five lakes of a nearly magical blue. The most accessible is Band-e-Haibat, held in 10-metre (33-ft) -high limestone walls laid down over millennia to form a natural dam. It's an Afghan tradition to drink the water for its curative powers, and there is a popular lakeside shrine for blessings.

Minaret of Jam

It's possible to traverse central Afghanistan from Bamiyan to Herat by road, although the rough crossing is only for the stout-hearted. Yet virtually in the geographical centre of the country is one of its greatest treasures (and its first Unesco World Heritage monument), the **Minaret of Jam**.

To reach the minaret takes almost three days of solid driving from Bamiyan through wild mountain terrain, yet its isolation is one of its attractions. Built in the 12th century by the Ghorids, the minaret stands around 65 metres (215ft) high, tucked into the crags of a narrow valley, the last visible symbol of the ancient city of Firuzkoh.

The minaret is a triumph. It has three tapering levels, each decorated in brick arranged into Koranic verses, with one band of blue glazed tile. The lovely views from the top reveal the minaret's hidden location (in a gorge where two rivers meet), which explains why the outside world was unaware of its existence until the 1930s.

An early start from Jam will take you on a long day's drive to Herat. Make a point of breaking the journey at **Chist** (Chest-e-Sharif) to see the domed Ghorid tombs, contemporaries to the minaret.

Herat

The western city of Herat, near the Iranian border, is a classic Silk Road city. Its roots predate Alexander the Great, and it flourished as a trading city continuously from the Kushans to the modern period, pausing only in the 12th century when the Mongol terror razed it to the ground.

Herat's heyday was during the Timurid Empire. Following Timur's death, Herat became joint capital of the empire with Samarkand. Shah Rukh and his queen Gowhar Shad packed the city with artists, poets and

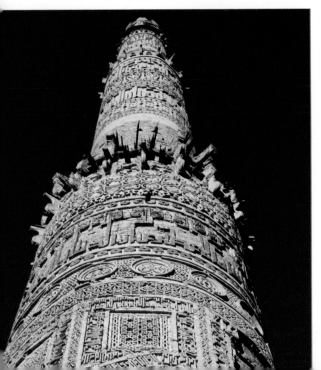

architects, turning Herat into one of the great cities of the age, before the rot of decadence set in. Herat played an early part in the Great Game when it was besieged by the Persians and Russians in 1838. An army mutiny 130 years later, suppressed with Soviet help, was an early marker on the path to full invasion.

The medieval **Old City** forms the core of Herat. Two great monuments are testaments to its history. The **Friday Mosque** (closed to visitors for Friday prayers) is deservedly the most celebrated in the country. The style echoes the Timurid revival, with its massive minarets rising from the ground flanking the great vault of the main prayer hall. The stunning mosaic work is from the mosque's own tile workshop, and restoration is ongoing. On the street running along the northern side of the mosque is a small workshop making traditional Herati blue glass.

A fort has sat on the mound of the **Citadel** (daily 8am–5pm; charge) since Alexander's time, although the current incarnation is Timurid. The complex was a military base until 2005. Now visitors can enjoy the fine views from the massive battlements.

Looking north from the Citadel lets you pick out the tottering minarets of the **Musalla Complex**. This was Gowhar Shad's finest commission, almost completely levelled by the British in the 1880s to clear a line of fire against a feared Russian invasion. Five minarets, their tiling almost lost, still stand, near the queen's tomb with its distinctive melon-ribbed dome.

An excellent new road leads from Herat to the Iranian border, and work has recently begun on a rail link to Mashhad. The roads northeast to Mazar-e-Sharif (a three-day drive via Meymaneh), or to Kabul via Kandahar, are not safe for overland travel.

Across the north

In Silk Road days, a caravan trail headed across the steppe of Afghanistan's north, via the Wakhan Corridor from China. This thin tongue of land separating Afghanistan from Tajikistan and Pakistan is part of the mountainous region of Badakhshan; a Wakhan permit and

A tradesman holds a necklace of lapis lazuli stones at a shop in Kabul.

LAPIS LAZULI

The mines of the northeastern province of Badakhshan have been producing lapis lazuli for export for over 7,500 years. Until recently, they were virtually the only known source of this semi-precious stone. Afghan lapis was an important trade good, found in everything from ancient Egyptian jewellery and Tutankhamun's funeral mask to the blue pigments of Michelangelo's paintbox. The Romans even ground it up to use as an aphrodisiac.

More recently, the lapis mines (found at Sar-e-Sang, south of Faizabad) were an important source of hard currency for the *mujahideen* fighting the Soviets, and for the anti-Taliban Northern Alliance. Usually flecked with pyrites and veins of white calcite, the best-quality stone is sold in Kabul and lacks such impurities.

permission from the border police are required to go there, theoretically arranged in half a day in Ishkashim.

Visitors might enter the Wakhan across the border from Tajikistan at **Ishkashim**, where there are a number of small guesthouses and the opportunity to collect a trekking guide. Two of the most popular areas for trekking, though still unfrequented by international standards, are **Noshaq Base Camp**, Afghanistan's highest peak, and routes heading east from **Sarhad-e-Boroghil**, the small town where the Wakhan's only road ends. For the hardy traveller, the Big and Little Pamir ranges offer the greatest – and most remote – scenery, including **Chaqmaqtin Lake**, Curzon's **ice cave** and even the possibility of spotting the elusive snow leopard or Marco Polo sheep in the **Wakhjir Pass.**

It is possible to trek on horseback and also to hire horses and yaks, in addition to human porters, to carry baggage. Accommodation is under canvas, in basic guesthouses or with Kyrgyz families in their yurts at **Bozai Gumbaz.**

The Bamiyan Valley and its eerily vacated Buddha niche.

Ai Khanoum

From **Ishkashim** the road leads westwards to the regional capital, **Faizabad**, which has a diverting bazaar, and then to **Kunduz**, but this area is often out of bounds due to the Taliban. An interesting diversion leads north to **Ai Khanoum**, presumed to be the site of Alexandria-Oxiana, founded by Alexander in 327 BC and the easternmost Greek city in the world. On the confluence of the Kokcha and Amu Darya rivers, the site itself was terribly looted during the civil war. The nearby town of Khoja Bahauddin has several Greek column capitals from Ai Khanoum in the town roundabouts.

Mazar-e-Sharif and Balkh

The city of **Mazar-e-Sharif** is the largest in the north, and is dominated by the turquoise domes of the **Shrine of Hazrat Ali**, dedicated to Muhammad's son-in-law, reputedly buried here. Rebuilt many times since the original was erected in the 12th century, the blue shrine has every square inch covered in patterned tiles. The shrine complex is the focus of Afghanistan's

DEMOLITION EXPERTS

The Bamiyan Buddhas survived for 15 centuries in the remote vastness of the Afghan Hindu Kush. Neither the ravages of time, nor the conquering armies of Islam – not even the scourge of Genghis Khan – had laid them low. Islam first came to Bamiyan with the conquest of the valley by Ya'qub ibn Leys in 871. Subsequently, iconoclasts painstakingly cut the eyes and nose off the large Buddha image, but left the figure standing. In the 17th century, the Persian ruler Nadir Shah is said to have "broken the legs" of the larger Buddha, though – this is less clear – the right leg, slightly bent at the knee, remained intact, while the left appeared to have sheared away at the hip.

In its prime, the figure was partly clad in stucco, and cords were draped down the body to simulate the folds and drapes of the robe. Although once brightly painted, time rather than religious vandalism had caused most of the outer coat to fall away, leaving rows of holes which once held wooden pegs to stabilise the stucco. Reports suggest that these very holes were packed with dynamite by the Taliban during their demolition.

By any standards, these towering images formed part of the common cultural heritage of mankind. Viewed in this context their destruction by Taliban was truly a mindless crime.

Nauroz celebrations every 21 March, and an important pilgrimage site.

Mazar-e-Sharif is a relatively new city, which has overshadowed the much older **Balkh**, just 20km (12 miles) away, only since the 19th century. Balkh was possibly the home of Zoroaster in the 6th century BC, and hosted Alexander's wedding party three centuries later. It grew rich off the Silk Road, and boomed again after the Arabs (who called it "the Mother of Cities") in the 9th century AD. Despite a Timurid renaissance, Balkh never fully recovered from the violent attentions of Genghis Khan, and is a small town today.

In a park in the centre of Balkh is the 15th-century **Shrine of Khoja Abu Nasr Parsa**, with its distinctive Timurid ribbed dome and delicate painted interior. To the north are the massive ramparts of **Bala Hissar**, Balkh's ancient fort – almost as big as the town itself. The view gives a good idea of the scope of the city walls, sections of which still stretch out to encompass the houses and fields. Down a track on the opposite side of the main highway in farmland is the 9th-century **Noh Gombad Mosque**, the oldest in Afghanistan. Although it is little more than a handful of columns and walls, the intricate stucco decoration clearly points to the Arabian traditions of the people who brought Islam to the country.

The road to Kabul

To the north of Mazar-e-Sharif the road leads to the Uzbekistan border at Termiz. Heading south to Kabul, the road passes through the Shomali Plain before crossing the mountains through the dramatic artery of **Salang Tunnel**, built in the 1960s. North of the pass, before the junction town of Pol-e-Khomri, is Samangan, where the rock-hewn stupa of **Takht-e-Rostam** is Afghanistan's most important intact Kushan site, dating from the 4th century AD. The massive structure has been dug out of the limestone, surrounded by a trench and topped with a carved reliquary. Just below the *stupa*, a series of caves has also been cut from the rock to form airy monks' quarters.

The Friday Mosque in Herat.

KYRGYZSTAN

Visitors can enjoy dramatic scenery, experience a nomadic lifestyle and seek out many historical sights connected with the Silk Road in this mountainous country.

The small mountain republic of Kyrgyzstan is often dubbed the "Switzerland of Central Asia" for its alpine valleys, flower-filled meadows and snow-capped peaks. Lake Issyk-Kul may indeed rival Lake Geneva, but the similarities end abruptly with the eagle hunters, yurts and nomads that make Kyrgyzstan a distinctly inner Asian country. Like its many lakes, it is a jewel hidden high in the mountain valleys of Central Asia, and more than amply rewards those who make the effort to explore it.

The Kyrgyz Republic is defined by its geography, specifically its mountains, which make up over 94 percent of the country. The north is dominated by the wild valleys of the Tian Shan – the "Heavenly Mountains" – or Tengir-Too in Kyrgyz, whose valleys offer some of the world's loveliest alpine scenery: a trekkers' paradise of rushing streams, juniper forests and glaciated peaks.

To the south, forming the southern wall of the Fergana Valley, are the remote towers of Turkestan and Pamir Alay, spurs of the great Pamirs. In between are the central highlands – rolling hills dotted with yurts and mountain lakes – Issyk-Kul, Song-Kol and Sary Chelek to name just three.

Life for the Kyrgyz

The Kyrgyz people arrived here in the 16th century, after migrating across inner Asia from homelands in the Yenisey Valley of Siberia. Today around 60 percent of the people are Kyrgyz, who remain close ethnic kin to their neighbours the Kazakhs. There are also significant numbers of Uzbeks and Russians, as well as pockets of Dungans, Koreans and others.

Despite years of Soviet collectivisation and modernisation, the remnants of a Kyrgyz nomadic culture remain.

Main Attractions

Tash Rabat
Saimaluu Tash Petroglyphs
Bishkek
Ala-Archa National Park
Burana Tower
Lake Issyk-Kul
Karakol
Alay Valley
Osh
Ozgon Mausoleum

Nomads play the traditional horseback game of Buzkashi.

All along the roadside in grazing areas you'll see locals selling Coke bottles full of *kymyz*, fizzy and bitter fermented mares' milk. The country's literary heritage rests largely in the memory of itinerant bards called *akyn*, and nomadic-inspired horse games are still played out annually in the summer pastures. Less desirable nomadic hangovers remain too, from the ongoing custom of bride-kidnapping to the system of clan-based politics. Islam remains a relatively thin veneer, especially in the north and centre of the country.

Central to the Kyrgyz definition is the *Manas* (see box), an oral epic poem 20 times longer than the *Odyssey* and *Iliad* combined. The epic chronicles the history of the formation of the Kyrgyz people through the exploits of the hero Manas, his wife Kanykei and son Semetei. A tomb, the Manas Gumbez, was built for the fictional hero in 1334, just southeast of the modern town of Talas.

Tulip Revolution

During the Soviet era, the mountains of "Kyrgyzia" remained off-limits

A young yurt-dweller.

thanks to its uranium mines, hydro-electric dams and prickly mountain border with China. Reluctant independence brought great economic hardship to the country, a problem compounded by the ensuing exodus of most of Kyrgyzstan's skilled and educated Russian population. President Akayev pushed through early reforms to turn the Kyrgyz economy into the most liberal in Central Asia. Increasingly corrupt and authoritarian, he was overthrown a decade later in the popular Tulip Revolution of March 2005.

The 2010 revolution and violence

Akayev's successor, Kurmanbek Bakiyev, came to power with significant support from the US, but he proved no better as a leader and corruption skyrocketed. In 2009 he announced the eviction of the US from their Manas airbase near Bishkek, purportedly in exchange for a $2 billion loan from Moscow, but the US was then able to renegotiate the lease and Bakiyev kept the Russian's money, losing him vital support from the Kremlin. The Russian

ENTERING AND LEAVING KYRGYZSTAN

Roads in Kyrgyzstan are often poor and the terrain difficult (see page 385). There are five crossing points into **Kazakhstan**. Buses and taxis run between Bishkek and Almaty, a journey that can take as little as three hours (excluding border formalities). In summer, frequent buses also run between Almaty and Cholpon-Ata.

There are two road crossings to **Uzbekistan** in the Fergana Valley, one near Andijan, the other near Namangan, although it is necessary to change transport at the frontier. Daily buses run between Bishkek and Tashkent but require a Kazakhstan transit visa.

A public bus runs twice a week from Osh to Kashgar in **China** by way of the Irkeshtam Pass. Tour operators in Bishkek and Kashgar can arrange travel up to the Torugart Pass, but travellers may be left stranded for hours at a freezing-cold frontier post waiting for a lift on the other side. Both borders are closed Sat and Sun.

A rough road crosses the Kyzyl-Art Pass to reach Murgab in **Tajikistan**, for which a GBAO (Gorno-Badakhshan Autonomous Oblast) permit is required. Shared taxis run between Batken in southwest Kyrgyzstan to Isfara in Tajikistan. However, reaching Batken itself may require an Uzbek transit visa and a multiple-entry Kyrgyz visa, as public transport between Osh and Batken travels through an Uzbek enclave. Private taxis can be persuaded to travel around the enclave, however.

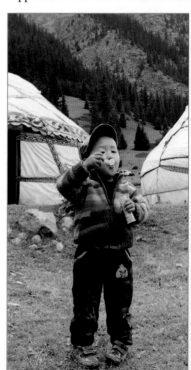

media, influential in Kyrgyzstan as well as at home, ran an anti-Bakiyev campaign, culminating in protests, bloody riots and an eventual coup in April 2010. Along with his son, Maxim, Bakiyev is alleged to have stolen more than $3 billion from Kyrgyzstan. Both men are wanted by Interpol.

Ousted from power, Bakiyev fled first to Osh and then with his family to Belarus. The vacuum of power was seized upon by the mafia to settle old scores, and the drug lords to pressurise the interim government into awarding them more favourable transit rates through the country. Under the guise of inter-ethnic violence, labourers in the south of the country were paid 2000 som (approximately $43) to kill both Uzbeks and Kyrgyz indiscriminately in a bid to destabilise the region. Violence between the communities inevitably escalated. At least 200 people died, 300,000 were internally displaced and 100,000 crossed the border into Uzbekistan as refugees.

Despite this, with its welcoming people, spectacular scenery and few of the visa and permit hassles that so dog tourism in the other Central Asian republics, Kyrgyzstan has huge tourism potential. Its network of fantastic community tourism projects unlocks the door to a unique world of yurts, nomads and mountain hospitality.

To experience fully the nomadic half of the schizophrenic Central Asian psyche you have to head up into the *jailoos* (pasturelands) of central Kyrgyzstan. Here the jagged northern Tian Shan soften into a landscape of rolling corduroy hillsides, rocky bluffs and high-altitude lakes that forms the border with China's Xinjiang province.

The road from Kashgar

The classic Silk Road route from Kashgar to Kyrgyzstan crosses the Torugart Pass. Logistically more complex than the other high road from China via Irkeshtam, though undoubtedly more photogenic, this crossing is one part of your trip that you need to arrange in advance through a travel agency. For one of Central Asia's most enthralling adventures, add overnight visits to Tash Rabat, Song-Kol and Kochkor and then arrange a yurt-stay excursion

Erkindik statue in Bishkek.

FATHER OF KYRGYZSTAN

The *Epic of Manas* is a traditional poem of more than 500,000 lines that has been transmitted orally through song for hundreds of years. Its exact origins are unknown, but what is certain is that in the 1920s and '30s the text was changed to reinforce a link between the hero, Manas, and the Kyrgyz people. The text is key to Kyrgyz national identity as it describes the unification of seven tribes into a single people. Consequently, the Kyrgyz government has promoted the epic heavily, celebrating its highly-debatable 1,000th anniversary in 1995 and building a Manas-themed park in Talas. The official line also claims it is the world's longest poem; it may have the most verses, but the Indian *Mahabharata* has more words.

Community-based Tourism

The best way to experience the nomadic flavour and natural hospitality of Kyrgyzstan is to stay with a mountain community.

The network of homestays, herders, yurt-owners and others that make up the Community-Based Tourism (CBT) organisation offers a unique chance to experience rural Kyrgyzstan. It was established in 2003 with Swiss assistance as part of measures to improve living conditions in remote mountain communities, by developing small-scale sustainable ecotourism initiatives. The family-based initiatives are not only sustainable but perfectly suited to the hospitality-rich but infrastructure-light nature of tourism in Kyrgyzstan. The CBT umbrella organisation provides training and marketing, but the bulk of the money (80–90 percent) goes directly to the service providers.

Making butter from milk outside traditonal yurts on the high mountain path from Osh.

Given some warning, the various branches of the CBT organisation can arrange everything from transport, homestays, yurt-stays and English-speaking guides to multi-day horse treks. For larger groups they can arrange workshops on yurt construction or felt-making, and can even arrange concerts of traditional Kyrgyz music.

A true adventure

Don't expect this to be a pampered, high-end experience. Your bed is likely to be a pile of duvets and a sheet: clean but simple. Transport will be a Soviet-era Zhiguli that's unlikely to start at the first attempt, and you may have to wait a few hours for your horses to arrive from the local pastures. However, this is a truly unique cultural experience.

One of the great things about the yurt-stays is the opportunity to try fresh dairy products, such as fantastic yoghurt, *kaimak* (fresh cream) and *airan* (yoghurt drink). For dinner expect such staples as *laghman* (noodles), *manti* (mutton dumplings) or *shorpo* (potato, carrot and mutton soup), plus plenty of *kok chai* (green tea) and snacks like *boorsuk* (fried dough pieces) and *kurut* (dried yoghurt balls). If you're lucky, you might get to try the traditional Kyrgyz dish *besh barmak* (noodles, meat and sauce), named "five fingers" because it is traditionally eaten with one's hands.

There are branches of CBT in almost every corner of the country: in Kyzyl-Oi (Suusamyr Valley), Arslanbob, Jalalabad, Kara-Suu (for Lake Sary-Chelek), Kazarman, Kochkor, Naryn, Aral, Kupuro Bazar, Talas, Bokonbayevo, Karakol, Tamchy, Batken, Alay, Kerben, Sary-Moghul and Chong-Kemin. Enquiries and bookings are best made online as the level of English spoken in the regional offices is sometimes limited.

CBT offers horse-riding through the walnut forests of Arslanbob, horse and foot treks to the alpine lakes of Sary-Chelek and Song-Kol, hikes into the Tian Shan mountains behind Karakol, jeep safaris through Central Kyrgyzstan and mountain bike cycling tours of Issyk-Kul and steppes (see videos on website). In rural areas their homestays are almost always the best places to stay. And with prices as low as $10 per night for accommodation and $10 for a day's horse hire, this is one of the Silk Road's best travel bargains. For detailed descriptions of the various options check out www.cbtkyrgyzstan.kg.

through the community-based organisation there (see page 232).

Torugart to Kochkor

Flush from the relief of clearing Kyrgyzstan immigration, you'll soon pass the beautiful lake and nature reserve of **Chatyr-Kol** before ascending to the Tuz-Bel Pass. After the desert scenery of Xinjiang, the rolling green hills and mountains come as quite a shock. The surrounding hills are often covered in snow as late as June, which makes for challenging driving conditions. The road crosses one final border-zone checkpoint to crest the Ak-Beyit Pass before descending into the Kara-Koyuk Valley. The only traffic you are likely to see along this stretch is the occasional truckload of scrap metal headed for China.

The one unmissable Silk Road site in central Kyrgyzstan is **Tash Rabat** (Stone Caravanserai), a fantastically atmospheric 15th-century caravanserai hidden up a side valley, 7km (4 miles) off the main highway. Restored in the 1980s, the stone interior includes stables and two dungeons. There is also basic accommodation, sleeping on the wooden benches that visitors sit on by day. Two yurt camps at the base of the site offer simple but cosy accommodation. It's possible to arrange a horse trek up to the pass behind the caravanserai for views over Chatyr-Kol, or you can continue over the pass to overnight in a CBT yurt on the silent shores of the lake.

About 20km (12 miles) past the turn-off to Tash Rabat the road temporarily expands into a three-lane superhighway, a former military airstrip, before passing the small fortress of Koshoy Kurgan to the left. The lonely ruins are connected to the great warrior-hero Manas, who allegedly built the site for his companion Koshoy.

The views north to the At-Bashy range open up as the highway bypasses the small settlement of At-Bashy and climbs up to the Kyzyl-Bel (Red Saddle) Pass, before finally descending into the Naryn Valley.

Naryn

Naryn is a popular overnight stop for Torugart travellers, though the long,

TIP

The CBT offices in Kochkor and Naryn can arrange transport, yurt-stays at Song-Kol lake and two- or three-day horse treks into the Song-Kol basin. They can also organise *jailoo* trips; two of the most popular locations are *Sarala-Saz*, 64km (38 miles) northwest of Kochkor, and the two- to four-day horse trek to *Kol Ukock* lake, to the east.

Yurts at Song-Kol.

strung-out Soviet town is fairly grim. On the western edge of town, past the army base, is a garish new mosque financed in the 1990s by Saudi Arabia. The regional museum is worth a quick look for its examples of yurts and *shyrdaks*, as is the art gallery on the main square displaying work from contemporary Kyrgyz artists. The Naryn River that flows through town is a major branch of the Syr Darya (Jaxartes).

From Naryn the main highway continues north to Bishkek, but a little-travelled dirt road branches west directly to the Fergana Valley, via Kazarman. It's a rough route that demands a reliable car. Along the route is a very remote collection of over 10,000 petroglyphs, at **Saimaluu Tash**. The 3,000-year-old petroglyphs (*saimaluu tash* means "Embroidered Stones" in Turkic) date from the Bronze Age to the Saka era, depicting ibex, shamanic ceremonies and warfare, and are a proposed Unesco World Heritage Site. The local CBT office can arrange a three-day return trip to the site on horseback, and this is undoubtedly the best way to see it.

On parade in Ala-Too Square, Bishkek.

A major highlight of central Kyrgyzstan is **Song-Kol**, a large and remote high-altitude lake cradled in a large bowl halfway between Naryn and Kochkor. Every year between June and August herders bring their flocks here to graze the lush pastures, and mushroom-like yurts sprout along the lakeshore. Visitors can reach the lake by road from the south or east, though the best way to visit is to follow the herders' example and make your way here on horseback. The views of the lake and mountains are unparalleled, and the overnight stay here in a simple yurt is a highlight of any trip to Kyrgyzstan.

Kochkor

Further north along the main highway, the town of **Kochkor** is the hub of tourism in central Kyrgyzstan. It's the epicentre of a remarkable experiment in community-based tourism (see page 232) that has spread like wildfire throughout the country, even into the neighbouring republics.

The CBT organisation can put you in touch with the town's 20 local

Bishkek

0 ___ 500 m
0 ___ 500 yds

homestays and also the **Altyn Kol** organisation, a co-operative of over 200 Kyrgyz women that produces and markets traditionally and locally made *shyrdaks* (Kyrgyz felt carpets). The quality is top-notch, and the association provides a much-needed additional source of income to a community that was hit particularly hard by the demise of the Soviet Union.

One of the best things you can do in Kyrgyzstan is take a trip out to the *jailoos*, summer pastures at an elevation of around 2,500–3,000 metres (8,200–9,800ft), where you can get a real taste of traditional Kyrgyz life. There are half a dozen locations around Kochkor where you can visit local herders, stay overnight in a yurt and ride horses. If you want, you can even take part in herders' chores, from milking and making yoghurt to herding the animals. You can string together locations to make a foot or horse trek of anywhere from two days to a week or more, visiting en route high-alpine lakes, petroglyphs, waterfalls and some dramatic scenery. You can also observe traditional horse games, especially in late July or August. Most exciting is *ulak-tartysh*, similar to the Afghan *buzkashi*, in which two teams compete on horseback to capture and then carry a 20kg (44lb) goat carcass into a designated goal. It's a wild, exciting game that takes great skill. Also popular is *kish-kuumai*, a form of kiss-chase, in which a male rider tries to catch a female opponent, despite her advantage of a head start and a faster horse. Rooted in the practice of bride-kidnapping, these days the race provides plenty of opportunities for flirting on the grasslands.

Bishkek

Kyrgyzstan's capital, **Bishkek**, is a pleasant city of around 1 million people. It is often described as the polite younger brother of the former Kazakh capital Almaty, just a couple of hours' drive to the north, and it certainly retains a relaxed, small-town feel. Unlike many of Central Asia's settlements, it's not a great city of antiquity. It started life as a fort guarding the trade routes at the fringe of the Kokand Khanate before becoming

The colourful shyrdaks, or felt rugs made by Kyrgyz women are used to decorate yurts and are given as wedding gifts.

SOUVENIR SHYDRAKS

If you only pick up one souvenir in Kyrgyzstan, make it a *shyrdak*, the felt carpets that are handmade in the highlands of central Kyrgyzstan. Kochkor, Bokonbaev and Bishkek are all good places to find a *shyrdak,* though purists claim the best examples come from Naryn.

Felt-making has long been an important summer activity for Kyrgyz women. The wool is first cleaned by beating it with sticks and is then spread over reeds as boiling water and soap are poured over it. The soggy wool is then rolled up into a tight tube and repeatedly rolled back and forth using opposing sets of ropes. The procedure is then repeated, before the felt is laid out to dry.

Shyrdaks are made from appliqué, not pressed, felt so the designs are cut out from the felt and then hand-stitched together, with a border sewn onto the sides as a final touch. The carpet motifs have their origins in the natural environment, with ibex horns, rams' horns, bird tracks and plant designs among the most popular. Brightly coloured Soviet chemical dyes supplanted traditional muted browns and greys in the 1970s, but these days natural dyes are making a comeback, particularly among NGO-supported *shyrdak* co-operatives. Crimson cochineal comes from the insect of the same name, and dark greens are extracted from motherwort.

The Burana Tower near Bishkek is all that remains of the city of Balasagun, once an important trading centre on the Silk Road.

An illustration of the traditional art of paper-making.

the Russian garrison town of Pishpek in 1878. Renamed Frunze in 1926 by the Soviets after the leader of the Red Army who was born here, it was only after independence in 1991 that it took the name Bishkek.

Bishkek's physical centre is **Ala-Too Square**, where locals gather to picnic and have their photos taken amongst the flowers and fountains, or to protest in more trying times. The central Lenin statue is gone, replaced by a statue of Erkindik (Freedom), but the capital has seen little of the mass-scale whitewashing of the Soviet era that is so apparent in neighbouring Uzbekistan. Lenin is still hanging around, after all; he's just been demoted to the back of the building, a short skip away from fellow ideologue Karl Marx.

Facing the square to the north is the **State Historical Museum** (Tue–Sun 10am–3pm; charge), worth a visit as an introduction to Kyrgyz culture and also for the mural of an American cowboy riding astride a Pershing missile. Fans of Lenin will not be disappointed – this was once the Lenin Museum, and many of the original

exhibits remain. On the west side of the square is the Kyrgyz government building known as the White House, from where snipers shot protestors during the 2010 coup.

To the east is leafy Dubovy (Oak) Park, where a second statue of Erkindik has replaced the image of Felix Dzerzhinsky, founder of the Soviet secret police. Another Soviet construction is the **Frunze House Museum** (Tue–Fri 9am–5pm, Sat–Sun 9am–4pm; charge), built around the supposed childhood home of the Red Army general. As the man who led the Soviet capture of Bukhara and Khiva and smashed the local *Basmachi* rebel movement, Frunze is not a likely hero of Bishkek, but locals still maintain the museum and his statue opposite the railway station on Erkindik nonetheless.

Also check out the Philharmonia to the west, fronted by a large statue of Manas, the World War II monument and the **Russian Orthodox Church**, the spiritual centre of Bishkek's large Russian population. The **Fine Arts Museum** (Tue–Thu, Sat–Sun

THE DEFINING BATTLE

Few pivotal moments in world history are as little-known as the Battle of Talas, in AD 751, when Arab and Chinese armies fought each other for five furious days in the middle of summer near the modern border of Kazakhstan and Kyrgyzstan.

In the end the Chinese armies were routed after their allies switched allegiances mid-battle. The clash defined the limits of Arab and Tang Chinese expansion and shaped the Islamic face of Central Asia for centuries to come. Samarkand became a great centre of papermaking thanks to skills learnt from Chinese prisoners of war. The spilled secrets of paper and silk production spread along the Silk Road from Samarkand to Baghdad and on to Europe, where they sparked an intellectual revolution.

9am–5pm, Fri 10am–4pm; charge) on Abdurakhmanov has a permanent collection of Kyrgyz folk art, including textiles, and also hosts temporary exhibitions of work from modern Russian artists. End the day with a performance at the charming neo-classical **Opera House** (charge for performances) or, alternatively, a shot of vodka and a brief flogging with birch branches at the sauna **Zhirgal Banya** (variable days 8am–9pm; charge) on Toktogul Street.

Around Bishkek

Wherever you stand in Bishkek the snow-capped range of the Kyrgyz Ala-tau frames the horizon to the south. Several travel agents in town can arrange treks, climbs, heli-skiing or picnics in the fine alpine valleys, just a short ride from the city.

The most popular trekking area is the **Ala-Archa National Park**, where trails lead up to a dilapidated ski centre or up the Ak-Say Canyon into a stunning mountain amphitheatre of snow-capped peaks. Climbers head here to ascend peaks Korona (4,860 metres/16,038ft) and Uchityel (4,572 metres/15,088ft). Other parallel canyons worth exploring to the southeast are the **Alameddin Canyon**, with its hot-springs sanatorium, and the **Kegeti Canyon**, where travel agents offer horse-riding and hiking trips.

The Chuy Valley

The most popular excursion from Bishkek is to the **Burana Tower** (open 8am–5pm; charge), Kyrgyzstan's only major Silk Road site, 80km (48 miles) east of the capital. The ruins have been identified as the 11th-century Kara-khanid city of Balasagun, though the Mongols called it Gobolik when they passed through in 1218. The collection of Nestorian crosses, Chinese coins and Buddhist carvings on display in the site museum point to the cosmopolitan nature of the city, though all that remains today is the heavily restored minaret, now half its original height of 44 metres (140ft). Climb the minaret for views of the city walls. Surrounding the site is a fine collection of 1,500-year-old *balbals*, man-shaped stone grave markers or totems.

Several other minor settlements litter the Chuy Valley, which once formed a popular side branch of the Northern Silk Road. Though little remains, they point to an intriguing meeting of the Sogdian, Turkic and Chinese worlds. Xuanzang recorded several of the sites during his trip through the valley in AD 620, and Chang Chun passed through in 1220 en route from China to the court of Genghis Khan.

Ak-Beshim, 7km (4 miles) southeast of Tokmok, is thought to be the ancient settlement of Suyab, a capital of the Western (Blue) Turks. Excavations have revealed a Buddhist temple and Nestorian church, along with a Chinese fortress raised here in AD 679, but there is sadly little to see today. The city was later eclipsed by Balasagun.

The 6th- to 12th-century remains of **Navekat** (modern Krasnaya Rechka) have recently come under Unesco

One of the many balbals surrounding the Burana Tower.

protection. Modern excavations have unearthed a golden burial mask, an 8-metre (26-ft) -long reclining Buddha, the remains of a Zoroastrian fire temple and also artefacts suggesting the presence of Manicheans and Nestorian Christians. Clearly, Navekat was once a cosmopolitan settlement, though the key discoveries made here have been removed to museums in St Petersburg and Bishkek.

The nearby town of **Tokmok** carries a certain infamy as the centre of a 1916 revolt against Tsarist Russian rule (and attempts at conscription) that resulted in 120,000 Kyrgyz deaths. Another 120,000 fled over the Tian Shan to Xinjiang, with thousands more dying en route. The event is now known as the *Urkhun*, or Exodus. You may want to stop for a photo alongside the **MIG fighter jet** on the outskirts of the town, and there is also a small **archaeological museum** with labels in Russian.

Lake Issyk-Kul

The pearl of the Tian Shan is **Issyk-Kul** (Ysyk-Köl in Kyrgyz), a great turquoise inland sea dusted with sandy shores and framed on both sides by snow-capped peaks. At 180km (108 miles) long, it is the world's second-largest alpine lake, after Bolivia's Lake Titicaca, and the second largest saline lake after the Caspian Sea. The local Kyrgyz named it "Warm Lake" because, despite the altitude, it never freezes, due to its slight salinity. Unusually, over 80 streams flow into the lake but none flow out. To the north rises the Kungey (Sunny) Ala-Too range; to the south is the Terskey (Dark) Ala-Too.

The lake's scenic shores have long been popular with visitors. The submerged Saka-Usun settlement of Chigu on the northern shore dates from the 2nd century BC, and Saka (Scythian) burial mounds dot the northeastern shoreline. Genghis Khan and Timur both led their armies nearby. Russian and Ukrainian settlers built their gingerbread Tsarist buildings on the lakeshore in the late 19th century, and Soviet apparatchiks flocked here in the 1970s to soak in its sanatoria.

It was near Issyk-Kul that Xuanzang came across the magnificent tented court of the Blue Turks, surrounded by lush summer pasturage. He described "riders mounted on camels or horses, dressed in furs and fine woollen cloth and carrying long lances, banners and straight bows". The multitude "stretched so far that the eye could not tell where it ended". It was the last-ever description of the great nomad confederation, which fragmented soon afterwards.

The northern shore

The northern shore of the lake is easily the more developed, with more frequent transport, sandier beaches and better tourist facilities. There are simple homestays at the villages of Tamchy and Cholpan-Ata, and the upmarket hotels and renovated sanatoria appeal to wealthy Kazakhs and Russians as well as domestic tourists. Trekkers will want to explore

Lake Issyk-Kul.

the network of trails that lead up the northern valleys, past verdant meadows and glaciers and over the high passes to Almaty in Kazakhstan.

One site worth a visit is the collection of 2,000-year-old **petroglyphs** at Cholpon-Ata. The hundreds of Scythian-era rock carvings depict ibex, wolves and hunting scenes.

Perhaps the most intriguing site on the northern shore is **Svetly Mys**, the location of eight Nestorian, Armenian, then Russian Orthodox monasteries, all built around the alleged burial site of St Matthew. Although little of the original buildings remain (the last monastery was burned and the monks killed in 1916), the church and almshouses have been restored for use as a children's home. There is also a craft workshop on site.

Karakol and the Tian Shan

Founded in 1869 by Tsarist military officers, the pleasant settlement of **Karakol**, at the southeast corner of the lake, is the biggest town in the region and an increasingly popular base for adventure tourists headed into the surrounding Tian Shan mountains. Time your visit for a Sunday and you'll get to catch both of the town's highlights – the bustling weekly animal market and the morning liturgy at the wooden **Holy Trinity Cathedral**. The town's excellent tourist information centre and network of homestays can help smooth out the logistics of your visit.

Worth checking out in the north of town is the Dungan mosque, built in 1910 by the town's community of Dungans, Muslim Chinese who crossed the border at the end of the 19th century, and also the **Regional History Museum** (daily 9am–5pm; charge) with its display of stuffed wildlife, musical instruments and, most interestingly, old photographs of the area.

One easy excursion from Karakol is to the Tsarist-era **Przhewalsky Memorial**, 7km (4 miles) northwest

from town. Famed for his expeditions to Mongolia, Tibet, Xinjiang and the Gobi between 1870 and 1885 and for the discovery of the diminutive brand of wild horse that still bears his name, Przhewalsky died in a nearby hospital after contracting typhus during the final preparations for an upcoming expedition. Lord Curzon wrote of Przhewalsky that he "deserved to be ranked with Livingstone and Stanley in this century as a pioneer of scientific exploration in an unknown and perilous continent". The interesting Soviet-era museum overlooks a former secret torpedo research centre.

Karakol's real draw is its proximity to the wild valleys of the Tian Shan. Local travel agencies and the CBT office can arrange transport, accommodation and yurt-stays, though nothing beats camping in these achingly beautiful valleys. The most popular destination is the **Altyn Arashan Valley**, a bone-shaking drive to the southeast, where you can soak in a hot spring while savouring views over alpine meadows and pine forests to the peaks of the Tian Shan. Equally

Coaxing a reluctant donkey across the river in Altyn Arashan Valley.

FACT

At 7,439 metres (24,510ft), Mount Pobedy (Tomur Feng) is the highest peak in Kyrgyzstan. It is located in the Tian Shan range in the far northeast of the country and marks the border with China. It is one of the five ex-Soviet 7,000 metre- (23,000 ft-) summits (including Lenin Peak) known as the 'Snow Leopards'.

An eagle hunter in action.

good for trekking is the **Karakol Valley**, just behind Karakol town.

Another good overnight excursion is the **Jeti-Oghuz** (**Seven Bulls**) **Valley**, southwest of town. Neither the Soviet-era sanatorium or the eroded rock formations that name the valley are really worth the fuss, but the yurt camps further upstream in the Valley of Flowers offer an opportunity for non-trekkers to get a taste of the fine alpine scenery.

The road east of Karakol winds over the mountains into the Engilchek (Inylchek) Valley, opening up trekking routes to the Engilchek Glacier and Khan Tengri base camp. This region offers some of the world's most spectacular trekking, but you need to arrange the trip well in advance with an experienced trekking company.

The southern shore

The southern shore of Issyk-Kul remains wilder, rockier and less visited than the northern route, but provides a useful loop route back to the eastern shore, and local travel companies offer some intriguing activities here, from regional food festivals to displays of eagle hunting and multi-day horse treks.

The Kyrgyz village of **Barskoon** is perhaps the most interesting stop along the southern route. Here you can shop for a yurt at the Ak Orgo Yurt Workshop on Lenina, track down ancient Tibetan rock inscriptions at nearby Tamga Tash or, best of all, arrange a multi-day horse trek through the company Shepherds Way (www.kyrgyztrek.com), which is based in the village. It's also possible to be put up at one of several local yurt-stays, if arranged in advance. The company Ecotour (www.ecotour.kg) has several eco-friendly yurt camps in the region, and the CBT can arrange accommodation. Silk Road fanatics can follow the paved road that leads south of town up the Barskoon River to a local waterfall. The road follows an ancient Silk Road branch that led over the Yshtyk Pass into the Ak-Shyrak region and then over the **Bedel Pass** (4,284 metres/14,136ft) into China. Xuanzang crossed this pass from Chinese Turkestan during his epic 7th-century voyage. Centuries later, thousands of Kyrgyz died along the route fleeing Russian troops in July

EAGLE HUNTING

For millennia the Kyrgyz and Kazakhs of the Tian Shan, Altai and Western Mongolia have used trained eagles to hunt for prey. Eagle hunting (*berkutchi*) as a way of life largely died out during the Soviet era, but a few hunters still keep the ancient skills alive. Training the eagle is an extremely labour-intensive exercise, and the resulting relationship between master and bird often lasts for 20 or 30 years. A trained golden eagle once cost as much as five camels.

Hunters hood the young eagles and use a *shyrga* (the skin of a hare or fox filled with straw) to train the bird slowly to hunt anything from marmots to foxes and hares. The other main tool of the trade is the *bardak*, a special wooden prop designed for a saddle and used to help support the weight of the huge birds.

1916. Today the road leads to **Kumtor**, the gold mine that provides 20 percent of Kyrgyzstan's total exports and a remarkable 55 percent of its industrial output. The pass to China is not open to foreigners.

Irkeshtam route

The latest international crossing to open between China and Central Asia is at Irkeshtam (Erkech-Tam), one of two routes that now cross into Kyrgyzstan from Kashgar, the other being the Torugart Pass (see page 231). Irkeshtam has quickly become the most popular mountain crossing into Central Asia, largely because it doesn't require the finicky transport arrangements that plague the Torugart crossing. It's a scenically spectacular Silk Road route that offers the most direct way into the Fergana Valley.

The road from the border descends into the Alay Valley, opening up superlative views of 7,134-metre (23,542-ft) Lenin Peak (also known as Pik Lenin and Koh-i-Garmo, "the Warm Peak"), one of the largest peaks in the Pamir range. At the crossroads village of Sary Tash, travellers can either follow roads south into Tajikistan along the Pamir Highway, west into the Alay Valley or north over the 3,615-metre (11,930-ft) Taldyk Pass to Osh and the Fergana Valley. Homestays are available in Sary Tash, a small town in a beautiful setting well over 3,000metres (10,000ft) above sea level.

The Alay Valley

The incredibly scenic **Alay** (**Alai**) **Valley** is located in one of the remotest corners of Central Asia and has more in common with the Pamir region of Tajikistan than with the rest of Kyrgyzstan. For climbers the valley offers easy access to Lenin Peak. The CBT branch at nearby Sary-Moghul can arrange trips to the mountain's base camp at Achik Tash. Extensive mountaineering experience is required to make the climb to the top, as are ice axes and crampons.

Further down the valley is the former fort of Doroot Korgan (Daraut Korgon), from where caravan routes once branched over the Pamir Alai range into the Fergana Valley. The main

TIP

Authentic eagle hunts only take place in winter, but the Tourist Information centre in Kadji-Sai and the CBT offices in Karakol and Bokonbaev can arrange summertime hunting displays at Tuura-Suu, Bokonbaev and Kadji-Sai on the southern shores of Lake Issyk-Kul. The August Bird of Prey Festival at Manzhuly-Ata, near Bokonbaev, features demonstration hunts and displays of falconry.

The beautiful landscape of the Pamir mountains in southern Kyrgyzstan.

river through the valley is the Kyzyl-Su, which continues into Tajikistan to become the Surkhob. Both names (in Kyrgyz and Tajik) mean "Red River".

Kyrgyz Fergana Valley

In many ways, the settled villages and towns of southern Kyrgyzstan have more in common with the oasis culture of Uzbekistan's Fergana Valley than with the rest of freewheeling northern Kyrgyzstan. With a significant Uzbek population, an Uzbek-style *chaikhana* and bazaar culture and a stronger Islamic identity, it's not surprising that there are occasional clan-based tensions with the more Russian-influenced north of the country. Ethnic tensions are ongoing here; in 1990 violence between local Uzbeks and Kyrgyz left over 300 dead and it spiralled out of control once again in summer 2010.

Osh

With a population of 220,000, **Osh** is Kyrgyzstan's second city and the administrative centre for the entire southern half of the country. The modern city has ancient roots as an early Silk Road city, and in 2000 celebrated its 3,000th anniversary. With the peaks of the Pamir Alai hanging tantalisingly in the distant haze to the south, the city is a starting point for trekkers and mountaineers headed into the high Pamirs.

Osh's main thoroughfare and central statue commemorates Kurmanjan Datka (1811–1907) – the "Empress of the Alay" – who became a rare female governor of the Alay district and oversaw the tricky transition from Kokandi to Russian overlordship. Look for her on the 50-som note.

Osh nestles at the base of the **Takht-i-Suleiman** (Throne of Suleiman), a huge slice of rock that ranks amongst Central Asians as Islam's third-holiest shrine, after Mecca and Medina, thanks to an early appearance by the prophet Suleiman (Solomon). Babur built a personal *chillakhana* (chamber for 40-day retreat) here in 1496, and the small shrine is still known as the Dom Babura (House of Babur). The shrine, which is sadly now no more than a metal hut dating from the mid-1990s, is a favourite among women

The Ozgon Mausoleum.

hoping to conceive. The view across Osh makes the climb worthwhile, particularly at sunrise or dusk.

At the base of the hill is the **Historical Museum** (9am–6pm; charge), next to what might well be the world's only three-storey yurt. Exhibits touch on the region's Silk Road history and offer glimpses of the petroglyphs at Saimaluu Tash and other local archaeological sites. Trails lead up from here to the Dom Babura and around the back of the hill, past an Islamic cemetery to the **Historical-Cultural Museum** (9am–6pm; charge), blasted into the side of the sacred hillside. This is not to be confused with the **Silk Road Museum** (9am–6pm; charge) at the bottom of the hill, whose range of archaeological and ethnographic displays contain pottery, handicrafts, weaponry and petroglyphs.

The other main sight is the huge central **Jayma (Friday) Bazaar**, which lines the churning Ak-Bura (White Camel) River. The lively bazaar, significantly damaged in 2010 but now on the road to recovery, is the one place in Osh that captures the spirit of the city's Silk Road past. It's also one of the best places in the country to buy the white felt Kyrgyz hat known as an *ak-kalpak*. It's the country's quintessential souvenir.

Other sights include the huge new central mosque and the **Lenin statue**, in the south of town by government offices, just one of several examples of Lenin memorabilia that still litter the town.

Around Osh

The best half-day detour from Osh is the 55km (33-mile) trip to **Ozgon** (Uzgen), a largely Uzbek town that is home to a heavily rebuilt 11th century minaret and a trio of ornate Karakhanid (11th–13th-century) mausoleums. The stunningly decorated tombs are noted for their fine incised terracotta decoration and probably provided inspiration for Samarkand's Shah-i-Zindah complex.

The local Ozgon branch of the CBT arranges homestays and horse treks into the **Kara-Shoro National Park** in the mountains above Ozgon. The nearby Kok-Art Pass is a more historically authentic Silk Road pass than either the Torugart or Irkeshtam crossings, but it's not open to international traffic these days.

Another excellent excursion is to **Arslanbap**, where another CBT branch office arranges horse treks through some of the world's largest walnut forests to a series of lovely mountain lakes.

The Uzbekistan border at Dostlyk is only 5km (3 miles) northwest of Osh. Much of the region is a victim of crazy jigsaw borders, delimited by Stalin, that have only gained an international solidity in the last decade. Kyrgyzstan's southern arm hosts several isolated enclaves, pockets of Uzbekistani and Tajikistani territory that are totally surrounded by Kyrgyzstan. The hardening of Uzbekistan's borders in the wake of terrorist activity here in the late 1990s has left much of the region out on a limb.

Lenin still proudly displayed in Osh.

YURTS

The nomadic lifestyle requires you to carry your home with you, and the humble yurt provides the perfect solution.

Along the length of the Silk Road, from the Kazakh steppe to the high Pamir and on into Xinjiang and Mongolia, wherever you find herders you'll see their curious felt houses known as yurts.

Described by travel writer Colin Thubron as resembling "badly done up parcels", yurts are in fact the ideal accommodation solution for any nomad on the move. Relatively portable, warm and spacious and made from raw materials supplied by the herders' own livestock, yurts can be constructed or taken down easily and quickly and carried away on the back of three camels (or more commonly these days, a truck).

It's no surprise then that yurts have been around for over a millennium. Genghis Khan reputedly had a yurt set on wheels and Tamerlane favoured the cosiness of his garden yurts to the cold grandeur of his stone palaces. The khans of Khiva built brick platforms for their winter yurts.

Travellers have the chance to stay in tourist yurts in Uzbekistan, Kazakhstan, Mongolia and parts of Xinjiang, though the most authentic are the yurt-stay programmes of Kyrgyzstan and Tajikistan, and a night in one of these yurts may just be a highlight of your Silk Road travels.

Intricate shyrdak decoration on a yurt exterior.

The wheel-shaped circular skylight, called a tunduk, is depicted on the national flag of Kyrgyzstan.

Time spent in a yurt gives you a ringside view of nomad chores – churning yoghurt, rolling out noodles, brewing up tea and even nursing sick or very young livestock.

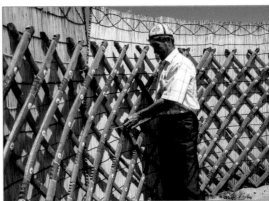

Constructing the yurt frame.

FUNDAMENTALS OF A YURT

All yurts have inherited a shared structure, though Mongolian yurts are generally bigger than their Central Asian counterparts. The main wooden skeleton of roof poles supports a collapsible concertina-like wooden lattice (*kerege* in Turkic) that forms the inner wall of the yurt. Reed mats form a middle wall, and thick grey or white felt is placed on top. The heaviest sections are the door frame and the circular skylight. The frame is tightened with woven strips and the floor is decorated with appliqué-felt carpets. The key to a yurt's success is felt – warm in winter, cool in summer and surprisingly waterproof.

The interior is divided into sections for the men and women of the yurt. As you walk in the front door, the kitchen is on the left, while hunting gear, horse tack and tools hang from the lattice walls of the men's section to the right. Guests are directed to the place of honour at the back of the yurt, in front of a large pile of bedclothes atop a wooden chest. The hearth and stove form the centre of the yurt, directly below an open skylight, which can be closed in bad weather by sliding a square of felt across the hole. Accessories generally include a shrine and a battery-powered radio.

Yurts are known by a variety of local names – buzoi in Kyrgyz, kiyizoi in Kazakh and ger in Mongolian – though we actually get the English term via the Russian word yurta.

...ven traditional ways of life can be brought into the 21st century, ...s here, where a yurt makes handy use of a solar energy panel.

...yurt can be assembled in a couple of hours. First comes the ...earth, then the floor, then the frame, the poles and finally the felt.

KAZAKHSTAN

From the sophistication of Astana and Almaty to the ancient sites at Turkistan, the Silk Road routes in Kazakhstan offer dramatic contrasts.

Main Attractions

Astana
Almaty
Almatinsky Nature
  Reserve
Bolshoe Almatinskoe
Taraz
Shymkent
Turkistan
Baikonur Cosmodrome

The dramatic Kazakh landscape.

Kazakhstan, the ninth-largest country in the world, covers an area greater than that of all the other Central Asian countries added together. Much of Kazakhstan is flat, arid steppe, but the southeast is home to forests and high mountains, which came within the sphere of influence of the main Silk Road settlements of modern-day Kyrgyzstan and Uzbekistan. A northern strand of the trade route passed along the Ili Valley in China through the Dzungarian Gate to continue west between Lake Balkash and the Zailiysky Alatau mountains. This summer route then followed the Chuy Valley of present-day Kyrgyzstan before reaching Taraz, where branches led southwest to Samarkand, via Shymkent and Otrar.

Kazakhstan has only really existed as a political entity since Soviet times; before that, it was a sparsely populated buffer zone between Russia and Central Asia. The exception was the far south.

The first settlers in the region were probably nomadic Scythians, whose *kurgans* (circular burial mounds) can still be seen dotting the countryside of southeast Kazakhstan and northern Kyrgyzstan. Various Turkic tribes followed, and by the early 10th century the cities of Otrar and Turkistan were developed in the south of the country. Karakhanid influence superseded that of the Bukhara-based Samanids in the 10th century, but Islam was temporarily replaced by Buddhism when Khitans invaded from Mongolia. The region returned to Islam when it was absorbed into the Khorezmshah Empire in the early 13th century.

As elsewhere, the arrival of Genghis Khan in 1218 would have fateful consequences. The leader's death in 1227 resulted in his empire being divided between his sons: the younger, Chagatai, inherited the land that included southern Kazakhstan, while the elder, Jochi, took on the territory to the north and the west.

Like the Kyrgyz, to whom they are closely related, Kazakhs have their roots in the Mongol tribes of southern Siberia. They first arrived around the turn of the 16th century, but became subjugated by the Oirats, another Mongol clan, at the end of the following century.

Russian influence began in the 18th century, and in the 1820s the Kazakhs swore allegiance to the Tsar in order to receive protection from the Kokand Khanate to the south. The Russians, who were active participants in the Great Game, were only too happy to establish a military presence in the region. Slavic settlers poured in throughout the late 19th and early 20th centuries, especially after the Trans-Aral Railway between Orenburg and Tashkent was completed in 1906, and Russians continued to arrive during the Soviet period. Even today, Kazakhstan has a considerable Russian population, with just 60 percent of the national total being Kazakhs and the remainder Russians and other races that include Tatars, Uzbeks and Uighurs.

Astana

Most visits will begin in the country's brash capital Astana, created in the 1990s along the Ishim River. Everything is brand new and built to impress, with enough sights for a couple of days. The **National Museum** (Tue, Thu–Sun 10am–6pm, Wed until 9pm; charge) opened in 2014 and houses the famous 'Golden Man' armour. The **Bayterek Tower** (daily 10am–9pm; charge), meaning "Tree of Life" offers wonderful panoramic city views. Shopping has a modern twist at the **Khan Shatyr** (Royal Marquee) designed by Norman Foster, who also created the Palace of Peace and Reconciliation glass pyramid. The guided tour fee includes a visit to the apex viewpoint

Almaty

Almaty remains Kazakhstan's largest and most sophisticated city – a metropolis of wide boulevards and leafy parks from where the snow-capped peaks of the Zailiysky Alatau range loom tantalisingly close to the south. It has a certain old-fashioned

Fresh, seasonal fruits for sale in Almaty.

Zenkov Cathedral.

ENTERING AND LEAVING KAZAKHSTAN

The train network in Kazakhstan is very useful, as most Silk Road sites lie on the main route linking Almaty with Moscow (see page 385).

A daily bus links Yining in Xinjiang, **China**, with Almaty, crossing at Korgas; a twice-weekly train operates between Urumqi and Almaty via the border post at Dostyk. There are two other road crossings at Koljat and Bakhty. There are five crossing points into **Kyrgyzstan**. The route between Almaty and Bishkek has regular bus and shared taxi services that take 3–5 hours. Further bus services link Almaty with Cholpon-Ata at Lake Issyk-Kul in summer.

A major highway leads south from Shymkent, west of Almaty, to Tashkent just across the **Uzbekistan** border at Yallama. Taxis go to the border, but walk across on foot. A railway link leads south to Tashkent from the junction at Arys, west of Shymkent. The rail crossing between Beyneu and Nukus is remote but efficient. A single border crossing with Turkmenistan at Bekdash/Yeralievo operates well.

Irregular ferries link Aktau with Baku in **Azerbaijan**.

Fifteen crossing points lead into **Russia** along Kazakhstan's northern border: north of Semey; north of Astana via Pavlodar and Petropavlovsk; west of Astana via Kostanai; north of Uralsk and west of Atyrau towards Astrakhan. Long-distance trains link Almaty with Moscow and with Novosibirsk, and Almaty and Astana with Moscow via Petropavlovsk.

Malus sieversii is a wild apple native to Central Asia.

charm and resembles a fairly typical Russian city, transported wholesale to remote Central Asia.

The city stands on the site of an old Silk Road settlement destroyed by Genghis Khan's hordes, and the present-day city – originally called Verniy – was established as a Russian outpost in 1854. It was badly damaged by earthquakes in 1887 and 1911, and renamed Alma-Ata in 1921. Following the construction of the Turkestan–Siberia Railway, it became the capital of Soviet Kazakhstan in 1927. Deported Koreans and Volga Germans swelled the existing Russian population during World War II and, even today, ethnic Kazakhs have only a marginal majority in a city that still has a very Russian character.

Around town

Most notable is the brightly painted, all-wood **Zenkov Cathedral**, that shines like a beacon through the pines of **Panfilov Park**. The cathedral, as any local will tell you, was constructed in 1904 without the use of nails. With its western tower standing 56 metres (185ft) tall, Zenkov Cathedral is one of the world's tallest wooden buildings, but it is more than a mere museum piece: the place resounds with the rich voices of its Russian congregation each Sunday morning. Panfilov Park is also home to a bold brass **war memorial** and eternal flame that celebrate the heroics of General Ivan Panfilov's division during World War II.

The **Museum of Musical Instruments** (Tue–Sun 10am–6pm; charge), is located in a curious wooden building near the park's eastern entrance. It houses a wide collection of traditional drum and string instruments, along with recordings of their sounds, with live concerts most evenings. For a taste of rural Kazakhstan a visit to nearby **Zelyony Bazaar** (Green Market), just north of the park, is also recommended.

The **Central State Museum** (Tue–Sun 10am–6pm; charge) has displays outlining Kazakhstan's history together with sections on natural history, ethnography and even space flight.

ORIGIN OF THE APPLE

There is a clue in the name of the Kazakh capital, Almaty, which, in its earlier form, Alma-Ata, translates as "father of the apple". It was originally thought that the 20,000 varieties of the domestic apple known today evolved from the chance hybridisation of several wild species, but recent DNA analysis has revealed that the progenitor of the modern apple is derived from a single species, *Malus sieversii*, that hails from the forests of southeast Kazakhstan's Dzungarian Alatau range, close to the Chinese frontier.

With this knowledge, US scientists are now returning to Kazakhstan to investigate the disease-resistant properties of the domestic apple's forefather. Almaty, it would seem, is a name well-chosen.

The **Kastayev Museum of Fine Arts** (Tue–Sun 10am–6pm; charge), west of the centre, has works by Soviet, Kazakh and European painters, and a collection of Kazakh handicrafts and carpets. Almaty also has a number of fine Soviet-period buildings, including the 1934 neoclassical **Abay Academic Opera and Ballet Theatre**, opposite the Hotel Almaty. Try to catch a bargain-price performance here.

Respublika Alangy, is the city's most prestigious square, with fountains, an independence monument and more neoclassical buildings. Next to the Palace of the Republic, a cable car climbs Kök-Tyube (Tobe or Green Hill) for sweeping city views, often through a pollution haze. There is an apple monument and appropriate Beatles statue.

Around Almaty

The picture-perfect Zailiysky Alatau mountains, spurs of the great Tian Shan range, offer city-dwellers a place to picnic, walk and escape Almaty's summer heat and pollution.

One easy excursion is to **Medeu**, an Olympic-sized ice rink that has trained generations of Soviet ice stars. Medeu is perfect for skating in winter, and in summer it serves as a good base for walks into the pine-clad foothills that lie immediately above it. There is also the option of a swimming pool just below the ice rink, though it is filled with chilly mountain water! Further along the same road, but considerably higher up, the **Shymbulak ski resort** is open from November to April and provides a useful base for hikes during the rest of the year.

East of Almaty, the **Almatinsky Nature Reserve** (Almatinsky Zapovednik) is home to Pik Talgar, at 4,979 metres (16,430ft) the highest point in the Zailiysky Alatau. Snow leopards are present in the reserve, but the likelihood of seeing one is extremely remote; however, you might see an arkhar, a large-horned wild sheep native to the region.

West of the city, **Bolshoe Almatinskoe** ("Big Almaty") lake is located high up in the gorge of the Bolshaya Almatinka River. This stunning blue

TIP

The dramatic Charyn Canyon lies 175km (109 miles) east of Almaty and is well worth a visit. Sculpted by the action of wind and the Charyn River flowing down from the Tian Shan, its sandstone cliffs and arches rise to several hundred metres. Downstream is the Red Canyon or Valley of the Castles, named after the spectacular rock formations.

Travellers hiking in the Tian Shan mountains.

Almaty

0 — 500 m
0 — 500 yds

TIP

Visits to Baikonur are possible if organised through a Kazakh or Russian tour company, but are expensive and tangled with red tape. Those fortunate enough to get in can visit the launch pad from where the Soviet cosmonauts rocketed into space, the cosmonauts' "hotel" and a museum that has displays of space food and some personal belongings of Yuri Gagarin.

alpine lake lies in the shadow of three towering peaks – Soviet (4,317 metres/14,240ft) to the southeast, Ozerniy (4,110 metres/13,560ft) to the south and Tourist Peak (3,954 metres/13,000ft) to the southwest – and serves as a starting point for treks into Kyrgyzstan.

Southen Kazakhstan

The city of **Taraz** (**Dzhambul**) went the way of many former Silk Road settlements when it was destroyed by Genghis Khan's Mongol army in the early 13th century. Hitherto it had been an important Karakhanid settlement. Taraz was eventually rebuilt as a frontier town of the Kokand Khanate before coming under Russian rule in the 19th century. A single Karakhanid monument, albeit a 20th-century Soviet reconstruction, still remains in a park just south of Park Lenina – the mausoleum of an 11th-century khan. The Daudbek Shamansaur mausoleum, built for an important 13th-century Mongol, stands nearby. The city's **History Museum** (Mon–Sat 9am–6pm; charge) has a collection

The tomb of Khoja Ahmed Yassawi in Turkistan.

of *balbals* (Turkic burial stones) and an exhibition on the history of the Silk Road.

The only remnants of ancient Taraz that still stand are to be found 18km (11 miles) west at Golavachovka, where there is the 12th-century Karakhanid **Mausoleum of Aishi Bibi**, conserved within a protective glass box next to the reconstructed 11th-century **Mausoleum of Babadzi-Khatun**.

Shymkent

Shymkent, an industrial city of half a million people, 200km (120 miles) southwest of Taraz, was yet another Silk Road caravan town that was razed to the ground by invading Mongols. The Kokand Khanate constructed a fort here in the early 19th century, which was subsequently annexed by Tsarist Russia in 1864.

Shymkent's busy bazaar and **Regional Studies and History Museum** (Tue–Sun 9am–6pm; charge), with its Silk Road exhibit, are the sights of most interest for present-day visitors. For those with an interest in the excesses of the Stalinist period, the **Museum for Commemoration of Victims of Political Repressions** does exactly what its name suggests.

Sayram

Sayram, 10km (6 miles) east of Shymkent, is far older, although there is little hard evidence of its supposed 3,000-year history other than a mention in the Zoroastrian holy book, the Avesta. This small town is best known as the birthplace of Sufi teacher Khoja Ahmed Yassawi (see page 251).

Otrar

Also known as Al-Farabi because it was the birthplace of the famous Islamic scientist and philosopher **Abu Nasr al-Farabi** (*c.*872–950), Otrar has unfortunate associations with Genghis Khan. Following the ill-advised murder of his envoy, the Mongol leader mounted a siege in 1219 that lasted for six months before

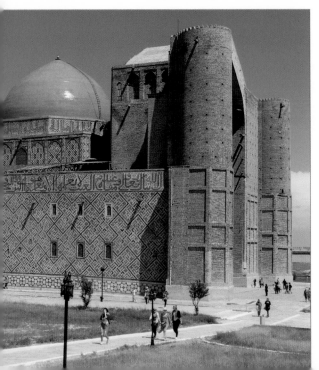

he finally breached the city walls and slaughtered almost everyone within. Prior to this, Otrar was a collection of oases that together formed one of the most flourishing settlements along the Silk Road.

These days Otrar, 170km (102 miles) northwest of Shymkent, is effectively just an archaeological site, although it has Unesco World Heritage status. Much is still to be excavated, but evidence of bathhouses, kilns, walls and a mosque can all be seen. Close to the site stands the **Mausoleum of Arystan-Bab** (an early tutor of Khoja Ahmed Yassawi), a 20th-century rebuild of an earlier 14th-century structure and an important pilgrimage site. The nearby village of Shauildir has a **museum** dedicated to the life and work of al-Farabi.

Turkistan

This university town on the fringes of the Kyzylkum desert, 60km (36 miles) north of Otrar, is home to Kazakhstan's most important Islamic monument and pilgrimage site: the 14th-century Timurid tomb of the Sufi saint **Khoja Ahmed Yassawi**.

Turkistan, formerly known as Hazrat-e-Turkestan, and as Shavgar or Yassi until the 16th century, was a Karakhanid trade centre before it came under the rule of the Kokand Khanate in the early 19th century. Khoja Ahmed Yassawi was a Sufi poet and scholar who spent much of his life in the town and died here in 1146. Local Muslims believed that three pilgrimages here were equal in spiritual value to going on Hajj, and so Timur commissioned this impressive mausoleum.

A smaller mausoleum faces the Yassawi tomb, that of **Rabiga Sultan Begimi**, the wife of an Uzbek leader and granddaughter of Timur. A restored 16th-century bathhouse stands west of the complex entrance, alongside a mosque. East of Rabiga Sultan Begimi's tomb, just beyond the gift shop, is the site **museum** (daily 9am–6pm; charge).

Baikonur cosmodrome

Located far from anywhere, this is where *Vostok 1*, the first manned space flight, piloted by Yuri Gagarin, was hurled into orbit on 12 April 1961. Gagarin led the way for a whole generation of Soviet cosmonauts to take off from here. The cosmodrome, which is central to a closed-off area that measures 90km (54 miles) east to west and 85km (51 miles) north to south, lies on the fringes of the Kyzylkum desert, just north of the garrison town of the same name (formerly Leninsk, but renamed Baikonur in 1995).

With the collapse of the USSR in 1991, Russia was left with the space programme's know-how, and Kazakhstan the prime launch site. An agreement was reached in 1994 in which Baikonur would be leased to Russia for a considerable annual rent – a lease that runs until 2050. Following the conclusion of the space shuttle programme, all flights to the international space station now depart from Baikonur.

A 2016 International Space Station rocket launch.

The Hindu Kush Range rises in the distance as mountain herbs flower by the roadside in the Pamir valley.

TAJIKISTAN

Visit ancient forts and cities that stood astride the
old Silk Road and enjoy the relative comforts of
Dushanbe, Tajikistan's attractive capital.

Squeezed between the upper reaches of the Oxus and Jaxartes rivers and bordering the most remote regions of Afghanistan and China, Tajikistan embraces the widest range of scenery of all the Central Asian republics. Most of it is defined by mountains, from the high rolling plateau of the eastern Pamirs to the remote, almost vertical gorges of the western Pamirs and the scenic central ranges of the Fan and Turkestan mountains.

The south is a sun-baked plain of small *kishlaks* (villages) and thirsty cotton fields that has more in common with the plains of northern Afghanistan and southern Uzbekistan than the rest of Tajikistan. The far northern finger of the country reaches into the Fergana Valley, where the bazaars and teahouses resemble those in the great trading centres of Uzbekistan.

History and people

With so many disparate parts, tied together by Soviet nation-building, it was unsurprising that the country imploded during the 1990s civil war. Over 70,000 Tajiks were killed, 500,000 were made homeless and 250,000 fled the country during the first decade of independence. After 10 years of relative peace the contrasts remain, and despite attempts to rebuild a shattered

economy, a certain amount of instability persists. Tajikistan is still the poorest of Central Asia's republics.

The Tajiks trace their roots back to the Sogdians and Bactrians, and define themselves as much by their Persian language and heritage than any shared ethnic traits. Ethnic Tajiks make up around 80 percent of the republic's population and consider as kin the Tajik-speaking peoples of northern Afghanistan and the Sarikol region of Tashkurgan in China's Xinjiang province. Many Tajiks live in neighbouring

Main Attractions

High Pamirs
Shokh-Dara Valley
Wakhan Valley
Dushanbe
Iskander-Kul
Penjikent
Fan Mountains
Khojand
Panchshanbe Bazaar
Istaravshan

*The Russian-made "Ural" brand of motorcycles
are a common form of transport.*

Uzbekistan, and in fact the towns of Bukhara and Samarkand are largely Tajik cities. Tajikistan's Persian heritage also gives it close ties to Iran.

The region has been at the fringes of empires (the Achaemenid, Kushan, Sogdian, Graeco-Bactrian and Samanid, and the Bukharan Emirate), but at the centre of none. Major branches of the Silk Road have long traversed the region, and the valleys of the Pamirs formed funnels as well as challenges for long-distance caravans. The popular caravan route across the Pamirs from Badakhshan to Tashkurgan was followed by, amongst others, Marco Polo, who described it as the highest place in the world.

Most travellers are drawn to Tajikistan by its spectacular mountain scenery. The tenuous infrastructure is luckily boosted by several excellent community tourism projects, whose homestays, guides and jeeps allow you to travel in basic comfort. Tourism is still very much in its initial stages here, but many people vote Tajikistan the most scenic, hospitable and exciting republic in Central Asia.

Transporting goods through the Pamirs.

The Pamirs

Known locally as the Bam-i-Dunya, or Roof of the World, the Pamir region occupies one of Asia's remotest corners. Perched at the high crossroads of China's Xinjiang province, Afghanistan's Wakhan Corridor and Pakistan's Chitral region, the high plateau once marked the furthest reaches of the Russian and British empires.

Chinese travellers such as Sung Yun, Fa Xian and Xuanzang referred to the region as "Pomilo", describing it as the "midpoint between heaven and earth". The Chinese attributed altitude sickness to the wild onions that grew here, going as far as calling the Pamirs "the Congling Shan", or Onion Mountains!

The word Pamir means "high rolling valley", and the region is indeed a high-elevation, treeless plateau, almost lunar-like in places, dotted with yurts, livestock and the occasional *tersken* bush. Curly-horned Marco Polo sheep, ibex and yak dominate the eastern half at altitudes of between 3,500 and 4,500 metres (11,500–15,000ft), while the deep, arid valleys, churning rivers and fragile alluvial settlements of the

ENTERING AND LEAVING TAJIKISTAN

Terrible roads, mountainous terrain and a sometimes awkward visa regime make Tajikistan a challenging country to travel (see page 385).

The border between Daroot-Korgon and Garm is currently closed to travellers, but the Pamir Highway south of Sary-Tash connects **Kyrgyzstan** with Tajikistan's Gorno-Badakhshan province. A special GBAO permit and private transport is necessary. A shared taxi service links Batken in southwest Kyrgyzstan with Isfara in northern Tajikistan. Crossing into Tajikistan is normally relaxed and trouble-free, providing your paperwork is already in order.

Tajikistan has a border crossing west of Penjikent that leads to Samarkand in **Uzbekistan** and another further south, just west of Dushanbe. In northern Tajikistan there are crossings at Oybek, west of Khojand, and at Kanimabad to the Fergana Valley. Dushanbe is connected to Termez by a regular rail link, and the circuitous route that links Dushanbe with Khojand also passes through Termez and Samarkand.

Two border crossings exist for **Afghanistan**, both little-used by Western travellers: between Panj-e-Payon and Kunduz, and between Ishkashim and Faizabad. Coming from Afghanistan, to cross at Ishkashim requires a GBAO permit in addition to a Tajik visa.

The Qolma Pass crossing that links Tajikistan's Pamir Highway with **China's** Karakoram Highway is not open for use by foreigners.

eastern ranges are strongly reminiscent of northern Pakistan.

Little-visited by travellers since the formation of the Soviet Union, the region was ironically one of the most travelled corners of Central Asia in the late 19th century, when the blanks in the map sparked a flurry of expeditions. British explorers like Francis Younghusband and George Curzon concentrated on the upper Oxus and the high passes into British India, while Russian explorers such as Kostenko, Svertsov and Fedchenko explored the Alai ranges and the great peaks of the northern Pamirs. Quintessential Silk Road explorers such as Sven Hedin (in 1894–5) and Aurel Stein (1915) explored the region's historical sites.

Access for today's travellers is via the Pamir Highway, a predominantly tarmac-surfaced version of the Silk Road built by the Soviets between 1934 and 1940 on top of ancient caravan tracks. The region is still widely known by its Soviet name, the Gorno-Badakhshan Autonomous Oblast, or GBAO, and remains a prickly border zone, crossed by Afghan drug-smugglers. For travellers it is simply one of the most scenic and adventurous corners of High Asia.

The High Pamirs

From the remote crossroads of Sary Tash in the Alay (Alai) Valley of Kyrgyzstan, the Pamir Highway swings past close-up views of Lenin Peak (Koh-i-Istiqlal, or Independence Peak), before entering Tajikistan, crossing the Kyzyl-Art Pass and finally descending to the spectacular blue inland sea of **Lake Karakul** (Qarokul). In good weather the lake reflects a radiant turquoise; but it is the overcast waters that give the lake its name "Black Lake" and moved Curzon to describe it as "a splendid spectacle, for its waters toss and boil like a seething cauldron". Formed 10 million years ago by a meteor, the lake is called *chong* (big) Karakul to differentiate from the *kichi* (small) Karakul across the border in China.

Behind the lake the high Pamirs rise majestically, concealing the 77-km (46-mile) -long Fedchenko glacier that tumbles off massive Ismoili

TIP

META (Murgab Eco Tourism Association) can organise a trip around the Pamirs, from jeep hire and English-speaking guides to both home- and yurt-stay, and they help you obtain the relevant permissions and registration with the touchy local KGB. The associated Yak House organisation supports minority Kyrgyz craft production by selling felt products to tourists and is well worth a visit.

Ney Elias, explorer extraordinaire.

THE BEST-TRAVELLED MAN IN ASIA

The political agent Ney Elias may just be the greatest British explorer of Central Asia that you have never heard of. Dubbed "the best-travelled man in Asia" after a series of epic journeys across Mongolia and the Karakoram, his most impressive achievement was his epic 1885 voyage across the Pamirs, from Kashgar to Badakhshan. His mission was to survey en route the Rang-Kul area and the Shughnan and Bartang valleys in an attempt to define the practical boundaries of China, Russia and Afghanistan. The solo traveller covered 5,000km (3,000 miles) and crossed over 40 passes in his 17-month trip, returning over the Hindu Kush to Chitral and Gilgit. Elias also held political posts in Mandalay, Sikkim, Ladakh and Yarkand, and was consul-general in Mashhad for a time. Francis Younghusband called him "the best traveller there has ever been in Central Asia".

While subsequent travellers to the region, such as Younghusband and George Curzon, shot to fame as imperial heavyweights, the self-effacing and hypochondriac Elias slowly sank into obscurity, and his political reports gathered dust in the locked vaults of the British Indian government, marked "Secret". As his nephew and biographer noted, "Few explorers have done so much and talked so little of what they have done."

Entrance to the transcaspian bridge on the Oxus.

Somoni (7,495 metres/24,700ft; formerly Pik Kommunizm). East of the lake the highway parallels the Soviet-era double-wire fences that mark the border zone with China. Marco Polo (1274) and the Chinese pilgrim Xuanzang (642) both passed by the lake, the latter believing it to be populated by dragons.

From the southeastern shores the main M41 continues south to Murgab, past a former Russian fort at Muzkol and over the Akbaytal (White Mare) Pass, the highest point on the highway at 4,655 metres (15,361ft).

Murgab

Murgab (**Murghob**) is a scrappy town of around 4,000 people, founded in 1891 by Russian Tsarist officers as a supply post at the furthest reaches of the Russian Empire. The town has a patchy bazaar and even patchier electricity, but it is a good base from which to make excursions to the surrounding high valleys. Most of the region's population is Kyrgyz, who pass the summers in remote herding camps, before moving their yurts

down into the warmer valleys during the harsh winter. On a clear day you can see the giant Pamiri peak of Muztagh Ata (7,546 metres/24,901ft) to the northeast across the border in China.

The most exciting excursion from Murgab follows the Aksu River (once considered the source of both the water and name of the River Oxus) into the remotest corner of Central Asia at Shaymak. Less than 84km (50 miles) from the border of China, Afghanistan and Pakistan, and with views over the Mintaka range, this is truly the meeting point of empires. The nearby Nazatash Pass (now closed) was a favourite with Silk Road travellers heading to the Stone Fort at Tashkurgan (Taxkorgan), just over the pass to the east. To the south is the Little Pamir and the important Silk Road passes of the Wakhjir (east into China) and the Kilik, Mintaka and Boroghil (south to Pakistan).

It was just southwest of here in August 1891, at Bozai Gumbaz in modern-day Afghanistan, that Francis Younghusband was thrown out of the Pamirs by his Russian counterpart

THE SOURCE OF THE OXUS

By 1872 a border agreement between the Russians and British had settled the Amu Darya, or Oxus, as the demarcation line. The snag was that no one was quite sure where exactly the Oxus was, at least in its upper reaches. As the rival empires inched ever closer, the problem became increasingly acute. A British public that had lapped up the drama surrounding the discovery of the source of the Nile suddenly turned its attention to the Oxus.

John Wood (a Navy officer, of all things) had made a famous trip in winter 1838 from Ishkashim and Langar up the Pyanj River to Zor-Kul lake, proclaiming it the source of the Oxus and renaming it Lake Victoria after the recently crowned young queen. Yet suspicions were soon voiced that the real source lay perhaps in the glaciers dividing Zor-Kul from the Little Pamir to the southeast. The trick was how to define the source of a river – the longest tributary, the highest source or the largest flow?

It was only when George Curzon discovered an ice cave in the Wakhjir region near the border with China in 1894 that the cave and the upper Wakhan River it flows into were agreed on as the true (highest) source of the Oxus. The border was finally demarcated in 1895, fittingly on the shores of Zor-Kul, relegating the debate to an obscure geographical conundrum.

Colonel Yanov in one of the remotest flashpoints of the Great Game. The two officers dined on such mountain luxuries as fresh vegetables and Kashgari brandy until the Cossack unit ordered the 28-year-old Younghusband to leave the region, claiming it as Russian territory.

The Chinese trucks you see parked on the outskirts of Murgab are heading to or from the **Qolma Pass** (4,362 metres/14,394ft), now once again an international Silk Road crossing. The pass is currently open to local traffic only, but may conceivably open before long to provide yet another remote border crossing into Central Asia. For the time being the pass is the preserve of Chinese truck drivers and Kashgari entrepreneurs driving Chinese-made minivans across the Pamirs for resale in Dushanbe.

Other excursions lead northeast to the glittering twin lakes of **Rang-Kul** and Shor-Kul, where META offers overnight Bactrian camel trips, or south to see the impressively fresh Neolithic paintings of **Shakhty**. It's possible to continue south by jeep from Shahkty to Jarty-Gumbaz (where you stand an excellent chance of spotting ibex and Marco Polo sheep, particularly during winter and the autumn rut), before continuing southwest to a string of spectacular Pamiri lakes, ending in Zor-Kul (Lake Victoria) at 4,126 metres (13,616ft).

Murgab to Alichur

Back in Murgab, the main Pamir Highway climbs south past a checkpoint to the low Naziatash Pass, to descend into the rich **Alichur Plain**, home to some of the best pasture in the Pamirs. Just past the huge tent-like rock of Chatyr Tash, a side road branches south for 6km (3.5 miles) to the enigmatic mud-brick **Bash Gumbaz tomb**. The main valley west of here is dotted with summertime yurts and the archaeological remains of past invaders and migrants, including the 11th-century silver mines and

2,000-year-old petroglyphs of Bazar-Dara, a tough day excursion from the main road.

Beyond the uninspiring modern settlement of Alichur, the river meanders through the lush Sumantash Plain while the road detours around a series of high-altitude salt lakes, among them Sassyk-Kul, Tuz-Kul and Yashilkul. You get a great overview of the first two of these lakes as the road climbs to a vantage point.

Just before the viewpoint, a side road branches left to the Wakhan Valley via the Khargush Pass. The main Pamir Highway continues west past a turn-off to the settlement of Bulun-Kul, which offers simple accommodation and a base from which to explore archaeological sites on the northeastern shore of Yashilkul lake. The nearby Mausoleum of Bekbulat marks the furthest extent of Chinese influence in the Pamirs.

Western Pamirs

The main road continues to climb slowly up to the 4,272-metre (14,097-ft) **Koitezek Pass**, the watershed that

The Bash Gumbez tomb sits on grazing land off the Pamir Highway.

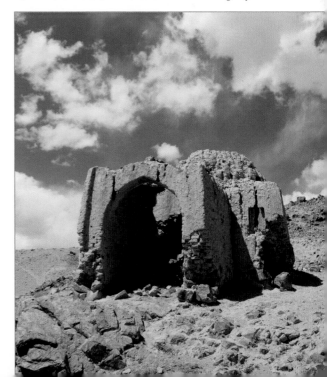

divides the eastern and western Pamirs. On the west side of the pass the mountains of the western Pamirs quickly become dryer and more jagged as the valleys deepen. Settled Pamiri culture replaces the semi-nomadic Kyrgyz lifestyle, and irrigated villages replace seasonal yurt camps. The intense flashes of greenery and the orchards of apricots, mulberries and apples could have been lifted directly from Pakistan's beautiful Northern Areas.

The highway descends past thermal hot springs near Jelondi and then the Gunt Valley enters from the right, draining the waters of Yashilkul lake into the historical district of Shughnan. A cliff above the village of Bogev, further down the valley, hides the ruins of the fire-worshipping centre of Kafir-Qala. Just before Khorog, the road passes a monument to the Pamir Highway in the shape of the first car ever to drive the route.

Khorog

The straggling administrative centre of **Khorog** (**Khorugh**) is the only town in the Pamirs. It is home to 30,000

locals, as well as government offices, several foreign NGOs and the ambitious new University of Central Asia, a multi-campus project financed by the Aga Khan Foundation. The region's former capital lies across the Pyanj River at Qala-i-Bar Pyanj.

The town is a good place to resupply, relax in one of the many Pamiri-style homestays and arrange your onward transport. The nearby Botanical Gardens are said to be the world's highest. The Regional Museum is worth a visit to see the first piano to arrive in the Pamirs, carried over the mountains from Osh over two months in 1914 for the pampered daughter of a Russian army officer. Also of interest are the recently restored **Central Park** and the actual first car to cross the Pamir Highway, which is kept on a plinth on the outskirts of the town.

Around Khorog

The valleys around Khorog conceal some stunning scenery and interesting archaeological sites, though the roads are bad and transport thin. Sporadically governed in name only by

An Afghan man in his traditional Pamiri house.

THE MOUNTAIN TAJIKS

Sometimes called "Mountain Tajiks", Pamiris are quite distinct from Tajiks in both language and religion. Speaking a handful of languages that are often incomprehensible even in the next valley, most Pamiris are Ismaili Muslims, followers of the Aga Khan. Local *khalifas* (village headmen) and *rais* (community leaders) take the role of imam, and there are no formal mosques, but rather shared meeting and prayer halls called *jamaat khana*.

If you are lucky you'll get to stay in a traditional Pamiri home. These unique houses have five pillars (representing the five prophets) arranged around a central recessed area, with a skylight (known as a *tsorkhona*) made from four concentric squares, representing the elements of earth, water, fire and air.

both Afghanistan and the Bukharan emirate, these remote valleys have long preserved their own cultures and languages. Western Pamiri valleys such as Yazgulum and Vanch remain unexplored by all but the hardiest trekkers.

The **Shokh-Dara Valley** to the east has several crumbling forts, at Roshtqala and more impressively further east at Shashbuvad and Deruj, which also has Saka tombs. The views of Engels Peak (6,507 metres/21,473ft) from Javshanguz are unparalleled. In a strong four-wheel-drive vehicle it's possible to continue up the Shokh-Dara Valley onto the plateau of the eastern Pamirs to remote Lake Turuntai-Kul, before joining the main Pamir Highway near the Koitezek Pass.

Equally stunning is the remote and elemental **Bartang Valley**, whose perilous road squeezes between the rocky valley walls and the churning leaden waters. The valley is famed for its music and dance, and you may be lucky enough to hear the strains of a locally made five-stringed *rabob*, accompanied by tambourine and Russian-influenced accordion. The

Bartangis are some of the most hospitable people in the Pamirs, and will need persistent persuading not to kill an animal in a visitor's honour.

The best excursion in this valley is to the lovely village of Bardara, 7km (4 miles) off the main road. Beyond here, the main road branches east to the village of Barchadev, where you'll need a special permit to continue the hike up to views of Lake Sarez, the spectacular body of water formed by a huge landslide on the Murgab River in 1911. There are fears that an earthquake could dislodge the plug, causing potentially the largest flood of modern times. An early-warning system was installed a few years ago by Swiss scientists.

The main valley branches northeast to Savnob, a lovely settlement that boasts a ruined *qala* (fortress) and cliffside caves, both built to protect against slave raids by Krygyz, Afghan or neighbouring Yazgulumi raiders. There's another fort at nearby Roshorv. The main reason to continue further up the Ghudara Valley is for trekking access to the Tanymas Valley

The Gunt River flowing through Khorog.

and Grum glacier. The upper valleys remain the wild habitat of ibex and snow leopards.

The road south of Khorog passes the **Kuh-i-Lal ruby mine**. Badakhshan has long been famed for both its lapis and rubies, a reputation that even Marco Polo noticed, noting that in "Syghinan" (Shughnan) "the stones are dug on the king's account, and no one else dares dig in that mountain on pain of forfeiture of life". Shortly before the mine is a turn-off marked to the **Garam Chasm** (hot springs), which makes a pleasant diversion en route.

The Tajik Wakhan

The spectacular **Wakhan Valley**, a major branch of the Silk Road, is shared between Tajikistan and Afghanistan, and offers fleeting views up southern side valleys to the snow-capped peaks of the Hindu Kush that form the border with Pakistan. Coming from the east, the poplar trees, well-tended fields and warmer temperatures come as a relief after the rigours of the high plateau.

Crossing flooded land in the Pamir valley.

The valley's main village is **Ishkashim**, which has the only border crossing with Afghanistan open to foreigners. The trade routes from China continued west from here to Faizabad, Kunduz and Mazar-i-Sharif. Marco Polo passed through Ishkashim in 1271 en route to the upper Wakhan, travelling via either Zor-Kul or the upper Sarhad region. A series of new bridges financed by the Aga Khan Foundation have retied many of the Silk Road connections that were severed by the formation of the USSR.

The strategic valley has long been contested by the Afghans, Pamiris, Kyrgyz and even Chinese, and it is dotted with *qalas*, which served to protect, supply and tax the trade caravans headed for Tashkurgan and Badakhshan.

The 2,000-year-old Kaakha Qala is one of the oldest of these forts, dating from the Kushan era and occupied these days by the Tajik army. Nearby is the Ismaili shrine of Shah-i-Mardan Khazrati Ali. East of here, above Darshai village, are some remote rock inscriptions in the 2,300-year-old Kharoshthi script, similar to ones found by Aurel Stein along China's Southern Silk Road.

The most spectacular of the Wakhan's forts is **Yamchun** (Zulkhomor), perched high above the valley floor, a 7-km (4-mile) winding drive off the main road. The massive 3rd-century curved buttresses lead from a narrow and easily defendable entrance into a large castle. The thick, powerful walls, rounded towers and loopholes perfectly fit every child's image of a medieval castle. Aurel Stein visited the fort in 1906 en route to China. The nearby natural hot springs of Bibi Fatima (named after the Prophet Muhammad's daughter) are well worth a visit.

Nearby **Vishim** (**Abrashim**) **Qala**, the "Silk Fort" of Zong, is also well worth visiting, just 4km (2.5 miles) before Langar, for its stunning views over the confluence of the Wakhan and Pyanj valleys. Paths on the Afghan side continue on to the Sarhad region of the upper Wakhan Corridor. One Silk Road reminder is the 7th–8th-century complex of Buddhist platforms and caves at **Vrang**, which may also have been a Zoroastrian site.

Further up the valley, near the junction of the Pamir and Wakhan rivers, the lovely village of **Langar** is a convenient place to overnight. The local *jamaat khana* acts as a House Museum, opposite the ageless shrine of Shoh Oftabi. Like most Pamiri *oston*, or shrines, it is adorned with ibex horns and holy stones, which the locals kiss while asking for good fortune. Thousands of petroglyphs are said to litter the pastures above town. Across the river on the Afghan side you can still see the hill of the Qala-i-Panj fort, which once controlled entry to the entire lower Wakhan.

Past Langar the road swings north, past the ruins of Ratm Qala and into the deep and dramatic Pyanj River Gorge. The border and customs post at Khargush marks the restricted turn-off east to Zor-Kul. The main road continues north over the Khargush Pass and past the salt lake of Chokur-Kul to the main Pamir Highway.

Khorog to Dushanbe

The 556-km (333-mile) M41 from Khorog to Dushanbe is another dramatic stretch of road that offers a two-day overland alternative to the scenic (but rather scary) hour-long flight back to Dushanbe.

From Khorog the road hugs the Afghan border for hours, following the twists and turns of the Pyanj River past the turn-offs to the **Bartang** and **Vanch** valleys, to arrive in **Kalaikhum (Qal'aikhum)**, headquarters of the Darvaz district. The valleys of the western Pamir have long been fought over, notably when the Afghan Murad Beg of Kunduz subjugated the valleys around Shughnan in 1820. The need for protection led to the construction of a string of forts, like those at Kalaikhum, Qala-i-Pyanj and Qala-i-Vomar. Most of the forts were later destroyed by the Russians.

From Kalaikhum there are two routes back to Dushanbe. The more scenic but poorly maintained route winds up to the Sagirdasht Pass before descending into the **Tavildara** and **Karategin** regions. The road is closed in winter as it goes over a high pass and snowfall blocks the way. Some of the worst fighting of the civil war took place in this remote clan-based area, and you can still see gutted tanks and troop transporters abandoned by the side of the road. The **Gharm Valley** joins the main road from the north as the mountains slowly peter out.

The other route choice, and the only wintertime option, is to follow the course of the **Pyanj River** as it makes a huge arc around the border with Afghan Badakhshan. The highway offers excellent views of amazingly remote villages across the river, which are only connected to the rest of Afghanistan by some incredibly stomach-tightening footpaths that sometimes consist of little more than

The spectacular 12th-century Yamchun fort in the Wakhan lies along the old Silk Road.

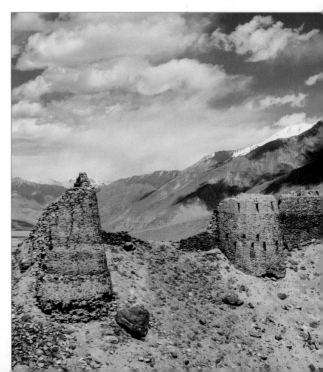

The Haji Yakoub Mosque in Dushanbe.

a few planks jammed with stones and suspended above sheer cliffs. The Turkish-built highway passes the lovely villages of Yogd and Zigar, at one stage on a surreal three-lane super-highway, before leaving the Pyanj Valley and climbing over the Shurabad Pass to the uninspiring southern Tajik city of Kulyab. From here it's an easy drive on to Dushanbe.

Dushanbe

Tajikistan's capital, a city of around 640,000, is an attractive, leafy city, built on a much more manageable scale than either Tashkent or Almaty. The town was known from 1929 to 1961 as Stalinabad, the capital of the Tajikistan SSR. After 1961 the name reverted to the traditional Dushanbe (Monday), named after the ancient weekly market. The emir of Bukhara stopped here briefly in 1920 en route to exile in Afghanistan, and the Turk Enver Pasha captured the town in 1922 as part of his attempts to raise a rebellion against Soviet rule.

There's an air of quiet prosperity in Dushanbe these days, and the streets are full of handsome Mediterranean-looking Tajiks, well dressed in traditional embroidered skullcaps and colourful psychedelic dresses. Most travellers stay only for a day or two, enough to finalise registration formalities and permits for the Gorno-Badakhshan region. Between leisurely lunches and people-watching in the many open-air cafés, there's more than enough to occupy your time.

The city's major points of interest line the main drag, **Rudaki,** named after the Persian poet that Tajikistan (along with Iran) claims as its favourite son. A stroll from north to south passes a statue of Rudaki, a few theatres and embassies and several neo-classical government buildings of salmon pink and canary yellow that remind one more of St Petersburg than inner Asia.

Buildings of note include the Majlisi Oli (Parliament), the Writers' Union Building (decorated with busts of famous Persian and Tajik writers), the attractive Turkish Embassy and the Ayni Opera and Ballet Theatre. The Oriental-Socialist architecture of the

Rokhat Teahouse is the perfect place to linger over a pot of green tea.

Dushanbe's main sights are its museums. The star of the **Museum of National Antiquities** (Tue–Fri 9am–5pm, Sat until 4pm, Sun 10am–2pm, closed Mon; charge) is the 12-metre (40-ft) -long Buddha excavated in 1966 from Adjina Tepe in southern Tajikistan. The 1,600-year-old statue is considered the largest intact Buddha in Central Asia. Also note the ivory carving of Alexander the Great, from Takht-i-Sangin in southern Tajikistan (see below).

Also worth a visit is the **Bekhzod National Museum** (Tue–Sat 9am–4pm, Sun 9am–3pm, closed Mon; charge), at the southern end of tree-lined Rudaki, home to wonderful examples of carved wood and Soviet art, alongside the Soviet obsession with mechanised agricultural achievements. The statue across the road is of Sadriddin Ayni (1878–1954), the famous Soviet Tajik writer.

Lunchtimes at the central **Haji Yakoub Mosque** offer one of city's few visible traces of Islam, as crowds of cloaked and bearded Tajiks stream in for daily prayers. The **Bagh-i-Markazi** (**Central Park**) is worth a visit at weekends and holidays for its funfair, pilau sellers and a statue of Lenin. The fallen leader's former plinth, a couple of hundred metres south, now houses a **statue of Ismail Samani** (pronounced Ismoil Somoni), the 10th-century Persian-speaking leader of the cultured Samanid dynasty, who also lends his name to the Tajik currency.

If Dushanbe appears at times disarmingly European, then its two main markets, the Shah Mansur and Barakat bazaars, are 100 percent Central Asian colour and bustle.

Around Dushanbe

The easiest excursion from Dushanbe is to **Hissar** (**Hisor**), 31km (18 miles) east, once an important *beglik* and outpost of the Bukharan Emirate. The eroded walls and giant mound of the fort remain, accessed through a restored gate. The fort was occupied by the Basmachi leader Ibrahim Beg until the Red Army destroyed it in 1921. Opposite are two madrassas and

Statue of Ismail Samani in Dushanbe.

the renovated foundations of an early 19th-century caravanserai. Buzkashi tournaments are often held here during Nauroz, the Persian spring equinox festival in mid-March.

Tursanzade to the west is the gateway to Uzbekistan and notable for its huge Soviet-era aluminium factory and for the 11th-century mausoleums of Khoja Durbod and Khoja Nakhshron, outside of town.

Southern Tajikistan

Amateur archaeologists keen to track down the faintest traces of the Silk Road may want to hire a car and invest a day or two exploring the hot and dusty cotton fields of **Southern Tajikistan**. Once known as Bactria or Tokharia, the scattering of archaeological sites here have revealed traces of a Graeco-Bactrian culture that incorporated both Greek and Iranian elements in quintessential Silk Road fashion. Unfortunately most finds of importance are housed in St Petersburg's Hermitage Museum.

A short 12-km (7-mile) drive southeast of Kurgonteppa (Qurghonteppa)

The flowing waters of the Varzob river.

(about 100km/60 miles south of Dushanbe) is the 7th–8th-century site of **Adjina Tepe** (Witches' Hill), where in 1966 archaeologists unearthed Central Asia's largest surviving Buddha statue. The "Sleeping Buddha" has stylistic elements that have much in common with the Gandharan art of Afghanistan and Pakistan. Wall paintings and sculptures housed in niches once surrounded the central monastic courtyard. The site is currently being restored by Unesco, though there's not a great deal to see.

The ancient site of Kobadiyan (7th to 2nd centuries BC), further south, is famed as the location for the discovery in 1877 of the **Oxus Treasure**, a stunning 2,500-year-old Achaemenid treasure-trove of 180 gold statues and over 500 coins that now resides in the British Museum, after it was bought piecemeal from Bukharan traders in Rawalpindi. In 2007 President Rakhmonov demanded the return of the treasure, but to no avail. Nearby is the ruined Graeco-Bactrian temple of **Takht-i-Sangin**, where archaeologists unearthed a famous ivory portrait of Alexander the Great, along with sculptures of the Greek god Apollo and an inscription in Greek to the local god of the Oxus.

It was close to here that Alexander crossed the Oxus on inflated hides over five days in 329 BC. These days modern travellers cross the Amu Darya at Panj-i-Payon, from where Afghan roads continue to Kunduz. The crossing was used to supply the Northern Alliance, headed by Tajik commander Ahmed Shah Masoud, during operations in 2001 against the Taliban.

Other sites include the 9th–11th-century baked brick cupolas of the Khoja Mashad Sayid Mausoleum and Madrassa in Sayot village, Shahrtuz district. Around 15km (9 miles) outside Shahrtuz are the 44 springs of Jilichor Chashma, a popular pilgrimage and picnic site.

Further east, near Vose, are the excavations of the 9th–11th-century Kulbek (Qulbuk) palace at Kurbanshahid (the ancient region of Kuttal). Inside Kulyab town is the 15th-century mazar of Sufi preacher Mir Sayid Hamadoni (1314–86).

Northern Tajikistan

The north of Tajikistan, cut off from Dushanbe by the towering Hissar, Zarafshan and Turkestan ranges, is in many ways a different country, more Uzbek in its culture and physically closer to Tashkent than to Dushanbe. The scenic drive between Dushanbe and Penjikent or Khojand takes you through some of the region's best mountain scenery.

The main M34 climbs north from Dushanbe past roadside *chaikhanas* and the gleaming villas of Dushanbe's dubiously rich, into the **Varzob Gorge**. As the canyon narrows, side valleys open to offer grand hiking, waterfalls, hot springs and even a ski resort at Takob. Traffic used to have to make the winding ascent to the 3,372-metre (11,128-ft) Anzob Pass, but a new 6-km (3.5-mile) -long Iranian-financed tunnel offers a shortcut through the Zerafshan range in what is viewed as a major attempt to tie the two halves of the country together. The tunnel is not, however, for the faint-hearted as despite being in use it is still incomplete: there are no lights, no proper road surface, and the tunnel regularly floods.

Somewhere in the remote mountains north of here, by the Polytimetus River (which is probably the Zarafshan), is the famed **Sogdian Rock**, where Alexander stormed the Sogdian forces under Spitamenes, his troops using rock-climbing techniques to capture both the Sogdians and his new wife, Roxanna.

Iskander-Kul

The best detour along this route is to scenic **Iskander-Kul**, a milky-blue mountain lake backed by a sleepy *turbaza* (Soviet holiday camp) and a dacha belonging to the president. Some great treks lead from here into the surrounding Fan Mountains, but it is highly advisable to have a four-wheel-drive vehicle if you plan to drive to the lake itself. Alexander (Iskander) the Great enjoys a cult in Tajikistan, and many lakes, mountains and stories are named after him. The main road follows the rushing river to **Ayni**, home to the heavily eroded 10th-century **Varzi-Minor Minaret**. From here roads lead west to Penjikent or north over the Shakhristan Pass to Khojand (Khujand, Khojent).

Between Ayni and Penjikent is **Mount Mug**, the site of the Sogdians' last stand against the Arabs in 721 (they lost and their leader Devastich was beheaded). Soviet archaeologists discovered a large cash of Sogdian documents here in 1932.

Penjikent

Northern Tajikistan's main archaeological site is the ancient Sogdian city of **Penjikent**, one of the great lost Silk

FACT

Not far from Penjikent, in the village of Panjrud on the route to Artush in the Fan Mountains, is the site of the mausoleum of the famous 9th-century Persian poet Rudaki. His small tomb complex lies just off the main street through the village. He was born nearby in the village of Rudak.

Looking out over Iskander-Kul.

Khojand is home to one of the largest statues of Lenin still standing in the former USSR.

The huge Panchshanbe Bazaar in Khojand.

Road cities of Central Asia. This rich, cosmopolitan place thrived on the banks of the Zarafshan River until destroyed by Arab invaders in 722. Silk cocoons were unearthed at the site during excavations.

Like most Central Asian cities, Penjikent consisted of a citadel, or ark, to the northwest, and an inner walled city, or *shakhristan*, which included a palace, temple platforms and streets of shops and workshops. To the south lies a necropolis. Copies of the fabulous Greek- and Iranian-influenced wall friezes, depicting scenes from the *Shahnameh* and local epics, are on display at the site and in the museum in the nearby town, as well as in Dushanbe and St Petersburg. The sensual pillars depicting swaying dancing girls and the Tantric images of the Indian gods Shiva and Parvati riding a buffalo highlight the cosmopolitan range of artistic influences that are so typical of Silk Road art.

The museum displays several *ossuaries*, pots used to store the bones of the deceased after their corpses were eaten by birds, in accordance with Zoroastrian tradition (and similar to Tibetan sky burial).

Just 20km (12 miles) west of Penjikent is **Sarawzm**, one of the oldest settlements in Central Asia, where archaeologists have unearthed a Bronze Age temple complex and the 2,500-year-old grave of a wealthy woman. From here roads continue west along the Zarafshan across the Uzbekistan border to Samarkand.

Fan Mountains

The main launching point for fantastic treks up into the craggy peaks and turquoise lakes of the **Fan Mountains** is the village of Artush, around 60km (36 miles) southeast of Penjikent. Popular trekking routes include to the Alauddin Lakes (four or five days), continuing over the 4,404-metre (14,500ft) Kaznok Pass to Iskander-Kul (total six days); or from the Marguzor Lakes to Iskander-Kul via the Tavasang, Munora and Dukdon passes (six days). Travel agencies in Dushanbe, Penjikent and Tashkent can arrange treks, as can international trekking companies.

Khojand

Khojand (Khujand, Khojent) is one of the oldest cities in Central Asia, though you'd be forgiven for not realising it these days. Alexander the Great founded his ninth city, Alexandria-Eskhate (Alexandria the Furthest), here on the banks of the Syr Darya (Jaxartes), marking the furthest extent of his exploits in Central Asia. The town developed as an important Silk Road depot, guarding and taxing the mouth of the Fergana Valley. The Mongols destroyed it in 1220 after a long siege made difficult by the local resistance leader Timur Malik.

The modern city is the second-largest in Tajikistan, and has more in common with the Uzbek cities of the Fergana Valley than with the Tajik towns of the south. The city (then known as Leninabad) was ceded to Tajikistan from the Uzbek SSR in 1929 solely to help Tajikistan reach the threshold 1 million population it required to become a full republic. The city briefly threatened to secede from Tajikistan during the civil war.

The original 10-km (6-mile) -long city walls are long gone and the military now occupies the old *qala*, whose eastern walls house a small **Museum of Archaeology and Fortifications** (daily 8am–5pm; charge). The impressive-looking new provincial **Historical Museum of Sughd Province** in the southeast corner of the *qala* has displays on Sogdian history and culture and local hero Timur Malik.

South of the *qala* is the huge **Panchshanbe Bazaar** (Friday Market), built in the 1950s as one of the largest in Central Asia. Across the plaza is the understated tomb-and-mosque complex of Sheikh Muslihiddin, dating from 1394 and a subsequent 16th-century renovation.

Khojand still has several Soviet-era monuments, including one of the largest Lenin statues left in the former USSR, on the north side of the Syr Darya. Look out also for the huge red hammer and sickle beside the bus stop in the centre of town and the bust of Lenin and Marx on nearby Komil Khojandy Street.

From Khojand roads lead northwest to Tashkent and east to Kokand, both in Uzbekistan. If you are heading to Kokand, consider a detour to the 12th-century **Hazrati Bobo Mausoleum** in Chorukh village, near Isfara, a rare wooden mausoleum carved with pre-Islamic symbols.

A worthy excursion from Khojand is to the town of **Istaravshan**, ancient Cyropolis, where you can still visit the citadel stormed by Alexander's forces in 328 BC. The old town conceals some beautiful Islamic tombs, including the Kok Gumbaz Madrassa, whose turquoise dome could have been lifted straight from Samarkand, and the Chor Gumbaz (Four Domes) Mazar, which boasts some lovely interior paintwork. The excellent Istaravshan bazaar is also well worth a visit. The town, known in Soviet days as Ura-Tyube, is 70km (42 miles) south of Khojand.

In Khojand's main square.

View from the Kalon minaret in Bukhara.

UZBEKISTAN

The great cities of Samarkand and Bukhara flaunt
their magnificent Timurid architecture, whilst
remote Khiva beguiles the Silk Road traveller.

For many travellers, Uzbekistan holds the very heart of the Central Asian Silk Road. Its three main historical centres – Samarkand, Bukhara and Khiva – all resonate deeply with the weight of history, and its bazaars and teahouses still carry echoes, albeit faint at times, of its fabulous past.

Uzbekistan – the "Land of the Uzbeks" – is just the latest name used to describe the ancient lands between the Amu Darya (Oxus) and Syr Darya (Jaxartes) rivers. The Greeks called the region Transoxiana; the Arabs knew it as Mawarannahr, the "Land across the River". It is here that the last mountain spurs of the Tian Shan and Pamirs yield to the desolate plains and forbidding desert sands of the Karakum and Kyzylkum deserts.

Cultural legacy

It is also in essence a cultural meeting point: of Turkic and Persian, nomad and settler, Uzbek and Tajik. This desert land, studded with caravan oases and made rich with plunder and trade, is above all the homeland of Timur (Tamerlane), who has bequeathed modern Uzbekistan with some of the Islamic world's most fantastic architecture. The Uzbeks themselves are relatively late arrivals, establishing themselves in the 16th century. Most of the madrassas and

mosques you see in Uzbekistan date from this era.

The teahouses of Uzbekistan are perhaps the best places in the region to soak up Central Asian culture. Factor in some time to stroll the bustling modern bazaars, sip green tea on a *tapchan* (tea bed) under the shade of a mulberry tree and dine on *shashlyk* (mutton kebabs) and freshly baked *naan* bread. Uzbeks everywhere wear the *doppi* skullcap with pride, and the fabulously photogenic elders, known respectfully

Main Attractions

Fergana Valley
Margilan
Tashkent
Samarkand
Shakhrisabz
Bukhara
Khiva
Khwarezm: Toprak Qala
Nukus
Karakalpakstan

Uzbek women.

as *aksakal* or "white beards", still wear the striped cloaks known as a *khalat* or *chapan*. The women of the region are a riot of colour, dressed in shimmering *ikat* cloth and sporting mouthfuls of gold teeth.

Landscapes are not Uzbekistan's strong point. In fact it has been said that Uzbekistan is two-thirds desert and one-third cotton. Certainly wherever you go in the country you'll pass the endless fields of "white gold" that make Uzbekistan one of the world's largest exporters of cotton. Yet in these fluffy white plants lie the roots of an environmental disaster. Decades of Soviet irrigation schemes has lead to chronic water pollution, soil degradation and the almost complete collapse of the Aral Sea Basin (see page 117). The damaged environment is just one hangover from the 70 years of Soviet rule, which moved seamlessly to become an independent country under hard-line president Islam Karimov in 1991. After 25 years in charge, he died in September 2016. Defining a new path for independent Uzbekistan remains a huge challenge.

For Silk Road travellers, Uzbekistan is easily the most exciting of the Central Asian republics. It has the region's most fabulous historical sites, its most outrageous architecture and its most stylish accommodations. Don't miss it.

Fergana Valley

After the rigours of the Tian Shan and Pamir mountains, the Fergana Valley must have appeared a paradise to weary travellers and traders. Hemmed in on three sides by the spurs of the Tian Shan, Pamir Alai and Turkestan ranges, the huge and hazy 330-km (200-mile) -long valley is warm, flat and fertile, and its bazaars overflow with fruit and produce.

The valley (known to the Chinese as Dayuan) played a key role in the opening of the Silk Road. Its famed "blood-sweating" horses (believed by the Chinese to be descended from dragons) were in such demand that China forced open the first transcontinental trade routes specifically to gain a supply of the steeds and thus a technical advantage over its marauding nomadic neighbours. The horse trade remained central to the Silk Road long after the secret of silk production had spread to the west.

The valley funnelled Silk Road traffic for centuries, though there's little evidence of this today. Little remains of the Buddhist temple of Kuva, the 7th- to 11th-century ruins of Kasan and Aksiketh outside Namangan and the Zoroastrian tombs of Pap except some neglected and dusty archaeological remnants.

The echoes of the Silk Road ring loudest in the valley's vibrant bazaars and in its crafts – the paper factories of Kokand, the knives from Chust and the blue-and-green ceramics of Rishtan. The valley is one of the world's oldest cultivated areas, and alongside the cotton fields there are orchards, vineyards, walnut groves and, of course, extensive mulberry tree plantations, which supply the valley's silk factories with their raw material. Cotton and silk milling and the manufacture of chemicals and cement are among the valley's most important industries; along the fringes are deposits of oil, natural gas and iron ore. The region's natural resources contributed to the industrialisation of all Soviet Central Asia.

Home to one-third of Uzbekistan's population, the modern Fergana Valley is the most densely populated part of Central Asia and its most religiously active centre. In recent years the valley has gained infamy as the centre of conservative Islam and of the government's increasingly brutal attempts to stamp its control on the country. Further pressure came with the influx of 300,000 refugees from Kyrgyzstan following violence there in 2010 and the situation can be volatile.

Watermelons from the fertile Fergana Valley.

Andijan

For travellers **Andijan** (Andijon in Uzbek transliteration) is the eastern gateway to the valley, a short hop and a skip from the Kyrgyz border near Osh. The city's huge Thursday and Sunday bazaars have been attracting traders for millennia, but these days Andijan is most famous (rather,

Merchants with toasted lochira flatbreads in Kokand.

ENTERING AND LEAVING UZBEKISTAN

Many visitors arrive first in Tashkent and then fly to Urgench or Nukus before backtracking through the Silk Road cities (see page 386).

Places to cross to **Kazakhstan** are between Tashkent and Shymkent by road (a main crossing and a smaller crossing primarily for lorries) or between Tashkent and Arys or Nukus and Beyneu by rail. The Nukus crossing involves a long and unpredictable rail journey.

There are two road crossings to **Kyrgyzstan** in the Fergana Valley, one near Andijan, the other near Namangan, although it is necessary to change transport at the frontier. Formalities tend to be more rigorous on the Uzbek side. Daily buses run between Bishkek and Tashkent but require a Kazakhstan transit visa.

A border crossing east of Samarkand leads to Penjikent in **Tajikistan**, and there is another further south that connects with Dushanbe. A further crossing point at Oybek (daily 24 hours), just south of Tashkent, leads to Khojand in northern Tajikistan, as does a crossing further east in the Fergana Valley just west of Kokand.

Two of the crossings to **Turkmenistan** (Bukhara to Turkmenabat and Urgench to Dashoguz) involve a long walk or taxi between border posts (open in daylight). Nukus to Konye-Urgench at Khodjeyli is walkable (9am–6pm). A border crossing into **Afghanistan** exists at Termiz but this is not always open to travellers.

The colourful ikat fabrics worn by Uzbek women are woven from yarns dyed using a resist-dyeing process similar to tie-dye.

A 16th-century miniature portrait of Zahir-ud-Din Muhammad Babur.

infamous) for the events of May 2005, when government troops massacred up to 1,000 unarmed demonstrators in the town's central square. There are several historical sites in town, such as the Babur Literary Museum, a former royal residence, but get advice on the current political climate before exploring too deeply. The Juma Mosque and Madrassa has long been a barometer of the shifting political tides, switching from Soviet-era museum to active madrassa and now back to secular museum.

Fergana Town

In the south of the valley, also within striking distance of the Kyrgyz border, is the city of **Fergana** (Farg'ona in Uzbek). Founded as a Russian garrison town in 1876, it was initially named Skobelov after the Russian commander who subdued Khiva and Kokand and conquered the Turkmen tribes at the battle of Gök-Tepe. The blue-hued Tsarist buildings and colonial Russian layout of the town initially seem at odds with the traditional rural architecture of the valley,

but the pleasant leafy boulevards, local museum and café-restaurants of the provincial capital make it a good base from which to explore the valley, and there are some good accommodation options, too.

Margilan

Located just 5km (3 miles) to the north of Fergana, **Margilan** (Marg'ilon) was an important stop on the Silk Road. The local mulberry trees have fed silk production for centuries – even during Soviet times – and the economic life of the town is still dominated by the enormous Margilan Silk Factory, which churns out 2.5km (1.5 miles) of silk every day and employs some 15,000 workers. For a fascinating glimpse of traditional production methods, head to the **Yodgorlik Silk Factory** (daily 8am–5pm). Individual families raise the fussy silkworms on home-grown mulberry leaves, before the cocoons are taken to the factory to be steamed and unravelled and the silk woven into thread and then dyed. The result is the *khanatlas*

BABUR

A descendant of Timur and grandfather of the Mughal Emperor Akbar, Zahir-ud-Din Muhammad Babur (1483–1530) is an intriguing figure. Born in Andijan in 1483, he was forced out of his beloved Fergana Valley by the rising might of the Uzbek Sheybanids and fled to Afghanistan, conquering Kabul, Kandahar and finally India, where he founded the Mughal Dynasty. Despite his great conquests, he was never able to return to Central Asia, and his major literary work, the *Baburnama*, is infused with wistful longing for his beloved Fergana Valley. Though little-known today, without Babur the Central Asian-inspired architectural genius of the Taj Mahal and numerous other Mughal splendours in Delhi and Lahore might never have come to pass.

(king of satin) or *ikat*, the brightly coloured blur that clads almost all Uzbek women. Also worth catching is the bustling Thursday and Sunday **Kuntepa Bazaar**, 5km (3 miles) west of the centre. Margilan's atmospheric bazaar was replaced by a giant covered market in 2007. The few architectural remnants in town include the Khonakah Mosque, the Turon Mosque and the Sayid Akhmad Khodja Madrassa.

Namangan

Namangan, in the north of the valley, is the third-largest city in Uzbekistan. It is also known as its most religiously conservative, and its streets contain the highest concentration of veiled women in the country. The many closed madrassas and strong police presence highlight the government's unease with the growth of Islam. If you are passing through the town, the terracotta facade of the Hadja Amin Kabri complex is particularly fine, as are the nearby ruins of Akhsykent, a 1st century AD settlement 25km west of the town.

Kokand

In the west, the Khanate of **Kokand** (Qo'qon in Uzbek) was long Central Asia's third regional centre of power, for centuries jostling for regional dominance with Bukhara and Khiva, until the arrival of the Russians forced them all into irrelevance. At its peak, this crossroads city boasted 600 mosques and 15 madrassas, and ruled territory from the Kazakh Steppe to the Pamirs.

Only 19 opulent rooms survive from the original 113-roomed **Palace of Khudayar Khan** (built 1862–72), but it's still worth a look (daily 9am–5pm; charge). The 100-metre (330-ft) -long *iwan* of the Juma (Friday) Mosque was built to house the city's male population during weekly Friday prayers. Nearby is the Amin Beg Madrassa. Fifteen minutes' walk east is the working Narbutabey Madrassa, behind which the royal cemetery houses the Modari Khan and Dakhma-i-Shakhon mausoleums – the tombs of Kokandi Khan Omar, his mother and his wife.

Routes west out of the valley lead naturally from Kokand to Samarkand

Enjoying the shady terrace of a Kokand teahouse.

via Khojand (in Tajikistan; see page 267); but today's convoluted jigsaw borders mean that travellers generally head first to Tashkent, a three-hour drive away over the 2,268-metre (7,484-ft) Kamchik Pass. The newly strategic highway passes endless hairpin turns and snaking lines of crawling truck caravans to cross the Chatkal range, a faint final echo of the mighty Tian Shan.

Tashkent

Uzbekistan's capital is a huge sprawling city of over 2 million people; the largest in Central Asia and the fourth-largest in the former USSR.

As a Soviet-era showcase of orderly boulevards, museums and monuments it's not a particularly inspiring place but it's worth a day or two's exploration.

The city's roots, at the foot of the Tian Shan, lie in the ancient caravan town that grew up at the border of the settled and nomadic worlds. Known initially as Chach, its name was changed by the Turkic-speaking Karakhanids to Tashkent, or Stone Village, in the 10th century. The Khanate of Kokand absorbed Tashkent in 1809, and in 1864 the Russian Tsarist General Chernaiev took the town with only 1,900 men,

TIP

The best way to get around Tashkent is on the metro, which is worth riding for its stylish stations, dripping in decoration (in particular Kosmonavtlar with its floating cosmonauts). The system opened in 1977. Don't take photos in the metro and watch out for policemen on the make, whilst acting as security guards at the entrances.

Tashkent

disobeying direct orders from his superiors in distant St Petersburg. The Russian military cantonment grew quickly under the first governor of Russian Turkestan, Konstantin Kaufmann.

The city became the capital of the Uzbek SSR in 1930, replacing Samarkand. World War II spurred rapid growth as evacuees and entire communities of deported Koreans and Germans were forcibly relocated here, along with much of western Russia's heavy industry. The modern face of Tashkent (Toshkent in Uzbek) was transformed by the Soviet reconstruction that followed a powerful earthquake in 1966.

Central Tashkent

Icons of independence litter the centre of the city. The prime real estate outside the Hotel Uzbekistan, currently known as Amir Timur Square, is occupied by a park with a **statue of Timur** in the centre – the latest in a long line of iconic statues that have included Konstantin Kaufmann, Joseph Stalin and Karl Marx. The pleasant, leafy park is an ideal place to kick off a stroll of the city, dotted with shady glades where locals gather to play chess.

The iconic theme continues in the **Amir Timur Museum**, on the north side of the square. The modern turquoise-domed building, opened on the 660th anniversary of Timur's birthday, is largely an exercise in propaganda, pairing the exploits of Timur with the cult of current president Karimov. The museum collection mainly consists of ancient manuscripts, paintings and engravings, but there are some fine wooden models of Timurid architecture from across Uzbekistan.

Further west, the huge Soviet-era parade ground of **Independence Square** (Mustikalliq Maidoni) was home to the Union's largest Lenin statue until 1992, when it was replaced by a large globe whose only country is an oversized Uzbekistan. The square is the focus of colourful Independence Day celebrations that take place here each 1 September. Surrounding the square is the

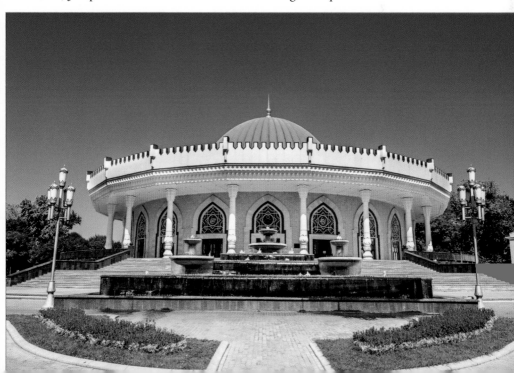

Tashkent's ornate Amir Timur Museum.

FACT

The chaos of the Bolshevik Revolution in Tashkent is described by F.M. Bailey in his book *Mission to Tashkent*. Bailey was in disguise when he passed through the city in 1918, and it must have been a pretty convincing one. At one stage the undercover British spy was given orders by the Russian secret police to hunt himself down!

Swimming in Tashkent's central canal.

new senate building, the president's office and various government ministries.

North from here is the **Tomb of the Unknown Soldier**, which commemorates the 400,000 citizens of Uzbekistan who died in World War II. Nearby is the **Earthquake Memorial**, a poignant spot that marks the exact time and date in 1966 that a major earthquake levelled the town and left 300,000 homeless.

Tashkent has the best museums in Uzbekistan, including the Museum of Applied Arts (daily 9am–6pm; charge) and State Fine Arts Museum (currently closed), which is based on the private collection and palace of Prince Nikolai Romanov. Most worthy of your time is the **Museum of the History of Uzbekistan** (Tue–Sun 10am–5pm; charge), which houses some 250,000 exhibits including a Kushan-era Buddha statue from Fayaz Tepe, a decorated bronze cauldron from the 4th century BC and impressive coins and manuscripts. Further west, the **Alisher Navoi Museum** (Mon–Fri 10am–5pm, Sat until 1pm; charge) celebrates the poet whose major work (*Khamsa*) put Chaghatai Turkic on the literary map in an age when poets generally wrote only in Persian.

Two metro stations north of Amir Timur Square on the green Yunusabad line take you to Minor station and the brand new Minor Mosque. Built in 2014 and a beautiful marble structure, it is now the largest in the country and welcomes visitors.

Old Town

Tashkent's Old Town (*eski shakhar*) doesn't compare to Samarkand or Bukhara in either scope or style, but it's worth a visit all the same. Start by taking the metro to the **Chorsu** (Four Roads) District and browsing the thunderous local bazaar, easily the city's best, offering the souvenir black-and-white Uzbek skullcaps, colourful mounds of spices, famously sweet melons and huge *naan* breads served hot out of the *tandur* oven. A short walk to the east is the traditional-style **Kukeldash Madrassa** and Juma Mosque.

North from Chorsu, the Soviet boulevards quickly wither to winding alleys of mud-walled houses, and traditional Central Asian culture reasserts itself. Hidden here in the Old Town is the religious heart of the city, the **Khast-Imam Square**, home to the Imam Ismail al-Bukhari Islamic Institute, the highest seminary in the USSR and one of only two that operated in Uzbekistan during the Soviet era. The Mufti of Tashkent (the country's top Islamic cleric) is based in the 16th-century Barak Khan Madrassa to the west.

Next to the nearby Tillya Sheikh Mosque, the affiliated Muyie Mubarek Library Museum (daily 9am–4pm; charge) holds an unexpected treasure, the **world's oldest Koran**. The Osman Koran dates from 655, and the blood of the Caliph Osman still stains several of its deerskin pages. The caliph was murdered while reading from the Koran, something that further fuelled the split between the Sunni and Shia branches of Islam.

Back on Navoi Street, and opposite the Literary Museum, is the 15th-century **Mausoleum of Yunus Khan**, grandfather of the Mughal emperor Babur, in the grounds of the Tashkent Islamic University.

Other sights

If you are in Tashkent outside the summer months, try to attend a performance at the lavish **Alisher Navoi Opera and Ballet Theatre**, designed by the same architect who built Lenin's tomb in Moscow. Performances range from Puccini to Uzbek folklore. Check also to see what is playing at the **Ilkhom Theatre**, the most progressive arts venue in the country.

The lonely onion-domed **Orthodox Russian Cathedral** is worth a visit on Sundays for its fine icons. Since independence, large numbers of Tashkent's Russian community have left Uzbekistan for a new life in Mother Russia.

Samarkand

More so than any other city in Central Asia, Samarkand's name drips with an exotic romanticism, whose resonance can be largely attributed to the

Original tiles on Samarkand's Gur-i-Mir.

Passing by a mosque in the Sheikh Tillya Mosque complex, home to the world's oldest Koran.

WORLD'S OLDEST KORAN

You won't be the only one surprised to hear that the world's oldest Koran resides in Uzbekistan, and its journey here was a convoluted one indeed. It is known as the Osman Koran, after the caliph who compiled it in Medina in the 7th century.

In the 14th century Timur brought the Koran to Central Asia, from Basra, to display it on the central marble lectern of Samarkand's Bibi Khanum Mosque. After the Tsarists took the city in 1868, the treasure was carted off to St Petersburg, until Lenin moved it on again, first to Ufa in Bashkaria and then to Tashkent's State Historical Museum. Finally, in 1989, at the height of *perestroika*, the Koran was handed over to Islamic clerics at the Sheikh Tillya Mosque, where it remains to this day.

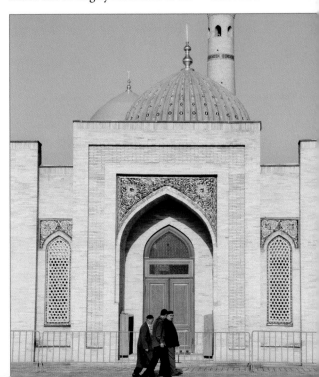

immortal lines of James Flecker's 1913 poem, *Hassan*:

> *We travel not for trafficking alone:*
> *By hotter winds our fiery hearts are fanned:*
> *For lust of knowing what should not be known*
> *We make the Golden Journey to Samarkand.*

Set at a trade crossroads and fed by the Zerafshan River, Samarkand (Samarqand in Uzbek) has been a Silk Road town for around 2,500 years. Alexander the Great visited in 329 BC, when it was the Sogdian city of Marakanda, part of the Achaemenid Empire. "Everything I have heard about Samarkand is true," he said, "except it is even more beautiful than I had imagined."

Sogdian wall murals recovered from Afrosiab in the northeast of the city depict the Silk Road heyday, when Tang China craved such exotica as Samarkand's golden peaches. Xuanzang described Samarkand (So-mo-kien) in the 7th century: "The precious merchandise of many foreign countries is stored up here... The inhabitants are skilful in the arts and trades beyond those of other countries."

The cosmopolitan city embraced Zoroastrian fire-worship and even

Samarkand

0 — 500 m
0 — 500 yds

became a Nestorian Christian bishopric until the arrival of the Arab armies changed everything in AD 712. The later invasions of the Khorezmshah and Mongol armies severely diminished the city. Marco Polo reported "a large and splendid city" at the end of the 13th century – but then he never actually saw it.

Samarkand is, above all, the city of Timur, and it is his turquoise domes and audacious building projects that draw visitors to this day. Timur forcibly relocated artisans from across his empire to embellish his capital, and it was in Samarkand that artisans from Persia, Azerbaijan, Syria and India saw "barbarism turned to beauty". For Timur himself, the city was "less a home than a marvellous trophy". Ever the nomad, he preferred the tents, camps and gardens outside the city walls to the epic bricks and mortar inside.

Silk Road traffic dried up from the 16th century, and Samarkand gradually took a back seat to Bukhara. The city was taken by the Russians in 1868 and shone briefly as the capital of the Uzbekistan SSR until sinking into obscurity as a remote corner of the Soviet Union.

The Registan

Samarkand's **Registan** (daily 8am–7pm; charge) is without doubt the single most dramatic architectural ensemble in Central Asia. Three towering madrassas, saturated from head to toe in mesmerising tilework, rise around open ground to form an irresistible symmetry. The British MP (and future viceroy of India) George Curzon called it "the noblest public square in the world".

The Registan ("Sandy Place") was originally a market area, where the six roads of the city met in a trade crossroads. It was later used for military parades and public executions, while the Bolsheviks used it for political rallies, trials and veil burnings. Now beautifully restored, it offers a fabulous and recently upgraded, high-tech evening sound-and-light show, much better than the previous version.

Ulug Beg built the first madrassa here (1417–20), on the west side,

The Bibi Khanum Mosque.

Tamerlane the Great

Few individuals shaped Central Asia as much as Tamerlane, a merciless leader who conquered lands from India to Baghdad.

Born into the Barlas clan of Turkicised Mongols only a century after the death of Genghis Khan, legend suggests that Tamerlane's palms were filled with blood, auguring a bloody life. He started his career as a bandit, and at the age of 27 he was shot with an arrow in his right shoulder and hip while rustling sheep. His wounds gave rise to his pejorative Persian nickname Timur-i-Leme (Timur the Lame) and the later Latinised version, Tamerlane.

Timur's ambitions were not easily contained, and by 1370 he had vanquished his former brother-in-law to be crowned ruler of Chaghatai – "Conqueror of the World". He proclaimed, "The world is not large enough for two kings", and for the next 35 years he tried to prove that claim. He defeated the Ottoman sultan Beyazid in Ankara, destroyed the Golden Horde on the Kazakh

Tamerlane, "Conqueror of the World".

Steppe, and wrested control of trade routes from Delhi to Damascus.

It has been estimated that Timur's merciless campaigns led to the deaths of 17 million people. Prisoners in Isfizar in Iran were cemented alive into giant towers. His troops bombarded the Christian armies at Smyrna with cannonballs made from the severed heads of their own knights. He boasted that his troops beheaded 10,000 Hindus in a single hour during the plunder of Delhi. In Baghdad in 1401 his forces killed 90,000 locals and cemented their heads into 120 towers.

A great legacy

Though he remains little-known in the West, his reputation alone was enough to inspire poetry by Edgar Allan Poe *(Tamerlane)*, drama by Christopher Marlowe *(Tamburlaine the Great)* and operas by both Handel and Vivaldi *(Il Tamerlano)*. Like all the great nomad leaders, Timur suffered the fate of being chronicled almost exclusively through the jaundiced eyes of his victims.

The man himself is in many ways a contradiction. Islamicised and Turkicised, he was a Muslim, though he never let his religion get in the way of his conquests. He spoke both Persian and Turkic fluently and had a great respect for learned men, yet he himself was illiterate. A nomad at heart who lived on the move, he also created some of the most beautiful urban architecture the world has ever seen. A chess fanatic, he invented a new game that employed twice the number of pieces (including camels, giraffes and war engines). Historians estimate that he had at least 12 wives.

Timur died in February 1405 in Otrar while planning his biggest campaign yet, the invasion of Ming China. His body was "embalmed with musk and rose-water, wrapped in linen, laid in an ebony coffin and sent to Samarkand". His body was interred in the Gur-i-Mir and his howls were allegedly heard nightly for a year after his burial. Today, Uzbekistan celebrates their most famous son with three giant bronze statues in the cities most associated with him. In Shakhrisabz, he stands defiantly in front of the remains of his Ak Sarai Palace; in Samarkand, he is in a more reflective seated pose near to his tomb; and in the middle of Timur Square in Tashkent, he proudly waves to the crowds riding his horse, near to his own museum. Perhaps his most fitting epitaph is inscribed on his tomb: "If I were alive," it reads, "people would not be glad."

flanked by 33-metre (109-ft) -high columns and richly decorated with star designs, *girikh* (geometric) patterns, and stunning mosaic and majolica tilework. If you tip the security guard downstairs, it is possible to climb the right-hand minaret and exit on to the roof, from where there is a superb view across Samarkand. It was a further two centuries before the **Shir Dor Madrassa** (1619–36) was erected to the east as a mirror piece. The madrassa gets its name from the mosaic lions (*shir*) that adorn the corners of the portal – anatomically incorrect, you'll be forgiven for thinking they're tigers. The flouting of the Islamic convention against the depiction of living beings is made doubly heretical by the beaming Zoroastrian-inspired sun faces painted on the lions' backs.

The ensemble is topped off by the **Tillya Kari Madrassa** (1646–60), wider than the other two and boasting a huge turquoise dome and magnificent gilded interior. The former *hujra* (student accommodation) cells now function as gift shops and you can watch artisans at work. The nearby four-sided Chorsu was once the city's skullcap bazaar.

The **State Art Museum** (daily 9am–6pm; charge) on the east side of the Registan displays copies of Afrosiab's murals and the famous Kushan-era Ayrtam frieze (discovered near the Afghan border), as well as Timur's wooden coffin.

Bibi Khanum Mosque

Timur made his true bid for architectural immortality with the **Bibi Khanum Mosque** (daily 8am–7pm; charge), a monumental building planned on a hitherto unseen scale, along the pleasant pedestrianised street northeast of the Registan. Financed from the spoils of a recent campaign to Delhi (1398) and built with the labour of 95 imported Indian elephants, the huge 35 metre- (116 ft-) entry arch was flanked by 50 metre- (165 ft-) minarets that led into a court paved with marble and flanked with mosques. But it was built in too much haste (Timur himself threw gold coins and scraps of barbecued meat to encourage workers), and the tottering

One of Bibi Khanum Mosque's three domes.

The Registan in Samarkand.

Ambassador to the Sogdian court depicted on the murals at Afrosiab.

The interior of Gur-i-Mir.

walls started to crumble almost as soon as they were finished. In the last decade, a similarly hasty programme of restoration has rebuilt the three main domes – "a shining blandness", in the words of Colin Thubron, "snuffing out the strange vitality of ruin".

The mosque was built in honour of Timur's chief wife, Saray Mulk Khanum, who was laid to rest in the nearby **Bibi Khanum Mausoleum**. A number of local women still come here to pray, although it is now considered a museum rather than a place of worship. Next to the mosque is the main **Siab Bazaar**, groaning with grapes, fruit and, yes, Samarkand's famed golden peaches. There is a pleasant picnic spot between the mosque and the market. A short walk north leads to the **Khazret Khyzr Mosque**, an elegant structure with carved wooden pillars and jewel-coloured paintwork, named after the pre-Islamic patron saint of wayfarers.

Shah-i-Zindah and around

Samarkand's other great artistic highlight is the **Shah-i-Zindah** (daily 8am–7pm; charge), a visually absorbing necropolis and one of the great masterpieces of Timurid art. The street of tombs, accessed from the main road or on foot via the city's modern graveyard, dates from 1372 to 1460 and houses a veritable "Who's Who" of Timurid aristocracy, including Timur's niece Shadi Mulk Aka, sisters Turkhan Aka and Shirin Bika Aka, and wives Tuman Aka and Kutlug Aka.

The tombs' real genius lies in their range of decoration, with carved terracotta and majolica tilework set into complicated floral designs framed with stylised calligraphy, everything saturated in a dozen intense shades of blue. The focus for local pilgrims is the tomb of the Arab leader Kusam ibn Abbas, who was beheaded after his attempts to convert locals to Islam and merged into the local pre-Islamic legend of the "Living King" (Shah-i-Zindah). Come shortly before dusk for the most atmospheric experience.

One of the few remnants of the early Silk Road are the ruins of **Afrosiab**, the Sogdian city that flourished from the 6th century BC until the arrival of Genghis Khan in 1220. It was here that the increasingly megalomaniac Alexander the Great killed his favourite general, Cleitus, in a drunken rage. Excavations of the dusty 120-hectare (300-acre) site have revealed Graeco-Bactrian and Kushan roots, Zoroastrian temples and a cult centre dedicated to the local god Anahita, though there's little to see these days except hot dusty trenches and low excavated walls. However, the **museum** (daily 9am–6pm; charge), housed in the modern Soviet-era building at the site, is fascinating, and guides (some speaking English) provide informative talks on the different periods.

Afrosiab is most famous for its wall murals (long since removed), which feature a royal bridal procession atop a white elephant, a series of bearded ambassadors to the Sogdian court and a ruler in magnificent clothes meeting with silk-bearing Chinese, Turkic and even Korean envoys. Copies of these murals are also on display at the museum. The site is named after the legendary king depicted in Firdausi's epic poem *Shahnameh* ("Book of Kings").

Adjacent to the site is the **Tomb of Doniyar** (Daniel), where a local legend claims that the bones of the Hebrew saint were interred after Timur brought them to Samarkand.

The most enlightened of the Timurid rulers was without doubt Timur's grandson, the "Astronomer King" Ulug Beg. Ulug Beg's penchant for astronomy, mathematics and science didn't go down well with the conservative court of the day, and he was eventually beheaded by his own son. In 1908 Russian archaeologists unearthed **Ulug Beg's Observatory**, commissioned in 1428 and destroyed by fanatics 21 years later. The underground chamber was excavated by the Soviets in 1938. You can still see the lower one-third of the arc of the great sextant cut into the rock, and the nearby museum helps to

explain how it all worked. A poignant inscription outside proclaims: "The religions disperse, kingdoms fall apart, but the work of science remains eternal."

Gur-i-Mir

Samarkand's final "must-see" is the Gur-i-Mir (Tomb of the Emir), the final resting place of Timur. The mausoleum was originally planned for Timur's favourite grandson, Muhammad Sultan (Timur had long wanted to be buried in Shakhrisabz), but Samarkand was deemed a more fitting resting place. The exterior of the building is dominated by a fine entrance portal and the hallmark ribbed turquoise dome that floats like a giant balloon above the central octagonal chamber. It's a beautiful but surprisingly modest monument for the world's greatest warlord. Timur is buried at the foot of his spiritual adviser, Mir Sayid Barakah, and surrounded by many of his family. His body lies under a tombstone that was at the time the world's largest slab of jade. The Persian invader Nadir Shah broke

Ulug Beg dispensing justice at Khurasan (15th-century miniature).

ULUG BEG

As the ruler of Samarkand, the Timurid ruler Ulug "Mirzoi" Beg (1394–1449), grandson of Timur (see page 280), built several of the city's most beautiful madrassas. However, it is his scientific patronage, and in particular his magnificent observatory, the Gurkhani Zij, for which he is most renowned. Like the Khwarezmian scientist al-Biruni 400 years before him (see page 112), Ulug Beg was the finest astronomer of his age, correctly repositioning 1,018 stars in an astronomical catalogue that was the first of its kind since Ptolemy. Tragically, within two years of his father Shah Rukh's death he was assassinated while on his way to Mecca, a martyr to science, and was laid to rest in his grandfather's tomb, the Gur-i-Mir.

Russian-made Ladas are still a common sight in Uzbekistan.

the slab while trying to steal it. The actual graves are in the crypt below.

Two other tombs are located within the Gur-i-Mir area: the 14th century **Rukhobod Mausoleum, which** is said to contain a hair of the Prophet, and the unrestored brick-built **Aksaray Mausoleum** on the street behind.

Other sights

Other architectural gems in the Samarkand suburbs include the **Mausoleum of Khodja Abdi Darun**, built by Seljuk Sultan Sanjar and renovated by Ulug Beg, and the nearby **Ishrat Khana** (House of Joy), a refreshingly unrestored pleasure dome built by Timur's wife and later converted into a mausoleum by one of Timur's descendants.

Shakhrisabz

South from Samarkand, modern roads follow a side branch of the Silk Road to the Oxus River. The route was popular with invaders and traders, and the latter were taxed at a defile en route known as the "Iron Gates".

The town of **Shakhrisabz**, 80km (48 miles) south of Samarkand over the Takhtakaracha Pass, is most famous as the hometown of Timur, who was born nearby in April 1336. His actual birthplace is in Khoja Ilgar Village, some 13km (8 miles) to the south, where a surprisingly unassuming cairn marks the spot.

Today Shakhrisabz is a charming, traditional Uzbek town, littered with the ruined monuments of its favourite son. The Chinese pilgrim Xuanzang visited when it was known as the Sogdian town of Kesh. Tajik-speakers later renamed it Shahr-i-sabz, the "Green City".

The White Palace

The main sight is the huge ruined complex of the Ak Serai, Timur's "White Palace". Built by slave artisans brought here from Khwarezm, the site was planned as a summer residence to complement Samarkand's Kok Serai, or Red Palace.

The restorers have again been hard at work here, trying to recreate the huge 65-metre (214-ft) entry towers

Bukhara

0   200 m
0   200 yds

that once supported Central Asia's largest portal. The incredible palace was visited in 1404 by the Spanish envoy Ruy González de Clavijo, who described the palace's blue-tiled walls, golden ceilings and the lush surrounding gardens of waterfalls and silk tents that were the site of epic Bacchanalian feasts of wine and horseflesh. By the time Clavijo arrived craftsmen had already been working on the palace for over 20 years.

A large statue of Timur dominates this newly pedestrianised and landscaped complex. Here the words of Timur resonate: "Let he who doubts our power look upon our buildings."

Timurid tombs

Other buildings worth visiting as you walk south are the 14th-century Malik Azhdar Khanaga and the Amir Timur Museum, housed in a former madrassa. The impressive blue dome in the south of the town belongs to the **Kok Gumbaz Mosque** (1435–6), built by Ulug Beg as part of the Dorut Tilovat complex. Timur's father Taraghay and his spiritual adviser Shamsaddin Kulyal are both buried in the nearby Timurid mausoleum.

A couple of minutes' walk to the east is the crumbling **Tomb of Jehangir**, all that remains of the Dorus Siadat, a Timurid family memorial that ranked as one of Timur's greatest creations. Timur's eldest son Jehangir and second son Umar Sheikh are both buried here, and Timur himself also planned to be interred here. The intended **crypt of Timur** was discovered nearby in 1943, and you can still see the empty underground marble casket.

From Shakhrisabz, the main M39 road continues southeast to the border city of Termiz, from where the Friendship Bridge leads across the Oxus to the Afghan cities of Mazar-e-Sharif and Balkh, themselves both ethnically Uzbek.

Bukhara

Known for centuries as Bukhoro-i-sharif (Bukhara the Noble), and the "Dome of Islam", the holy city of Bukhara (Buxoro in Uzbek) is one of the oldest cities in Central Asia, stretching back some 2,500 years. At its peak the city boasted 250 madrassas, 200 minarets and a mosque for every day of the year.

According to the Persian epic *Shahnameh*, the hero Siyavush founded the city after marrying the daughter of neighbouring Afrosiab. The town thrived as a transit spot and a crossroads town, with city gates pointing to Merv, Gurganj, Herat, Khiva and Samarkand.

In the early days Bukhara was eclipsed by great cities now lost in the surrounding deserts. All that remains of Varakhsha, once the richest caravan stop in the region, are the superb Sogdian murals, now preserved in local museums, of hunters battling leopards and a court scene flanked by winged griffins. The Hephthalite capital of Paikend, another of the great regional trading

Ceremonial daggers made by artisans in Bukhara.

Ak Serai in Shakhrisabz.

QUOTE

"A stranger has only to seat himself on a bench of the Registan, to know the Uzbeks and the people of Bokhara. He may here converse with the natives of Persia, Turkey, Russia, Tartary, China, India, and Cabool. He will meet with Toorkmuns, Calmuks, and Kuzzaks, from the surrounding deserts, as well as natives of more favoured lands."

Alexander Burnes on 19th century Bukhara

centres, was destroyed during the Arab invasion.

Bukhara hit its high point in the 9th and 10th centuries under the Samanid Dynasty, when the city became a great centre of Persian culture and science. Thinkers such as al-Biruni, the poet Rudaki and the medic Ibn Sina (Avicenna), Bukhara's grand vizier for a time, enjoyed access to Bukhara's "Treasury of Wisdom", a library surpassed in the Islamic world only by the House of Wisdom in Baghdad.

The city was largely destroyed by the Mongols in 1220. Genghis Khan addressed the trembling citizens of Bukhara with a perverse sense of logic: "If you had not committed great sins," he said, "God would not have sent a punishment like me." When the Moroccan traveller Ibn Battuta arrived in Bukhara a century later in 1333, the city was still in ruins.

The khanate (and later emirate) was revived in the 16th century under the extensive building programmes of Abdullah Khan, but by the Astrakhanid Dynasty the decline of the Silk Road had isolated Bukhara, and the city began a gradual slide into decay and fanaticism.

The 19th century brought intrepid travellers to the city. The great traveller William Moorcroft arrived in 1825 in search of horses but left empty-handed, only to be murdered on the return journey to Balkh. Alexander "Bokhara" Burnes, later to write his classic travelogue *Travels into Bukhara*, visited the city in 1832. The city gained true notoriety abroad when the British officers Conolly and Stoddart were executed in Bukhara in 1839. Bukhara's glory days were coming to an end. Even in the 19th century foreign travellers described the city as wearing "a halo of departed glory".

Today the quiet and largely Tajik town offers plenty of scope for exploration. If you have only one spare day in your itinerary, spend it here. The domes and minarets of the sun-dried city glow golden in the afternoon light, and although a little lacking in spice, exhausted by its long Soviet rule, the city's twisting backstreets still provide plenty of Silk Road atmosphere.

A city within a city: Bukhara's ancient Ark.

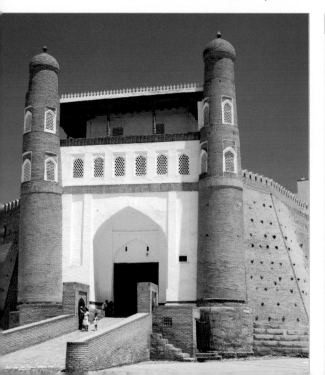

RESTORATION WORK

War, neglect and an extreme climate have taken a heavy toll on Uzbekistan's architectural gems. By the end of the 19th century, many of Samarkand's domes and Bukhara's minarets had started to collapse. Early Soviet archaeologists painstakingly restored Bukhara's Ismail Samani Mausoleum, and Samarkand's Registan to their former glory, but sadly these monuments are again under threat. A rising water-table is driving salt into Bukhara's brickwork, it's common to see grass growing and birds nesting amongst the tiles, and the clumsy reconstruction of sites like the Bibi Khanum Mosque in Samarkand is damaging Uzbekistan's golden cities. Scaffolding, though essential to repair work, regularly blights domes across the skyline.

The Ark

The heart of ancient Bukhara is the **Ark** (daily 9am–6pm; charge), the 2,000-year-old fortress around which the city formed. Fortified, destroyed and rebuilt many times over the years, the "city within a city" became home to the emirs of Bukhara, evolving into a complex warren of chambers, mosques, reception rooms, servants' quarters, mint, jail and armoury. What remains today is only about 30 percent of the original; peek around the back to see the ruins left by the Red Army artillery of General Frunze in 1920.

The main entrance leads up a ramp into the great 18th-century gatehouse, or *darvazkhana*, above which the emir's retinue would watch executions and public events in the square below. The **Bukhara State Art and Architectural Museum** occupies the Friday mosque and the former 17th-century coronation room, and displays 18 permanent exhibitions of paintings, manuscripts, coins and ethnographic items.

Outside the Ark, at the foot of the baked brick walls, is **Registan Square**, home to the city's slave market, parade ground and, when a drumbeat pulsed from the depths of the Ark, its flogging and execution ground. The elegant colonnaded *iwan* of the Bolo Hauz Mosque rises to the north.

Around the back of the Ark is the **Zindon**, the former city jail, where important prisoners were held, often for years at a time. You can still see the notorious "Bug Pit" where the British officers Conolly and Stoddart were held for months before being executed.

South of the Registan are the Abdullah Khan Madrassa (1588) and Modari Khan Madrassa (1567), the latter built for the mother (*modar*) of the Uzbek Khan Abdullah Sheybani (1533–97). Further south is the multicoloured Balyand Mosque, noted for its gilded *kundal* paintings.

Samanid Mausoleum

A five-minute walk west of the Ark brings you to Samani Park, which is home to one of Central Asia's great architectural highlights, the **Ismail Samani Mausoleum**. The 10th-century gem houses the tomb of Ismail Samani, founder of the cultured Samanid Dynasty that oversaw Bukhara's cultural highpoint. The genius of the cubed building lies in its elegant basket-weave brickwork, which glows in full glory in the afternoon light.

Nearby is the **Chashma Ayub**, built in 1380 around the spring of the Old Testament prophet Job (Ayub in Arabic). The conical cupola, unique in Bukhara, was designed by artists relocated from Gurganj (Kunya-Urgench) by Timur. The town bazaar is next door.

The use of all-over brickwork on the Ismail Samani Mausoleum represented an architectural innovation. Its ornate exterior reflects the light in different ways during the day.

Poi Kalon ensemble

Bukhara's most impressive building is the **Kalon Minaret** (Kalon meaning "great" in Tajik). Built in 1127 by the Karakhanid ruler Arslan Khan, the tower was probably the world's tallest building at the time of its construction. Even Genghis Khan was

The imposing Kalon Mosque in Bukhara.

FACT

In 1938 Fitzroy Maclean arrived into Bukhara almost a century after the Conolly and Stoddart incident. In *Eastern Approaches* he wrote, "I could have spent months in Bokhara, seeking out fresh memories of its prodigious past, mingling with the bright crowds in the bazaar, or idling away my time under the apricot trees in the warm sunlight of Central Asia."

View of the Kalon Minaret from the Ark.

awestruck, ordering the building spared from the Mongol destruction. It is the only building of this period to survive in Bukhara.

The minaret rises 48 metres (158ft) through bands of intricate brick patterns and is connected to its mosque roof by a bridge passage. The single turquoise band towards the top is thought to be the earliest example of glazed tilework in Central Asia. The minaret was nicknamed the "Tower of Death" in the 19th century, when criminals were tied in sacks and hurled off the skylight by orders of the Emir.

The attached **Kalon Mosque** (admission charge) was for centuries Bukhara's main Friday mosque, built to accommodate over 10,000 worshippers. The town's first Arab governor built the earliest mosque on this spot. A later 12th-century building was set ablaze by the Mongol forces but was rebuilt in 1514. When Genghis Khan arrived at the holy site he turned the mosque into a stable and uttered "The hay is cut. Give your horses fodder", the signal for his troops to pillage the city. The mosque still has its 288 cupolas, of which the largest is the gorgeous Kok Gumbaz (Blue Dome) at the west end. The mosque was used as a warehouse during the Soviet era.

Across from the mosque are the twin turquoise domes of the **Mir-i-Arab Madrassa** (1535), one of only two such institutions to function in Uzbekistan during the Soviet era. The building was financed by Ubaidullah Khan from the sale of 3,000 Persian slaves and is named after the khan's Yemeni spiritual adviser (Mir-i-Arab means "Lord of the Arabs"). Both adviser and Khan are buried inside. This is still a working madrassa, and so the fine interior is off-limits to tourists.

To the south of the madrassa is the small **Emir Alim Khan Madrassa**, now a children's library.

To the east is the **Ulug Beg Madrassa** (1417), Central Asia's first madrassa and the prototype for the version that Ulug Beg was to build three years later in Samarkand's Registan Square. Ulug Beg's love of astronomy and science is revealed in the star-shaped motifs and the inscription above the portal that states: "It is the sacred duty

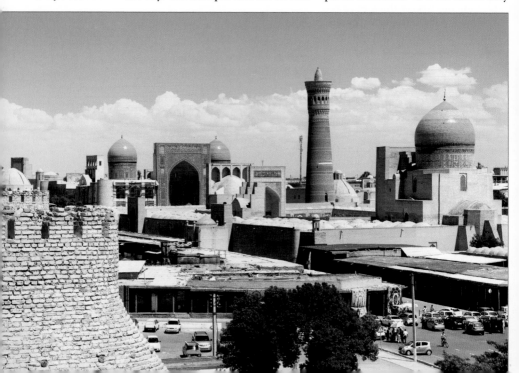

of every Muslim man and woman to seek after knowledge." The madrassa was renovated during its 500th anniversary in 1994.

The unrestored **Abdul Aziz Madrassa** (1652) across the road boasts fine Chinese-influenced interior decoration and a woodcarving museum. Both madrassas follow a standard design, with a mosque and lecture hall on either side of an entrance portal and a series of student cells arranged around the inner courtyard.

Bukhara's bazaars

The heart of any Silk Road city lies in its bazaars and Bukhara once boasted 40 of them, along with 24 caravanserais, six *tims* (trading houses) and three *toks* (multi-entried bazaars that straddle major intersections). Though the turbaned traders of old have been replaced by souvenir-sellers, the cool, domed covered bazaars still offer a glimpse of the bones of a medieval Central Asian bazaar. Most of the buildings in this part of town house small exhibitions, craft workshops or souvenir stands, sometimes all three.

The main thoroughfare leads south from the **Tok-i-Zargaron** (1570, Jewellers' Bazaar), which once cornered the local market in lapis and rubies from Badakhshan, past the long-vanished Indian caravanserai to the Abdullah Khan Tim, which once specialised in wool and silk, and now, appropriately, sells carpets.

South of here is the 16th-century **Bazori Cord Hammam**, a bathhouse still open for men and tour groups who reserve it in advance. Also here, dominating the five-spoked intersection, is the **Tok-i-Tilpak Furushon**, or Cap Makers' Bazaar, which once specialised in gold-embroidered skullcaps, fur hats and illustrated manuscripts, all of which had to be protected from the glare of the sun. Inside the bazaar is the tomb of holy man Khoja Ahmed I Paran.

To the side, between the two domed bazaars, is the **Magok-i-Attari Mosque**, one of the earliest religious shrines in the city and the site of a former herb, spice and perfume (*attar*) bazaar. Excavations in the depression (*magok* means "in a

A Bukhara carpet-seller.

SHOP

These days most of Bukhara's bazaars and architectural sites are home to souvenir stalls. One of the best local buys are Bukharan-style miniature paintings, reproductions of court scenes, medieval folk tales and famous vignettes taken from such Central Asian literary classics as Navoi's *Khamsah* and Firdausi's *Shahnameh*. Visitors can often watch the artists painting new works.

The bathing pool at the Emir's Summer Palace.

pit") have revealed a shrine to the local moon god, a Zoroastrian temple, a Buddhist monastery and an Arab mosque, stacked on top of each other in layers of history. To the south is the 12th-century mosque portal, stunningly decorated with incised alabaster *girikh* (geometric designs). A carpet museum occupies the interior, but a portion of the excavations lie revealed in the far corner.

To the west of the Tok-i-Sarrafon is the 16th-century **Gaukushan Madrassa**, now a metal-chasing workshop and named after the slaughterhouse (*gaukushan* means "cow-killer") that used to occupy the site.

Lyab-i-Hauz

With its traditional architecture and ancient mulberry trees set around a central stepped pool, the *mahalla* (district) of the Lyab-i-Hauz ("Around the Pool") is in many ways the town's most attractive. The *hauz* (pool) dates from 1620 and was one of 200 that supplied Bukhara with its drinking water (as well as many of its infectious diseases). The shady

poolside chaikhana (teahouse) is a great place to relax over a bowl of *plov* and a pot of green tea, though tourism has forced out most of the *aksakals* who gave the place much of its character.

The *hauz* was commissioned by Grand Vizier Nadir Divanbegi, who also initiated the **khanagha** (pilgrim hostel) and mosque to the west. East of the pool, the **Divanbegi Madrassa** was originally built as a caravanserai, but when the khan mistakenly inaugurated it as a madrassa it had to be hastily converted (once uttered, the edicts of the khan could never be rescinded). Two mythological birds decorate the portal, grasping white doves in their talons. The Mongol-faced sun recalls the Shir Dor Madrassa in Samarkand. The madrassa hosts a colourful nightly folklore and fashion show in summer, and the nearby puppet show is also worth a visit.

To the south is a statue of Khoja Nasreddin, the Sufic holy fool, whose humorous sayings and anecdotes are much loved throughout the Islamic world. Finishing off the ensemble to he north is the **Kukeldash Madrassa** 1568), the largest in Central Asia, with 160 student rooms.

The town's **Jewish quarter** stretches south from the Lyab-i-Hauz. Legend has it that the Jews were given this land in exchange for the area now known as Lyab-i-Hauz. Bukhara's Jews trace their arrival in Bukhara from the 14th century and they long played an important role in trade with the Khazaria region in the Russian Volga. The community once numbered 4,000, but since 1991 many have opted for a new life in Israel. It's possible to visit the nearby synagogue and Jewish cemetery.

A few hundred metres east of he Lyab-i-Hauz is the **Chor Minor** 1807), one of Bukhara's quirkiest buildings. This architectural oddity, which resembles an upside-down chair, is actually the gatehouse of a destroyed madrassa. The blue domes of the eponymous four minarets (*chor minor*) were once topped by storks' nests and fell into disrepair but have since been restored by Unesco. A souvenir seller occupies the ground floor

and will allow visitors to climb onto the roof (charge).

Suburban Bukhara

If you have a spare few hours, head into the northern suburbs to the Sitorai Makhi Khosa, otherwise known as the **Emir's Summer Palace** (Wed–Mon 9am–5pm, Tue until 2.30pm; charge). Built by the Russians in 1911, the kitschy half-European, half-Oriental palace was home to the last emir of Bukhara, Alim Khan, until he fled to Afghanistan in 1920. The first Congress of the Bukharan Soviet was held in the palace that same year, heralding the dramatic political changes to come.

The wedding-cake-like complex leads into an inner courtyard of reception halls, where you'll find the **museums of Applied Arts, National Costume and Needlework**. The examples of gold embroidery and *suzani* (wall hangings) here are particularly fine. The last museum is housed in the former palace harem, where a voyeuristic emir would watch his concubines bathing, before

Colourfully-attired Uzbek women.

The Chor Minor once opened into a large madrassa complex. Its name means "The Four Minarets" in Tajik, although its sky-blue turrets have little in common with ordinary minarets.

The Islam Khoja Minaret.

throwing an apple to his passing favourite. The complex is fascinating in its depiction of an emirate straddling the medieval and the modern and was the first place in the Bukharan emirate to have electricity.

Around Bukhara

About 12km (7.5 miles) from Bukhara in Kasri Orifon village is the **Bakhauddin Naqshbandi complex**, centred around the tomb of the 14th-century saint who is Bukhara's spiritual protector. With its "wishing trees", holy stones and sacrificial offerings, the site offers a glimpse into Central Asia's brand of popular or "parallel" Islam, which has its roots as much in an animist past as in the formal teachings of Islam. Apart from the saint's tomb, the complex includes two mosques, a huge *khanaga* (1544) and the tombs of two khans, Abdul Aziz and Abdullah II.

The other main Sufic site is the **Chor Bakr**, whose street of tombs is centred around the graves of Sayid Abu Bakr and three brothers (*chor Bakr* means "four Bakrs"). The term

The unfinished Kalta Minor minaret.

sayid denotes a direct descendant of the Prophet Muhammad, and the sanctity this brought the complex made it the preferred burial place of the Bukharan aristocracy. The quiet complex of mosque, pilgrim accommodation, *chillakhanas* (meditation rooms) and *takharatkhanas* (place for ablutions) remains a pilgrimage site and its gardens are a tranquil spot for picnics. It is 6km (3.5 miles) west of Bukhara.

Khiva and Khorezm

Hiddenin the deserts of northwest Uzbekistan, an 18-day journey by camel from Bukhara (or 45-minute flight from Tashkent), the oasis caravan town of **Khiva** (Xiva in Uzbek) has long been the remotest of the three khanates.

Though local legend has the town founded by Shem, son of Noah, Khiva is not the most ancient town in the region. Like its great brethren the Indus, Nile and Euphrates, the Oxus Delta has long nourished one of Asia's great centres of antiquity. Most of these ancient cities lie neglected, lost

Khiva

Mustaqillik
DISHAN KALA
Bagcha Darvaza (North Gate)
Toshpolatov
Toshpolatov
Toshpolatov
Hotel Islambek
City Wall
Abdulla Boltaev   ICHAN KALA
Abdulla Boltaev
Rakhimov
City Wall
Abdulla Boltaev
Toshpolatov
Hotel Asia Khiva
★
Viewing platform
Zindon
Kukhna Ark Citadel
Dost Alimjob Madrassa
Allah Kuli Khan Bazaar and Caravanserai
Muhammed Rakhim Khan Madrassa
Dost Alyam Madrassa
Tash Hauli (Stone) Palace
Matinyaz Divanbegi Madrassa
Arabhana Madrassa
Ata Darvaza (West Gate)   Kalta Minor
Kalta Minor (Restaurant Khiva)
Matpana Bay Madrassa
Kutluq Murad Inaq Madrassa
Allah Kuli Khan Madrassa
Al-Khwarizmi
Pakhlavon Mahmud
Sayid Allauddin Mausoleum
Polvon Darvaza (East Gate)
Muhammed Amin Khan Madrassa (Orient Star Hotel)
Juma Mosque
Abdulla Khan Madrassa
Aq Mosque
Tinchlik
Pakhlavan Mahmud Mausoleum
Islam Khoja Minaret
Madrassa of Shir Ghazi Khan
Islam Khoja Madrassa
City Wall
0   100 m
0   100 yds
N
Islam Khoja
South Gate

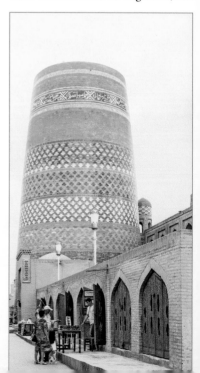

and baking in the desert sands, though the former capital of Gurganj (Konye-Urgench) can still be visited in neighbouring Turkmenistan.

Khiva prospered after both the Mongols and Timur flattened Gurganj, and it eventually became the region's capital in 1592. The oasis town provided a vital pit stop for caravans headed to Merv. Trade with the Russian Volga, particularly Astrakhan, added to the city's wealth and filled its caravanserais with samovars, furs, guns, karakul pelts and Turkestani melons. Isolated and lawless, the city also grew rich on plunder and, importantly, the slave trade.

It was the slave trade, specifically the 3,000 or so Slavic slaves, that gave the Russians the excuse they needed to attack its troublesome neighbour. Things did not go well at first. The first expedition ended in the slaughter of 4,000 Russian troops and the despatch of the expedition's head, literally, back to St Petersburg. The second winter expedition faltered in the frozen desert and never even reached Khiva, with the loss en route of 8,500

camels. In a move typical of the Great Game, the British officers James Abbot and Richmond Shakespear rushed to the city in an attempt to release the slaves and pull the rug from under the Russians' feet. But it was too little, too late. Khiva was living on borrowed time and by 1873 Kaufmann had engineered the absorption of the khanate into the Russian Empire.

Today Khiva is the most architecturally intact and tightly packed of Uzbekistan's Silk Road cities. Its intense green-and-blue tilework ranks as some of the most opulent in Central Asia, but it also has the feel of a movie set or a museum city, frozen in time and without the lived-in feel that makes Bukhara so fascinating.

The main points of interest are in the **Ichan Kala**, or inner city, encased in 17th-century **city walls** with rounded bastions and punctured by four entrances. These gates were once sealed dusk to dawn to keep marauders out. These days most tourists enter through the western **Ata Darvaza gate**. The city walls sadly no longer rise from

The imposing city walls of Khiva.

The skeleton husks of rusting ships on what was once the Aral Sea.

All but one of the columns in the Juma Mosque are carved of black elm wood.

the wind-whipped desert sands but rather from a tarmac car park.

The Ichan Kala

As you enter the inner town, on the right (south) is the **Muhammad Amin Khan Madrassa** (1855), the largest in the city and named after one of the city's more impressive khans. The madrassa's 125 *hujra* cells, once housing the madrassa's students, are currently home to the atmospheric Orient Star Hotel. Above the main entrance there is an inscription in Arabic calligraphy that reads: "This wonderful building will stay here forever to descendants' joy".

Beside the madrassa is a glowering statue of al-Khwarizmi (783–840), the brilliant Khorezmian mathematician after whom the word "algorithm" is named (he is also considered the father of algebra – another Arabic word, *al-jabr*). Khwarizmi was born in Khiva but spent much of his working life in Baghdad.

Outside the madrassa is the bright green stub of the **Kalta Minor**, commissioned by Amin Khan to be the

world's tallest minaret, but abandoned as too costly after the khan was murdered three years later. It is consequently rather squat in appearance.

To the left is the **Kukhna Ark**, the oldest core of the original fortress, whose roots stretch back some 1,500 years. The complex is notable for ice-blue tilework and tall *iwans* that face north to catch the prevailing summer breezes, with great views of the old city from the viewing platform on the roof. The royal rooms include a summer mosque, mint, harem and a throne room where the khan would meet winter guests in a felt yurt erected on a brick base (the yurt was easier to heat than the draughty brick halls of the palace). Just outside the Ark is the *zindon*, or city jail.

To the east is the **Muhammad Rakhim Khan Madrassa** (1871), now home to a crafts centre. A museum is dedicated to the khan, who was also known for his poetry, written under the name Feruz Shah. Feruz was the last khan of Khiva. An interesting figure, his notable achievement was to bring the khanate's first telephone

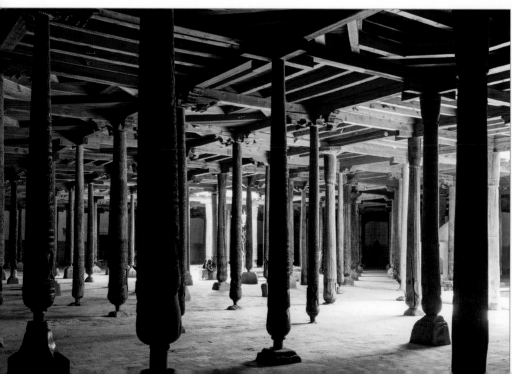

from St Petersburg, with little thought to the fact that there was no telephone line for hundreds of miles in any direction.

One of Khiva's holiest sights is the **Pakhlavan Mahmud Mausoleum**, which commemorates the poet, wrestler and patron saint of Khiva who died here in 1325. The 19th-century tomb contains some of the city's best tilework and also the largest cupola in Khiva. The Soviets spent years trying to dislodge the cult of Khiva's local *pirs* (holy men), but the spot is still madly popular with pilgrims and wedding parties who come here for blessings.

Opposite the tomb is the **Madrassa of Shir Ghazi Khan**, built with the sweat of 5,000 Persian slaves who, sensing that their promised freedom was not forthcoming, lynched the unfortunate khan inside his new building. The inscription on the portal reads stoically, "I accept death at the hands of slaves."

Khiva's tallest minaret, the 45-metre (148-ft) **Islam Khoja Minaret**, is named after the enlightened early 20th-century grand vizier who built several public schools and hospitals before being assassinated by outraged religious conservatives. Built in 1908, it is the last Islamic monument to be built in the city before the arrival of the Soviets. The attached madrassa hosts the city's best museum, featuring some wonderful silk clothing amongst the other applied arts.

If the heat is getting too much, dive into the deliciously cool gloom of the nearby **Juma Mosque** (1788), supported by a dense forest of 213 wooden pillars that are cleverly arranged to allow the entire congregation a view of the *mihrab* (niche pointing the direction to Mecca). Aptly, the mosque holds an exhibition of carved *karagacha* (elm) wood.

Follow the 60-metre (200-ft) -long tunnel of the eastern **Polvon Darvaza** gate (built in 1806) into the main bazaar, where you can pick up one of Khorezm's fantastic hats, brightly coloured *ikat* fabrics and hand-painted ceramics. Be prepared to haggle hard.

Before you leave the old city, don't miss the 19th century **Tash Hauli Palace** (Stone Palace), home to the court of Allah Kuli Khan (1826–42) and a highlight of the city. A secret corridor connects the fabulously decorated inner harem to the reception court (*ishrat hauli*) and law courts. The intricately carved columns are particularly fine, as are the majolica tiles in the harem's inner courtyard.

Excursions from Khiva

Several ruined and crumbling fortresses in the deserts of the Khorezm oasis make for a great overnight trip from Khiva or Urgench. En route to the desert, near the town of Beruniy, the road crosses a rickety pontoon bridge to offer an unassuming glimpse of one of Asia's most historically and geographically important defining points: the Oxus River (Amu Darya). Bled almost dry at this point by the thirsty cotton fields of Turkmenistan and Uzbekistan, the

The walls in the harem courtyard of Tash Hauli Palace are decorated with beautiful Islamic glazed tiles.

sluggish river is today only a faint echo of its former self.

Most popular is the enormous 4th- to 7th-century **Ayaz Qala**, where you can stay overnight in a traditional nomadic yurt. It's also possible to make camel trips from here and even swim in the desert at the nearby Ayaz Lake.

Of most archaeological interest is the Kushan-era **Toprak Qala**, the region's biggest city until the destruction of irrigation canals left it marooned in the desert sands. The Russian archaeologist Tolstov excavated the palace friezes in 1938, unveiling a blend of Classical Roman and Gandharan styles dating from the 2nd or 3rd century AD, a time when the transcontinental Kushan Empire dominated the entire middle leg of the Silk Road.

The other main excursion is to the white salt-caked former shores of the **Aral Sea**, where you can visit the iconic beached fishing trawlers rusting in the sand, 150km (90 miles) away from the nearest water. In what is perhaps the greatest environmental disaster of recent times (see page 117), the dying sea has lost half its area and 75 percent of its volume within a single generation, bled dry by the Soviet obsession with cotton monoculture. A visit to the ruins of the sea and the rusting skeletons of ships is a sobering reminder of the dangers of environmental recklessness.

The trip leads first to **Nukus**, the environmentally blighted capital of Karakalpakstan, where art-lovers should stop at the impressive **Igor Savitsky Art Gallery** (Mon–Fri 9am–5pm, Sat–Sun 10am–4pm; charge), home to one of the finest collections of Soviet avant-garde art from the 1920s and 1930s. Much of the museum's collection, which numbers some 90,000 items, as well as detailed biographies of represented artists, is available to view online at www.savitskycollection.org. The **Karakalpak State Museum** and the **Museum of Amet and Aymkhan Shamuratiev**, a local artist and writer who came to prominence in the early 20th century, are also worth a brief visit.

Ayaz Qala.

Conolly and Stoddart

Bukhara was the setting for one of the most notorious incidents in the Great Game, when two British agents held prisoner by Nasrullah "The Butcher" met their fate.

The emir of Bukhara from 1826 to 1860 was the highly unstable Nasrullah, fondly known amongst his subjects as "The Butcher", a nickname he received when he killed 28 of his relatives in a bloodstained scramble to become ruler.

In 1837, a Sandhurst-trained British envoy, Colonel Charles Stoddart, arrived at the gates of the emirate in an attempt to build a political alliance between Britain and Bukhara, and to assure the emir that Britain's push into Afghanistan would not threaten Bukhara. A soldier rather than a diplomat, he quickly offended the volatile emir with his ignorance of Bukharan protocol by arriving in front of the Ark to salute the emir on horseback, rather than first dismounting. Neither did he bring any gifts or a letter of introduction from Queen Victoria.

Stoddart was taken to the Zindon and thrown into Bukhara's notorious vermin-filled "Bug Pit", a 6-metre (20-ft) -deep subterranean dungeon, accessible only by a length of rope, where he was held on and off for the next two years.

Nasrullah played with Stoddart like a cat with a mouse, alternately releasing him and then sending him back into the pit, until Stoddart was convinced he was quite mad. At one point the emir's executioner descended into the pit to behead the British officer on the spot, whereupon the desperate Stoddart converted to Islam in exchange for a modicum of freedom. Amazingly, whilst staying in the police house, he managed to smuggle several letters back to his family in which he put on a brave face, despite the ghastly conditions.

Doomed rescue mission

Then in the winter of 1841 another agent, Arthur Conolly of the Sixth Bengal Light Cavalry, arrived outside the gates of Bukhara on a one-man rescue mission.

Conolly was certainly well equipped to accomplish the release. A veteran Central Asian political officer who travelled in disguise under the name Khan Ali, he was the quintessential Great Game player, and is even credited as the first person to coin the phrase.

Conolly was treated cordially at first, but when the British Army was routed in neighbouring Afghanistan it dawned on the unstable emir that he had little to fear from a British reprisal and he once again threw both officers into the pit. The emir was convinced that the men were spies, a suspicion not helped by the British government who had already disowned the two men as "private travellers".

It became clear to the snubbed emir that Queen Victoria was never going to reply to his earlier personal letter. As part of the celebrations over the defeat of his rival the Khan of Kokand, Conolly and Stoddart were led bound into the Registan Square and forced to dig their own graves. Stoddart was beheaded and Conolly was given one last opportunity to convert to Islam, before he too was killed. It was the 24th of June 1842, and one of the darkest days in the Great Game.

Within the museum inside the Ark Citadel are copies of the paintings of both men, the originals of which are held in London's National Portrait Gallery.

Emir Nasrullah, the "Butcher of Bukhara".

TURKMENISTAN

Unknown to most people, Turkmenistan is an isolated police state, but offers visitors fascinating ruins to discover at Nisa, Merv and Konye-Urgench.

Main Attractions
Merv
Konye-Urgench
Ashgabat
Nisa
Darvasa Crater

In Ashgabat's Independence Park.

Turkmenistan is the most isolated of Central Asia's five republics. Largely comprised of desert, a formidable chain of mountains separate it from its southern neighbour Iran. The economy is largely based on oil and natural gas from the Caspian Sea. The number five (and the pentagon shape) appears everywhere – columns, statues, stars, motifs – representing the five regions (or *velayats* – Ahal, Balkan, Dashoguz, Lebap and Mary) and unity of the Turkmen nation. The symbol of each tribal area is shown in a vertical line on what must be one of the most intricate and attractive national flags. Independence from the old Soviet Union was on 27th October 1991, not that most people noticed, as the new country retained the old hardline regime more than any other. Saparmurat Niyazov moved seamlessly from being Chairman of the Turkmen Soviet Socialist Republic to President of Turkmenistan, taking the name Turkmenbashi (Father of all Turkmen) and declaring himself President for Life in 1999.

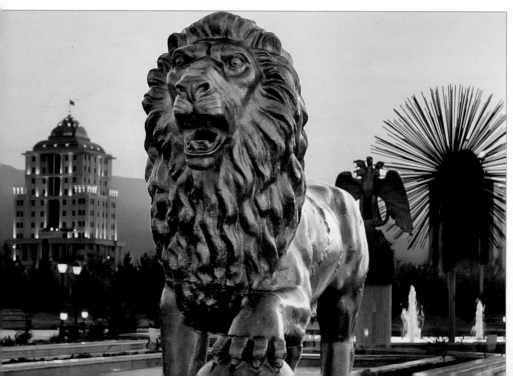

An authoritarian dictatorship, Turkmenistan remains largely shut off from the outside world. Media are tightly controlled and speaking against the government is a serious crime. Restrictions have been loosened since the death of Niyazov in 2006, but his successor Berdymuhamedov shows little sign of bowing to international pressure on human rights.

Turkmenistan maintains tightly controlled borders and strict visa regulations and requires that all foreign visitors have an official minder, factors that keep through traffic to a bare minimum. But it wasn't always so: 800 years ago this barren land was at the epicentre of Silk Road trade.

Merv

Merv (daily 9am–8pm; charge), located in the southeast near the city of Mary, was once Central Asia's lynchpin for caravan traffic, renowned for its artisans, scholars and religious institutions to rival Samarkand and Bukhara. Founded within the Murgab river delta in the 6th century BC by the Achaemenids, the city had several names as invaders took turns to occupy and expand, as witnessed by its enormous size. From the 11th century the city was known as Marv-i-Shahjahan – "Merv, Queen of the World" with a population exceeding 200,000, but soon ended with the Mongol invasions.

A long half-day is needed to see the main highlights, driving around by vehicle: the most rewarding is a climb to the rim of Erk Kala, the oldest section, possibly of Zoroastrian origin. From the top are views across the large Greek Gyaur Kala area, which contain a later Buddhist stupa and Nestorian church. Arab expansion turned Merv into the capital of Khurasan ('eastern land') as the Abbasids developed a new city across the water channel known as Sultan Kala – later expanded by the Seljuk Turks, whose final ruler Sultan Sanjar was buried in his famous domed mausoleum in 1157. Other sites of note are the ruined brick Great and Little Kiz Kalas and the pilgrimage site of the Mausoleum of Muhammed ibn Zayd.

Konye-Urgench

Konye-Urgench (daily 9am–8pm; charge) is in the northwest of the country, located along the northern branch of the Silk Road towards the Caspian Sea, and was the ancient capital of Khorezm.

In the 12th century, it was renowned for its libraries, mosques and madrassas, but its glory days ended with the Mongol onslaught when the invaders diverted the waters of the Amu Darya to flood the streets. The most striking sights amongst the ruins are the Gutlug Timur minaret, a precarious 60-metre (197-ft) brick structure and the nearby monument of Torebeg Hanum, which is probably a ruined palace dating to the 12th century. There is an important Sufi shrine, the Mausoleum of Najmuddin Kubra, where colourfully dressed pilgrims pray in front of its worn facade.

From Konye-Urgench the road heads south across the Karakum

ENTERING AND LEAVING TURKMENISTAN

Visitors must first acquire a Letter of Invitation (LOI), which can be issued by a travel agency and can take two to three weeks to process. Bring a copy of the LOI to obtain the actual tourist visa at point of entry and pay the registration fee (US$14). Travellers must be accompanied by a licensed guide unless they have a five-day transit visa. Pre-arranged guides meet their clients at the border and help register passports with police within 3 days of arrival.

The three border crossings with **Uzbekistan** are straightforward and operate well. The most popular is Farap/Alat, between Bukhara and Turkmenabat in the south, and Dashoguz/Shavat, near Urgench in the north (long walk or taxi between posts). Further north between Nukus and Konye-Urgench is Khodjeily crossing.

The nearest **Iran** crossing to Ashgabat is Howdan/Badjigiran. The 20km/12 miles of no-man's-land between the borders is linked by taxi for US$10. In winter the best choice is at Sarakhs, linking Mary with Mashhad in Iran. Nearer to the Caspian Sea is Gudurolum crossing.

A single border crossing with **Kazakhstan** at Bekdash/Yeralievo is open daily from 9am–5pm and operates well, but the one into **Afghanistan** at Serhetabat is often closed to tourists. Irregular ferry services link the port of Turkmenbashi to Baku, **Azerbaijan**; it is advisable to arrive with a few days left on one's visa as ferries only sail when full of cargo.

Ruins at Merv.

Desert towards the capital Ashgabat. The burning gas crater of Darvaza is a must-see en route, but requires 4WD and an overnight camp, as it is best seen at night when the fiery inferno ignites the desert sky.

Ashgabat

Old **Ashgabat** (Asgabat) was levelled in an earthquake on 6 October 1948 and rebuilt in a thoroughly Soviet manner. But President Niyazov also left a significant imprint on the city, gracing it with lavish government buildings, vast museums and self-glorifying statues. The first-time visitor is often amazed at how such a remarkable show-piece city can be unknown to the outside world. The city continues to expand at an impressive rate with remarkable white marble-clad buildings and attractions appearing every few months. Most museums and sites of interest are situated along the city ring road.

The **National Museum of History** (Wed–Mon 9.30am–5pm; charge) has a slightly sterile feel, but does boast a remarkable collection. Official guides are optional but do accompany groups.

Their knowledge and language skills will greatly enhance your visit, but you can also split off and wander around alone. It is sometimes compulsory to visit the hall dedicated to the cult of the current president, interesting in its own way. The collection of ivory *rhytons* (royal drinking vessels) is superb, as are the objects from the ancient pre-Silk Road trading centre of Gonur and the nearby Parthian capital, including the beautiful statue known as the 'Aphrodite of Nisa'. Models and plans usefully explain the layouts of Gonur, Nisa and Merv. Photography is allowed upon payment of an expensive camera fee.

The quality of Turkmen carpets is world renowned, with the greatest collection now held at the **Turkmen Carpet Museum** (Mon–Fri 9.30am–5pm, Sat 9.30am–12.30pm; charge). There are hundreds of examples of colourful regional designs, almost all with English captions showing the location, date, size and the number of knots. The use of an official guide is optional and only one general view photograph is permitted inside, with a hefty charge for subsequent photo.

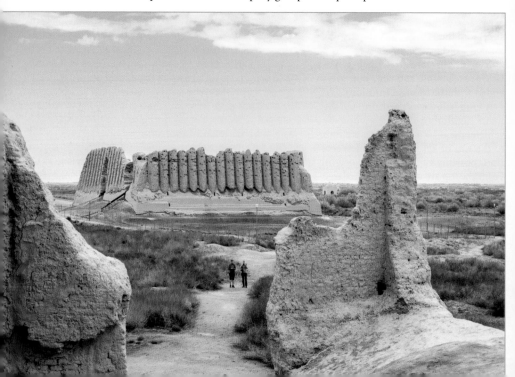

Sprawling through the southern part of the city is **Independence Park**, a relaxation and entertainment area of manicured gardens, fountains and marble walkways. Of interest is the great white column of the Independence Monument, resting on a giant white yurt which houses the jewellery and sculptures of the **Museum of Turkmen Values** (Wed–Mon 9.30am–5pm; charge). Five-headed eagles and Turkmen heroes pop up everywhere, as do reminders of Niyazov in the form of a great golden statue or a huge version of his "Rukhnama" (Book of Soul), which opens up into a large screen for nighttime projected images. Another golden statue of Niyazov stands atop the **Arch of Neutrality** (daily 9am–8pm; charge), now removed from the centre to its own park on the outskirts of the city. His figure no longer rotates to face the sun, but his outstretched hands encompass a grand sweep of his remarkable vision of a modern city.

The world's largest enclosed Ferris wheel can be found at the **Alem Centre**, which also has a planetarium, cinema and bowling alley.

An interesting half day excursion from Ashgabat is to the Nisa ruins and the nearby Niyazov mausoleum and mosque. Nisa (daily 9am–8pm; charge) was the initial capital of the Parthians when it probably functioned as a sanctuary for early Arsacid kings, with evidence of a shrine, temple, palace and treasury. Much of their art was influenced by the Greeks, as exemplified by the classical gods and goddesses adorning many of Nisa's carved ivory *rhytons*, now in the National Museum. The site also seems to have some connection with the local Zoroastrian religion, but was abandoned during the 1st century BC after a severe earthquake. Later Parthian burials seem to have taken place here amidst sacrificial offerings and festivals. Much of our present knowledge comes from the ongoing Italian excavations. From the top of Nisa's walls, a large mosque can be seen in the nearby village of Gypjak, birthplace of Niyazov. His mausoleum and showpiece **mosque** (daily 9am–8pm; free) are of the highest-quality workmanship. There is no admission during prayer times.

WHERE

The Path of Health in the foothills of the Kopetdag Mountains encourages a fitness lifestyle, with various walks along the foothills and the chance to see herds of Marco Polo sheep. The longest route zigzags 18km (11 miles) through the foothills from the edge of the city to the ruins of Nisa.

Visitors at Darvaza Crater.

Cappadocia's distinctive landscape.

WESTERN ASIA

The Near East is struggling with instability,
but there are rewards for the intrepid
traveller to Iran, Lebanon and Turkey.

Gateway at ancient Persepolis.

Traders along the western end of the Silk Road pass over countless layers of history, in a region referred to as "the anvil of civilisation" by historian Sir Leonard Cottrell. This is land touched by ancient Egyptians, Hittites, Sumerians, Assyrians, Babylonians, Greeks, Phoenicians and the later Persians and Romans, who developed and extended skills of warfare, communication and architecture. Despite being best known for the westward trade in silk, there was an equal exchange of goods and knowledge from Western Asia going east, with items including gold and other precious metals, ivory and glass. Add to this the domestication of the camel from Arabia and the flow of Christian and Islamic ideas from the Holy Land, and it can be seen as a true trade of commercial goods and ideologies. The era of the Silk Road was just one of the many historical highlights of the Near East which greatly influenced the region, and still does today.

A Persian rose.

Deserts and rivers

Compared to China and Central Asia, the distances involved are relatively small, yet there is a surprising variety of terrain. Approaching the Mediterranean, the deserts are smaller, the mountains less intimidating, but this is a region where political diplomacy and economic manoeuvring play more important roles.

Any map will show the importance of the two great rivers of Mesopotamia, the Tigris and the Euphrates, which run almost parallel from the Turkish mountains to the head of the Persian Gulf. The Euphrates, in particular, could be exploited by traders, as it virtually connects the Indian Ocean to the Mediterranean Sea. It was a natural waterway that became more important in the later centuries of the silk trade, when the sea route from China was more practical than the arduous overland crossing, which often became embroiled in petty disputes for control. Even the Syrian Desert was not as tough to cross as those further east, thanks to natural water springs, particularly at Palmyra.

Stability of empires

Under a series of great warrior-kings in the 5th and 6th centuries BC, the Persian Empire was the largest the world had ever seen. During this period the development of the Royal Road from Mesopotamia to Turkey literally paved the way for the later Silk Road, but it was the controlled distribution of water into arid areas that was their greatest legacy. The Persian *qanat* system of underground channels, carrying precious water from mountain to desert, was copied throughout Asia and beyond, and was arguably the single most important factor in making the route initially viable and then sustainable for over a thousand years.

Following the collapse of Greek control, the Parthians re-established Persian authority, and it was they who became the first distant consumers of silken fabric. But once the Romans saw those Parthian silk banners unfurled in battle, a greater market was opened that almost ruined the Roman economy. The stability of the Parthian Empire for 350 years allowed the Silk Road to develop and link China with Rome.

Silk routes

Hemmed in by the desolate Iranian plateau on one side and the rugged mountains at the southern end of the Caspian Sea, the route worked its way through northern Iran to the ancient city of Rey, now a suburb of modern Tehran. From here a seasonal northerly route struck directly towards the Black Sea and Turkey via Tabriz, but was more difficult and only passable in summer. The main highway, however, ran west through the Zagros Mountains, before dropping down into the fertile valleys of the Tigris and Euphrates rivers. More trade goods now appeared from the south, having travelled along the parallel sea route around the Indian Ocean before entering the Persian Gulf, where Palmyrene agents and envoys had established themselves. The ancient cities of Damascus, Aleppo and Antioch were the western crossroads of other trade routes that brought frankincense and myrrh from Arabia and gold from Africa. Everything was then shipped around the Mediterranean, from a series of ports stretching from Tyre in the south to Seleucia Piera in the north.

The Euphrates near Dura Europa.

Travel today

Relative to recent decades, Iran has reached a sort of normality with the West and is open for visitors. Once inside the country it is possible to travel around relatively freely and follow the route from the Turkmenistan border to Turkey, and almost completely to Iraq. However, the political situation can change rapidly and it is necessary to liaise fully with a local agency in Iran.

Syria and Iraq have descended into chaos and both countries are off limits. Lebanon always has its own problems, making travel there uncertain, but it is improving. Turkey, the most familiar country in the region to many, thanks to its well-developed tourist industry, has seen a recent upsurge in terrorism and failed military coup in 2016. For most of the time, it is a question of timing your visit wisely and keeping abreast of the current situation via reliable news sources.

Carpet in a bazaar.

Sunset over Baghdad.

IRAN

Famous ancient cities stretch across this proud land between East and West, and names like Persepolis, Shiraz and Isfahan resonate down the centuries.

The Iranian plateau effectively controls the overland Silk Road, with the only other option to go north around the Caspian Sea. Persian rulers, in whatever form, have always had the power to help or restrict this trade. For centuries they produced very little themselves, knowing that luxury goods would pass across their land, from which they could grow wealthy. But it was not just overland trade from the East that made Persian cities prosperous: their unique position meant that they could also benefit from the parallel sea trade.

The Persian Gulf is the closest that the Silk Road comes to the open sea and was often used as a method of bypassing Central Asia completely. From the earliest times even simple boats could navigate along the Indian Ocean coastline into the Gulf and land their goods on Persian shores. Great inland cities such as Isfahan, Yazd and Shiraz developed along these routes linking the Gulf ports with the Silk Road proper, trading in silk and other valuable Eastern commodities such as spices. This trade control has always been envied from outside, making Persia a land to invade and control.

But sometimes the Persians themselves became invaders, using the Royal Road of Darius to stretch their borders to the Adriatic and then east to India. After the short interlude of Alexander and his successors, the Parthians improved roads and water supplies, acting as the linchpin between Rome and China. Sassanids continued to improve the infrastructure, but their constant battles with the late Romans and Byzantium left them too weak to resist the Arab conquest in the mid-7th century. Islam became the dominant religion and Arabic its language.

Main Attractions

Ribat-i Sharaf
Mashhad
Nieshapur
Tehran
Persepolis
Pasargadae
Isfahan
Kashan
Shiraz
Tabriz

A Bandari woman wearing thei traditional burqa.

FACT

Many slogans on Iranian buses are variations on "Dear Lord, make this a safe journey for us, praise be upon Muhammad and his tribe". And there is good reason, as Iran has one of the worst road safety records in the world. Around 25,000 people are killed each year, blamed on poor driving, bad roads and minimal vehicle safety features.

The 12th-century Ribat-i Sharaf.

Turks, Assassins, Mongols and the even more barbaric Timur ravaged Persia for centuries, until the stability of the Ottoman Empire and its Persian counterparts – the Safavids – brought an age of enlightenment, culture and art. But still the invaders came, this time from Afghanistan and Russia, until eventually the British ruled through puppet shahs. The Islamic Revolution of 1979 in part shapes the country as we see it today, but it by no means defines Iran or the Iranian people.

Relations between Iran and the rest of the world remain strained, but there was an easing of tension in 2013 when a new President was elected. Hassan Rouhani is seen as a moderate when compared to the outgoing Mahmoud Ahmadinejad and it is no coincidence that the 2015 nuclear deal (lifting crippling economic sanctions on Iran, in exchange for limiting its nuclear ability) was agreed under Rouhani. He is up for re-election in 2017. Tourist visas are not so difficult to obtain nowadays and the country has seen a sharp increase in visitor numbers.

Despite ongoing international political tensions, Iran is still a fascinating and largely safe country in which to travel. Historical sites are well-preserved and the museums of Tehran world-class. The Iranian people are cultured, hospitable and often keen to distance themselves from the hardline policies of their government. Visitors are required to show respect for Islam in their dress and behaviour, and avoid criticising the regime, but travel in Iran is nonetheless an exceptionally rewarding experience.

The border to Damghan

The modern road from the Turkmen border towards Mashhad is busy with trucks and containers, many carrying expensive stolen cars from Europe and the Emirates across the Persian Gulf to Russia and Central Asia where buyers are less concerned about their provenance. This road follows some sections of the old caravan routes, but eases itself around the rolling hillsides and craggy escarpments. Being traversed on foot and with animals, the old Silk Road was more direct,

ENTERING AND LEAVING IRAN

You must have a visa for Iran before you arrive, and visitors will usually be met by a car, driver and guide. You are more likely to have your visa application accepted if it is submitted via an agent. Tourist itineraries must be agreed in advance and overnight accommodation booked by an Iranian agent, but after that is put in place, there is not much to stop you travelling alone for a few days. (See Travel Tips, page 400, for more information on transport in Iran.)

The weekly train to/from Tehran to Istanbul in **Turkey** is temporarily suspended due to Kurdish unrest within Turkey. There are three crossings with Turkey at Bazargan/Gurbulak, Razi/Kapikoy and Serow/Esendere. Turkey now requires online e-Visas to be obtained in advance.

Visitors are not allowed near the **Iraq** border and will be turned back east of Kermanshah, from where it is possible to fly back to Tehran.

The border crossing to **Pakistan** at Taftan is often out of bounds, as is the border with **Afghanistan** between Mashhad and Herat.

The Turkmenistan crossing to Ashgabat is at Howdan/Badjigiran at 1,700m/5,600ft altitude. The 20km/12 miles of no-man's-land between the borders is linked by taxi for US$10. In winter, the best choice is at Sarakhs, linking Mashhad with Mary. Nearer to the Caspian Sea is the Gudurolum crossing.

with many old caravanserais still to be found in the desolate countryside, the first of which is known as **Ribat-i Sharaf**, one of the largest and most important. This recently renovated *ribat* (meaning "fortified caravanserai"), 6km (4 miles) from the village of Shorlog, lies serenely in a wide valley of barley crops, with the old Silk Road clearly visible through a narrow gorge a few kilometres away. Built in 1140 by the last Seljuk ruler, Sanjar, it is an impressive display of the art of brick construction and decoration, much of which would have been covered by stucco and paint. Inside are vast camel stables, drinking troughs, rooms for fodder and baggage areas, all worked with intricate brick designs and Kufic inscriptions.

This region is home to groups of semi-nomads of Baluchi and Afghan stock, interbred with local families, who sometimes assist with the trafficking of opium from Afghanistan. In spring these gentle mountains are often layered by thin blankets of cloud and completely covered in a haze of vivid reds, yellows and purples from a carpet of wild flowers. This is the time when herders prepare their animals to move into the mountains for three months of grazing, the men living on bread, sheep butter and the occasional hunted boar.

Old and new Silk Road transportation lie side by side where the old caravanserai at Marhee lies ruined alongside the modern railway bridge. This new line was built in 1993 to link Mashhad with Sarakhs and promote trade along the old Silk Road, but is currently for freight trains only.

Mashhad

Mashhad was a small village called Noqan when the Silk Road passed to the south, but after it became the resting place of Imam Reza, the Eighth Imam, it gained importance. Born in Medina in AD 765, Imam Reza was a direct descendant of the Prophet Muhammad and died in suspicious circumstances while with the Abbasid Caliph Ma'mun. Imam Reza was buried next to Ma'mun's father, the famous Caliph Harun al-Rashid, and the shrine became a centre of

FACT

The English word "paradise" is derived from the Persian *pairi-dis*, meaning "walled enclosure", describing the luxurious walled gardens of pomegranates, almond trees, damask roses and turquoise-tiled pools of water, dating back to the Achaemenid era. Fabulous gardens divided into four-sections became famous as *chahar bagh* (four gardens) as far away as India and Andalusia.

Mashhad and the shrine of Imam Reza.

Persian Carpets

Persian carpets are famous around the world for their high quality of workmanship, richness of colour and intricate Islamic designs.

Carpet-making has been at the heart of Iranian culture for hundreds, if not thousands, of years. Carpets can be valuable documents covering particular periods of everyday life. Persians even wrote love poems about their carpets.

An ancient skill

It was the Persians who pioneered the art of carpet-weaving, with a history stretching back nearly 2,500 years. The sheep and goats herded by the nomads of the Persian plateau provided the basic materials with which to make carpets. Increased workmanship and quality turned them from simple doorway and floor protection into works of fine art, brought to the attention of kings and rulers, who commissioned more luxurious versions. But unless specifically preserved, an old carpet soon

A local vendor displays a typical design of carpet for sale in Isfahan.

disintegrates, unlike artefacts such as metal plates or coins, so there are seldom remains of carpets from archaeological digs.

Documents from these periods indicate that, for example, the floor of the tomb of Cyrus the Great at Pasargadae was covered with luxurious carpets. A thousand years later Chinese texts mention the amount of carpets looted from Ctesiphon and then later by the Arabs. One of these is the famous Winter Carpet, made for Khosro I (AD 531–79), woven in silk, gold, silver, pearls, rubies and diamonds, and later described by Muslim scholar al-Tabari. It is also known as Khosro's Spring because it represented the most beautiful spring garden, designed to make the king forget about winter. The Islamic garden (*char bagh*) is a popular design for carpets, with weavers replicating their geometric layout and symmetry.

When the Seljuk Turks entered Persia in the 11th century, they introduced the Turkish knot. In East and West Azerbaijan and Hamadan where Seljuk influence was greatest, the Turkish knot is still used to this day. The palace of the Ilkhan leader Ghazan Khan (1271–1304) in Tabriz is reputed to have had paved floors covered with precious carpets.

Safavid highlights

Two of the most famous carpets in the world come from this region and are now in the Victoria and Albert Museum in London and the Los Angeles County Museum respectively. Dated 1539 and known as the Ardebil carpets, the design is typical of Tabriz, when it was still the Safavid capital. The so-called 'Chelsea rewoven carpet' is possible older and on show in Tabriz. The height of Persian carpet-weaving was during this Safavid Dynasty in the 16th century. Trade with Europe prospered, and the new capital, Isfahan, became one of the greatest cities in the world, with skilled weavers creating wonderful silk carpets with gold-and-silver thread.

Towards the end of the 19th century under Qajar rule, trade with Europe revived and a new period of craftsmanship and carpet-making flourished. Today, carpet-weaving is the most widespread handicraft in Iran and still a huge industry, with the major centres being Hamadan, Isfahan, Kashan, Na'in, Tabriz, Tehran, Shiraz, Yazd, Mashhad and Qom. The Carpet Museum in Tehran (see page 322) has some of the finest examples of the last 450 years.

pilgrimage for Shia Muslims (Mashhad means "place of martrydom").

Every road seems to lead to the golden minarets and dome of the **Mosque of Gohar Shad**, which lies in the heart of the city. As the holiest site in Iran, any visit must be under strict conditions and tight security – women must wear the *chador* and photography is forbidden. The Foreign Visitors Centre will explain the site to non-Muslims, and a visit is truly memorable. The entrance to the library is a large sculpted piece of artwork showing a gold-and-blue bound Koran sitting upon a pile of books. Inside is a wonderful wooden replica of the first mosque of the Prophet Muhammad – underneath a palm tree in the Arabian Desert. The pure golden entrances to the courtyards are reassuringly dull in lustre, not gaudy, exuding exquisite workmanship of the highest quality. Cream-and-gold tiling creates harmonies with turquoise and dark-blue mosaics that are simply amazing.

The minarets on each side of the mosque are stunning examples of tilework – cream-coloured with small diamonds of dark-blue detail. The light-blue dome is a masterpiece of simplicity with yellow detail spelling out the creed of the faith. Broken mirror work reflects every point of dark blue and purple light from the countless ornate chandeliers, impossible to focus upon, within the vast shimmering, dazzling landscape. Huge car parks and access roads running below the complex show the massive organisation associated with the shrine. All this is not just paid for by charitable donations, as the theological colleges, carpet and sugar factories, transport companies, shops and land around Mashhad, are all under the control of the clerics.

The village of **Tus**, 18km (11 miles) away, is famous for the tomb of the poet Hakim Firdausi (or Ferdowsi) who lived here in the 10th century. His great poem, *Shahnameh* ("Epic of the Kings"), is still read today 1,000 years later. His tomb takes inspiration from the great Cyrus tomb at Pasagardae, but here you can go underground to pay respects amid

The Tarikhaneh Mosque in Damghan is one of Iran's oldest mosques. It was built in the 8th century, but its structure reflects earlier Sassanid styles.

The face of the Ayatollah Khomeini on an Iranian bill.

CALIPHS AND IMAMS

These two words appear in many different contexts, and it is often difficult to fully understand their uses. Caliph means "successor" (of the Prophet Muhammad), and as such is the title of a Muslim chief, civil and religious ruler. The Omayyid Caliphate was the dynasty of Sunni rulers based in Damascus just a few years after the death of Muhammad.

An imam can be a religious leader within a mosque or community, or one of the leaders of the Shia sect known as the Twelve Imams, greatly revered in Iran, Iraq, Syria and Lebanon. The great split in Islam occurred after the Battle of Karbala in AD 680, when Caliph Yazid killed Imam Hussein, the 3rd Imam. This is commemorated by Shia followers each year on the 10th day of the month of Muharram, known as the day of Ashura (meaning ten).

marble friezes of scenes from Firdausi's poem.

Sang Bast

South of Mashhad, traders heading west along the Silk Road stopped at the caravanserai of **Sang Bast**, now a prison and rehabilitation centre for drug addicts and HIV sufferers. Drug addiction is a growing problem in Iran. Situated on the main road and railway looping around the mountains from Mashhad to Neishabur, Sang Bast also has the remains of a mosque and minaret, the oldest in Khorasan province, and the tomb of Arsalan Jadheb, governor of Tus in the 10th century. This rich agricultural land, all owned and controlled by the clerics in Mashhad, was famous for the quality of its produce, originally irrigated by a system of *qanats* stretching from the continuous line of mountains to the north. But much of this land now lies fallow due to poor rainfall and the illegal drilling of wells, which has reduced the water-table level by some 20 metres (66ft), making the *qanats* useless.

A herdsman near Sang Bast.

Nieshapur

One of the most famous locations on the Silk Road used to be **Nieshapur** (**Neyshabur**), but the town is now just a shadow of its former self, having been destroyed and rebuilt many times. Started by the Sassanids under Shahpur I (hence the name), it became a wealthy trading city in locally produced turquoise and a thriving intellectual centre. The main caravanserai in the city centre has been heavily restored, offering a glimpse of the past, with a natural history museum, atmospheric teahouse and artisan shops. In the 10th and 11th centuries, as the capital city, it produced some of the finest ceramics and pottery ever made in Persia. Omar Khayyam, one of the world's most famous poets, lived here, working as a mathematician and astronomer, devising an extremely accurate solar calendar called the *Jalali*. He died in 1131, and his modern tomb looks like a giant net being stretched towards heaven. Across the road a new scientific and cultural centre is dedicated to him.

Down the road is the tomb of Farid Ud-Din Attar, a 12th-century

PERSIAN POETS

As Islam spread beyond its Arabian roots, new forms of interpretation and verse appeared in the Persian language, later cherished around the Islamic world for its brilliance, richness and scope. One of the original poets was Firdausi, born in AD 940, who wrote *Shahnameh* (Book of Kings), the national epic of 60,000 couplets.

The 11th-century poet Omar Khayyam is the most renowned of the Persian poets through his work *Rubaiyat*, which is popular in many cultures, while the Sufi *qazals* of Jelaleddin Rumi still resonate with Western followers. Sa'adi became the greatest poet of the medieval period with *Golestan* (Rose Garden), but even he was eclipsed by Hafez in the 14th century, whose great body of work is lovingly quoted today.

Sufi mystic who was eminent in the fields of literature and philosophy. This area is Old Nieshapur, of which almost nothing remains, but nearby excavations at Shadyakh have revealed a span of occupation from the Arab conquest. West from here are the wide open plains that catch the full force of seasonal thunderstorms heading towards the distant northern mountains.

Damghan

Damghan was a major trading centre connecting with the route from Hormuz on the Gulf to the Caspian Sea. Not only has it suffered like Nieshapur from invaders, but it is also prone to violent earthquakes. The oldest section of town is Tepe Hessar, with evidence back to Zoroastrian times and the recently discovered body of a woman buried 7,000 years ago. Meanwhile, in the centre of the pleasant town is possibly the second-oldest mosque in Iran, known as the Tarikhaneh (www. tarikhaneh.com), meaning "House of God", which dates back to the 8th century. The stout columns and simple lines of the prayer hall and courtyard are dominated by the 25-metre (82-ft) Seljuk minaret, of which more is said to be underground, including the original doorway.

South to the Gulf

As the main Silk Road passed across the northern Iranian plateau, there is an obvious trade route connection to the south. Before reaching the Mediterranean, the closest that the Silk Road comes to the open sea is the Persian Gulf, connecting with the sea trade running between Asia and Africa. Incense and spices had already been traded around the Indian Ocean for over 1,000 years before silk appeared.

The islands of Hormuz and Qeshm have always been important maritime centres, controlling the entrance to the Persian Gulf through the Strait of Hormuz. Directly inland from Hormuz is the town of **Bam**, an important textile centre, with an impressive 2,000-year-old citadel. This mud structure controlled the overland route from southern Pakistan but was badly

TIP

Yazd has always had a problem securing a reliable supply of water on the edge of the desert. The Yazd Water Museum is located near the main crossroads and documents the digging of *qanats* up to 40km (24 miles) in length and explains the many water systems of the region.

Detail on the tomb of Farid Ud-Din Attar, Nieshapur.

damaged in the December 2003 earthquake, which killed over 26,000 people. Rebuilding the modern city and sympathetic restoration of the site is underway. Skirting around desert and some of the highest peaks in Iran, the difficult route reaches the city of **Kerman**, where the great mosque and the atmospheric Regent's Bazaar are the main attractions. Poor agricultural land has meant that the taxing of trade and weaving carpets have always been the main industries.

Yazd

A look at a map of Iran shows **Yazd** in the centre of the country – a meeting place of trade routes from every corner. Throughout its long history, the inhabitants have prospered from trade and have a great Silk Road tradition. But it has suffered from a less than ideal location on the southern edge of the Dasht-e Kavir Desert, which the main Silk Road skirts to the north.

The large Jameh Mosque (daily; charge) has the typical Yazd double minarets, cavernous prayer hall, central courtyard, deep *qanat* access and interesting museum. The entranceway is similar to the remarkable facade of the Amir Chakmaq, used as a grandstand for watching the religious plays during the holy month of Muharram. In this square are also some of the best examples of *badgirs* – wind-towers that catch the slightest breeze to cool houses in the stifling summer temperatures. In recent years, some of the ornate merchants' houses have been modernised into hotels and restaurants.

Yazd is the best place in Iran to see the influence of modern Zoroastrianism. Near the city centre is the serene setting of the Ateshkadeh or Fire Temple (daily; charge), where the holy flame is said to have been burning for over 1,500 years. The pleasant rose garden is a good place to view the beautiful bright-blue-and-yellow symbolic representation of Ahura-Mazda, above the doorway.

One peculiarity of this faith is the ancient method for disposing of dead bodies. In order not to contaminate the earth, air, fire or water, the deceased are laid out in Towers of Silence (daily; charge) – walled areas on hilltops where scavenging birds and animals slowly reduce them to bones. There are two such towers on the outskirts of Yazd beyond the Ateshkadeh. A dome-covered well, which received water by *qanat* from the surrounding mountains, is one of the buildings at the foot of the hills, where the bodies were initially prepared before being taken up to the top to be torn apart. Restrictions on such practices by the Imams has meant that many of the 25,000 or so Zoroastrian followers of Yazd have to be buried in the modern cemetery nearby. Have a wander and look at a newly prepared grave, to see how the hole is lined with concrete to stop contamination of the earth.

From Yazd there was a longer but easier route to the northwest around the Dasht-e Kavir Desert through

Intricate tilework on the Jameh Mosque.

Na'in and Kashan (both still important carpet-weaving centres). But the most direct route towards the Caspian Sea and the main Silk Road was heading due north across the inhospitable desert to Damghan, a feasible crossing in spring and autumn.

West of Damghan

West of Damghan lie the southern folds of the rugged Elburz mountains. Routes either climb over some tough terrain near the 5,671-metre (18,605-ft) Mount Damavand (Iran's highest peak) or veer further south along the edge of the Dasht-e Kavir Desert. This strategically important narrow corridor of land between the desert and the Caspian Sea has always physically separated eastern and western Iran, while at the same time linking them together by trade.

Roughly 20km (12 miles) beyond Damghan, a large caravanserai can be seen beside the road at Qodratabad, from where a strange cylindrical mountain rises above the hills to the north. This is Gerdkuh, "the round mountain", as mentioned by early poet Firdausi and site of a famous Ismaili fortress belonging to the Assassins (see page 330).

Shahr-e Qumis

Midway between Damghan and Semnan is Qosheh, from where small mounds can be seen away to the left, generally agreed to be the scant remains of the Parthian capital of **Hecatompylos** (meaning "hundred gates"). Now called Shahr-e Qumis, a restored caravanserai can be inspected along with rough buildings identified as a royal palace and remains of a possible Tower of Silence. Proper excavation in future years might reveal this to be an important centre along the Silk Road.

Leaving these deserted plains, the route passes through the wealthy provincial capital of **Semnan**. Much of the modern success of Semnan comes from mining in the surrounding mountains, mainly the extraction of silicates (insoluble metal salts) needed for the production of cement, brick and glass. A monumental gateway is all that remains of the citadel, and the Jama Mosque dates from the time of Timur's son Sharokh in 1424.

A restored caravanserai at the foot of a low pass near the village of Lasgerd shows how well protected the traders were. West of here eroded and mined mountains expose their multicoloured bands of striations from creamy browns to rusty purple, beyond which rises Mount Damavand. The pass at Eyvanakey is thought by many experts to be the **"Caspian Gates"** mentioned by classical writers, but for the modern traveller it is notable for a series of reddish-brown bluffs that look like giant heaps of melted chocolate pouring down from the mountains into the meandering streams. The fast highway sweeps into modern Tehran past the new suburbs, but in antiquity the main centre in the region was Rey, 12km (7.5 miles) to the southeast of the capital.

Hiking up Mount Damavand.

Tehran's futuristic Azadi Monument.

Rey

Below a large isolated mountain, Rey still manages to keep its identity despite the onslaught from the expanding capital. Rey certainly has a long history, with evidence of occupation back to Neolithic times and pottery dated to the 5th millennium BC. These early settlements were centred around the famous **Cheshmeh Ali** water spring (still producing bottled mineral water today), where there is a 19th-century Qajar period bas-relief and a section of early Islamic mudbrick wall, now rebuilt.

This was an important centre for the Medes, and some experts believe that Zoroaster himself was born here in the middle of the 7th century BC. The city appears to have been abandoned and rebuilt several times, and used by Parthians and Sassanids, before becoming an Abbasid town under Caliph al-Mahdi, whose son Harun al-Rashid was born here in AD 763.

The main attraction today is the Imamzade of three great religious figures, known as the sacred **Shrine of Shah Abdel Azim**. The golden dome is flanked by two golden-topped minarets featuring beautiful spiral tile designs. Gold doors decorated in blue lead straight to the tomb of Hussein, great-grandson of the Second Imam,

Carpet Museum

Contemporary Art Museum

Tehran Grand Hotel

Reza Abbasi Museum

LALEH PARK

Keshavarz

Valisar

Meydan-e Vali Asr

Karimkhan Zand

Negatollahi

Mofateh

TEHRAN GARDEN

Kargar

Hejab

Vesale Shiraz

Ghods

Felestin

Valisar

Taleghani

Atlas Hotel

Hafez

Qarani

Taleghani

Taleghani

Taleghani

16 Aza

Taleghani

Tehran University

Amir Kabir University

Negatollahi

Sommaye

Sommaye

Enghelab

Ferdowsi

Enghelab

Meydan-e Enghelab-e Eslami

Enghelab

Enghelab

Teatr-e Shahr

Ferdowsi

Darvazeh Dowlat

Enghelab

Azadi Monument

Kargar

Jomhuri

Eslami

Valisar

Jomhuri

Eslami

Ferdowsi

Lalehazar

Sa'di

Darvazeh Shemiran

Ebne Sina

Jomhuri

Glass and Ceramics Museum

Si Tir

Sa'di

Eslami

Hafez

National Jewels Museum

Meydan-e Horr

Jami

Jami

Sabt

Baharestan

Hor

Imam Khomeini

National Archaeological Museum

Ferdowsi

Museum of the Islamic Period

Lalehazar

Sa'di

Mellat

Daneshgah-e Emam Ali

Hassaabad

Hassan Abad

Imam

Mellat

Iran

MONIRIYEH

Fayyazbakhsh

Khomeini

Imam Khomeini

Valisar

Moniriyeh

Moniriyeh

Moniriyeh

SHAHR PARK

Behesht

Naser Khosro

Pamenar

Mostafa Khomeini

Kargar

Eslami

15 Khordad

Golestan Palace

PAMENAR

Vahdate

Panzdah-e Khordad

15 Khordad

Rey

Ghazvin

AMIRIYEH

Valisar

Mosjed Imam Khomeini

N

Tehran

0 ___ 500 m
0 ___ 500 yds

Railway Station

Holy Shrine of Imam Khomeini

Khayam

BAZAR
Tehran Bazaar

Hassan, and inside is some of the finest inlaid woodwork to be found anywhere. A series of prayer rooms and antechambers lead around the complex, each more dazzling than the last. Every step across the marbled floor to the tomb of Taher, a descendant of the Fourth Imam, and Hamzeh, brother of the Eighth Imam, shifts the viewpoint of a million pinpoints of pastel-coloured lights from the fabulous angled mirrors. Muslims come here for a variety of reasons: some are deep in prayer or concentration, while others read the Koran or local newspapers, all in the most ornate of surroundings.

If you are allowed inside, this is a fine alternative to the holier shrines at Mashhad or Qom. Women must wear the *chador* and then have access to their own section. The gateway opposite the main entrance leads into the long covered atmospheric bazaar under a series of brick arches with skylight domes. Across town is the strange bulk of the **Toghrul Tower**, a tower tomb dating from the middle of the 12th century. It might once have

had a conical roof, but now, open to the elements, it is like walking into a giant cooling tower.

Away from the centre is a mountain slowly being eaten away by massive mining projects, which once had a Zoroastrian Tower of Silence on top. Below is the 10th-century **Shrine of Bibi Shahrbanu**, a place of pilgrimage especially for women, containing the body of the mother of Sajjad, the Fourth Imam. She was the eldest daughter of the last Sassanid king, Yezdegird III, who was defeated in his series of battles against the invading Arabs. He escaped to Merv and died in 651, whilst his son Firuz is said to have continued east to seek asylum at the court in China. His daughter Bibi Shahrbanu remained behind to become the wife of the Third Imam, Hussein, grandson of the Prophet Muhammad. A nearby cave celebrates the legend that when Bibi Shahrbanu was in danger of losing her life, she prayed to God, who opened the mountain for her to enter for safety, and then closed it behind her.

The Cheshmeh Ali spring in Rey.

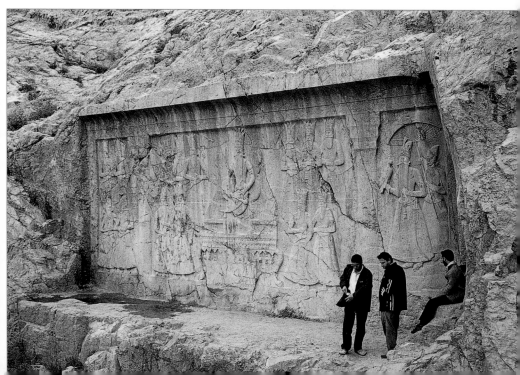

Tehran

The Iranian capital, **Tehran**, has only been a major centre for the last two centuries, and here we start to lose the flavour of the East and find more Middle Eastern and Arab influence. The northern suburbs are home to wealthy apartments, exclusive designer shops and restaurants. Higher up the mountainside, they look down on the traffic and smog choking the rest of the city.

Museums

Tehran is the place to see the best items unearthed along the Silk Road in Persia, and most organised tours include city sightseeing, visiting a selection of relevant museums.

The **National Archaeological Museum** (Tue–Sun 9am–6pm summer, 9am-5pm winter; charge) contains world-class objects from important sites around the country, such as the famous frieze of Darius, fragments of the *Tachra* staircase taken from Persepolis and the imposing bulk of the 2nd-century BC bronze warrior. Salt was an important commodity, as shown by the remains of a preserved miner from the 3rd or 4th century BC, in a salt mine near Zanjan.

The **Museum of the Islamic Period** (Tue–Sun 9am–6pm summer, 9am–5pm winter; charge) is nearby and houses both temporary exhibitions and a permanent collection. The illustrated Korans and textiles are particularly fine.

While many world-famous museums display a single Persian carpet, such as the Ardabil carpet in London, the **Carpet Museum** (www.carpetmuseum.ir; Tue–Sun 9am–5pm; charge) has an extensive collection of some of the finest Persian carpets, sourced from weaving centres such as Hamadan, Kashan and Tabriz. The styles of design include Garden of Paradise, Prayer Niche, Tree of Life, Zodiac, Hunting Scenes, Koranic and Historical Figures. Quality is indicated on the label by *radj* – the number of knots over a measurement of about 7cm (3 inches) – and varies between 30 and 120 knots. One of the oldest in the collection is a large blue-and-white carpet from Taft, near Yazd, dating from 1556.

Alongside is the Contemporary Arts Museum (Sun–Thu 10am–6pm, Fri 3–6pm; charge) with its unexpected collection of western art. Assembled by the last Shah's wife, there are works by Pollock, Rothko, Kandinsky, Gauguin, Picasso (more than 25), Bacon, Warhol and Lichtenstein.

Located downtown in the former Egyptian Embassy, is the **Glass and Ceramics Museum** (www.glasswaremuseum.ir; open Tue–Sun 9am–noon and 1–7pm; charge). Behind a beautiful facade and grand staircase are rooms dedicated to pottery, ceramics and glass stretching from the 3rd century BC to the 18th century AD. Here are 11th-century ceramic bowls from Nieshapur; the original 13th-century ceramic tiles from Takht-e Suleiman, and 12th-century pottery from Kashan and Rey decorated with Firdausi poems. The golden age of glass in Iran

The ornate facade of the Golestan Palace.

was around the 12th century, when decorative effects for necklaces, vases and bottles were produced by blowing into the mould, engraving, carving in relief and enamelling.

The **Reza Abbasi Museum** (www.rezaabbasimuseum.ir; Tue–Sun 9am–5pm; charge) has a great selection of items starting with a wonderful bronze horse bit of the 8th century BC, through to later illuminated manuscripts and folios. On the third floor are the oldest objects including Achaemenid gold plates and beakers, a Parthian gold-and-turquoise necklace, as well as an amazing gold *rhyton* (royal drinking vessel) in the shape of a horse's head. The second floor is dedicated to everyday items influenced by the Islamic period – bowls, tiles, figures, vases and plates. On the first floor is the beautiful calligraphy of manuscripts and books decorated with gold and lapis lazuli, and early versions of famous Persian poems such as *Golestan* by Sa'adi and *Shah-nameh* by Firdausi.

Not to be missed is the **National Jewels Museum** (Sat–Sun and Tue 2–4pm; charge). The equivalent of the British Crown Jewels are kept in a high-security vault under the central branch of Bank Melli, only open to the public for a few hours each week. Here are some of the most exquisite items in the world, including jewellery and royal regalia of the utmost quality. Of special note is the Darya-e Nur, the largest pink diamond in the world, and the Globe of Jewels, an extraordinary piece of craftsmanship that uses over 50,000 precious stones set into a mounted golden sphere. Oceans are depicted by emeralds, the land as rubies, with certain countries like Iran and England indicated by diamonds. Bands of diamonds show the tropics.

Other sights

One of the city's most pleasant areas is the **Golestan Palace Complex** (Mon–Wed, Fri-Sat 8.30am–3.30pm; charge), which is set around well-kept gardens in the centre of the city. The name translates as "Rose Garden". Each building requires a different entry ticket, but certainly worthwhile is the Marble Throne of Fath Ali Shah, used for the coronation of Reza Shah in 1925. The tall Shams al-Emirah tower, covered with colourful decorative and figurative tilework, stands beside art galleries and photographic archives.

Tehran Bazaar, the mother of all bazaars, is more than just a labyrinth of buying and selling. At crucial times in Iran's history, the power of the *bazaris* has helped to support or reject the ruling authority, and it certainly has a great influence over the national economy to this day. With no room to expand, rent at a premium and commuting a nightmare, many wealthy traders are today basing themselves in the more pleasant suburbs and doing all their business online.

The **Holy Shrine of Imam Khomeini** (daily; free) was begun in 1989 upon the death of Ayatollah Khomeini, situated outside the Martyrs' Cemetery for those killed in the war with Iraq. This massive building

A pottery statue from Lorestan in the National Archaeological Museum in Tehran.

Schoolgirls outside the mausoleum of Imam Khomeini.

has a central dome, four minarets and four outer blue domes. Past the X-ray and security checks is a vast hall with the tomb placed inside a large glass shrine, slowly filling up with money pushed through the panels. The whole area is a vast parkland and a popular place for visiting families and schoolchildren.

The **Azadi Monument** (Sun–Fri 9am–2pm; charge) is a major landmark en route to Mehrabad airport. This large modern gateway controls the routes to the west. A small museum and viewing platform can be accessed inside.

The Persian Gulf

The Silk Road was not just for the overland transport of goods across Asia, as plenty of routes connected with trade coming by sea. The nearest access was with the Persian Gulf at the easily defended island of **Kharg**, 30km (18 miles) off the Iranian coast. Excavations have shown occupation for at least 5,000 years, and there are two large tombs similar to those at Palmyra in Syria. Kharg Island is still an

The prayer hall in the Nasir al-Molk Mosque, Shiraz.

important trading centre, but as one of the world's largest oil terminals, access is restricted. To the north of the Gulf, trade also brought prosperity and wealth to a whole string of cities.

Shiraz

A major settlement even before Persepolis existed, **Shiraz** continues to be the great centre of Fars province. It developed after the Arab conquest and became the sanctuary of Iranian poetry and philosophy in the 13th and 14th centuries. The great poet Sa'adi was born here at the end of the 12th century and travelled extensively around the Levant as a dervish and was even taken prisoner at one point by the Crusaders in Syria. A man from Aleppo paid for his release on condition that he marry his daughter, which left him far from happy, as retold in his most famous work, *Golestan* (Rose Garden).

Sa'adi is well known in the West – one of his verses even adorns the Hall of Nations entrance of the United Nations building in New York. But in Iran he is not venerated quite as much as the later poet Hafez – a name given to someone who can recite the Koran by heart. Born around 1320, Hafez wrote love verses that endeared him to the Iranian people and are still quoted and interpreted in everyday conversations today. Works of both poets flow lyrically with roses, love and wine – the famous Shiraz grape and wine are named after the city.

The compact **Nasir al-Molk Mosque** and the more central **Vakil (Regent's) Mosque** both have beautiful ceiling designs in the prayer halls. Throughout the day mottled colours sweep across the walls and floors as the sun passes the stained-glass windows.

For some retail therapy, try the enormous **Bazaar-e Vakil**, which sprawls through the city.

Driving north from Shiraz is probably the best opportunity for observing some of the semi-nomadic tribes, such as the *Qashgai*, who still

migrate into the mountains searching out new pastures for their herds
of sheep and goats.

Persepolis

The world-famous site of **Persepolis**
(daily 7.30am–7pm; charge) lies 45km
(27 miles) northeast of Shiraz on the
edge of the Marvdasht Plain. Founded
by Darius I after he rejected nearby
Pasargadae, it took a further 120 years
of continuous building by his successors to cover the site that we see
today. While the other capitals of the
Achaemenid rulers at Susa, Babylon
and Ecbatana were well known to the
outside world, Parsa, as it was called
at the time, was a secret ritual city.
The important ancient Zoroastrian
spring festival of *Nauroz (New Year)*
was celebrated here. The entrance to
the great city is through the Gateway
of Xerxes, perched on the edge of the
terrace, flanked by two human-headed
bull colossi. Stepping between the
colossi, notice the graffiti scrawled by
visitors over the past 150 years, notably "Stanley – New York Herald 1870",
presumably the year before he found

Livingstone in Africa. On the left, now
at ground level, are examples of the
strange double-headed griffin capitals.
    The tall, narrow entrance into the
Hall of One Hundred Columns has
some of the finest carvings to be seen
anywhere; the fine detail on the clothing and footwear is remarkable. The
famous **Apadana** staircase shows the
conquered nationalities bringing
offerings to the king, from Ethiopi-
ans and Libyans to Armenians and
Indians. An explanation chart nearby
helps to identify the peoples and their
gifts including kudu, lions and Bactrian camels. The great Apadana, or
Audience Hall, is laid out along the
massive terrace, designed to accommodate over 10,000 people. Entry
was originally through huge wooden
doors covered with gold plate leading
to a columned portico, and then the
central hall of 36 columns with double bull protomes. The roof beams of
Lebanese cedar were inlaid with ivory
and gold, from which heavy curtains
hung, the walls decorated with blue-
and-yellow glazed tiles showing lions
and bulls.

*The remains of the
Apadana Hall at
Persepolis.*

The mythological griffin figure known as Homa is the pagan guardian of travellers – and the company logo for Iran Air.

Relief of a Persian soldier at the entrance to the Hall of One Hundred Columns.

The compact **Palace of Darius** is decorated with exquisite carvings along the side of the lower courtyard. Again there are offerings being brought by conquered peoples, frozen in time, shown climbing the steps forever up to the palace. Returning towards the Apadana, the Tripylon has an excellent carving of Darius on his throne, with his son Xerxes in attendance. On the lower level is the museum, which has a unique collection of items peculiar to this site, such as an extraordinary 2,500-year-old bronze trumpet used in the *Nauroz* ceremonies.

Behind the Royal Treasury is a path up to the two rock-cut tombs overlooking the site. The tomb on the right is for Artaxerxes III, the one on the left for his father Artaxerxes II. Both are set back on a small platform, and each facade is carved with the winged symbol of Ahura-Mazda above the king worshipping before a fire altar. The views from these platforms across the entire terrace and Marvdasht Plain are superb. Having been used for over 200 years, the site

was destroyed during Alexander's Persian campaign, but opinion is divided if this was deliberate or accidental.

Naqsh-e Rustam

Darius and his three successors are buried a few kilometres away at a place called **Naqsh-e-Rustam**. Only the Darius tomb has been positively identified, but the others are thought to be, from right to left: Xerxes, (Darius), Artaxerxes and Darius II. Below the tombs are panels of bas-reliefs from later Sassanian times, the most important of which is below the Darius tomb, showing Shapur I holding two captives, thought to be Roman Emperor Valerian and Philip the Arab. The "Cube of Zoroaster" that stands half buried in front of the tombs is probably not a fire temple, but possibly a deposit of holy texts or a resting place of the royal bodies before entombment.

Pasargadae

The earlier Achaemenid capital of **Pasargadae** (daily 7.30am–7pm; charge) lies a further 80km (48 miles)

DARIUS THE GREAT

Following a period of unrest, the Achaemenids found their greatest leader in Darius, who ruled from 522 to 486 BC. During this time he extended the frontiers of the Persian Empire to Afghanistan, Ethiopia, Libya and the banks of the Danube. Tributes from all these peoples can be seen on the famous Apadana staircase at Persepolis.

Communications and movement of troops over such a vast territory was facilitated by the building of the Persian Royal Road, running from Persia to western Turkey, sections of which certainly evolved into the Silk Road. Rebellions were frequent and ruthlessly put down, but it is the battles with his Greek neighbours for which he is mainly remembered, for example when he was defeated at Marathon in 490 BC.

to the north, and was the site of Cyrus' victory over Astyages the Mede in 550 BC. Aurel Stein is mainly associated with his work further east, but he excavated this site in 1934 and concluded that prehistoric communities were settled here at least 6,000 years ago. The most impressive structure is the remarkably well-preserved tomb of Cyrus the Great (559–530 BC), built like a small ziggurat and similar to Lycian tombs found in Turkey. Early historians tell us that the body of the founder of the Achaemenid dynasty lay in a gold sarcophagus on a golden couch, surrounded by treasure. The structure was later developed into a mosque and then a caravanserai.

Some distance away are the remains of the Audience Hall or Pavilion, with fragments of carved mythical animals and a trilingual inscription that reads "I, Cyrus, the King, the Achaemenid". Further still are the heavily supported walls of "Solomon's Prison", maybe a tomb or possibly a fire temple and forerunner of the one at Naqsh-e Rustam. Dominating this area is the citadel, known as the Throne of the Mother of Solomon, whose walls were possibly an early version of the Persepolis stone platforms, upon which a great temple was planned but never completed. Having been superseded by Persepolis, Pasargadae seems to have retained some importance as a place to confirm a king's coronation. The names of early Islamic prophets like Solomon were sometimes attributed by local people to these ancient structures, in order to avoid destruction by the invading Arabs.

Isfahan

Roughly midway between the Persian Gulf and Rey is a highlight of any visit to Iran – **Isfahan** (**Esfahan**), one of the great cities of the world. Its name in Sassanid times was Sepahan (meaning "Place of the Army"), an oasis for caravan trade heading around the Dasht-e Kavir Desert. The fortunes of the city might simply have ebbed and flowed with the passing trade had it not been chosen by Shah Abbas to be his well laid-out capital in 1598. Armenians were brought from Jolfa on the Azerbaijan border to build

The incomparable Imam Mosque, Isfahan.

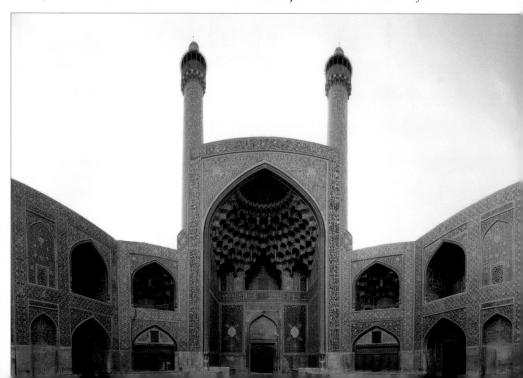

the mosques and palaces and create the spacious new city. The developing Safavid Dynasty attracted European East India Company agents wanting to influence the court. This zenith of Persian art and architecture lasted for little more than a century and ended abruptly with the Afghan invasions, when Mashhad became the new capital instead. Isfahan slumbered until it re-emerged as the modern centre of the cotton-spinning and wool-weaving industry, and is now the second-largest city after Tehran.

The great open centre of the city is the **Imam Khomeini Square**, around which are the most famous grand buildings. At the southern end is the beautiful **Imam Mosque** with its ornate blue, turquoise and white stalactite work and honeycomb decoration on the porch. Through the imposing portal, the axis shifts by 45 degrees to allow the *mihrab* to be in line with Mecca, before facing the graceful twin minarets and the most beautiful turquoise-blue dome resting on a large circular drum with windows. The space inside this large

iwan is impressive as is the incredible subdued blue-and-gold decoration on the inside of the cupola. When caught by the sunlight, a beam of golden light breaks the continual circle into a multicoloured peacock's-tail display. Beyond the galleries that surround the courtyard are madrassas, flower gardens and a winter gallery used in cold weather. This masterpiece of Persian art is a testament to the vision and commitment of Shah Abbas, who saw it completed within his lifetime.

On the eastern side of the square is the **Sheikh Lotfollah Mosque**, built at the same time as the Imam Mosque and named after a respected Lebanese scholar. Here the dome is a delicate cream with turquoise, black and white arabesque detail, which sits perfectly on the blue entrance portal. Again there is amazing stalactite work and delicate lettering above the doorway, which leads to a small corridor. There is no courtyard or minaret, just a simple, small prayer hall beneath the double cupola. The decoration is a series of blue-green ellipses receding into the golden centre, and is more harmonious than the Imam Mosque.

The western side is dominated by the tall **Ali Qapu Palace**, initially a monumental gateway into the royal palaces, which once stood behind. It is spread over six floors, and the grandest view is from the open pillared terrace from where the king would watch games of polo in the square. The throne room is full of frescoes, and towards the top of the building is the amazing "music room" whose intricately cut decorations aided the acoustics.

Beyond Imam Square

A couple of blocks behind the Ali Qapu Palace is the tranquil setting of the **Chehel Sotun Pavilion**. Twenty slender wooden columns on lion bases hold up an elaborate wooden ceiling stretching across an open terrace. The name means "40 columns" – which can be seen when the 20 are

The great hall of the Chehel Sotun Pavilion.

reflected in the elongated pool in front. Inside the throne room are large historical frescoes and other paintings depicting more intimate themes. A similar ornate pleasure palace called Hasht Behesht (Eight Paradises) is a few blocks further south.

The northern entrance of the Imam Square leads into the maze that is the Esfahan Bazaar, a labyrinth of narrow covered alleys snaking through the suburbs. Here, under the high stone vaults, are some of the finest pieces of work from Persian craftsmen, each in its own section – finely engraved metalwork, gold and silver jewellery, delicate inlaid wood with mother-of-pearl and patterned fabrics.

Seemingly detached from the city-centre bustle is the quiet ambience of the **Friday Mosque** – a place truly to appreciate Islamic art and architecture. The low-key entrance is between a series of fabric shops, which eventually leads to the courtyard with four *iwans*. This is not a Safavid construction, but a sublime piece of work from the 15th-century Mongol–Timurid period that is more associated with destruction.

The south porch, with two slender minarets on the left as you enter, has some of the finest mosaic work in the Islamic world and became a template for later Safavid buildings.

Most of the Zayandeh riverbank area has been turned into pleasant gardens and walkways. A stroll across the **See-o-se Pol** (Thirty-Three Arch Bridge) is a popular evening pastime, as is a wander beneath the arches, when the river is dry. Built in 1600, the bridge connected the city with the Armenian Christian enclave of Jolfa and its interesting Vank Cathedral. Further downstream are the Khaju Bridge, built in 1650, and the Shahrestan Bridge, with some sections dating to the 12th century. All these old bridges are pedestrianised and illuminated at night, making for irresistible night-time photos.

Isfahan to Rey

The old city of **Kashan** developed around the permanent water spring at Fin Gardens – the archetypal Persian Garden with water channels, fountains, pleasure pavilion and a

Many of the wall paintings inside the Chehel Sotun Pavilion depict scenes of Safavid court life.

In the "house of strength".

THE HOUSE OF STRENGTH

The evening is the time to witness the unique Iranian pastime of a visit to the *zurkhaneh*, or "house of strength". There are many around the country, but those in Isfahan and Yazd are more used to foreign visitors coming to experience the earthy odours of a bunch of sweaty men being put through their paces by an old man banging a drum and hitting a bell.

Based on Sufi principles, the idea of the experience is to build up the body and mind, within the structure of a group or club of like-minded men. This is achieved through spiritual, mental and physical activity, helping to overcome the difficulties of modern life. Beginning and ending with prayers to Imam Ali, a respected elder leads the younger men in trials of strength and concentration, all to the swaying rhythms of drum and bell. Suddenly it all stops and there is a discussion for five minutes about the application of religion to everyday healthy living or respect for elders. Then all the frantic activity starts again, until another break for a piece of Persian poetry, perhaps.

Some of the elders are 80 years old and former sporting champions, whose fading photos and old patched leather shorts adorn the walls of the *zurkhaneh*. There is nothing quite like it anywhere else in the world, and it is certainly an unforgettable, if somewhat smelly, experience.

Mausoleum of Oljaitu in Sulteniyeh.

bathhouse dating from the Safavid period. Sialk Hill is the remains of countless settlements at the site dating back at least 4,000 years, as proved by important pottery fragments now in the museums of Tehran and the Louvre in Paris. The town grew rich on silk carpet-weaving and became one of the most prosperous towns in Iran. Some merchant's houses and *hammams* have recently been restored and are wonderful examples of local architecture.

Qom

The route from Isfahan to Rey passes around the city of **Qom**, which together with Mashhad are the main sites of Shia pilgrimage in Iran. Non-Muslims must make strict observances to be permitted to the holy site in the centre of Qom – the tomb of Fatima, sister of Imam Reza (he is buried at Mashhad). Developed by the Safavids as an alternative to the holy sites in Kerbala and Najaf, then under Ottoman control (now in Iraq), Imam Khomeini studied here and Qom was always at the forefront of the

Alamut, a mountain fortress.

revolution against the Shah. Today it is the centre of Shia Islamic study, with a great variety of nationalities for the many clerics. Security is high, and photographs are not permitted at the shrine or any of the many seminaries and theological colleges. Women wearing the *chador* and men suitably dressed can sometimes enter the shrine complex into a large courtyard with three *iwans*, where there is access for clerics to pray. Beyond this is a beautiful honeycombed ceiling gateway leading to a second and third courtyard with the dazzling mirrored entrance to the shrine itself to the right, and tombs of respected clerics. Fatima is buried below a simple gold dome resting on a high drum with a single band of Islamic text running around the top.

Tehran to Tabriz

At different times throughout its history, the Silk Road from Rey went north through Tabriz towards Turkey and the Black Sea. Difficult in winter, but feasible in summer, this is the shortest overland route to

THE ASSASSINS

The legend of the Assassins was brought to Europe by the Crusaders and Marco Polo, and popularised by Freya Stark in her book *The Valleys of the Assassins*.

It is thought that Hassan-i Sabbah was born in Rey around 1040 and possibly studied in Nieshapur with Omar Khayyam. His beliefs and teachings are somewhat obscure as his great library at Alamut castle was destroyed, but he taught his recruits to conceal their particular Shia belief, loosely based on Ismaili principles, and protect their location at all costs. Any Sunni religious or political figures opposing them were likely to be assassinated by his drug-crazed killers, known as the *hashisheen* (hashish-users), from which the word "assassin" derives.

Hassan's method of training involved taking his followers into a garden paradise of wine, honey, music and young maidens, getting them high on hashish before sending them out on their murderous missions – promising them more of the same if they died fulfilling their duty. Hassan died at Alamut in 1124, but the cult spread around the Near East, and at the height of their power there were over 100 Assassins' castles from Gerdkuh in eastern Iran to Masyaf in western Syria. They were forced out of their remote fortresses by the Mongols in 1256 and the majority of their Persian castles were completely destroyed.

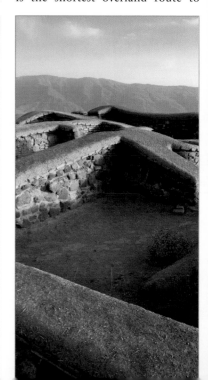

Constantinople and Italy. Today, the quickest way out of Tehran is on the smart new commuter trains to **Karaj**, running alongside the main highway with forests and the mountains to the north, industrial units to the south.

Qazvin

Qazvin was founded by King Shapur I in the 3rd century AD, and became a later Safavid capital under Tahmasp I. Later still it traded locally produced silk cocoons from the Gilan region along the nearby Caspian coast. A series of earthquakes has destroyed much of old Qazvin, but the Imamzade Hussein (son of the Eighth Imam), Jama Mosque and museum are worthwhile for the Safavid period decorative arts.

Alamut

It can take up to four hours by car and foot to reach the ruins of **Alamut (Gazor Khan)**, the great centre of Hassan-i Sabbah. Originally built in 860, the fortress was taken by the Assassins in 1090, who ruled for over 150 years, but it was destroyed by the Mongol leader Hulagu in 1256 and little remains today. The journey should not be undertaken lightly, as the weather can be bad and the castle sometimes closed. This region is the homeland of the Dailamites, a fierce fighting tribe who enlisted into the armies defending Persia against any invader. This strategic location saw them initially fight the Byzantines, who were constantly at war from the 4th to the 7th centuries, and later they strongly resisted the invading Arabs. A few centuries later, many of these fighting Dailamites became Assassins.

Sulteniyeh

The Mausoleum of Oljaitu is all that remains of **Sulteniyeh**, summer capital of the Ilkhanids, descendants of Hulagu. The Spanish ambassador from the court of Henry III passed through the city in the early 15th century and noted that every summer, caravans of camels arrived with many kinds of cloth woven of silk or cotton, brought by ship from China, via Hormuz. Merchants from Genoa, Venice, Turkey, Syria and Baghdad flocked here, and in 1318 the pope even established an archdiocese. This large tomb was originally built for the first Shia Imams, but instead only became the resting place of Sultan Oljaitu himself in 1316. The brick dome stands 52 metres (172ft) from the ground and is of complex design, modelled after the 1157 tomb of Sultan Sanjar in Merv, serving as the template for all later large mausoleums around the country. Major reconstruction is taking place, but there are glimpses on the walls supporting the dome of the beautiful glazed tile and brickwork that once covered the interior.

Further up the valley is the Sassanid-era town of **Zanjan**, with a fine covered bazaar and many caravanserais in various states of disrepair. Metalworking has turned Zanjan into the knife capital of the country, with every type of blade, dagger and sword available.

EAT

The town of Zanjan is a small regional centre formed on the metal industry, where old buildings from the Silk Road era can often struggle to find new uses. However, Caravanserai Sangi has been converted into a pleasant restaurant, which often hosts live local music in the evenings, with many of the songs originating from northern Iran.

Locally produced rose-water for sale in Kashan.

Takht-e Suleiman

One diversion from here is to the impressive ruins at **Takht-e Suleiman** (Throne of Solomon), an intriguing site spread around a "bottomless" lake on a sediment plateau. An outer wall with 38 towers dates from the 3rd century, but this was already an important site centuries earlier. Details are obscure, but it may have been the centre of one of the four holy fires for the Zoroastrians, because one of the more substantial ruins is of an ancient fire temple made entirely from fired bricks and lime mortar. It remained a ceremonial centre as Sassanid kings travelled here after their coronation at Ctesiphon to make offerings, and there are later buildings from the Ilkhanid period.

Entry to the site is through the large Ilkhanid gateway, but notice the impressive earlier Sassanid gateway just to the right, which some experts believe influenced Roman arch construction. Follow the outflowing water channel up to the level of the lake from where the site can be viewed. The most striking monument directly across the lake is the Western (Khosro) Gallery, held up by a mass of scaffolding. Foundations and walls have been identified as the fire temple, dining room, hypostyle hall and courtyard, but it is hard to imagine what it could have looked like during any one period. Excavated finds include Sassanid coins and glazed tiles and ceramics, examples of which are in the site museum. The name of the site appears to have nothing to do with Solomon of the Bible; legend says it was invented to stop the invading Arabs of the 7th century destroying the site of one of their early prophets. A few kilometres away is the spectacular volcanic cone known as Zendan-e Suleiman (Solomon's Prison), which was inhabited as far back as 900 BC, and also seems to have been a place of religious significance.

Returning to the road north from Zanjan towards Tabriz, the road climbs a pass to reach Mianeh and then up to Tabriz, set along the Aji Chay Valley below beautiful ranges of mountains, well supplied by *qanat* water.

Statue of Avicenna.

Tabriz

The Azeri capital of **Tabriz** feels completely different to other major Iranian cities, with Turkey and the Black Sea not far away. Strangely, the Mongols who destroyed many Persian cities treated Tabriz kindly and built a lot of fine buildings under Ilkhan Ghazan. It was the first capital of the Safavids, but suffered from its proximity to the Ottomans and was replaced by Qazvin and then Isfahan, which has also more recently replaced Tabriz as the second-largest city in Iran. Tabriz has regularly been attacked, especially from Russia, as well as suffering from major earthquakes. The climate does not favour its location either, being stiflingly hot in summer and carpeted in snow for long winter months, but it is good for skiing. The majority of the population speak Turkish and have strong ties to the neighbouring countries of Azerbaijan, Armenia and Turkey.

Built in 1465 by Jahan Shah, the **Blue Mosque** is a masterpiece of Mongol–Timurid architecture and the finest building in the city. Entry is through a great central portal, the only part to survive the earthquake of 1779, and decorated with glazed tilework of arabesques and intertwined flowers, framed by heavy cable-moulding. The layout is unusual, with the open courtyard covered by a huge dome, probably to combat the severe winter weather. Pass below a small archway of extremely intricate stalactite mosaic work into the second domed chamber, to be dazzled by magnificent cobalt-blue glazed tiles and gilded gold work. Some hexagonal pieces are displayed in a glass case in the centre and are truly exquisite. The Mongols brought Chinese artists with them who added Buddhist influences to the designs such as delicate flower work and strange peacocks. The overall cream, turquoise and cobalt blue is a reminder of the decoration on the two minarets at the holy shrine in Mashhad, on the other side of the country.

Next door is the **Azerbaijan Archaeology Museum** (Sat–Thur 8am–8pm, Fri 8am–1pm; charge), with a fabulous collection of pottery stretching back to 10th-century Nieshapur, rivalling the Glass and Ceramics Museum in Tehran (see page 322). There are Achaemenid *rhytons*, gold necklaces and jewellery from the 1st millennium BC, pottery from the 5th millennium BC and carved stone "hand ingots" (which resemble modern handbags) from the 3rd millennium BC. Upstairs is the so-called "Chelsea rewoven carpet", which has unsubstantiated claims to be older than the silk and wool Ardebil carpets in London and Los Angeles. Ardebil lies 230km (138 miles) to the east, but the London Ardebil carpet was probably woven in Tabriz in 1539 and shows Chinese influence with *tchi* cloud bands on the border. This smaller "Chelsea" design is of animal figures on carmine red with dark-blue medallions and, with 462 knots to the square inch, it has about 30 percent more knots than the equivalent Ardebils.

Sabzi seeds grown to celebrate Nauroz (New Year).

Aerial view over the fortress, lake and ruins at Takht-e Suleiman.

As you can imagine, carpets are the main items in the bazaar, and you can find them at every stage of the commercial process – being bought, traded, inspected, cleaned, repaired and ultimately sold. Individuals often wander around with smaller carpets looking for an opportune sale. Ibn Battuta commented in the 14th century that he had never seen such a riotous scene as he did inside the Tabriz bazaar.

Behind the impressive municipality building and clock tower on Shahrdari Square are a few streets of important merchants' houses, about 10 of which have been recently restored, including the wonderful **Ghadaki** and **Behnam houses** now within the Arts Faculty of the university. Nearby is the 160-year-old **Salmasi House**, home to the Sanjesh Measurement Museum, containing instruments for measuring time, distance, volume, weight and pressure all displayed within fabulous restored rooms of distinct red and white brickwork.

From here the road tackles the mountains to Maku and eventually, after more than 300km (180 miles), reaches the Turkish border at **Bazargan**.

Tehran to Iraq

From Rey, the route to the Iraqi border follows the ancient Royal Road, used by conquerors and invaders to and from Mesopotamia, and later still by the overland merchants and caravans making straight for the Mediterranean. The route to Hamadan runs through **Saveh**, a town that suffered greatly when the Mongols arrived. But it is associated with a tradition from the times of Marco Polo, that the Magi set out from here and were later buried in three great tombs. True or not, there is nothing to be seen of this today in the modern town. The windswept open plains west of Saveh lead to Mt Alvand (3,571 metres/11,780ft), stunningly snow-capped in winter, with Hamadan nestling at its base.

Hamadan

Modern **Hamadan** is located on top of the ancient trading capital of Hagmatana (meaning "Assembly Point", referring to a free meeting place for the various tribes), called Ecbatana by the Greeks. The history of this important city is as great as any on the entire Silk Road, and dates back to at least the 8th century BC, when it was the capital of the Medes. As power shifted to the Achaemenids, it became the summer capital of Cyrus the Great, while Susa was his winter base. The modern city can be quite disappointing, as almost all traces of its great history have been destroyed or looted by a succession of invaders from Alexander and the Seleucids to the Parthians and Seljuks. But there are wonderful stories, such as the account by Herodotus in the 5th century BC (*Histories* 1.98–9), who describes the Royal Palace and treasure house defended by seven walls, each one taller than the next and painted in different colours, the last two being of silver and gold. It is possible that he was translating

A statue of the poet Khaqani outside the Blue Mosque.

an account of a ziggurat, an ancient stepped construction in the centre of the city.

As one city has been destroyed and another built on top, the majority of ancient objects have come from illegal digging rather than supervised excavations. Gold and silver tablets, gold *rhytons* and jewellery are mainly to be found in the National Archaeological Museum in Tehran (see page 322). But a new museum beside the excavations of old Ecbatana, just to the north of the city centre, is displaying more recent finds, including inscriptions, carvings and a fountain from Safavid times.

The centre of the modern city radiates from Imam Khomeini Square, not far from the tomb of **Esther and Mordecai**, a site of great Jewish historical interest, but of unproven credibility. Esther of the Bible was possibly the wife of Xerxes, who together with her cousin Mordecai sought permission for the Jews to return to Jerusalem from exile. There are many suggestions as to who is really buried here, but it is still the main place of Jewish pilgrimage.

One of the most ancient sites is at **Ganj-Nameh** (meaning "Treasure Book"), a few kilometres away on the lower slopes of Mt Alvand, where two Achaemenid cuneiform inscriptions list the lineage and conquests of Darius I on the left and Xerxes I on the right. Both are written in three scripts – Old Persian, Elamite and Neo-Babylonian. It is a pleasant summer excursion for city-dwellers, especially on Fridays, who crowd the parks and teahouses.

A later addition in the city centre is the 1950s tomb of the famous Persian philosopher and scholar Ibn Sina, known in the west as **Avicenna**.

Heading west from Hamadan, lush green plains stretch away to distant snowy mountains in all directions. Through this magnificent stark scenery rumble modern traders carrying new commodities – truckloads of cement, fabricated steelwork and oil, while an optimistic signpost indicates "Kerbala 615km". An early morning sun burns off the overnight moisture, wrapping the fields in thick mist, out of which ghostly figures emerge struggling to control their herds of sheep and goats across the lanes of fast-moving traffic. Beyond a tough mountain pass, often closed by snow in winter, is the largely forgotten site of **Kangovar**, a ruined collection of impressive cut stones and huge columns dominating the surrounding flat landscape. Remains of a temple dedicated to the guardian of water, goddess Anahita, lie on a series of platforms, which have been compared to Persepolis in layout, but this requires a lot of imagination.

It would be only natural that conquering heroes would carve their successes on the spectacular rocky outcrop of **Bisotun**, around which every trader and invader has had to pass for thousands of years. The old main road running along the base of the mountain has thankfully been closed, allowing a safer view of the strange 2nd-century BC reclining statue

A girl dressed up for Nauroz (New Year) in Kermanshah.

Imam Khomeini Square in Hamadan.

of Hercules holding a wine goblet. Just beyond is a Parthian relief from slightly earlier, but the main interest is to be seen high up on the mountain. On a prepared piece of rock is a carving of Darius (the largest figure, third from the left) standing on his opponent Gaumata, recording that the decisive battle took place here at Bisotun. In front of Darius is a line of eight vanquished rulers paying homage. A ninth figure (in pointed hat at the end) was added after a few years in order to celebrate his later victory over the Scythians. The winged symbol of Ahura-Mazda hovers above the figures and is surrounded by 1,200 lines of text in three languages. So important was this inscription at the time that it was copied and distributed to all the provinces – fragments of it in Aramaic were even found on Elephantine Island at Aswan in Egypt.

Kermanshah

This is the last provincial capital before Iraq, which suffered greatly in the Iran–Iraq War, with an important oil refinery close to the centre of

Tilework on the Takiyeh Muavin al-Molk.

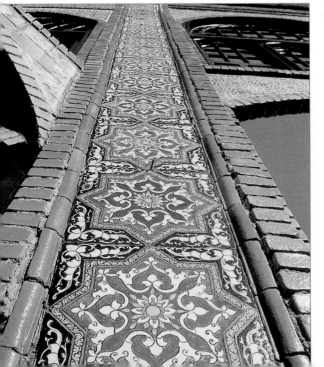

town. Kermanshah, meaning "City of the Kings of Kerman", was founded in the 4th century around **Taq-e Bustan** (meaning "Arch of the Garden"), a pleasant suburb of garden cafés and a boating lake fed by a sacred spring. To the left of the entrance are archaeological finds from the region, including carved capitals possibly from an unknown temple at Bisotun. Cut into the base of the cliff are two grottoes and a bas-relief panel. The larger grotto is the greatest of the Sassanid period, showing two winged figures, similar to carvings depicting Nike at Ephesus, but here holding the royal diadem. The rear wall is carved in high relief and shows an investiture at the top, whilst below is a remarkable armour-clad king on horseback. The intricate hunting scenes on the two side walls are quite different in style and execution, and would once have been completely coloured. Higher up on the left wall, some colour remains on a much later relief from Qajar times. The older, smaller cave has reliefs of Shahpur III and his relatives soon after the founding of the city. Further along is a bas-relief panel showing the investiture of Ardashir II. Ahura-Mazda is represented by the god Hormizd on the right, with Mithra on the left

On the opposite side of Kermanshah is the **Takiyeh Muavin al-Molk**, a Shia mourning site for pilgrims heading for Kerbala. This 19th-century Qajar period building celebrates the martyrdom of Imam Hussein in a series of stories depicted in beautiful coloured tilework in the front courtyard and rear garden. Some of the themes are unusual, such as the bloody flagellations during the month of Muharram.

The change in scenery is abrupt as palm trees start to appear in marked difference to the Iranian plateau as the highway runs down towards the Mesopotamian plain. The border with Iraq is at **Khosravi**, but access to this whole region is subject to security restrictions.

Magian Spells

Zoroastrian philosophy was the main religious belief system of the ancient Iranians and formed the basis of modern Iranian culture.

It is uncertain exactly where the early prophet Zoroaster (Zarathustra to the Persians) came from, but it was somewhere in northern Persia, between 1000 BC and 600BC.

He preached that there was just one God, called Ahura-Mazda (Wise Lord) and, pre-dating Judaism, Christianity and Islam, Zoroastrianism is therefore one of the world's earliest monotheistic religions. Ahura-Mazda and his creation represent truth and order and through good thoughts and good deeds his followers can keep chaos at bay. Zoroastrians believe that Ahura-Mazda will ultimately triumph over Angra Mainyu (the embodiment of evil), the world will end and the souls of the living and the dead will be reconnected with God.

The Magi

Ahura-Mazda communicated with his devotees in their dreams. The meaning of his messages was not always clear, so the priests of the Median Empire (known as Magi, from the Greek *magoi* or wise men) were required to interpret such dreams. The Greek historian Herodotus, writing in the 5th century BC, records that the Magi had appeared some 200 years previously and were particularly skilled at reading dreams. The historical Magi were part of Persia's elite and valued advisors to their rulers, which gave them the credibility required to successfully spread their faith and other ideas.

The Magi tried to explain and understand the world around them by calculating time, developing calendars, predicting tides and studying the early sciences – medicine and alchemy – as well as poetry, art and religion. It has been credibly suggested that the Magi referred to in the Christian nativity story were these same Zoroastrian priests.

Early astrologers

Their speciality was studying the night sky, because they believed that whatever they observed in the heavens would be reflected in events on earth. By monitoring movements in the sky, they could make predictions about what would happen on earth. They developed their own astrology using the twelve signs of the Zodiac that are recognised today. The Magi were not astrologers or astronomers as we would know them today; rather they were "searchers of wisdom" and regarded as scholars in their time.

Zoroastrians today

Today it is estimated that the worldwide population of Zoroastrians is about 200,000. The largest group belong to India's Parsee (meaning Persian) community, who became successful during the time of the British Raj in India as middlemen between the elite ruling British and diverse Indian nationals; the Tata name is one of the most famous. The population in Iran is significantly smaller, having been driven out or converted to Islam during the 7th century. Iran's Zoroastrians are concentrated in Tehran and Yazd, where there is still an operational Zoroastrian fire temple (fire being a ritual purifier). Their practice of laying out dead bodies inside Towers of Silence is now restricted, and many Zoroastrians are instead buried in concrete-lined graves to prevent the decaying corpse poisoning the earth.

Zoroastrian Towers of Silence, Yazd.

IRAQ

From Baghdad to Babylon, Ninevah to Nimrud, Iraq's cultural heritage is one of the greatest along the entire Silk Road.

Main Attractions
Baghdad
Karbala
Ctesiphon
Babylon
Uruk

A lithograph shows the Assyrian palaces of Nimrud, along the Tigris River.

Throughout its ancient history Iraq was known as Mesopotamia – literally "the land between the rivers", referring to the fertile valleys of the Euphrates and the Tigris. As the cradle of the highly developed early civilisations of the Babylonians and the Assyrians, this region has always been envied by neighbouring emerging empires. With the Arab invasion and the spread of Islam, Baghdad became one of its earliest capitals under a dynasty known as the Abbasids. Mongol destruction and Ottoman control eventually led to British rule and reorganisation, until independence in 1932 when it was renamed Iraq.

The monarchy was overthrown in 1958 by a military junta, after which military coups and Ba'ath Party in-fighting dominated politics until 1979, when Saddam Hussein took control. As a minority Sunni, Saddam had ruthlessly juggled control of the Shia majority, together with other minorities of Kurds, Christians, Yazidis and Assyrians. The fallout from his ousting by allied forces in 2003 is a continuing part of Iraqi and international history, with repercussions felt across the region and the world, and cultural ramifications, including the destruction of the Babylon archaeological site.

Following Shia victories in elections and the withdrawal of US troops in 2011, sectarian violence ensued in the country, creating a chaos into which stepped Daesh (also known as ISIS, ISIL and IS 'Islamic State') in 2014. For a few years the Kurds had managed to stem the flow of regional unrest into their relatively quiet areas, but Daesh's incursions have changed this. Daesh took on Kurdish forces (known as the 'Peshmerga') in 2014, and the conflict is on-going. At the time of writing, the Iraqi government was in control of the south and centre of the country; the Kurds had sections of the north and a major offensive by was underway by pro-Iraqi government forces and allies to retake Mosul, the last remaining bastion of power for Daesh in Iraq.

Baghdad

Baghdad has always been an important trading and economic centre. When the Abbasid Caliphate was based here in the 8th and 9th centuries AD, goods from the Silk Road filled the bazaars and warehouses along the banks of the Tigris. It was the entrepôt of the Middle East, trading incense and pearls from Arabia; gold and slaves from East Africa; spices and dyes from the Indies. Baghdad became the richest city in the world, with a wealth of Islamic mosques and shrines, including the Kadhimain Shrine (tombs of the Seventh and Ninth Shia Imams), constructed in AD 1515.

The most important Islamic shrines for Shia believers worldwide are to be found in the holy cities of Kufa, Karbala and Najaf to the south, and Samarra to the north. Kufa (Al Kufah) was the city where Ali, son-in-law and cousin of the Prophet Muhammad and the First Shia Imam, was murdered in AD 661. His tomb in nearby Najaf (An Najaf) is a great centre of pilgrimage.

The **Iraq Museum** (www.iraqmuseum. org) housed what was probably the finest collection of Mesopotamian artefacts in the world. About 15,000 items, including 5,000 unique cylinder seals, were looted in 2003, but following the

Glazed brick from the Ishtar Gate in Babylon, now in Berlin.

return of some of its most important treasures and an ambitious renovation project, it has since been periodically open to the public. It is hoped the museum will soon reopen permanently and, in the meantime, a large part of the collection is online.

Karbala

Situated south of Baghdad, the holy city of **Karbala** is where Hussein, the son of Ali, was martyred by the Umayyad Caliph Yazid in AD 680. This conflict over the succession of the Caliphate has distinguished the Shia from the Sunni sects of Islam ever since. Shia followers make pilgrimages here known as *Ashura* ("ten" in Arabic) commemorating the date of Hussein's death. The head of Hussein is said to rest in a shrine inside the Umayyad Mosque in Damascus.

Due to unrest in Baghdad in AD 833, the capital of the Caliphate moved further up the Tigris to Samarra, during which time it was the centre of the Islamic world, until AD 892. It is most famous for its wonderful ziggurat-style spiral minaret, constructed in AD 847. Sadly this unique building was also

badly damaged recently when the US military used it as a look-out position, and it became a target for attacks. Samarra also has great significance to Shia Muslims, as the final resting places of the Tenth and Eleventh Imams.

Ctesiphon

Droppingdown from the Iranian plateau, the main city established by the Parthians on the eastern bank of the Tigris was **Ctesiphon**, about 30km (18 miles) downstream from Baghdad. The great arch of the banqueting hall of the Palace of Shapur I (the 3rd-century AD Sassanid king, seen carved into the rock facade at Naqsh-e Rustam in Iran) is one of the most famous of Iraqi monuments. The slender, fragile arch is thought to be the largest single span ever constructed from baked bricks. Here, the Euphrates and Tigris rivers bend within a few kilometres of each other.

Babylon

South along the Euphrates is one of the most famous ancient cities in the world, Babylon. Most of the buildings to be seen are remnants from the rule of King

The Kadhimain Shrine in Baghdad.

STOLEN TREASURE

In just a few days of chaos during April 2003, it was reported that an estimated 170,000 items were looted from the Iraqi National Museum in Baghdad – though still shocking, the true figure was closer to 15,000. Exactly what is missing will probably never be known, as many of the catalogue details have also been lost or destroyed. Some pieces had been stored away safely in advance, but it was not possible to save more in the time available. The Iraq Antiquities Department has now issued identification cards for many of the artefacts and handed them to Interpol. Neighbouring countries such as Syria, Jordan and Lebanon have seized thousands of smuggled items on their borders. Despite an amnesty, however, not all the recovered pieces have been handed back.

Nebuchadnezzar II in the 6th century BC. Some of the ruined constructions are said to have been part of the famous Hanging Gardens, one of the Seven Wonders of the Ancient World.

Most prominent are the two palaces of the king, the ziggurat (an early tiered building) and the Ishtar Gate. Dedicated to the goddess Ishtar, the Gate was constructed of blue glazed tiles with alternating rows of bas-relief *sirrush* (dragons) and *aurochs* (ancestors of our domesticated cattle); the roof and doors of the gate were of cedar. Through the gate ran the Processional Way, which was lined with walls covered with glazed bricks of lions.

The magnificent Ishtar Gate can now be admired in the Berlin Museum, and the black diorite *stele* with the inscribed *Code of Hammurabi* is one of many items to be found in the Mesopotamia Room at the Louvre in Paris.

Recently, American forces used the ancient site as a military command centre named Base Alpha. A helicopter pad was constructed inside the site and vibrations from landings led the roof of one building to collapse.

Uruk

Further south along the old course of the Euphrates are two more important cities. Uruk (also known as Akkad) was the first major city of the Sumerians, and arguably the world's first city. The *Epic of Gilgamesh* celebrates the king of the first dynasty and is one of the first works of literature. Beyond that are the ruins of Ur, close to the modern town of Nasiriya (An Nasiriyah). Mentioned several times in the Bible, Ur has an impressive large ziggurat dedicated to the moon God Nanna.

Northern Iraq

Ninevah was an ancient capital of the Assyrians until the death of their last great king, Ashurbanipal, in the 7th century BC, killed by the Medes. Some of the great gateways and walls have been reconstructed, but most of the original bas-reliefs are now held in the British Museum.

Even older are the ruins at **Nimrud**, the previous capital of the Assyrians, known as Calah in the Bible.

Statue of King Ashurnasirpal II, king of Assyria from 883–59 BC, holding the symbols of sovereignty.

ENTERING AND LEAVING IRAQ

Despite the unsettled situation over the past decade, there have been a surprising number of tourists opting to visit Iraq. The main thing to understand is that the Kurdish area in the north has been virtually autonomous from the rest of the country since the overthrow of Saddam Hussein, but since the incursions of Daesh, this Kurdish region is now affected by violent unrest. Apart from the extreme northeast, most of northern Iraq is now too dangerous for visitors.

There are crossing points along the border with **Turkey**, but all are out of bounds for tourists, with serious consequences for attempting to cross. Most of these border posts have strict checks to control who is coming in and out of Iraq.

The entire border with **Syria** is out of bounds, as is the case with **Jordan**, even though the border crossing between Baghdad and Amman is open.

The border with **Iran** is generally open, but foreigners are not allowed near it from the Iranian side. Large numbers of Iranians cross the border mainly as pilgrims to visit the major Shia shrines in Iraq.

The only option for entering at present is to fly into Baghdad with MEA, Emirates, Royal Jordanian, Qatar Airways, Gulf Air, EgyptAir or Turkish Airlines. Visas can be obtained upon arrival if all permissions are obtained well in advance.

SYRIA

Every place along the Silk Road has had periods of prosperity, alternating with destruction. Today Syria, until recently one of the richest repositories of Silk Road culture, is being destroyed.

Syria has always benefited from its unique position at the end of the Asian trade route, controlling overland access to both Europe and Africa. The classic Silk Road reached the Mediterranean after surviving the tough desert crossing via Palmyra, from where goods were sent on to Rome. After Palmyra's demise, the desert crossing became impossible, and so a secondary route became more important which skirted north around the desert by following the Euphrates upstream and then through Aleppo and Antioch.

Until relatively recent national and political divisions, "*Syria*" referred to all the land known as the Levant at the eastern end of the Mediterranean and its hinterland to the Euphrates, of which the modern country is just a small part. Syria is where the world's first written scripts originated, and there is a continuing argument about whether Damascus or Aleppo is the world's oldest city. Until the recent war, Damascus was always the religious and political capital, whilst Aleppo bustled with the lifeblood of trade – but no longer.

Syria's central position made it an easy target for any expanding empire, from Hittite and Egyptian to Assyrian and Persian. These and many other ancient civilisations have battered and rebuilt the country for thousands of

years, leaving a rich cultural heritage that was unlike anywhere else. Buildings separated by centuries leant side by side, ancient ruins recalled distant empires, and Bedouins with mobile phones kept society moving forwards, but always with one foot in the past. People continually adapt to the changes around them, and Syrians are some of the best at doing that, especially today.

Throughout the latter part of the 20th century, Syria had a no less turbulent time politically. A succession of military coups and more than 40 years

Main Attractions

Dura Europos
Damascus
Krac des Chevaliers
Resafeh
Apamea

Local farmers in Apamea.

under emergency law effectively suspended the constitution. Disappearances and incarceration without trial were commonplace, and there was no effective opposition to the Assad regime (first Hafez al-Assad and then his son, the Western-educated ophthalmologist Bashar al-Assad).

Near the Iraqi border

The undefined and unstable Iraqi border with Syria crosses the Euphrates at Abu Kamal, where the river swings in a more northerly direction. Almost immediately on the western bank is the ancient settlement of **Mari**, at a place called Tell Hariri (meaning "Hill of the Silk-Weaver"). Despite its great importance as an early city-state comparable to Ur in the east and Ebla and Ugarit further west, there is little to see from 6,000 years ago. Some of the excavated items found at the central Palace of Zimri-Lim are in the Louvre in Paris. A cache of clay tablets in Akkadian script tell us that the city thrived on the tax of passing trade between Mesopotamia and Anatolia around 4,000 years ago.

Dura Europos

Only 15km (9 miles) further north is the later city of **Dura Europos**. Dura means "fortress" in Aramaic, hinting at a time before this Hellenistic city became a regional melting pot for East and West, with temples to satisfy all persuasions. The ruins have suffered further destruction over recent years. Little remains of the important synagogue to the left, but this is where the wonderful frescoes were found that are reconstructed and still hopefully protected in the National Archaeological Museum in Damascus. Beyond the extensive site are the major buildings spectacularly located on the banks of the Euphrates, including the Strategion Palace and the **Palace of the Dux Ripae** (meaning "riverbank commander") with the best views across the river and surrounding farmland.

Two main routes then took the silk trade westwards from Dura Europos to the Mediterranean, the first going straight across the Syrian Desert to Damascus via Palmyra. When Palmyra collapsed into the sands, its desert trade route was replaced with one

Syria and Lebanon

continuing up the Euphrates towards Aleppo, which shifted the balance of control to places further north, like Resafeh, leaving Dura Europos to "disappear" until British troops stumbled across it in the 1920s.

Across the Syrian Desert

The route from Dura Europos to Damascus is the classical route that strikes straight across the Syrian Desert, the route that many people think of as the Silk Road in the Middle East. It passes through the once-extraordinary city of Palmyra that blossomed briefly in the desert, and the imposing city of Damascus.

Palmyra

Images most closely associated with the Silk Road in the Middle East are the evocative vistas of **Palmyra** (Tadmur) in the middle of the Syrian Desert. Even many years after its heyday, it was a great adventure to travel to this city spread across the desert sand, whose monuments changed shade and texture subtly throughout the day.

A small settlement developed here at a natural water spring almost 4,000 years ago when it was known as Tadmor (a name mentioned in texts from Mari). It grew wealthy by taxing passing traders and charging them for water. After the Romans gained Syria in 64 BC they seemed quite happy to grant autonomy to places like Antioch and Palmyra – its new name derived from the many date palms. But then the Romans saw the silk banners of the Parthians for the first time and the marvellous new material started to flow to the Mediterranean. By the 1st century AD Palmyra was not just trading silk from east to west, but had become the independent centre of desert routes radiating in all directions to Damascus, Homs, Hama, Antioch, Resafeh, Seleucia (on the Tigris), Dura Europos, Ctesiphon and even Petra.

Through this wealth it became a destination and financial centre in its own right, where luxurious items were bought and resold. Palmyrene merchants arranged much of this trade in advance by setting up agencies in Rome and Egypt, and throughout

Engravings on the entrance to the Temple of Bel.

ENTERING/LEAVING SYRIA

There are many crossing points along the border with **Turkey**, but all are out of bounds for tourists, with serious consequences for attempting to cross. Most of these border posts have strict checks to control who is coming in and out of Syria, and some are closed due to the unprecedented numbers of refugees trying to leave the country.

Since 2015 **Lebanon** has introduced a strict visa system to control the huge numbers of Syrian refugees entering the country at the Masnaa crossing..

Battles for control over the two crossings with **Jordan** are ongoing. Both have been shut since a suicide car bomb exploded at Rukban in June 2016, near to a large refugee camp on the Syrian side.

It is not possible for foreigners to travel overland from Syria to/from **Iraq**.

The Syrian Conflict

Today's tragic war in Syria is having major consequences for the world, with no immediate end in sight.

On the back of uprisings in other Arab countries in the so-called 'Arab Spring', pro-democracy protesters took to the streets of Deraa in southern Syria in March 2011. The fierce crackdown on such opposition by President Assad's Ba'ath party government forces stimulated even more protests in many other towns and cities across Syria, inspired by the dramatic events unfolding in Libya and Egypt. Some members of the Syrian Army refused to obey orders to fire on civilians and defected, to eventually form the Free Syrian Army (FSA) fighting alongside the protesters.

By 2012 the fighting had spread across the entire country and into the main cities of Damascus and Aleppo. Essentially, by now, it was a civil war. It became clear that this president would not flee his country (as in Tunisia, Egypt and Yemen) and would hold onto control by whatever means. Syria was suspended from the Arab League and sanctions were imposed on Assad and other high-ranking officials.

Tragically, Aleppo now lies in ruins.

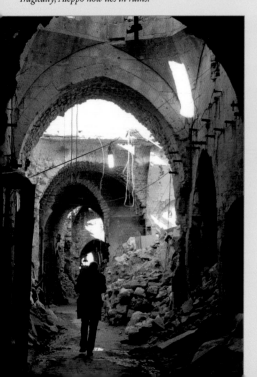

The complex web of religions, sects and tribal allegiances unravelled down to the most basic of levels, not just internally, but through the complicated network of connections within the region. Assad's ruling Alawite elite are a relatively small Shia sect, whilst the majority of the Syrian population are Sunni.

The huge uncontrolled border with Iraq meant that opportunist jihadist fighters could now join this volatile mix by easily entering Syria from the east. Factions of Daesh (also known as ISIL, ISIS or 'IS' Islamic State) moved in from Iraq, extending their controlled territory across parts of Syria, with a de facto capital at Raqqa. Into this already confusing mix were added the Kurds who had been striving for their own Kurdish homeland in the north for many years, which brought in more tensions with neighbouring Turkey, already struggling to control Kurdish ambitions in its own country.

As the battles for control intensified, more distant powers were drawn into the conflict to support their allies. The government was able to call upon help from other Shia groups such as Hezbollah in neighbouring Lebanon, the Shia republic of Iran and Syria's great ally Russia. Despite western governments calling for Assad's removal, their air strikes against Daesh strongholds and other rival jihadist groups such as al-Nusra Front, based at Deir ez Zor, can be seen, confusingly, as aiding Assad's grip on power.

An ongoing fight

By 2016 the devastated country was a patchwork of different controlled areas linked by dangerous corridors of communication. The Assad government/Hezbollah/Iran/Russia grouping have superior air power over the opposition FSA/rebel/Daesh/Kurd forces, who are often engaged in fighting amongst themselves for local control, as well as confronting Assad. Against this backdrop, Christian, Druze, Syrian Turkmen and Yazidi minorities all survive as best they can. None of the UN-sponsored peace talks has yet reduced the fighting, which appears to be hardening into yet another Shia versus Sunni proxy war. The latest ceasefire deal at time of writing came into effect on 30 December 2016.

In 2006 Aleppo was the Capital of Islamic Culture, attracting millions of visitors. Ten years later it is totally destroyed and millions of its inhabitants have fled or somehow survive in the ruins. The country remains deeply unstable and tourists are not advised to travel to anywhere in Syria at this time. Only when some sort of normality returns to Syria will it be possible to investigate the use of chemical weapons, mass killings and war crimes, attributed to all sides in the conflict.

Mesopotamia. Their presence is recorded on Kharg Island at the head of the Persian Gulf by the great burial tombs they created, almost identical to the sunken mausoleums here in their home city. Rome used Palmyra to defend itself against the Sassanids, but ended up battling the new Palmyrene Empire itself, under the control of Queen Zenobia. Rome retaliated and Palmyra never recovered, losing its silk trade to the Euphrates route towards Aleppo. It was only in the 17th century that the West became aware of this great abandoned city in the middle of the desert.

If any city developed, blossomed and faded so acutely on the strength of trade, then it is this one. Palmyra developed its own unique culture, influenced by, but independent of, Rome. It was designed by Roman and Greek architects, which gives the effect of a classical city in the desert, but follows no great plan, as everything fits into the available space. The **colonnaded street** shifted axis to bend around existing buildings as the city expanded from below the castle towards the modern roadway. One difference from a pure Roman city is the absence of stone paving, apparently to ease the feet of the vast numbers of loaded camels.

To the left is the small (by Roman standards) restored **theatre**, site of brutal killings during the first period of Daesh control. Almost in the centre of the city is a quartet of four-columned structures known as the **tetrapylon**, each one previously containing a large statue. A funerary temple lies at the end of the colonnaded street, with a nearby Temple of Allat and the area known as Diocletian's Camp, installed to reaffirm Roman control after Zenobia's revolt (see box). The most substantial of the ruins at Palmyra was the impressive **Temple of Bel**, until its recent destruction by Daesh.

Dominating the city is the distant 17th-century **Qalaat ibn Maan** (Arab Castle), attributed to a Lebanese leader, Fakhr al-Din Mani, who grew wealthy on silk in Ottoman times. His construction is perched on a rocky outcrop, and was probably built upon earlier 12th-century fortifications.

Valley of the Tombs

In 2015 it was reported that Daesh had blown up the major tomb structures to the west of the city including the Tower Tomb of Elahbel and the Tomb of the Three Brothers. However, some elements within these tombs had already been removed for safety by the antiquities service. The site museum has been completely ransacked by iconoclast Daesh militants, culminating in the murder of museum director Khaled Asaad, who had given us permission to take photographs in the museum for an earlier edition of this book.

Towards Damascus

The most direct route from Palmyra to the Mediterranean is on to Homs and through the Homs Gap, passing close to Krac des Chevaliers, but the most common routing was southwest to Damascus.

Touring Palmyra by camel in days gone by.

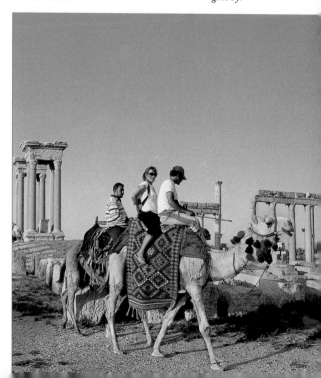

Desert Irrigation

For centuries, desert settlements have relied on underground tunnels to bring water for traders and their animals, and to irrigate crops.

The town of Palmyra owed its existence to the natural Efqa spring that bubbles sulphurous water to the surface. Without it, it would not have been possible to supply enough water for traders en route to Damascus, and their only choice would have been to travel up the Euphrates Valley.

Without a natural supply, water has to be brought in artificially, and for centuries desert settlements have relied on underground channels, known as *qanats*, to supply the water they need. The history of the *qanat* is uncertain, but goes back about 3,000 years to ancient Persia, or even possibly Oman, where the first channels were dug by hand to bring water from the mountains up to 40km (24 miles) away. Vertical shafts allowed for ventilation as well as the removal of silt and stones carried down the channel.

Hama's waterwheels.

The use of this system spread along the early Silk Road routes – east to Central Asia and China, and west to Syria and Jordan. Arab expansion in the 7th century took this same system to North Africa and Muslim Spain. Because the *qanats* were so vital, they had to be well protected, especially in times of invasion, as a whole city could easily be taken by cutting off its supply of water.

Re-using the canals

Today, there are an estimated 22,000 *qanats* in Iran carrying water some 300,000km (186,000 miles). These systems require continual skilful maintenance and can soon become blocked and useless if left. Only about 10 percent of Syria's *qanats* are thought to be working, mainly in the mountains around Damascus and the Dead Cities region to the west of Aleppo. Many others were abandoned after Independence in the 1950s, when land reform created large cooperative farms requiring more water than the *qanats* could supply and diesel pumps were introduced.

Ancient *qanats* from Roman and Byzantine times are still being discovered. The job of digging and repairing a *qanat* is highly skilled, requiring nerve and agility to work underground in small tunnels full of dust – skills that are being lost as few people want to do this work, while the conflict of recent years has also had an impact.

A method of irrigation popular with the Romans was to have a series of small dams along watercourses and *wadis*, which held rainwater temporarily, but long enough to irrigate fields via canals. These could fill large water cisterns at desert cities such as Qasr al-Hayr al-Gharbi from its dam at Harbaqa. The modern Assad Dam astride the Euphrates does a similar job on a much larger scale. The large old wooden waterwheels of Hama were a small-scale solution to water distribution along channels, raised up from the Orontes River.

Qanats in the future

A consistent and plentiful water supply is still a major concern in these areas today. When the conflict in the country has subsided, Syria will have problems meeting those demands because of Turkish dam-building projects on both the Euphrates and Tigris rivers, so it may be that more 2,000-year-old *qanats* will be brought back to life in the future.

Damascus

Along its great length, the Silk Road passes through some famous old centres, but **Damascus (Dimashq)** claims to be the oldest continuously inhabited city in the world. Proving this is extremely difficult, as there have been few opportunities to dig through the layers of this ancient city. Tablets from Mari 4,500 years ago mention Dimashq, "well-watered by the Barada River", lying on the way to the early ports of Tyre and Sidon. Egyptians, Hittites, Babylonians and Persians, in fact every civilisation of the region, has needed to take the city to confirm its authority. Early Christian sites are associated with St Paul, and later the emerging Arab civilisation naturally chose the city as its first capital. After ridding the region of the Crusaders in the 12th century, Saladin turned Damascus into an intellectual centre of poets, artists and philosophers.

Generally the city has survived the centuries rather well, as generations of traders have prospered from new opportunities and adapted to the downturns. From the mid-17th century the Ottoman silk-weaving industry boomed in both Aleppo and Damascus, using silk cocoons produced in the nearby mountains.

Despite the continued fighting, there is some sort of normality and the city centre still works reasonably well, as it is the base of the Assad regime. Most inhabitants have already fled, but some remain due to their support of the government, or are unable to get out. The further from the centre, the greater the damage, with many rebel-controlled suburbs almost completely destroyed as the fighting and bombing continues relentlessly.

The Jesus Minaret of the Umayyad Mosque.

The Old City

The area known as the **Old City** has been continually shaped and adapted over thousands of years – a process that is still continuing. It will only be possible to fully analyse the damage to the hundreds of sites of antiquity when the fighting finally ends.

In the heart of the old city is the **Umayyad Mosque**, the latest in a long line of religious buildings on this ancient sacred site. There is evidence

The Tower Tomb of Elahbel.

QUEEN ZENOBIA

Under threat from the Sassanids in AD 256, Rome entrusted Palmyra's defence to family clan leader Odenathus. Upon his death 10 years later, his widow Zenobia assumed leadership, styling herself as "Queen of the East", but she was to become even more troublesome than the Sassanids, that she was supposedly protecting Rome from.

A beautiful and courageous woman, she defeated a Roman force sent to subdue her, invaded Egypt and set up her own Palmyrene Empire. Minting coins in Alexandria with herself as "emperor" proved too much for the new emperor Aurelian, who needed to restore Rome's faltering grip on its empire. His forces defeated her army twice and she was captured trying to flee across the Euphrates River.

FACT

Weaving knowledge was transferred along the Silk Road, with one of the five basic techniques associated with a particular centre – Damascus. Fabric woven with raised patterns known as brocade became synonymous with the city. Figured woven material, especially with silk, took its name as "damask". The other four techniques are tapestry, twill, lampas and tabby.

of worship here from over 3,000 years ago, and each successive civilisation has adapted the area for its own use. In the first century of Islam, a great centre for worship was needed, and negotiations took place to occupy the site of the church. Despite invasions, earthquakes and fires, the structure has remained remarkably intact and any repairs have been well conducted. Recent damage includes a shell that blasted into the world-famous golden mosaic above the main entrance.

The **prayer hall** is essentially the old Byzantine cathedral, which being aligned to the east was long and narrow. The Muslims placed a *mihrab* (prayer niche) in the southern wall and so the room became unusually short and wide instead. The pretty green-domed marble shrine to the left of the *mihrab* is said to contain the head of **John the Baptist**. Beyond is a doorway to the small golden **Shrine of Hussein**, containing the head of the Third Imam.

Another famous shrine is through the entrance underneath the Minaret of the Bride, in the centre of the

northern wall. The simple tomb in the garden belongs to **Saladin**, the great Muslim warrior and adversary of the Crusaders. His body is in the 19th-century white marble tomb, which replaced the original dark wooden sarcophagus beside it.

National Museum

Many objects are still laid out in the garden of the **National Archaeological Museum** but the building itself has been closed since the fighting started. This is the only museum out of the 25 in Syria where the objects should be safe and not looted. The objects are world-class, including the first complete alphabet of 30 cuneiform signs on a small clay tablet found at Ugarit, near Latakia. From the same period (around 1300 BC) is an extraordinary carved ivory inlaid table-top. The museum staff are well aware of the countless items looted from Baghdad's museums a decade ago, and have already taken many of the prized exhibits to secret locations. However, as these staff are part of the Assad regime itself, it is not

The basalt theatre of Bosra.

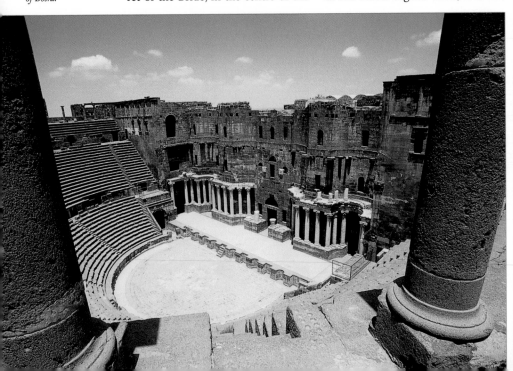

beyond the realms of possibility that some items are also disappearing, much as happened during the previous Assad regime.

Across the road is the delightful **Takiyeh as-Suleimaniyeh**, with its two thin Ottoman minarets, built by the architect Sinan, who also designed the Khusuwiye Mosque in Aleppo and Istanbul's famous Suleiman Mosque. It was constructed to aid the passage of pilgrims to Mecca, with a hostel area (now the National Army Museum) and madrassa.

Around Damascus

To the south of Damascus, the Hauran landscape is a fertile but stark region of extinct cones and rugged volcanic debris that has resulted in some unusual constructions, such as the black basalt **Bosra Theatre**. The city was known to the ancient Egyptians and Nabataeans because of its position on the route connecting Palmyra with Petra, and was a strategic centre for the Romans. The Arabs swept in quickly from the south and took Bosra from the Byzantines, in the same year as the death of the Prophet Muhammad. Serious damage to the theatre has been reported in the recent conflict.

The language spoken by Christ and the merchants of Palmyra was Aramaic, which is now only used in a few remote villages. One of these is **Ma'alula**, a tight collection of pretty pastel-coloured houses built across a mountainside. Two buildings indicate this to be an early and important Christian centre – the Monastery of St Sarkis, high up on the cliff face (the same Sarkis or Sergius who was martyred at Resafeh, see page 353), and the lower Convent of St Takla. This town has seen heavy fighting since the Battle of Ma'alula in 2013 with many buildings destroyed, and it is unclear how many Christians remain.

Homs

The city of **Homs** (**Hims**) developed at the point where the overland route from Palmyra crosses the Orontes River. It grew in importance in Roman times when it was known as Emesa, especially when Emperor Septimius Severus married Julia Domna,

The mummy of a man from Palmyra, over 2,000 years old.

SILK IN MUMMIFICATION

The rows of ornate tower tombs which were constructed outside Palmyra indicate the importance of the death ritual in the 1st–3rd centuries AD. All the major organs were removed from the body, which was filled with straw to maintain a natural shape. The brain was extracted in pieces through the nose or removed whole if the head was severed. The head was then replaced and held by wooden clasps at the base of the neck. These organs were then discarded, unlike the ancient Egyptian practice of storing them in canopic jars beside the body. At this stage the bodies were wrapped in layers of fabric such as linen or, in the case of wealthy families, imported Chinese silk which were cut into long strips. The use of silk appears not just to be an economic indicator, but also a pagan spiritual one.

Each layer of fabric was coated with spices and bitumen, a natural asphalt obtained from the Euphrates Valley, and allowed to dry for up to 70 days. Completed mummies were placed inside family tombs along with their personal jewellery and luxuries, ensuring their continued high status in the afterlife. One of the Chinese silk fragments from the face of a mummy is decorated with geometric patterns. An example of silk polychrome design found in the Kilot Tower Tomb of AD 40 has survived with remarkable details depicting Chinese dragons.

A handmade carpet featuring a traditional design.

The ablutions fountain in the Umayyad Mosque.

the daughter of the local high priest, in AD 187.

Al-Zenar Church (Church of the Virgin's Belt) in the east of the city is of particular interest, but was badly damaged by government forces in 2012 and then burned by fleeing rebels who were forced out of the city in 2014. According to the legend, the Virgin Mary died in AD 56, and as the angels were carrying her body to heaven, St Thomas asked for a sign that he could show the other Christians, so she gave him her belt *(zenar)*. Thomas took this with him to India until his relics were returned here, deposited in this church and subsequently forgotten until rediscovered in 1953. The light-beige belt is 74cm (30 ins) long and 5cm (2 ins) wide, and made of wool, possibly with flax and silk. The belt was coiled into a circular reliquary, in its original box, in a small shrine inside the church. In one of the few glimmers of hope during the current conflict, the church has recently been restored and the venerated relic of the belt was reportedly returned to the church in August 2014.

Krac des Chevaliers

Recognised as a Unesco World Heritage Site since 2006, Krac des Chavaliers was the greatest Crusader castle ever built, controlling the Homs Gap, the easiest and shortest route from Palmyra to the sea. Initially constructed by the Emir of Homs around 1030, it was known as Hisn al Akad – the castle of the Kurds. It was given to the Knights Hospitaller by Raymond II, Count of Tripoli, in 1142 and the Crusaders expanded the structure as part of a line of hilltop castles, while they sought to reclaim Jerusalem from the Muslims.

Krac des Chevaliers is what every castle should look like – massive, brooding and impregnable. The fortifications are feats of engineering, and the concentric design allowed defenders to protect themselves on all sides. The distances between the inner and outer walls maximize the accuracy of bow shots, and the angling of the outer walls makes them almost impossible to mine. 1,000 years after its construction, the severity of modern warfare has

HUMANITARIAN CRISIS

Around a quarter of a million people have died and at least half of Syria's population has been displaced to date in the Syrian war. Those still within Syria are often denied even basic food and water. Almost 5 million have fled to safety in neighbouring countries, causing huge pressures on Jordan, Lebanon and Turkey. At the western end of Turkey, just a small stretch of the Mediterranean Sea separates it from a few Greek islands that offer safety within the European Union, and many have undertaken the perilous journey, prompting a crisis within the EU on how to handle the million people requesting asylum. Less than five percent of these refugees have been offered permanent resettlement through UNHCR. The displacement of the Syrian people looks likely to be one of the major human tragedies of our times.

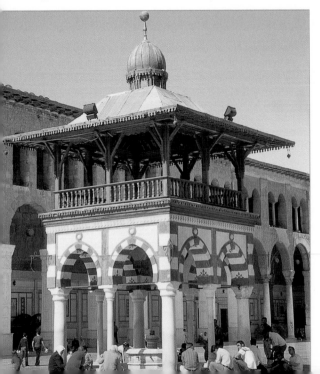

gone beyond what a crusader castle can withstand. Heavily fought over by Syrian Army and rebel forces, the extent of damage will only be known when hostility ceases.

Assassin castles

The Assassins originated in Iran (see page 330), but they had a strong presence in Syria as well. Rashid al-Din Sinan, who was known as the "Old Man of the Mountain", was in charge of the network of 10 Assassins' castles in Syria at the end of the 12th century, all of which controlled lucrative trade and communications routes running to the Mediterranean. As the Assassins' Shia influence in Persia faded and ultimately disappeared, Syria held out for much longer by making allegiances with the Crusaders who were attempting to take Jerusalem by fighting the Sunni Muslims. This Shia/Christian alliance was much to the annoyance of the Ayyubid Dynasty Sunni followers of Saladin. Many of these Assassin fortresses are in stunning locations, but most are now in ruins.

Along the Euphrates

Following the destruction of Palmyra by Emperor Aurelian in AD 242, an alternative route from Dura Europos went up the Euphrates to Aleppo and Antioch. **Resafeh (Rusafah)** was a relatively small caravan halt between Damascus and northeastern Syria until the Romans withdrew from Dura Europos and re-established their garrison here, building a supply road across the desert from Palmyra. Its location seems strange, being some distance from the river, but this was the route the traders were forced to take, away from the riverbank during times of flood. Unusually, this also became a place of great pilgrimage for early Christians when a Roman soldier by the name of Sergius was martyred here for refusing to make sacrifices to Jupiter. The town became known as Sergiopolis and benefited from lavish gifts of churches, water cisterns and strong walls to defend itself from the desert Arabs. From Resafeh, the original course of the Euphrates (now under Lake Assad) swung

A few conical mud houses are still to be found in rural areas south of Aleppo. Known as "beehive houses", the walls are half a metre (1.5ft) thick, keeping the locals warm in winter and cool in summer.

Glassware for sale in the old town of Bosra.

north, leaving just a 70-km (42-mile) run west to Aleppo.

Aleppo

Tucked into the northwest corner of Syria, **Aleppo** (known locally as Halab, a name possibly derived from Aramaic) is one of the oldest cities in the world. Between the Euphrates and the Mediterranean, the city controls access to the sea, Africa and Europe. This strategic centre was coveted, attacked and sometimes destroyed by all the major powers in the region: Egyptian, Hittite, Assyrian, Achaemenid, Greek, Roman, Byzantine, Sassanid, Arab, Turk, Crusader, Mongol, Mameluke, Ottoman and French.

On the edge of the now ruined Old City is the barricaded **National Museum**, whose staff have defiantly sought to protect as many of the valuable objects as possible, given the situation. It holds the fabulous collection uncovered at Mari, including the wonderful 4,000-year-old statue of an Amorite spring goddess holding a pot from which water once flowed, as well as the strange statue of a bearded man wearing a layered dress of feathers.

Dominating the eastern end of the **Old City** is the **Citadel**, built on a natural mound around which the city developed. Evidence only goes back to 1000 BC, but it has been the site of countless temples and palaces destroyed and rebuilt by each new conqueror. The moat and sloping stone glacis completely enclose the structure. Such a strategic location has always been important to control, as shown in the latest conflict when most of the Citadel was been destroyed by aerial bombing. At the foot of the Citadel are the ruins of the burned and bombed souk, with its warehouses and factories, once the most atmospheric of all Silk Road market places. The Great Mosque located within the souk is now in ruins, its great minaret finally felled after 900 years.

Just west of the city is one of the most important Shia sites in Syria. The 12th-century **Mashhad al-Hussein** embodies the Shia traditions of the local dynasties in Aleppo during the time of the orthodox Sunni rule of the Ayyubids. The shrine contains a piece of marble impregnated with the blood of the Third Imam, Hussein, whose head and those of his 15 followers were carried here from Karbala in Iraq, where they were martyred in AD 680. The heads were taken on to Damascus, but the stained marble remains here, placed on red silk inside a gold-and-silver shrine venerated by Shia pilgrims from around the world, especially Iran.

Around Aleppo

Named after the Persian wife of Seleucus, **Apamea** became a great military base, with thousands of trained horses and reputedly 500 war elephants imported from India. But the location was not well chosen, as it constantly suffered from earthquakes throughout the Roman, Byzantine,

The blend of modern life and ancient structures in Damascus.

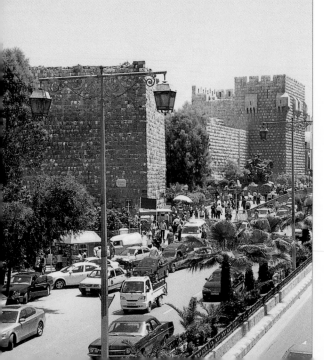

Persian, Arab and Crusader conquests. A beautiful colonnaded road still runs the length of the ancient city, but the lack of security during the current conflict has meant that the site has been completely ransacked by illegal digging. The fate of the beautiful Roman and Byzantine mosaics in the museum at the foot of the hill is uncertain, but reports are that many have been protected.

Between Aleppo and Apamea is **Ebla** which has also suffered from recent illegal digging. Ebla is a much older site, possible dating to the 3rd millennium BC and was an important city of palaces and temples. Excavations at the ancient library in the 1960s unearthed the remarkable Ebla tablets, shedding light on the society, trade and beliefs from around 5,000 years ago.

Church of St Simeon

Religious tourism is not a new phenomenon. In the 5th century AD early Christian pilgrims travelled great distances to seek out the ascetic **Simeon the Stylite** (*stylos* is Greek for "pillar"), probably the most famous person in the world during his lifetime, who dedicated his life to the worship of God by rejecting all basic comforts. Seeking solitude, he retreated to the top of an 18-metre (60-ft) -high stone pillar, where he survived for around 35 years, giving daily religious pronouncements. Even after his death, people still visited the site, and this great church was built for worship, unusually centred on the remains of his pillar, rather than the altar. It was the largest Christian building erected for 500 years, until the great cathedrals of Europe. His body was initially buried in nearby Antioch, but was considered to be such an important relic that it was later removed to the Byzantine capital, Constantinople. The church, known as **Qalaat Semaan** (Fortress of Simeon) is reported to have been badly damaged by a Russian airstrike in May 2016.

To the Turkish border

Idlib is the region of the so-called **Dead Cities**, over 700 sites of occupation between the 1st and 8th centuries AD. The completeness of the stone buildings, including entire villages, has puzzled experts for years, but it would seem that the reason for the sudden exodus was a downturn in olive oil demand, traded through Antioch. Following the collapse of this lucrative market to the Roman Empire, farmers were immediately forced to grow grains in the more fertile river valleys to become self-sufficient. The most impressive Dead Cities are Serjilla and Al-Barah to the south of Idlib.

The sites are currently under threat for several reasons. Being near the Turkish border, they are on the weapons supply route for various opposition fighting groups and make a useful supply dump. Airstrikes by pro-government planes not only target the weapons, but also destroy the ancient sites. The ruined cities also provide temporary shelter for displaced Syrians fleeing the fighting or heading to the border.

Aleppo's Citadel was an important landmark.

LEBANON

For a small country, Lebanon has had a turbulent and colourful history, as much as any other along the Silk Road.

The ruins of the Great Mosque at Aanjar

Long before silk arrived in Tyre, the Phoenicians traded from these ports all around the Mediterranean. Beirut was never as important as Tyre and Sidon in the south, or Byblos to the north, but it did become a centre for intellectual thinking, law and philology, with no equal in Roman times. Chinese silk dyed in purple from Tyre became the most sought-after luxury garment in Rome, at the culmination of this epic Silk Road overland journey.

Encouraged by the Byzantines, silk-weaving became a major industry, whose skills were passed on to Greece and Sicily. Arabs and Crusaders took control and then moved on, until the Ottoman silk industry boom in the mid-19th century, which transformed the mountainous hinterland.

War-torn and battered through the 1970s and '80s, Lebanon emerged briefly in the late '90s with new hope and enthusiasm for the future. Sadly it has descended back into armed conflict both internally and with its two neighbours, Israel and Syria. Hezbollah and Amal forces seized western Beirut in 2008 following the government's declaration that Hezbollah's communications network was illegal, and 62 people died in the ensuing violence. The porous border with Syria has meant that Lebanon has become embroiled in Syria's civil war as the Shia group Hezbollah helps to prop up President Assad in Damascus.

Today Lebanon is reeling under the double pressures of the armed conflict overflowing from Syria, and the huge numbers of fleeing Syrian refugees, who now total approximately one quarter of Lebanon's population. The job of governing Lebanon has never been easy with its balancing act of Sunni, Shia, Maronite Christian and Druze communities, and often too difficult for even the most flexible of politicians, with a rapid turnover of Presidents and Prime Ministers. Most tour operators are avoiding Lebanon, but there is a small, thriving, local tour industry catering for independent travellers, who report trouble-free visits. Check your own government advice and time your visit wisely. As always with Lebanon, whatever the troubles, life is lived to the max. As some of the locals say "History, hedonism and hummous – what more do you need?"

Syrian border to Beirut

The ruins of **Aanjar**, are an 8th-century Omayyid town built to control the caravan trade along this route from Damascus. Interestingly, it was the only ancient trading centre in Lebanon to be inland, so it also doubled as a summer hunting lodge for the caliph. The town is laid out as a perfect square, divided into quarters by two main central roads with gateways at each end. At the upper part of this quiet site is the famous restored palace with graceful arches on two storeys.

Baalbek

Only 35km (21 miles) up the Bekaa Valley is Lebanon's greatest Roman site at **Baalbek**, a name taken from the worship of the Phoenician god Baal in the Bekaa.

The site seems to have been continuously inhabited for about 4,000 years, with traces of Phoenician, Greek (when it was known as Heliopolis), Byzantine and Arab dynasties, as well as the major Roman buildings to be seen today. The temples of Jupiter and Bacchus are two of the largest in the world, which dominate the site with their giant columns, entablatures and carvings. Nearby is the smaller Temple of Venus and unusual Hexagonal Court. Visiting advice often depends on your home nation. On one hand, this is a stronghold of Hezbollah and continues to be an area of high tension, but equally the Baalbeck International Festival celebrated 60 years in August 2016 with concerts by Jean Michel Jarre amongst others.

Getting to the coast means climbing out of the Bekaa up a southern spur of the Lebanon Mountains. The views back across the southern Bekaa to Mount Hermon (Jebel al-Sheikh to the locals) can be stunning in good weather.

Silk Museum

High in the hills above Beirut in the village of **B'sous** is a small museum

View towards Beirut from B'sous.

ENTERING AND LEAVING LEBANON

The current situation means that all land border crossings to and from Lebanon should be considered closed for the immediate future. This is due to the ongoing conflict in Syria together with the usual tensions with Israel. It is possible to obtain a Lebanese visa before arrival but as the only logical entry point is Beirut airport, it's best to make use of the VOA (visa on arrival) system, which works well and at least safeguards unused visa fees if the situation suddenly flares up and a trip has to be cancelled. (See Travel Tips, page 400, for more information on transport in Lebanon.)

There are a suprisingly large number of airlines flying to Beirut, but this keeps changing. Major European airlines usually include British Airways, Lufthansa, Air France, Alitalia, Aegean Airlines, Vueling Airlines, Czech Airlines, LOT and TAROM.

From the Middle East region there are also MEA, Emirates, Royal Jordanian, Qatar Airways, Etihad Airways, Gulf Air, Oman Air, Kuwait Airways and Turkish Airlines. From further afield are Qantas, Aeroflot and Ethiopian Airlines.

You must check the security situation before arrival as there have been serious incidents in the southern Beirut suburbs between the city centre and the airport, but all agency taxis and official drivers would know which roads and areas are safe to travel into the city centre.

in a converted silk mill dedicated to the manufacture, trade and use of silk. From the main Damascus road go through the village of Aley, marked "Musée de la Soie", or ask for *mathaf harir*. The **Silk Museum** (May–Sept Tue–Sun 10am–6pm; charge) was founded in 2001 by George Asseily and his wife Alexandra. Despite the lack of tourists, the small team strive to preserve the silk legend with an informative video presentation. The museum highlights the 19th-century Lebanese silk industry, which used this mill and many others, when Mount Lebanon was known as the "Mountain of Silk".

Beirut

Beirut (Beyrouth) has an amazing early history that has seen the headland protect fleets of Phoenician biremes, Greek triremes, Roman galleys and Ottoman galleons. Once a hotspot for celebrities in the 1960s, Beirut is just a shadow of its former self, but despite many difficulties, it is striving yet again to be a top resort and a financial centre of the region.

Beirut has become synonymous with the troubles in the Middle East, an image that it is struggling to shake off, but on a calm day there is nowhere better to have a sumptuous restaurant meal with magnificent views, promenade along the bustling Corniche and party in the myriad nightclubs till the early hours.

The **National Museum** (www.bei rutnationalmuseum.com; Tue–Sun 9am–5pm; charge) suffered as much as any building during the civil war, being located along the Green Line separating the warring factions. An unnerving video presentation shows how the collection was protected during this time.

Of particular interest are the objects from Tyre, including 2nd-century BC marble sarcophagi, one with fabulous details of Greek battles and another known as the "Drunken Cupids". The "Legend of Achilles" is decorated with amazing figures on the frieze carved almost in the round. A much earlier connection with ancient Egypt is the black basalt stele of Pharaoh Ramses II from the 13th century BC – an example of the strict formality that ruled art

Weaving at the Silk Museum.

SILK INDUSTRY

The Silk Museum in B'sous is located inside one of the many redundant silk factories on the Lebanese hillsides. Mulberry trees grow easily here, and silk production was the major activity during Ottoman control in the Middle Ages, employing people of all age groups from the peasant farming communities.

By the late 19th century, there were over 3 million mulberry trees growing in the area. In the industry's heyday, silk accounted for half the income from the Mount Lebanon region, traded through Beirut and Tripoli. Many investors came from France to set up cocoon-reeling factories for the export of yarn to Lyon. Some of the old silk factories, such as Deir al-Qamar and Beit Eddine, have become famous sites in their own right.

here until the arrival of the Achaemenids in the 6th century BC. The 5th-century BC capital with bull protomes found at Sidon would not look out of place at Persepolis. The Anthropoid Sarcophagus, found in Sidon, shows all the cultural influences of the great empires in the region – Egyptian, Persian and Greek.

Reopened in 2006 after extensive renovation is the impressively modern **American University of Beirut (AUB) Archaeological Museum** (www.aub.edu.lb/museum_archeo; Mon–Fri 9am–4pm; free) in Hawra District, which originally opened in 1868. Of interest is a section about purple dye from Tyre, a small loaded camel statue from the Achaemenid period and a fascinating photo of Lebanon from space showing the major archaeological sites and trade routes.

Two wonderful mansion/museums in downtown Beirut are open to the public, showing private collections in sumptuous surroundings. The mission of the **Nicholas Sursock Museum** (Wed–Mon 10am–6pm Thu noon–9pm; free) is to collect, preserve and exhibit local and international art. The **Robert Mouawad Museum** (daily 9am–5pm; charge) has a remarkable collection of valuable historic artefacts covering a wide period.

Sidon

It is only 40km (24 miles) from Beirut to **Sidon** (Saida), an important trading and shipbuilding centre from Phoenician times, which reached prominence under the Persians, for whom it became a renowned glass-making centre. Most of what can be seen dates back to Crusader times, including the quaint Sea Castle, built to defend the harbour using blocks pillaged from nearby Roman buildings.

Tyre

For more ancient sites covering the period of silk trade, we must head for the ultimate destination on our journey, the port of Tyre, now called

Sour. Tyre (Sour) has been shaped by all the major civilisations of the region – Egyptians, Phoenicians, Assyrians, Greeks and Romans. It lent its name to the royal purple dye created from the tiny sea shells, a heap of which, known as Murex Hill, has survived inland from the harbour. The town is often out of bounds due to its proximity with the Israeli border.

Byblos

Locally known as Jubayl, **Byblos** has a history stretching back at least 7,000 years and today has a very attractive, small natural harbour. The name Byblos comes from Phoenician via Greek, meaning 'Papyrus' (our word Bible means 'Papyrus book'). It is only 42km (26 miles) north of Beirut and was used by all the major regional civilisations, with monuments today from Phoenician, Roman and Crusader periods, all Unesco protected. Pleasant cafes, bars and restaurants ring the small harbour, but it will struggle to regain the glory days of the 1960s and 70s when it partied with Hollywood A-listers.

TIP

Lebanon is a small country and nowhere is more than 130km (80 miles) from the centrally-placed capital Beirut. Every site can be visited in a day trip from Beirut, but you must make sure that you have the correct paperwork and permissions to get through the many roadblocks and security checkpoints.

Smoking nargiles on Beirut's Corniche.

Interior of the Blue Mosque, Istanbul.

TURKEY

The final route choice was towards ancient Antioch, the Black Sea, or across the Anatolian plateau to Constantinople – modern-day Istanbul.

O nce they crossed into Anatolia – in modern Turkey – the weary travellers on the Silk Road may still have had hundreds of kilometres to go. They might take the northern route west, threading along the Black Sea coast via Trebizond (Trabzon) to reach the Byzantine and Ottoman capital of Constantinople, which was to become Istanbul. Another way of reaching the city's fabulous bazaars was by continuing right across the central Anatolian plains, following the Persian Royal Road and avoiding the steep mountains to the north and south, heading to the major cities where they could trade along the way – Diyarbakır and Mardin, Konya and Bursa.

The east

Entering Turkey from the east, specifically from modern Iran, Armenia and Georgia, is now easier than it has been for decades. Far from the standard tourist trail there are also a number of significant sites, not least among them **Mount Ararat**.

The Ararat massif is 40km (25 miles) in length and includes the highest peak in Turkey: Mount Ararat itself. Known most widely as the place where Noah's ark came to rest, the mountain is also the national symbol of Armenia, featuring on the country's coat of arms and bank notes. A

Time for lunch in Antakya.

climbing permit and certified guide are required should you wish to climb the peak.

15km (9 miles) southwest of Ararat is Dogubeyazit, the unprepossessing town that marks the border with Iran. Two things make Dogubeyazit worth a visit: the views of Ararat (5,137m/16,854ft), Little Ararat (3,896m/12,782ft) and Tendurek Dagi (3,533m/11,592ft); and the spectacular **Ishak Pasha Palace** (charge). Begun in 1685 by Colak Abdi Pasha and completed a century later by his

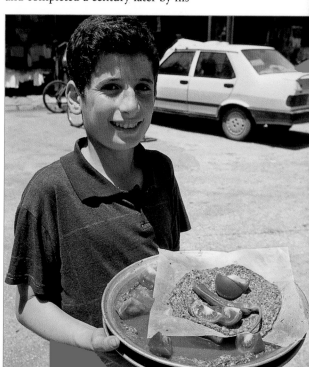

grandson Ishak (Isaac), the palace and administrative complex is one of the most impressive examples of Ottoman architecture. The vast entranceway, courtyards, mosque and harem are well preserved and the site is rarely crowded.

The inland routes

Inland, the Silk Road effectively followed the same route for much of its distance as the Persian Royal Road, which connected Ephesus and İzmir on the Aegean seaboard through Zeugma, crossing the Euphrates near Gaziantep to Babylon, as early as the 5th century BC. In later Roman times, there were military camps every 30–40km (20–25 miles), where travellers were welcome to rest in safety, while the later Byzantine Empire spaced its camps out every 50km (30 miles). But it was the Seljuks who really went to town on travellers' facilities.

By the 12th century, when the sea routes were in the hands of the West, the Seljuks enticed traders to use the land routes by offering foreign

The distinctive green minaret of the Mevlâna Tekke Müzesi in Konya.

merchants guarantees that they would be free from robbery. These were the world's first insurance deals, and, to ensure the safety of the travellers, tax was levied only in areas where crimes occurred – no crime, no tax. So it was in local interests to keep the neighbourhood clean. Good roads were built, with caravanserais no more than a day's travel apart. Some 200 of these magnificent *hans* (travellers' inns) survive in varying states of decay and restoration across Turkey, some now back in business as hotels, restaurants, nightclubs and museums, and others in ruins or used as barns.

Just across the Syrian border, **Mardin** rears up from the Mesopotamian plain, a city of mellow, pale golden stone known for its filigree jewellery, pistachio nuts and as the home of popular Turkish TV series *Sıla*, a glamorous family drama.

The town, whose magnificent warren of old stone houses and alleys cascades down the cliff like golden lace in the evening light, began to thrive in the 3rd century AD with the arrival of the Syriac Christians, who built

ENTERING AND LEAVING TURKEY

Turkey was until recently a very easy country in which to travel, but since the increase in terror attacks in 2016 the situation has changed rapidly. Most people could buy their visas at the airport or land border on arrival, but the need for tighter security now means visitors need to pre-register and paying online for an e-Visa, with some temporary overlap in systems. There are many international flights to Istanbul, Ankara and elsewhere, with the major airlines. For longer domestic distances, you may want to consider taking some internal flights – the network of local airports is excellent – or take the train along limited sections of the route such as Istanbul–Ankara. There are good coach services and plenty of taxis or shared taxis (*dolmus*) for local travel (see page 400).

There are many crossing points along the border with **Syria**, but all are out of bounds for tourists, with serious consequences for attempting to cross. Similarly, the border with **Iraq** into Iraqi Kurdistan has almost completely shut down for tourists, due to increased tension between Turkey and its own Kurds in the region. Check the security situation before travelling.

The weekly train to/from Tehran in **Iran** to Istanbul is temporarily suspended, also due to Kurdish unrest in the east of Turkey. However, the three crossings with Iran at Bazargan/Gurbulak, Razi/Kapikoy and Serow/Esendere appear to be operating normally.

numerous monasteries and churches and lived on trade and as jewellery-makers. The last of them emigrated to Sweden in the 1980s, leaving only a few priests to man the cavernous churches. There are five former inns and caravanserais.

From here the road heads north. This whole vast area of southern Turkey is part of the GAP Project, a massive feat of water engineering that is creating a sequence of dams along both the Tigris and Euphrates rivers for hydroelectric power and irrigation.

If the Kurds had a capital, it would be solid, black **Diyarbakır**, about four hours' drive north of Mardin. The Old Town of this grimly workaday city on the Tigris lies behind vast charcoal-black basalt walls 5km (3 miles) long, with a ring of 82 defensive towers, built during the reign of Constantinus but frequently restored over the centuries, with numerous inscriptions, geometrical and animal designs. It is possible to climb some of the towers and walk sections of the wall, from where there are fine views across the city and the Tigris Valley.

Known in classical times as Amidiya, the city was annexed to Islamic rule in AD 639 when it became the property of the Arab clan of Baqr (hence the name "abode of the Baqr", or Diyarbakır). Within the walls are a number of mosques and ancient Orthodox churches, the grandest of them the Ulu Camii (Grand Mosque; İzzet Paşa Caddesi), which is the oldest in Anatolia and once the Syriac Cathedral of Mar Touma (St Thomas). Stripy black-and-white Syrian-style architecture is found in many of the city's public buildings, not least the huge Hotel Grand Kervansaray, built in 1521 as a *han* for travellers on the Silk Road with 72 rooms, 17 shops and stabling for 800 camels. It is once again working as a hotel and restaurant, though without the camels.

Birthplace of Abraham

The main route now heads southwest, along the Euphrates Valley and past what is now the huge **Ataturk Dam**, centrepiece of the whole GAP Project, to reach the ancient city of **Sanlıurfa**.

Seljuk palace at Ani, northeast Anatolia.

THE SELJUK TURKS

First mentioned in Chinese writings in 1300 BC, the Turks are people of Central Asia, their language belonging to the Ural-Altaic family, which includes an eclectic selection from Finnish and Hungarian, to Japanese and Korean. Traditionally they married outside their tribe, and, as renowned horsemen, were hired as mercenaries by empires from the Mongols to the Abbasids. In the mid-11th century, a small Turkmen tribe, the Seljuks, recent converts to Islam and in the service of the Abbasid caliph, set up a state in Iran, with their first capital at Rey, later transferred to Isfahan (and an eastern capital at Merv). Impatient for greater power and with evangelising zeal, they decided they were the true heirs to all the lands once conquered by the Prophet Muhammad and set off to fight, negotiate and buy their way to an empire.

At the Battle of Manzikert in 1071, the Seljuks won a decisive victory against Byzantine Emperor Romanus IV Diogenes, who was captured and ransomed in exchange for much of eastern Anatolia. From here they built themselves an empire and a civilisation, but it came to an abrupt and untimely end in 1243 when they were themselves destroyed in battle by Genghis Khan and his Mongol hordes, in spite of help from the Byzantine emperor, leaving the field clear for the rising power of the Ottomans.

Some scholars believe that Sanlıurfa, or Urfa, was the biblical town of Ur, but Iraqis have a similar claim. Here not only are you swept straight back into the Old Testament, with references to prophets abounding, but far beyond, to the dawn of civilisation. The world's first domesticated grains (dating back to c.9500 BC) were recently found here, while the world's oldest known temple stands on a windswept hillside overlooking the plains of Harran at Goblekitepe, about 20km (12 miles) out of town.

According to Islamic tradition, it was in Urfa that Abraham was catapulted off the cliff into the fire, to be saved by God, who turned the fire into water and the logs to fishes – both sacred pool and fishes still survive beneath the citadel and are a place of pilgrimage and great beauty in the town centre. The cave where Abraham was supposedly born is in the same park.

To the south of the city, the green, irrigated Mesopotamian plains are littered with ancient history, much of it as yet unexcavated. Of all the villages,

the most important is **Harran**, an ancient city and site of the original Temple of Sin, now buried deep beneath centuries of other archaeological gold. Known throughout the ancient world for its astronomers and savants, it was here that Ruth poured water for Jacob, and where the Roman emperor Crassus supposedly died by having liquid gold poured into his mouth.

About three hours' drive further west, **Gaziantep** (formerly Antep) dates back to the Hittite period. Home of pistachios, copperware, *lahmacun* (meat with dough) and the best *baklava* in Turkey, it is a thriving industrial city and a major producer of silk and cotton textiles. A 6th-century Byzantine fortress, remodelled by the Crusaders, tops an artificial mound near the city centre, and there are numerous fine old houses, mosques and caravanserais in the winding city streets. The **Archaeological Museum** (Istasyon Caddesi; Tue–Sun 8.30am–noon, 1–5pm; charge) has a few of the many magnificent mosaics rescued from the rising dam waters at nearby

Detail of a mosaic from the Hatay Regional Museum in Antakya.

Zeugma. The major crossing point of the Euphrates on the eastern edge of the Roman Empire, Zeugma was a city of enormous wealth, as these world-class mosaics attest. Half the site has been flooded by the new lake, but archaeological excavations continue on the other half.

Antakya, ancient Antioch

Many travellers would also arrive in the northwest corner of Syria and head for the nearby city of Antioch, now Antakya, in Hatay, a finger of Turkish territory between Syria and the sea. The Turkish border post at **Reyhanlı** is continually being extended to deal with the rapid increase in overland trade between the two countries and also, for the time being, the flood of refugees fleeing violence in Syria. Beyond the hills that form the border, the land flattens into an endless panorama of wheat fields. The dark outline of the Amanus Mountains looms ahead, but the ancient traders took an easier route south along the base of the mountains following the Asi (Orontes) River, itself having run

across the border from Homs and Hama. Long before any towns are visible, there are the unmistakable pencil-thin Ottoman minarets piercing the landscape.

The modern town of **Antakya** (ancient Antioch) lies astride the pleasant Asi (Orontes) Valley a few miles from the sea. It is fitting that, with the spread of Christianity along the Silk Road, there is a direct link from this western end, where St Peter resided a few years after the death of Christ. His simple grotto church, known as **Sen Piyer Kilisesi** (Tue–Sun 8.30am–noon, 1.30–7pm; charge), overlooks the town from the side of Mount Staurion ("Cross Mountain") and is worth a visit for this view alone. One of the first secret prayer places for followers of Christ, this was possibly the first church where the disciples were called "Christians". Drops of water seeping into the cave serve for baptism and are believed to have special properties.

The houses, mosques and bazaar in the Old Town are interesting, but there is little to see from antiquity, other

TIP

As well as visiting the amazing historical sights, the spectacular landscape around the Cappadocia region is a fabulous playground for outdoor activities. Local operators can equip and advise on gentle walks, hiking, multi-day trekking, mountain biking, horse riding, quad-biking, white-water rafting, helicopter flights and even hot-air ballooning. Check the safety arrangements for all adventure activities.

Mardin at night.

than in the excellent **Hatay Regional Museum** (Tue–Sun 8.30am–noon, 1.30–5pm; charge) by the banks of the river, where the vast range of high-quality mosaics is well presented.

This branch of the Silk Road ends at the coast near **Samandagı**, at the ruins of the old harbour of Seleucia Piera, the port of Antioch. History has been swallowed by sand and overgrown by coastal vegetation, but it is an interesting, if forgotten area. Near the village of Çevlik, the large, white, stone walls creating field barriers are parts of the old harbour wall.

Road signs indicate the "Ancient City of Seleucia Piera and Cave City" behind a seaside restaurant. The site map shows the extensive area stretching inland, but the main sites are the tunnel and caves, an easy 90-minute walk away. The route is along the floodwater channel (Titus Tunelı) built by Emperors Titus and Vespasian in the late 1st century AD. The most remarkable section is where the sky becomes a thin slit of light, until finally a square tunnel the size of an underground railway cuts through solid rock. It is extremely dark, but a good adventure. Retrace your steps to the small bridge, and follow the signs to the Bezikli Megara, leading to the area of limestone rock-cut tombs, some dating from the 1st century AD.

Cappadocia

Far to the northwest, **Kayseri** is one of the oldest cities in Anatolia and was always an important Silk Road centre at the junction of a number of historic routes. It was the capital of the Graeco-Roman province of Cappadocia from 380 BC to AD 17, and, from 1071, a Seljuk city. Many fine Islamic monuments remain, and the 1,500-year-old castle, built initially by the Romans, still stands at the central square of the city. Nearby, the **Karatay caravanserai** (see box) is one of the finest restored caravanserais in the country.

Kayseri is the gateway to **Cappadocia**, an otherworldly and impossibly beautiful landscape of twisted limestone towers, crevasses and canyons. Dominated by Erciyes Dağ (ancient Mt Argaeus), the third-highest mountain

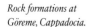

Rock formations at Göreme, Cappadocia.

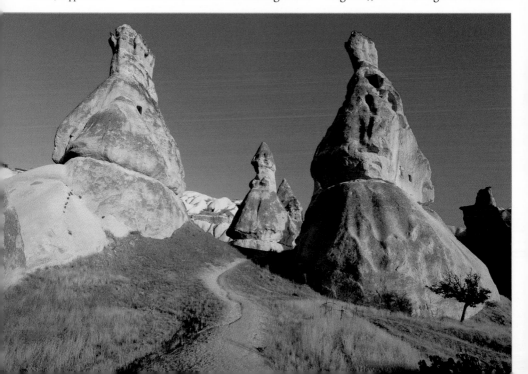

in Anatolia (3,917m/12,848ft), the whole area was covered in soft limestone when the mountain erupted millions of years ago, since when the weather has carved it into these tortuous shapes, seen at their most fantastic in the fairy 'chimneys' of Zelve and the towering rock citadel of Üchisar.

There are also troglodyte houses, cave churches and huge underground cities seven and eight storeys deep. There are over 400 of these, the largest and most spectacular at Derinkuyu and Kaymaklı (both daily 8am–5pm, to 6pm in summer; charge), once capable of housing up to 20,000 people. But perhaps even more fabulous than the cave houses are the churches, of which there are some 3,000 known so far. The best are in the Ihlara Valley, with over 60 churches in the walls of the 10-km (6-mile) -long gorge, and in the fabulous **Göreme Open Air Museum** (daily 8am–6pm, to 5pm in winter; charge with additional fees for Buckle Church and Dark Church), which encloses over 30 of the finest churches in Cappadocia, most dating from the 9th–11th centuries.

The villages of Ürgüp, Ortahisar and Göreme are where most tourists stay.

Seljuk capital

For the medieval traveller, arriving in **Konya** was like arriving in New York or London. From 1071 to 1308, it was the capital of the Seljuk Empire and a vastly important political and commercial hub. Overlooking the city's many Seljuk monuments is a huge mound, Alâeddin Tepesi, on top of which stand the last remaining walls of the Sultani Sarayı (Palace of the Seljuk Sultans) and the Alâeddin Camii (12th and 13th centuries); some of the world's oldest carpets were found here, dating from the 13th century.

Of far greater importance, however, is the **Mevlâna Tekke Müzesi** (Kısla Caddesi; daily 9am–5pm, Mon from 10am; charge), the monastery and **tomb of Mevlâna Jelaleddin Rumi**, an Afghan-born Islamic mystic who wrote mystical poetry in Persian (the court language of Seljuk Konya) and founded the Sufi monastic order of Dervishes who aimed to achieve

Whirling dervishes.

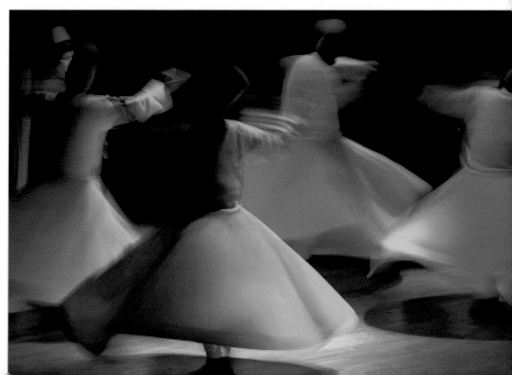

mystical union with God through music and dance. The Whirling Dervishes still pray in stately pirouettes, although you can see the *sema* (ritual dance) performed at tourist shows. The monastery is a place of pilgrimage, also supposedly housing hairs from the Prophet Muhammad's beard as well as a magnificent collection of art, ancient manuscripts and rare 13th-century *kilims* (woven carpets). The wonderful Karatay Medresi, an Islamic school built in 1251, now houses a fine **Ceramics and Tile Museum** (Hastane Caddesi, Alâeddin; daily 9am–noon, 1–5pm; charge).

From Konya, some traders would turn south to the coast at Antalya to trade through the port, but most would trudge on to the west, heading towards **Eğirdir Gölü**, the second-largest freshwater lake in Turkey. The pretty town of **Eğirdir** on its shores became a regular stop for travellers, with a fine collection of old Greek and Ottoman houses, the ruins of a Seljuk fort and a 15th-century Ulu-camii (Great Mosque). St Paul gave his first sermon at **Yalvaç** (ancient

A placid lake, Eğirdir Gölü.

Antioch ad Pisidiam; open 9am–5pm; charge), further up the eastern shore of the lake.

Centre of the silk industry

Bursa was supposedly founded by the Bithynian King Prusias I Cholus "the Lame" (r.228–185 BC), who chose the site, in the shadow of 2,554-metre (8,377-ft) Uludağ, with the help of the great Carthaginian general Hannibal. However, the city really came into its own in 1326, when it was conquered by Orhan Gazi, described by 13th-century traveller Ibn Battuta as "the greatest of the Turkmen kings, and the richest in wealth, lands and military forces".

Bursa became the Ottoman capital upon the fall of Constantinople in 1453. From the first, it was a trading centre – Orhan issued his first coins here in 1327 and set up a *bedesten* (combination inn, market and secure lock-up) in 1340. Today, it is the fifth-largest city in the country, and its lovely architectural heritage is slowly being submerged beneath a sea of concrete.

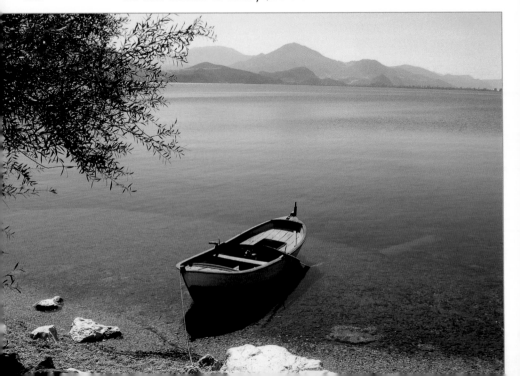

The Çarsı (Bazaar) is still the commercial centre of the city; the Bedesten, built by Sultan Beyazıt I on the site of Orhan Gazi's earlier building, is still used for storing and selling gold and silver jewellery. Around it stand a group of *hans* (inns), each built with courtyards shaded by trees and cooled by fountains, the rooms used as shops, storage and dwellings. The earliest of them was the Emir Han, the grandest the Koza Han, today the centre of the Turkish silk industry, with vivid bolts of cloth festooned over counters and piled high against the walls of the tiny shops. You can buy silk shirts, suits, ties and scarves or even have your dress made, for a fraction of what you might pay elsewhere.

Profits from the bazaars went to support a network of mosques and charitable institutions, many of which are architectural masterpieces.

Outside the city centre, three of the early emperors have fine complexes and, just to the south of Çekirge Caddesi, the Muradiye Külliyesi (1425–6) has several royal tombs, including the tomb of Murat II (1421–51). Nearby are the 17th-century **Ottoman House Museum** (Tue–Sun 9am–5pm; charge), and the **Hüsnü Züber Müzesi** (Uzunyol Sok 3, Kaplıca Caddesi; Tue–Sun 10am–5pm; charge), a restored Ottoman guesthouse, built in 1836.

Tile town

There was one more significant stop en route: **İznik** (formerly **Nicaea**), 80km (50 miles) northeast of Bursa, was founded in 316 BC by Antigonus I (the One-Eyed) and named Nicaea in 301 BC by Lysimachus, after his deceased wife. An important Roman city, it was here that Constantine convened the First Ecumenical Council in AD 325, which formulated the Nicaean Creed, the expression of faith still used by most Christians. A Byzantine refuge during the 13th-century Crusader occupation of Constantinople, it was conquered by the Ottomans in 1331. Potters brought in from Tabriz in Persia created the ceramic industry, which sent magnificent İznik tiles across the empire.

The main portal to the ruins of Karatay Caravanserai.

KARATAY CARAVANSERAI

The certificate of foundation of the Karatay Caravanserai, built in 1237 near Kayseri, offers a fascinating glimpse into how these institutions operated. No matter what time they arrived, travellers were welcomed, given a place to wash (with soap), stable and feed their animals, store their goods safely and sleep. Food and medical services were provided, shoes mended or new shoes given if the old ones were too worn. Animals were re-shod, oil and candles were provided for light and firewood for heat. And all this was completely free of charge. In the morning, once everyone had packed and was satisfied that all was present and correct, the manager would ceremonially throw open the doors and send them on their way with the blessing "Bismillah" (in the name of God).

Beyond İznik the route lay around the shores of the Sea of Marmara, and to the Bosporus – the end of Asia. On the far side, over 2,500km (1,500 miles) since crossing the Syrian border into Anatolia at Mardin, after a journey that would take even a modern tourist with a good car at least two days, the foot-sore camel caravan stood at the gates of one of the greatest cities on earth.

Istanbul

Whether it is called Constantinople or **Istanbul** depends on the date, but the city still has one of the most tumultuous bazaars the world has ever known, the prize for which weary travellers have crossed a continent to reach. The domes and spires of Aya Sofia (Hagia Sophia in Greek), the Blue Mosque and Topkapı Palace rising above the Bosporus remain a stunning, welcoming site. Cross this remarkable waterway and you step from Asia to Europe.

At the city's heart is Sultanahmet, between the Bosporus and the Golden Horn, centred around At Meydanı, the Hippodrome. Nearby is Aya Sofia, the Church of the Holy Wisdom (Tue–Sun 9am–5pm, May–Oct until 7.30pm; charge) constructed in AD 632–7 on the orders of Emperor Justinian, turned into a mosque and then a national museum in the 1930s, when its beautiful medieval mosaics were uncovered. Its splendid design has been followed by mosque-builders ever since. The **Blue Mosque** (open outside prayer times) opposite dates from 1616. With six minarets, 260 windows, madrassa, caravanserai and kitchen, it was a complete social centre. In front of the Blue Mosque is the **Museum of Turkish and Islamic Arts** (Tue–Sun 9am–5pm; charge), specialising in carpets.

The extraordinary underground water cistern, **Yerebatan Sarayı** (daily 9am–5pm; charge), should be visited, also the **Archaeology Museum** (Tue–Sun 9am–5pm; charge).

Most intriguing of all is **Topkapı Sarayı** (Topkapı Palace; Tue–Sun 9am–6pm, in winter until 5pm; charge). Here, among the courtyards and kiosks, libraries and gardens, sultans reigned in glory. The harem and its incumbents were swathed in the finest silks that money could buy.

The stunning skyline of Istanbul.

The Grand Bazaar

The Silk Road ended in the fantastic warren of Istanbul's bazaar, where anything could be sold or bought – and can still.

By the time of Mehmet I's conquest, Constantinople was a sorry place – the real money had been in Ottoman hands for decades, while the Byzantine emperors cowered fearfully behind the city walls. What the city and the empire needed was a hard injection of cash, and that would come from trade. By 1461, building was under way, just beside the old Forum of Constantine, the commercial centre of the city since it was built in the 4th century AD. A trading centre fit for an empire began to take shape, with *bedestens*, *hans*, restaurants, water fountains and teahouses, banks, storerooms, workshops, mosques, a bathhouse, school and literally thousands of shops. It even had its own fire brigade.

The modern market

Today, the Grand Bazaar remains one of the largest buildings in the world, with 22 gates leading to 61 streets covering 31 hectares (76 acres). No one knows exactly how many shops there are, and even though some have combined into larger spaces, there are estimated to be up to 4,500 shops and 30,000 traders working in the bazaar at any one time, attracting more than a quarter of a million shoppers and visitors each day, both regulars and tourists.

Right at the centre, the Iç Bedesten is the oldest building in the bazaar, adapted to be the market's first lock-up and also used for slave auctions. It is still used for the bazaar's most precious sales, from fine jewellery to antiques and icons. The silk market is the 15th-century Sandal Bedesten in the southeast corner. Beneath a roof of 20 brick domes, there remains a silk auction here every Wednesday at 1pm. A silk carpet is a fitting souvenir.

Traditional crafts

Around the *bedestens*, the grid of streets is named after the craftsmen and traders who once plied their trade there – silk-thread makers (*kazazcilar*), fur-makers (*kürkçüler*), slipper-makers (*terlikçiler*), shoemakers (*kavafçilar*), mirror-makers (*aynacilar*), fez-makers (*fesçiler*), quilt-makers (*yorgancilar*), polishers (*perdahçilar*) and jewellers (*kalpakcilar basi*). Although few names still reflect their origins, with every alley piled with *lokum* (Turkish delight) and chess sets, leather bags and stained-glass lanterns, gleaming copperware and twinkling inlaid wood, the Jewellers' Street, on the south side of the bazaar, still burns with polished gold and silver, the sparkle of diamonds and the deep lure of sapphires. The finest carpets are found deeper into the maze or in some of the 40 former *hans*, such as Zincirli Han.

And if the vast array within the covered market is insufficient, the streets around are crowded with stalls, leading to the Book Bazaar near the university, down through the very workaday market of plastic buckets and cheap saucepans, to the water's edge at Eminönü, where the Mısır Çarsısı (Egyptian or Spice Market), built in the mid-17th century, is the place to buy every kind of spice and herb. During a spate of bomb attacks in the summer of 2016 there was one blast near to the bazaar which killed 11 people. Nevertheless, the Grand Bazaar remains one of the major sights of Istanbul and an evocative Silk Road experience.

In the heart of the Grand Bazaar.

TRAVEL TIPS
THE SILK ROAD

TRANSPORT

GETTING THERE AND GETTING AROUND

GETTING THERE

By air

On arrival, passengers from international flights must fill out arrival cards, and customs and health declarations. On departure, passengers must fill out a departure card. Some airports levy a departure tax.

Beijing

Beijing's modern Capital Airport, 25km (16 miles) from the centre, connects China to the world's major cities and the city to all parts of China (for details see http://en.bcia.com. cn). The journey into the city centre takes 30 minutes if the traffic is light but can take an hour at busier times. Airport bus services (15–30 Rmb) operate regularly to downtown Beijing, and many of the leading hotels offer limousine or minibus services.

Taxis can be found between international and domestic arrivals; ensure that the meter is turned on and ignore the hordes of taxi touts who wait inside the terminal building: these taxis are illegal.

You must check in at least two hours before departure for an international flight, as security measures in China are now very tight. Hotels usually have flight booking services, and most major airlines have offices in Beijing.

Hong Kong

Hong Kong is a major international air-traffic hub for the region, so there is no shortage of flights. Hong Kong's international airport (www. hongkongairport.com) is at Chek Lap Kok, a small island to the north

of Lantau Island and about 34km (21 miles) from Central (the main shopping and banking area).

The Airport Express (AEL) is a comfortable train service that runs every 12 minutes and takes 24 minutes into town; it offers the most convenient and cost-effective way to get to and from the airport (the journey by road via taxi or bus takes around 40 minutes and costs about HK$90 to Kowloon, HK$100 to Hong Kong Island).

Departure taxes

There is a departure tax of around HK$120 (US$15) to be paid on flights from Hong Kong, and 90 Rmb (US$12) on flights from Shanghai. For passengers departing from Beijing, the airport tax is now included in the price of the ticket.

There are numerous buses linking the airport to the city and to destinations in Guangdong. The Airbus services (prefixed "A") run at regular intervals from 6am to midnight and cost HK$19–48. Slower commuter buses are prefixed "E", and there are shuttle buses to Tung Chung MTR station. There are also direct ferry services from the airport to Macau and Shenzhen.

Flying out, you can check in at the AEL Central and Kowloon stations 90 minutes before departure.

Kashgar (Kashi)

The airport is located 11km (7 miles) north of the city. There is a shuttle bus between the airport and the CAAC office on 95 Jiefang Nanlu (tel: (0998) 282 2113). China Southern

Airlines and Hainan Airlines have daily flights between Kashgar and Urumqi, and seats are not usually difficult to come by.

Lanzhou

The airport is at Zhongyuan, 70km (44 miles) north of Lanzhou. CAAC (tel: (0931) 888 9666) runs an infrequent shuttle bus (30 Rmb) to and from its office at 520 Donggang Xilu. Unfortunately, there are no fixed times for the buses; they vary according to departing and arriving flights on any given day, so be sure to check with the office ahead of time.

Taxi drivers charge around 200 Rmb for the trip. As with most things in China, bargaining is in order. Beware of taxi drivers who mill around the CAAC office and offer to take you to the airport for significantly less. Travellers with early-morning flights may want to spend the night before at one of the airport hotels, such as the Lannzhou HNA Express Hotel (tel: (0931) 841 5926).

Shanghai

Shanghai is one of China's main transport hubs, connected to a number of foreign destinations and almost all domestic locations, and is one of only two cities in China to have two airports (Beijing being the other). Most domestic and some international flights use the old airport at Hongqiao (tel: (021) 81 8888, http://en.shairport.com/ hongqiaoair.html), about 15km (9 miles) west of the city centre. The international airport (tel: (021) 9608 1388, http://en.shairport.com/ pudongair.html) in Pudong is 70km (44 miles) east of downtown.

From Hongqiao Airport it can take from 30 minutes to an hour to the city. Most hotels have shuttle buses available. Otherwise, plenty of taxis are available right outside both terminals. Don't hire drivers who tout their services at the terminal entrances; their cars don't have meters, and they will try to charge you exorbitant rates. To get into the city, most drivers use the expressway that connects to the Ring Road. Expect to reimburse the driver for the toll.

From Pudong a taxi will take you approximately an hour (reckon on 130–160 Rmb) to the city, but the high-speed Maglev train can rocket you to Longyang Road underground station in Pudong in under eight minutes for 50 Rmb (single fare). There are eight airport bus lines. Airport Shuttle No. 1 connects Hongqiao and Pudong airports. The No. 2 metro line will eventually run east–west between Hongqiao and Pudong airports, and numerous stops in between, but it is yet to be completed.

If leaving on an international flight, you are expected to arrive at the airport two hours before takeoff.

Urumqi

The airport (tel: (0991) 3804224) is 17km (11 miles) north of the city. China Southern Airlines has its main office at 62 Youhao Nanlu, tel: (0991) 451 4668, and is open 7am–5pm daily. The airline has a number of booking offices around the city.

A taxi to the airport will cost around 30–40 Rmb, or you can take either the airport bus (20 Rmb) or bus No. 51 (5 Rmb).

Urumqi is connected via international flights to Almaty (Kazakhstan), Bishkek (Kyrgyzstan), Islamabad (Pakistan), Novosibirsk and Moscow (Russia), Tashkent (Uzbekistan) and Tehran (Iran). Foreign airlines in Urumqi include Siberian Airlines (tel: (0991)

The Karakoram Highway in Xinjiang.

2864327) and Kyrgyzstan Airlines (tel: (0991) 231 6333).

Xi'an

The airport is about 40km (25 miles) northwest of Xi'an at Xianyang. Most major hotels offer limousine or bus transfers, which have to be arranged ahead of time. China Southern Airlines runs a shuttle bus (6am–6pm) between the Melody Hotel (86 Xi Dajie), just to the west of the Bell Tower, and the airport, which is timed to its arriving and departing flights.

Otherwise, a taxi will cost around 120–130 Rmb to go into the city, but you may have to bargain hard as overcharging is common. The trip takes around 50 minutes.

Xi'an's airport connects it to most of the big cities in China, as well as to Nagoya and Hiroshima in Japan. In Xi'an, China Southern Airlines has a number of ticket offices dotted around the city. One of its main offices is located at the corner of Laodong Nanlu and Xiguan Zhengjie, 1km (0.6 mile) outside the west gate of the old city (tel: (029) 8870 2299). Other airlines flying to Xi'an daily include Air China, China Eastern Airlines, Hainan Airlines and Shanghai Airlines.

Overland routes

See also Central Asia Travel Tips, page 385, and Entering and leaving panels in each chapter.

Kazakhstan

There is a daily bus service and a twice-weekly train service between Urumqi and Almaty in Kazakstan (you will need to obtain a visa in advance).

Kyrgyzstan

Although it is, in theory, possible to take a bus from Kashgar to Bishkek

in Kyrgyzstan over the Torugart Pass, foreigners are not permitted to do so. You can travel as far as the border but must arrange private transport on the other side. You need to obtain a Kyrgyz visa in advance.

Pakistan

It is possible to travel the Karakoram Highway between Kashgar and Islamabad. Visas are required for entering Pakistan and cannot be obtained at the border for either Pakistan or China. Officially the border is open between April and October, though even those dates are weather-dependent. During this time there are daily buses, weather permitting, going from Kashgar to Tashkurgan (five hours), which is the last outpost in China where immigration and customs checks are performed. The bus stops here overnight before continuing over the Khunjerab Pass to Sost. In summer there are daily departures for the two-day, 500km (310-mile) trip. On both the Pakistani and Chinese sides of the border the roads may be blocked by landslides, and you may have to walk a fair distance, carrying your luggage. Accommodation en route is relatively modest, and closed completely out of season.

GETTING AROUND

By air

Flying within China is a quick and relatively cheap way of getting around the country. There are more than 175 airports in the country, and the number of regional airlines connecting these airports has grown dramatically over the last few years. Two of the larger domestic carriers, China Southern (CZ) and China

Border crossings

Western China shares international frontiers with Mongolia, Kazakhstan and Kyrgyzstan, as well as shorter international frontiers with Russia, Tajikistan, Afghanistan, Pakistan and India. At time of writing, international land crossings are only possible between Xinjiang and Kazakhstan, Kyrgyzstan and Pakistan. See individual Places chapters for information on entering and leaving China.

CHINA

CENTRAL ASIA

WESTERN ASIA

Eastern (MU), cover most destinations throughout the Shaanxi, Gansu and Xinjiang regions.

Xinjiang is China's largest province, and there are regular air links from its capital, Urumqi, to cities across China, including Beijing, Chengdu, Chongqing, Guangzhou, Hong Kong, Kunming, Lanzhou, Shanghai and Xi'an.

Xi'an, the capital of Shaanxi province and eastern terminus of the Silk Road, is a major Chinese city and is readily accessible by air from most provincial capitals as well as from Beijing, Chengdu, Guangzhou, Shanghai and Urumqi.

There are regular flights from Lanzhou and Dunhuang in Gansu province to destinations including Beijing, Guangzhou, Urumqi and Xi'an.

By train

China's rail network covers 121,000km (75,186 miles) and includes numerous destinations along the Silk Road. There is no first or second class on Chinese trains, but four categories or classes: *ruanwo* (soft-sleeper), *ruanzuo* (soft-seat), *yingwo* (hard-sleeper) and *yingzuo* (hard-seat). The soft-seat class is usually only available for short journeys. Long-distance trains normally only have soft-sleeper or hard-sleeper facilities. The soft-sleeper class has four-bed compartments with soft beds, and is recommended, particularly for long journeys. The hard-sleeper class has open, six-bed compartments. While you can reserve a place for the first three classes (you always buy a ticket with a place number), this is not always essential for the hard-seat category.

A train passes by the Tian Shan mountains in China.

Train travel along the Silk Road

One of the most romantic ways to travel over large distances is by train, for which the Silk Road is particularly well suited the further east you go. Almost half of the length of the Silk Road is within China, and it is an unforgettable train journey across the vast open expanses from Xi'an to Urumqi and Kashgar, via Lanzhou, Jiayuguan and Turpan. However, some of the ancient Silk Road sites are not along the modern railway. For Dunhuang the nearest station is Liuyuan, whilst the station for Turpan is actually Daheyan, about 30km (19 miles) away.

Reservations can be made at ticket offices in the town centre, through travel agencies or at your hotel. Be on time, as trains tend to be punctual.

As a rule of thumb, train services tend to operate less frequently but take less time than buses to reach their destination. The excellent website http:/trains.china.org.cn provides up-to-date train timetables and seat prices for all inter-city routes, and allows for booking tickets online.

By bus

Overland buses are the most important means of transportation in many parts of China where there is no railway line. All travel along the southern section of the Chinese Silk Road can conveniently be achieved using the regular bus services between the towns. Distances are not too great, and reasonably comfortable buses ply these routes. Buses are the cheapest means of transport, but are also correspondingly slower. There are regular breaks during journeys. Many overland buses have numbered seats, and it is advisable to book a ticket well in advance. Modern air conditioned buses are

usually available between the larger cities.

Kashgar (Kashi)

The long-distance bus station is on Tiannan Lu, just south of Renmin Lu. There are daily buses from Kashgar to Korla, Kuqa, Aksu, Hotan, Daheyan, Urumqi and Yengisar.

Lanzhou

The south bus station is on Langongping Lu, and from here there are several buses serving Linxia, but only three direct buses to Xiahe each day. The main long-distance bus station on Pingliang Lu serves Tianshui, Wuwei and Zhangye. The west bus station is at the western edge of town on Xijin Xilu, where buses depart regularly for the trip to Binglingsi.

Urumqi

Urumqi is the hub of bus travel throughout Xinjiang. The south bus station is some way south of the city and serves destinations including Hami, Hotan, Korla, Kashgar, Kuqa and Turpan. The north bus station on Heilongjiang Lu serves Yining and other points north and northwest.

Xi'an

There are three major bus stations scattered around the city. The most convenient, the long-distance bus station, is located opposite the main train station just off Jiefang Lu.

By taxi

Taxis are certainly the most comfortable form of transport, and drivers will agree a fixed rate for longer journeys and excursions, with prices usually starting at around 300–400 Rmb. Taxis are plentiful in all cities, and if you don't speak the language, it is a good idea to carry details of your destination written in Chinese.

Be wary of people offering taxis away from taxi ranks. Before setting off in a taxi, agree on a price for the journey, or ensure that the driver agrees to use the meter.

A – Z

A HANDY SUMMARY OF PRACTICAL INFORMATION

A

Accommodation

Choosing a hotel

China's large cities have numerous modern hotels, most of them at the high end of the market, including many of world-class calibre. Many belong to international hotel chains, and their management and staff have been trained abroad. The prices of these better hotels are in line with hotel prices in the West. Tour groups are usually accommodated in well-appointed tourist hotels. Except in the first-class hotels, take caution with laundry services, particularly with delicate clothes.

Booking rooms at hotels in the middle and lower price ranges can sometimes be difficult, particularly during Chinese New Year (a week or two in January or February) and during the May and October holiday periods, when hotels are often completely full.

Rates at all but the cheapest hotels are subject to 10–15 percent service surcharge. Rates for each price category are shown in the yellow boxes in the listings and are for a standard room.

Guesthouses

Some guesthouses or simple hotels refuse to take foreign guests, usually because of rules imposed by Chinese travel agencies or the local police, who often determine where foreigners may stay.

However, individual travellers may be able to find lodgings in guesthouses in smaller towns off the tourist track. They usually have rooms with two or more beds, or dormitories, shower and washing facilities, and are recommended for those on a budget.

Other accommodation

It is difficult for foreigners to find accommodation outside of hotels and guesthouses, although some universities and institutes have guesthouses where foreign visitors can find good, cheap lodging. YHA China is a member of the International Youth Hostels Federation, with online booking at www.hihostels.com.

If you are going on a long trip or hike in the countryside, especially in Tibet or in areas around the sacred mountains of China, you will probably come across various types of "long-distance travellers' lodgings". It is advisable to carry a sleeping bag.

In Beijing and some provinces, restrictions have been eased as to where foreigners can stay. Not all hotels are aware of the ruling, however, and may still shun foreigners. It is to be hoped that a more relaxed regime will eventually cover the whole of China, so that tourists are no longer restricted to the more expensive hotels and barred from countless budget options.

B

Budgeting for your trip

Travelling in China remains relatively cheap for foreign travellers as the Chinese government controls the renminbi exchange rate, ensuring it stays competitive for exports. In a country as vast as China prices still vary considerably, however, not only between city and countryside but also between provinces. For budget travellers, daily costs including accommodation and food (but excluding transport) range from US$25 to US$40 per day. Travellers wishing for a higher degree of comfort should allow US$40–75 per day. Travellers planning to stay in top-end accommodation should allow US$75–200, although, increasingly, the sky is the limit, especially in Xi'an, Lanzhou, Dunhuang and Urumqi.

Remember that if you are travelling with your own vehicle in China, you will require incur not only the fee but also the travel, food and accommodation expenses of your government-approved guide, significantly driving up your costs.

C

Climate

Chinese Central Asia, which includes not just Xinjiang, but also the neighbouring provinces of Gansu and Qinghai, as well as

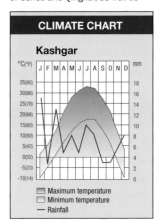

nearby Tibet and Inner Mongolia, is an area of climatic extremes, being very hot in summer and often well below zero, even at midday, in winter. **Shaanxi** is marginally warmer in winter, but more humid and uncomfortable in summer, when **Xinjiang** and **Gansu** can be very hot but with dry heat. Another climatic problem unique to the Northwest within China is dust. All of the Northwest, but Xinjiang in particular, can suffer from blinding, choking sandstorms, especially in spring and early summer. Rainfall is virtually non-existent for most of the year – but when the heavens do open, the downpour can be heavy.

Crime and security

There is still less crime in China than in many countries, but crime is an increasing problem. Take the same precautions applicable anywhere, on the street and with valuables in hotels and on public transport. Pickpockets and bag-slashers can be a problem, especially on crowded trains and buses, and in stations.

The **Public Security Bureau** (gongan ju) is the ever-present police force. They are usually friendly towards foreigners. With serious travel-related disputes – for example, with taxi drivers or hotels – they are usually able to resolve the problem.

Customs regulations

On arrival each traveller must complete a health declaration form. Tourists can freely import two bottles of wine or spirits (four bottles if you staying more than six months), 400 cigarettes and a reasonable amount of perfume, as well as foreign currency and valuables for personal use without restrictions. The import of weapons, ammunition, illicit narcotics and pornographic literature is prohibited. On departure, antiques such as porcelain, paintings, calligraphy, carvings and old books must be certified by an official antique shop, or they may be confiscated.

D

Disabled travellers

Only in recent years have the needs of disabled people received attention in China. Now, regulations regarding rooms and other facilities for the disabled will be met in the new hotels. In general, though, towns,

Electricity

The electricity supply is 220 volts, 50 cycles AC. Supplies in outlying areas can be erratic, but the larger towns and cities are usually well powered. There are a number of different plugs used in China, but generally you'll find either the three-pronged angled pins or the two-pronged flat pins in hotels. It's a good idea to carry a conversion plug with you, especially if you are travelling with a laptop computer or mobile phone.

institutions, public transport and sights offer little accessibility.

Travelling in a group for the disabled certainly reduces these problems considerably. The China National Tourist Offices and CITS have information about special trips for the disabled.

E

Eating out

What to eat

Eating along China's Silk Road is surprisingly varied and good. Most visitors would agree that the choice and quality of cuisines available between Xi'an and Kashgar are markedly superior to those available elsewhere in Central Asia, and travellers heading westwards along the Silk Road will have to wait at least until Iran, and probably until Turkey, to find a comparably sophisticated choice of cuisine.

In large part this is, of course, due to Chinese culinary influence dating back at least two millennia. In the two decades since China began its gradual but inexorable opening to a free-market economy, even relatively remote areas like Gansu and Xinjiang have become more prosperous than ever before, and restaurants serving all China's great schools of cuisine – but most especially Sichuan – are to be found in every major city and oasis town between Xi'an and Kashgar. Even night stops for truckers in transit points like Anxi and Hami spell out regional specialities in neon lights, encouraging drivers to patronise this Northeastern diner or that Cantonese dim sum establishment.

Nor is Chinese culinary influence limited exclusively to Chinese cuisine. Most visitors to Xinjiang would agree that Uighur food is superior to any other indigenous Central Asian tradition. From the delicious flat breads and rich, locally grown fruits,

to the unusually succulent lamb and noodle stews, Xinjiang leaves the various "Stans" standing.

Other cuisines available along the Eastern Silk Road include Tibetan fare, mainly along the Gansu–Qinghai frontier, and Mongolian – the latter not terribly sophisticated, but quite acceptable in an Urumqi hotpot restaurant (especially in winter), if less so at an isolated Mongol yurt erected somewhere in the endless Gobi steppe. The latter is no place for vegetarians!

Uighur and Hui cuisine

The Northwest differs from other regions of China in that pork – though still popular among Han Chinese and widely available in Han Chinese restaurants – is not the staple it has become elsewhere in China. Gansu province, with its substantial Hui Muslim population, tends to favour beef as an alternative to pork, and Xinjiang is definitely mutton country.

Uighur food features the usual Central Asian specialities, combined with some South Asian elements derived from the region's Mughal past and current Pakistani influence. The difference from the various countries of former Soviet Central Asia is that Uighur food seems to be fresher, better-quality, better-cooked, spicier and more varied.

The staples of Uighur cuisine are **mutton** (or beef, or chicken) **kebabs**, served with delicious *naan* breads baked in a tandoori oven and sprinkled with fennel, poppy seeds, sesame, garlic or onion. They vary in size, shape and flavour from oasis to oasis, but are uniformly delicious and make excellent long-distance snacks, especially when eaten with local grapes, melon or other luscious fruits with which Xinjiang abounds in season.

Also enduringly popular are **pilaf**, known locally as *polo*, *chuchura* (**dumplings**) and *samsa* (**samosas** stuffed with minced meat and vegetables). Uighurs are great noodle cooks (and eaters), specialising in "hand-pulled" *laghman* **noodles** (*lamian* in Chinese) served with a rich stew of mutton, peppers, tomatoes, aubergines, garlic and spring onions. Noodles fried with meat and vegetables are called *suoman*. The vegetarian variant is called *suoman gush siz* – nutritious and delicious.

Uighurs sometimes end their meals with locally made **ice cream**, sweetened sticky rice desserts or fresh or dried fruits – it's even possible to dry strips of Hami melon in the hot, arid summer months.

Hui (Chinese-speaking) Muslim cuisine is much closer to Han Chinese than to Uighur, but is always halal, never using pork or other forbidden foodstuffs. As Han Chinese can eat in Hui Muslim restaurants (but it is much less usual for Hui Muslims to eat in Han restaurants), Hui restaurateurs have traditionally dominated much of the culinary scene in Xi'an, Gansu and Xinjiang, as well as being enduringly popular further afield in Beijing, Shanghai and other great cities of eastern China.

Where to eat

Chinese meals are generally better shared between several people who can dip into a variety of dishes placed in the centre of the table. Most better-quality hotels have a variety of restaurants that offer good food at reasonable prices. Chinese snack foods such as noodles, dumplings and dim sum are readily available at stalls in night markets or near bus and train stations. Chinese (including Hui Muslims) generally eat using chopsticks.

The main oases in Xinjiang, notably Turpan, Korla, Kashgar and Khotan, all have good speciality Uighur restaurants. Similarly, better hotels in Xinjiang often have a Muslim restaurant offering halal food to Muslim guests, as well as a Chinese restaurant and a restaurant serving international dishes. Finding Uighur food at the plethora of street stalls in and around bus and train stations and in local bazaars is simplicity itself, as these stalls are found just about everywhere. Uighurs don't usually eat with chopsticks, but may employ fork, knife, spoon and of course fingers – though only of the right hand, which is reserved for communal eating, while the left hand is considered "impure" and used for ablutions.

Drinks

Bottled **water** is available everywhere at reasonable prices. Most hotel rooms (as well as railway sleepers) provide thermos flasks filled with hot water and a small selection of bags of black and green **tea**. Chinese also drink lots of **hot water**, which is surprisingly refreshing and good at quenching thirst. Chinese **beer**, in dozens of different brands, is available everywhere – even in the most Muslim of towns like Linxi and Khotan; cheap, plentiful and low in alcohol content, it makes an excellent accompaniment to both Chinese and Uighur food. Better yet, especially around Dunhuang and Turpan, are the excellent **wines** made from locally grown but nationally celebrated grapes. One of the best brands is Loulan, named for the ancient lost city at the heart of the Lop Desert. Sorghum,

barley and millet are widely grown throughout the Northwest, and from these, as well as from rice, a surprisingly large choice of Chinese **spirits** are on offer – try, for example, the 55 percent wheat and sorghum spirit called maotai jiu. Imported spirits, wines and beers are increasingly available across the Northwest. Drinking alcohol – even in front of Muslims, far from all of whom are teetotallers – is acceptable behaviour. Being drunk or rowdy in public is not.

Embassies and consulates

Beijing

Australian Embassy
21 Dongzhimenwai Dajie Sanlitun, tel: (010) 5140 4111, www.china.embassy.gov.au
British Embassy
11 Guanghua Lu, Jianguomenwai, tel: (010) 5192 4000, www.ukinchina.fco.gov.uk/en
Canadian Embassy
19 Dongzhimenwai Dajie, Chaoyang District, tel: (010) 5139 4000, www.beijing.gc.ca
Irish Embassy
3 Ritan Donglu, tel: (010) 8531 6200, www.embassyofireland.cn
New Zealand Embassy
Sanlitun East 3rd Street, tel: (010) 8532 7000, www.nzembassy.com/china
US Embassy
55 An Jia Lou Lu, tel: (010) 8531 3000, http://beijing.usembassy-china.org.cn

Shanghai

Australian Embassy
22/F, CITIC Square, 1168 Nanjing Road (W), tel: (021) 2215 5200, www.shanghai.china.embassy.gov.au
British Embassy
Shanghai Centre, Suite 301, 1376 Nanjing Rd (W), tel: (021) 3279 2000.
Canadian Embassy
ECO City Building, 8th floor, 1788 Nanjing Xi Lu, tel: (021) 3279 2800, www.shanghai.gc.ca
New Zealand Consulate
2801-2802A & 2806B-2810, Corporate Avenue 5, 150 Hu Bin Road, tel: (021) 5407 5858, www.nzembassy.com/China
US Embassy
1038 West Nanjing Road, Westgate Mall 8th Floor,, tel: (021) 6433 6880, www.shanghai.usembassy-china.org.cn

Hong Kong

Australian Embassy
23/F, Harbour Centre, 25 Harbour Road, Wan Chai, tel: (0852) 2827 8881, www.hongkong.china.embassy.gov.au

British Embassy
1 Supreme Court Road, Admiralty, tel: (0852) 2901 3000.
Canadian Embassy
8th floor, Berkshire House, 25 Westlands Road, Quarry Bay, tel: (0852) 3719 4700, www.hongkong.gc.ca
US Embassy
26 Garden Road, Central, tel: (0852) 2523 9011, http://hongkong.usconsulate.gov

Emergencies

If you have a mobile phone with roving capacity, you may be able to SOS. Check with your service provider. If you have an accident, emergency services are called by dialling **110** for police, **119** for fire services, or **999** for the ambulance service (**120** if you are in Beijing or Shanghai) .

Etiquette

The dominant **Han** culture is very self-confident. Chinese can be polite as individuals, but sometimes seem collectively impolite to visiting Westerners. Concepts of maintaining face and level tempers are highly valued. Belching, shouting loudly into mobile phones, smoking and spitting are all openly frowned upon by the Chinese authorities, who are doing their best to reform such "outdated, antisocial" behaviour.

F

Festivals

Holidays such as National Day and International Labour Day are fixed on the modern calendar, but most traditional festivals and events are determined by the lunar calendar, which means the date varies slightly from year to year. Each region has its own special days and events.

Muslim festivals

The main festivals specific to Xinjiang and other predominantly Muslim areas along the Silk Road are Eid al-Fitr (Turkish: Bayram, the "Festival of the Breaking the Fast"), held at the end of the Muslim fasting month of Ramadan; and Eid al-Adha (Turkish: Kurban, the "Festival of the Sacrifice"), held to mark the culmination of the Hajj pilgrimage to Mecca. Since the Muslim calendar, like the traditional Chinese, is lunar, these festivals fall on different dates each year. It's worth noting that the fasting month of Ramadan – which is observed by many Muslims in

China – is easier on the non-Muslim visitor than it would be, for example, in Iran or Saudi Arabia, as Han Chinese restaurants, at least, remain open everywhere.

Buddhist festivals

Labrang Monastery, at Xiahe in Gansu, is the most important Tibetan monastery in China outside the Tibetan Autonomous Region. Between approximately 14–17 January and 26 June–15 July (according to the lunar calendar), major festivals are held here each year involving merit-making, sutra-chanting and devil-dancing. The most important festival of all, known as Monlan or "Great Prayer", falls sometime in February or March, with pilgrims dressed in their finest clothes visiting from all over the Tibetan-speaking world.

The most important festival time is the Lunar New Year, or Spring Festival, which usually falls in late January or early February. Public buildings are festooned with coloured lights, people from all over China travel to reunite with family and friends, debts are settled and food is consumed. In recent years, a more relaxed atmosphere has brought the revival of old Spring Festival traditions, such as giving *hongbao* – small, red envelopes containing money – to children and young adults. Temple fairs feature martial arts demonstrations, stand-up comedy and home-made toys.

On the 12th day of the third lunar month, at the beginning of April, the Chinese honour their deceased ancestors by observing Qingming, sometimes referred to as the "grave-sweeping" day. It is much less impressive nowadays, as people are cremated instead of buried. Qingming is a time for remembering ancestors, but also for revelling in a warm spring day.

The Mid-Autumn Festival usually takes place around mid-September. Shops do great business in "moon cakes" – pastries filled with gooey sesame paste, red-bean and walnut filling. *Tang yuan*, glutinous rice-flour balls with sweet fillings in sugar syrup, and *yue bing*, a cake baked specifically for this occasion, are also eaten. In the tradition of poets, this is the time to drink a bit of wine and toast the moon.

G

Gay and lesbian travellers

In the past two decades gay people of both sexes have increasingly asserted their presence and rights, especially in such big and go-ahead cities as Shanghai, Beijing and Guangzhou. In western Xinjiang, where Central Asian Islamic mores are more apparent, homosexuality may be more readily accepted than in years gone by, but is still not flaunted.

H

Health and medical care

A yellow fever vaccination certificate is required if coming from an infected area less than six days prior to entering China. Vaccinations for hepatitis A and B, diphtheria, tetanus, typhoid and polio should be up to date.

The most frequently reported health problem in China is diarrhoea. The best prevention is to ensure maximum hygiene while travelling, especially in restaurants and road-side snack bars. Never eat raw, uncooked or partially cooked food, including salads, other than in the top hotels. Animal or human excrement is still frequently used as fertiliser, so bacteria on uncooked vegetables can easily be ingested. It is also suggested if travelling outside a tour group, to acquire chopsticks and a tin bowl with lid for train journeys and meals in small road-side restaurants. Drink only boiled or bottled water, even though the tap water is drinkable in some places, and reduce exposure to insects as far as possible.

There is a big difference in China between urban and rural medical services. If travelling in the countryside, there may be no appropriate medical services beyond primary health care, which is good in China. Some hospitals in cities have special sections for foreigners where English is spoken. Many of the large hotels have their own doctors. Payment must be made on the spot for treatment, medicine and transport.

National holidays

1 January New Year's Day
January/February Chinese New Year (lunar)
8 March International Women's Day
1 May Youth Day (4th May Movement)
1 June Children's Day
1 July Founding of the Chinese Communist Party
1 August Founding of the People's Liberation Army
1 October National Day

I

Insurance

Travel and medical insurance is essential, including evacuation cover. Bring copies of documentation and all necessary phone numbers with you.

Internet

Internet cafés are to be found just about everywhere. Even the smallest towns on the Silk Road have their own cafés, usually close to the centre, and rates are very reasonable. One word of warning: they can be smoky and noisy, and often unpleasant to sit in for too long. Most four- and five-star hotels have their own business centres with internet access, but rates can be considerably higher than the ordinary cafés.

M

Maps

A significant number of English-language maps have been produced for China in recent years, which is a real boon for tourists. City maps, provincial maps and regularly updated road maps are all readily available abroad, and can also be purchased from English-language bookshops and tourist centres in major Chinese cities.

Media

An English-language newspaper, the *China Daily*, is published every day except Sunday. It is often obtainable from the big hotels for free. Same-day editions are available only in large cities; elsewhere, it'll probably be several days late. International newspapers and magazines can usually be found in the larger hotels.

Money

The Chinese currency is called the renminbi or "people's currency", usually abbreviated to Rmb. The basic unit is the yuan (colloquially, kuai). Ten jiao (colloquially, mao) make one yuan; ten fen make one jiao. Thus, 100 fen make one yuan. Notes are currently issued for 1, 2, 5, 10, 20, 50 and 100 yuan. Coins come in 1 yuan, 5 jiao, 1 jiao and 5 fen.

Major currencies are accepted in banks and hotels. Global network-connected ATMs (Cirrus, Plus) can be found in major cities – try branches of the Bank of China.

John's Information Café

In 1988 John Hu set up the first café and travel service for Western tourists in Kashgar. Today there are several branches of **John's Information Café** (www.johncafe. net) conveniently spread along the Chinese section of the Silk Road. They are excellent places to pick up the latest information on all forms of transportation, organise a bewildering number of treks and tours, especially out of Kashgar. Onward travel arrangements can also be arranged.

Dunhuang
22 Mingshan Lu (next to the Feitian Hotel)
Tel: (0937) 882 7000
Turpan
2 Qingnian Lu (next to the Turpan Hotel)
Tel: (0995) 852 4237
Kashgar
337 Seman Lu (next to the Seman Hotel)
Tel: (0998) 258 1186

Don't expect to use credit cards much outside of Xi'an, except in the very top hotels. Also, most transport costs (e.g. domestic air and train tickets) are paid in cash. Cash advances may be obtained from major branches of the Bank of China in Xi'an, Lanzhou, Kashgar and Urumqi.

O

Opening hours

Shops are open every day, including public holidays. Opening hours are usually 8.30am or 9am to 8pm. Government offices and banks are usually open Mon–Fri, 8.30am to 5.30pm, with a lunch break from noon to 1.30pm. Note that these times can vary slightly from place to place. In Xinjiang and parts of Gansu, for example, offices often open later as they are on Beijing time, rather than the local, unofficial time.

P

Photography

Taking photographs or videos of bridges, government buildings, military installations and railway stations is strictly prohibited. As in other countries many museums, palaces or temples will not allow photographs to be taken, or will charge a fee. At other times, photography is allowed, but without using either a flash or a tripod. A good example of this is the Terracotta Warriors in Xi'an: photography was banned completely until a recent easing of restrictions. No special permit is necessary for a video or movie camera, as long as it is clearly not for professional use.

Photographic film, memory cards and batteries are widely available.

Postal services

Express mail (EMS) is available to the majority of international destinations, as are private international courier services. Note that large parcels must be packed and sealed at the post office.

For general delivery and poste restante services you should visit the central post office.

Public holidays

In addition to China's national holidays, 1–7 May and 1–7 October are week-long public holidays for the majority of Chinese. It is not advisable to plan a trip during these times. Most shops are open during holidays. School holidays in China are between 1 August and 30 September. This also applies to universities.

Don't plan on travel or border crossings during holidays unless reservations have been made and confirmed a long time in advance. It is especially wise not to make any travel plans during the Spring Festival, which is three days long and is the period when everyone is travelling to their hometown.

R

Religion

The various Muslim peoples of the Northwest are – with the exception of a handful (41,000) of isolated Shia Ismaili Tajiks in the high Pamirs – uniformly Sunni Muslims of the moderate Hanafi school, much given to trade and commerce and little interested in fundamentalism. Visitors are welcome to enter mosques and religious schools, but should dress modestly and remember to remove their shoes.

Officially, the People's Republic encourages atheism. However, there are Buddhist and Daoist temples and places of worship throughout the country, as well as mosques in the Muslim areas and in all large cities, which have regular prayers at the prescribed times. Catholic and Protestant churches can also be found in most big cities.

S

Shopping

Many of the larger towns will provide ample opportunity for shopping. Xi'an in particular is full of antique, handicraft and souvenir shops. It is worth looking for local products in the smaller towns or in places where ethnic minorities live, as these will be difficult to find anywhere else.

Antiques that date from before 1795 may not be legally exported. Those that can be taken out of China must carry a small red seal or have one affixed by the Cultural Relics Bureau. All other antiques are the property of the People's Republic of China and, without the seal, will be confiscated without compensation. Do not buy "antiques" that the vendor claims are over 100 years old, as they are probably fake.

T

Telecommunications

Domestic long-distance calls are cheap; international calls are relatively expensive. Local calls in China from hotels are usually free of charge, but international calls made from hotels typically have high surcharges added to China's already high IDD rates. IP (Internal Phone) cards are the cheapest way to phone abroad; these can be purchased at news-stands and hotels in the larger cities. The international dialling code for China is +86.

Domestic area codes

Add 0 to the codes below if dialling from within China:
Beijing 10
Dunhuang 937
Hotan 903
Kashgar 998
Kuqa 997
Lanzhou 931
Tianshui 938
Turpan 995
Urumqi 991
Xi'an 29
Zhangye 936

Tipping

Tipping is still not common in the majority of restaurants and hotels,

Time zones

The whole of China officially runs on Beijing time (GMT + 8 hours), although Xinjiang time is unofficially GMT + 6 hours.

although it is accepted in the top-class ones. Note that as part of the ritual any gift or tip will, at first, be firmly rejected.

Toilets

Public toilets in China are usually best avoided. Squat toilets are the norm, privacy cannot always be counted on, toilet paper is rarely provided and standards of sanitation are generally low. Some international fast-food chains provide Western-style facilities, but by far the best option is to head for a good hotel.

Tourist information

The **China National Tourist Office** (www.cnto.org.uk) is a useful source of information on travelling in China and has 19 offices in several countries across the world.
Some of these include:
Australia
11th Floor, 234 George Street, Sydney, New South Wales, 2000.
Tel: +61 (2) 9252 9838.
Canada
480 University Avenue, Suite 806, Toronto, Ontario, 91203.
Tel: +1 (416) 599 6636.
United Kingdom
71 Warwick Road, London, SW5 9HB.
Tel: +44 (20) 7373 0888.
United States
370 Lexington Avenue #912, New York, NY 10017.
Tel: +1 (212) 760 8218.
France
15 Rue De Berri, 75008, Paris.
Tel: +33 (1) 5659 1010.

V

Visas

All foreigners must acquire an entry visa before arrival in China. If you are part of a group, the tour operator will often obtain this. Individual travellers can apply at any Chinese embassy or consulate. The process is straightforward, taking about five days depending on current regulations and on your own country's regulations for issuing visas to Chinese nationals. A 30-day single-entry visa is usually issued. Your passport must be valid for

six months after the expiry date of the entry visa.

It is possible for residents of 45 countries, including the UK, USA, Australia, New Zealand and Canada, to obtain a free 72-hour visa to visit China while in transit to other destinations. This only applies for entry to specific ports and for visits of 3 days or less. See http://www.cnto.org/plan/go/visa-info/#72hour for more information.

If your visa expires while you are in China, it can be extended once (or sometimes twice) by the local Public Security Bureau (gongan ju). It is essential to apply for an extension before your current visa expires, or you risk paying a substantial fine.

Public Security Bureaux
Beijing
2 Dongdajie, Qianmen.
Tel: (010) 8402 0101.
http://www.bjgaj.gov.cn/web/
Kashgar (Kashi)
111 Youmulakexia Lu.
Tel: (0998) 282 2048.
Lanzhou
482 Wudu Lu.
Tel: (0931) 871 8114.
Shanghai
1500 Minsheng Lu.
Tel: (021). 2895 1900.
Urumqi
Jiefang Beilu.
Tel: (0991) 282 4629.
Xi'an
136 Xi Dajie.
Tel: (029) 8675 1111.

W

Weights and measures

China uses the metric system.

What to bring and wear

Nowadays it's increasingly easy to buy just about anything you require in China, and not only in great cities like Beijing, Shanghai and Xi'an, but also in lesser provincial centres like Lanzhou, Urumqi and Kashgar. That said, it's a good idea to bring your own medication (the Chinese traditional pharmacopoeia is extensive but very different), tampons etc. Travellers might also consider bringing a small torch and a multiple adaptor for three-pin sockets.

In the summer months, take light cotton clothes that are easily washed and not too delicate. For winter in the Northwest, take some really warm clothes – insulated thermal underwear and warm socks are a good idea – as well as gloves and a hat,

though the latter are readily available at reasonable prices locally. Much of the Eastern Silk Road runs through arid country where rain rarely falls, but an umbrella (together with a hat) will shield you from the very powerful sunlight. Good walking shoes are essential for visiting ancient cities and Buddhist cave temples.

When to go

Given the climatic constraints of Chinese Central Asia, the best times to visit the Chinese sections of the Silk Road are late spring and early summer (approximately April–June), as well as late summer and early autumn (approximately September–November). In midwinter passes are often snowed-in or iced-up, travel is difficult and many restaurants and hotels close for the duration of the cold season.

Women travellers

Women travellers are, generally speaking, remarkably safe travelling in China. The usual precautions have to be taken, especially in remote areas or rough districts of large cities, but no more so – indeed rather less so – than in many Western countries. Xinjiang, especially among the Uighur and other Muslim minorities, is a little different. Here excessive displays of female independence, revealing clothing and sexually explicit talk can lead to trouble, though to a far lesser extent than in neighbouring India or Pakistan. In all instances, it's better to dress discreetly, especially when visiting temples or mosques, and to avoid noisy behaviour and public tipsiness.

Websites

The following websites are a useful source of information on China and the Silk Road.
http://blogs.wsj.com/chinarealtime/ Daily commentary about China, written by correspondents at Dow Jones and Wall Street Journal magazine.
http://idp.bl.uk/idp.a4d The International Dunhuang Project run by the British Library.
http://depts.washington.edu/silkroad Silk Road Seattle Project, sponsored by the University of Washington.
http://www.orgs.muohio.edu/silkroad/ The Miami University Silk Road Project.
www.wildcamels.com The Wild Camel Protection Fund.

LANGUAGE

UNDERSTANDING THE LANGUAGE

MANDARIN CHINESE

Mandarin is a collection of dialects spoken across north and southwestern China. With more than 1.3 billion speakers, it has more native speakers than any other language in the world.

Mandarin relies on word order and participles to provide information such as person, number, tense and case. The basic word order of subject-verb-object is generally used but there are regional variations, in particular preceding the direct object with the indirect object. Post-verbal participles denote the aspect of the action, but again there is variation in their usage.

The vocabulary of Mandarin is vast and it includes loan words from other languages with which Mandarin has interacted, notably Mongolian and Manchurian. New words are commonly formed with the addition of prefixes and suffixes or by compounding two words with similar meaning.

Pronunciation of Mandarin tends to terrify non-native speakers. Syllables are comprised of an initial consonant, followed by a glide, a vowel, a final and a tone, and there are several hundred syllables in regular usage. Tones vary between regions but regardless of the area in which they are spoken, they tend to fall into four tonal categories: the level tone, rising tone, falling tone, and a final stop.

Key phrases

Hello. 你好。 *Nǐ hǎo.*
How are you? 你好吗？ *Nǐ hǎo ma?*
Fine, thank you. 很好, 谢谢。 *Hěn hǎo, xièxie.*

Please. 请。 *Qǐng.*
Thank you. 谢谢。 *Xièxiè.*
Excuse me. 请问 *Qǐng wèn.*
I'm sorry. 对不起。 *Duìbùqǐ.*
I can't speak Chinese. 我不会说中文。 *Wǒ bú huì shuō zhōngwén.*
Is there someone here who speaks English? 这里有人会说英语吗？ *Zhèlǐ yǒu rén huì shuō yīngyǔ ma?*
Help! 救命！ *Jiùmìng!*
I'm lost. 我迷路了。 *wǒ mílù le.*
Goodbye 拜拜。 *Bai-bai.*

UIGHUR

Uighur is a Turkic language with an estimated 10 million speakers, who are split largely between Xinjiang and Kazakhstan. It was first written down in the 5th century and is usually written in Perso-Arabic script, though you will occasionally also see Uighur in Latin or Cyrillic script.

Uighur grammar has a number of interesting features. Whilst the word order is subject-object-verb as in many European languages, there is no difference in inflection for masculine and feminine nouns, and six different cases. Verbs are conjugated for both tense and mood.

Although the core Uighur vocabulary is Turkic, Uighur also features a number of loan words. Kazakh, Uzbek and Chagatai are dominant donors due to the geographical proximity of their speakers as well as their linguistic similarity, but words of Arabic, Persian and Tajik are also prominent due to the spread of their respective literatures (including religious texts) in areas where Uighur is spoken.

Key phrases

Hello. (Greeting) *Ässalamu aläykum*
Hello. (Response) *Wä'äläykum ässalam*
How are you? *Yakshimasiz?*
Fine, thank you. *Yakhshi.*
Thank you. *Rakhmat.*
You're welcome *Tuzut Qilmang!*
I'm lost! *Man ezip Qaldim.*
Can you help me? *Manga yardam Qlarsizmu?*

Example of Chinese script on black bamboo.

FURTHER READING

HISTORY

Foreign Devils on the Silk Road by Peter Hopkirk. Thoroughly readable account of Stein, Hedin and other explorers' search for the lost treasures of Central Asia.

Life along the Silk Road by Susan Whitfield. A fascinating and erudite collection of historical "short stories" based on characters – the merchant, the soldier, the courtesan etc. – chiefly based on first-hand information derived from the archives and murals of Dunhuang.

Silk Road: Monks, Warriors and Merchants on the Silk Road by Luce Boulnois. Lavish, well-illustrated and researched account of the Silk Road.

Southern Silk Road: In the Footsteps of Sir Aurel Stein and Sven Hedin by Christoph Baumer. Account of the exploration and identification of lost cities along the Southern Silk Road between Kashgar and Dunhuang.

The Silk Road: 2000 Years in the Heart of Asia by Frances Wood. The story of the Silk Road in its broadest possible scope, with illustrations taken largely from the collections of the British Museum and British Library.

The Travels of Marco Polo translated by Ronald Latham. Tried and tested English translation of Polo's Il Milione, including travels in Xinjiang and along the Eastern Silk Road.

TRAVEL WRITING

Danziger's Travels: Beyond Forbidden Frontiers by Nick Danziger. An overland journey via Turkey,Iran and Afghanistan to Xinjiang, Gansu and Tibet.

From Heaven Lake: Travels through Sinkiang and Tibet by Vikram Seth. In this well-written travelogue Seth describes his unusual journey through remote areas of China, Tibet and Nepal.

In Xanadu: A Quest by William Dalrymple. An overland journey approximately following the tracks of Marco Polo from the Middle East, through Xinjiang, to Mongolia.

News from Tartary by Peter Fleming. Travels in the 1930s across Northwest China and Xinjiang.

Shadow of the Silk Road by Colin Thubron. Sublime account of a journey from Xi'an in China to Antakya in Turkey, with plenty of detail on Gansu and Xinjiang.

The Road to Miran: Travels in the Forbidden Zone of Xinjiang by Christa Paula. Intrepid and ultimately successful attempt by an art historian to reach the (then) forbidden city of Miran near Charklik.

OTHER INSIGHT GUIDES

Other **Insight Guides and Insight City Guides** that highlight destinations in China include: *Beijing, China, Hong Kong* and *Shanghai*. Insight's **Explore** series includes titles on *Beijing, Shanghai* and *Hong Kong*. These books pack information into an easily portable and convenient format, with a series of itineraries that reveal the best of the destinations. Insight **FlexiMaps** are designed to complement our guidebooks. They provide full mapping of major destinations, and their easy-to-fold, laminated finish gives them ease of use and durability. The range of titles features the following destinations: *Beijing, Guangzhou, Hong Kong* and *Shanghai*.

TRANSPORT

GETTING THERE AND GETTING AROUND

GETTING THERE

By air

Central Asia's main hubs are Almaty (Kazakhstan), Tashkent (Uzbekistan), Bishkek (Kyrgyzstan) and Karachi (Pakistan). Although there are some direct flights from Western Europe, many stop over at Moscow, Istanbul or Dubai en route. There are few direct transatlantic flights to the region, so a transfer is necessary in London, Istanbul, Moscow or Dubai. It is possible to reach Central Asia from the US West Coast by flying west via Tokyo or Seoul. The best approach for travellers from Australasia is via Bangkok.

Kyrgyzstan

Bishkek is close enough to Almaty, in Kazakhstan, to use it as a gateway, but the Kyrgyz capital has direct flights to Moscow with Aeroflot and to Istanbul with Turkish Airlines. KLM provides a free transport service to Bishkek for its Almaty-bound flights. The national carrier, Air Kyrgyzstan, flies to ten destinations, which include Urumqi, Moscow, and Tashkent. China Southern Airlines flies to Urumqi, which is useful if you are connecting to other destinations in China.

Tajikistan

Dushanbe has few connections outside Central Asia other than regular flights to Moscow. Tajik Air and private Somon Air airlines fly to Dushanbe from St Petersburg, and these sometimes connect with London flights. It may be more convenient to take a regional flight from Bishkek or Tashkent. The national carrier, Tajik Air, currently flies to 14 destinations, including Urumqi,

Delhi and Tehran, but its poor safety record prevents it flying to Europe.

Uzbekistan

Tashkent is reasonably well connected. Uzbekistan Airways has flights to European destinations that include London, Rome, Frankfurt and Istanbul, as well as various Asian destinations.

Kazakhstan

Almaty has regular flights to Istanbul, Frankfurt and Amsterdam with Lufthansa, KLM and Turkish Airlines. The Kazakhstan national carrier Air Astana also flies direct from Astana to Paris and from Almaty to Asian destinations including Beijing, Delhi, Bangkok, Kuala Lumpur and Seoul. Air Arabia links Almaty with Sharjah (UAE) twice a week and China Southern flies to and from Urumqi, in Xinjiang, most days of the week.

Pakistan

Most flights arrive at Karachi. There are also direct flights from London to Lahore. Emirates, Gulf Air and Etihad Airways fly from London to a variety of destinations in Pakistan via Dubai, Bahrain, Doha and Abu Dhabi.

Afghanistan

The refurbished Kabul International Airport is the main way of getting in

Departure taxes

With the exception of Afghanistan, departure taxes are included in the price of the air ticket. Passengers flying from Kabul airport will be charged a departure tax of AFN10 for domestic flights and AFN20 for international flights.

and out of Afghanistan, and there are a surprising number of flights each day, including to neighbouring capitals. Ariana, the national carrier, flies to Moscow, Istanbul, Ankara and Dubai, but for most international connections you need to fly via Dubai, from where there are several flights a day to Kabul.

Turkmenistan

The brand new 'Oguz Khan' terminal at Ashgabat airport is shaped like a giant winged bird and is the largest in Central Asia. Turkmenistan Airlines has flights to Paris, Frankfurt, London, Birmingham and other Central Asian capitals. You can travel to and from Europe/USA via Baku with Lufthansa/ United, and Turkish Airlines connect most places through Istanbul. Belavia connects with Minsk, S7 with Moscow daily and FlyDubai to Dubai.

By bus

International bus routes connect **Kazakhstan** with Xinjiang province in China. A daily morning bus service runs in both directions between Yining (Ili), in China, and Almaty, in Kazakhstan, crossing at Khorgos. This takes 10–12 hours, including a minimum of two hours at the border where luggage has to be unloaded and X-rayed. It is also possible to take an overnight sleeper bus to the Khorgos border from Urumqi, cross on foot and then pick up Almaty-bound transport on the other side.

To reach **Kyrgyzstan** from China by bus there is just one option, via the Irkeshtam Pass. This route is fairly straightforward, as there is an overnight bus service between Kashgar in Xinjiang and Osh in southern Kyrgyzstan. However, timetables are sporadic, and the bus runs infrequently during the winter months. The journey takes around 18 hours as long as there are no breakdowns or delays at the border. To cross the 3,752-metre (12,381-ft) Torugart Pass further north requires the hire of private transport, as foreigners are not allowed to use the public bus that runs between Kashgar and Naryn. Tour agencies in Kashgar can arrange Chinese transport as far as the pass and for a Kyrgyz vehicle to be waiting on the other side for onward travel to Naryn.

There is a through service between Kashgar in China and Gilgit in **Pakistan** along the Karakoram Highway, via the Khunjerab Pass. This is open from 1 May to 31 October for groups and up to 15 November for individual tourists. It takes about five hours to travel from Tashkurgan (the last town in China) to Sost (the first village in Pakistan) – not including the time taken for the formalities at the border. Bus, van and jeep services from Tashkurgan to Sost are run by the PTDC (Pakistan Tourism Development Corporation) and NATCO (Northern Areas Transport Corporation).

There is a direct daily bus service between Mashhad in Iran and Herat in **Afghanistan**, which takes about seven hours. There are no cross-border bus services entering or leaving Turkmenistan.

By car

For the experienced and strong-stomached motorist, driving to Central Asia can be a rewarding challenge. There are four main overland routes to reach Central Asia. Crossing Russia, motorists require both a visa and a "Green Card", which is proof of motor insurance. This costs about $110 if purchased at the border but is cheaper bought in advance. An international driving permit and translations of your documents into Russian will speed up any encounters with traffic police or border officials. Driving from Moscow to the Kazakh border takes two days (more if you plan to enter Kazakhstan further east) and four border crossings are open: those at Uralsk, near Kostanai, at Petropavl and at Omsk.

Approaching from the southwest, a *carnet de passage* is required for both Turkey and Iran. The cost of the carnet is dependent on the value of your vehicle, and the fee is non-refundable. UK nationals should request a carnet from the RAC (www.rac.co.uk), and other nationalities can get one from the equivalent motoring club in their country of residence. The Iranian border with Turkmenistan is open between Mashhad and Ashgabat, and, for those unable or unwilling to pass through Iran, an alternative route exists from eastern Turkey through the Caucasus and by boat across the Caspian Sea, entering either into Turkmenbashi in Turkmenistan or Aktau in Kazakhstan. The ferry from Baku (Azerbaijan) to either destination is unscheduled, but departures take place approximately twice a week. It is not possible to make a reservation in advance as vehicles and passengers take lower priority than cargo. Sailings typically take 14–16 hours and cabins are allocated on a first-come-first-served basis.

Driving into Central Asia from China is challenging and expensive. Although a carnet is not necessary, you must apply for a foreign vehicle permit in addition to your visa. You will also require an official guide or escort for the duration of your trip, and must pay not only his salary but also his transport (if there is no space in your own vehicle) and accommodation. Allow at least $50 a day. If your visa application is accepted but your vehicle permit is declined, it is sometimes possible to arrange to ship your vehicle to the border as "goods in transit". This is, however, time-consuming and costly as you must travel separately from your vehicle. The main crossing from China into Kazakhstan is Khorgos near Almaty, and there are also open borders further north at Bakhty and Maikapshagai. The Irkeshtam and Torugart Passes both permit foreign tourists to enter Kyrgyzstan by private vehicle, though resolving red tape at the latter can take as much as eight hours. China's border crossing with Tajikistan, although a standard international crossing since 2014, is currently not open to foreigners .

Afghanistan

Motorists require a Ministry of Foreign Affairs vehicle import permit from an Afghan consulate ($100). An additional $100 may also be payable at the border for a Ministry of Finance vehicle permit. The quality of roads in Afghanistan is extremely poor, meaning that driving speeds rarely exceed 20km/h (12mph) away from highways. Motorists can enter Afghanistan from Tajikistan at Ishkashim, or from Uzbekistan at Termiz. The road into Iran via Herat is also open though less secure.

Pakistan

Motorists must have a valid carnet or pay import duty. The Khunjerab Pass into China is closed in winter but a relatively straightforward drive from April through October. It is not advisable to enter Afghanistan or Iran from Pakistan without a police escort.

Kyrgyzstan

No permit or import duty is payable. There is, theoretically, a three-month import period for foreign vehicles, after which you must get foreign plates, but in practice this is usually overlooked. The main border with Kazakhstan is at Kordai and it is also possible to enter past Taraz. Sary Tash serves as the main entry point when driving to Tajikistan and, when open, Dostlyk is the main border crossing with Uzbekistan.

Kazakhstan

No permit or import duty is payable. A Russian translation of vehicle documents is highly advisable. Expect a thorough vehicle check by customs. Allow at least four days to drive north to south across Kazakhstan. Failure to present all vehicle documents on request by the police may result in a fine.

Uzbekistan

No permit or import duty is required, but expect to pass through quarantine as well as customs and immigration. Until recently, the only border with Kazakhstan officially open to foreigners was Shymkent. This appears to have changed, with the lorry crossing at Ahay also open to foreign cars, but this may not be permanent. The land borders with Kazakhstan and Kyrgyzstan may be shut without warning. Fuel shortages are common. When leaving Uzbekistan, motorists must get an exit stamp costing $4.

Tajikistan

Motorists pay a temporary import fee on arrival. The exact cost seems to be dependent on the customs official in charge, but is approximately $50. You must keep this receipt or you will be charged again on departure. There is a $10 vehicle exit fee. Fuel shortages are common and it is almost impossible to get spare vehicle parts unless you are driving a Toyota. Road conditions are exceptionally poor, as is the standard of driving.

Turkmenistan

Importing anything into the country is not easy, especially cars. As well as all paperwork, permits and large import fees, you will need liability insurance, as the green international insurance card is not valid. There will also be a tax to be paid at the border for estimated fuel used inside the country to compensate for the subsidised fuel prices. Most rural roads are in a terrible condition. Dark coloured cars are frowned-upon, especially in the 'white city' of Ashgabat.

By train

Train is an interesting way to reach Central Asia for those happy to contemplate the Kazakh steppe for days on end. Coming from the west, Moscow is the main departure point, and Russian and Kazakhstan transit visas are necessary.

The most convenient train is probably the **Moscow–Almaty** service (train number 8, Kazakhstan), which leaves Moscow every other day and takes approximately 77 hours to reach the Kazakh capital. This route comes via Orenburg in Russia, and Aralsk and Kyzylorda in Kazakhstan. A longer route runs down to Almaty from the Trans-Siberian route to the north at Novosibirsk.

The twice-weekly **Moscow–Bishkek** direct service (train number 18, Kirgizia) follows the same route through Kazakhstan and takes around 74 hours.

Tashkent is best reached on the thrice-weekly train number 6 (Uzbekistan), which takes a branch line south of the main Moscow–Almaty route just west of Shymkent. The overall journey time is 69 hours.

Train classes are based on the Russian system in which *spalny vagon* is a sleeping compartment with two beds, *kupe* is a four-berth sleeping carriage and *platskartny* an open-plan carriage with dormitory-style bunks. Kupe is adequate in most circumstances. Precise train times and days of running can be found at www.russiantrains.com.

Coming from China, a twice-weekly "Zhibek Zholy" (Silk Road) service runs between Urumqi and **Almaty**, which takes around 36 hours, including a lengthy bogie-changing procedure at the Kazakh frontier in which the carriages are winched above the tracks. A daily train service links Urumqi with Beijing. There is a monthly express train from Zahidan in Iran to **Quetta** (via Taftan) in

Pakistan, which takes 30 hours or more. Passenger train services from Moscow to Tashkent weave across the Turkmenistan border but are essentially 'sealed units' as nobody is allowed on or off.

GETTING AROUND

By air

Given the often poor road conditions, air travel in the region is a viable option, especially for long distances.

Kyrgyzstan has connections that link the capital with a handful of towns with Air Kyrgyzstan (www.air.kg) and Air Bishkek. Most useful is the regular service between Bishkek and Osh, which reduces a 14-hour road journey to less than an hour and costs little more than a place in a shared taxi. Somon Air (www.somonair.com) has a service betwwen Dushanbe and Khojand in the north of the country. See more ar http://caravanistan.com/transport/flights/khorog-dushanbe.

Uzbekistan has a fairly efficient national network with Uzbekistan Airways (www.uzairways.com) that stretches across the country from Tashkent to far-flung destinations like Nukus and Urgench.

Kazakhstan is well covered by Air Astana (www.airastana.com), whose network centres on Almaty, and to a lesser extent, Astana, which link the main cities with domestic destinations like Aralsk and Semey. Scat Air (www.scat.kz) also operates domestic flights. The price of some airline tickets is subsidised by the Kazakh government.

Flying within **Pakistan** is a quick way of getting around the country, and is often very cheap. Shorter journeys are subsidised by the government, so a flight to Gilgit on the Karakoram Highway from Islamabad is not that much more expensive than taking the bus. PIA (www.piac.com.pk) produces a timetable listing all its flights. Apart from PIA, there are several other internal air services, notably Air Blue (www.airblue.com), Aero Asia, Bhoja Air and Shaheen Air (www.shaheenair.com), though these are not as extensive as PIA's.

Afghanistan's two airlines – Ariana (www.flyariana.com) and Kam Air (www.kamair.com) – offer domestic services from Kabul to major cities, including Herat, Mazar-i-Sharif (there are also connections between these two cities) and Bamiyan. Many foreign embassies ban their staff from flying

on Afghan airlines owing to safety concerns. The UN operates more reliable flights and, although primarily for NGO staff, remaining seats may be sold to other travellers.

Turkmenistan Airlines (www.turkmenairlines.com) has a modern fleet, handling all internal flights from Ashgabat to five destinations – Mary, Dashoguz, Turkmenabat, Turkmenbashi and Balkanabat. Flights are heavily subsidised and are great value.

By train

Central Asia's rail network is a Soviet legacy and operates in much the same way as the current Russian system. Rail is a useful means of getting around in Uzbekistan and Kazakhstan, but hardly registers as an option in Kyrgyzstan and Tajikistan. There is no functioning passenger railway in Afghanistan.

Kyrgyzstan has almost no domestic services, apart from very slow holiday services between Bishkek and Kaindi, and Tokmok and Balykchy on Lake Issyk-Kul.

Tajikistan's Dushanbe–Moscow service no longer runs, although irregular trains link Khojand with Samarkand, and Dushanbe with Termiz in southern Uzbekistan. There is also a limited rail service from Dushanbe to Kurganteppa and Kulyab in the south.

Uzbekistan has a reliable rail service that links Bukhara and Samarkand with Tashkent – slower than shared taxis but cheaper and more comfortable. The website www.seat61.com lists the current timetables for Uzbekistan's internal rail routes as well as international services. In **Kazakhstan**, where vast distances separate the major centres, overnight train travel is the only real alternative to flying, and the rail services that link Almaty and Astana with Moscow are useful for long-distance east–west or north–south travel.

The trains in **Pakistan** are slow but convenient, serving the major towns and sites of interest.

Rail services in Turkmenistan are unpredictable, with varying quality and timetables. Useful routes across the country run from the Caspian Sea to the Uzbek border and from Ashgabat to Dashoguz in the north.

By bus

Buses vary enormously in Central Asia, ranging from comfortable long-distance coaches to decrepit **regional** services. The former mostly run between larger urban centres and the latter between country towns and villages, where they tend to stop on demand. Long-distance bus stations are commonly located some distance from the town centre and often require a minibus or taxi ride to reach them. Long-distance tickets are usually bought from the station office or an agent prior to travel, whereas fares are normally collected by a conductor on local buses. On long-distance buses luggage is normally stored in the baggage compartment or on a roof-rack, while on local services it usually has to go inside the vehicle along with the sacks of vegetables.

Kyrgyzstan has a limited number of buses running long-distance routes from the capital, mostly east to Lake Issyk-Kul, and a fair number of local services connecting Bishkek with the towns of the Chuy Valley. Those buses donated by China Aid (clearly marked with the donor's logo) tend to be the newest and therefore most reliable. Most people travel by minibus or shared taxi. There are no bus services between Bishkek and Osh because of tunnel restrictions at the Töo-Ashuu Pass. In the south of the country there are limited bus services for destinations like Batken and Kyzyl-Kiya, but nothing that goes beyond the border into Uzbekistan.

Tajikistan has a limited bus service that mostly operates between Dushanbe and the south of the country, though the service is at best erratic. Given the mountainous terrain and terrible roads, shared taxis and minibuses are a more practical means of transport, though breakdowns and blown tires are an inevitability.

In **Uzbekistan**, the state bus service is in decline, and many routes have been taken over by private bus companies that offer a more comfortable service. These usually do not leave until full, which can mean a lengthy wait. Shared taxis are a swifter option, particularly if you are prepared to pay for un-filled seats to get the vehicle moving.

Long-distance, inter-city buses are most common in eastern **Kazakhstan**, particularly between Almaty, Astana and the cities of the southeast. Western Kazakhstan generally relies more on rail services.

In **Pakistan**, private operators run regular air conditioned coach services between towns and cities, often referred to as "big buses". Daewoo Intercity is highly recommended. NATCO (Northern Areas Transport Company) runs more decrepit buses up the Karakoram Highway (KKH) to Gilgit and beyond. A good new addition to Northern Areas transport is the Silk Route Bus Service, air conditioned coaches that ply direct routes between Rawalpindi and Kashgar via Hunza.

There are no organised bus companies in **Afghanistan**, rather a collection of small operators with mainly minibuses plying the routes between cities.

There is a good network of long-distance buses in Turkmenistan between the major towns and cities. It is difficult to use these for visiting the major sites, but they are great value.

By minibus

Minibuses – usually referred to as *marshrutki* or *marshrutnoe* – run on fixed routes throughout Central Asia, often following a bus route but providing a faster service at a slightly higher price. Other routes ply where bus services do not exist at all. Minibuses usually leave when full, and it can be hard to pick them up midway between destinations because of lack of seats. They usually operate from outside bus stations but may sometimes have a separate stand. The minibuses typically have a poor safety record due to a combination of lack of maintenance and bad driving, so try to get a seat rather than standing if you have the option.

By taxi

Taxis fall into two categories: **private taxis** hired for a specific journey and **shared taxis** that run on fixed routes. With private taxis it is imperative that a price is agreed before setting off, as well as details regarding tolls to be paid and charges for waiting time. Long-distance private taxis are most useful in **Kyrgyzstan**, where costs are low and few alternatives exist to reach off-the-beaten-track destinations. Shared taxis are an important mode of transport throughout much of the region, especially in **Uzbekistan**. They run on regular routes between cities and leave when all seats are full. It is always possible to leave earlier by buying all of the remaining seats.

In **Pakistan**, Suzuki pick-ups, three-wheeled scooter rickshaws and private taxis are the most common transport options in towns.

Border crossings

Very few bus services cross international boundaries in Central Asia, and so it is a matter of taking local transport to a border point, walking across and then looking for onward transport. See individual Places chapters for information on entering and leaving.

Taxis are plentiful in and around the main towns and cities in Turkmenistan and are good value. Get a rough idea of the cost from a local first and bargain if necessary.

Driving

Self-drive car hire is available in some of the larger cities like Almaty, Tashkent and Islamabad, which have local agencies or international franchises. However, insurance may be difficult to arrange, and this, coupled with poor roads and erratic driving standards, is probably enough to put off most would-be drivers.

Hiring a vehicle with driver is an altogether better option. It does not cost that much more (with the exception of Tajikistan), and the driver, who will know the region and the road conditions, can sometimes also act as a guide. The Community Based Tourism (CBT) organisation in **Kyrgyzstan** can provide knowledgeable local drivers at a fixed per-kilometre rate.

In **Afghanistan** it is not possible to hire a car without also hiring a driver – Afghan roads are not for the faint-hearted anyway. Paved highways are a rarity, there are no road signs, few road rules, but plenty of police checkpoints. The Kabul–Kandahar–Herat road passes through Taliban country and is highly dangerous. Large hotels can usually offer cars with drivers, or contact tour operators in Kabul.

In **Pakistan**, cars with drivers can be hired from some larger hotels. Though more expensive, they may be worthwhile, as the drivers usually speak some English. Avis has offices in Karachi, Islamabad and Lahore (www.avis.com.pk) and Europcar has an office in Lahore and Karachi (www.europcar.com).

Hiring a car is forbidden in **Turkmenistan**, so the only option is a taxi for shorter trips, or to hire an agency car and driver for longer journeys.

A – Z

A HANDY SUMMARY
OF PRACTICAL INFORMATION

A

Accommodation

There is a wide range of accommodation in Central Asia, from simple B&Bs to five-star hotels. Hotels fall into three categories: Soviet-period hotels whose designated star-rating may demand something of a leap of faith; modern, international-style hotels with standards similar to those anywhere else in the world; and smaller boutique hotels that offer character and a more personal touch. Soviet-style hotels may be the only choice in towns that lie off the beaten track, especially in **Kazakhstan** and much of **Tajikistan**. Although these are sometimes reasonable, more often than not they fulfil all the stereotypes of the former USSR, with bleak, anonymous rooms and grumpy staff who welcome guests with a scowl. Most hotels in this category follow the Soviet system of having a woman *(dezhurnaya)* responsible for each floor whose job it is to look after room keys and ensure that guests do not get up to any mischief.

Uzbekistan probably has the best options in terms of variety and comfort, particularly in the Silk Road cities of Samarkand, Bukhara and Khiva. **Kazakhstan** is mostly geared towards business visitors, and away from Almaty and Astana, Soviet-style hotels may be all that is available.

There is a good range of hotels in Bishkek, **Kyrgyzstan**, some of which can be booked online at www.bishkek-hotels.net, and new places have opened for business in provincial centres like Karakol, Naryn and Osh in recent years.

In smaller towns and villages, often the only option is to stay with a local family. Fortunately there is an excellent network of homestays under the auspices of the CBT programme.

Tajikistan is probably the least geared up for visitors, with mostly run-down Soviet-period accommodation and just a few private hotels outside of Dushanbe. There is, however, a fledgling Community-Based Tourism (CBT) programme in operation that offers basic homestay accommodation in the remote Gorno-Badakhshan region of the southeast.

Pakistan has some excellent up-market hotels, including the home-grown Avari (www.avari.com), Pearl Continental (www.pchotels.com) and Serena chains (www.serenahotels.com), in both the cities and smaller tourist centres. In addition, there are some beautiful hotels run by the PTDC (Pakistan Tourism Development Corporation), as well as numerous recommendable options in out-of-the-way places – particularly in the north.

Turkmenistan is in the process of completely renewing its hotels in Ashgabat, with amazing new Vegas-style hotel structures dotted around the city, to compliment the older-style city centre offerings. In Mary and Dashoguz it can still be a problem to find a bed for the night at any level of comfort or service.

Along with affordability, the most important consideration in **Afghanistan** is security. The best accommodations operate to the UN's Minimum Operating Security Standards (MOSS), offering the most secure environment – particularly important in Kabul.

Homestays

For those willing to rough it a little, homestays offer a viable alternative to hotels, and in some areas may be all that is available. Found mostly in **Kyrgyzstan** and **Tajikistan**, homestays are generally fairly basic, and have facilities that usually include a shared living area, an outside toilet and makeshift shower. This offers simple but comfortable accommodation for a very reasonable price – an excellent choice for backpackers and independent travellers.

The Community-Based Tourism (CBT) organisation coordinates and monitors homestays throughout Kyrgyzstan, but there are others that work outside these networks. Homestays in Tajikistan, mostly in Gorno-Badakhshan, tend to belong to META, the Tajik equivalent to CBT.

The homestay experience is one of the joys of travelling in the region as it enables the traveller to get close to the everyday life of the country. English is not generally spoken, and so it requires an effort from both host and guest to make each other understood. Having to clean one's teeth in the garden and share a squat toilet is a small price to pay for a memorable experience, fierce hospitality and tasty home-cooked food.

Yurt camps

Yurt camps can be found throughout the region, but they are by and large a Kyrgyz speciality. In **Kyrgyzstan**, yurt-stays may be arranged with Bishkek tour companies, local CBT groups or informally with local Kyrgyz willing to rent out a spare yurt. Yurt camps are found in various upland areas, most notably at Lake Song-Kol, around Lake Issyk-Kul and at Tash-Rabat.

In **Tajikistan** there are yurt camps in the Pamir region of the southeast; in **Kazakhstan**, in the mountains of the southeast near the Chinese border; and on the edge of the Kyzylkum Desert in **Uzbekistan**.

Most yurt camps are simple affairs where guests sleep on bedding on the floor and make use of a basic toilet and washstand outdoors. There are more luxurious ones, too, with proper beds, flush toilets and high-class cuisine.

Turbazas

These Soviet-era holiday camps are still a popular choice with some Central Asians. They are usually found near water (Lake Issyk-Kul, Kyrgyzstan) or at beauty spots with a reputation for fresh mountain air (Arslanbob, Kyrgyzstan; Iskander-Kul, Fan Mountains, Tajikistan). Despite the professed health benefits of a *turbaza* stay, the routine, for many Central Asian men at least, often revolves around lengthy vodka and karaoke sessions rather than bracing mountain hikes.

Camping

Wild camping is the only option in mountainous areas of **Kazakhstan**, **Kyrgyzstan** and **Tajikistan**. It is sometimes possible to camp next to a *turbaza* or yurt camp and make use of the facilities. Some of the more well-trodden trekking routes in Kyrgyzstan and Kazakhstan have basic campsites scattered along the trail, but these tend to be cramped and litter-strewn.

Camping is part and parcel of the trekking scene in the Karakoram and Hindu Kush in **Pakistan**, with some dramatically situated sites in the Hunza Valley. The same applies in the Wakhan Corridor, where a tent may be your only accommodation option. There are two designated campsites (both signposted but without electricity and a water tap) but otherwise be prepared to pay a small fee direct to the landowner if camping in a field. All camping equipment should be brought with you.

B

Budgeting for your trip

Flights to and from, and the numerous visas and permits required to travel across, Central Asia drive up the cost of travelling in what is otherwise a relatively inexpensive part of the world. Local incomes tend to be low, and this is reflected in the cost of the most basic accommodation, food and transport options.

Capital cities and also the oil towns of Turkmenistan and Kazakhstan are atypically expensive, however. Hotels and restaurants are aimed at expats and business travellers, all of whom are using their expense accounts, and so double rooms start at around $120 and rocket up from there. Likewise, a meal in a reasonable restaurant, excluding alcohol, will set you back at least $30 per person. If you plan to drink alcohol, remember that imported brands are markedly more expensive than local ones because of the import taxes.

If you are travelling on a more modest budget and in remoter areas, it is usually possible to find homestay or guesthouse accommodation for $10–15. Afghanistan is the notable exception, where bed and breakfast will set you back around $25. Eating where the locals eat – usually road-side stalls – is cheap providing you can live on *shashlyk*, *shorpo* and tea, and supermarkets and corner shops tend to stock a range of affordable local brands. Shared taxis or minibuses are cheaper than private cars; even if you are hitchhiking you will be expected to contribute towards the cost of fuel.

C

Climate

Extreme continental: Uzbekistan can get very hot – above 40°C (104°F) – in the summer months, while the mountainous areas of central Kyrgyzstan can dip to −25°C (−14°F) in the dead of winter. The Central Asian capitals, which are all relatively low-lying, are warm and humid in summer (30–35°C/85–95°F) but often sub-zero in the winter months. Astana in Kazakhstan has the greatest temperature swing. Spring receives the highest precipitation, which may fall as snow as late as April.

CLIMATE CHART

Samarkand

☐ Maximum temperature
☐ Minimum temperature
— Rainfall

Crime and security

Most of Central Asia is generally safe for travellers. The Islamist insurgencies that took place in southwest **Kyrgyzstan** in 2010 appear to be a thing of the past, though communal violence is not uncommon. The greatest threat of robbery tends to be in the big cities, especially at night outside bars and nightclubs in Bishkek and Almaty, and also while travelling by public transport. If you lose any items, contact the police. Crooked officials pose less of a problem than they used to, although there are still a few who attempt to extort money from foreigners. This is particularly true of the transport police. Keep calm, make sure you have copies of all important documentation (including your driving license), and try to avoid handing over money on the street. Ask to be taken to the nearest police station, and always demand a receipt.

Afghanistan is a somewhat different country to the other destinations in this guide. The ongoing Taliban insurgency in the south and east continues to affect the country profoundly, while the weakness of the Afghan government and rule of law in general add further to instability. Even the areas we cover in this guide are not immune from trouble, and Kabul in particular has been the target of repeated Taliban terror attacks, including suicide bombings. The British government advises against non-essential travel to Afghanistan, though this warning is reduced for the Wakhan Corridor. Even if conditions permit a visit, we advise against independent travel in favour of using a Kabul-based tour operator (or local operator in the case of the Wakhan), who will have access to current security information, risk assessments and contingency planning.

In **Pakistan**, there is a risk from random terrorist attacks on the northwest frontier, due to the recent problems in Baluchistan and the fallout from the "war against terror", which has spawned Taliban activity in NWFP and certain areas outside it. It is therefore advisable not to venture beyond Quetta in Baluchistan, and one should check with local officials before venturing out in West Punjab – or indeed anywhere in Federally Administered Tribal Areas (FATA) of NWFP. Except for people arriving overland from Iran by car, the authorities are unlikely to provide police escort to ordinary tourists. Local and intelligence officials are also very suspicious of cameras (video, especially), and Western documentary

Cinemas

Many English-language films are shown in Central Asian cinemas, but they are often badly dubbed into Russian. Russian movies are more popular, and the occasional Kazakh- or Uzbek-language film also sometimes makes it onto the big screen. Pakistani cinemas show imported films from various sources, including blockbusters from the West, and home-grown Lollywood movies are growing in popularity. There are only a couple of cinemas in Kabul, mainly showing Bollywood-style films to exclusively male audiences.

filmmakers have been locked up for months. As for the rest of Pakistan, it should be pretty safe, and that includes Peshawar and the Settled Areas of NWFP. Inevitably, one explosion in Karachi or a shooting in Gilgit leads to stern travel advisories being issued by foreign governments, with the result that the whole local tourism industry collapses for several months. Note these advisories by all means, but also bear in mind that sectarian violence in Gilgit and Karachi is nothing to do with tourists, and they are therefore never targeted. When trouble does occur, visitors are protected rather than threatened.

Statistics show that Pakistan is a very safe place to travel for foreigners; visitors are much less likely to get mugged here than in London or New York. However, you should still keep your personal belongings on your person or lock them in the hotel safe. Some hotels request that you deposit your valuable articles like jewellery and cash with the receptionist.

Customs regulations

There are no major restrictions other than for weapons, drugs and the export of artefacts, which require an export licence. The import of liquor into Pakistan is not permitted, though foreigners can drink in hotel bars. Customs declaration forms need to be filled out when entering some of the countries in the region and presented when leaving. Cash is also supposed to be accurately accounted for, so anything undeclared is best stashed away in case an over-vigilant customs officer wants to count it.

Uzbekistan is particularly vigilant with the amount and types of medication being brought into the country, even for personal use. This is

important at border crossings where some foreigners have been detained carrying medicines that are perfectly legal in most other countries. Try to obtain an up to date list of allowed and banned medications, especially codeine-based drugs.

D

Disabled travellers

Little concession is made to disabled travellers in the region outside the top hotels and, sadly, wheelchair access is extremely problematic. In the former Soviet "Stans", disabled children have typically been left in the care of the state, and attitudes are slow to change.

E

Eating out

Where to eat

In the larger cities there is a choice of restaurants to suit all pockets and tastes, from expensive international-standard restaurants to cheap kebab places. Away from the major centres, the choices will be fresh and tasty Central Asian or Russian dishes, although Korean food can sometimes be found in the most unlikely places. Written menus will usually be in the local language and/or Russian.

In a region where the fat-tailed sheep is king, vegetarians may have a hard time finding something suitable, vegans even more so, as some sort of meat finds its way into most dishes, even salads. Homestays and guesthouses more familiar with Western ways are sometimes able to provide vegetarian meals on request.

A chaikhana is traditionally a place that serves only tea but they often have a shashlyk (kebab) griddle out the front and may serve a couple of other dishes. The more traditional ones are characterised by takhta – low tables on raised platforms around which customers sit cross-legged. Chaikhanas are found throughout the region, but most commonly in Uzbekistan, Afghanistan, southern Kyrgyzstan and northern Tajikistan. Shoes should be removed before sitting down.

If hygiene appears to be dubious it is wise to avoid salads or food that has been inadequately reheated. Kebabs, piping hot from the griddle, and freshly boiled noodles are invariably safe.

What to eat

Mutton is by far the commonest meat, beef less so. Chicken is sometimes available, while pork, forbidden to Muslims, is served mostly in Russian restaurants. Horse meat is common in some areas, especially Kazakhstan, where chuchuk (horse-meat sausages) are seen as the ideal accompaniment to vodka. As ubiquitous as mutton dishes is plov, an Uzbek speciality that is a sort of rice pilaf made with carrots and stock.

Laghman – chunky noodles with chunks of mutton and a spicy stock – is another very common dish, although the best is undoubtedly made by Uighurs in Chinese Xinjiang. Shorpo – a thick soup of boiled mutton and root vegetables – is also very popular, particularly in Kyrgyzstan. Other Kyrgyz staples include samsa, baked pastry-like parcels stuffed with fatty mutton, and manti, steamed dumplings. Beshbarmak, made from flat noodles and a spicy mutton sauce, is a dish for special occasions in Kazakhstan and Kyrgyzstan and is not usually sold in restaurants.

Russian dishes that are commonly served in the region are pelmeni (small ravioli in broth), blini (pancakes) and borscht (beetroot soup). Most Russian dishes usually come served up with a dollop of smetana (soured cream) and a dill garnish.

Pakistan shares its culinary heritage with India, so menus overlap, although the food is generally less hot than traditional Indian fare. Classic dishes include korma (meat in spicy yoghurt gravy) and roghan gosht (garnished meat). Meals are usually accompanied by breads such as naan, kulcha and paratha, which are sometimes stuffed with minced meat or vegetables.

Afghan cuisine relies on a handful of dishes that, while individually tasty, can become quickly monotonous. The two main dishes are pulao (rice cooked with lamb or beef, usually with raisins and carrot), and kebabs with bread. A popular northern dish is mantu, a steamed ravioli with yoghurt sauce. Vegetables can be thin on the ground, but there is usually a surfeit of excellent fruit, including grapes, melons, pomegranates, apples and cherries, plus nuts.

Electricity

220 Volts AC, 50 Cycles. Countries in Central Asia use European-style two-pin rounded plugs. Power cuts are the norm and generators ubiquitous.

Drinks

Chai (tea), both green and black, is found everywhere. Drinking either is an excellent way to hydrate cheaply and safely. Unboiled tap water is best avoided, but bottled water is usually easy to find.

As in the rest of the former Soviet Union, vodka is a way of life for some in Central Asia, despite Islamic prohibition, and the notion of "just a small glass" is an alien one. Once a bottle is opened it is meant to be finished, and to stop drinking once a session is under way is seen as very bad form. Beer is very popular, and Russian Baltika of varying strengths is widely available. In Kyrgyzstan and Kazakhstan, *kymyz*, slightly alcoholic fermented horse milk, is the tipple of choice in mountainous areas. Other popular drinks include bozo, made from millet, and *maksym*, from wheat. In Uzbekistan, *katyk*, a thin yoghurt drink, is common, and in drier parts of Kazakhstan *shubat*, fermented camel's milk, is the local equivalent of *kymyz*.

Non-Muslim visitors who wish to drink alcohol in Pakistan require a permit that enables them to buy alcohol from hotels or authorised vendors. Similarly in Afghanistan, alcohol is only available at restaurants catering to foreigners, almost all in Kabul.

Embassies and consulates

Kyrgyzstan
British Embassy
21 Erkindik Boulevard, Office 404, Bishkek, tel: (312) 303 637 ,
https://www.gov.uk/government/world/organisations/british-embassy-bishkek
US Embassy
Prospect Mira 171, Bishkek, tel:(0312) 597 000,
http://bishkek.usembassy.gov

Tajikistan
British Embassy
Mirzo Tursunzade 65, Dushanbe, tel: (0372) 242 221,
www.ukintajikistan.fco.gov.uk
US Embassy
Ismoili Somoni 109A, Dushanbe, tel: (0372) 292 000,
http://dushanbe.usembassy.gov

Uzbekistan
British Embassy
Gulyamov 67, Tashkent, tel: (071) 120 1500,

www.ukinuzbekistan.fco.gov.uk
US Embassy
Moyqorghon 3, 5th Block, Yunusobod, Tashkent, tel: (071) 120 5450,
http://uzbekistan.usembassy.gov

Kazakhstan
Australian Embassy
Al-Farabi 5/2A, 9th Floor, Almaty, tel: (0727) 777 879.
British Embassy
6th Floor, Kosmonavtov Street 62, St. Chubary District, Astana, tel: (07172) 556 200,
www.ukinkz.fco.gov.uk
US Embassy
Rakhymzhan Koshkarbayev Avenue 3, Astana,, tel: (07172) 702 100,
https://kz.usembassy.gov

Pakistan
Australian High Commission
Constitution and Ispahani, Diplomatic Enclave, No. 1,Sector G-5/4, Islamabad, tel: (051) 835 5500,
www.pakistan.embassy.gov.au
British High Commission
Diplomatic Enclave, Ramna 5, Islamabad, tel: (051) 201 2000,
https://www.gov.uk/government/world/organisations/british-high-commission-islamabad
US Embassy
Diplomatic Enclave, Ramna 5, Islamabad, tel: (051) 208 0000,
http://islamabad.usembassy.gov

Afghanistan
Australian Embassy
The Australian Embassy in Kabul operates from a number of locations that are not publicly disclosed due to security reasons. tel: (061) 2 6261 3305
http://afghanistan.embassy.gov.au
British Embassy
15th Street Roundabout, Wazir Akbar Khan, Kabul, tel: (0700) 102 000,
www.gov.uk/government/world/organisations/british-embassy-kabul
Canadian Embassy
House 256, Street 15, Wazir Akbar Khan, Kabul, tel: (0799) 742 800,
www.afghanistan.gc.ca
US Embassy
Kabul, tel: (0700) 10 8001,
http://kabul.usembassy.gov/

Turkmenistan
British Embassy
3rd floor office building, Four Points Ak Altyn Hotel, Ashgabat, tel: 012 36 34 62/64,
www.gov.uk/government/world/turkmenistan
US Embassy
9 1984 Street (formerly Pushkin St), Ashgabat, tel: 012 94 00 45,

http://turkmenistan.usembassy.gov/contact.html

Emergencies

It is advisable to carry the telephone number of the nearest embassy or honorary consul of your country at all times. Emergency numbers for ambulance, fire and police are respectively **01**, **02** and **03** in **Kazakhstan**, **Uzbekistan** and **Tajikistan** and **101**, **102** and **103** in **Kyrgyzstan**. In **Turkmenistan** call **03** for medical emergencies only.

Emergency services in **Pakistan** are contacted by dialling **15** plus a local number for police, **16** plus a local number for fire services, and **115** plus a local number for the ambulance service. Of course, you need to get the local number.

There are no country wide emergency numbers in **Afghanistan**. In Kabul, dial **100** for the police, **0799 357 049** for ambulance and **020 210 1341** for the security department.

Etiquette

Although not always on the surface deeply religious, the Central Asian countries are socially conservative and predominantly Muslim, particularly in more rural areas, and visitors should therefore behave sensitively. Particular in the former Soviet states you may well see the young, urban population skimpily dressed, but this is not recommended for foreigners as it may be seen to be disrespectful by older generations. In Afghanistan, men must wear long trousers and long-sleeved tops. Women should wear tunic-style blouses that cover their body shape, and a headscarf. The same dress code should be applied when visiting mosques and other religious sites in the region.

Handshaking is a widespread ritual, often accompanied with a gesture to the heart, and it is common for men to continue holding hands as they talk. Women do not usually shake hands, but foreign women may be invited to do so with Central Asian men. Do not take offence if your hand is declined.

Shoes should be removed whenever entering a home or a mosque. In more conservative areas, particularly in Afghanistan and Pakistan, homes are strictly divided by sex and male guests will not encounter female members of the family. Foreign women have a hybrid status and are sometimes allowed to participate in both male and female spheres.

CHINA

Eating is always done with the right hand, especially when sharing a communal bowl, as the left hand is used for washing oneself and therefore is considered dirty. Bread is considered sacred and should never be discarded on the floor. Hospitality is of prime importance, even in the poorest communities, so you should always show gratitude to your host and bring a gift or an item of food if invited to share a meal.

F

Festivals

The spring equinox festival of Nauroz (also known as *Nauryz, Nooruz, Nawroz* or *Navrus*), widely celebrated in the region, is an excuse for traditional games like *buzkashi* and much partying. Horse game fairs are also staged in the summer *jailoos* (seasonal pasture) of **Kyrgyzstan**, in particular the annual Central Asia Horse Festival.

In **Pakistan**, there are a great many *melas* (festivals), jolly occasions with fairs, circuses, pilgrimages, religious frenzy, people in catatonic trances, beating of drums and bagpiping. The most exciting religious *melas* are those marking the *urs* of the Sufi saints. The dates for most of these *melas* depend on the sighting of the moon and therefore vary from year to year. Most of them, however, occur during the spring period.

Two important festivals in **Afghanistan** are the Gul-e Sorkh International Music Festival, in Mazar-e-Sharif in March, and Kabul's AgFair Agriculture Festival in October.

G

Gay and lesbian travellers

Male homosexuality is legal in Kyrgyzstan and Kazakhstan, but illegal in Uzbekistan, Tajikistan,

Pakistan and Afghanistan. Female homosexuality is not sanctioned either way, presumably because it is not considered an issue. Because of social mores, public displays of affection between same-sex – and also straight – couples is best avoided. There is a nascent gay scene in Almaty but otherwise the Soviet rhetoric that homosexuality is a mental disorder is widely accepted.

H

Health and medical care

A yellow fever vaccination certificate is required if coming from an infected area less than six days prior to entering Kazakhstan or Pakistan. Vaccinations for hepatitis A and B, diphtheria, tetanus, typhoid and polio should be up to date for all countries.

A malaria risk exists across all non-mountainous parts of Afghanistan and parts of Pakistan. There is also a slight risk in southern Uzbekistan and Tajikistan in summer. Diseases such as leishmaniasis and brucellosis, common in some local populations, are rarely contracted by travellers to the region. Rabies is present, but only poses a risk to those spending long periods in rural areas. HIV and STDs are fairly widespread.

However, despite the risks listed above, diarrhoea is the illness visitors are most likely to suffer from.

Air pollution in large cities can cause severe problems to anyone suffering from breathing difficulties, so remember to bring inhalers and suitable medication.

I

Insurance

Travel and medical insurance is essential, including evacuation cover. Check before purchasing, however,

as some insurers won't cover for travel to Afghanistan. Bring copies of documentation and all necessary phone numbers with you.

Internet

Internet cafés are widespread throughout the region, although connections can be slow. Many of the better hotels offer Wi-Fi access.

M

Maps

Good maps of Central Asia are frustratingly hard to come by. The Soviets did produce detailed topographical maps of the region but they do not tend to be commercially available, even in the countries themselves. The same applies to trekking maps, which should be purchased abroad, if indeed they are in print.

Hotels and tourism offices in capital cities and towns with a significant inflow of tourists often produce maps of their local area. These may be photocopies of print-outs from Google, but they are often all that is available.

Media

Kyrgyzstan, **Tajikistan**, **Uzbekistan** and **Kazakhstan** have a range of newspapers in Russian and the national language. Kazakhstan has the English-language *Almaty Herald* and *Kazakhstan Monitor*, and Kyrgyzstan the *Bishkek Observer* and *The Times of Central Asia*, which covers all of Central Asia. Turkmenistan has a weekly newspaper in English called *Neutral*. Neither **Uzbekistan** nor **Tajikistan** has any English-language print media.

In **Afghanistan**, newspapers are sold in the cities. The international press can be hard to find even in Kabul, although the *Kabul Times* is published in English. *Afghan Scene* is an English-language monthly aimed at expats.

In **Pakistan**, there are many Urdu publications, and also publications in regional languages. The major Urdu newspapers are *Nawa-i-waqt, Jang* and *Wafaq*. International newspapers and news magazines are available in the cities, at bookshops and in the foyers of high-class hotels. English-language newspapers, such as *The Nation, The News* and *The Leader*, are published in the major cities.

CENTRAL ASIA

WESTERN ASIA

Turkmen president Saparmurat Niyazov depicted on the Turkmenistan 50 tenge coin.

Television and radio are tightly controlled in **Uzbekistan** but more liberal in the rest of the region, with privately owned channels supplementing state-controlled ones.

In **Afghanistan**, local television and radio broadcasts are mainly in Dari and Pashto, but the BBC World Service broadcasts on FM in Kabul, and across the rest of Central Asia. International English-language satellite channels are provided for guests at many hotels throughout the region.

Money

The **Kyrgyzstan** currency is the som, which comes in notes of 1, 5, 10, 20, 50, 100, 200, 500 and 1,000 som and a few rarely used coins.

In **Uzbekistan**, the official currency of sum comes in notes of 1, 3, 5, 10, 25, 50, 100, 200, 500 and 1,000, but because there are currently around 1,300 sum to the dollar, smaller denomination notes are rarely seen. **Tajikistan**'s currency, the somoni, has notes of 1, 5, 10, 20, 50, 100 somoni and coins of 5, 10, 20, 50 diram and 1, 3 and 5 somoni.

Kazakhstan uses the tenge, which comes in notes of 200, 500, 1,000, 2,000, 5,000 and 10,000 tenge, and 1, 2, 5, 10, 20, 50 and 100 tenge coins.

Turkmenistan uses the Manat, in notes of 1, 5, 10, 20, 50, 100 and 500. Coins are 1, 2, 5, 10, 20, 50 tenge.

Afghanistan's currency, the afghani, has bank notes of AFA5, 10, 20, 50, 100, 500, and there are coins of AFA1, 2 and 5. Pakistan's unit of currency is the rupee, with 100 paisas to a rupee. Notes are in denominations of Rs1,000, 500, 100, 50, 10 and 5. Coins are in denominations of Rs2 and 1, and 50 and 25 paisa.

By far the best currency to carry is US dollars as sterling and euros are a struggle to exchange. Dollars used for exchange must be in pristine condition and preferably of high denominations, otherwise they will be refused. Traveller's cheques are generally more trouble than they are worth. ATMs are relatively numerous in the towns and cities of Kazakhstan. In Kyrgyzstan, they are currently only found in Bishkek, Osh and Jalalabad. Tajikistan has very few, mostly in Dushanbe, and in Uzbekistan they are unreliable, even in Tashkent. There are a limited number in Kabul accepting Visa and MasterCard, and increasing numbers in Pakistan.

Credit cards are usually accepted for payment in top hotels and some up-market restaurants and shops, except in Afghanistan, where US dollars or afghanis are preferred.

National holidays

Kyrgyzstan

1 January New Year's Day
7 January Christmas (Russian Orthodox)
8 March Women's Day
21 March Nauroz
9 May Victory Day
5 May Constitution Day
31 August Independence Day

Tajikistan

1 January New Year's Day
7 January Christmas (Russian Orthodox)
8 March Women's Day
21 March Nauroz
1 May Labour Day
9 May Victory Day
27 June National Unity Day
9 September Independence Day
6 November Constitution Day

Uzbekistan

1 January New Year's Day
7 January Christmas (Russian Orthodox)
8 March Women's Day
21 March Nauroz
9 May Victory Day
1 September Independence Day
8 December Constitution Day

Kazakhstan

1 January New Year's Day
7 January Christmas (Russian Orthodox)
8 March Women's Day
21 March Nauroz
9 May Victory Day
10 June Capital Day
30 August Constitution Day
25 October Republic Day
16 December Independence Day

Pakistan

23 March Pakistan Day
1 May Labour Day
1 July Bank Holiday
14 August Independence Day
6 September Defence of Pakistan Day (commemorating the Indo-Pakistan War of 1965)
11 September Anniversary of the death of the Quaid-e-Azam, M.A. Jinnah
9 November Iqbal Day (anniversary of the birth ofAllama Iqbal)
25 December Anniversary of the birth of Quaid-e-Azam
31 December Bank Holiday

Afghanistan

21 March Afghan New Year (Nauroz)
28 April Victory Day
1 May National Labour Day
4 May Remembrance Day for Martyrs and the Disabled
19 August Independence Day
9 September Ahmad Shah Massoud Day

Turkmenistan

1 January New Year's Day
12 January Memorial Day
19 February National Flag Day
8 March International Women's Day
21 March National Spring Holiday
9 May Victory Day
18 May Constitution Day
6 October Earthquake Remembrance Day
27 & 28 October Independence Days
12 December Neutrality Day

O

Opening hours

Opening hours are normally Monday to Friday from 9am until 5pm or 6pm. Banks are normally open from 9am to 4pm, except in Pakistan where they close at 1pm. Shops often stay open later, until around 8pm or 9pm.

Friday is the official holiday in Afghanistan. Museums and galleries are usually closed on one day of the week, often on Mondays. Restaurants tend to close early outside the larger cities. Shops and businesses may change their opening hours during Ramadan, particularly in Pakistan and Afghanistan.

P

Photography

Avoid taking photos of military installations, bridges and airports, especially in Uzbekistan, Pakistan and Afghanistan. Turkmenistan is very strict in banning photography along many central avenues in Ashgabat, especially around the Presidential Palace. In general, it is unwise and unkind to photograph people unless they give their consent. Do not attempt to take photos of women in the street in Afghanistan. Women visitors might have the opportunity of taking photos of Afghan women, in an all-women environment.

Ensure that you bring sufficient photographic materials, including film/memory cards and chargers.

Postal services

Kazakhstan, Kyrgyzstan and Pakistan probably offer the most dependable services. For important parcels and documents it is probably best to make use of an international courier service like DHL. There is a Datapost service from Pakistan to some countries, including the UK and US. All items sent by this service are registered and covered against loss. In Afghanistan, use only postal services in Kabul, Herat and Mazar-i-Sharif.

Public holidays

Islamic holidays are based on the Hejiri calendar. The months are lunar months, so the year is 13 days shorter than the Western calendar. Thus dates of certain holidays may vary from year to year. It is best to find out whether any of these dates fall within the time period of your projected visit. In Afghanistan and Pakistan, Ramadan or an Eid (religious feast) will mean that places are closed at certain times and that food may not be readily available because everyone else is fasting.

The two main holidays, **Eid al-Fitr** and **Eid al-Adha**, are also observed throughout Central Asia, but other Muslim holidays are mainly observed in Pakistan and Afghanistan.
Eid al-Fitr, three days marking end of Ramadan (fasting month)
Eid al-Adha, four days at the end of Hajj
1st of Muharram, Islamic New Year
9th of Muharram, Ashura
12th of Rabe'a al-Awwal, Prophet Muhammad's birthday

R

Religion

In **Kyrgyzstan, Tajikistan, Uzbekistan, Turkmenistan** and **Kazakhstan** most people are Sunni Muslim, nominally at least, while many Russians follow the Orthodox Christian faith. Uzbeks from the Ferghana Valley tend to practise a more conservative Islam, while the Pamir region of Tajikistan has many Ismailis, a unique and tolerant sect of Shia Islam that follows the Aga Khan. Many people, particularly Kyrgyz,

observe a syncretic version of Islam that is suffused with elements of shamanism.

Islam is the main religion of **Pakistan**. Some 97 percent of the total population are Muslims, with less than 1.5 percent Hindus and about the same number of Christians, and considerably fewer Sikhs. The Muslim population is divided mainly between Sunnis (77 percent) and Shias (20 percent).

Afghanistan is almost entirely Muslim, with 85 percent of the population being Sunnis. The Shia minority includes the Hazaras. There are small numbers of Sikhs and Hindus in urban areas.

S

Shopping

What to buy

Both Bukhara and Samarkand in **Uzbekistan** have an enormous number of gift shops that sell a range of items including traditional clothing, wall hangings, pottery and leather goods. **Kyrgyzstan** has less choice, but *shyrdaks*, the felt carpets used in Kyrgyz yurts, are widely available. There are other felt goods besides *shyrdaks* that may be purchased, such as slippers and wall hangings.

Traditional hats make good, inexpensive souvenirs: the white felt *kalpak* worn by Kyrgyz men, the square doppi of Uzbekistan or the well-known woollen *pakol* caps of **Pakistan** and **Afghanistan**.

In the bazaars of Islamabad, Rawalpindi and Peshawar you will find silverware, woodwork, embroidered items, *namdah* rugs (made from chain-stitch embroidery on felt with colourful designs), kaftans, Kashmiri shawls, *salwar kameez* and woollen *weskits* (waistcoats). One item to look for is Peshwari chappals – sturdy and comfortable men's sandals.

Afghan carpets are deservedly famous, from the richly decorated Bokhara styles of the Turkmen north to the tribal Baluchi style. Chicken Street is Kabul's most famous shopping address and sells wool or silk embroidered *suzani* bedspreads, carved lapis lazuli, *pakol* hats and pottery from Istalif. Herat is famous for its handmade blue glass. **Turkmenistan** is proud of its weaving heritage and has some high quality carpets and rugs for sale.

T

Telecommunications

The best place to make international calls is the local telephone office, as surcharged hotel rates tend to be sky-high. Phonecards are available in Pakistan and can be used to make cheap overseas calls. The landline network in Afghanistan is extremely limited but mobile coverage is reasonable. Main post offices have international phone facilities, otherwise look for PCOs (Public Call Offices) or phone stands – a guy with a phone, stopwatch and calculator. Calls between neighbouring Central Asian countries are considered to be international and charged accordingly.

Many Western mobile phone networks have roaming arrangements in Central Asia but these are quite costly. Buying a local SIM card is a good idea if staying for any length of time.

International dialling codes
Kyrgyzstan +996
Tajikistan +992
Uzbekistan +998
Kazakhstan +7
Pakistan +93
Afghanistan +92
Turkmenistan +993

Tipping

Tipping is not common in Central Asia, except in larger cities where a 10 percent service charge may be added to your restaurant bill.

Toilets

Modern, sit-down toilets are found in most hotels and restaurants, with squat toilets elsewhere. In rural areas, even quite wealthy private homes will often just have a hole-in-the-ground earth toilet. Carry your own toilet paper.

Tourist information

The websites of tour and trekking companies operating in the region are a good source of information. KCBTA (tel: +996-312-443 331; www.cbtkyrgyzstan.kg), **Kyrgyzstan**'s community-based tourism coordinators based in Bishkek, can give helpful advice on Kyrgyzstan.

The **Pakistan** Tourism Development Corporation (PTDC; www.tourism.gov.pk) has information offices in every city and can help organise trips and transport. The provincial governments also have their own tourism bodies, which offer similar assistance as well as running their own trips. The Afghan Tourist Organisation in Kabul (tel: (075) 201 6907, http://afghan-tours.com) is eager, but offers little of practical use to visitors.

V

Visas

This is a complex area that is continually in flux. Visas are necessary for all of the Central Asian republics, although some are more difficult to obtain than others, and some embassies require a "letter of invitation" (LOI) before they will issue a visa. An LOI can be obtained by post or email from a reliable Central Asian agency.

In terms of difficulty, a visa for **Kyrgyzstan** is the easiest to obtain at the current time. A one-month tourist visa can be obtained by posting a downloaded application form to a branch of the embassy (www.kyrgyz-embassy.org.uk or www.kgembassy.org), or by buying one on arrival at Bishkek Airport. Visas for **Kazakhstan** are a little more difficult, and the embassy (www.kazembassy.org.uk or www.kazconsulny.org) may want to see an LOI, although this requirement appears to have stopped for the time being for British and EU passport-holders.

Uzbekistan visas are relatively easy to obtain (see www.uzbekembassy.org or www.uzbekconsulny.org) but an LOI is currently necessary for British passport-holders. It is usually possible to get a **Tajik** tourist visa on arrival at Dushanbe airport, but applying in advance at a Tajik embassy (www.tajikembassy.org.uk) may be a more reliable option. A **Turkmenistan** visa is fairly difficult to get as you

first need a LOI from the person to be visited and have it certified by the State Migration Service (http://uk.tmembassy.gov.tm). Be very specific with dates and places to be visited.

A visa for **Pakistan** can be obtained from one of its embassies or consulates, and an application form can be downloaded from www.phclondon.org or www.embassyofpakistanusa.org.

All visitors to **Afghanistan** require a valid passport and an entry visa, which should be obtained prior to departure, from Afghan consulates and embassies. More details and a downloadable visa application form can be found at http://afghanistanembassy.org.uk, or www.travcour.com. Single-entry visas are valid for one month.

W

Websites

Some useful websites:
www.times.kg The Times of Central Asia.
www.eurasianet.org Regional news.
www.uzbekistan.com General information on Uzbekistan.
www.tourism.uz Tourism in Uzbekistan.
www.pamirs.org Travel and trekking in the Pamir region.
www.pakistan.gov.pk Official website of the government of Pakistan.
www.kabulguide.net Useful site for those staying long-term in Kabul.
www.kabulcaravan.com General travel information.
www.iwpr.net Institute for War and Peace Reporting.
www.fco.gov.uk UK Foreign Office advice.

What to bring and wear

A torch (flashlight) is handy for power cuts and late-night trips to the

Weights and measures

Countries in Central Asia use the metric system.

bathroom. Bringing photocopies of your passport, visas and essential documents is a wise precaution, and a supply of passport photos will be necessary if applying for visas.

Comfortable, hard-wearing clothing is best. Loose-fitting clothes are ideal for most of the year, but be prepared for extremes of temperature, especially if trekking. Visitors to the more conservative countries should respect religious sensibility. Sun lotion and sunglasses are essential and if you are a spectacle-wearer, bring along a spare pair of glasses just in case.

When to go

Central Asia is a seasonal destination whose upland areas (much of **Kyrgyzstan** and **Tajikistan**) are best visited between late May and October. Because of blistering summer temperatures, lowland areas such as **Uzbekistan**, **Turkmenistan** and much of **Kazakhstan** are best visited between April and June and September to early November.

The northern mountains of **Pakistan** can be visited from spring through to autumn, although in high summer the heat in the valleys can still be oppressive.

Spring and autumn are the ideal times to visit **Afghanistan** as summers can be brutally hot, and the winter freeze brings whole areas of the country to a standstill. The warm seasons are shorter in the mountains, with winter arriving early and snow melting late.

Women travellers

Women travellers do not face any particular problems, although those travelling alone will come across examples of unapologetic sexism from time to time. It is advisable to dress and behave modestly and avoid situations that may turn out to be compromising. When travelling by public transport it is best to seek out fellow Western or local female travellers for company.

Women can have a difficult time in Afghanistan, however, and will find travelling with a male companion will help avoid unnecessary hassles. Non-revealing clothes to cover your body shape are essential, along with a headscarf.

Tajikistan is best visited between late May and October.

LANGUAGE

UNDERSTANDING THE LANGUAGE

Central Asia has a *smorgasbord* of languages, with each community championing its own tongue and literature. Russian, however, remains the *lingua franca* for inter-ethnic communication in the "Stans", and English or a smattering of Persian will serve you well in Afghanistan and Pakistan.

RUSSIAN

Russian is a Slavic language spoken by an estimated 171 million native speakers in Russia and the former territories of the USSR. It is written in the Cyrillic alphabet.

Russian grammar is challenging, but native speakers recognise this and will be understanding if you get it wrong: it is the vocabulary and pronunciation that is most important. Nouns and adjectives have six cases (which are dependent on their grammatical function in a sentence) and verbs are conjugated on the basis of gender (masculine, feminine or neuter) and tense. Pronouns are often omitted in the present and future tenses.

Syllables in Russian can be hard or soft and this largely (though not always) depends on the following vowel. Russian is thankfully phonetic (ie words are pronounced how they are spelled), though putting the stress in the wrong part of a word can change the meaning.

Key phrases

Hello Привет. *pree-VYEHT*
How are you? Как дела? *kak dyeh-LA?*
Fine, thank you Хорошо, спасибо. *kha-ra-SHO spa-SEE-ba*

Please Пожалуйста. *pa-ZHAL-sta*
Thank you Спасибо. *spa-SEE-ba*
Yes Да. *da*
No Нет. *nyet*
Excuse me Извините. *eez-vee-NEET-yeh*
I can't speak Russian Я не говорю по-русски *ya nye guh-va-RYOO pa ROO-skee*
Do you speak English? Вы говорите по-английски? *vi ga-va-REE-tya pa ahn-GLEES-kee?*
Help! Помогите! *pa-ma-GEE-tyeh!*
I'm ill (man) Я болен *ya-BOH-lyen*
I'm ill (woman) Я больна *ya-bahl-NAH*
I need a doctor Мне нужен врач. *mnyeh NOO-zhen vrahch*

DARI/TAJIK

Dari and Tajik are both closely linked to Persian, and speakers of either language can easily understand the other. Although Tajik is sometimes written in Cyrillic, both languages are normally written using the Perso-Arabic script due to their largely Islamic cultural heritage. Perso-Arabic scripts are written from right to left. You will find speakers of Dari and Tajik not only in Afghanistan and Tajikistan but also in large numbers in Uzbekistan: Bukhara and Samarkand were once both Tajik literary centres.

Key phrases

Hello سلام *Salaam.*
How are you? چی حال داری؟ *Chi hal dari?*
Fine, thank you خوب تشکر *Khob, tashakor*
Please. لطفاً *Lotfaan*
Thank you تشکر *Tashakor*

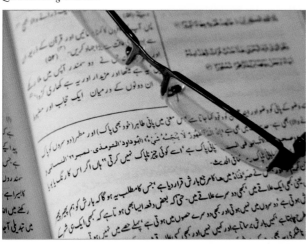

Quran showing Urdu text.

CHINA

CENTRAL ASIA

WESTERN ASIA

Detail from an Uzbek stamp.

KAZAKH

Kazakh is a Turkic language closely linked to Nogai and Karakalpak. Approximately 10 million speakers live within the borders of Kazakhstan itself, and there are another 3 million outside the country. Today the language is written in Cyrillic, though it has historically also been written in Perso-Arabic and Latin.

The greatest proponent of literature in Kazakh was Abay Kunanbayev (1845-1904), who wrote extensively about folk culture as well as producing his own poems. Many Kazakh streets are named in his honour.

Key phrases

Hello Сәлем. *sa-lem.*
How are you? Қалыңыз қалай? *khaly-ngyz-qalai?*
Fine, thank you Рақмет, жақсы. *rakh-met, jaq-sy.*
Thank you Рақмет. *rakh-met.*
Yes иә. *ee-ah.*
No жоқ. *joq.*

KYRGYZ

Kyrgyz is a Turkic language that is similar enough to Kazakh for speakers to understand one another. Originally written in Turkic runes, then Perso-Arabic and, for a short period, Latin, the Cyrillic alphabet has been in use since the 1940s. There are an estimated 4.5 million Kyrgyz speakers spread between northern

Afghanistan, eastern China and Uzbekistan, though the majority are in modern Kyrgyzstan.

Nouns in Kyrgyz take one of six cases, and this is shown in their endings. There are eight possible pronouns (including variations for formal and informal addresses), which can be declined in all six cases, and a possible 42 morphemes indicating those same people!

Key phrases

Hello *Salam*
How are you? *Kandaisiz?*
Fine, thank you *Jakshuh, rakhmat*
Please *Suranych*
Thank you *Rakhmat*

TURKMEN

Turkmen is yet another Turkic language, but also heavily influenced by Persian due to being spoken in not only modern Turkmenistan but also northeastern Iran and parts of northwestern Afghanistan. Turkmen today is written in a variant of the Latin script known as *Täze Elipbiý*, or the "New Alphabet". The political opposition, however, continues to use Cyrillic.

The structure of Turkmen is characterised by vowel harmony: words of native origin consist either entirely of front vowels or of back vowels, and this is dictated by the infinitive form of the verb. Prefixes and suffixes take the same pattern as the words they are attached to, but foreign loanwords are unaffected by this grammatical quirk.

Key phrases

Hello *Salam*
How are you? *Ýagdaýyňyz niçik?*
Fine, thank you *Bolýar*
Please *Baş*
Thank you *Sag bol*

URDU

Urdu is an Indo-European language that is akin to Hindi but takes the majority of its loanwords from Persian rather than Sanskrit. It is spoken by almost 70 million people across Pakistan and northern India, as well as amongst the South Asian diaspora. Urdu's grammatical structures are relatively easy to learn, though the tendency to miss out vowels when writing the Perso-Arabic script can make it tricky to read for beginners.

The long interaction between Urdu and English in colonial India has created a large shared vocabulary: listen out for familiar words such as bungalow, pajamas, polo and Raj.

Key phrases

Hello سلام *salaam*
How are you? کیا آپ کیسے ہیں؟ *Aap kaise hain?*
I am fine میں ٹھیک ہوں *main theek hoon*
Please براۓ مہربانی *barai mehrbaani*
Thank you شکریہ *shukriya*

UZBEK

Uzbek is a Turkic language written in the Cyrillic script. There over 28 million native Uzbek speakers, who live not only in Uzbekistan but also across the rest of Central Asia and in western China. Its vocabulary and grammar are closely linked to Uighur, but Persian, Arabic and Russian have also had a significant influence on the language's development and its modern usage.

Uzbek has a number of different dialects originating in different regions. The dialects you are most likely to hear are those used in Afghanistan, Fergana and Khorezm.

Key phrases

Hello *Salom*
How are you? *Qalay siz?*
Fine, thank you *Yakshi, rakhmat*
Please *Markhamat*
Thank you *Rakhmat*

FURTHER READING

HISTORY AND CULTURE

Asia Overland: Tales of Travel on the Trans-Siberian and Silk Road by Bijan Omrani.
A History of Inner Asia by Soucek Svat. Accessible introduction to the history of Central Asia.
Everyday Life in Central Asia: Past and Present by Jeff Sahadeo and Russell Zanca (editors).
Afghanistan: A Companion and Guide by Leeming and Omrani. A richly illustrated history of Afghanistan and its peoples, authoritative and written with flair.
The Great Game by Peter Hopkirk. A gripping account of the exploits of young soldiers and other players engaged in a shadowy struggle along distant frontiers.
Younghusband by Patrick French. A superbly researched biography of Sir Francis Younghusband, last of the great imperialists and key player in the Great Game.
Where Three Empires Meet by Knight. Travels in Kashmir and the British invasion of Hunza and Gilgit, 1891.

MODERN HISTORY

Beyond the Oxus: The Central Asians by Monica Whitlock. An incisive look at the region from a former BBC correspondent.
The New Central Asia: The Creation of Nations by Olivier Roy. An analysis of the emergence of national identities in post-Soviet Central Asia.
Murder in Samarkand by Craig Murray. The memoirs of a British ambassador fired after drawing attention to human rights abuses in Uzbekistan.
The New Great Game: Blood and Oil in Central Asia by Lutz Kleveman. An investigation into the international struggle for dominance over the region's oil and gas reserves.

Tamerlane's Children: Dispatches from Contemporary Uzbekistan by Robert Rand. A short but perceptive look at modern-day Uzbekistan.
Taliban: Militant Islam, Oil and Fundamentalism in Central Asia by Ahmed Rashid. The Lahore-based journalist's authoritative account of the causes and effects of the Taliban's rise to power.
Afghanistan: A Modern History by A. Rasanayagam.

ART AND ARCHITECTURE

Kyrgyzstan by Klavdiya Antipina and Rolando Paiva. A lavishly illustrated book about the costumes of nomadic Kyrgyz.
Monuments of Central Asia: A Guide to the Archaeology, Art and Architecture of Turkestan by Edgar Knobloch.
Three Women of Herat by Veronica Doubleday. A musician's account of her experiences in 1970s Afghanistan.

FICTION

Tales Told in Tents: Stories from Central Asia by Sally Pomme Clayton and Sophie Herxheimer.
Jamilia by Chingiz Aitmatov. A love story set in the Caucasus.
The Railway by Hamid Ismailov. An imaginative portrayal of the fortunes of a fictional Uzbek village.
The Kite Runner by Khaled Hosseini. A captivating story of friendship and betrayal in 1970s Kabul.
Earth and Ashes by Atiq Rahimi. A tale of three generations of an Afghan family during the Russian occupation.
The Far Pavilions by M.M. Kaye. A good old romance with a kick at the end and a grand account of the Second Afghan War.
Kim by Rudyard Kipling; various editions. Classic novel, not just for children.

TRAVEL NARRATIVES

Out of Steppe by Daniel Metcalfe. A vivid travelogue combined with a sensitive discussion of Central Asia's declining minorities.
Silk Dreams, Troubled Road by Jonny Bealby. A fascinating account of an epic journey along the Silk Road on horseback.
A Game of Polo with a Headless Goat by Emma Levine. An interesting book about the game of buzkashi and other traditional Asian sports.
The Lost Heart of Asia by Colin Thubron. The inimitable travel writer's account of his journey through Central Asia in the early 1990s.
In Search of Kazakhstan: The Land That Disappeared by Christopher Robbins. A fascinating insight into this vast and varied country.
A Ride to Khiva by Frederick Burnaby. A classic Victorian travelogue.
Eastern Approaches by Fitzroy MacLean. This new edition reveals to a new generation the real-life Soviet adventures of super-spy MacLean, the original inspiration for James Bond.
The Road to Oxiana by Robert Byron. Byron's classic account of his travels in Persia and Afghanistan in search of the region's architectural treasures.
The Sewing Circles of Herat by Christina Lamb. A fascinating glimpse into life under the Taliban and the heroic resistance of a women's sewing group.
A Short Walk in the Hindu Kush by Eric Newby. Newby's account of his journey with a friend from London to the wild mountains of the Hindu Kush. One of the best travel books ever written.

OTHER INSIGHT GUIDES

Other **Insight Guides** that highlight destinations in and near Central Asia include India, Russia and Estonia, Latvia & Lithuania.

TRANSPORT

GETTING THERE AND GETTING AROUND

GETTING THERE

By air

Iran

The national airline, Iran Air, flies direct from many European and Asian cities to Tehran. British Airways, Lufthansa, Austrian Airlines, KLM, Turkish Air and Gulf Air also fly to Tehran. Tehran's aged airport at Mehrabad is located only 10km (6 miles) west of the city centre, but the new Iman Khomeini Airport south of Tehran is now handling more international flights.

Lebanon

Rafik Hariri International Airport to the south of Beirut is the home of Middle East Airlines (www.mea.com.lb). It operates flights to Europe, the Middle East and Africa. Some European airlines, including British Airways and Air France, also fly into Beirut.

Turkey

Air transport is excellent and cheap, with regular scheduled international flights into Istanbul, Ankara and Antalya, several low-cost carriers serving both Istanbul and Antalya, and numerous charter flights into Antalya in summer.

By bus

The days of the "hippie trail" which wound its way from Europe to Afghanistan, via Iraq and Iran, are long gone, but theoretically it is still possible to follow a similar route. Turkey and Turkmenistan would be the modern entry and exit points, and some overland tour buses and trucks

still manage to make the crossings. If entering and departing across these land borders, the maximum length of a transit visa is 10 days, which can normally be extended in the major cities. All visas and paperwork should be completed in advance of reaching the Iranian border.

Iran

Express coaches run almost daily between Tehran (and Tabriz) and Istanbul, Ankara and Erzurum in Turkey. There is also a daily service into Azerbaijan.

Turkey

There are coach services across Europe to Istanbul with Eurolines (www.eurolines.co.uk), plus coaches linking towns in the far east of the country with Georgia, Armenia and Iran.

By train

Many of the countries of Central and Western Asia are keen to promote the idea of rail travel along the Silk Road, but any serious journey soon gets bogged down in impracticalities. Irregular and uncertain train services (some only for freight or non-foreigners), not to mention different gauges and border restrictions, mean that crossing between countries can be extremely difficult. Having said that, rail travel within each country can be a real delight. The overnight trains through Uzbekistan are always great fun, and if you can get tickets, the ride across northern Iran is great value. There are two weekly train services leaving Tehran that are useful. The Trans-Asia Express goes between Ankara and Lake Van by train, then ferry over Lake

Van and onwards from Van pier by train Tehran, but it was currently suspended at time of writing due to security concerns in Eastern Turkey. See www.seat61.com for updates, more information and timetables.

Iran

The only passenger railway connection operates across the Turkish border from Tehran to Lake Van and beyond.

Turkey

There are rail links to Istanbul from Europe via Bulgaria, and the famed Orient Express passenger train (www.orient-express.com) even goes back there once or twice a year. Rail Europe can provide timetables and tickets for travel in Turkey. In the UK, contact (08448) 484 064 or www.raileurope.co.uk; in the US, contact (1-800-622 8600) or www.raileurope.com.

GETTING AROUND

By air

Iran

Iran Air (www.iranair.com) operates internal services to Ahvas, Bandar

Border crossings

Travel between Western Asian countries is generally straightforward, although it is advisable to organise visas in advance, because of the unpredictable political situation. See individual Places chapters for information on entering and leaving Western Asian countries.

Abbas, Isfahan, Mashhad, Shahrekord, Shiraz and Tabriz among other destinations. These and many other destinations are also served by newer, smaller airlines such as Caspian Air, Iran Aseman (www.iaa.ir), Taban (http://taban.aero/en/), Saha Air, Eram Air, Qeshm Air (www.qeshm-air.com) and Mahan Air (www.mahan.aero). Many Iranians use the internal airlines as their primary means of transport over longer distances, so flights are often booked up well in advance. Be aware, however, that international embargoes have had a detrimental impact on the upkeep of Iranian aircraft and, consequently, Iran's air safety record.

Lebanon

There are no internal flights in Lebanon due to the small size of the country.

Turkey

There is a wide network of domestic flights operated by Turkish Airlines (www.thy.com), Onur Air (www.onurair.com.tr), and Atlas Jet (www.atlasjet.com).

By train

Iran

The railway service is not extensive, and all lines radiate inconveniently out from Tehran. The services generally run on time and are at least comparable with express coach journey times. Men and women are sometimes in separate compartments, but mixed tourist groups are allowed. The two metro lines running underneath Tehran may also be useful.

Lebanon

There is currently no rail network in operation in Lebanon.

Turkey

The train network in Turkey is limited, with few lines and infrequent services, although these do happen to coincide with some Silk Road destinations. Inter-rail, Eurodomino and Balkan Flexipass tickets are valid in Turkey; Eurail passes are not. A cheap 30-day Train Tour Card (www.tcdd.gov.tr) offers unlimited travel throughout the country.

By bus and minibus

Iran

Express coaches serve many towns and cities and are a popular, quick and reliable way to get around the country. Bus stations are usually located along ring roads on the outskirts of towns, which often require a taxi journey into the centre. Tehran has several huge bus terminals in the suburbs, generally located in the direction of travel. In rural areas men and women are sometimes seated apart, but on longer coach journeys both sexes sit together.

Lebanon

Distances are small and easily covered in a day. Buses and minibuses are good options around the towns and cities.

Turkey

Coaches are the main form of long-distance inexpensive travel in Turkey, and every town and city has a bus station. With every competing company running its own booking kiosk, it's probably easier to go via a travel agent who will book you onto the service that fits with your timings.

Taxis

There are plenty of taxis in all larger towns and cities. Try to get the meter activated, but as many drivers will refuse to do so it is best to agree the fare beforehand. No journey within a city should cost more than a few US dollars, except in Turkey where fuel is more expensive. If visiting out-of-town sights, don't forget to arrange for the return trip as well or you could get stranded.

Shared taxis

These are great fallbacks should you fail to get a bus ticket or miss a departure. The large taxis leave (usually not far from the bus station) when they are full and are faster, but more expensive. If the waiting proves too much, you can offer to pay the set fare for the "empty" seats to get it moving. Within cities, shared taxis run along set routes, picking up and dropping off as they go. Should you be the last person in the taxi, the drivers will sometimes take you direct to your destination, such as a hotel.

Driving

Vehicles can be brought into all the countries in this region with the correct paperwork, or hired through international companies like Hertz, Europcar, Avis and Sixt. Drivers must be at least 21 years old and hold an International Driving Permit and national driving licence.

However, unless you are staying for an extended period, speak and

A battered Merc in Yazd.

read good Arabic, Farsi or Turkish, and know exactly where you are going, it makes more sense to hire a car and driver for about the same rate as a self-drive car.

Iran

Vehicles can be brought in and driven around Iran, but this is a serious undertaking in such a dangerous traffic-accident country. Some of the major car-hire companies advertise at arrivals halls, but these would tend to be for Iranian or Arab nationals rather than Western tourists. Europcar advertises through Iran Tour (www.irantour.org), but the prices include a driver. To drive in Iran you would need an International Driving Permit (check which sort), national licence and suitable insurance cover.

Lebanon

All the major international car-hire companies and many local ones will rent vehicles to foreigners.

Lebanon is a small country with all the major routes radiating from Beirut. The main highway is along the coast, from where roads reach inland to the mountains. During periods of unrest in Lebanon you might be stopped at roadblocks along the coast road, which passes close to the many Palestinian refugee camps.

Turkey

You can hire a car through Hertz, Europcar, Sixt and Avis or any number of local companies. Car hire is not particularly cheap, and fuel is extremely expensive (diesel is cheaper than petrol).

The condition of the roads in Turkey is usually reasonable, although if you can avoid driving at night, you would do well to do so. The roads are not well lit, nor well enough signposted, so it is advisable to drive defensively. It is also a good idea to have your address written down to help when asking passers-by for directions.

A – Z

A HANDY SUMMARY OF PRACTICAL INFORMATION

A

Accommodation

Choosing a hotel

The tourist infrastructure in **Iran** is still undeveloped, with a few four- and five-star hotels, basic hostels for local travellers and not much in between. In many cases the choice of hotel will have already been made for you as part of a tour package. The lack of good quality two- and three-star accommodation means that most organised tours are either quite expensive, limited in the itineraries they offer or stay in hotels that might not come up to Western standards. Experienced tourists acknowledge that the standard of a five-star hotel in Iran is not quite the same as in Europe or the US.

While tourism tries to establish itself, hotel facilities such as room service or the quality and range of breakfast might be less than visitors expect because staff are relatively inexperienced and do not speak much English, so be patient and flexible.

Lebanon can be a popular tourist destination, with a range of hotels from five-star luxury to rural B&Bs. Luxury hotels and resorts are concentrated in and around Beirut, along the coast and at the main ski centres. Most hotel staff speak fluent English, French and Arabic.

In **Turkey** there is a huge selection of excellent hotels in Istanbul and Cappadocia, from international chains to delightful historic boutique hotels. Elsewhere along the route the choice is strictly limited. In many places, however, there are restored historic houses that offer excellent accommodation, some with restaurants, at prices of around US$75–250 per night for a double room.

A Turkish *pansiyon* is somewhere between a simple hotel and a bed and breakfast, popular with Turkish holiday-makers. They can be lovely places to stay, especially if run by a family. The more expensive will have en suite facilities in every room.

Hostels

There are no youth hostels in **Iran**. There are basic hostels, known as *mosaferkhunehs*, for local travellers, but these do not always permit foreigners. A better option for budget travellers is to stay at one- and two-star hotels, some of which are decent and reasonably priced.

One of the main developments in **Lebanon** over the past few years is the rise of eco-tourism and the opportunity of spending a few nights in local communities. Some families are opening their homes to visitors on a B&B basis (typically US$10–40) to offer an authentic Lebanese experience.

Accommodation is so reasonably priced in **Turkey** that there are very few youth hostels as such. It is possible, out of term-time, to stay in empty student dormitories or halls of residence or in teachers' accommodation *(ogretmen evi)*, but the rooms will be spartan and often no cheaper than the cheapest ordinary *pansiyon* or hotel.

Camping

The authorities in **Iran** are not keen for tourists to stay too far off the beaten track, and certainly not in tents. Iranians have recently taken to camping, and now take every opportunity of pitching a tent on any piece of open ground. If camping is a part of your tour, then this will be arranged through your tour operator, who will get the necessary permits.

There are few official campsites in **Lebanon**, but there are some on the outskirts of cities. On the coast there are numerous seasonal tourist camping sites and chalets of various categories and prices.

You can actually camp anywhere in **Turkey** except designated historic or natural sites, provided you don't damage farmland or light fires in forests. For most trekking activities camping is necessary. The best camping areas are close to the seaside resorts, and have all the necessary facilities, including showers, shops, restaurants and activities. They generally cost around as much as staying in a cheap hotel.

B

Budgeting for your trip

Iran is a good-value destination, where eating out is cheap by Western standards, as are most transport costs. If on a group tour, accommodation and travel costs will already be covered, so it is just extras like additional food and drink, further sightseeing and souvenirs that you will need to pay for. Meals in local restaurants should cost no more than US$10 per day, or about US$20 in better hotel restaurants. Remember that foreign travellers cannot use their credit/debit card in Iran, whether for payment or at ATMs: you must bring all your money with you in cash, ideally as US dollars.

Lebanon is likely to cost around US$50–75 a day, particularly for eating, drinking and accommodation.

In **Turkey** you can set your budget where you want to (within limits) with low-cost airlines, buses and pensions offering low-cost options, and five-star deluxe hotels and private chauffeurs catering for higher budgets. Allow a minimum of US$75 a day, then work upwards to your required level of luxury.

C

Climate

Summer can be very hot (as high as 50°C/122°F) in the south and central regions of **Iran**. Northwest Iran is always about 10–15°C cooler than the rest of Iran, and winters can be very cold. The wettest months almost everywhere are March and April.

Syria has a moderate Mediterranean climate with four distinct seasons. Temperatures in autumn and spring range from 20°C to 25°C (70–77°F), but the weather can be changeable, especially in the mountains along the coast. Winter is generally moderate, but wet in the coastal region and cold inland: 5–15°C (40–60°F). Summer is hot everywhere (around 35°C/95°F), dry inland, humid on the coast and scorching in the desert.

Lebanon's Mediterranean climate enjoys 300 sunny days per year. Winters are moderate on the coast and cold in the mountains, with snow covering the highest peaks. Summer is hot and humid along the coast, but refreshingly cool in the mountains.

Turkey has three distinct climatic regions – the Mediterranean coast, the Anatolian plain and the Sea of Marmara. The Mediterranean remains relatively mild in winter, although there is snow on the mountains, with hot dry summers. Inland, the winters can be bitterly cold and the summers searingly hot. In the Istanbul region, the weather tends to be damp and grey in winter and warm in summer.

Crime and security

Most of the concern about visiting **Iran** will be before actually arriving. But once inside the country, the visitor soon realises how friendly most Iranians are, compared with the vision conjured up by the Western media. With such strict Islamic penalties for even minor offences, most visits are trouble-free, but there are still opportunists in every bazaar and market. Beware pickpockets (both local males and females) who seek out solo tourists by jostling them in crowded places while reaching into bags and pockets, especially in the bazaars of Shiraz, Isfahan and Tehran. The authorities take allegations of spying and drugs possession particularly seriously, and it's these rules where foreigners tend to fall foul.

Due to the current political situation as of late 2016, it is not safe for tourists to visit **Syria**. Most foreign embassies have closed and withdrawn their staff.

Security is a constant worry for those visiting **Lebanon**. In Beirut, as in other towns and villages, streets are generally safe day and night, and the culture encourages the community to watch out for all locals and visitors alike.

Crime is very low in **Turkey**, although there is inevitably some pickpocketing in the cities. Sadly, terrorism is a risk, but most visits are trouble-free. The police go out of their way to be polite to Westerners, but will deal harshly with drugs offences.

Customs regulations

Alcohol is prohibited in Iran, but you are allowed to import 200 cigarettes and 50 cigars duty-free. Books and magazines might be inspected, and any unsuitable literature will be confiscated. DVDs and videos can be seized if the officials suspect that they may contain offensive or pornographic material.

Elsewhere, alcohol and cigarettes are usually limited to 200 cigarettes and 1 litre of wine or spirits. Expensive electrical equipment such as laptops, DVD and MP3 players, digital and video cameras could be of interest to customs and might be written into your passport, ensuring they depart with you. DVDs and tapes might be viewed for content.

Cinemas

Cinema screens in Western Asia are dominated by Hollywood blockbusters, although home-grown dramas and comedies are occasionally shown.

Iranian films and their directors often hit the headlines at the major film festivals, but these art films are of little interest to Iranian audiences, who prefer more high-action films. Some Western films do get released in censored form and there is a steady trickle of acceptable Iranian movies.

D

Disabled travellers

There are few concessions for disabled travellers, who unfortunately have to get by as best they can. Hiring an extra carer to look after a disabled traveller would not be expensive, and it is advisable to alert hotels and destinations well in advance.

Some museums and newer buildings are equipped with ramps for wheelchairs, but most of the ancient sites are not, so there are still many steps, staircases and rough surfaces to be negotiated. Local blind people are often accompanied.

E

Eating out

What to eat

Other than the major hotels in **Iran** there are surprisingly few restaurants to choose from, even in a large city like Tehran. A few offer Persian dishes like the excellent *fesanjan* (chicken or duck in rich pomegranate and walnut sauce), and some specialise in international fare such as Indian, Korean, Chinese or Lebanese. Most Iranians socialise with their family and apart from business meetings would eat at home, so there is little trade to keep many restaurants in business. Persian food is generally very good and healthy, with many regional specialities prepared from fresh

CLIMATE CHART

Istanbul

	Maximum temperature
	Minimum temperature
—	Rainfall

CHINA

CENTRAL ASIA

WESTERN ASIA

Electricity

220 Volts AC, 50 Cycles. Countries in Western Asia use European-style two-pin rounded plugs. Some remote areas still get power cuts, but often these are confined to the early hours of the morning.

ingredients consisting of rice, meat, nuts, fruits, vegetables and herbs. For convenience, many of your meals are likely to be variations of lamb, mutton or chicken kebabs, which Iranians know how to prepare and cook very well.

In **Lebanon**, Beirut is well served with high-quality restaurants, and its food is rightly famous around the world as a blend of Western and oriental flavours. Top restaurants in the Central District are frequently fully booked, especially over weekends. Along the coast are many local places specialising in fish and countless others offering a wide range of Western and Middle Eastern dishes. The area of Achrafiye has many trendy restaurants, while the coastal views over Pigeon Rocks at Raouche are popular sunset eateries.

A typical quick breakfast in Lebanon is a bowl full of *foul madames*, consisting of beans, olive oil, lemon and herbs. In the city centres there are countless fast-food outlets ranging from sliced *shawarma* (meat served with salad in local bread) and *falafel* sandwiches to Western burgers, fries and pizzas. Also look for *börek* (savoury pastries), *gözleme* (pancakes, usually served with a tomato sauce), and *lahmacun* (thin pizzas).

Everything is on offer in **Turkey**, from grand palaces to modern chic restaurants and backstreet cafés. A *restoran* will usually specialise in either *et* (meat) or *balık* (seafood); all offer a wide range of *meze* with salads and dips, such as *hummus*, which can be a meal in themselves. Fish costs at least twice as much as meat. Lower down the scale, the *lokanta* can be anything from a cheerful self-service cafeteria to an atmospheric brasserie.

Drinks

Tea *(chay)* is undoubtedly the national drink of **Iran**, and always served hot, black and strong. Some of the most memorable places are the atmospheric teahouses, known as *chaykhanes*. Coffee beans

are an expensive import, and the local replacement coffee mixtures are unlikely to stimulate much appreciation, apart from thick, rich Turkish coffees. Delicious fruit and vegetable juices, milkshakes and yoghurt drinks are all freshly made throughout the country. Alcohol is strictly forbidden, though it is permitted for religious purposes, such as communion wine in churches, and to non-Muslims with special permission, but not tourists.

Lebanon's café and bar scene rivals that of any major European city. The recently restored Beirut Central District and Gemmayzeh area are usually buzzing with activity well into the night with lively music and theme bars. Here the Mediterranean aniseed drink is called *arak*, to be sipped with a splash of iced water, while the Lebanese climate is perfect for making high-quality wines. Traditionally, at the end of the meal, black Turkish coffee is offered.

Bottled water is freely available in **Turkey**, which also produces reasonable beer and wine, although they are not available in all restaurants. There are plenty of bars in main cities and tourist centres, but elsewhere, the tea *(çay)* shop is the social centre. There are also excellent fresh fruit juices, according to season.

Embassies and consulates

Iran

Australian Embassy
No. 2, 23rd Street, Khalid Islambuli Avenue, Tehran, tel: (021) 8386 3666, www.iran.embassy.gov.au
British Embassy
198 Ferdowsi Avenue, Tehran, tel: (021) 6405 2000, www.ukiniran.fco.gov.uk/en
Irish Consulate
Honorary Consul of Ireland, S.J. Assadabadi Avenue, Corner of 50th Street, No. 2/6, First Floor, Tehran, tel: (021) 8804 1925, e-mail: feizollahi@arfconsult.com
New Zealand Embassy
1, 2nd Park Alley, 34 Sosan Street, North Golestan Complex, Aghdasiyeh Street, Niyavaran, Tehran, tel: (021) 2612 2175, www.nzembassy.com/iran
US Embassy
The Swiss Embassy (39 Shahid Mousavi Street, Golestan 5th, Pasdaran Avenue, Tehran, tel: (021) 2254 2178, www.eda.admin.ch/tehran) has a US Interests section.

Lebanon

Australian Embassy
Embassy Complex, Serail Hill, Beirut, tel:, (01) 961 600, www.lebanon.embassy.gov.au
British Embassy
Embassy Complex, Serail Hill, Beirut, tel: (01) 960800, www.gov.uk/government/world/organisations/british-embassy-beirut
Canadian Embassy
43 Jal Al-Dib Highway, Coolrite Building, 1st floor, Jal Al-Dib, Beirut, tel: (01) 726 700, http://www.canadainternational.gc.ca/lebanon-liban
US Embassy
Awkar facing the Municipality, PO Box 70-840, Antelias, Beirut, tel: (04) 542 600, http://lebanon.usembassy.gov

Turkey

Although the embassies are in Ankara, the consulates in Istanbul handle visa and passport matters.
Australian Embassy
MNG Building, Ugur Mumcu Caddesi 88, 7th Floor, Gazi Osman Paşa, Ankara, tel: (0312) 459 9500, www.turkey.embassy.gov.au.
British Embassy
Sehit Ersan Addesi 46/A, Çankaya, Ankara, tel: (0312) 455 3344, www.ukinturkey.fco.gov.uk
Canadian Embassy
Cinnah Caddesi 58, Çankaya, Ankara, tel: (0312) 409 2700, www.turkey.gc.ca
Irish Embassy
MNG Binasi, B Blok Kat 3, Ugur Mumcu Caddesi 88, Ankara, tel: (0312) 459 1000, www.dfa.ie/irish-embassy/turkey
South Africa Embassy
27 Filistin Street, GOP, Ankara, tel: (0312) 405 6861, www.southafrica.org.tr
US Embassy
110 Atatürk Blvd, Kavakıdere, Ankara, tel: (0312) 455 5555, http://turkey.usembassy.gov

Emergencies

In **Iran** the initial call should be to the police on **110**. Explain (in Farsi only!) what has happened and they will then alert any other emergency services if needed. Otherwise, you can contact services directly on **115** (ambulance) or **125** (fire). No payment is required for any medical assistance provided by an ambulance, but a hospital or clinic would need payment. Obtain a receipt for claiming against insurance.

The following emergency numbers are used in **Lebanon**: police **160**, internal security forces **112**, Red Cross **140**, civil defence **125**.

The general emergency telephone number in **Turkey** is **115**. Others are: Police **155**, Ambulance **112**, Fire **110**. In major tourist areas there are also specialist tourist police (Istanbul, tel: (0212) 527 4503 and Ankara, tel: (0312) 384 0606).

Etiquette

Iran is a deeply religious country that follows Islamic code. For both men and women, it is best to cover up as much as possible. In an effort to be friendly, the male tourist will often extend a hand of friendship, which will be warmly accepted by an Iranian man, but politely refused by an Iranian woman. Always be aware that shoes need to be removed, not just inside mosques, but also some tombs, mausoleums, madrassas and private homes. In holy places like Mashhad or Qom, women must wear the *chador*, which can be obtained from the site guardian.

The days when an unmarried couple were not allowed to sleep in the same room seem to be over, but there may still be some small local hotels (particularly in holy centres) where this could be a problem. Men and women, even if they are married, should not show affection for each other in public. Most Iranians will politely indicate if a visitor is doing something unacceptable, albeit unknowingly.

Whilst more moderate than Iran, both **Lebanon** and **Turkey** are still Muslim countries, and visitors should respect religious sensitivity, particularly in the matter of dress and public conduct, and when in the towns and away from the beach. Eating, drinking and smoking in public during the holy month of Ramadan should be avoided.

F

Festivals

Most celebrations are connected to Islamic holidays (see page 407). Others include:

Iran

February Fajr Film Festival, Tehran
March 21 Nauroz (New Year)
October Tehran Short Film and Iran International Documentary Festival

Lebanon

February Al-Bustan Festival
July/August Baalbek Festival, Beiteddine Festival, Byblos International Festival, Tyre Festival, Aanjar Festival

Turkey

June traditional Kirkpinar Oil Wrestling Tournament (Edirne)
June–July Istanbul Arts & Culture Festival
September International Grape Harvest Festival (Ürgüp)
Sept–Nov Istanbul Bienal (odd-numbered years)
December Mevlâna Commemoration Ceremony (Konya)

G

Gay and lesbian travellers

Homosexuality is illegal in **Iran**, **Syria** and **Lebanon** (although there is a lively gay scene centred on a few bars in and around Beirut). However, both male and female travellers will not have any problems, as long as there are no outward signs of a gay relationship. As in many Middle Eastern countries, local men might well hold hands in the street, but this is usually just a sign of friendship. Istanbul has a more open gay scene, and details of the latest fashionable locations will be in the press and online.

H

Health and medical care

No vaccinations are compulsory, but there are recommendations for protection against tetanus, typhoid, hepatitis B, rabies, cholera and polio. Consult a travel clinic for advice about prophylaxis against malaria, which can a problem in southeastern Iran between March and November and northeastern Syria between May and October. A yellow fever certificate is required if entering from an infected area. For latest advice consult a doctor or visit www.fitfortravel.nhs.uk.

Large towns and cities on the tourist trail are well served by

Oil wrestling in Turkey.

hospitals and clinics. Doctors are generally well qualified and most medical personnel speak English or French. For minor ailments and problems, such as breathing difficulties due to air pollution, refer to one of the pharmacies in all towns and cities. The pharmacist can often speak a European language and will advise treatment.

Intense heat and sun can cause problems during the summer months, so ensure you take sun protection for skin, eyes and head and drink plenty of bottled water.

I

Insurance

Every traveller should have some form of travel and medical insurance. Small medical costs should be paid direct and reclaimed, but for a major medical problem consult the 24-hour emergency number. Bring all your details of insurance cover.

Internet

Modern **Iranians** are proud to tell you that Farsi is the fourth most widely used language on the internet, indicating just how much they have taken to the service, with internet cafés all over major cities.

There are many internet cafés in the main centres in **Lebanon**.

The **Turks** love the internet and, unusually, almost every hotel offers free broadband.

M

Maps

Good maps of Iran are hard to obtain, and very few of these have detailed information. The vast majority of visitors arrive as part of a group through local tour operators, who often give away free maps of Iran upon arrival. Tourist cities such as Tehran, Isfahan, Shiraz and Yazd have good street maps indicating the main points of interest, obtainable free at hotels or tourist information offices.

Good-quality maps of Lebanon and Beirut are available from larger bookstores in the capital. Tourist information offices can also provide free, but less accurate, maps.

Maps and signs in Turkey are fairly clear, but it is difficult to get hold of decent street maps of towns and

National holidays

Iran
1 January New Year's Day
6 January Army Day
11 Feb Victory of Islamic Revolution
20 March Oil Nationalisation Day
1 May Labour Day
14 July National Day
17 July Republic Day
8 August Ceasefire Day (End of Iran–Iraq War)

Lebanon
1 January New Year's Day
9 February Mar Maroun Feast
1 May Labour Day

6 May Martyrs' Day
15 August Assumption of Mary
22 November Independence Day

Turkey
1 January New Year's Day
23 April National Sovereignty and Children's Day
19 May Youth and Sports Day
30 August Victory Day
29 October Republic Day
The dates for religious holidays (which change from year to year as they are based on the lunar calendar) are available at www. godweb.org/IslamCalendar.htm

cities outside Istanbul before you get there.

Media

The media in **Iran** is firmly in the control of the ruling authorities, with many previously independent publications and websites forced to close over recent years. Print media seem to offer a vast choice of almost 30 newspapers and 80 magazines, but they are mainly variations on the official line. Several newspapers are in English, with some offering better coverage of overseas news or international sport. See www.iran-daily.com and www.tehrantimes. com but beware that both sites are periodically blocked or suspended.

State television runs two government channels as well as dedicated religion, news, science and sports channels. There is also a local TV channel for each province.

The more up-market hotels have (theoretically illegal) satellite dishes with access to BBC, CNN and Euro News channels. Some TV channels and internet sites are occasionally blocked due to perceived outside bias in the reporting (such as the BBC Persian-language website www. bbcpersian.com), but radio signals, including the BBC World Service, from around the world remain intact. Illegal satellite dishes are installed on most rooftops, and the general population has an informed view of international politics.

Arab and local newspapers and magazines are sold everywhere in **Lebanon**, while foreign newspapers are found at the international hotels. The *Daily Star* (www.dailystar.com.lb) is the English-language newspaper in Lebanon. Local television and radio broadcasts mainly in Arabic, but there

are some wildlife programmes in French and English. Satellite dishes can access all the major international news channels, provided by all the top hotels.

Sabah and *Hürriyet* are **Turkey**'s best-selling national newspapers, while the left-wing *Cumhuriyet* is considered the most serious newspaper. *Milliyet* is a well-established liberal paper. The English-language *Hürriyet Daily News* (www.hurriyetdailynews.com) provides coverage of local and international events. International newspapers and magazines can be bought at news-stands and bookshops in tourist areas. Turkey has over 12 television channels, plus additional regional channels, the majority of which are privately owned. Satellite and cable channels are available in major hotels.

Money

Iran
It will take a few days to get used to the incongruities of the Iranian currency, because even though notes and coins indicate rials, most prices are written and spoken as tomans (1 toman = 10 rials). So initially, the confusion of so many zeros is heightened by exactly which price is being referred to. A bottle of mineral water costing 3,000 rials (about 30 US cents) could be indicated as 300 tomans or even a verbal or finger sign for "3", leaving you to figure it out. Most sellers are genuinely honest and will rectify any mistakes or misunderstandings.

Exchanging money can be a problem, especially off the main tourist trail. In the main cities, exchange offices and some souvenir/

carpet shops speedily change cash in major currencies, but banks can be choosy about what currencies they take and are often slow. Credit cards and traveller's cheques are not generally accepted, except for some tourist shops in large cities, so travellers should carry US dollars to cover their needs.

Lebanon
The official currency is the Lebanese pound, but US dollars are widely used. Many shops, hotels and restaurants accept credit cards and there are many ATMs. Traveller's cheques can be exchanged at some banks.

Turkey
The Turkish lira (TRY or TL) notes come in denominations of TL 5, 10, 20, 50, 100 and 200 notes and 1, 5, 10, 25 and 50 kuruş plus TL1 coins. TL1 is split into 100 kuruş. Make sure you have plenty of small change and small denomination notes, as people rarely seem to have change. ATMs are plentiful if you need to top up. Most tourist shops take credit cards and are prepared to deal in US dollars, euros or sterling.

O

Opening hours
Friday is the official holiday in **Iran**, where government and bank official hours are roughly 8am–2pm Saturday to Thursday. In **Lebanon** many offices close early on Friday, and bank hours are 8.30am–12.30pm Monday to Saturday. Banks in **Turkey** are open Monday to Friday 8.30am–noon and 1.30–5pm, and a few larger branches also open Saturday morning; all have 24-hour cash

dispensers. Most places are closed on Sunday.

Shops and stores in Iran are open 9am–1.30pm and 5–8pm, later in summer. In Lebanon and Turkey stores tend to remain open all day, but shut at around 6pm. Museums are usually closed one day of the week – either Monday or Tuesday. Historical sites are open every day, and sometimes stay open later in summer.

The fasting month of Ramadan and the two-week New Year holidays are rules unto themselves, but generally places are open in the mornings.

P

Photography
Photographers should take care of exactly what their camera is pointing at, especially outside the main tourist sites. It is forbidden to take photos of any government or official building, police station, military site, airport, harbour, dam, train station or any place deemed to be strategically important. Avoid taking shots of anything that has a uniformed presence outside, or aerials on top. Photography is banned in some religious sites in Iran, such as Mashhad and Qom, although many locals do not seem to be aware of this.

Taking photographs of individuals also requires caution; whilst most local men seem agreeable, almost all women are not. Women visitors might have the opportunity of taking photos of local women in an all-women environment. Observe any signs where photography is forbidden and certainly do not attempt to photograph any police, soldiers or other security forces. Some

mosques and most museums allow photography while others charge an extra camera fee. Bring as many memory cards as you need, as the quality of local supplies is limited.

Postal services
Every town and city has a main central post office, and stamps can also be bought at some tobacco kiosks. Post office hours generally follow official opening hours, but some main post offices stay open late.

Public holidays
Islamic holidays are based on the Hejiri calendar. The months are lunar so the year is 13 days shorter than the Western calendar. Thus dates of certain holidays may vary from year to year. It is best to find out whether these fall within the time period of your projected visit. Ramadan or an Eid (religious feast) will mean that places are closed at certain times and that food may not be readily available because everyone else is fasting. The ancient Iranian New Year celebration called Nauroz (also Now Ruz) starts on 21 March and lasts for two weeks, during which time many people are absent from work. Christmas and Easter are also celebrated in Western Asia, and each country has its own national holidays.

Islamic holidays
Eid al-Fitr three days marking end of Ramadan (fasting month)
Eid al-Adha Four days at the end of Hajj
1st of Muharram Islamic New Year
9th and 10th of Muharram Ashura – martyrdom of Imam Hussein
12th of Rabe'a al-Awwal Prophet Muhammad's birthday
27th of Rajab Ascension of Prophet Muhammad

R

Religion

Iran
Iran is the only country where Shia Islam is the state religion. Almost 99 percent of the population are Muslims, with only a small percentage belonging to the Sunni sect. Followers of Sunni Islam live along the coast of the Persian Gulf, with many links to the Sunnis of UAE. Three minority religions are officially recognised – Zoroastrianism, Judaism and

Turkish newspapers for sale in Istanbul.

PTT is the logo for Turkey's Post Office.

Christianity – and each is concentrated in certain traditional centres.

There are Zoroastrian temples in Yazd, Isfahan and Tehran. For thousands of years, Jews have traded in the region, and since the time of Cyrus the Great have settled as artisans. There are still Jewish synagogues in Tehran, Hamedan and Isfahan. Christian churches are mainly from the Armenian branch and are found in all main towns and cities, with especially strong communities around Tabriz. Religious minorities that are not recognised include Buddhists, Sikhs and Baha'is (whose founder came from Shiraz). For these followers there can be no outward sign of community or places of faith, so worship is carried out in the privacy of the home.

Syria

Almost 90 percent of Syria's population are Muslims, with the majority being Sunni. This also includes many Kurds, whose homeland straddles the Turkish and Iraqi borders. There are small concentrations of Shia, Druze, Ismaili and Alawite. Syrian Christians make up about 10 percent of the total and are also split into many diverse groupings.

Lebanon

Around 60 percent of the population are Muslims, of which Shia are the majority, followed by Sunni and Druze. Christians make up approximately 39 percent and are also split into many diverse groupings, and the remaining 1 percent are classified as "other".

Turkey

Almost 99 percent of the population are Muslim. Turkish Islam is generally moderate, and the country prides itself on its secular government, but religious sentiment should still be respected.

S

Shopping

What to buy

Iran

Persian handicrafts include silks, gold, silver, brassware, ceramics, hand-blown glass, inlaid wood and carved or painted miniatures. Carpets and *kilims* are always good value, especially in Hamadan, Isfahan, Kashan, Na'in, Tabriz, Tehran, Shiraz and Yazd. Saffron, caviar and pistachios also make good gifts.

Syria

Syrian handicrafts represent an ancient tradition of skilled workmanship, including hand-woven silk brocades, embroidered tablecloths, carpets, engraved brass and copper, leather goods, glass vases, hand-printed cotton garments, jewellery, furniture inlaid with mother of pearl, as well as preserved fruit and Turkish delight.

Lebanon

Locally produced goods include carpets, brassware, silver jewellery, pottery and fossils.

Turkey

Turkish bazaars are a shopper's paradise, filled not only with traditional

Time zones

Iran is GMT +3.5 hours from 22 September to 21 March and GMT +4.5 hours from 22 March to 21 September. Syria, Lebanon and Turkey are GMT +2 from November to April and GMT +3 from May to October.

crafts but chic modern design. Carpets and cushions are of course king, but other items include leather, cotton, silk, jewellery, ceramics and inlaid chessboards. Edible gifts include saffron, nuts and Turkish delight.

T

Telecommunications

International 24-hour phone and fax services are available in most hotels in **Iran**. The use of mobile phones is also spreading fast, but as of yet there are no international roaming agreements.

Elsewhere in Western Asia, there is good mobile phone coverage, and many networks have international roaming agreements, albeit at costly rates. If staying for a long time, consider buying a local phone and SIM card offering better rates. International calls from hotels can be extremely expensive. Telephone booths offer local and international calls with payphone cards bought from post offices and kiosks. Some post offices have good-value international phone facilities but short opening hours, while nearby there is usually an enterprising shop or café owner with a phone and calculator.

International dialling codes

Iran +98
Syria +963
Lebanon +961
Turkey +90

Tipping

In **Iran**, restaurant staff expect a small gratuity from tourists, around 10 percent, and hotel staff should be tipped small notes for any help they give. Try to keep as much small change as possible for taxi drivers, porters and toilet attendants too.

In **Lebanon**, it is customary to tip 10–15 percent in restaurants, plus service charge.

If there is no service charge (*servis dahil*), leave 10 percent in restaurants in **Turkey**; if there is a service charge, leave a little small change. Allow YTL1–2 for porters and about YTL5 per day for the room cleaners in hotels. *Hammam* attendants will generally expect up to 25 percent of the price. Do not tip taxi drivers.

Toilets

There is absolutely no problem in using the toilets belonging to a hotel or restaurant even if you are just passing by, but try to leave a tip for the attendant. There are some toilets in public parks, service stations and modern shopping malls. It should always be possible to use the toilets in a mosque if necessary, but remember to carry toilet paper at all times.

Tourist information

In **Iran**, tourism falls within the duties of the Ministry of Culture and Islamic Guidance, but the best you can hope for are maps and smiles at a few tourist offices. Most of the active promotion comes from the private tour operators, who supply guides, transport, maps and itineraries for their incoming tour groups.

The main **Lebanese** tourist office is on Rue Banque du Liban in Beirut's Hamra District, and can provide maps and information. The Ministry of Tourism's website (www. destinationlebanon.gov.lb) is also a useful source of information. Much of the tourism promotion is done by the many tour operators, who have good information and travel advice on their websites.

Almost every town with anything to offer tourists has a small tourist office or kiosk in **Turkey** and, in most, the person behind the counter will have a rudimentary grasp of English. Whether they have any useful information depends on what you are asking. Try the Ministry of Culture and Tourism website (www. hometurkey.com) as a first step.

V

Visas

To get a visa for **Iran** you must first be invited into the country by an Iranian company or institution or, in the case of tourists, an approved Iranian travel agent. They will take your personal details to the Ministry of Foreign Affairs in Tehran, who issue an authorisation number, which will be faxed to the Iranian consulate in your country. At this point you get a visa application form from the consulate and lodge your passport, photographs (women must wear a headscarf in photos), letters and application forms with the visa number they give you. It may take up to five days for the consulate to issue your visa, and the whole process might take three to six weeks. Passports must be valid

for at least six months. A transit visa lasts for a maximum of 10 days, but extensions can be obtained once inside Iran. See www.travcour.com for more details.

Visitors to **Lebanon** can obtain a visa in advance from the nearest embassy or consulate, or at Beirut Airport, but check details. For updates on visa information, contact the Lebanese embassy or consulate in your country. Passports must be valid for at least six months. Travellers with passports containing visas or entry/exit stamps for Israel are unlikely to be allowed into Lebanon.

All visitors to **Turkey** require a valid passport and an entry visa, obtained at the airport on arrival – keep hard currency handy: UK (£13), Canada (US\$60), Australia (US\$20), USA (US\$20) and Ireland (E15). E-visas are now available in advance.

W

Websites

Some useful websites:
www.iranchamber.com Iranian history, art and culture.
www.chnpress.com/tourism Cultural Heritage News agency.
http://www.irpedia.com Official tourism website.
www.lebanon.com General website with hotel and restaurant listings.
www.mfa.gov.tr Turkish Foreign Ministry
www.istanbul.com Official Istanbul tourist office website.
www.kultur.gov.tr Turkish Ministry of Culture and Tourism.
www.turkeytravelplanner.com Definitive US-run website.

What to bring and wear

Be sure to bring appropriate clothing if travelling in **Iran**. Men should wear shirts and long trousers; shorts are not acceptable. Women must not draw attention to the shape of their body or expose any flesh except their face and hands. At its simplest, women should arrive in a pair of loose trousers, long shirt and compulsory headscarf, then see what the local fashion is and buy accordingly in the shops. Elsewhere in Western Asia, women should not wear short or revealing clothing in mosques or souks.

Between October and May, winter clothing is recommended – at least a fleece and waterproof jacket. The desert can be freezing

in winter, as are sites in the higher mountains, and you'll need to keep warm and dry. In the summer (May–September), clothing should be light and loose-fitting. Always bring sunglasses, suncream and a hat. Mosquito repellent, plasters, a torch (flashlight), camera and an extra bag to take home your shopping complete the kit.

When to go

Spring (April–June) and autumn (September–November) are the best times to visit Western Asia, when it is hopefully not too hot or cold, with warm days and pleasant evenings. Try to avoid Easter, however, when hotels can be fully booked with tour groups, and Ramadan, when everything slows down a bit. Skiers should plan a visit between November and March.

It can be unbearably hot in southern **Iran**, so a winter/spring tour of the southern half of the country is ideal, but not for the main Silk Road sections of the north, where winter weather can be severe. The route from Mashhad across the north of Iran to Rey is good apart from the winter months, and the northern route through Tabriz is best undertaken from late spring to early autumn. Rain can be a problem at any time of the year in the north.

Women travellers

As long as you are prepared to observe the strict codes of female behaviour and dress, most women have no problems travelling around **Iran**. But it is always advisable to keep to well-lit and busy parts of towns and cities. As an "honorary man", a woman tourist is accepted in public places such as teahouses, but can also go into female enclaves of a private house, which are forbidden to men. If you can overcome the communication barrier, most local men are extremely helpful, and the women will be interested about your life and family.

The same applies to **Lebanon** and **Turkey**, although women may be gazed at. Turkish men are great flirts, but if in doubt, shout and every man in the vicinity will rush to your rescue.

Weights and measures

Countries in Western Asia use the metric system.

LANGUAGE

UNDERSTANDING THE LANGUAGE

Western Asia has a rich linguistic heritage that encompasses everything from Aramaic, Assyrian and Babylonian through Latin and Greek, Kurdish, Armenian and classical Persian. While not all of these languages are spoken today, you will see their inscriptions in archaeological sites and historic manuscripts, and their grammatical structures, words and literary ideas have significantly influenced three of the modern languages widely spoken in the region today: Arabic, Persian and Turkish.

ARABIC

Arabic is a Semitic language, closely related to Hebrew, and its various dialects all stem from the Classical Arabic of the 6th century AD. Today's written Arabic (Modern Standard Arabic) is derived from the Arabic of the Koran and is the official language of 26 states, even though their various spoken dialects can be mutually unintelligible.

Arabic verbs are marked for person, gender and number, and conjugated for the past or non-past, an active or passive voice, and one of five different moods. Nouns have three grammatical cases, three numbers (singular, dual or plural), two genders and three states (indefinite, definite and construct). Adjectives are marked for case, gender, number and state but interestingly, non-human nouns are always combined with a singular feminine adjective.

Arabic has three short vowels (a i u), three long vowels (ā ī ū) and two diphthongs (aj and aw). A vowel at the end of a word is often not pronounced. Consonants can be plosive or fricative, and either voiced or unvoiced.

Key phrases

Hello ابحرم. *marhaba*
How are you? كيف حالك؟ *Kayfa Haaluka?*
Fine, thank you بخير, شكرا *bi-khair Shukran*
Please من فضلك. *min faDlak*
Thank you شكرا *shukran*
Yes نعم *na`am*
No لا. *laa*
Excuse me لو سمحت *min faḍlak*
Goodbye مع السلامة *ma`a as-salaamah*
Do you speak English? هل تتكلم الجليزية؟ *Hal tatakallam al-ingliziyyah?*
Help! مساعدة! *Musaa`adah!*

PERSIAN

Persian (often also referred to as Farsi) is an Indo-Iranian language and so has close grammatical and structural links with European languages such as Latin and French. It has around 60.6 million native speakers who reside across modern Iran, Afghanistan and Tajikistan, and it has significantly influenced the structure and vocabulary of other regional languages including Hindi, Urdu and Armenian.

Persian grammar is pleasingly straightforward. Normal sentences are structured with the subject-object-verb word order and, if the object is specific, it precedes a prepositional phrase. The declension of verbs expresses the tense and aspect of an action, and they agree with number and person of the subject.

The Persian vocabulary has been significantly widened through the compounding of existing words and also the addition of prefixes and suffixes to the stems of verbs and also to nouns and adjectives. Persian has also adopted loanwords from a variety of sources: Mongolian and Turkic words are present in large numbers due to the political role of successive Turkic dynasties in Persian history; French and Russian

Learning a few words of Persian for bartering in the bazaars will come in handy in Iran.

Taxi rank in Turkey.

words (and their adaptations) were absorbed into Persian in the 19th and early 20th centuries; and English is also now making its presence felt, particular in technical vocabulary.

Persian has six vowels (three long and three short) and 23 consonants, of which two are nasal. The majority of consonants are labial (pronounced on the lips, for example m, p, b) or alveolar (pronounced with the tongue just behind the top teeth, for example n, t, d). Only j is spoken with the tip of the tongue on the palate. Syllables always begin with a consonant sound, and it is usually the last syllable of a word that is stressed.

Key phrases

Hello. مالَس *Salâm*
How are you? چطورید *chetorid?*
Fine, thank you خیلی مـنون ،مبوخ *xubam, xeyli mamnun*
Please افـطل *lotfan*
Thank you مرسی *mersi*
Yes بـلھ *bale*

Mosque door with Persian text.

No نَ *na*
Excuse me ببخـشیـد *bebaxšid*
Goodbye ظفاحادخ *xodâhâfez*
Do you speak English? میتوانید
Mitavânid بزنیـد؟ حـرف انگلیـسی
Engelisi harf bezanid?
Help! کُمَک *komak!*

TURKISH

Turkish is the native language of more than 71 million people, not only in modern Turkey but also in parts of Cyprus, Iraq, Greece and Bulgaria. The language originated some 1,300 years ago in Central Asia, but the standard version spoken today is known as Istanbul Turkish because of the region in which it is primarily spoken. As late as 1928 Turkish was written in the Perso-Arabic script, but Ataturk introduced a variant of Latin script so that Turkey would be more closely aligned with Europe and also to break with the country's Ottoman past.

In Turkish the standard word order is subject-object-verb, though this can be altered to stress the importance of a specific word or phrase. Nouns do not have a specific gender, but there is an extensive use of honorifics and second-person pronouns (with their respective verb endings) to denote the status of the person and also the level of familiarity the speaker has with the subject.

The Turkish alphabet has 29 letters, seven of which have been modified from their original Latin forms. There are eight vowels (a, e, i, ı, o, ő, u, ű), and no letters for q, w and x. Turkish words never contain two vowels next to each other, so if you do see two vowels together you know that it's a loanword from another language. The language is entirely phonetic, which definitely aids pronunciation.

Key phrases

Hello Merhaba *mehr hah bah*
How are you? Nasılsınız? *na suhl suhn uhz*
Fine, thank you İyiyim, teşekkürler. *ee yee yeem teh shek ür lerr*
Please Lütfen *Luet fen*
Thank you Teşekkür ederim *teh shek uer eh der eem*
Yes Evet *eh vet*
No Hayır. *Hah yuhr*
Excuse me Bakar mısınız? *bah kar muh suh nuhz*
Goodbye Hoşçakalın. *Hosh cha kaluhn*
Do you speak English? İngilizce biliyor musunuz? *Eengleez jay bee lee yor muh suh nuhz*

FURTHER READING

HISTORY AND CULTURE

The Heritage of Persia by Richard N. Frye. Academic analysis of Persian civilisation, history and art.

Damascus: Hidden Treasures of the Old City by Brigid Keenan. A tour through the wealth of Roman, Christian and Islamic relics of the Old City.

Monuments of Syria by Ross Burns. In-depth descriptions of all the major historical sites.

Travellers History Turkey Chastleton Travel. A potted guide to the history of one of the oldest and most complicated countries in the world.

Byzantium by John Julius Norwich. Three-volume definitive guide to the magnificent Byzantine empire.

Lords of the Horizons: A History of the Ottoman Empire by Jason Goodwin. A concise but lively run through the Ottoman period.

Storm on Horseback: The Seljuk Warriors of Turkey by John Freely. Book about the original Turks by one of the great writers on Turkey.

Istanbul, The Imperial City by John Freely. Illustrated introductory biography of the city and its social life through 27 centuries.

Daughter of Persia: A Woman's Journey from Her Father's Harem Through the Islamic Revolution by Sattareh Farman-Farmaian. With honesty and humour, Farman-Farmaian describes her upbringing in the home of a Persian prince and her ringside seat on the turbulent political events of Iran's 20th century.

MODERN HISTORY

Behind Iranian Lines by John Simpson. Views of the Islamic Revolution from inside Iran.

Out of Iran: A Woman's Escape from the Ayatollahs by Sousan Azadi. A westernised Iranian woman's account of life under the ayatollahs.

The Truth about Syria by Barry Rubin. Placing ancient Syria in the political jigsaw of the modern Middle East.

Hedjaz Railway by R. Tourret. All you ever needed to know about the railway that Lawrence of Arabia blew up.

Pity the Nation: Lebanon at War by Robert Fisk. Continually updated accounts of Lebanon's political problems both internal and external.

ART AND MUSIC

Islam: Art and Architecture edited by Markus Hattstein and Peter Delius.

Introducing Persian Architecture by Arthur Upham Pope.

A History of Ottoman Architecture by Godfrey Goodwin. Comprehensive and definitive, covering every kind of building all over Turkey.

FICTION

Fragments of Memory by Hanna Minah. A look at the changing silk industry a century ago.

Send Us Your Thoughts

We do our best to ensure the information in our books is as accurate and up-to-date as possible. The books are updated on a regular basis using local contacts, who painstakingly add, amend and correct as required. However, some details (such as telephone numbers and opening times) are liable to change, and we are ultimately reliant on our readers to put us in the picture.

We welcome your feedback, especially your experience of using the book "on the road". Maybe we recommended a hotel that you liked (or another that you didn't), or you came across a great bar or new attraction we missed.

We will acknowledge all contributions, and we'll offer an Insight Guide to the best letters received. Please write to us at:

Insight Guides
PO Box 7910
London SE1 1WE
Or email us at:
hello@insightguides.com

The Prophet by Gibran Khalil Gibran. A guide to life by Lebanon's most celebrated author.

The White Castle, The Black Book, The New Life. Novels by Orhan Pamuk, translated by Güneli Gün. Three of many books by introspective, perceptive, sometimes over-complex Nobel-prize-winning Turkish writer.

Modern Syrian Short Stories by M.J.L. Young, Three Continents Press. A view of life in the changing Syria of the 1980s.

TRAVEL NARRATIVES

Adventures in Persia by Reginald Teague-Jones. Amazing account of a car journey through Persia in 1926.

The Valleys of the Assassins: And Other Persian Travels by Freya Stark. Wonderful descriptions of all the major sites as seen in the early 1930s.

The Hills of Adonis by Colin Thubron. The famous travel writer witnesses the Lebanon of the 1960s.

A Fez of the Heart by Jeremy Seal. Travels around Turkey in search of a real fez, the felt hat banned in 1925; a perceptive, alternative view of modern Turkey.

Istanbul: Memories and the City by Orhan Pamuk. An evocative biography of the city, drawing upon Pamuk's own childhood and a rich understanding of its history.

OTHER INSIGHT GUIDES

Other **Insight Guides** that highlight destinations in Western Asia include *Jordan*, *Israel* and *Turkey*. Discover Istanbul's hidden corners with the award-winning **Select Guide** *Istanbul* – a stylish guide to the city, offering a selection of unusual and quirky ideas to suit your mood. **Insight Guide Explore** titles provide walks and itineraries in the world's most exciting destinations, in a pocket-sized format with pull-out map, and the list includes a guide to *Istanbul*. Insight **FlexiMaps** provide full mapping of major destinations, and their easy-to-fold, laminated finish gives them ease of use and durability.

CREDITS

Insight Guide Credits

Distribution
UK, Ireland and Europe
Apa Publications (UK) Ltd;
sales@insightguides.com
United States and Canada
Ingram Publisher Services;
ips@ingramcontent.com
Australia and New Zealand
Woodslane; info@woodslane.com.au
Southeast Asia
Apa Publications (SN) Pte;
singaporeoffice@insightguides.com
Hong Kong, Taiwan and China
Apa Publications (HK) Ltd;
hongkongoffice@insightguides.com
Worldwide
Apa Publications (UK) Ltd;
sales@insightguides.com
Special Sales, Content Licensing and CoPublishing
Insight Guides can be purchased in bulk quantities at discounted prices. We can create special editions, personalised jackets and corporate imprints tailored to your needs.
sales@insightguides.com
www.insightguides.biz

Printed in Poland by Pozkal

First Edition 2008
Third Edition 2017

Editor: Sarah Clark
Author: Chris Bradley
Head of Production: Rebeka Davies
Picture Editor: Tom Smyth
Cartography: original cartography Stephen Ramsay, updated by Carte

Contributors

This new edition of *Insight Guide The Silk Road* has been carefully and comprehensively updated to account for the major events that continue to unfold in the countries covered by this book. While it explores a major historical "highway", history is being written every day and please note that some information contained here is particularly subject to change.

Responsible for bringing the book up to date is author and lecturer **Chris Bradley**, a pioneering tour leader who took groups along the Chinese and Central Asian Silk Road during the 1980s and has since led many tours to Uzbekistan, Turkmenistan, Iran, Syria, Lebanon and Turkey, amongst others. Chris also worked on the first edition of the book. Other original writers include **Tony Halliday**, **Andrew Forbes**, **Bradley Mayhew**, **Laurence Mitchell**, **Philippa Scott** and **Melissa Shales**, amongst others.

This new edition was commissioned and edited by **Sarah Clark**.

About Insight Guides

Insight Guides have more than 45 years' experience of publishing high-quality, visual travel guides. We produce 400 full-colour titles, in both print and digital form, covering more than 200 destinations across the globe, in a variety of formats to meet your different needs.

Insight Guides are written by local authors who use their on-the-ground experience to provide the very latest information; their local expertise is evident in the extensive historical and cultural background features. All the reviews in **Insight Guides** are independent; we strive to maintain an impartial view. Our reviews are carefully selected to guide you to the best places to eat, go out and shop, so you can be confident that when we say a place is special, we really mean it.

Legend

City maps

	Freeway/Highway/Motorway
	Divided Highway
	Main Roads
	Minor Roads
	Pedestrian Roads
	Steps
	Footpath
	Railway
	Funicular Railway
	Cable Car
	Tunnel
	City Wall
	Important Building
	Built Up Area
	Other Land
	Transport Hub
	Park
	Pedestrian Area
🚌	Bus Station
ⓘ	Tourist Information
✉	Main Post Office
✝	Cathedral/Church
☾	Mosque
✡	Synagogue
🛆	Statue/Monument
⚲	Beach
✈	Airport

Regional maps

	Freeway/Highway/Motorway (with junction)
	Freeway/Highway/Motorway (under construction)
	Divided Highway
	Main Road
	Secondary Road
	Minor Road
	Track
	Footpath
	International Boundary
	State/Province Boundary
	National Park/Reserve
	Marine Park
	Ferry Route
	Marshland/Swamp
	Glacier Salt Lake
✈	Airport/Airfield
∴	Ancient Site
⊖	Border Control
🚡	Cable Car
🏰	Castle/Castle Ruins
🞈	Cave
🏠	Chateau/Stately Home
✝	Church/Church Ruins
⌒	Crater
🗼	Lighthouse
▲	Mountain Peak
★	Place of Interest
※	Viewpoint

INDEX

Silk Road